D0918893

PRINCIPLES AND TYPES OF SPEECH COMMUNICATION

Eighth Edition

PRINCIPLES AND TYPES OF SPEECH COMMUNICATION

Eighth Edition

Douglas Ehninger
The University of Iowa

Alan H. Monroe

Bruce E. Gronbeck
The University of Iowa

Scott, Foresman and Company
Glenview, Ill.
Dallas, Tex. • Oakland, N.J. • Palo Alto, Cal. • Tucker, Ga. • London, England

All hand-drawn illustrations in
this book are by Ron Bradford.

Photographs in Chapters 2, 5,
16, and 20 are by Paul Sequeira.

Photographs in Chapters 2, 14,
and 22 are by Perry Riddle.

Library of Congress Cataloging in Publication Data

Ehninger, Douglas.
Principles and types of speech communication.

Seventh ed. by A. H. Monroe and D. Ehninger published
in 1974.

Includes bibliographies and index.
1. Public speaking. 2. Oral communication.
I. Monroe, Alan Houston, 1903-1975   joint author.
II. Gronbeck, Bruce E., joint author.   III. Title.
PN4121.M578   1978   808.5'1   77-15588
ISBN 0-673-15118-2

1 2 3 4 5 6-VHJ-84 83 82 81 80 79 78 77

Preface

The Eighth Edition of *Principles and Types of Speech Communication* presents in a thoroughly revised and revitalized form many of the basic concepts, principles, and practices that have so richly proved their worth through seven previous editions and more than four decades of classroom use. At the same time, it affirms its continuing awareness of recent developments in the field of speech communication by introducing five entirely new chapters reflecting current trends which influence the teaching of the basic course. The result, we believe, is a highly practical and genuinely modern public communication textbook, concise in presentation, well balanced in content, compact in aspect.

Among the new or extensively redeveloped chapters are those on Listening, Alternative Patterns of Speech Organization, Language, Paralanguage, Proxemics and Nonverbal Communication, Audio-Visual Resources, Group and Conference Presentations, Public Argumentation and Advocacy, Speech Evaluation and Rhetorical Criticism. The chapters on Audience Analysis, Forms of Supporting Material, and Motive Appeals have been considerably recast to relate more directly to the role that beliefs, attitudes, and values play in shaping the communicative transaction. The instruments of Voice, Bodily Expression, Language, and Audio-Visual Support have been placed in new perspective in the section on Modes of Communicating Meaning. The materials on the Speech Communication Process, the Motivated Sequence, Factors of Attention, Speech Structuring, and Basic and Special Types of Speeches reflect important new research findings in those areas. The four sections of the Appendix—"Finding and Recording Speech Materials," "Making Your Speaking Voice More Effective," "Evaluating and Criticizing the Speeches of Others," and "Communicating in Small Groups"—are directly pertinent to a number of the chapters in the text proper and further extend their usefulness.

Throughout, special care has been taken to maintain clarity and conciseness in the language used to describe basic concepts and processes; and the organization of the chapters has been tightened to ensure an economical, phase-by-phase discussion of all of the essential steps in speech planning, preparation, and presentation. Each of the major topics covered, although forming a part of a carefully integrated instructional program, also stands as a self-contained unit, thus enabling the instructor to alter the order in which chapters are studied, or to omit portions less suited to students' immediate needs and capabilities. In sum, without sacrificing a sound balance between theoretical and pragmatic concerns, this new edition of *Principles and Types of Speech Communication* presents in updated form the same conventional wisdom which has for so long been the book's hallmark.

Uniquely characteristic of this new edition is the increased attention paid to the speaker's total personality or *self* as a wellspring of communicative effectiveness. Care is taken not only to identify and describe the materials out of which speeches are constructed, but also to consider how these materials may be most effectively used to reflect the speaker's individual traits, the end which he or she seeks, and the audience addressed. Also increased is the emphasis given to the physical settings and psychological contexts in which various kinds of communicative transactions occur.

Further enriching the pedagogical thrust of the text itself are the study materials which round out each of the book's twenty-two chapters, and which have been updated and made more selective and accountability-oriented. The Study Problems and Probes are designed to stimulate and extend the students' learning experiences *outside* the classroom; the Oral Activities and Speaking Assignments are aimed at guiding and making more effective their work *inside* the classroom; and the Suggestions for Further Reading are intended to broaden their understanding of the speech communication process and to encourage pursuit of topics that prove of particular interest. Additional suggested speaking and study assignments, lists of supplementary books and films, instructional procedures, speech-evaluation forms, and sample test questions for each chapter are available in an instructor's manual, *A Guide to Using Principles and Types of Speech Communication, Eighth Edition,* and may be obtained from the publisher on request.

To vivify the contemporary character of the text, increase the ease with which it may be read, and heighten its visual appeal, the book has been completely redesigned typographically and more illustrations added. Abundant and originally conceived drawings, diagrams, and charts illustrate key concepts and processes and help ensure comprehension and retention. The photographs have been selected with an eye to depicting some important facets of public communication as they function in real-life situations and settings.

Overall, as coauthors we have striven to carry forward the basic philosophy, ideas, and aspirations for effectiveness in oral communication which characterized the life and work of the book's original author, Alan H. Monroe, who died January 25, 1975, at a time when this edition of *Principles and Types of Speech Communication* was still in an early planning stage. We trust that it continues to reflect the profound influence which Professor Monroe had upon us and upon the entire field of speech communication.

We have been greatly aided and encouraged in the preparation of this revision by the critical insights and sound advice of a goodly number of speech communication scholars and fellow educators, most of whom were familiar with the text in one or more of its earlier editions. Among these are Gail W. Compton, Eastern Michigan University; Walter Fisher, University of Southern California; James Gibson, University of Missouri; Michael McGuire, University of Georgia; Michael Osborn, Memphis State University; Sharon Ratliffe, Ambassador University; Stanley Schmidt, Portland Community College; J. Michael Sproule, Indiana University Southeast; Hermann Stelzner, University of Massachusetts; David L. Swanson, University of Illinois; and Elaine Tompkins, State University of New York at Albany. David W. Addington, Bowling Green State University; Eleanor M. DiMichael, Queens College; and Howard H. Martin, University of Iowa, provided assistance and valuable advice relative to the materials on Voice. Some fifty others, users of the Seventh Edition of the book, also provided suggestions and recommendations for this new edition by responding to our detailed questionnaires. Richard Cherwitz and Jefferson Bass of the University of Iowa reviewed illustrative examples and bibliographical material for several of the chapters. To all of these we are deeply grateful. We wish to thank, too, the many teachers and students who—over the years—have generously provided ideas and suggestions for the enhancement of successive editions.

If students using this latest edition of *Principles and Types of Speech Communication* draw from its pages an enlarged understanding of speech communication and a fuller realization of the potential of public speaking as a personal, positive, and productive force in contemporary society, our intention in preparing this revision will have been richly fulfilled.

D.W.E.
B.E.G.

Contents

Part One
Speech Communication
as Process and Transaction

Part Two

Public Communication:
Preparation and Adaptation to the Audience

Part Three

Public Communication:
Modes of Communicating Meaning

Part Four
Public Communication:
Basic Types

Part Five
Public Communication:
Special Types

Appendix
A
B
C
D

Sample Speech Material for Study and Analysis

Illustrations, Diagrams, and Charts

PRINCIPLES AND TYPES OF SPEECH COMMUNICATION

Eighth Edition

Part 1

SPEAKER AUDIENCE INTERACTION

Speech Communication
as Process and Transaction

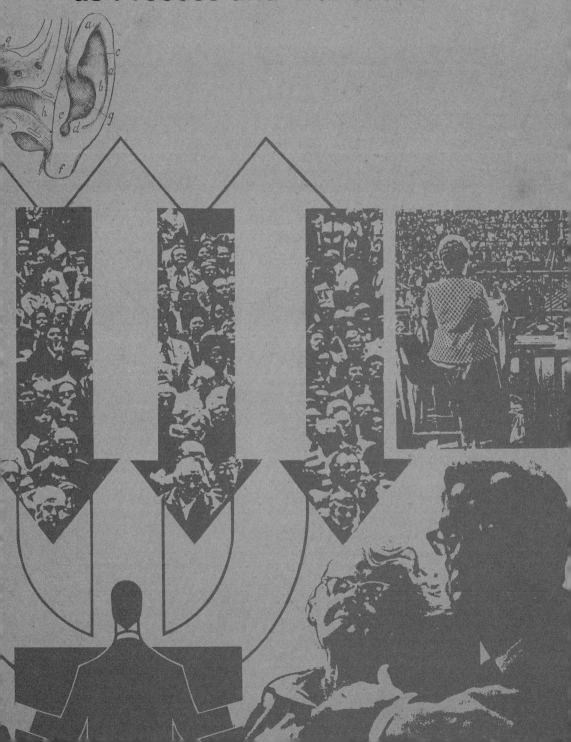

Speech Communication: Process and Forms

Different as these two declarations appear to be, if we take them apart to see what makes them tick, we will find that they are alike in a number of significant respects. Both spring from a *communicative impulse*—a desire on the part of one person to "say" something to somebody else. In both, *a speaker* attempts to transmit *a message* to *a listener*. Both

4

recognize that the message may not be received or, if received, may not be understood. Both reflect an implicit awareness that at least two *channels* exist: a visual channel and an aural channel ("what we see, and what we hear . . ."). Neither declaration is made in a vacuum; each is "embedded" in a communicative *situation,* if not a physical setting, then certainly a social or psychological context. In sum, both contain all of the elements essential to the functioning of the *speech communication process.*

The Process and Its Elements

Holding these illustrations in mind, pause for a moment to review the speech "transactions" in which you yourself have participated during the past few days. Doubtless they were a varied lot. On some occasions they probably involved only you and one other individual. On others you may have been a member of a small group engaged in a social conversation or a committee work session. At still other times you may have listened to a speech or report presented to a dozen or more persons. The behavior which the speakers and listeners exhibited in these situations also is likely to have differed. Sometimes you and your companions spoke in an informal or casual manner; sometimes you were more restrained or formal. Sometimes you stood; sometimes you sat. The speaker may have continued to speak for a period of time without interruption, or may have been interrupted frequently by questions, comments, or heckling.

In spite of these differences, however, all of these speech transactions had in common those same elements or factors inherent in the two declarations we cited at the outset: a *speaker* situated in a particular physical *setting* and social *context* originated a *message* which was transmitted over a *channel* to one or more *listeners* who then responded by "feeding back" reactions to the speaker visually or verbally. Indeed, had any one of these factors been absent, no speech transaction could have occurred. These factors and their inherent relationships are suggested in the diagram on page 6.

Let us now examine each of these factors more fully, beginning where a speech transaction normally begins—with the speaker.

The Speaker

So far as the speaker is concerned, all speech transactions are shaped by <u>four</u> important influences: communicative purpose; knowledge of <u>subject; command of speech skills; and attitudes toward self, listeners, and subject.</u>

The Speaker's Purpose in Communicating. Except in the rarest of instances, we speak in order to achieve some purpose or attain some goal. Our purpose may be as simple as the wish to be sociable or be-

Figure 1. / THE SPEECH COMMUNICATION TRANSACTION:
    Basic Elements and Factors

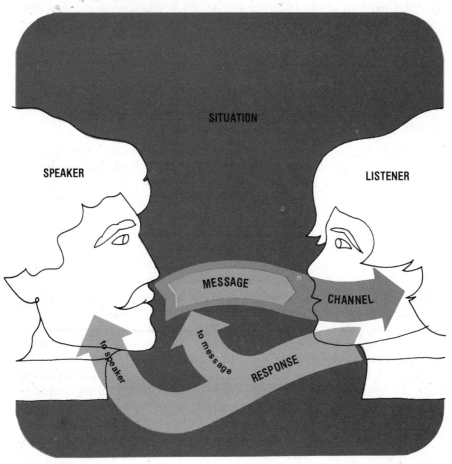

friend a stranger. We may, at the other extreme, seek to alter our listeners' most cherished values or move them to an action fraught with
dangers. Our purpose may be to reinforce an existing attitude, to resolve a conflict, or to pose a question. We may wish to provide entertainment, explain a problem, test an idea, refute an assertion, ward off a
threat, establish or maintain status, or achieve any number of similar
ends. Sometimes our communicative purposes are *defensive;* sometimes they are *aggressive.* In every case, however, we communicate with
others because there is an end we seek or a desire we wish to fulfill.

   To say that whenever we speak we have a purpose is not, of course, to
assert that in all cases our audience is aware of what that purpose is.
Sometimes what we want listeners to regard as an objective statement
of fact is actually a subtle piece of propaganda designed to influence
their beliefs or behavior. At other times, remarks we intended ironically

are interpreted literally. Even we ourselves may not always be aware of the purpose our message is designed to serve, or we may subconsciously delude ourselves concerning the motives that prompt it. In speech communication, no less than in other kinds of behavior, each human being is a complex creature whose motives often remain hidden. But if we will look deeply enough into any speech transaction, we nearly always will discover the desire to achieve some end or fulfill some purpose.

The Speaker's Knowledge of the Subject and Command of Speech Skills. Whenever we speak, our knowledge of the subject and our command of speech skills affect the nature of our message and the effectiveness with which it is transmitted. Unless we have a thoroughgoing *knowledge of the subject* of our discourse, we cannot hope to communicate clearly and cogently the beliefs, attitudes, or values we hold for it. In casual conversations, no less than in formal speeches, if we have only a surface knowledge of what we are talking about, our ideas will be few and thin. When, on the other hand, we have a breadth and depth of information about a subject, we are likely to present significant ideas in a well-developed and more orderly fashion.

Besides a knowledge of subject matter, a command of the fundamental skills of *vocal and bodily delivery* is important regardless of the situation in which a speech transaction occurs. Mumbled or inaudible words, a monotonous pitch pattern, and a harsh or breathy voice detract from, or even alter the meaning of, any oral message. The ability to use our voices and bodies to express ideas orally and visually facilitates the understanding and acceptance basic to successful functioning of the speech communication process.

The Speaker's Attitudes. Whenever we speak, our attitudes toward ourselves, our listeners, and our subject affect what we say and how we say it.

Attitude Toward Self. All of us carry about a picture of ourselves as persons—a self-concept or image of the kind of individual we are and how others perceive us. We think of ourselves as successful or unsuccessful, as liked or disliked, as someone whose opinions are respected or discounted, as competent or incompetent to discuss a given topic or make a given judgment.

Our self-image influences how we are likely to behave in a given speaking situation. If we have a low estimate of our abilities, we tend to advance ideas diffidently and often in a random or confused manner. Usually, our voices are unsteady, our bodies stiff, and our gaze directed toward the floor or ceiling rather than toward our listeners. In contrast, if we have an exaggerated idea of our knowledge or abilities, we may adopt an overbearing manner, disregard the need for facts and proofs, and state our ideas without regard for the feelings of others.

A previously formed self-image is not, however, the only factor that affects our speaking behavior. What happens during the course of the communicative encounter also has a significant influence. If, on the one hand, we find that what we say is well received, that our listeners are interested and attentive, our fear and reluctance gradually are replaced by a growing sense of assurance. When, on the other hand, we find the listeners uninterested, annoyed, or hostile, our thinking becomes scattered and our manner less poised and forthright. Because outward speech behavior is a faithful mirror of inner thoughts and feelings, our self-image — as challenged or confirmed by *feedback* from listeners — has quite correctly been called "the starting point or base line from which all communication proceeds."[3]

Attitude Toward Listeners.   Another important influence on our speaking behavior is *our attitude toward our listeners.* Each time we speak, we do so from a certain *status-* or *role-position* — that of seller or buyer, parent or child, teacher or student, boss or employee, stranger or friend. And as our role-positions change, so also do our attitudes toward the persons we are addressing. We talk in one way to individuals we know well and in quite a different way to casual acquaintances or strangers. Similarly, our speaking manner changes as we communicate with those who stand above or below us in a social or professional hierarchy. Most students, for example, contest the opinions of other students more vigorously than they contest the opinions of a professor whom they respect.

How we regard the person or persons we are talking to also influences our speaking behavior in other subtle but unmistakable ways. Admiration or contempt, sympathy or indifference, love or hatred, patience or impatience, approval or annoyance are mirrored not only in the tone and inflectional patterns of the voice, but also in facial expression, muscle tension, and bodily posture. Although we may for a time dissemble or conceal these states of mind, sooner or later listeners usually are able to read the telltale signs we are attempting to hide.

Attitude Toward Subject.   Finally, our behavior as speakers is influenced by our attitude toward the subject we are discussing. Whether we regard it as interesting or boring, pertinent or irrelevant, crucial or trivial, whether we believe or disbelieve what we are saying, our attitude colors and conditions the ideas we present and the language in which we express them. Our attitudes toward our subject are reflected in the same subtle cues of voice and body behavior that disclose our attitudes toward ourselves and our listeners.

The Speaker's Credibility.   Whenever we speak, our success in winning agreement, inspiring confidence, or promoting action depends in large measure upon the listeners' estimate of our worth and competence. Knowledge of the subject matter, though important, is not the only factor on which personal effectiveness in speaking depends. If we wish to have our ideas believed or our proposals endorsed, we must possess qualities which audiences perceive as *reputation, character, competence, trustworthiness, dynamism, sociability* or *friendliness,* and *sincerity.* These are important dimensions of *credibility* and strongly determine the degree to which audiences accept what the speaker says.*

Speakers who are known to be unreliable, whose personalities are drab, or whose motives are suspect have little hope of winning adherents. On the other hand, speakers who are known to be of good character, who have warm and colorful personalities, who are alert and energetic, and who seem to be genuinely interested in the well-being of their listeners are more readily attended to and believed.

The Message

Whenever we speak, the messages we transmit are made up of the same three variables of content, structure, and style.

Content. It is self-evident that the messages which we transmit to listeners have a content — are about something we want them to be aware of. What we say may take the form of an assertion, a question, or an exclamation; it may report an observation, express a feeling, or prescribe a course of action; it may or may not be accompanied by visual or auditory cues that enhance our meaning. In every case, however, the message has a thought-content or subject matter.

Structure. Often less evident is the fact that all messages have a structure. Any message we transmit, whether a single sentence or many, whether long or short, simple or complex, is of necessity structured or organized in some way. Its structure may be dictated by the nature of the ideas themselves or may, as in the case of the marriage ceremony or pledge of allegiance, be imposed by a socially or institutionally approved formula. The structure may be direct or circuitous, loose or compact, clear or confusing, progressive or redundant. It may, at one extreme, entail no more than the ordering of a few sentences, or — at the other — require the strategic structuring of large-scale units of thought. But because we can express only one idea at a time, we inevitably give every message a certain sequence or structure.

---

*Useful discussions of *source credibility* and the role it plays in successful speaking may be found in Frederick P. Hart, Gustav W. Friedrich, and William Brooks, *Public Communication* (New York: Harper & Row, Publishers, 1975), pp. 87–110; James C. McCroskey, Carl E. Larson, and Mark L. Knapp, *An Introduction to Interpersonal Communication* (Englewood Cliffs, N.J.: Prentice-Hall, Inc., 1971), pp. 78–92; Herbert W. Simons, *Persuasion: Understanding, Practice, and Analysis* (Reading, Mass.: Addison-Wesley Publishing Company, Inc., 1976), pp. 108–129, 160–166. Research on the subject is summarized in Stephen W. Littlejohn, "A Bibliography of Studies Related to Variables of Source Credibility," *Bibliographic Annual in Speech Communication; Volume II, 1971 Annual,* ed. Ned A. Shearer (New York: Speech Communication Association, 1972), pp. 1–40.

Style. The third variable in every spoken message is style. Although language is not the only medium which speech communication employs, it is a very important one. When we communicate solely by gestures or other visual, nonvocal, or nonverbal means, we are said to be employing sign language. But insofar as language is involved, just as we make choices in the selection and arrangement of units of thought, so also we make choices in the selection and arrangement of words or symbols to express those thoughts. Depending on the choices we make, our style may be plain or ornate, smooth or awkward, rhythmical or jumpy, pleasing or irritating. In communicating ideas through the use of words, however, we always must choose and arrange them in one way rather than another.

The Listener

How listeners will respond to a message varies according to (1) their purpose in listening; (2) their knowledge of and interest in the subject; (3) their listening skills; and (4) their attitudes toward themselves, the speaker, and the speaker's message.

The Listener's Purpose. Whenever we listen, we do so in order to achieve some purpose or satisfy some desire. We do not listen—really listen—to anybody or anything unless we have a purpose. As listeners, no less than as speakers, we seek rewards of some kind. We may listen to be amused, to be informed, to be persuaded, or to be moved to action. When in Chapter 6 we examine human needs and motives, we will see that both listeners and speakers are influenced by the same physical needs and psychological priorities. By this, we do not mean to imply that the purposes of listeners and speakers always are identical. Rather, we wish merely to emphasize here that listener purpose—like speaker purpose—is an indispensable element in the making of speech communication transactions.

The Listener's Knowledge of the Subject and Command of Listening Skills. Whenever we listen, our knowledge of and interest in the speaker's subject and our skill in listening influence our reception of the message and the way in which we respond to it. Whether we find a speaker's ideas easy or difficult to understand depends in part upon how much we already know about the subject. Whether we find the ideas interesting depends, in part, upon our ability to associate and relate these ideas with information or experiences we have previously acquired. When we already have some knowledge of and interest in the subject matter or when that subject touches upon other subjects important to us, our task as listeners is easier; in proportion as these elements are lacking, it becomes more difficult. Indeed, at times our previous knowledge of a subject may be so deficient that we are unable to receive the speaker's message, much less respond to it intelligently.

Listening skills are not inborn or "automatic"; they must be cultivated, consciously refined, and practiced. As you are doubtless aware, people differ considerably in their skill as listeners.[4] Some of us are able to follow the speaker's ideas more easily than others; some of us are quicker to catch errors in inference or to note deficiencies in evidence. The important point to note here is that listening skills do differ considerably from person to person and are, therefore, a significant variable in shaping and conditioning all kinds of speech transactions.

The Listener's Attitudes.   Whenever we listen, our attitudes toward our self, the speaker, and the subject affect what we hear, how we interpret it, and how we respond. We have said that our behavior as a speaker in sending a message is influenced by our attitudes toward our self, our subject, and the other person or persons involved in the speech transaction. These same factors influence how we respond as listeners to a message. If as listeners we have little confidence in our own judgments, we tend to be swayed more easily than those whose self-esteem is higher. Also, as listeners we tend to be more readily influenced by views which confirm our own opinions and values. More often than not, we deliberately seek out speakers whose positions we already agree with, and retain longer those ideas of which we approve. The relationship between speaker and listener is, therefore, not one-dimensional, but reciprocal or bi-directional. This is why listeners' purposes, knowledge of the subject, listening skills, and attitudes toward themselves and the speaker and the subject must always be regarded as essential influences upon the speech transaction.

The Channel

All speech communication is affected by the channel over which the speaker's message is transmitted. For our purposes, a channel may be defined as the pathway over which a message travels in reaching its destination. When the participants in a communication interchange meet face to face, they usually employ two channels: the *aural* and the *visual*. That is, the message is communicated in part by what is said (the aural channel) and in part by what is shown by gestures, facial expression, posture, etc. (the visual channel). When the speaker cannot be seen (as in sending messages by radio or telephone), the vocal mechanism alone must do the work it normally shares with the rest of the body. A "clear" channel is one relatively free of obtrusive sights and sounds — anything that might block or interfere with the free flow of the message to or from a destination. When such blockage or interference is present, the channel is said to be "noisy." The fact that a channel may be either "clear" or "noisy" requires that appropriate adjustments be made in the message. If the channel is free of noise in the form of physical or psychological distractions, the volume or loudness of the voice may remain at its usual level, and ideas may need to be stated only once. When, on the other hand, distractions and noise interfere with the free flow of the message through the channel, vocal volume must be raised, sounds articulated more sharply, and ideas repeated or given more than the customary amount of elaboration.

The Communicative Situation

All speech communication is affected by the physical setting and social context in which it occurs.

Physical Setting. Listeners' anticipations or expectancies, as well as their readiness to respond, are influenced by the physical setting in which the speech communication process occurs. Persons waiting in the quiet solemnity of a great cathedral for the service to begin have quite a different expectation than do theatergoers gathered to witness the opening of a new musical revue. Similarly, listeners at an open-air political rally have a different expectation than they would have if they were about to hear a scholarly lecture on political theory. The furniture and decor of the room in which speaker and listeners find themselves also make a difference. Words of love are best spoken in secluded, intimate settings, in soft light, or before an open fire. Comfortable chairs and pleasant surroundings tend to put the members of a discussion group at ease. The executive who summons an employee to an impressively furnished office with the title "President" on the door gains a natural advantage not only because of a superior position in the corporate hierarchy, but also because of the setting in which the conversation occurs.

Social Context. Even more important than physical setting in determining how a message will be received is the social context in which it is presented. Custom and good manners often decree the kind of message and the style of presentation that are appropriate. At many social events, for example, to engage in "shop talk" or to dwell on a subject that is of interest to only a few of those present is considered poor taste. Committee meetings frequently are opened with a few moments of general conversation of a personal or incidental nature. Memorial services and award dinners are not considered proper places at which to launch attacks upon a political opponent or to engage in discussions of abstract philosophical questions.

Social context also decrees that there be a difference between what people consider appropriate to say in private or in the company of a few close friends and what is acceptable when talking to strangers or addressing a large audience. This, of course, is not to suggest that the rules of custom and good manners are never violated. What is important is the extent to which these sociocultural constraints usually influence the content of the messages speakers send, the manner in which such messages are transmitted, and the feelings of uneasiness or disapproval which departures from them may arouse.

Besides influencing the structure and content of messages transmitted by speakers, social context also is influential in determining how these messages will be received by listeners. Messages that win the evident approval of respected individuals sitting or standing near a listener are more likely to win the approval of that listener also. Persons standing or sitting elbow to elbow tend to react as a unit; a handful of listeners scattered at random throughout a large auditorium show less uniformity of response. Facts reported or opinions expressed at a party often are taken less seriously than the same facts or opinions stated at a congressional hearing or as part of a formal lecture. Advice offered in moments of crisis may be endorsed more readily than the same advice offered under less pressing circumstances.

The overt responses that individuals make as they listen to a message likewise vary from situation to situation. Persons who listen patiently and without discernible objection to a long speech or lecture with which they thoroughly disagree may be among the first to register their disapproval in a business or social conversation. At a political rally, vigorous applause or shouted approval of the speaker's ideas is expected; at a church service, such overt forms of response generally are avoided. In these and similar ways, the behavior of listeners, no less than that of speakers, is conditioned by the physical, psychological, and sociocultural circumstances surrounding the speech transaction.

Interaction of the Speech Communication Elements

All speech communication entails a complex pattern of interaction among the communication elements: speaker, message, listener, channel, and situation. These five factors or elements are, as we have emphasized, basic to the speech communication transaction regardless of the form that it takes. In describing these factors, we have suggested that there is a continuous interplay among them — an influencing and counter-influencing, a shaping and reshaping. To further an understanding of these cross-currents of influence, let us now look more closely at this matter of interaction.

Because it is affected not only by forces playing upon it from without, but also by an interaction among the elements of which it is composed, any speech transaction is an extremely complex phenomenon. The personality, values, and aims of the speaker, together with the physical surroundings and social context in which the transaction occurs and the channel over which it is transmitted, influence the content, structure, and style of the message. The message as thus framed and communicated alters or fails to alter the listeners' knowledge, beliefs, or behavior, and changes or confirms their attitudes toward the speaker and the message. The listeners' responses, as fed back to the speaker during the course of the interchange, influence the way in which subsequent portions of the message will be presented. But besides influencing the content of the message transmitted, the physical and social contexts influence the language or style in which the content is couched and how the speaker's ideas will be received by the listener. The aural and/or visual channels, in turn, limit the kind of message that can be transmitted, determine the range of auditory and visual stimuli which the speaker may utilize, and affect the listeners' expectations and patterns of response.

Numerous and intricate as they are in themselves, these patterns of interaction are rendered still more complex by the fact that an act of speech communication, while in itself a discrete unit of thought or action bounded by a definite beginning and ending, has antecedents that stretch into the indefinite past and consequences that reach into the indefinite future. What the speaker says and how he or she chooses to say it are influenced both by the demands of the immediate speaking situation, and also by the accumulation of many years of personal growth and conditioning—years in which knowledge has been acquired, judgments formed, attitudes toward other persons shaped, and speech skills and habits learned. The knowledge and attitudes which listeners bring to the speech encounter likewise are the result of a long process of conditioning. Even the structure that a message takes and the channel over which it may appropriately be transmitted have histories that influence both its content and the manner in which it is presented. Sermons, for example, have for centuries opened with a reference to a Biblical text and then proceeded to an explanation of the text's significance or a hortatory appeal based upon the ideas it contains. In social introductions younger persons are presented to older ones and men to women. Whenever possible, news of the death or serious injury of a loved one is communicated to closely concerned individuals in a face-to-face meeting rather than over the telephone.

In sum, no speech transaction is an isolated event. It is heavily conditioned (1) by outside forces operative at the time the transaction occurs, (2) by the past experiences of the communicators—experiences extending back into their life histories almost from the moment of birth, (3) by what follows the communicative interchange, (4) by the way other persons visible to the speaker and listener are reacting during the communication, etc. Viewed thus, a communication transaction is merely a moment in an ongoing process, a single, discrete occurrence within a total universe of experience. It is embedded in a situation that affects the expectancies of those who hear it, and is in many instances governed by a convention or custom of long standing.

A Communication Transaction: A Detailed Model

Now that we have examined in some detail the basic elements and relationships involved in a communicative transaction, let us review them by considering a more detailed version of our earlier model:

Figure 2./ THE SPEECH COMMUNICATION TRANSACTION:
A More Fully Developed Model.

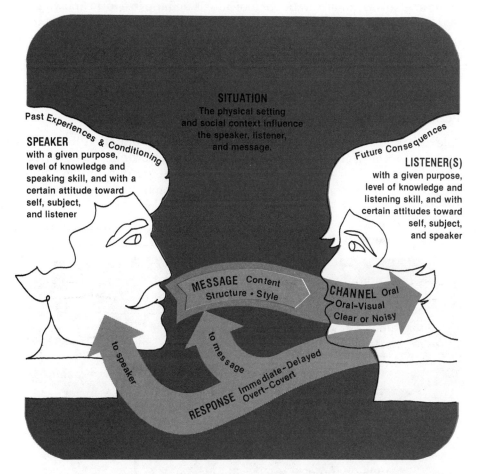

A SPEAKER, influenced by past conditioning, present SITUATION, communicative purpose, level of knowledge and speaking skill, and attitudes toward self, subject, and
listener(s), transmits a MESSAGE which has content, structure, and style, over a CHAN-
NEL which limits or shapes the messages to one or more LISTENER(S) whose reception of
the message is, in turn, influenced by conditioning, purpose, situation, and attitudes
toward self, subject, and speaker. The LISTENER(S) responds to the speaker and message
with cues that cause the speaker to modify subsequent portions of the message or to
alter his or her verbal or nonverbal behavior. Insofar as a communication transaction affects the beliefs or behaviors of speaker or listener(s), it has consequences for their future
thought and action.

The Basic Forms of Speech Communication

As we suggested earlier, the communication encounters of daily life fall
into three major forms or classes. Some involve only two persons who,
alternately assuming the role of speaker or listener, exchange ideas

about a subject of mutual interest. This form of encounter is generally referred to as *interpersonal* or *dyadic communication.* On other occasions a relatively small number of individuals engage in a form known as *small group communication* to discuss a matter of common concern in a more or less informal manner. On still other occasions a single individual presents a speech to an audience of some size or complexity in a form known as *public communication.* (See diagrams below and at right.)

Public Communication: The Focus of This Book

A textbook in which all three forms were given the attention they deserve, however, would be of inordinate length and probably would not be a very effective teaching instrument. For these reasons, in this book we propose to concentrate mainly on public communication. Consider-

Figure 3./ COMMUNICATING WITH ANOTHER PERSON

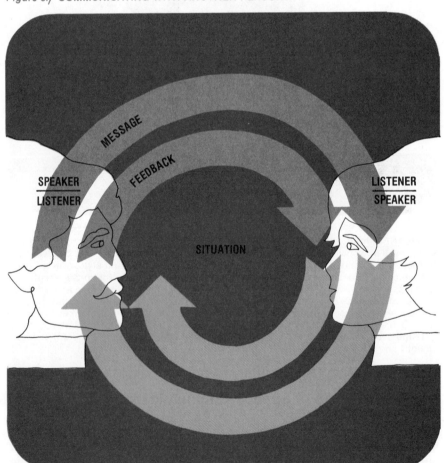

Figure 4./ COMMUNICATING IN A SMALL GROUP

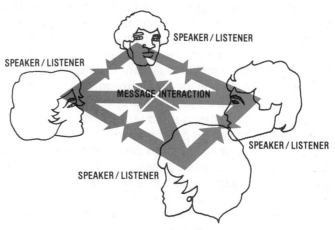

Figure 5./ COMMUNICATING IN PUBLIC

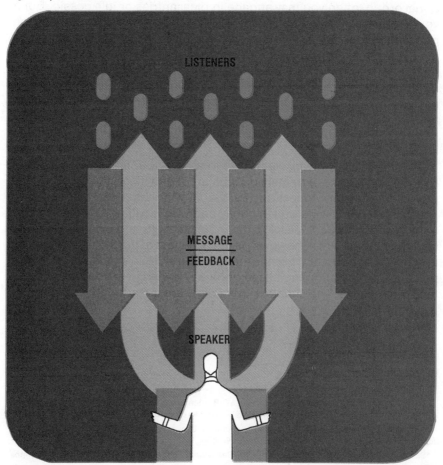

ations of length and efficiency are not, however, the sole reasons we have chosen this focus. A public communicator characteristically is called upon to transmit to a comparatively large number of listeners a continuous and uninterrupted message or discourse lasting from a few minutes to an hour or more. This creates problems in selecting and organizing materials and in maintaining listener interest that normally are not present in dyadic or small-group communication. Moreover, for most persons formal speechmaking is a relatively new or unfamiliar activity, and for this reason often tends to be viewed by the potential public speaker with some apprehension. Most important, however, communicating in the public situation deserves special consideration because it places upon the speaker a measure of responsibility that interpersonal and group transactions do not always carry. And this is to present within a relatively broad framework and in patterns that are readily understandable information and ideas that are of genuine significance to an audience having diverse backgrounds and varying emotional and intellectual states of mind.

When you speak to another individual or as a member of a conversational group, often you may engage in pleasantries or idle gossip. But if you speak to an audience of fifty people for a period of as little as ten minutes, you consume five hundred minutes of the world's collective time. If a speech lasts for an hour and you present it to an audience of a thousand, that audience will spend ten thousand hours or well over four hundred full days of the world's time listening to you. Obviously, under such circumstances, you have a responsibility to offer more than pleasantries. You must set forth fresh ideas and relevant information worth listening to, and you must do it in such a way that they may be grasped and remembered.

All this does not mean, we hasten to assure you, that speaking effectively in public is an extremely difficult art or one that only a few persons are able to master. Almost any individual who has a genuine desire to speak interestingly and well in public and who is willing to work systematically at the task can develop the requisite skills and proficiency to do so. What it does mean, however, is that for most of us to gain proficiency as a public speaker and master the required skills, we must follow a systematic course of training based upon a knowledge of sound and time-tested principles. The chapters that follow are intended to provide such a course.

Reference Notes

[1]Text from poster courtesy of Steffen & Gaines, Inc.

[2]From "Beyond the Campus Gate" by Waldo W. Braden, from *Vital Speeches of the Day*, Volume XXXVI, July 1971. Reprinted by permission of Vital Speeches of the Day.

[3]George A. Borden, Richard B. Gregg, and Theodore G. Grove, *Speech Behavior and Human Interaction* (Englewood Cliffs, N.J.: Prentice-Hall, Inc., 1969), p. 101.

[4]See, in particular, Larry L. Barker, *Listening Behavior* (Englewood Cliffs, N.J.: Prentice-Hall, Inc., 1971).

Problems and Probes

1.   Identify and describe three speech transactions in which you personally participated during the past week. In at least two of these encounters, you should have been the speaker initiating the interaction. Formulate answers to the following questions:

  a.   In which of the three situations — person-to-person, small group, or public communication — did each of these three transactions take place?
  b.   What channel or channels did you use?
  c.   What was your communicative purpose in each case?
  d.   To what extent do you feel you accomplished your communicative purpose in each transaction? Why?
  e.   What was the extent of your message-preparation in each of the three instances? If preparation was more mandatory and/or more extensive for one situation than for others, explain why this was so.
  f.   Show how, in one of these transactions, the physical setting probably influenced what happened. In another, explain how the social context tended to affect the outcome.

2.   Select at least two speech transactions which you observed, but in which you did not yourself participate. Evaluate these transactions, showing *(a)* how the speaker's knowledge (or lack of knowledge) of the subject affected the accomplishment of his or her purpose, and *(b)* how the speaker's skill (or lack of skill) in vocal and bodily communication influenced the transaction.

3.   In a notebook set aside for the purpose, start a Personal Speech Journal. The contents will be seen only by you and your instructor, who will call for the journal at intervals during the term. After thoughtful analysis, prepare an inventory of your personal speech needs and your abilities as a speaker. Include an evaluation of your past experience in individual and group situations. Outline your personal goals and desires for the course.

Oral Activities and Speaking Assignments

1.   Participate actively in a general class consideration of the subject "Things That I Like (Dislike) in a Speaker." As you and the other members of the class mention your likes and dislikes, your instructor may want to list them in two columns on a chalkboard. At the conclusion of this oral consideration, help your instructor summarize by formulating a composite picture or list of those speaker traits or qualities to which the majority of the class members would respond favorably and those traits or qualities to which the majority would respond unfavorably. Finally, if you (as a class — collectively) find many traits or qualities which you cannot classify in some absolute manner, ask yourself why. Are there variables within situations or contexts, within our perceptions of "proper" social roles, etc., which make absolute categorization impossible? What are some of these variables?

2.   Working in pairs, present pertinent biographical information about yourself to another member of the class. This person, in turn, will prepare a short speech introducing you to the group. You, of course, will do likewise for the student with whom you are paired. When these speeches have been completed, draw up a composite picture of the audience to whom you will be speaking during the remainder of the term.

Suggestions for Further Reading

A. Craig Baird, Franklin H. Knower, and Samuel L. Becker, *Essentials of Speech Communication,* 4th ed. (New York: McGraw-Hill Book Company, 1973),

Chapter 1, "Your Communication Environment"; Chapter 2, "You the Communicator: A Complex of Roles."

Theodore Clevenger, Jr., and Jack Matthews, *The Speech Communication Process* (Glenview, Ill.: Scott, Foresman and Company, 1971).

Gerhard J. Hanneman and William J. McEwen, eds., *Communication and Behavior* (Reading, Mass.: Addison-Wesley Publishing Company, Inc., 1975), Chapter 1, David K. Berlo, "The Context of Communication"; Chapter 2, Gerhard J. Hanneman, "The Study of Human Communication."

C. David Mortensen, *Communication: The Study of Human Interaction* (New York: McGraw-Hill Book Company, 1972), Chapter 2, "Communication Models."

Thomas M. Scheidel, *Speech Communication and Human Interaction,* 2nd ed. (Glenview, Ill.: Scott, Foresman and Company, 1976), Chapter 1, "The Speech Communication Process."

Anita Taylor, Arthur C. Meyer, and B. Thomas Samples, *Communicating* (Englewood Cliffs, N.J.: Prentice-Hall, Inc., 1976), Chapter 1, "Relating to Your World: The Communication Process."

2

Listening: Speaker-Audience Interaction

Too often we assume that the speaker bears the major, if not the entire, responsibility for effective oral communication. But, as we stressed in Chapter 1, speech communication is a two-way transaction between speaker and listener, not a one-way oral bombardment by speaker on listener. Without good listeners and good listening, there can be no feedback; and without feedback, speakers would be compelled to voice their messages aimlessly and to no purpose. Therefore, when you find yourself in the role of listener (as you very often do), you have to know how to listen and what to listen for; when you find yourself in the role of speaker, you have to know what facilitates and what impedes effective listening and prepare your messages accordingly. Thus what we have to say in this chapter about the process and skills of listening is applicable more or less equally to the public speaker and the public listener—since you cannot communicate fully and transact meaningfully without being both.

Listening Versus Hearing

In a given day, more than 40 percent of the time the average adult spends in communicative activity is spent in listening. In fact, an estimated 85 percent of all learning takes place aurally.* Among all of the stimuli which the human body receives from its environment, those received by ear are second in volume and complexity only to those ab-

---

*See studies reviewed in Larry L. Barker, *Listening Behavior* (Englewood Cliffs, N.J.: Prentice-Hall, Inc., 1971), pp. 3–4.

sorbed by the eye. To understand the significance of this in terms of oral communication, we need to consider briefly the kinds of mechanisms with which we receive and process information aurally.

Hearing is a physiological process whereby sound waves are transformed into auditory nerve impulses. These nerve impulses, in turn, travel through both the voluntary and involuntary nervous systems. The voluntary nervous system (the central nervous system or CNS) processes messages directed to the primary level of hearing—the messages that you "think about," absorb, sift through, interpret, store, or forget. The involuntary nervous system (the autonomic nervous system or ANS) works with aural stimuli on the tertiary level of hearing. Thus, when you hear a gunshot at close range, you do not say to yourself: "That is a loud sound in my right ear; it is scaring me, and I'm going to jump." You simply jump, perhaps with a scream added for good measure. On the tertiary level of hearing, you respond to aural stimuli reflexively, via involuntary nerve centers in the hindbrain or spinal column. In between these two levels is the secondary level of hearing, which seems to be controlled through a sophisticated interaction between the voluntary and involuntary nervous systems. Consider, for example, the background music played at your doctor's or dentist's office. You know, of course, that the music is present with all of its soothing strings and mellow trombones. But only occasionally do you really think about what is playing, for such music purposely avoids stimuli strong enough to make it stand out. It is there to settle nerves, not raise adrenalin levels. You hear such music only half-consciously or intermittently.

These distinctions among the primary, secondary, and tertiary levels of hearing are important in themselves, for they provide a basis for diagnosing the audiological and neurological problems which can beset hearing. In this book, however, we are concerned with the distinctions because they can help us understand "listening," which is the psychological counterpart of the physiological process referred to as hearing.

Listening is a complex psychological operation by which the bits and pieces of coded symbols and signals perceived by the central nervous

Figure 1./ THE THREE LEVELS OF HEARING

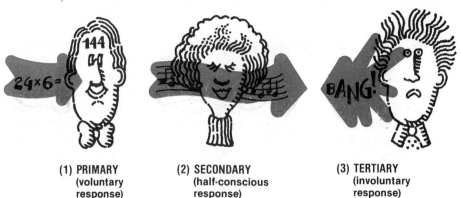

| (1) PRIMARY (voluntary response) | (2) SECONDARY (half-conscious response) | (3) TERTIARY (involuntary response) |

system and the autonomic nervous system are converted into comprehensible messages. Note, however, that these bits and pieces are not those carried exclusively by words and sentences. A rasping voice, a vigorous gesture, tenseness of the facial muscles, a body stiff and slightly bent forward—all such stimuli are processed by your mind to produce the possible message: "This speaker is talking about Subject X and is very serious in his accusations." Thus listening, while principally an aural event, can involve almost all of your senses. It is, in short, *the whole interpretive process whereby your body makes sense out of communicative stimuli.* How, then, do we go about listening? And, more importantly, why do we listen closely at one time, but only intermittently at another?

How We Listen

The answer to the first of these questions involves the parallels between hearing and listening suggested earlier. That is, just as you hear on three different levels, so also you can listen on at least three different levels. At times, you may listen with full discrimination. That is, you fully concentrate your sensory equipment upon as many of the auditory, visual, olfactory, and even tactile stimuli as you can in order to understand what a speaker is saying. Listening with full discrimination, however, is very tiring. No matter how much you may wish to hang on someone's every word and gesture, you usually find that you cannot do so. Your body tires, and your mind demands rest. At other times, you listen without discrimination, a communicative activity which is analogous to the secondary level of hearing. You simply let the stimuli emanating from the speaker's utterances and movements "wash over" you without making any serious attempt to sort through every word, syllable, and gesture and translate them into messages. Very probably you often listen to music in this way, for instance, or occasionally listen to a verbal message without discriminating sharply among ideas or subpoints.

Most of the time, however, you listen with partial discrimination. That is, you normally tune in and out of messages. For one thing, you have little choice because your physiological hearing equipment is not perfectly efficient. Scientists estimate that the human organism, unless it is in a state of hypnotic trance, must break concentration or focus every two to five seconds.[1] Your electrical circuits, it appears, cannot tolerate neurological stimulation for periods longer than that. Hearing, therefore, is intermittent and partial—and so, consequently, is listening. At each physiological breakpoint, the temptation to listen to something else—to other sounds in the room or other thoughts floating around in your mind—is almost overwhelming. What Wayne Minnick has termed your *internal and external perceptual fields* come into play each time you try to listen, as other stimuli (external) and other thoughts (internal) compete with the speaker and message to draw your attention.[2] These perceptual fields and the roles they play are suggested in Figure 2.

Figure 2./ THE PERCEPTUAL FIELDS OF THE LISTENER

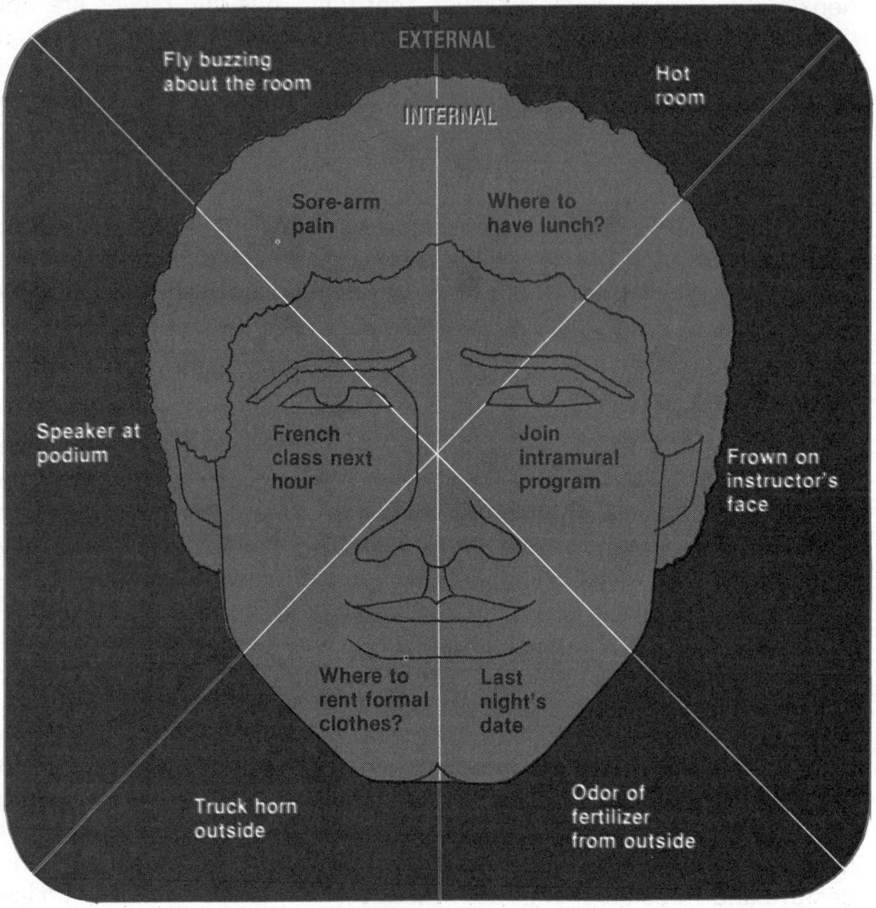

Competing demands upon our attention guarantee that you and I usually listen with only partial discrimination. That is, we literally hear and symbolically process only part of a given speaker's message. Listening with full discrimination occurs rarely.

Remember, then, that hearing—the physiological apprehension of aural stimuli—and listening—its psychological counterpart—are both highly complex processes which seem to guarantee that you seldom, if ever, will absorb, retain, and ultimately remember a speaker's message in all of its fullness and detail. As a result, you must work extremely hard at listening. It is difficult work, demanding concentration and a knowledge of listening techniques. However, as an almost constant consumer of oral messages, you should practice such techniques diligently, no matter how difficult, until you are an accomplished listener. You are constantly caught up in public and private communicative activities, and you must learn to listen in order to survive.

Why We Listen

The listening techniques you should practice will vary with your reasons for listening. Sometimes, you listen for enjoyment, sometimes for understanding or comprehension, and sometimes for evaluation.

Listening for Enjoyment

Of these three main reasons, listening for *enjoyment* usually is the easiest goal to achieve. Sometimes, during an after-dinner speech or a television monologue, you recognize that a speaker wants merely to entertain you, and you want to be entertained. So you listen because it is pleasurable to do so. Or, again, you may simply appreciate special or unusual speaking skills—listening to a William F. Buckley, Jr., use the English language or a Martin Luther King, Sr., rhythmically beat out English syntax. Listening for enjoyment, in other words, occurs when you desire or expect an aural experience to be entertaining, exciting, humorous, or otherwise pleasurable and a speaker tries to provide you with it. Listening for enjoyment also occurs when you find yourself fascinated, amused, or a bit bedazzled by, say, the verbal agility, the nonverbal expertise, or the overall communicative skills of a particular speaker. At such times, whether it is the substance of the speech or the skills of the speaker which attract you, you make a mental contract with yourself and with the speaker to relax, sit back, and enjoy the oral performance.

"Sit back and enjoy," indeed, is the key phrase because in listening for enjoyment, your body and your mind lose some of their tension and acuity. Some—but not all. You must remain alert. Often the content material of the enjoyable speech—be it the build-up of humor, the suspenseful yarn, or something else—will require that you make at least some small commitments of "intellectualized" energy. The full appreciation of a speaker's communicative skills will exact a measure of your concentration. A good listener does not completely sag into a blob or fully turn off all critical faculties. Listening for enjoyment involves at least partial and occasionally almost full discrimination. But the concentration you exercise when listening for enjoyment is focused on the immediate present, the here-and-now, and is unlike the other kinds of listening that we shall discuss in a moment—listening that demands that you constantly review what has been said and continuously anticipate what will come next. When you are listening for enjoyment, these few "rules" should prove rewarding:

1. *Relax physically and mentally.* Sit in a comfortable, relaxed position. Insofar as possible, empty your internal perceptual field of worries and other interests, giving yourself completely to the humor and other diverting materials presented by the speaker.

2. *Cultivate a receptive attitude.* In the case of a speech to entertain, this means engendering feelings of friendship and warmth toward the other listeners and the speaker. Also try to anticipate the pleasure which you believe will characterize the event; for this will, in turn, usually increase your actual enjoyment. When listening to enjoy the performance of the speech as much as, if not more than, its substance, maintain an alert, receptive attitude—a purposive concentration upon the speaker's sounds, rhythms, pitch, tone, gestures, movements, etc.

3. *Use imagination and empathy.* When trying to appreciate either the entertainment values of the material or the techniques of the speaker, allow your mind to enter into the occasion unfettered. Visualize the stories told, "feel" the gestures that are made, or bounce along with the assonance and alliteration of the linguistically accomplished speaker.

4. *Critically examine your own reactions after you have heard the speech.* Even though you may have spent an evening listening simply for enjoyment, you may want to mentally review the communicative event. What did you laugh at? Which of the speaker's verbal or nonverbal skills did you particularly appreciate? Could you imagine yourself using language with similar facility and effect? Such questions, if answered, will give you insight into your own psychological workings, and will help you formulate your own standards for communicative excellence.

Listening for Understanding

Listening for understanding or comprehension is a much more difficult task than listening for enjoyment. Listening for understanding requires a grasp of the speaker's central theme or message, a feeling for its overall structure, an ordering of the subsidiary notions, an identification of the kinds of supporting materials, a sense of what is most important and least important in the speech, and an assessment of how the speaker's ideas fit into your own beliefs, attitudes, and values.

Listening for understanding is more difficult also because you do not receive every stimulus the speaker sends. Listening for comprehension thus requires that you partially reconstruct the speaker's message from the bits and pieces—the mosaic—of ideas, sounds, images, etc., you have received. Gestalt psychologists term this process *completion* or *resolution.* If you see a series of short lines all equidistant from a central point, you mentally fill in the spaces to make a completed circle. If some one starts counting "1, 2, 3, 4, ..." you mentally continue the sequence, "5, 6, 7, 8 . . . ."[3] In a similar but more abstract way, you tend to complete oral messages. An illustration of how such completion works is shown in Figure 3 on page 27.

This inner drive for message completion is, in one sense, of great help to you as a listener. It ensures—almost automatically—that you will try

Figure 3./ THE PROCESS OF MESSAGE COMPLETION.

"Today, I want to talk... seriously... about this country... Journalism (journalism? My gosh! I have an examination next hour in Journalism!)... about political candidates around the country, states in counties and cities, telling us... political lies... about good issues and bad issues, rhetorically clever moves ... sophomores (is tonight the sophomore dance? should I ask her?) than candidates who stand for taxes, social security, jobs, inflation, and morals."
[Message for Person A: Some candidates tell us lies about anything, while others promise more taxes, inflation, and stuff. Obviously, there are no good politicians.]

"Today I want to talk with you about a serious problem facing this country: the problem of political journalism. I am disturbed that the journalists who follow political candidates around the country, around the states, around the counties, and around the cities spend more time telling us what the various candidates' statements mean *politically* (was it a good or a bad issue, a rhetorically clever move or a sophomoric tactic, good for your party or good for the opposition?) than what the candidates stand for in terms of taxes, social legislation, jobs, inflation, and public morality."

"Today I want to talk... about a serious problem —political journalism. I am disturbed that journalists... follow political candidates around the country... telling us what... the various candidates mean politically (what does that mean?)... than what their stands are on taxes ...legislation for the party or opposition (what does that mean?), inflation, publicity, morality."
[Message for Person B: Political journalists twist what politicians are saying so that we don't really know what they are standing for. I still am not sure what is being said here, but...]

Speaker

Person A

Person B

Person A, listening to the message, completes it by filling in the missing pieces in one way; and Person B, listening to the same message, completes it in quite another way. Neither has received the *actual* message, but at least Person B has picked up the gist, thanks to an acquired habit of listening to the key ideas and of resolving problems of incompleteness in ways consistent with the speaker's intent.

to fill in what you have missed or glossed over. It also, however, can be a detriment. If you are listening to a speaker discuss a topic familiar to you—for example, a college's grading policy—it is all too easy to complete the message imperfectly. That is, you may assume the speaker said something he or she did not say, or you may ignore a novel idea because it does not fit easily into your pre-established framework of ideas on the topic. When listening for understanding, therefore, to ensure accurate perception and reasonably full reception of messages, take the following precautionary steps:

1. *Identify the speaker's major or leading ideas, and concentrate closely on each as it is presented.* Unless you carefully identify each

major idea as it is stated, and separate it from its developmental material, you may fail to grasp the speaker's dominant thesis, as did Listener A in Figure 3. Don't listen for "just the facts," but constantly focus on the major ideas to which those facts are closely connected. Often, speakers will use phrases such as "My main point is . . . ," "Secondly, we find that . . . ," "To sum it all up . . . ," etc. Listen carefully for these and similar signals.

2. *Identify the dominant structure or arrangement of the major points.* Determine whether the speaker is organizing ideas chronologically, in terms of causes and effects, or is perhaps following a problem-solution pattern.* Not only will identification of the overall structure help you remember the speech, but it also will help you understand the direction and nature of the mental path through which the speaker wishes to lead you. When a speaker, for example, first tells you what happened in 1925, then in 1936, next in 1942, and finally in 1957, you are assisted in at least two important ways. Your recognition of this chronological pattern (1) helps you recall the dates; (2) helps you realize that the speaker probably is emphasizing cyclical events or is laying out the progressive development of ideas, institutions, or peoples because these matters are most often thrown into a chronological pattern. When listening to a speech, constantly look backward and think forward to make sure you understand where you have been and where you may be going.

3. *Examine critically the details used to develop and support the major ideas.* Supporting materials—statistics, illustrations, comparisons, etc.—help both to prove central theses and also to clarify major ideas. Look closely, therefore, at how the supporting data are being used. Does the speaker's use of a specific instance to illustrate an abstract notion significantly clarify the idea? Does the speaker's statistical analysis of current trends actually support the principal thesis? Or are the numbers thrown in merely to impress you? Is the quoted testimony of the authorities relevant to the problem and useful in comprehending it? By asking yourself such questions, you can appreciably increase your understanding of the idea and its place within the speech as a whole.

4. *Relate the speaker's major ideas to your own beliefs, attitudes, values, and behaviors.* Ask yourself why you are attempting to comprehend this message. Will the ideas be important to your life (or only to your ability to survive the next test in class)? Is this a speaker whose reputation and credibility are such as to make it worth your while to listen no matter what he or she may be saying? Is the occasion itself so memorable that it alone should color your recollections of the speech? In thus asking yourself what there is about this speech, this speaker, and this occasion that is important to you, you are search-

---

*For a full discussion of such alternate patterns of speech organization, see Chapter 10.

ing for a mental pigeonhole—or trash can if you want to forget this speech—in which to store this communicative experience.

Listening for understanding or comprehension, Socrates insisted, was a skill which would disappear with the spread of written language. Perhaps to some degree we have lost the skill to listen discerningly. However, in a day when the electronic, aural-visual media have become so powerful and pervasive and appear in many respects to be gaining ascendancy over the printed media, listening for comprehension does seem to be a skill much in demand again.

Listening for Evaluation

Evaluative listening represents the most sophisticated kind of listening you can engage in. Like listening for understanding, it demands that you mentally absorb, sift through, process, and file a message. *In addition,* however, you must attach a value, a judgment, a critical commentary to it. Thus your attention necessarily is split between the need to perceive and fully understand the communicative event itself and the need to make an evaluative reaction or a judgment of its comparative worth.

How you evaluate a speech, a speaker, and an occasion depends, again, upon why you want to evaluate them. Are you interested in the worth of the ideas? in the strength of the arguments offered? Do you wish to verify whether the speaker, purported to have certain qualities or abilities, demonstrates those abilities when addressing an audience? Or is it the occasion itself that calls for evaluation? Suppose, for example, you are interested in deciding (evaluating) for yourself whether the congressional seniority system is good or bad. You attend a public gathering likely to produce defenders and denigrators of the system, whose ideas you can listen to and evaluate. You might go to another meeting primarily to judge the personality and possible persuasiveness of a particular speaker, say, a colorful Common Cause lobbyist dedicated to denouncing deficiencies and inefficiences of the system. Or, you might decide to witness firsthand an occasion in which congressional seniority is operative—a hearing before the Senate Administrative Practices Committee. Evaluation of communication events thus can involve a variety of standards and viewpoints.*

When listening for evaluation—when trying to form fair and necessary judgments and affix comparative worth to ideas and messages, use the following questions to guide your efforts in productive directions:

1. *What seem to be the speaker's general and specific purposes?* Does the speaker seek to entertain you, to present information and

---

*We shall treat these standards and perspectives more fully in Appendix C, where we discuss the systematic evaluation of public speeches.

increase your understanding, to reinforce your existing beliefs and attitudes, to change your opinions, or to move you to overt action? To what degree is this purpose appropriate to this speaker, this audience, and this occasion? Does this speaker have a hidden agenda,* or at least an important personal gain which might be realized in this speech if this audience reacts as desired? Does this audience expect certain ideas or issues to be presented; and, if so, did those expectations guide the construction of this speech?

2. *How does the speaker arouse and maintain attention and interest?* Has this speaker relied upon such factors of attention as conflict, suspense, curiosity, action, novelty, and humor? Has he or she heightened your interest by using analogies, narration, vivid descriptions, contrasts, factual and hypothetical examples, and illustrations? Especially in a longer speech, is this speaker able to sustain and renew your attention and interest?

3. *Does the speaker try to guarantee that you the listener will understand the message clearly?* Has this speaker employed proper vocal emphasis and gestures, enough repetition and restatement, illustrations relevant to your experience, analogies which ensure clarification, needed definitions and explanations, an appropriate organizational pattern, carefully built transitions and summaries, visual or aural aids, and concrete language? Has this speaker used enough of these modes, materials, patterns, and devices and in the proper proportion so that the message you receive inside your head seems sufficiently similar to the message shaped and transmitted from inside the speaker's head?

4. *What do you perceive to be the speaker's attitudes toward you as a listener?* Are there vocal, physical, or verbal signs that this speaker is thinking more of himself or herself than of the central idea and the audience? What are these signs? Do you sense that this speaker is treating you and the rest of the audience with condescension? fear? contempt? love? respect?

5. *Do you perceive the speaker to be a credible source on this subject?* To what degree and in what ways do you find this speaker competent, trustworthy, sincere, expert, educated, informed, honest, friendly? Do the central ideas, organization of thoughts, choice of language, voice, gestures, and physical stance tend to strengthen or weaken your impression of his or her credibility?

6. *Do you view the speaker's proposals as reasonable?* Are the central ideas, the supporting materials, the reasoning, and the language in which these are phrased appropriate to the audience, the occasion, and the speaker? Are the proposals feasible, despite such potentially limiting factors as finances, time, or manpower?

---

*A hidden agenda is a covert purpose, covered or protected by an announced or overt purpose. The telephoner who tells you you are on a quiz program when he or she actually is trying to sell you a merchandising coupon book has a hidden agenda.

Listening . . .

whether engaged in primarily for
enjoyment, full comprehension, or
evaluation and even though an
intensely private and internal affair,
is ultrabasic to the accurate
reception of public messages and
meaningful feedback.

7. *Do you feel there is a convincing connection between the speaker's central idea or purpose and your own beliefs, attitudes, and values?* Besides being generally sound in substance, does the speech appeal directly to your so-called standards and tastes and (presumably) to those of the other listeners? Were you made to feel that you had a personal stake in the outcome? If so, what did the speaker do to make you feel that way?

8. *Can you discern important unstated assumptions in the speech?* What unspoken beliefs, attitudes, values, premises, stereotypes, etc., implicitly undergird the speaker's ideas and demand examination? (In searching for these assumptions, listen for such give-away phrases as "All upright Americans know . . . ," "The moral members of this audience . . . ," "Anyone can see . . . ," "Unquestionably . . . ," "Our forefathers . . . ," "What could be more natural than . . . ?" etc.) How do these assumptions reflect the speaker's conceptions of reality, truth, knowledge, goodness, and the essential nature of humankind as you define them? Do the assumptions hold up under close examination? Are they indicative of a particular school of thought or philosophy?

9. *In what ways does the speaker's language (style) contribute to clarity and persuasiveness?* Do the words used fall within the audience's vocabulary? Is the language lively, concrete, simple—but not simplistic? In what ways do the linguistic choices intensify your reaction as a listener? Do they add color and point? reflect the speaker's deep-seated concerns? arise out of the demands of the setting or occasion? Is any of the language, especially the phrasing of key notions, memorable—and, if so, in what way?

10. *Do the nonverbal messages sent by the speaker reinforce the verbal message, or do they stand in contrast to it?* Is this speaker's body saying something different from the words? (Often, a speaker will talk confidently, but physically show fear or lack of confidence; or the words will say "This is the truth," but the eyes will say "I am stretching the truth.") Do you tend to believe the words or the body? Why? Or, more positively, does this speaker use a good delivery—strong voice, well-timed gestures, an active body, and a communicative face—to reinforce key points in the verbal message?

11. *What function does the speech serve within the context of some larger campaign or movement?* Is this merely one communicative event among a series of others, both oral and written, verbal and visual, that collectively aim at accomplishing some attitudinal and/or behavioral change on a society-wide basis? If so, how does this message fit in with the messages that preceded it, and how will it, perhaps, fit with those that are likely to follow? What do you as a listener have to know about the campaign or movement as a whole in order to make sense out of this speech?

12. *Ultimately, what demands does this speech make upon you as a*

thinking, feeling human being? Assuming that this speaker's message has found in you a receptive heart and mind, what adjustments will you have to make? Will you have to change your mind about the speaker? Will you have to adjust certain beliefs, intensify or redirect certain attitudes, view your values in somewhat different ways, replace certain planks in your philosophy of life, and alter some of your behaviors accordingly? Are you strong enough to make these adjustments, whatever they are, without trauma or discomfort? In short, what are you going to do with and about this speech? In what specific ways will the speaker's message affect how you think, feel, and act?

This list of a dozen difficult-to-answer questions demonstrates the degree to which listening for evaluation is a major communicative undertaking. We all can listen with relatively little critical awareness when listening for pure enjoyment. But few of us can successfully listen for evaluation without hard and continued practice. Indeed, one of the principal contributions a course in speech communication may make to your real-life experience is the opportunity it provides to practice listening for evaluation in the relative security of a classroom. As you listen critically to speech after speech throughout the term, you will be honing critical listening techniques that might take years to sharpen outside of the classroom. Take full advantage, therefore, of this rare learning opportunity.

Listening from the Speaker's Perspective

Before leaving the subject of this chapter, let us return briefly to this book's principal concern—the speaker's role in public oral communication. That role, of course, significantly affects the public speaker's attitudes toward, responsibilities to, and relationships with public listeners. Conceivably, a sensitive speaker could draw one of two conclusions from the foregoing pages: (1) either a speaker can say anything he or she pleases because no one is listening too well anyhow; or (2) the careful builder of oral messages can do much to guide, even control, listeners' reception of messages. Actually, both conclusions carry some serious implications for the concerned speaker. Admittedly, your messages seldom, if ever, will get through to any audience in all of their completeness and complexity. The physiological-psychological processes of hearing-listening make it probable that you will be heard in fits and starts, a few words here, some partial thoughts there. But this does not mean that you can say anything you wish, for even with partial discrimination an audience can grasp an amazing amount of material. The silver-tongued orator who hopes that glibness and guile can frost over a host of half-formed ideas, errors, or lies more often than not is caught by alert members of the audience, and even upon occasion publicly exposed. On the contrary, the fact that an audience catches only snatches of a speech means that as a speaker you must always weigh carefully everything that you say. The very imperfection of the hearing-listening process places great demands upon the speaker desiring successful communication with an audience. The chapters which follow will focus more fully upon the nature of these demands, and will provide detailed advice on what to do about them.

Reference Notes

[1]From "Time Perception" by Herbert Woodrow from *Handbook of Experimental Psychology*, ed. S. S. Stevens. Copyright © 1951 John Wiley & Sons, Inc. Reprinted by permission of John Wiley & Sons, Inc.

[2]Adapted from *The Art of Persuasion* by Wayne C. Minnick. Copyright © 1957 by Houghton Mifflin Company. Reprinted by permission of Houghton Mifflin Company.

[3]Reprinted by permission of Hawthorn Books, Inc. from *Theories of Learning* by Ernest R. Hilgard, copyright © 1956 by Appleton-Century-Crofts. All rights reserved.

Problems and Probes

1.   In your journal, make an objective analysis of yourself as a listener: *(a)* Are you able to keep your own thoughts and prejudices from interfering with your reception of the speaker's message? *(b)* Do you listen for signposts the speaker sets up, for the main ideas and transitions around which the content of the talk is organized? *(c)* Are you able to subordinate supporting material so as to keep the speaker's dominant ideas clearly in mind? *(d)* Are you sensitive to the emotional overtones provided by specific kinds of phrasing? *(e)* Do you include reactions to delivery and voice in your overall judgment of the speaker? When you have answered these questions, prescribe for yourself methods by which you can improve your listening ability—methods drawn along the lines suggested in this chapter. With the assistance of your instructor, try to work out a day-by-day program which will help ensure your implementation and mastery of these methods.

2.   With several other members of the class, attend a speech or lecture. Attempt to determine individually *(a)* the speaker's purpose, *(b)* the major ideas of the speech, and *(c)* the types and adequacy of the supporting materials that are used. Compare your findings with those of others in the class. On what kinds of judgments is there unanimity of opinion? On which, divergence? Why?

3.   Attend the presentation of a public speech, and seat yourself where you can observe closely the reactions of various members of the audience as they listen to the speaker. Do some appear to listen intently throughout? Do others seem to allow their attention to wander and, if so, at what points in the speech? Does the speaker appear to react or adjust to such audience feedback? How? What kinds of physical cues or signs did you rely on in answering these questions? Do you as a speaker rely on similar cues when adjusting to the listeners' feedback?

4.   What, to your mind, is the importance of physical setting in good listening? How do you react to noises, uncomfortable temperatures in a room, seating which makes a view of the speaker difficult? Does the arrangement of chairs

(pews in church, circles of chairs in classrooms, across-the-desk seating for conferences) affect your listening habits? Do you listen in one manner when seated in front of a lecturer, in another when talking to a friend at a crowded party? Make some useful generalizations regarding the ways in which the speech situation affects the ease or efficiency with which you listen.

Oral Activities and Speaking Assignments

1.   As a check on listening abilities, participate in a class discussion on a highly controversial topic which generates strong disagreements among members of your class. Conduct the discussion with a single rule: Before anyone can speak, he or she must summarize — *to the satisfaction of the previous speaker* — what that speaker has said. As a result of the activity, what conclusions can you draw about: *(a)* people's ability to summarize accurately and satisfactorily, and *(b)* the manner in which good listening and feedback reduce the amount and intensity of disagreement?

2.   Participate in a general class discussion on the question "In what ways may aspects of the physical setting affect how listeners respond to a message?" Focus your attention on this question by considering the following examples:

> *(a)*   Delegates attending national political conventions are expected to vote on platforms, select major candidates, and charge themselves up for the hard work of vote-mongering. They meet in bars, hotel caucus rooms, committee rooms, and on the convention floor itself. They discuss candidates, issues, group and individual stands, and their chances for victory in the upcoming election; they listen to supportive, patriotic, actuative, and celebratory messages as they move from setting to setting, from intimate conversation to the mass hysteria of a floor demonstration.
>
> *(b)*   In a church, the congregation usually sits in pews facing the front; liturgical ceremonies are carried out on a raised platform, and a sermon or message is delivered from an elevated pulpit or lectern. The members of the congregation are surrounded on all sides by religious symbols, paintings, and/or icons; often they engage in songs, chants, and/or responsive readings.

As a group, attempt to arrive at generalizations about the effects of these settings on listening habits.

Suggestions for Further Reading

Larry L. Barker, *Listening Behavior* (Englewood Cliffs, N.J.: Prentice-Hall, Inc., 1971).

Linda Costigan Lederman, *New Dimensions: An Introduction to Human Communication* (Dubuque, Iowa: Wm. C. Brown Company, Publishers, 1977), Chapters 10 and 11, "The Receiver: As Listener" and "The Receiver: Listener Plus."

Charles M. Kelley, "Empathic Listening," in *Concepts in Communication,* ed. Jimmie D. Trent et al. (Boston: Allyn & Bacon, Inc., 1973), pp. 263–272.

Brent D. Peterson, Gerald M. Goldhaber, and R. Wayne Pace, *Communication Probes* (Chicago: Science Research Associates, Inc., 1974). "Your perceptions may be a prime obstacle to effective communication," pp. 24–34.

Carl Weaver, *Human Listening: Processes and Behavior* (Indianapolis: The Bobbs-Merrill Company, Inc., 1972).

Part 2

IDEAS SPEAK!

Self-confidence

Communicative skill

Integrity
Knowledge

Sensitivity to people
and situations

Willingness to
learn from others

ron bradford

Public Communication:
Preparation and Adaptation to the Audience

1. Achievement and Display
2. Acquisition and Saving
3. Adventure and Change
4. Companionship and Affiliation
5. Creativity
6. Curiosity
7. Deference
8. Dependence
9. Destruction
10. Endurance
11. Fear
12. Fighting and Aggression
13. Imitation and Conformity
14. Independence and Autonomy
15. Loyalty
16. Personal Enjoyment
17. Power, Authority, and Dominance
18. Pride
19. Reverence or Worship
20. Revulsion
21. Sexual Attraction
22. Sympathy and Generosity

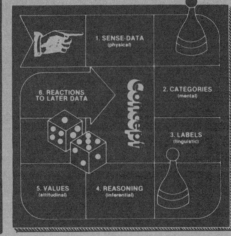

1. SENSE-DATA (physical)
2. CATEGORIES (mental)
3. LABELS (linguistic)
4. REASONING (inferential)
5. VALUES (attitudinal)
6. REACTIONS TO LATER DATA

Concept

Activity or movement
Realty
Proximity
Familiarity
Novelty
Humor
The vital
Suspense
Confli

3

The Public Communicator and the Speechmaking Process

In Chapter 1 we distinguished among three basic forms of speech trans-actions — *interpersonal, small group,* and *public* — and surveyed certain characteristics or properties common to all. In this chapter we begin to look more specifically at public communication, the kind of speech transaction we shall be concerned with throughout the remainder of this book. What properties set it apart from other forms of oral inter-change? What special problems or challenges does it present to the speaker? How should you go about preparing to speak in public? These are some of the matters to which we shall now direct attention.

The Public Communicator

In a sense, any utterance — whether heard by a single individual, by a few persons, or by many — may be said to be "public." As we shall here use the term, however, *public communication involves a single speaker who, employing a relatively formal tone or manner, presents a continu-ous discourse of some length to a sizeable number of listeners.* Under this definition, most popular and classroom lectures, political speeches, and church sermons may be regarded as public communications. So may the speeches made at professional and trade conventions, com-mencement exercises, sales meetings, dedication or memorial services, and remarks made at large dinners or banquets. Indeed, as we em-phasized in Chapter 1, almost every educated man or woman is likely to be called upon quite frequently to make a public speech of one kind or another.

Opportunities and Responsibilities

Because, in normal circumstances, the public communicator is able to present an uninterrupted message of some length to a sizeable number of listeners this not only spreads the message more widely, but also gives the speaker obvious advantages over persons speaking in interpersonal or group situations. In large measure, at least, the public speaker may plan in advance what to say and how to say it, and may thus deal with complex subjects in a systematic rather than piecemeal fashion. He or she may present in some detail and usually without interruption the evidence or documentation necessary to support a contention, and may do so at that point in the presentation when it will have maximum effect. Finally, except under unusual conditions, people who come to listen to a speech tend to have at least some advance interest in the subject and at least some respect for the knowledge or competence of the speaker.

At the same time, however, public communication also imposes challenges and responsibilities that other forms of oral communication usually do not — or at least not to such a high degree. Public speaking, as we are about to see, poses special problems in organizing ideas, maintaining interest, and adapting arguments to a variety of listener attitudes. Moreover, as we emphasized in Chapter 1, it places upon the speaker the responsibility of presenting ideas of genuine and lasting significance — of saying something that will reward the audience.

In the interpersonal and group situations, all of the participants share equally the responsibility for making a speech transaction interesting or productive. Each of the participants is, as a rule, not only expected to listen and understand, but also to contribute worthwhile ideas or aid in solving the problem at hand. In public communication, however, these responsibilities rest principally upon you as the speaker. You *alone* must produce and present the information or provide the insights necessary to make the speech interchange a worthwhile experience. For this reason, as a public speaker, more than as an interpersonal or group speaker, you assume a greater risk — the risk of not being able to supply the facts and ideas needed to make the transaction worth the time and effort of your listeners. It is this accentuated risk rather than the relative size of the audience involved that distinguishes public communication from most dyadic or one-to-one and small group communications.

Public communication, in short, is not characterized simply by external signs or appearances. While it is, by and large, characterized by the properties of audience size and composition that we have noted, it also entails internal or psychological factors that deserve special recognition and should be considered in their own right.

Characteristics and Competencies

Bearing in mind these opportunities and responsibilities of the public communicator, let us move on to consider the qualities you must possess or acquire if you are to fulfill this role effectively. Six, in particular, merit attention in this brief overview: (1) *integrity*, (2) *knowledge*, (3) *self-confidence*, (4) *communicative skill*, (5) *sensitivity to people and situations*, and (6) *a willingness to learn from others.*

Integrity. More than two thousand years ago, the Greek philosopher Aristotle emphasized a truth even then already old and widely recognized: *An effective speaker must be an effective person.** Success as a public speaker, he declared, involves more than a ready vocabulary, pleasing diction, and coordinated gestures. To succeed, you must, in addition, be intelligent, well informed about both the immediate subject and human affairs in general, and possess a high degree of poise and self-control. But above all, if your ideas are to be publicly accepted, you must be respected as a person of character and moral worth.

This emphasis upon character or *ethos* as an essential element in public speaking has been echoed by major writers on the subject from Aristotle's time to our own. People do not listen merely to a speech, but to a *person speaking.* Because a speaker's words and manner mirror what that person is, the *self* and the *expression of the self* can never be divorced. "What you are," maintains the ancient proverb, "speaks so loudly that I cannot hear what you *say.*" If you have a reputation for speaking the truth and for supporting your views with sound arguments, you will be listened to because people believe in your integrity. A speaker of poor character may win temporary success, but will soon become known as one who seeks unfair personal advantage or who warps or suppresses evidence to prove a case. Such a person will quickly lose the ability to convince or convert audiences to a cause. As we have earlier emphasized, your reputation for reliability and high motives is perhaps your single, most powerful means of exerting influence. Certainly it is one of the most important ingredients of any successful speech transaction.**

Knowledge. When Daniel Webster was asked how he was able to prepare his famous reply to Senator Robert Y. Hayne on such short notice, he said that the ideas had come to him like thunderbolts which he needed only to reach out and seize, white hot, as they went smoking by. This store of thunderbolts was no accident. Over many years Webster's constant study of law, literature, politics, and human nature had filled his mind with an abundant supply of facts, illustrations, and arguments at his instant command. Successful public communicators in all ages have had a similar arsenal upon which to draw.

If you would broaden your knowledge and enhance your understand-

---

*Aristotle, *Rhetoric*, 1356a.

**A fuller discussion of the role that personal integrity plays in successful public communication may be found in Otis M. Walter, *Speaking to Inform and Persuade* (New York: The Macmillan Company, 1966), Chapter 8, "The *Ethos* of the Speaker."

ing of the world and the ideas and values of people within it, you, too, must read widely and observe carefully. The background you already have, when carefully considered and supplemented by additional study, will provide sufficient material for your practice speeches. Selecting and organizing that material will help you marshal and clarify your thinking. Indeed, you will do well to begin in just this way—by talking about things that are vivid parts of your own personal experience. As you grow in skill and confidence, you will want to reach beyond immediate and familiar topics. You may wish to investigate and speak about ideas and developments relevant to your personal future—your job, your chosen career, or profession. Be careful also to acquire knowledge and develop interests *outside* your work, however. To become a well-rounded and interesting speaker, you must know about more than a single subject. Keep abreast of current happenings in your world, your country, your community by reading at least one responsible daily newspaper, listening frequently to reputable news broadcasts, and watching informed and well-documented telecasts. Cultivate a hobby. Widen your horizons. Take notes. Jot down your observations. Build up an easy-reference file of cartoons, clippings, and articles. In public speaking, as in any other activity, there is no substitute for knowledge that is thorough and varied.

Self-Confidence. So central is self-confidence to effective public speaking that, in a sense, much of what we say in this book is aimed toward developing or strengthening this valuable quality. Self-confidence is, of course, characterized by certain physical behaviors and mental attitudes. Usually, if you are a confident communicator, you will evidence—among other things—an erect but comfortable posture, easy movements free of fidgeting or jerkiness, direct eye contact with your listeners, vocal earnestness and energy, and an alertness which enables you to adapt your remarks readily to the nature of the audience and the demands of the occasion. Among the major enemies of self-confidence are self-consciousness and excessive nervousness. Here, briefly noted, are some steps you may take to reduce an undue consciousness of self and to strengthen your poise and self-control in the public situation:

1. *Realize that some tension or nervousness is natural.* If you feel tense when you arise to speak, you are no different from other people. Surveys have shown that from 60 to 75 percent of college students experience tension and nervousness when standing before an audience, and more than 30 percent consider it their most serious problem. Rather than regretting your nervousness, *use* it productively. Much of the sparkle and alertness we admire in good speakers comes from the controlled employment of the nervous energy the speaking situation generates. Instead of giving a dull and uptight speech, they dissipate their tensions through physical actions that vitalize, invigorate, and emphasize their ideas.

2. *Talk about something from your own experience—at least in the beginning.* Select a topic that really grabs you, that makes you want to speak out and communicate with others. Usually this will stimulate you to talk more freely and confidently. If you lose yourself in your subject, you are sure to lose some of your self-consciousness.

3. *Know—really know—what you're talking about.* Think about your topic. Study it until you know more about it than anyone in your audience. Subject-mastery is closely akin to self-mastery, and can increase your feeling of poise and self-control.

4. *Keep your main ideas few in number—and in a simple, easy-to-remember order.* You will feel more confident if you are thoroughly familiar with the direction you want your speech to take. So master for instant recall your major ideas and the sequence in which you plan to present them.

5. *Speak in public as often as you can.* Confidence is born of trial-and-error experience. Repeated experiences with audiences of different sizes and types will reduce your apprehension, strengthen your self-assurance, and increase your poise.

6. *Focus your attention on your audience.* Make sure that the goal of communicating ideas and feelings to others dominates your efforts. Instead of concentrating on yourself, concentrate constantly on your listeners to see if you are getting across to them.

7. *Learn to use physical activity purposefully.* Properly employed, bodily movement serves two important functions in public speaking: *(a)* it helps you communicate ideas, and, *(b)* it tends to work off your tensions. In most cases, the moment you start to speak, that tense, uptight feeling will begin to fade, especially if you make a conscious effort to channel the overcharge of nervous energy into constructive, meaningful communicative behavior. As you speak, move purposefully in relation to your audience. Use bodily gestures to help present your ideas more clearly and forcefully. Supplanting nervous rigidity and random actions with purposeful physical activities will stimulate more energetic thought and expression while —at the same time—giving you greater assurance and confidence.*

Communicative Skills. Fluency, poise, control of the voice, and coordinated movements of the body mark the skillful public speaker. Combined with qualities of integrity, knowledge, and self-confidence, such skills can significantly increase your effectiveness by enabling you to communicate your ideas forcefully and attractively.

Skill in speaking is gained principally through practice. Practice, however, proceeds best when based on a knowledge of sound principles and carried on under the direction of a competent instructor. Moreover, care must be exercised that in practicing you do not develop

---

*For additional suggestions on gaining confidence, see Roderick P. Hart, Gustav W. Friedrich, and William D. Brooks, *Public Communication* (New York: Harper & Row, Publishers, 1975), pp. 38–43.

distractive habits or acquire an unnatural or artificial manner of delivery. Good public speaking is animated, but it is also natural and conversational. It commands attention not through the use of tricks and techniques, but because of the speaker's earnest desire to communicate. Indeed, many successful public speakers seem merely to be conversing with their audiences. In the chapters that follow we shall extend our consideration of these and other communicative skills and suggest how you may develop, refine, and implement their use in practical speaking situations. Also, at the end of most of the chapters in this textbook we have provided some "Oral Exercises and Speaking Activities" designed to encourage and guide your practice in mastering and habituating these necessary skills. The decision to participate seriously in these activities and the determination to engage in continued and extensive practice are, of course, ingredients which only you can supply.

Sensitivity to People and Situations. A speaker who is obviously a person of integrity and one who knows his subject well may still be oblivious to the fact that he is boring his listeners or in some way alienating or offending them. Perhaps he continues to talk long after their attention and interest have waned. Perhaps he tells embarrassing stories, treads on religious scruples, or ridicules ethnic origins. Perhaps his delivery is cold and dignified when the circumstances call for warmth and informality.

In contrast, the competent communicator is sensitive to the needs, values, and reactions of listeners and to the demands of the speech occasion. The sensitive speaker has a highly developed ability to read and adapt to signs of attention or inattention, agreement or disagreement, approval or disapproval — to the feedback — which the audience provides. Sensitivity of this kind consists of a number of relatively independent characteristics and differs considerably from individual to individual in much the same way that intelligence does.* As research has shown, you can improve your sensitivity through training and conscious effort. Begin by trying to put yourself mentally in the shoes of your listeners. Carefully consider in advance whether they are likely to think and feel as you do — or quite differently. Try to form a mental image of what turns them on — and off. When you speak to them, try to make them want to understand you and your ideas. Watch carefully the signals your listeners send to you as you talk, and do not be afraid to depart from your speech plan in order to adapt to their reactions. Watch other speakers also, noting in particular how they reveal their awareness and sensitivity to audiences, and how they succeed or fail in making the necessary adaptations. These are at least some of the ways by which you can begin to develop that sensitivity to persons and to communicative contexts which is indispensable to success as a public speaker.

---

*See, for example, Henry Clay Smith, *Sensitivity to People* (New York: McGraw-Hill Book Company, 1966), pp. 175–180.

Willingness to Learn from Others.   Every time you have an opportunity to hear a speaker address an audience, take advantage of it. Go to hear speakers of all kinds. Study their delivery and use of language. Notice how they organize ideas and develop arguments. Observe the kinds of explanations, examples, illustrations, statistics, and comparisons they choose, and how they use them. Compare the performances you observe with the rules and principles we describe in the following chapters. Pick out one or two speakers whom you have a chance to hear frequently. Make a detailed study of their speaking behaviors and techniques. Decide if any of their methods would be good ones for you to adopt—or adapt. But do not take any speaker as a model to imitate in a servile fashion. Remember that one of your greatest assets as a speaker is your own individuality and distinctness as a person.

Figure 1./ PUTTING TOGETHER THE PARTS OF A COMPETENT COMMUNICATOR

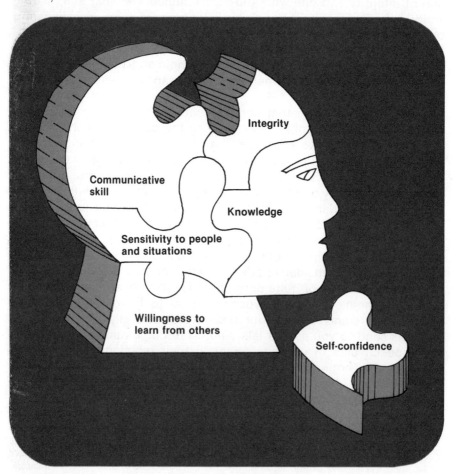

The Public Speechmaking Process

Let us turn now from our brief overview of public communication and the competent public speaker and direct our attention more specifically to a *preview* of the speechmaking process, especially as it concerns the preparation of the first speeches you may be asked to present in class. We use the term *preview* to stress that the ideas and procedures we are about to outline will be developed at greater length later. Our purpose here is to introduce you to the presentational methods and the essential steps in the making of public speeches and, at the same time, to provide a foundation for the remaining chapters in Part Two—to lay out some useful groundwork for what is to come.

Presentational Methods of Speaking

In the strictest sense, the presentational methods of public speechmaking are an aspect of delivery—the eighth and final step in the process. However, because the method of speaking you choose significantly affects many of the other choices you must make in all of the other seven steps, it requires first and immediate attention. In choosing a method of presenting a speech you have four options. That is, you may present a speech in (1) impromptu, (2) memorized, (3) manuscript, or (4) extemporaneous format.

An *impromptu speech* is one delivered on the spur of the moment with no specific preparation. Hence, you must rely entirely on your existing knowledge and speaking skills. The impromptu method is useful in an emergency, but should be restricted to situations which cannot be anticipated. Too often the "moment" arrives without the informed and inspired "spur." Whenever possible, therefore—if you only think you *might* be called upon to speak—it is better to plan ahead than risk the rambling, incoherent, fumbling presentation which the impromptu method so often produces.

A *memorized speech* is planned, structured, written out word for word, and then committed to memory. Except in rare instances, avoid this method. When speaking memorized words, you will unavoidably concentrate on them rather than on *ideas,* thus producing usually a stilted, inflexible speech. If you forget a word or a phrase, you are in danger of losing the entire thread of your thought. Your delivery tends to become excessively formal and oratorical, and you are likely to hurry your words, sacrificing meaning for empty utterance and losing the naturalness and spontaneity so fundamental to good speaker-listener interaction. Even worse, perhaps, the memorized speech makes it impossible for you to adapt to your audience's reaction or feedback.

The *speech read from manuscript,* like the memorized speech, is also written out word for word, and the speaker *reads it aloud* to an audience. When extremely careful wording is required—as in the President's

Figure 2./ THE PRESENTATIONAL METHODS OF SPEAKING

messages to Congress, for example, where a slip of the tongue could upset domestic politics or undermine foreign policies, or in the presentation of scientific reports where exact and concise exposition is required—the manuscript method is appropriate, even necessary. Many radio and television speeches also are read because of the strict time limits imposed by broadcasting schedules. Viewed as a specialized method useful only in certain situations, the ability to read effectively a speech from manuscript is important. But you should not resort to it when it is neither useful nor necessary, because its use—like that of the memorized speech—inevitably diminishes the freshness, spontaneity, and adaptability vital to meaningful oral communication.

The *extemporaneous speech,* like the memorized and the read-from-manuscript speeches, is carefully planned, systematically structured, and outlined in detail. There, however, the similarity ends. Rather than writing out the speech word for word, the extemporaneous speaker — following a carefully prepared plan or outline — orally "pre-phrases" the speech several times and, if possible, practices it orally in private prior to presentation. With this method, you memorize only the structure or the major-idea sequence. Then, working from this sequence or outline, you practice phrasing the speech, feeling free to express yourself somewhat differently each time you talk it through. You use the outline only to fix the order of the main ideas in your mind, and you practice various wordings to develop the flexibility of expression which may be necessary when you eventually deliver the speech.

If you use the extemporaneous method carelessly or without adequate preparation, the result may resemble the impromptu speech — an unfortunate fact which sometimes leads to a confusion of these two terms. If you use the extemporaneous method properly, however, you can produce a speech nearly as polished as one that is read aloud from manuscript, and one which is certainly more vigorous, spontaneous, and flexible. For this reason, the extemporaneous method of presentation is superior to both the memorized method and the manuscript method in most public communication situations. Without sacrificing solidity of content or cogency of organization, it makes possible easy adaptation to feedback from your audience. The extemporaneous speech may, within reasonable limits, be shortened or lengthened; ideas not understood when first stated may be repeated; and examples and other illustrative materials may be altered as the need arises. The speeches you present in class will usually be extemporaneous. Quite aside from this fact, however, strive to make it your preferred and most frequently used format. The ensuing discussion of the speechmaking process is based primarily on the extemporaneous speech.

Previewing the Eight Essential Steps

Preparing almost any speech for public presentation normally entails three phases consisting of the following steps: (1) selecting and narrowing the subject, (2) determining the specific purpose, (3) analyzing the audience and the occasion, (4) gathering material, (5) making an outline, (6) wording the speech, (7) practicing aloud for clarity and fluency, and (8) delivering the speech. (See illustration of this process on page 48.) These eight steps or progressive tasks, you will find, need not be performed separately and in exactly the sequence indicated. As you gain additional experience you may be able to dispense with one or more of the steps, or you may even develop a way of working that better fits your needs. For your first speeches, however, we strongly recommend that you perform *all* of the steps in the process in the order given. The result probably will be a more effective presentation than you otherwise would be able to make.

Figure 3./ EIGHT ESSENTIAL STEPS IN THE FULL DEVELOPMENT OF A SPEECH

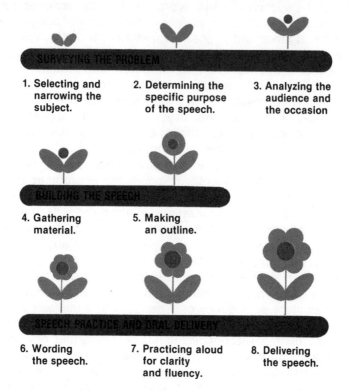

SURVEYING THE PROBLEM

1. Selecting and
   narrowing the
   subject.

2. Determining the
   specific purpose
   of the speech.

3. Analyzing the
   audience and
   the occasion

BUILDING THE SPEECH

4. Gathering
   material.

5. Making
   an outline.

SPEECH PRACTICE AND ORAL DELIVERY

6. Wording
   the speech.

7. Practicing aloud
   for clarity
   and fluency.

8. Delivering
   the speech.

Selecting and Narrowing the Subject. Ordinarily, in this first phase of your preparation you start by drawing together what you already know that might be worth talking about and tentatively deciding whether any of your ideas might be developed into a speech. Sooner or later, you select a subject that you are interested in and one you think is likely to interest your listeners. Narrow this subject so that it fits within the time limits specified or assigned. One of the commonest faults of beginning speakers is to select a topic too broad to be treated adequately in the time available. The narrower your subject, the more fully you will be able to expalin or prove the essential points and the more interesting you can make your speech by including a variety of illustrative incidents and instances, supportive statistics, comparisons, etc.

Determining the Specific Purpose of the Speech. It is not enough that you be able to center your speech in a well-defined subject and have at least a general notion of how you will narrow it. You must decide what you want it to do to and for your listeners—why you want to talk about it. *You must have clearly in mind the exact response of understanding, belief, or action that you want from your audience.* Think of each speech you make as an instrument for winning a definite response from your listeners. Once you know exactly what your specific purpose is and can state it in a very short, simple sentence, it will serve you admirably as a framework in which to further narrow your topic and — equally important — as a constant guide to selecting and organizing the ideas and points to include in your speech.

For speechmaking in the classroom, a specific purpose has an added dimension: the fulfillment of the particular goal for which the instructor has assigned the speech. If, for instance, your speech is supposed to demonstrate that you know how to organize ideas, or to prove a point, or to maintain interest, make that a part of your special and specific purpose.

Analyzing the Audience and the Occasion. Listeners, as we noted in the preceding chapter, are the essential target of all speeches that are purposeful — and of some that are not. A good public speech, therefore, not only reflects your interests and enthusiasms as the speaker, but also reflects the interests, enthusiasms, preferences, priorities, and limitations of the audience to whom it is given. As you plan and prepare your speech, then, continually put yourself in the place of your audience and ask how *you* would feel about the facts and ideas being presented. In order to do this successfully, you have to analyze it. Learn as much as possible about the people who compose it: their age, sex, social-economic-political status, origins, backgrounds, prejudices, etc. Try to find out how much they know about your subject, what they probably believe in and value, and what their probable attitude is toward you and your subject. Analyze the *occasion,* too. Consider the setting and circumstances in which you will be speaking: What is bringing the audience members together? What rules or customs will prevail? What will precede and follow your speech? And what will the psychological climate and the physical environment be like?

Gathering the Speech Material. As you move into the second phase of preparation, you start by assembling the materials needed to build your speech. Probably, at some point in the first phase you will have sorted out and assessed your *existing* knowledge of the subject and made some tentative decisions regarding material you can usefully draw from your personal experiences. Nearly always, however, you will find that this knowledge and material are not sufficient. You will need to gather *additional* information with which to develop, expand, and reinforce your major points. You may gather valuable materials from conversations and interviews, and from newspapers, magazines, books, government documents, and radio or television programs. Regardless of the time and labor involved, do your research thoroughly. Good speeches are packed with examples, illustrations, stories, figures, and quotations you can discover only by careful search. Appendix A of this book (pages 397–407) describes in some detail how you may conduct this search to find the precise kinds of material you seek.

Making an Outline.   Early in your preparation, make a preliminary list of the ideas to be included in your speech and tentatively indicate their arrangement. Do not attempt, however, to draw up a complete outline or final speech plan until you have gathered all of the necessary supporting and illustrative materials. Keep the plan or outline flexible, and continue to adjust it as you feel the need to do so. Only when you have assembled ample data of these kinds should you attempt to set down in final order the main points you expect to make, together with such subordinate ideas as are necessary to explain or to prove these points fully.

Later we will consider a number of specific patterns for arranging ideas within a speech. We will consider, too, the various forms an outline may take. (If you feel the need at this time to see some sample outlines, turn to Chapter 11, pages 174 – 188). For now, however, remember two rules: (1) *arrange your ideas in a clear and systematic order,* and (2) *preserve the unity of your speech by making sure that each point is directly related to your specific purpose.*

Wording the Speech.   As you approach this third phase of the public speechmaking process, hold in mind that there are at least two useful ways to develop the wording of your speech: talk it through or write it out. In the former, with your detailed outline before you to fix the major ideas in your mind, talk it through several times, composing your sentences orally in a variety of ways until you find the most effective way of stating them. At first, you may need to refer to the outline, but put it aside just as quickly as you can, and do not plan to use it while actually giving your speech. With each repetition you will become increasingly sure of yourself. Do not attempt to settle upon the exact words you will use in final delivery. The purpose of these talk-throughs is to master the *ideas,* not the language. At this point, if your speech is to be read aloud from manuscript for an audience, commit it to writing, being careful now that each word and sentence express exactly the ideas you wish to communicate.

Which of these two ways of phrasing your speeches is the better will, of course, depend upon your individual style as a speaker and upon the type of occasion. Beware of assuming, however, that written "speech" and spoken "speech" are one and the same. One is created primarily for the eye, the other for the ear; and the differences between them are vast. For most of the speaking you will be doing, we recommend the oral method of composition because of its greater naturalness and flexibility. To be safe, however, seek the preference of your instructor on this point.

Practicing Aloud for Clarity and Fluency.   In this step, you practice the presentation of your speech as you hope to deliver it to an actual audience. Working in privacy, speak the speech aloud several times from beginning to end, following the ideas as you have previously ordered and phrased them. A tape recorder and, if available, a large mirror are useful here. The first time through, you will probably leave out a good deal, so go over the speech again and include what you left out. This kind of practice will serve to fix even more firmly in your mind the plan and substance of your speech and give you a fairly clear idea of how the whole will sound to your listeners. Stand rather than sit. Move about as your ideas and feelings dictate. Take care not to develop a planned set of gestures and movements, but keep your delivery as spontaneous as possible. If you are practicing a speech to be read from manuscript, glance up from the page frequently; for in actually delivering your remarks, you must maintain eye contact with your listeners. Throughout, try to maintain a mental image of the audience you expect to face. Decide whether the situation which will confront you can best be handled by a vigorous, lively presentation, or by a quiet, dignified one. Above all, practice making your manner of speaking seem personal. Remember that you will be speaking to people — not at them.

Delivering the Speech. Let's assume that you have prepared and practiced your speech, and that in this concluding and climactic step you now stand before your audience, ready and eager to communicate. "How," you ask, "should I deliver my message? What can I do that will help me communicate what I want to say while I am saying it?" Three simple rules should guide the delivery of your early speeches: (1) be yourself; (2) look at your audience; and (3) communicate with your body as well as your voice.

1. *Be yourself.* Act as you would if you were engaged in an animated conversation with a friend. Avoid an excessively rigid, oratorical, or aggressive posture; but don't lean on a lectern or table or a wall. When you speak, you want the minds of your listeners to be focused on the ideas you are expressing, not on your delivery of them. Anything unnatural or unusual — anything that calls attention from matter to manner — is a distraction and should be avoided.
2. *Look at your listeners.* As we continue to emphasize throughout, watch the faces of your listeners for clues to their reactions. Without this feedback, you will be unable to gauge the ongoing effectiveness of your speech — to know whether you are putting your message across or whether you should make some prompt adjustments. Moreover, people tend to mistrust anyone who does not look them in the eye. So, if you fail to do so, they are likely to misjudge you and undervalue your ideas. And, finally, they nearly always listen more attentively if you look at them while you are speaking.
3. *Communicate with your body as well as your voice.* Realize that as a speaker you are being seen as well as heard. Movements of the body, gestures of the arms and head, changes in facial expression and muscle tension — all can help to clarify and reinforce your ideas. Keep your hands at your sides, so that when you feel an impulse to gesture, you can easily do so. Let other movements of your body

also respond as your feelings and message dictate. Do not force your actions, but do not hold them back when they seem natural and appropriate to what you are saying. Earnestly attempt to transmit your ideas to others, and sooner or later you will be motivated to bodily responses of some kind, for such responses are an integral part of the desire to communicate.

These, then, are the eight basic steps in the public speechmaking process. If carefully followed, they can help you attain the comunicative competencies we have described and can guide well your initial efforts to prepare and present meaningful messages to audiences. Do not expect them, however, to produce instant success. It is hard to force the development and organization of a good speech. Good speeches, like stout trees, must grow over a period of time. To postpone beginning the preparation of even a short and comparatively simple speech until the night before you are to give it invites disaster. As soon as you know you are to speak, begin thinking about the audience response you desire. In so doing, you can best utilize your background and knowledge and seek additional material to fill in the gaps. Work on your speech as frequently as possible, even if only for a few minutes at a time. Your confidence and effectiveness will increase in direct proportion to your mastery of your plan and your material. And do not be discouraged if your first attempts at public speechmaking fall short of your expectations. In succeeding chapters, as we have noted, we will consider in greater depth and detail all of the essentials we have previewed only briefly here.

Problems and Probes

1.   Comment critically on the contention that a public speaker, more than most interpersonal or group communicators, is faced by a special set of responsibilities and risks. Are there situations in which, though a speaker confronts a large audience, these responsibilities are absent? Are there interpersonal or group situations in which the responsibility for making the interchange productive rests principally on only one speaker? Can you think of a more satisfactory conception of public communication than the one here developed?

2.   Give one or two examples from your own experience of how some man or woman has exerted influence over others because of strong personal or ethical appeal. Did this person have a comparably strong influence over you personally? Why or why not?

3.   Which factor—the speaker's knowledge of the subject or skill in speech delivery—would you say is more important in determining how a speech is received by the listeners? Explain and defend your answer.

4.   At this point in the course, you have probably taken part in a number of different oral activities: speeches, class discussions, and the like. Refer to your Personal Speech Journal and look again at the inventory of your *speech needs and abilities* that you prepared at the conclusion of Chapter 1. Now enter in the Journal your views of yourself—written from an oral communication perspective, of course—and describe the extent and ways in which your speaking abili-

ties and goals may have changed or been reinforced. You might use as a general guide in this analysis "Characteristics and Competencies of the Public Communicator," which we considered on pages 39–44.

5.   Make a list of five subjects drawn from your own personal background or experience which you think would be interesting and informative to your classmates. Take some class time to circulate the lists to the other members of the class and have them rate their preferences by number. Keep your marked list in your Journal for future use in choosing speech subjects.

Oral Activities and Speaking Assignments

1.   Choose a subject for a brief speech three or four minutes in length. The chief criterion of your choice should be that talking on this subject will, you believe, be likely to put you at ease as you speak to the other members of the class. After you have your instructor's go-ahead on the chosen subject, proceed to prepare and present this speech, following the suggestions offered in the "Eight Essential Steps" previewed on pages 47–52 of this chapter.

2.   Following the principles and procedures set forth in this chapter, prepare and present a three- or four-minute speech on a subject chosen by you and approved by your instructor. Narrow the focus of your speech by selecting the one or two aspects of the subject that you believe would be of greatest interest and appeal to the other members of the class. (Consult Appendix A for suggestions concerning printed and other sources of speech materials.)

3.   Hold a class discussion in which you consider as objectively as you can why people often become nervous when speaking in public. Trade ideas about what can be done to combat this problem. If time allows, consult persons in the community—ministers, public officials, and others—who do a good deal of public speaking, and find out what their experiences and recommendations are.

Suggestions for Further Reading

Aristotle, *Rhetoric,* 1356a, "The Character of the Speaker as a Means of Persuasion"; 1378a, "A Certain Character in the Speaker."

Waldo W. Braden and Mary Louise Gehring, *Speech Practices: A Resource Book for the Student of Public Speaking* (New York: Harper & Row, Publishers, 1958), Chapter 2, "How Speakers Prepare Their Speeches," pp. 14–26.

Roderick P. Hart, Gustav W. Friedrich, and William D. Brooks, *Public Communication* (New York: Harper & Row, Publishers, 1975), Chapter 1, "Communicating in Public."

Raymond S. Ross, *Speech Communication: Fundamentals and Practice,* 4th ed. (Englewood Cliffs, N.J.: Prentice-Hall, Inc., 1977), Chapter 4, "Emotion and Confidence."

John F. Wilson and Carroll C. Arnold, *Dimensions of Public Communication* (Boston: Allyn & Bacon, Inc., 1976), Chapter 2, "First Considerations."

Choosing Speech Subjects and Purposes

In Chapter 3 we surveyed, in abbreviated form, the steps or tasks involved in preparing a speech. In this chapter we discuss more fully the first two of these steps, namely: selecting a suitable subject and determining the speech purpose. The first step in preparing to speak consists of deciding what you are going to speak about and what reaction you want from your audience as a result. Subject and purpose are thus intimately related, the former having to do with the *central concern* or *thesis* of your speech and its substance, and the latter relating to the *response* you hope to evoke from your listeners as or after they hear what you have to say. Although in practical terms, subject and purpose are thus closely interdependent, for our analysis here we will arbitrarily separate one from the other and consider each in turn.

The Subject of the Speech

Selecting Your Subject

Often, the subject of your speech will be predetermined for you—at least in part—by the group you are invited to address. You are, for instance, a water-resources expert asked to speak to a local service club on means of controlling pollution in a nearby river. Or, after a trip through China, you are invited to describe for a study group the social and economic conditions in that nation. At other times, the subject on which you will speak is left to your discretion, and nearly always you will have considerable freedom in selecting the particular facet or aspect of the subject you wish to emphasize.

When confronted with the task of choosing a subject or determining which aspect of a general topic to stress, beginning speakers frequently experience difficulty. Sometimes they choose a subject on which their background of knowledge or experience is inadequate. Often they fail to pay due attention to the needs and interests of their audience, or they greatly underestimate the amount of time necessary to develop their message adequately. To avoid mistakes of this kind and to make your selection of speech subjects more appropriate and systematic, observe the following guidelines:

Select a subject about which you already know something and can find out more. Base your speeches on jobs you have held, places you have visited, or on your hobbies or special interests. Then supplement this information with additional reading and research. You always speak best on subjects you know best or are actively studying. In speaking, as in other human endeavors, knowledge is power.

Select a subject that is interesting to you. If you are not interested in what you are talking about, you will find preparation a dull task, and your speaking is likely to be listless and ineffective.

Select a subject that will interest your audience. The more interest your listeners already have in the subject, the less you will have to worry about holding their attention when you speak. A subject may be interesting to an audience for one or more of the following reasons: it vitally concerns their health, happiness, prosperity, or security; it offers a solution to a recognized problem; it is new or timely; and there is conflict of opinion concerning it.

Select a subject you can discuss adequately in the time at your disposal—an important rule that, as we shall see, affects the speechmaking process in a variety of contexts. In a ten-minute speech, do not attempt to review "The Causes and Consequences of Civil War in Angola." Instead, describe some of the reasons the Communist nations became involved, or discuss the reasons that led to their withdrawal.

In sum, remember that even though you are assigned a subject, you will probably still need to limit it—to select some phase or aspect that you can discuss effectively within the time limits you have been given. If you experience difficulty in selecting a suitable speech subject, we suggest that you study the list of subject categories at the end of this chapter, pages 64–65.

The Title of the Speech

Closely related to the subject of the speech is its title. The subject identifies the material content of the speech: the problem to be discussed, the objects or activities to be described. The title, on the other hand, is the *specific label* given to the speech—usually announced by the chairman—for the purpose of arousing the interest of the audience. Hence, the title is a kind of advertising slogan—a catchword, phrase, or brief statement which epitomizes the subject and spirit of the speech in an attractive or provocative form. When Ernest A. Jones, president of MacManus, John & Adams, Inc., discussed the effects of advertising techniques in influencing the consumer's buying habits, he titled his speech "The Man with the Split-Level Head." A college student used the title "The Eleventh Commandment" for a speech denouncing our modern-day tendency to condone crime in high places.

What, then, are the requirements of a good title? There are at least three; it should be relevant; it should be provocative; it should be brief. To be *relevant,* a title must be pertinent to the subject or to some part of the speaker's discussion of it. The relevancy of the title "The Eleventh Commandment" was made clear when the speaker pointed out that the commandments "Thou shalt not steal" and "Thou shalt not cheat" have been supplemented by a new one, the eleventh, "Thou shalt get away with it." In this example, notice that while the title is not a prosaic restatement of the subject, it clearly is pertinent to the idea the speaker seeks to communicate. Make sure your title does not mislead.

To be *provocative,* a title should make the audience sit up and listen. Sometimes the subject of the speech itself is of such compelling interest that a mere statement of it is provocative enough. In most instances, however, you must find a more vivid or unusual phrasing. At the same time, you must take care not to give away the entire content or message of your speech in the title. Especially if the audience is hostile to your purpose, you must avoid wording your title in a way that makes that purpose too obvious. To entitle a speech for a women's political group "Down with the ERA" is provocative, but unlikely to gain a fair hearing.

Finally, the title of a speech should be *brief and simple.* Imagine the effect of announcing as a title "The Effects on Non-Target Classmates of a Deviant Student's Power and Response to a Teacher-Exerted Technique." Such a title can only be excused when the discussion is a technical one to be presented before a professional audience that has a specialized interest in the subject. In circumstances of that nature, the precise statement of the subject matter may be important. Even so, the title should be as short and simple as possible.

Usually the exact phrasing of the title can best be left until the speech has been completely built. To devise a title that is both relevant and provocative will be much easier after you have developed your central ideas and gathered much of your supporting material. The phrasing of titles has been considered here, rather than later, because of its close relation to the subject and purpose of the speech and not because it is done early in the speech-building process.

The General Ends of Speech

Regardless of the subject or title, as we have emphasized, *the aim of every speech is to win a response from an audience.* You must never lose sight of this aim or purpose, for it lies at the foundation of the entire process of speechmaking. The question immediately arises, then: What kinds of responses do you as a speaker commonly seek to elicit?

Writers on practical speaking, from classical times to the present, have grouped speech purposes into a few fairly definite types and—for the last two centuries at least—have classified them according to the *kind of reaction* the speaker seeks from the listeners. Many such classifications, varying in scope and detail, have been used. You will find the following classification, identifying four general purposes or ends of speech—(1) to *entertain,** (2) to *inform,* (3) to *persuade,* and (4) to *actuate*—functional as well as convenient to use. See Figure 1 on page 58.

A *general end,* as the term is used here, denotes a broad, general class or type of speech purpose directed toward the response a speaker desires from an audience. Merely because your purpose coincides chiefly with one of these general ends or aims, however, does not imply that you will be unconcerned with the others or that you can afford to neglect them. You usually must inform the audience of certain facts or problems before you can hope to create belief; and ordinarily you will need to persuade in order to secure action—to stir your listeners to behave as you desire. One of these general ends should, however, always be your major objective, and the others only means to that goal. For this reason you must take care that the contributory purposes do not detract from the central objective of the speech—that they are included only when they advance the principal aim, and only to the extent that they do so. Let us now briefly examine each of the general ends in its role as a primary aim.

To Inform

When your purpose is to clarify a concept or a process for your listeners, when you endeavor to explain terms and relationships, or strive in other ways to widen the range of your listeners' knowledge, the objective of your speech will be to inform. This is the purpose of the foreman who instructs a worker how to operate a new machine, of the teacher who lectures to a class, of the business executive who reports on the last quarter's earnings to the board of directors, or of the county's farm agent who explains the results of tests carried on at an agricultural experiment station. Informative speeches and lectures also are common at meetings of luncheon clubs and of trade or professional associations.

All this—we again emphasize—does not mean that clear explanation is useful only when speakers have the creation of understanding as their

---

*Note that three of these general ends or purposes—to inform, to persuade, and to actuate—as they affect the organization and types of speeches, are developed in depth in Chapters 17, 18, and 19 respectively. Although we do not give full-chapter treatment to the speech to entertain *as such,* considerable attention is devoted to it in "Using Supporting Materials to Amuse or Entertain" (Chapter 7, pages 122–125), and in "Humor" as a factor of attention (Chapter 8, pages (134–135). See also the sample speeches, "A Case for Optimism" (pp. 124–125) and "The Comic Spirit and the Public Speaker" (pp. 282–288).

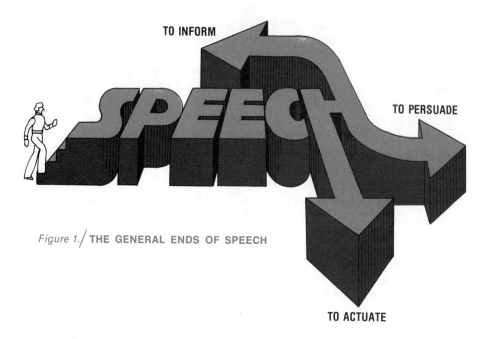

Figure 1./ THE GENERAL ENDS OF SPEECH

general goal. In a persuasive speech, for example, you can rarely induce an audience to accept a proposition that you have not first made completely clear. But in a speech which aims to inform, you urge no specific belief or action. Your central purpose is *to make the listeners understand and to provide them with the information needed for this understanding.* To achieve this end, you must relate new ideas to the existing knowledge of your listeners, structure the message clearly in order to enhance retention of the information, and present an abundance of concrete examples and specific data so that they will fully understand the leading ideas of your message.

To Persuade

When your purpose is to alter the beliefs or deepen the convictions of your auditors, the general end of your speech will be to persuade. Many speeches have this general end. Political speakers urge their constituents to believe in the platforms and performances of their respective parties; salespersons attempt to create belief in the superiority of certain products or services; philosophers debate the validity of their hypotheses; ministers urge their congregations to accept certain attitudes and values. In all these cases, however, where the general end of the talk is only to *persuade* (and not to actuate through persuasion), no overt behavior, act, or performance is requested of the audience. They are asked merely to agree with the speaker. Many times, in fact, listeners are incapable of taking definite action because the authority for action lies with some other person or group, or because a time for social or political action has not yet arrived. But they can form opinions by which to judge and sometimes change the actions of those who are in authority.

This important distinction can be drawn more sharply, perhaps, by the following example. A great many public speeches are made to the electorate, even in non-election years, about the foreign policy of the administration. The actual authority for controlling this policy lies with the President and with Congress, yet speakers outside the administration attempt to influence the beliefs of the ordinary citizen. Why? Because these beliefs, through the influence they can exert upon public opinion, ultimately will affect the government's foreign policies and help shape the nation's future course of action abroad. The immediate purpose of the speakers, however, is not to prompt performance, not to gain action in the form of a vote, but merely to win agreement in belief. Later, of course, the candidates for President and Congress may speak on these same subjects in an attempt to actuate—to urge or to impel people to exert a direct influence on foreign policy by voting in a certain way at the next election. In the first case, the speaker's purpose is merely to persuade the audience; in the second, the purpose is to secure action based upon persuasion—the purpose to which we now turn our attention.

To Actuate

When your purpose is to cause your listeners to perform some definite observable act, the general end or aim of your speech will be to actuate. This performance may be to vote "yes" or "no," to contribute money, to sign a petition, to form a parade and engage in a demonstration; or it may be any one of a hundred other types of observable public actions. Underlying and prompting this behavior, however, will be strong belief, aroused emotion, or both. For this reason the development of the speech which aims at producing action follows closely the methods suggested for speeches which seek simply to persuade. Sharply distinguishing the actuating speech, however, is the fact that it goes beyond the persuasive one; in it *you openly ask your listeners to perform some overt act at a specified time and place.* The relationship between the speech to persuade and the speech to actuate may be summarized as follows: When the general end of a speech is *to actuate,* the speaker's purpose is *to persuade* as a necessary step *toward* causing listeners to engage in some definite, observable behavior. (See diagram on page 60.)

The Specific Purpose of the Speech

In addition to a clearly defined general end or goal, a good speech also should have an immediate or specific purpose. *The specific purpose always is narrower in focus than the general one and states precisely*

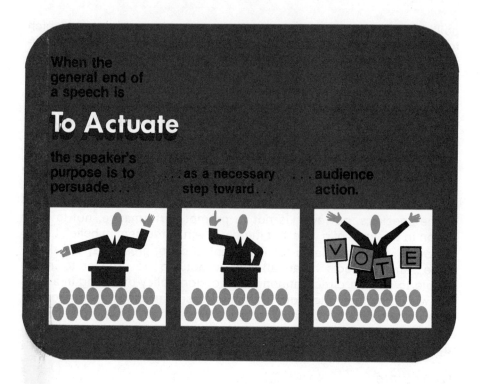

When the
general end of
a speech is

To Actuate

the speaker's
purpose is to ...as a necessary ...audience
persuade...   step toward...   action.

what the speaker wishes the audience to understand, believe, feel, or do. The following examples will illustrate the relationship between the subject, the general end, and the specific purpose of what we term the three basic types of speeches—informative, persuasive, and actuative:

1. *Subject:* Why Drugs?
   General end: To inform.
   Specific purpose: To help the audience understand some of the causes of drug addiction.

2. *Subject:* Equality for All.
   General end: To persuade.
   Specific purpose: To convince the audience that sex discrimination is still widespread in business and the professions.

3. *Subject:* Health Insurance for College Students.
   General end: To actuate.
   Specific purpose: To get members of the student council to vote in favor of the group policy offered to the student body by the ABC Health Insurance Company.

Additional examples of a specific speech purpose might be to ask the audience to:

—understand how safety matches are made *(inform).*

—believe that nuclear power plants pose a health hazard *(persuade).*
—vote for Jones for Congress on November 4 *(actuate).*

Selecting the Specific Purpose: Determining Factors

If you will think of communication as terminating in a specific mental or behavioral response, you will realize immediately that the selection of the specific purpose of a speech should be guided not only by the speaker's own aims or wishes, but also by the nature of the audience and the speaking occasion. In choosing and framing the specific speech purpose, therefore, keep in mind the following factors:

Your Private or Ultimate Aim as a Speaker. Suppose that an assistant vice-president of a large firm is presenting a reorganization plan to the executive committee or board of directors. Her *immediate* purpose is to secure the plan's adoption; but her *ultimate* aim—her "hidden agenda"—may be to enhance her own reputation, authority, or salary. Keeping this in mind, she may modify her proposal somewhat, or she may strive to get someone else to urge its adoption so that if the attempt does not succeed, the responsibility will not be entirely hers. The point is: *do not try to win from your listeners an immediate, positive response which will have a negative effect upon your ultimate objective.*

The Authority of the Listeners or Their Capacity to Act. For a speaker to demand of a group of students that they "abolish all required courses" would be foolish if the final decision concerning course requirements is in the hands of the faculty. But students do have the right to bring pressure on the faculty toward this end. Therefore, a more logical purpose for a speaker in this situation would be: "Petition the faculty to make all courses elective." As a speaker, *carefully limit your specific purpose to urging an action or behavior that is clearly within the domain of your listeners' authority.* Do not ask them to do something they would be unable to do even if they wanted to.

The Existing Attitudes of the Listeners. A group of striking workers who believe they are badly underpaid and unfairly treated by their employer probably would be hostile to the suggestion that they return to work under the existing conditions. They might, however, approve submitting the dispute to arbitration by a disinterested person whose fairness and judgment they respect. If you are speaking to an audience having an attitude hostile to your point of view, you might—by presenting only one speech—convince your listeners that there is something to be said on the other side of the question; but you would probably find it impossible to persuade them to take positive action on it. *Your specific purpose, in short, must be adjusted not only to the authority but also to the attitudes of your listeners.* Do not ask them for a response you cannot reasonably expect from persons holding their particular feelings or beliefs. (These attitudes are considered in detail in Chapter 18.)

The Nature of the Speech Occasion. To ask people to contribute money to a political campaign fund might be appropriate at a pre-election rally, but to pursue this specific purpose at a memorial service would be decidedly out of place. An athletic awards ceremony is hardly the occasion on which to seek an understanding of how a catalytic converter works. The members of a little theater association would not want to engage in a discussion of finances between the acts of a play, though they might respond to a brief announcement urging their attendance at a business meeting where the budget will be discussed. *Be sure that your specific purpose is adapted to the mood or spirit of the occasion on which you are to speak.*

The Time Limits of the Speech. You may be able in a few minutes to induce an audience that opposes your proposal to postpone action until a later time, but you almost certainly will need a much longer time if you hope to change your listeners' feelings and convictions enough to favor your position. Similarly, if your subject is complex, you may be able to inform your hearers, to get them to understand your proposal, in a fifteen-minute speech; but you may need much more time to convince them of its desirability. *Do not, in short, attempt to get from your audience a response or outcome impossible to attain in the time available.*

When you have formulated the specific purpose of your speech on the basis of the five foregoing factors, your speechmaking will be off to a sound start. Once determined, use this purpose as a constant guide throughout the remaining steps of your preparation. Write it out in a clear, simple sentence, making sure you state it in terms of the response you want from your audience. Then fix that sentence firmly in your mind. Whenever you encounter an idea or a piece of information that will help you advance and *fulfill* this specific purpose, work it into your speech plan. Otherwise, forget about it, no matter how interesting or attractive it may be. By thus using a carefully framed purpose as a yardstick for determining the relevance of possible materials, you can make certain that your speech will be unified and coherent, and that everything you say will be directed toward the precise response you seek.

Your study of this chapter should have made clear the importance of choosing a strong subject and defining both your general end and specific objective early in the process of speech preparation. Also, you should be aware now of certain key questions you will need to answer more or less simultaneously in these first two steps of the speechmaking process; namely: (1) What *subject* should I talk about, and to what aspect of it should I *limit* myself? (2) What *general end* should I try to attain—to inform? to persuade? to actuate? (3) What specific response shall I seek—what is my *specific purpose* in speaking to this audience? And (4) eventually—after I have built my speech in detail—how shall I phrase a *title* for it which will make my audience want to hear it?

Problems and Probes

1. List at least five different subjects on which it might be appropriate to give a speech *to inform*. Do the same for speeches *to persuade* and *to actuate.* In an informal survey, pool your suggestions with those of the other students and construct a master list of at least twelve subjects for which each type of speech might be used.

2. Select a subject with which you are familiar, one drawn from your major in college, from work experience, from travel, from your hobby, etc. Assume that during the semester you will be asked to present three five-minute speeches on this subject—one *to inform,* one *to persuade,* and one *to actuate.* Select and frame a specific purpose for each speech. Then repeat the experiment, but this time assume that in each case you will be presenting a fifteen-minute speech to a local service club. Let the other members of the class evaluate the appropriateness of your choices.

3. Read three printed speeches selected from such sources as *Representative American Speeches* (edited annually by Waldo W. Braden) or the magazine *Vital Speeches of the Day.* Try to determine the general and specific purpose of each speech and to evaluate how well these purposes were fulfilled.

4. Refer to the list of subject categories on pages 64–65. Rank-order the ten categories which are potentially the most interesting to you. Devote part of a class period to compiling a master list representing the preferences of the class as a whole. Record the results in your Personal Speech Journal, and consult them when selecting topics on which you will present future speeches.

Oral Activity and Speaking Assignment

1. Select a subject with which you are well acquainted and about which you have much you can say. Write a specific purpose for each of four or five speeches which you would like to give on this subject. Select from these the purpose that seems best adapted to the interests of your classmates, and deliver a five-minute speech aimed at accomplishing this purpose. At the close of your speech, read aloud the specific purposes which you rejected, and let your classmates and instructor evaluate the appropriateness of your choice.

Suggestions for Further Reading

Bower Aly and Lucile F. Aly, *A Rhetoric of Public Speaking* (New York: McGraw-Hill Book Company, 1973), Chapter 2, "Searching the Mind: Discovery."

Donald C. Bryant and Karl R. Wallace, *Fundamentals of Public Speaking,* 4th ed. (Englewood Cliffs, N.J.: Prentice-Hall, Inc., 1976), Chapter 3, "Subjects and Basic Materials."

Linda C. Lederman, *New Dimensions: An Introduction to Human Communication* (Dubuque, Iowa: Wm. C. Brown Company, Publishers, 1977), Chapter 4, "The Sender: Dynamics Affecting the Sender's Message Making."

Loren Reid, *Speaking Well,* 2nd ed. (New York: McGraw-Hill Book Company, 1972), Chapter 5, "Choosing Subjects for Speaking."

Subject Categories:

Aids to Choosing Speech Topics

The beginning speaker often has difficulty in selecting a suitable speech subject. If you find yourself in this situation, we suggest that you study the following list of subject categories. These categories are not speech subjects; rather, they are *types or classes of material in which speech subjects may be found.* To decide upon a suitable subject for a public speech, consider them in terms of your own interests and knowledge, the interests of your audience, and the nature of the occasion on which you are to speak.

PERSONAL EXPERIENCE

1. Jobs you have held.
2. Places you have been.
3. Military service.
4. The region you come from.
5. Schools you have attended.
6. Friends and enemies.
7. Relatives you like— and dislike.
8. Hobbies and pastimes.

FOREIGN AFFAIRS

1. Foreign-policy aims. What they are. What they should be.
2. The implementation of policy aims.
3. History of the foreign policy of the United States (or of some other nation.)
4. Responsibility for our foreign policy.
5. Ethics of foreign-policy decisions.
6. How foreign policy affects domestic policy.
7. War as an instrument of national policy.
8. International peace-keeping machinery.

DOMESTIC AFFAIRS

1. Social problems.
   Crime.
   The family: marriage, divorce, adjustments.
   Problems of cities.
   Problems of rural areas.
   Problems of races and ethnic groups.
   Problems of juveniles or the aged.
   Traffic accidents.
   Abortion.
   The drug culture.
   Sex mores.
   Pollution.
2. Economic problems.
   Federal fiscal policy.
   Economically deprived persons and areas.
   Fiscal problems of state and local governments.
   Taxes and tax policies.
   Inflation and price controls.
   International monetary affairs.
3. Political problems.
   Powers and obligations of the federal government.
   Relations between the federal government and the states.
   Problems of state and local governments.
   Parties, campaigns, and nominating procedures.
   The courts and court procedures.
   — Delays in justice.
   — The jury system.
   Congress versus the President.
   Democracy as a form of government— advantages and disadvantages.
   Careers in government.

THE ARTS

1. Painting, music, sculpture.
2. Literature and criticism.
3. Theater, cinema, and dance.
4. Government support of the arts.
5. The artist as a person.
6. History of an art form.
7. Censorship of the arts.

EDUCATION

1. Proper aims of education.
2. Recent advances in methods and teaching materials.
3. The federal government and education.
4. Courses and requirements.
5. Grades and grading.
6. Athletics.
7. Extracurricular activities.
8. Meeting the demand for education.
9. Fraternities.
10. Student marriages.
11. Students' role in educational decision making.
12. Parietal rules.
13. Alternatives to college.

MASS MEDIA

1. Radio, television, and film.
2. The press.
3. Censorship of mass media.
   - To protect public morals.
   - For national security.
4. Use of mass media for propaganda purposes at home or abroad.
5. Ways to improve mass media.
6. Effects on children.
7. Cable television (CATV).

SCIENCE

1. Recent advances in a particular branch of science.
2. Science as method.
3. Pure versus applied research.
4. Government support of science.
5. History of science.
6. Science and religion.
7. Careers in science.

BUSINESS AND LABOR

1. Unions.
   - Benefits and/or evils.
   - Regulation of unions.
   - "Right-to-work" laws.
2. Government regulation of business.
3. Ethical standards of business practice.
4. Advertising in the modern world.
5. Training for business.
6. Careers in business.
7. Blue-collar and white-collar status.
8. Wages: hourly or annually?
9. A guaranteed lifetime income.
10. Portable pensions.

PERSISTENT CONCERNS

1. "The good life"— what and how.
2. Man and God.
3. Beauty.
4. The ideal society.
5. Life-style—what it is and how to develop it.
6. Parents and children.
7. The tests of truth.
8. Love.
9. Discovering one's self.

5

Analyzing the Audience and the Occasion

Effective communication is *audience-oriented.* No speaker should engage others in a communicative transaction without something interesting, instructive, or persuasive to say.* No speaker can be successful and no idea has power unless an audience accepts the speaker and absorbs the idea. Short of seeking such success by saying whatever others want to hear, as a speaker you have a responsibility to adapt your message to the audience and to the specific speech occasion. The nature of that audience and that occasion, therefore, should guide the selection of the subject matter and specific purpose, the claims advanced, the kinds of supporting material, the patterns of arrangement, the language, and the modes of vocal and physical encoding you employ. In this chapter—the third step in the speechmaking process—we will examine the factors to be considered when you analyze in advance the audience for whom you are designing the public speech and the occasion on which you are to offer it.

Analyzing the Audience

In an important sense, the concept of *audience* is an imaginary construct, for in reality there is no such entity. Each person sitting in an auditorium is an individual; and no matter how people are crowded together, arranged in rows, or reached electronically by a message, they

---

*For some interesting ideas about what it means for one *self* to engage another *self* in complete communication existentially, see Georges Gusdorf, *La Parole* [Speaking], trans. Paul T. Brockelman (Evanston, Ill.: Northwestern University Press, 1965).

never lose that individuality. But, while the place of individuality in communication events is receiving widespread attention of late, as a public speaker you are often forced to operate as if collectives of people do have some degree of homogeneity, of *entity*—as if audiences do exist. The concept allows you to think analytically about the collective backgrounds and psychological states of your listeners, and to form useful generalizations about ways audiences probably will behave when confronted with certain messages.

What kinds of generalizations about the backgrounds and personalities of audiences are warranted?* Although we do not as yet have definitive answers to this question, thanks to extensive research we do have a considerable body of information concerning audience behavior. When you combine this social-scientific research with common sense, examples from great communicative events of the past, and personal experience, you can improve considerably your abilities to analyze audiences.

Viewed analytically, an audience is a *social animal* and a *thinking animal*—a *cultural structure* and a *cognitive structure.* The social or cultural factors of audience behavior we shall term *external* in that they represent social or behavioral guidelines generated by other members of the listener's society. The intellectual or cognitive factors of audience behavior we shall term *internal* because they represent prods-to-action uniquely built into each listener's head.

External Factors in Audience Behavior

It is, of course, impossible to list everything in your listeners' environment which conceivably affects the way they react to spoken messages. There are, however, several variables important in determining this reaction, namely, the size, age, sex, education, group membership, and cultural and ethnic backgrounds which characterize your audience.

Size. In general, the larger the audience, the more heterogeneous or dissimilar its constituent parts, and hence the more diverse its collective beliefs, attitudes, and values. Bearing upon the size factor are these two useful generalizations:

1. *The larger the audience, the more general and comprehensive your appeals may have to be.* If you are offering a list of reasons why an audience should take action, for larger audiences you must attempt to make those reasons more abstract. For example, the ads in mass-

---

*The following sources enlarge upon our discussion of backgrounds and personalities of audiences: Paul D. Holtzman, *The Psychology of Speakers' Audiences* (Glenview, Ill.: Scott, Foresman and Company, 1970); Marvin Karlins and Herbert I. Abelson, *Persuasion: How Opinions and Attitudes Are Changed* (New York: Springer Publishing Co., Inc., 1970); Stephen W. King, *Communication and Social Influence* (Reading, Mass.: Addison-Wesley Publishing Company, Inc., 1975); Howard H. Martin and C. William Colburn, *Communication and Consensus: An Introduction to Rhetorical Discourse* (New York: Harcourt Brace Jovanovich, Inc., 1972); C. David Mortensen, *Communication: The Study of Human Interaction* (New York: McGraw-Hill Book Company, 1972); and Wayne C. Thompson, *Quantitative Research in Public Address and Communication* (New York: Random House, Inc., 1967).

circulation magazines such as *Reader's Digest* have much more general appeal than ads in smaller-circulation magazines such as *Ms.* (women's market), *Popular Mechanics* (men's market), or *Humpty Dumpty* (children's market). Often, as a speaker you can use the same kind of strategy.

2. *The larger the audience, the more you may need to create sub-audiences.* If, in a given situation, making your appeals general and abstract will weaken their impact, try analyzing your audience in terms of smaller sub-audiences or sub-groups. Proponents of abortion reform, for example, when confronting a large and diverse audience, often direct specific arguments to specific segments of that audience, telling *women* that they have a right to control their own bodies, *religious people* that they have no right to dictate their beliefs to others, *humanitarians* that they ought to relieve the suffering which results from population explosions, and *cost-minded auditors* that abortion reform is cheaper than expansion of social services. A barrage of such different appeals arises from attempts to analyze an audience in terms of sub-groups, each having a strong and readily identifiable vested interest, and each of which may frequently overlap the interest of some other sub-audience.

Age. Ever since Aristotle described the behavioral patterns of young, middle-aged, and old men, there has been a continuing recognition that a person's age affects the way he or she receives messages.[1] While the age factor in communication has not been fully investigated, enough has been done to suggest a few generalizations useful in analyzing audiences:[2]

1. *People's interests vary with age.* In matters of government, for example, younger people as a group are generally more isolationist than older people; those in their forties and fifties are especially concerned with taxes, business, and the economy; and older persons are more interested in pensions, medicare, and the availability of social services.
2. *Middle-aged people generally are less self-centered than either younger or older people.* The young, it would seem, are seeking a place in society, and the elderly are watching their group ties deteriorate; hence, both groups are especially susceptible to appeals addressed to the well-being, satisfaction, and security of the self.
3. *People tend to grow more cautious with age.* This tendency is reflected in their buying and living habits, their social and political attitudes, and the degree to which they are open to innovation.
4. *People's social-political activism varies with age.* Across the U.S. population, for example, the least active voters are those in the 18–24 age bracket; the most active, 45–54. The speaker delivering

an actuative speech to both young and old simultaneously has an especially difficult task.

5. *Older people are more conservative and pessimistic than younger people.* Generally, according to today's social scientists, older persons seem less willing than the young to believe in humanity's ability to solve the world's problems. This finding reflects an observation Aristotle made over 2000 years ago. "The old," he said, "have lived long, have been often deceived, have made many mistakes of their own; they see that more often than not the affairs of men turn out badly. And so they are positive about nothing; in all things they err by an extreme moderation. They 'think' — they never 'know.'"[3]

Sex.   The question of whether intellectual, attitudinal, and behavioral differences between men and women are genetically, biologically, or culturally derived is much discussed these days. As the rise of feminist consciousness in our society suggests, these differences are increasingly attributed to *cultural conditioning.* The following generalizations, therefore, as they bear upon the analysis of audiences, must be viewed as extremely tentative and subject to frequent revision. But, at the moment at least, social scientists seem to agree that:

1. *Women are more persuasible than men.* A number of studies appear to document the greater susceptibility of women to various kinds of persuasive appeals. Note, however, that this difference can be somewhat mitigated by education, so that the difference in persuasibility between well-educated males and females is less pronounced.

2. *Generally, women seem more susceptible to group pressure than do men.* This kind of susceptibility, it seems, has to do with the comparative number and strength of the roles the person can identify with. In general, Western society has allowed men to fulfill a large variety of roles, and hence males have many role models. This, in turn, affects the degree of permissible individuality and susceptibility to group influence. Women, on the other hand, have been relatively restricted in the number of roles they can fulfill, and hence have a greater susceptibility to pressures exerted by the group. Appeals to peer-group thought are, therefore, probably more effective with a female audience.

3. *Women, in general, have greater humanitarian concern than men.* Women seem more prone to analyze an issue in terms of its so-called "human" values rather than in terms of its political expediency or financial costs. Women tend usually to be more pro-peace and anti-war. They appear to be more interested in social welfare programs for the real betterment of people rather than for the vote-gathering potential of such measures. But, of course, as more women enter the field of professional politics, this may very well change.

4.   *In general, social interests of both men and women seem to be gov-
     erned by the social roles they play.* These roles, as we have suggest-
     ed, have been largely determined — historically at least — on the basis
     of sex. Thus women audiences are presumed to be more interested
     in children, fashions, and the home, whereas men are more interest-
     ed in the economy, business, and sports.

Overall, since socially determined sex roles are changing at a perceptible rate, the usefulness of the sex factor in analyzing audiences may be
fading. With changes in educational opportunity, employment practices, and increasing awareness of the effects of sexism, some of the
foregoing generalizations are gradually being undercut. Consequently,
before putting them to use, you should attempt first to assess the degree to which male and female segments of a specific audience may be
conscious of sex roles and likely to be affected by the sex-role factor.

Education.   As we already have suggested, the amount and kind of listeners' education affect how they will react to a message. Specifically:

1.   *The greater the education, the less likely the listener is to be affected
     by outright emotional appeals.* Simply put, well-educated people are
     more difficult to persuade than less well-educated people.
2.   *Well-educated people have more stable, more consistently held be-
     liefs, attitudes, and values than do the less well-educated.* Moreover,
     when they do change their minds, they are more likely to be influ-
     enced by new information. Overall, better-educated people defer
     more often to verifiable information and arguments rooted in proven
     factual data, whereas poorly educated persons defer more often to
     expert judgment and to group pressures.
3.   *Educational background affects the listener's (a) desire to keep up
     with current events; (b) sense of fatalism or pessimism; (c) partici-
     pation in community affairs; and (d) willingness to express interests,
     offer opinions, and react from an articulated philosophy or ideolo-
     gy.* Better-educated people usually are more active socially and po-
     litically, more often see possible good coming from such activities,
     and are more willing to talk about their activities than are less well-
     educated people.

Group Membership.   Being a member of reference groups, solidarity
groups, or just plain interest groups influences the way listeners react to
public messages. Even though you may feel separated from family or
estranged from church, or even though you may think you have out-
grown the old high-school gang and neighborhood clique, each of
these groups makes unmistakable claims on what you think and how
you act. Some of these groups have taught you right from wrong; some,
how to resolve puzzling experiences; others, how to greet and get ac-

quainted with strangers, and so on. The influence of experiences you have had with these reference groups, even after you have disassociated yourself from them, lingers on, affecting your behavior in subtle ways.* Therefore, when you are analyzing an audience for the purpose of adapting your message effectively, find out first who belongs to which reference group; then try to ascertain what its members do and how they are likely to think and feel about your subject and point of view.

Cultural and Ethnic Background.   While most of us long ago rejected the notion that races and sub-groups within races differ basically, we all recognize that *culturally induced* differences among races, societies, and peoples are facts of social life. To paraphrase Adele Davis, "We are whom we've lived with." Our cultural or ethnic backgrounds not only determine what foods we like and what forms our recreation takes, but, more importantly, what *social rules* we operate by. Because the number of these social rules affecting our thought and behavior is nearly infinite, we cannot begin to list all of those which affect the reception of oral messages. This does not, however, relieve us from our responsibilities as speakers to try to identify and adjust to the social rules—traditions, if you prefer—which may affect our audience.

Given what the audience knows about you, the occasion, the subject, etc., are there some ethnic traditions or culture-based rules which could affect your listeners' reception of you and your message? If, for example, you are a member of a sorority or fraternity, will a group of "townies" or "dormies" receive your speech on the rush system more skeptically than a group of "brothers" and "sisters"? Or, if you are a black athlete addressing a white audience, are there old cultural prejudices—or at least behavioral expectations—you will have to deal with because of both your race and your avocation? You must constantly address such questions to yourself as you seek to unearth the elements of the cultural and ethnic backgrounds of your listeners in order to determine how you can best shape your message to earn their acceptance and belief.

Cultural and ethnic background, group affiliation, educational level, sex role, age differential, and audience size—these, then, are the *external* factors which can serve you when, as preparers of public messages, you need to know what an audience is like. Recognizing the transitory nature of certain of the generalizations we have made regarding these matters, the tentativeness of others, and the overall caution with which we have advanced them, you will understand that they are intended only as *possible guides* to audience analysis, not an infallible set of rules to be inflexibly applied.

---

*See Irving L. Janis, *Victims of Groupthink* (Boston: Houghton Mifflin Company, 1972).

Audiences . . .

for public messages come in an infinite number of mindsets, sizes, and transactional settings. They may be indifferent or apathetic, antagonistic, enthusiastic or derisive, or downright bellicose. Their motivations may be simple or complex, their value systems obvious or obscure. Taken together, they constitute the challenge of "audience analysis."

Internal Factors in Audience Behavior: Belief-Attitude-Value Systems

When you turn to analyzing the *internal* factors prompting audience behavior in the acceptance or rejection of messages, your task becomes more complicated. Now you often must deal with factors having greater complexity and less visibility. One commonly used approach to the task—and the one that we will take—is through listeners' beliefs, attitudes, and values. To arrive at that understanding, you need to consider first the notion of *concepts* and their *formation.* You need to know how the people in your audiences—and you—*generalize* concepts to evolve beliefs, *weight* concepts to generate attitudes, and *structure* concepts to attribute values.

All of your experiences, and especially those that made a difference in your life—bits of informal and formal schooling, moments of great highs and oppressive lows—ultimately make up the beliefs, attitudes, values, and behaviors that constitute you as a unique individual—a self. Moreover, by the time you are thirty, you probably will have organized these elements into a relatively rigid *belief-attitude-value system.* To understand the importance of such a system, we need to back up a bit and review the ways most of us learn about ourselves, our acquaintances, and our world.

Forming Concepts.   The process of concept formation is highly complex and usually occurs in fits and starts throughout our lives. In general, it involves the six-step operation depicted in Figure 1 on page 75. As the figure suggests, in the physiological activities of attending to your world, you (1) take in *sense-data*—sights, sounds, smells, tactile impressions, tastes—through your various sense perceptors. Then you (2) mentally *categorize* those data, storing some alongside others you have gathered in the past, building new data-banks for unique experiences. Next, you (3) *label* these concept-categories, normally getting such labels from family, friends, acquaintances, and teachers. Once you have categorized and labeled these sense-data, you (4) learn to build connections between categories; that is, you learn to infer or to *reason.* You learn to connect certain concepts so as to form statements in reasoning chains. The next step in the process is (5) *valuation;* you not only sense, categorize, label, and reason in terms of concept-categories, but you also attach positive or negative judgments to propositions and experiences. Finally, when you have evaluated the concepts, you are ready for the last step—(6) using your backlog of categorized sensory experiences, concepts, and feelings to *react to future data.* When this happens, you have acquired a basis for *judging* and a basis for *predicting*—you've learned to learn new facts about yourself and your environment.*

---

*For a somewhat different but expanded discussion of these notions, see Thomas M. Scheidel, *Persuasive Speaking* (Glenview, Ill.: Scott, Foresman and Company, 1967), Chapter 2.

Figure 1./ STEPS IN CONCEPT FORMATION

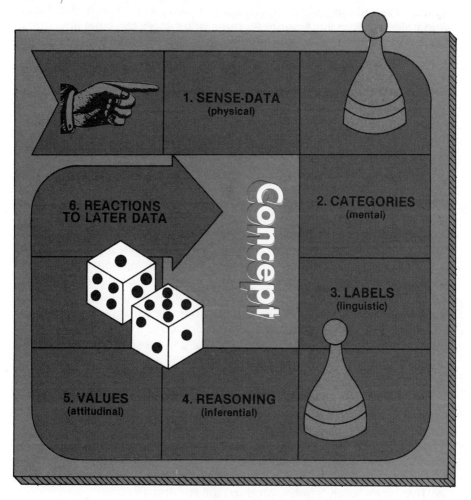

Note two important aspects of this six-step process: *(a)* For the most part, *it is a private affair.* The way you sense the world is your own; your mental categories are your own; to some extent, you reason independently of all others; and, of course, your values are the product of complex interactions among your *selves,* your families, your experiences, etc. *(b)* Because concept formation is such a private activity, *misunderstandings occur regularly.*

For example, suppose that I learned about cows by growing up on a farm where cows were important economic entities, valued friends I guided through sickness and health, and even the source of my sex education. As a result, my concept of "cowness" would be quite different from that of a person raised in inner-city New York, who may have seen cows only in zoos and picture books, who thinks of cows alongside all of the other animals locked in cages. And, of course, we both would have radically different visions of cowness from a child of India, who holds cows in veneration. All three of us apply the label *cow* to the same quadruped, but each brings to the object far different conceptual associations.

Such a process of concept formation, then, accounts for the individuality of each member of an audience. Moreover, because the process occurs in roughly the same way from person to person, it is useful in accounting for the *rationalistic* side of human motivation. The operational result of this six-step process — this belief-attitude-value system — is a kind of psychological grid of concepts and feelings which fuels and feeds each person's cognitive or intellectual processes.

Generalizing Concepts: Beliefs.*   The cornerstones of your cognitive structures are your beliefs. A belief is a proposition which asserts a relationship between two things or between a thing and some attribute of it. Beliefs can be singular ("John is six feet tall"), or general ("All crows are black"). Beliefs can be primitive (based directly upon your own experience or senses) or derivative (learned from someone else: an authority, a book, etc.). Beliefs can be structured vertically (i.e., generated causally from higher-order beliefs or generated inductively from specific instances) or horizontally (if you are against war, you are likely also to be for national self-determination, because beliefs in these two subject-areas often have a side-by-side relationship and are thus aligned horizontally).

Thus, a series of *singular, primitive* beliefs —
"John Jones is six feet tall."
"His brother Hank is five feet, eleven inches tall."
"His sister Janet is six feet, one inch tall." —

can be combined *vertically* (via induction) to form a *general* belief —

"The Jones family's genes produce tall children."

This belief, in turn, can be related to any number of other beliefs *horizontally,* depending upon the individual holding it. For example, this belief could be generalized even further to a belief about genetic engineering ("Genetic engineering or control will produce a race of stronger, more healthy people"); and that belief, in its turn, could be related to others concerning the biological sciences ("Biological research will save the world") or to government's role in genetic research ("Only under the sponsorship of a government can we as a nation make genetic progress"). This succession of horizontal beliefs could conceivably be extended even further to beliefs about government spending, the roles of universities in training biologists, etc.

---

*Based on Chapters 2 and 3 of *Beliefs, Attitudes, and Human Affairs,* by Daryl J. Bem. Copyright © 1970 by Wadsworth Publishing Company, Inc. Used with permission of the publisher, Brooks/Cole Publishing Company, Monterey, California.

Thus, we have termed beliefs the cornerstones of our cognitive structures because they represent *the factual-type statements* we hold to be true. We say "factual-type" because of course not all beliefs are true. For example, humanity long believed that the earth was flat and that the universe revolved around it. These propositions were beliefs; they just happened to be false, even though they worked perfectly to explain the phenomena of nature. Indeed, insofar as the communicator is concerned, one of the most important characteristics of beliefs is that they are *falsifiable.* One of the great weapons of the persuader, therefore, is the use of facts capable of undermining faulty beliefs.

Weighting Concepts: Attitudes.   Beliefs, especially important beliefs, are not merely neutral statements which float around in our heads. Those beliefs which are central to our lives usually are weighted with feelings. That is, we attach positive or negative feelings to a belief, thus creating an attitude. Statements which express positive or negative feelings are *attitudinal statements.* An attitudinal statement can take one of three forms. (1) It can take the form of a *belief-plus-attitude:*

"The U.S.S.R. has more defensive missiles than the U.S., and *I think that's bad.*"

Or (2) it can directly attach a *value-word* ("good," "bad," "right," "wrong," "beautiful," "ugly," etc.) to a concept:

"This road is *lovely.*"

"Black is *beautiful.*"

"Socialized medicine is *bad.*"

Or (3) it can include a *value standard* or *criterion for judgment* (sometimes classified as a *normative statement*):

"*If* you want to get to Des Moines quickly [i.e., if your *value standard* is efficiency], take Interstate 80."

"*If* you want to get to Des Moines along a scenic route [i.e., if your *criterion for judgment* is a highly held aesthetic value], take Highway 6."

Attitudes, at any rate, express our preferences: those things which we approach and those which we seek to avoid. Attitudes are important to the speaker for two reasons: (1) Attitudes themselves often are the targets of persuasion. Indeed, social scientists have devised many theories of *attitude-change,* some of which we shall review in Chapter 6. Because attitudes conceptually lie midway between our beliefs and our values, attitude-change in many ways represents the core of persuasion: if you can change someone's attitudes, you often can affect beliefs, valuative alignments, and behavior directly. (2) Attitudes also provide the persuader with clues to understanding deep-set values and even *motives* (see the next chapter), which in turn can help you determine what appeals to employ in a speech. For example, suppose over a period of time you heard someone say, "Gimme an interstate highway any time!" "What's the quickest way to get a charcoal fire going?" "Looking around the room for something else to carry will save you three hundred steps a day," etc. These statements and questions implicitly or explicitly express a preference for efficiency. The person, therefore, probably is susceptible to an appeal to pragmatic values, and especially to ideas which promise to save time, space, money, or physical effort. In addressing a speech to such a person, say, on agribusiness (increasing the size of and formally incorporating the farm industry), appeals to efficiency, cost saving, and increased production—all based on a pragmatic value—might work well. In this case, a series of attitudinal statements is used as a clue to a utilitarian, persuasive strategy, a particular motive appeal. Understanding a person's attitudes, therefore, provides the speaker with key points of attack.

Structuring Attitudes: Values. Whereas beliefs are statements about the world that are capable of being judged true or false, and attitudes are positive or negative preferences, *values* are congregations or clusters of beliefs to which attitudes have been attached. Psychologists Milton Rokeach and Seymour Parker discuss two kinds of values: (1) *terminal values,* that is, end-states of existence such as "comfortable life," "sense of accomplishment," "world of beauty," "family security," etc.; and (2) *instrumental values,* that is, preferred modes of behavior which allow you to reach terminal ends, such as "ambition," "cheerfulness," "courageousness," and "honesty."[4]

Eduard Spranger, a German scholar, has another useful system of values. He maintains that human beings can be typed or classified according to their dominant *value-complexes.*[5] Thus, in Spranger's system, some people are "economic" types, in that they usually think in terms of usefulness or practicality; others are "political," in that they value competition, power, and influence; still others are "theoretical," in that they are intellectualized, concerned with abstract "truth" and logical rigor. With some modification, Spranger's notion of value-types is a useful one because it allows speakers in a general way to identify— for purposes of audience analysis—six basic value-complexes:

1. *Pragmatic values*—values predicated on the assumption that the end justifies the means, that efficient solutions to problems are more important than abstract considerations.
2. *Political values*—values which seek to establish hierarchical and power relationships between peoples and institutions.
3. *Psychological values*—personalized values which stress the care of the individual's own mind and body, aiming at personal satisfaction with the individual's self.
4. *Sociological values*—values which stress the virtues of human relationships in and of themselves, for whatever personal or group sacrifice is necessary.
5. *Philosophical-theological values*—values which stress the power of commitment to abstract systems of thought and ethics, and to the notion that ideologies ought to dictate behavioral standards.

6. *Aesthetic values* — values which emphasize the importance of form, ritual, and inner/subjective appreciation of beauty.

The usefulness of this analysis of values will become increasingly apparent in the following chapters. Here, we wish chiefly to emphasize that the belief-attitude-value systems (BAV systems) are the rational or cognitive aspects of human motivation. Understanding how they operate in an audience provides you as a speaker with a goodly number of ways to adapt an idea or a proposal and its supporting materials in order to give them maximum impact. Moreover, when you combine an understanding of these internal-factor systems with a careful analysis of the external factors (age, sex, education, group membership, etc.) which influence listeners' behavior, you should be able to analyze with considerable accuracy the nature of a given audience.

Analyzing the Speech Occasion

Occasions can be analyzed in any number of ways — for instance, as *communicative* occasions (a time to argue, a time to persuade, a time to conciliate, etc.), as *ritualistic* occasions (weddings, funerals, inaugurations, etc.), or as *spheres-of-influence* (political occasions, social occasions, religious occasions, etc.). For our purposes here, however, we take a less inclusive and somewhat simpler view. As we define it, *an occasion is any situation which contains rules for expected or traditional modes of physical and symbolic behavior.* That is, an occasion is a time when more or less established rules for acting or modes of conduct tend to affect audience expectation.

The Demands Occasions Can Make

The demands which occasions can make upon speakers may involve four aspects of the speechmaking process: (1) selection of topics, (2) organization of messages, (3) choice of language, and (4) modes of delivery.

Selection of Topics. The occasion can in part control what the speaker can properly say. For example, in an inaugural address the President of the United States is expected to (1) greet the gathered citizenry, (2) suggest that the time for partisan bickering is past, (3) indicate what ills on the domestic scene must be cured, (4) suggest what aspects of foreign affairs will occupy this administration, and (5) ask divine and human help in carrying out the administration's mandate from the people. Other instances in which the list of topics to be covered in whole or in part by the occasion include labor rallies, the monthly meeting of an investment club, opening-day lectures in most classes, football coaches' fall prognostications, etc.

Organization of Messages.   The way messages are put together also may be strongly influenced by the occasion. We expect history lectures to be organized chronologically, political speeches to be organized in a problem-solution format, sermons to explicate a text and then discuss its implications. Such demands for organizational patterns are the products of occasions and their long-established customs or rules.

Choice of Language.   As you are probably well aware, you speak one way in front of close friends, and in quite a different manner when presenting a speech in class. Although you do not become a totally different person in these two situations, communicatively at least you tend to emphasize different aspects of your selfness; and those differences manifest themselves in your language. Similarly, all occasions to a greater or lesser extent influence the linguistic choices a speaker must make. Some speech occasions (for example, a funeral eulogy) demand formal language; others (for example, a football rally) require a casual, informal use of language. Slang often is permissible in a sales speech, but seldom is appropriate in a graduation address. We expect intensely partisan language at a political rally, but want our biology lecturers to use more neutral language. *How* you say what you say, then, is to a considerable extent a product of *where* you say it.

Modes of Delivery.   What is true of language is also true of paralanguage — your use of voice, gesture, and body. We would not expect evangelical fervor from a President addressing the Congress, even though we did expect that same person as a Presidential candidate to pound the podium or to use vigorous gestures and exaggerated vocal force. Nor do we expect a lawyer addressing a jury to stand, eyes affixed to the ceiling; although we would be less disturbed if a philosophy professor were at times to talk to her students in this manner. *Occasions,* in other words, can significantly affect your modes of presentation.

Of course, traditions are sometimes violated intentionally to achieve a particularly powerful effect. Thus, George Whitfield, the eighteenth-century evangelist, moved a great many New Englanders with language much more colorful and flamboyant that any of them had heard from preachers previously. F. D. Roosevelt's so-called fireside chats in the 1930s achieved some of their reputation because he spoke much less formally than his predecessors had. If Demosthenes had not reordered and shuffled the charges placed against him by Aeschines, his personal defense of his public career in his "On the Crown" speech would have lost much of its interest and persuasibility. So if traditions or expectations for a given occasion can be changed by the right speaker at the right time, they can be violated with great success. But, more often than not, most of us follow the rules to gain entry to the minds of an audience and to make sure we do not inadvertently offend anyone.

Ways to Probe the Demands of Occasions

"But," you may well ask, "how can I find out what the rules and prevailing customs in a given speaking situation are? How am I to know what occasions demand of speakers?" Usually, you can find answers to these questions by examining three sources: (1) formal records, (2) observation, and (3) informal learning.

Formal Records. Sometimes the rules for speaking are written down. A book on parliamentary procedure indicates how you can get the floor and propose a motion. For example, if you are elected to your school's student governing body, you will want to examine the constitution and the written rules for parliamentary procedure used by that body. Or, somewhat less formally, if you are going to address a community service club (Lions, Rotary, Optimists, etc.), you may inquire about the club's traditions and expectations: How long do speakers usually talk? Should they be completely serious, or is some humor expected? Do they customarily use visual aids; and, if so, are facilities for them available?

Careful Observation. Sometimes, you can discover the rules for speaking simply by observing how other speakers adjust to the demands of occasions. Politicians, for example, spend a good deal of time analyzing the successes and failures of candidates for public office. John F. Kennedy not only wrote a biography *(Profiles in Courage)* which compelled him to examine the speeches and actions of other politicians, but he also kept detailed files of quotations, rhetorical strategies attempted by previous Presidential campaigners, and random observations on political speaking. You, too, can learn what audiences and occasions demand of speakers by listening and watching evaluatively.

Informal Learning. Fortunately, you can familiarize yourself with a great many of the occasional demands of speaking simply by living. In traversing childhood, puberty, and early adulthood, you moved from occasion to occasion, and both consciously and subconsciously you learned the approved modes of communicative conduct. Thus you can learn how to address a local school board by attending school-board meetings, analyzing what happens there, and watching others present speeches and proposals. Much of this learning occurs randomly, of course, but it is one of the most effective means of discovering the rules and prevailing customs in a given speaking occasion.

In summary, to maximize your speaking effectiveness, often you will have to probe the nature of the occasion to find out if there are special rules for communicative conduct and modes of speechmaking normally followed on that occasion. Such probing, however, will not be exhaustive because of who you are and of how complicated occasions can be. You will want to check out whatever formal rules are available, however; and to better meet the expectations of your audience, you probably will want to note at least generally what other speakers have done on the occasion.

A Sample Analysis of an Audience and an Occasion

Keeping in mind the foregoing guidelines for analyzing audiences and speech occasions, study the following step-by-step analysis prepared by a student for a speech on behalf of an intercollegiate athletic program for women. Observe how the speaker used the facts at her disposal to draw a picture of the persons making up the audience, and how she planned to adapt her remarks to their concerns and attitudes:

   I. *Title:* FROM SPECTATOR TO PARTICIPANT: ATHLETICS FOR WOMEN.
  II. *Subject:* Intercollegiate Athletic Competition for Women Students.
 III. *General Purpose:* To actuate.
  IV. *Specific Purpose:* To get the Board in Charge of Intercollegiate Athletics to institute a program of intercollegiate sports for women students.
   V. *Specific Audience:* The Board in Charge of Intercollegiate Athletics, consisting of the Director of Athletics, the Assistant Director of Athletics, Director of Men's Intramural Sports, Director of Women's Intramural Sports, six coaches of men's varsity sports, five elected faculty members, and five elected student representatives. One intramural director, one faculty member, and one student representative are women.
  VI. *Analysis of Occasion:*
       A. *Nature:* Annual meeting of the Board to approve the budget for the coming year.
       B. *Prevailing Rules:* A strict time limit of five minutes for every speech made to the Board, plus any time needed for questions by Board members.
       C. *Precedents and Consequences:* Speech will be given late in the afternoon, after Board has heard many other requests. Board members probably will be tired. After all requests have been heard, the Board will still have to draw up the budget.
       D. *Physical Environment:* Board will meet at tables set up in an auxiliary gymnasium, surrounded by athletic equipment.
 VII. *Analysis of Audience:*
       A. *Composition:*
            1. *Size:* Twenty Board members, plus additional spectators.
            2. *Age:* Five members are of college age; fifteen members are between 30 and 55.
            3. *Sex:* Seventeen males, three females.
            4. *Occupation:* Collegiate personnel with special interests and qualifications in athletics.
            5. *Education:* One third were physical education majors in college, most with advanced degrees; one third are under-

graduates; one third are Ph.D.'s in arts or sciences.
  6. *Membership in groups:* All are members of Board as well as of general academic community. The factors influencing both groups can be made salient in the speech.
  7. *Cultural-Ethnic Background:* Two Board members are black (but this not a factor here).
B. *Knowledge of Subject:* Board members have:
  1. Specialized knowledge of nature of intercollegiate competition in sports.
  2. General knowledge of present women's intramural athletic program.
  3. Probable knowledge of current campus controversy over question of an intercollegiate sports program for women.
C. *Beliefs, Attitudes, and Values:*
  1. *Political:* Board is undoubtedly aware of general charge of sexism in the athletic program and wishes to avoid politicizing its functions.
  2. *Theoretical:* Board members believe strongly in values of college athletics generally.
  3. *Economic:* Board undoubtedly is worried about increased cost of intercollegiate athletic program, yet well aware that a portion of its money comes from student fees.
D. *Attitude Toward Speaker:* Probably suspicious.
E. *Attitude Toward Subject:* Interest mixed with uneasiness and uncertainty about extent and nature of program to be proposed.
F. *Attitude Toward Speech Purpose:* Most Board members are probably undecided; a few may be hostile.

VIII. *Proposed Adaptation to Audience and Occasion:*
A. Introduce speech with thanks for fine intramural program now available to women. Make reference to surrounding facilities and equipment.
B. Keep language of speech positive, but not so strong as to alienate neutral or undecided listeners.
C. Stress primarily the values of intercollegiate competition for women. Mention — but with this predominantly male audience, do not overemphasize — the matter of equality between the sexes.
D. Show a knowledge of the financial problems faced by the Board. Ask only for women's field and track competition for coming year, with more sports to be added later. Demonstrate how maximum participation may be realized at minimum cost.
E. Be prepared to answer Board's possible questions concerning number of women interested, neighboring schools which could furnish competition, estimated cost of proposed program, available locker-room facilities, equipment, etc.

Reference Notes

[1] Aristotle, *Rhetoric,* p. 1389b.

[2] Alfred Hero, "Public Reaction to Government Policy," in John P. Robinson, Jerrold G. Rusk, and Kendra B. Head, *Measures of Political Attitudes* (Ann Arbor: Survey Research Center, Institute for

Social Research, 1969); Leonard Broom and Philip Selznick, *Sociology,* 4th Edition (New York: Harper & Row, Publishers, Inc., 1968); James N. Morgan and others, *Productive Americans* (Ann Arbor: Survey Research Center, Institute for Social Research, 1966); Angus Campbell and others, *The American Voter* (John Wiley & Sons, Inc., 1964); A. W. Bowden and others, " 'Halo' Prestige," *Journal of Abnormal and Social Psychology* 28 (January-March 1934); S. E. Asch, "Studies of Independence and Conformity: A Minority of One Against a Unanimous Majority," *Psychological Monographs* 70 (1956), No. 9; Janet L. Wolff, *What Makes Women Buy* (New York: McGraw-Hill Book Company, 1958); Theodore M. Newcomb and others, *Social Psychology* (New York: Holt, Rinehart & Winston, Inc., 1965); David Krech and others, *Individual in Society* (New York: McGraw-Hill Book Company, 1962); C. E. Swanson, "Predicting Who Learns Factual Information from the Mass Media," in *Groups, Leadership and Men: Research in Human Relations,* edited by H. Guetzkow (Pittsburgh: Carnegie Institute of Technology Press, 1951); and E. J. Brown, "The Self as Related to Formal Participation in Three Pennsylvania Rural Communities," *Rural Sociology* †8 (December 1953); all as cited in Howard H. Martin and C. William Colburn, *Communication and Consensus: An Introduction to Rhetorical Discourse* (New York: Harcourt Brace Jovanovich, Inc., 1972), Chapter 4, 74–79.

[3]Aristotle, *Rhetoric,* p. 1389b.

[4]Reprinted from "Values as Social Indicators of Poverty and Race in America" in volume no. CCCLXXXVIII of *The Annals* of The American Academy of Political and Social Science. © 1977 by The American Academy of Political and Social Science. All Rights Reserved. See also Milton M. Rokeach, *Beliefs, Attitudes, and Values: A Theory of Organization and Change* (San Francisco: Jossey-Bass, Inc., 1968), and his *The Nature of Human Values* (New York: Collier-Macmillan, Free Press, 1973).

[5]From *Types of Men,* 5th Edition by Eduard Spranger. Reprinted by permission of Max Niemeyer Verlag.

Problems and Probes

1. Think of three hypothetical speaking occasions, envisioning audience composition, subject matter, and speaker purpose. Explain how such factors as sex, educational level, geographical region, occupation, and age might affect the persuasive message of the speaker in each of the hypothetical instances.

2. Study your own class in terms of audience composition. Analyze the members of the class according to the internal and external factors discussed in this chapter. Attempt to generalize on the basis of the following questions: As a persuasive speaker, what assumptions can you make about your audience's values, expectations, and beliefs? How must you as a speaker adapt to this audience? Check with the other members of the class to see how well your generalizations coincide with their actual expectations, values, and beliefs.

3. Read or listen to a speech in which the values, beliefs, and attitudes of the listeners are hostile toward the purpose of the speaker. Analyze the speech to ascertain as well as you can how the speaker has endeavored to overcome the hostility or apathy and influence the audience to accept his or her purpose and message.

4. Select a suitable subject and use it to frame a specific purpose for a five-minute speech to persuade *(a)* an audience that is favorable, but not aroused; *(b)* an audience that is interested, but undecided; *(c)* an audience that is apathetic; *(d)* an audience that is hostile toward the proposition or recommendation; and *(e)* an audience that is opposed to any change from the present situation.

Oral Activities and Speaking Assignments

1. After your instructor has divided the class into four-person groups, meet with the other members of your group, and discuss with them the next round of speeches to be presented: the actual topic you are intending to use, your general and specific purpose, development of your idea or proposition, your speech plan or outline, useful kinds of supporting materials, etc. Criticize each other's

plans and preparation, offering suggestions for changes and more specific adaptations to this particular classroom audience. After discussing and evaluating the potential of your speech with a portion of your audience, you should be able subsequently to develop and present a better and more effectively adapted message to the class as a whole.

2. As a student of speech communication, you can learn something about the principles of audience analysis by observing how such public-opinion pollsters as Dr. George Gallup analyze "the great American audience" to derive the samples upon which they base their predictions. Together with several other members of your class (as your instructor may designate), investigate these methods as described in books, magazine articles, newspaper surveys, etc., and report on them orally, either in individual presentations or in an informal discussion with the class as a whole.

 Suggestions for Further Reading

James W. Chesebro, "Cultures in Conflict: A Generic and Axiological View," *Today's Speech* XXI (Spring 1973): 11–20.

Paul Holtzman, *The Psychology of Speakers' Audiences* (Glenview, Ill.: Scott, Foresman and Company, 1970).

Kathleen M. Jamieson, "Generic Constraints and the Rhetorical Situation," *Philosophy and Rhetoric* VI (1973): 162–170.

Mary Lystad, *As They See It: Changing Values of College Youth* (Cambridge, Mass.: Schenkman Publishing Co., Inc., 1973).

Thomas M. Scheidel, *Speech Communication and Human Interaction,* 2nd ed. (Glenview, Ill.: Scott, Foresman and Company, 1976), Chapter 7.

Richard E. Vatz, "The Myth of the Rhetorical Situation," *Philosophy and Rhetoric* VI (1973): 154–161.

Determining the
Basic Appeals

In the preceding chapter we emphasized the importance of analyzing your audience in order to discover its social and cognitive structure. In this chapter we will examine the *motivational foundations* underlying that structure. In order to do this, however, we must first establish the relationship between cognitive structure and motivation; then we can examine motives and motivational appeals; and, finally, we will be able to describe ways in which a speaker can unite analyses of BAV systems and motives concretely. Again, this chapter, like the previous one, is fundamentally preparatory to the actual construction of messages.*

Motivation and Belief-Attitude-Value Systems

In the pages that follow we shall pursue what is commonly called a *functional approach to cognitive change.* That is, we are taking the view that human beings develop their curiosities, form their belief-attitude-value systems (BAV systems), and alter their perceptions of the world in accordance with and to the extent that these psychological phenomena or constructs fulfill or frustrate their basic needs. These needs, in turn, are

---

*For other discussions of the relationships between cognitive and motivational structures, see Richard V. Wagner and John J. Sherwood, *The Study of Attitude Change* (Monterey, Calif.: Brooks/Cole Publishing Company, 1969), and Daryl J. Bem, *Beliefs, Attitudes, and Human Affairs* (Monterey, Calif.: Brooks/Cole Publishing Company, 1970), esp. Chapters 2–5. And, for fuller treatments of motives and the roles they play in communication generally, see William V. Haney, *Communication and Organizational Behavior: Texts and Cases* (Homewood, Ill.: Richard D. Irwin, Inc., 1967), Chapter 4; and Thomas M. Scheidel, *Speech Communication and Human Interaction,* 2nd ed. (Glenview, Ill.: Scott, Foresman and Company, 1976), pp. 164–178.

rooted in the very animalness of humans, in their tendencies to protect themselves, reward themselves, reproduce themselves physically, interact with others, band together for common defense and reward, etc. Thus, we do not change our BAV systems solely on the basis of new information and abstract, valuative concerns, but primarily as a result of changes in our substructure of motives. Human cognitions are driven or acted upon by feeling-impulses which function to solidify or change our cognitive structures. Consider these examples:

Example A. You are walking through a woods on a fall afternoon. You hear a gunshot, and you jump. Then you say to youself, "That must have been a gunshot."

Example B. You know nothing about glaucoma. One day a doctor tells your grandmother that she has the eye disease. You immediately go to the library to find a layman's explanation of it.

Example C. You have been dating a person for some time, going together to films, concerts, picnics, etc. Finally, you decide that tonight you will ask the big question, "Do you love me?" You know you will do it toward the end of the evening. Every half hour or so during the earlier part of the evening, you notice that your palms become clammy, beads of sweat appear on your forehead, your heart seems to race, and an unmistakable knot twists in your stomach.

Example D. You have never been much on going to church. One evening, however, you agree to attend a religious gathering; and you become convinced of the truth of the claims offered. Thereupon, you devote at least ten hours a week to explaining those truths to anyone who will listen.

These examples illustrate four important aspects of the relationships between BAV systems and motives:

1. *Motives are bio-basic and often precognitive.* In Example A, you jumped without thinking; the thought—"That must have been a gunshot"—came after the physiological reaction. Like any other animal, the human being must protect itself, and in many situations can do so without "using its head."
2. *Motives often manifest themselves physiologically.* The sweat, increase in blood pressure, and stomachache in Example C attest to the power that fear of the unknown has in our lives. Lie detectors, for example, work because motives manifest themselves physiologically. A lie normally is accompanied by a rush of guilt which, in turn, causes minute but recordable changes in galvanic skin response, heart rate, blood flow, etc. The study of "body language"—of the observable signs and signals we give off unconsciously in the presence of others—rests on similar ground. Body language experts or readers assume that your inner states are manifested in eye-pupil dilation, posture (for example, crossing your arms or legs), nervous gestures, and on and on—matters we shall take up in Chapter 14.

3. *Motives can affect beliefs.* In Example B, you sought information—that is, you wanted to construct generalized beliefs—about glaucoma because you feared for your grandmother (or yourself). Motives affect beliefs in very powerful ways. Thus, a motive (thirst) can make you believe you see something (the mirage of water) even when it does not exist.

4. *Conversely, beliefs can affect motivation.* In Example D, once you had acquired the strong set of beliefs-attitudes-values which represent religious conversion, the motivation to confront even strangers with those beliefs, attitudes, and values was almost overwhelming. On a smaller scale, you can see this principle illustrated every time you go to a county fair. In a booth, a huckster stands slicing vegetables with a clever little machine, working on the assumption that once you know (that is, have a belief about) what the machine can do, you will buy it (that is, be motivated to act positively on it).

What we have been saying, therefore, is that there exists a highly complex relationship between motivation and BAV systems, that is, between feelings/emotions and ideas/values. For our purposes as speakers, the most important fact about motives is that they can function to alter beliefs, attitudes, and values. Indeed, because they are so deeply rooted in often unconscious aspects of the human psyche, they represent *the principal tool for changing people through public speech communication.*

Motive Needs

In each of the four examples we have just cited, an inner aim or goal impelled you to act; a deeply seated or felt need or desire motivated you to do something. You experienced both need and motive; and because of this *motive need,* you tended to move or act in a certain direction. Depending upon their particular point of view, psychologists have called such action-tendencies by different names: instincts, emotions, prepotent reflexes, purposive or wish-fulfilling impulses, inner drives, and so on. Despite these differences in labels, however, certain propositions are quite commonly agreed upon: (1) In all human beings there are certain universal action-tendencies; the organism, that is, has within it the capacity and tendency to move in different directions. (2) Much human behavior is need-motivated and goal-directed. And (3) a human being's locomotion toward some goal is activated by physiological needs, psychological impulses, and environmental prods, or some combination of such forces.

The importance of these three propositions is that with such simple notions we can conceptualize the function of speech communication in terms of an inertia principle: *The normal condition of people in an audience is one of physical relaxation, mental inertia, and emotional equilibrium, unless something has already happened to stir these people into motion or unless the speaker does so through verbal and/or nonverbal cues.* In other words, if you are to accomplish the purpose of your speech, you must *(a)* overcome the inertia of your listeners; or *(b)* if they are already moving mentally in a direction *away* from your objective, you must counteract that tendency by setting in motion some fundamental reaction or motive need which will move them in the direction of your goal. But before you can do so, you must understand what these basic urges or reaction-tendencies are, and you must know how to make them salient—how to cause them to stand out in the thinking of your listeners.

Motivational Appeals

Recognizing that a *motive need* is an impulse to satisfy either a biological urge or a psychological-social want, you may well ask: How can I as a public speaker go about creating, using, and/or satisfying such needs? How can I translate these basic needs/wants/desires into linguistic acts—into effective public communication? The answer to both of these question is: with the use of motivational appeals.

Briefly, *a motivational appeal is either (1) a visualization of some desire and a method for satisfying it, or (2) an assertion that some entity, idea, or course of action can be or ought to be linked with an impulse-to-human-action—that is, a motive.* Thus, in Example C above, sweaty palms, a fluttering heartbeat, and stomach cramps probably were produced by visualization. Earlier in the evening, both before and while you were with your date, you created little pictures—perhaps even full pieces of dramatic dialogue—of what declaring your love would be like. Will you be suave, casual, or a stuttering fool? Will you find the words, the looks, the actions to move your beloved? Will the object of your affections respond verbally or nonverbally, with tears or laughter, flippantly or seriously? Will you be accepted or rejected? In visualizing various scenarios, you play-acted yourself through a variety of motivational appeals: Is the *fear of rejection* worth the possibility of mutual *declarations of love*? Will *aggressiveness* work better than a quiet expression of your need for closer *companionship*? Should you profess *independence* or *dependence*? You probably made decisions on such tactics by trying them out in your head, creating little vignettes with various moves and countermoves. By a process of *intrapersonal* visualization you thus assembled a group of motives potent enough—you hoped—to move your date in the direction of the decision you wanted. That is, you carefully sorted out and selected the motivational appeals you deemed most effective.

At other times, instead of visualizing courses of action for yourself or your listener, you may simply try to attach motivational concepts directly to other concepts. In Example D, perhaps you had long associated such motivational concepts as *conformity, authority, dominance, revulsion,* and *destruction* with the institution of the church. Then, following the evening of the religious meeting, you came to see that the institution ought to be associated with *adventure, endurance, loyalty, beauty, reverence,* or *generosity.* That is, you decided that you had misconstrued the church's motivation and even misanalyzed your own. Conversion was effected, and your behavior changed.

Motivational appeals, therefore, are verbal attempts to make salient and relevant a series of motives within an audience, within an idea or proposal under discussion, or within a countervailing force that is stopping listeners from accepting that idea or proposal. Such appeals work *visually* (through verbal depiction) or *assertively* (through verbal propositions of association).

Some Types and Examples of Motivational Appeals

Present in every listener and every audience, of course, is an infinite number of specific human wants and needs to which you can direct your appeals. Any attempt to specify or enumerate them, therefore, must of necessity be incomplete and overlapping to some extent. However, the list in Figure 1 can — because of its applicability and practicality — provide a useful starting point. In it you will find a number of specific desires, drives, feelings, and sentiments to which motivational appeals have often proved effective. By mastering the list and achieving a thorough understanding of the meaning and import of each of the items, you can begin immediately to use them in your analysis of your listeners' attitudes, beliefs, and values. This, essentially, is what we meant when we said at the outset of this chapter that we are taking a *functional approach to motivation and attitude-formation/change.*

To open up just a few of the many possibilities of these motivational appeals, let us briefly examine a number of them:

Achievement and Display.   Ordinarily, people want to do their best. They yearn to achieve success or distinction. They are willing to work hard to accomplish tasks in which they can display their skill and expertise, to *have,* to *do,* or to *be* something that sets them apart, that makes others willing to acknowledge their uniqueness.

Acquisition and Savings.   Most of us like to earn money, to keep it, and to spend only as much as necessary to acquire the other things we want. Discount stores are filled with people trying to get as much as possible at the lowest price. Advertisements for airlines and resort hotels frequently feature special "off-season rates." But this acquisitive or thrift-conscious motive extends to many things besides money. Stamp collecting, the keeping of photo albums, the gathering of art treasures or rare books, and similar hobbies reflect the same tendency.

Adventure and Change.   Nearly everyone likes the thrill of mild danger — the adventure of diving beneath the surface of the sea, of scaling a mountain, or of exploring strange lands and cities. Basic to a yen for

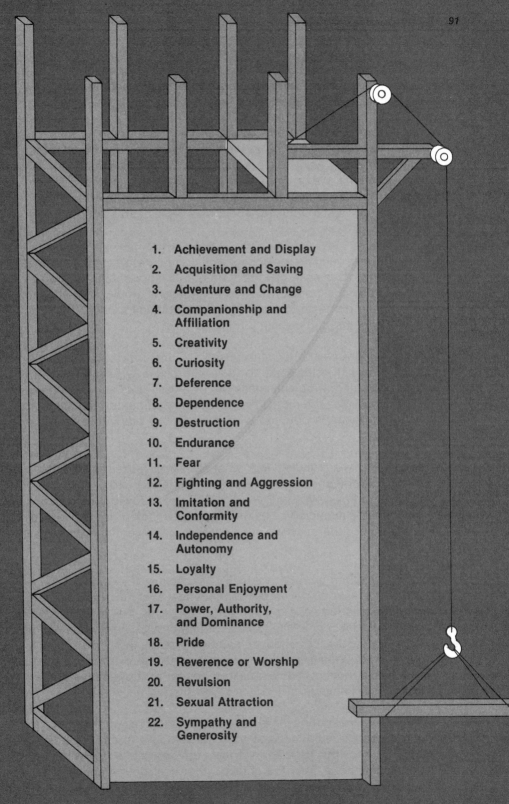

1. Achievement and Display
2. Acquisition and Saving
3. Adventure and Change
4. Companionship and Affiliation
5. Creativity
6. Curiosity
7. Deference
8. Dependence
9. Destruction
10. Endurance
11. Fear
12. Fighting and Aggression
13. Imitation and Conformity
14. Independence and Autonomy
15. Loyalty
16. Personal Enjoyment
17. Power, Authority, and Dominance
18. Pride
19. Reverence or Worship
20. Revulsion
21. Sexual Attraction
22. Sympathy and Generosity

Figure 1. / BUILDING MOTIVATIONAL APPEALS

adventure is the longing for *change*. Change is the impetus that drives us to seek out new and different things, to meet other people, to try new jobs, or participate in the latest fads.

Companionship and Affiliation.   A few people prefer to be hermits, but most of us like company. We cross the street to walk with a friend rather than walk alone. We want to be a part of a group, to share, to make strong attachments. We go to parties, join clubs, write letters to absent relatives, and prefer to live in a dormitory or share an apartment with friends. Even the most tedious task becomes more bearable if others are sharing it with us.

Creativity.   The urge to create shows itself in many ways: in inventions, books, buildings, business organizations, and empires. In addition to building with physical objects such as bricks, steel, or wood, we like to organize human beings into working units—political parties, business firms, athletic teams, and the like.

Curiosity.   Children tear open alarm clocks to find out where the tick is, and adults crowd the sidewalks to gaze at a celebrity passing by. But curiosity is not mere inquisitiveness or nosiness, as is sometimes implied. It also provides the motivation for the experimenter, the scholar, and—when curiosity is coupled with the love for adventure—the explorer.

Deference.   There are times when most of us recognize the advantage of deferring to someone whose wisdom, experience, and expertise are greater than our own. We sense the benefit of following instructions and doing what is expected of us. In the spirit of deference, we accept the leadership of others, conform to custom, and even learn to praise other people.

Dependence.   When people *over*-defer, especially for extended periods of time, they tend to develop a dependence. Everyone is, of course, born dependent; and this is a feeling not altogether lost in adulthood. Whatever their age, people like to have others provide help when needed. In proper measure, dependence can be a healthy thing; overdone, it can quickly erode initiative and destroy other necessary drives and action-tendencies. Indeed, many speakers appeal to its negative consequences in urging change.

Destruction.   In most of us there seems to be an occasional impulse to tear apart, to break, to bulldoze over, to batter down, to cut to pieces—to destroy. Perhaps this urge springs from the desire to show our superiority, our dominance, over the object of our destruction and thus expand our ego. In any event, we are all destroyers at times. Build a house of blocks for a baby, and he knocks it down. Let someone present a theory or an argument, and someone else delights in picking it full of holes and tearing it apart.

Endurance.   Stick-to-itiveness in a highly mobile and impermanent age may seem something of an incongruity, but it is nevertheless a strong motivating force which tends to keep most of us steadily at a job until it is finished. On a larger scale, the motive of endurance is responsible for our sense of timelessness and institutional sanctity; people sometimes sacrifice their lives to guarantee that social institutions will endure.

Fear.   If the other person is bigger than you are, you hesitate to attack him. Instead, you go home and put a lock on the door to keep him out. Physical injury, however, is by no means the only thing we fear. We are also afraid of losing our jobs, our property, our friends, our future. Especially do we fear the dangerous power of what is strange or hidden: *the unknown.* If the members of an audience are needlessly fearful, your first task is to reassure them — to allay their anxieties and dreads. If they are unaware of a danger that confronts them, your duty is to warn them.

Fighting and Aggression.   Much has been spoken and written in an effort to explain why human creatures fight one another — why they engage in acts of aggression and violence. Here we shall concern ourselves with only two facets of this multifaceted manifestation of human conflict: *anger* and *competition.* We become angry at people who cheat or insult us, challenge our ideas or values, destroy our property, or interfere with our rights or efforts. The form in which we fight back against these intrusions may vary from physical attack to subtly destructive gossip, but normally it has for its purpose protecting our safety or restoring our self-esteem. The impulse to fight or to struggle also evidences itself in *competition.* Even though we are not angry with antagonists, we enjoy matching wits and muscles with them for the sheer pleasure of the struggle or for the sake of demonstrating our superiority. Participation in games is based on this tendency, and many people argue or debate for this reason. Business and scholastic rivalries are manifestations of the element of competition. The prevalent phrase "We *beat* them" suggests the combative nature of such efforts.

Imitation and Conformity.   Both consciously and subconsciously, people tend to imitate others. From earliest childhood, all of us try to emulate those whom we most greatly admire; and as we grow older, the range of the people, ideas, and behaviors we imitate steadily increases. We copy the garb, attitudes, actions, and even the pronunciations of other persons — especially of those we respect or envy. Do not suppose, however, that imitation is exclusively volitional; much of it is *imposed.* Oftentimes we feel compelled to imitate — to *conform* — because of subtle or overt pressures from peers, parents, and professors. "They say" and "Everybody's doing it" are clearly conformative in their motivation.

Independence and Autonomy. In spite of the tendency to imitate or conform, we do not like to lose our independence, to be bossed about, to have to attend class, or to be prohibited from acting as we like. If you can influence your hearers to believe they are doing something of their own volition, they will be much more likely to do it than if the act is forced upon them.

Loyalty. The feeling of loyalty, based upon our tendency as individuals to identify with other persons or groups, sometimes provides strong motivation. The strength of the loyalty appeal will vary, however, with the degree to which the individual has become identified with a particular person or group of persons. Hence, a person's loyalty to family is usually stronger than loyalty to a college or a social club.

Personal Enjoyment. Pleasures are many and varied, and people usually act to prevent their curtailment or to enhance their effect. Among the pleasures almost universally desired we find the enjoyment of comfort and luxury, beauty and order, sensory satisfactions, and relief from burdensome restrictions and restraints. Other pleasures are more personal in nature and vary from individual to individual.

Power, Authority, and Dominance. Most of us like to exert influence over others. In search of power, people have given up lucrative positions to enter government service at a much smaller salary, hoping thereby to increase their dominance over other human beings and to influence the course of events. If you can combine an appeal to increased power with an appeal to self-advancement in the form of a larger income or a higher social status, many of your listeners are likely to find your message exceedingly persuasive.

Pride. One of the most powerful single appeals that can be made is to pride, especially when you are dealing with young people. A varsity letter has little intrinsic value, but an unbelievable amount of work often will be done to earn one. Election to an honorary society has more importance to the average student than a cash award. But the influence of pride is not limited to the young; from childhood to old age, we all are extremely careful to protect our egos. Pride manifests itself in numerous ways, including intensive efforts to earn a *reputation, self-respect,* and recognition as a person of *sound judgment.*

Reverence or Worship. There are times when all of us sense our own inferiority in relation to a superior person, idea, or thing. If we admire this sufficiently, we may grow to revere it. Reverence combines a feeling of humility and a willingness to subordinate ourselves. It takes three common forms: *hero worship,* or the deep admiration of other persons; *reverence for traditions and institutions;* and *worship of a deity,* whether it be conceived religiously or as a philosophical concept.

Revulsion. The fragrance of a flower garden attracts people; the odor of a refuse heap repels them. Just as pleasant sensory experiences evoke enjoyment, so unpleasant sensations and perceptions arouse disgust or loathing. By showing the unsanitary conditions in a city's slums, you may create sentiment to clean them up. By picturing the horrors of war in bloody detail, you may influence hearers who could not be reached by reasoned arguments alone. While doing these things, however, beware of rendering your descriptions so gruesome that your speech itself becomes revolting. Restraint is required to make a description of repulsive conditions vivid enough to be impressive without, at the same time, offending the sensibilities of the listeners.

Sexual Attraction. In the vast majority of cases, men strive for the attentions of women, and women seek to attract men. The importance of this force in human life needs no emphasis here. Whatever promises to make us more attractive in the eyes of the opposite sex, or to remove an obstacle to that attraction, usually gains our support. The taboos that society has placed upon sexual matters, however, require that the speaker use care in referring to them. Stories, anecdotes, or jokes which treat sex in vulgar ways, or language too heavily freighted with sexual terms and innuendos may repel rather than attract your listeners. Properly used, however, the appeal to sexual attractiveness itself is strong; and when employed with the appropriate restraints, it strongly supports other appeals a speaker may employ.

Sympathy and Generosity. Just as we are likely to identify ourselves with the groups to which we belong or aspire to belong, so we tend to see ourselves in the plight of those who are less fortunate than ourselves. This feeling of compassion for the unhappy or the unlucky, which we here call sympathy, makes us want to help them. We pause to aid a blind man or to comfort a crying child. Out of generosity we give money to feed people whose homes have been ravaged by flood, earthquake, or fire. As a speaker, you may influence your audience by rousing in them the sentiment of sympathy or pity. To do so, however, remember that you must make it easy for them to identify themselves with the unfortunate ones, to put themselves in the other persons' shoes. You cannot accomplish this with statistics and abstractions; you must describe specifically, sympathetically, and compassionately the individuals to whom you refer, and you must depict their plight vividly.

Motivational Appeals and Valuative Orientations

Having examined valuative orientations in the previous chapter and motivational appeals here, we are now in a position to consider how these matters are related. As we suggested earlier, the relationships between BAV systems and motives assuredly are complex. Sometimes beliefs, attitudes, and values seem to determine what our motivations are; at other times the obverse appears true. And at still other times, it is almost impossible to determine what motivates individuals to believe or to act, for human beings can at times be highly capricious, with no seemingly coherent patterns of behavior. Despite these difficulties, however, it is still possible to discern certain relationships between values and motives which seem to hold for a relatively large number of people in many important situations. Figure 2, page 97, suggests what some of these relationships may be.

The world of human thought and action is not necessarily as neat as Figure 2 indicates. And we must stress that crossover is certainly not unusual. For the person who loves money, for instance, "monetary worth" becomes a more personally satisfying motive than a pragmatic motive; for others, political activity is more a search for affiliation and companionship than for power; and so on. But the chart at least suggests some possible relationships between valuative orientations and motivational appeals — relationships you reasonably may want to examine when preparing a speech. Moreover, it can serve to remind you of a truth often lost in waves of abstract analysis: While it is possible for us *analytically* to separate BAV systems (cognitive or rational structures) from motive needs (impulsive or emotional structures), *in reality,* as a communicator you must deal with the whole human being, with the complex bundle of ideas, impulses, attitudes, aspirations, values, and ideologies which comprise each person in your audience. As you approach actual audiences made up of actual people, then, you may want to use Figure 2 to explore some or all of the following questions:

1. On my particular topic, is my audience more likely to be reached through appeals to pragmatic, political, psychological, sociological, philosophical-theological, or aesthetic values?
2. If, say, psychological values probably will dominate, what aspects of personal gain should I emphasize? Adventure? Curiosity? Fear? Independence?
3. If I need to stress two or more values, how should I integrate my motivational appeals? Should I make the pragmatic values stand out by mentioning them first and last, and thus make the sociological values secondary by placing them in the middle of my speech or giving less time to their development?
4. May I have to be careful in reconciling certain potentially conflicting motivational appeals? For example, if I decide pragmatic values are important and hence appeal to efficiency and monetary gain, and yet also seek to emphasize philosophical-theological values by an appeal to lasting qualities and future reward, potentially I have a conflict within the motivational structure of my speech and am liable to the charge of inconsistency.
5. In the final analysis, in what ways do my own valuative orientation and motivational structure limit what I may legitimately say to my audience? If, for instance, I despise religion, I undoubtedly would be untrue to myself if I were to make an appeal to divine judgment

Figure 2. / VALUATIVE ORIENTATIONS AND THEIR PRINCIPAL MOTIVATIONAL FOUNDATIONS

VALUES HELD

PRINCIPAL MOTIVATIONAL FOUNDATIONS FOR THE VALUE HELD

PRAGMATIC VALUES
- acquisition and savings
- efficiency
- monetary worth
- progress
- technological ease

POLITICAL VALUES
- dependence upon others
- fighting/aggression
- competition
- power/authority dominance
- loyalty to country or other high authority

PSYCHOLOGICAL VALUES
- achievement and display
- adventure
- curiosity
- endurance
- fear/anger
- independence and autonomy
- personal enjoyment
- pride
- revulsion

SOCIOLOGICAL VALUES
- affiliation and companionship
- deference to others
- imitation and conformity
- loyalty to other people/groups
- sexual attraction
- sympathy and generosity

PHILOSOPHICAL THEOLOGICAL VALUES
- authority of ideas
- loyalty to ideas and ideologies
- coherence of action
- reverence and worship
- future reward

AESTHETIC VALUES
- beauty
- creativity
- form and organization

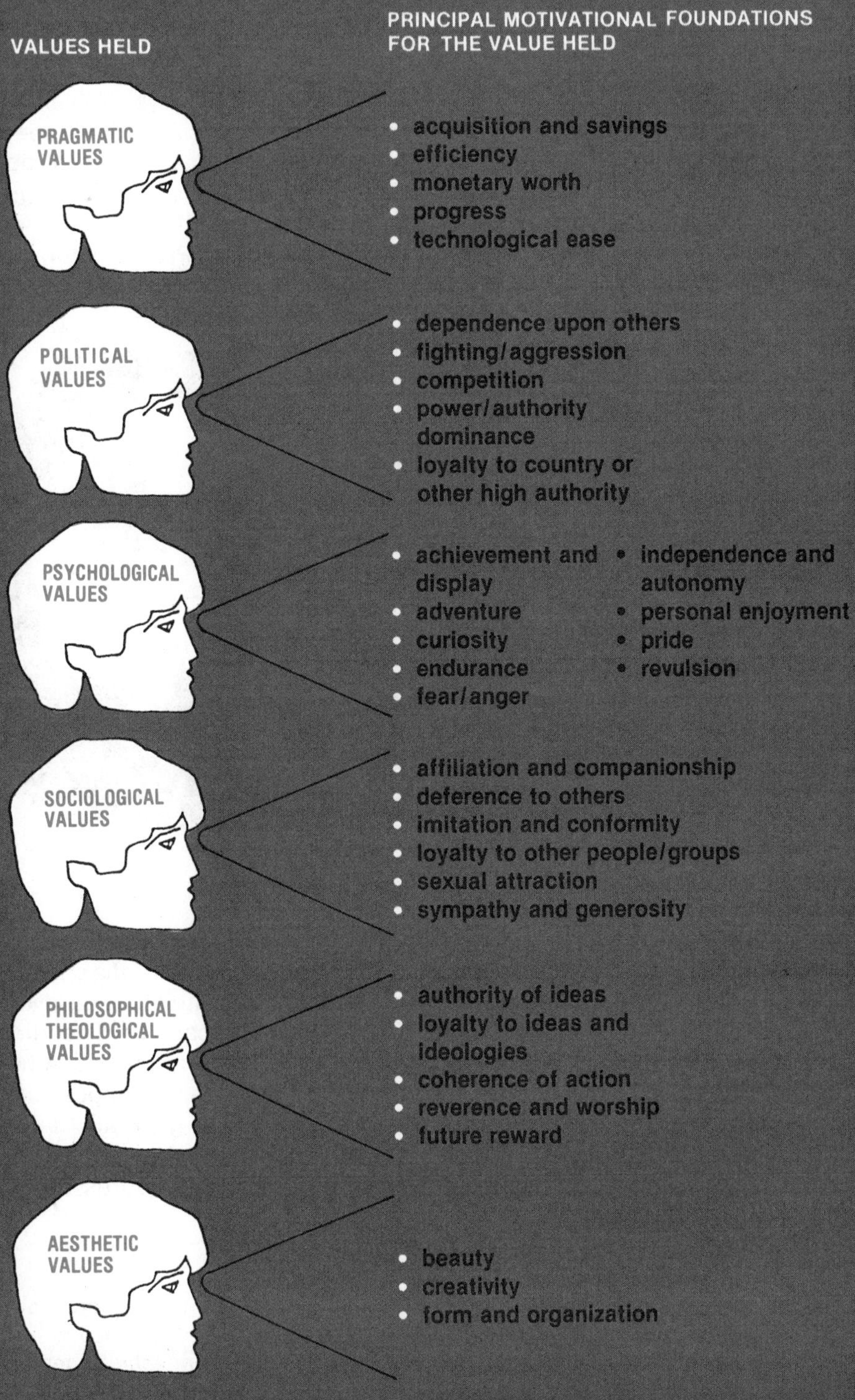

when urging a course of action, just as I could not tolerate myself if I appealed to sexuality while personally abhoring people who read "sex" into everything. In selecting motivational appeals, my own ethic always must constitute a final court of judgment.

These questions will merely get you started in your analysis of valuative orientations and motivational appeals. Given a specific topic, a specific audience, and a specific speaker (yourself), you can of course go much further in the analysis of values and motives. The diagram shown below provides an example of the way in which a specific motivational appeal—fear—can be used to relate your message ("Protect yourself with 'Fire Alert'") to your audience.

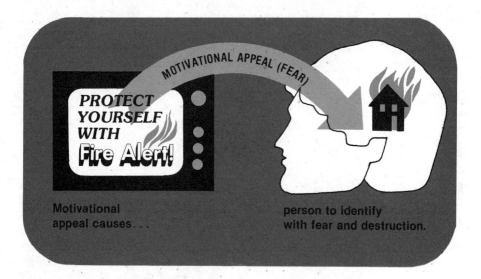

Using Motivational Appeals to Extend an Audience Analysis

In the previous chapter we presented a step-by-step analysis of a speaking situation in which a speaker proposed to get an athletic board to expand women's competitive sports programs on her campus. The title of that speech, you will recall, was "From Spectator to Participant: Athletics for Women"; and Points I through VIII of that analysis appear on pages 82–83. Point VIII and its subpoints A, C, and E generally dealt with motivational appeals. In light of the new information presented in this chapter, we now can suggest more specific appeals addressed to this end; specifically:

VIII. *Proposed Adaptation to Audience and Occasion*
   A. Introduce speech with thanks for fine intramural program now available to women *(appeal to previous generosity)*. Make reference to surrounding facilities and equipment *(appeal to current achievements)*.

    C.   Stress primarily the *theoretical* values of intercollegiate competition for women. *(Such an appeal to professionals often ridiculed as "jocks" and anti-intellectuals can emphasize personal worth, adventure, creativity, competition, pride, etc.)* Mention — but with this predominantly male audience, do not over-emphasize — the matter of equality between the sexes *(allay fears, and only gently move into questions of dominance).*

    E.   Be prepared to answer Board's possible questions concerning number of women interested *(indirect appeal to political power),* neighboring schools which could furnish competition *(appeal to competition),* estimated cost of proposed program *(appeal to ease of acquisition),* available locker-room facilities *(visualization of proposal's workability),* etc.

Overall, therefore, this speech stresses a theoretical (that is, psychological) value, with secondary appeals aimed at political and economic value-orientations. As an initial proposal, it maintains a firm, but conciliatory, stance. If the proposal were unreasonably rejected, of course, the next speech might make the political and economic values more important, especially if the speaker believes a mini-confrontation is the only route to persuasion.*

Some Cautions for Using Motivational Appeals

You must develop skill, tact, and good judgment in your use of motivational appeals. *Do not be blatant, objectionably obvious, or patently aggressive.* Such behaviors create resistance in listeners — not acceptance or commitment. Do not say, as an extreme example, "Mr. Harlow Jones, the successful banker, has just contributed handsomely to our cause. Come on, now. *Imitate* this generous man!" Or, "If you give to this cause we will print your name in the paper so that your *reputation* as a generous person will be known by everyone." Instead, in making an appeal of this kind, respect the intelligence and sensitivities of your audience and suggest — through the use of descriptions and illustrations of desired actions — that contributors will not only be associated with others in a worthwhile and successful venture, but will also have the sincere appreciation of many who are less fortunate than they.

    Remember, also, that listeners generally are reluctant to acknowledge, by word or action, certain motives which privately may exert a very powerful influence upon them: acquisition, fear, imitation, attraction, self-pride, etc. Therefore, when you elect to use such appeals, be careful to present them objectively and tastefully, and — above all — supplement or combine them with *other* motivational drives or desires which your hearers will probably be less reticent to have others recog-

---

*For an interesting attempt to rank-order, in terms of rhetorical sophistication, possible strategies for proposers of significant change, see John Waite Bowers and Donovan J. Ochs, *The Rhetoric of Agitation and Control* (Reading, Mass.: Addison-Wesley Publishing Company, Inc., 1971), esp. Chapter 2.

nize as the causes of their actions. This involves, of course, constant evaluation of the appropriateness of these appeals. (For a detailed consideration, see "To Evaluate the Ethics of Communication," page 437.)

From a functional standpoint, then, and to sum up the thrust of this chapter, *the choice and phrasing of your motivational appeals should always be adapted to the beliefs, attitudes, and value-orientations of your listeners.* Keep in mind, however, that certain beliefs, attitudes, and values will be more deeply and firmly embedded than others in the thought and behavior patterns of your listeners. Crystallized attitudes and opinions usually are based on a combination of basic wants and sensed needs, and often are tenaciously held. Therefore, with respect to any particular subject and purpose about which you wish to speak, you must consider not only the controlling motives of your audience, but also the specific attitudes, beliefs, and value-orientations which these motives have produced. By associating your ideas and proposals with the positive attitudes of your audience and by avoiding negative associations, you can make your appeals stronger, more direct, and more truly functional. Do not expect, however, to be able to accomplish this with complete success on your first attempt. Skill in selecting and phrasing motivational appeals must be the product of painstaking analysis, careful thought, and repeated practice.

Problems and Probes

1. Bring to class three examples of speeches which incorporate motivational appeals as discussed in this chapter. Explain what kinds of appeals are used in each, and why. Do these motive appeals add to or detract from the speaker's persuasive effort? What other appeals could the speakers have utilized? Combine your examples and your analysis in a brief written report and hand it to your instructor.

2. Assume that you are going to *(a)* sell a set of encyclopedias to a stranger; *(b)* persuade an instructor to raise a grade; and *(c)* convince a dormitory, fraternity, or sorority corridor to elect you to the dorm or house council. In each instance, which of the following methods do you deem the more persuasive: impressing your listeners with a *motive* for believing what you want them to believe, or showing them the *logic* of your proposal by presenting well-supported information and well-reasoned arguments? In writing, develop and defend your choice in each case.

3. Prepare a list of the motivational appeals you would employ when attempting to persuade an audience of college students to take the following actions: *(a)* contribute to the campus charity drive, *(b)* enlist in the army, *(c)* study harder, *(d)* give up their automobiles, *(e)* have an annual physical examination, *(f)* learn to speak Russian, *(g)* drop out of college.

4. Clip and bring to class ten magazine advertisements which contain one or more motivational appeals. In preparing this assignment, identify each appeal, write a brief statement telling why you think it was selected to sell this particular product, and evaluate its effectiveness. Note that often a motivational appeal may be used both in an illustration and in the printed text to reinforce each

other and the motivational appeal(s) of the advertisement as a whole. Hand your analyses to your instructor, and also be ready to talk about them informally in class if that should be requested.

5.   Using the examples of speeches which you gathered for Problem 1, determine whether the motivational appeals employed constituted ethical and legitimate means of persuasion. How do you distinguish between those appeals which are ethical and legitimate and those which are not? Can you specify a few universal principles which allow us to make future distinctions between ethical and unethical motivational appeals? In answering these questions, consider the subject matter of the speeches analyzed and the situation in which they were made, as well as the nature of the appeal itself.

Oral Activities and Speaking Assignments

1.   Present a three- or four-minute speech in which, through the combined use of two or three related motivational appeals, you attempt to persuade your audience to a particular belief or action. (For example, combine appeals to *adventure, companionship,* and *personal enjoyment* to persuade them to take a conducted group tour of Europe; or combine *sympathy* and *pride* to elicit contributions to a charity drive.) At the conclusion of your speech, ask a classmate to identify the motive appeals you used. If other members of the class disagree with that identification, explore with the class as a whole the reasons why your appeals did not come through as you intended, and what you might have done to sharpen and strengthen them.

2.   In a group discussion with other members of your class, attempt to construct a list of principles which help differentiate ethical from unethical appeals. In the course of discussion, answer the following questions: *(a)* Under what conditions would you consider a motive appeal to the wants or desires of listeners an entirely ethical and legitimate means of persuasion? *(b)* Under what conditions might such an appeal be unethical? *(c)* Where does the ethical responsibility rest: with the speaker? with the audience? or in adherence to a list of external criteria?

Suggestions for Further Reading

Walter Fisher, "A Motive View of Communication," *Quarterly Journal of Speech* LVI (April 1970): 131–139.

Ralph N. Haber, Ed., *Current Research in Motivation* (New York: Holt, Rinehart & Winston, Inc., 1966).

Abraham Maslow, *Motivation and Personality,* 2nd ed. (New York: Harper & Row, Publishers, 1970), Chapter IV, pp. 35–58.

Gerald R. Miller and Murray A. Hewgill, "Some Recent Research on Fear-Arousing Message Appeals," *Speech Monographs* XXXIII (November 1966): 377–391.

Ivan L. Preston, "Relationships Among Emotional, Intellectual, and Rational Appeals in Advertising," *Speech Monographs* XXXV (November 1968): 504–511.

Thomas Scheidel, *Speech Communication and Human Interaction* (Glenview, Ill.: Scott, Foresman and Company, 1974), Chapters 8 and 9.

7

Supporting the Major Ideas

Consider the typical day of an ordinary, middle-aged American, working in a city, living in a suburb with 2.3 kids, a dog, a station wagon, and a patio. He arises at 6:15 a.m., to the voice of a local disc jockey exhorting him to purchase a new car. He has breakfast while news people fill him in on the events of the day, warning him of three labor strikes and two international incidents. His daughter demands that he buy a ticket for her school play, while his son pleads for money to attend wrestling camp, and his wife tells him that he will have to eat supper alone that evening because she has a League of Women Voters' workshop on wetlands drainage. He then heads for work on a commuter train, surrounded by fifteen posters asking for contributions to charitable causes and by three friends urging him to vote for three different candidates for the city council.

At work, he first meets three salespersons who want his business; he then has a session with a secretary wanting a raise, next with an employee begging not to be released, and then lunch with two associates who are competing for an elevation in rank. In the afternoon, he makes two presentations to board members as he seeks to diversify the company's markets, and by late afternoon is on his way home in a car pool as he listens to another deejay selling trips to Jamaica and reading the radio station's daily editorial.

After a TV dinner, he spends his evening with five situation comedies and thirty commercials for everything from lawn mowers to cold remedies. He finishes off his day with "The Johnny Carson Show," where guests are promoting an animal protection society and a new political party.

Most of us have been similarly bombarded: so many messages and causes make so many claims and offer so many general and often contradictory solutions that we cannot easily sort out the plausible explanations or legitimate propositions without referring to the specific materials which underlie them. Therefore, both as consumers and producers of informative, persuasive, and actuative messages, we need to know what these specific materials are and how they affect the rational aspects of communicative transactions. Because they provide the explanation and proof upon which understanding and belief rest, they are called *supporting materials.* That is, their function is to clarify, amplify, or prove the major beliefs, attitudes, and values which speakers wish to communicate. They are also the flesh and blood which bring your leading ideas to life and sustain them once you have implanted them in the minds of others.

In this chapter, then, we will consider first the various *forms* of supporting materials; then we will talk about some of the *decisions* you have to make when choosing and using these different forms; and finally we will *illustrate* such decision making in some sample speech outlines.

The Forms of Supporting Material

There are seven forms of supporting material (see illustration, page 104) which you may use to develop or prove the major ideas in a speech:

1. *Explanation*
2. *Analogy or comparison*
3. *Illustration (detailed example)*
4. *Specific instances (undeveloped examples)*
5. *Statistics*
6. *Testimony*
7. *Restatement*

Explanation

By definition, an explanation is an expository or descriptive passage which seeks (1) to make clear the nature of a term, concept, process, or proposal; or (2) to offer a supporting rationale for a contestable claim. Three types of explanations are especially useful to you as a speaker: *explanations of what, explanations of how,* and *explanations of why.**

Explanations of What. Some explanations serve to delineate more specifically what a speaker is discussing; they make ideas clearer and

---

*For an informative analysis of explanation, see W. V. Quine and J. S. Ullian, *The Web of Belief* (New York: Random House, Inc., 1970), Chapter 8, "Explanation." These authors also have helpful chapters on "Testimony" (Chapter 4) and "Analogy" (Chapter 6).

Figure 1./ MATERIALS FOR VERBALLY SUPPORTING AN IDEA

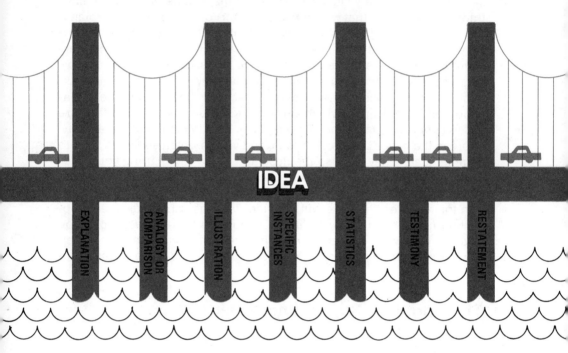

more concrete, giving audiences enough details so that they can "get their minds around" the concept. For example, Scott Andrews, University of Iowa, offered this explanation of a type of literature called the *fantasy novel* in a speech on that subject:

> One of the most popular forms of literature in recent years is the fantasy novel. Like its first cousin, science fiction, "fantasy" is a difficult term to define. But usually the term is applied to a work which takes place in a non-existent and unreal world such as a fairyland or which concerns incredible and unreal characters, or which employs physical principles not yet discovered or even contrary to present existence. Tolkien's world in the "hobbit," Katherine Kurtz's "Deryni," and the vision of Arthurian England in Walter Munn's *Merlin's Ring* are universes with these characteristics.[1]

Explanations of How.   A second class of explanations tells audiences "how"—how something came to be, how something is done, etc. Explanations of *how* frequently recount the processes or steps involved in carrying out an operation. P. Dorothy Gilbert used such an explanation in introducing a speech on chair-caning:

The intricate patterns of cane or reed you see on chair seats make the process seem mysterious and all too artistic for most of us. On the contrary. As I will demonstrate to you today, anyone can learn to cane a chair in order to restore a valuable antique or to save a family heirloom. Chair-caning involves five easy-to-learn steps: First, soak the cane to make it pliable; then, clean out the holes through which the cane will be stretched; next, weave the cane or reed through the holes in four to seven operations; fourth, tie off the pieces of cane underneath the chair; and finally, lace a heavier piece of cane over the holes to cover them. Let me describe each step, one at a time.[2]

Explanations of Why. Explanations which account for a thing's existence or present state can be called explanations of "why." They appear often in academic lectures, as when a history professor explains *why* a series of events caused a war or a revolution. But this type of explanation also is useful when you wish to explain why a certain problem requires a solution. In a speech delivered to the World Food Conference in Rome, November 5, 1974, U.S. Secretary of State Henry Kissinger offered the following explanation of why a threat of famine exists worldwide:

> During the 1950s and '60s, global food production grew with great consistency. Per capita output expanded even in the food-deficit nations; the world's total output increased by more than half. But at the precise moment when growing populations and rising expectations made a continuation of this trend essential, a dramatic change occurred: during the past three years, world cereal production has fallen; reserves have dropped to the point where a significant crop failure can spell a major disaster.[3]

Valuable as explanations are in making ideas clear, processes understandable, or causes specific, two cautions must be observed in their use: First, *do not allow your explanations to become too long or involved.* You may be interested in all of their twistings and turnings, but they may bore or confuse an audience. And, second, *do not talk in vague or abstract terms.* If an explanation does not make a concept clearer or more concrete—that is, if it replaces one difficult term or concept with a host of others—it will be impossible for the listeners to follow. Keep your explanations brief, simple, and orderly. Combine them with some of the forms of support to be discussed below—often, with specific instances or illustrations. In this way, you will help your audience rather than mislead or confuse them.

Analogy or Comparison

In an analogy or comparison, similarities are pointed out between something that is already known, understood, or believed by the listeners and something that is not. Thus, you might explain the game of cricket to an American audience by comparing it with baseball, or tell how a thermostat works by comparing it with a simple temperature thermometer. Analogies or comparisons may be either *figurative* or *literal.*

Figurative Analogies. Figurative analogies involve phenomena which, though basically different in nature, exhibit comparable properties or relationships. They are used principally to make ideas or distinctions clear to an audience. Dr. Louis Hadley Evans, minister-at-large for the Presbyterian Church, drew these figurative analogies to distinguish between the terms *deist* and *theist:*

> To you the world is what: a clock or a car? Is it a huge clock, that God once made, that He wound up at the beginning and left it to run of itself? Then you are a *deist.*
>
> Do you believe that it is rather a car that God once made, but that does not run without His hand on the wheel, without His ultimate and personal control? Then you are a *theist.*[4]

Literal Analogies. Although analogies which compare things that are unlike—the world with a clock or a car, for example—may be excellent means of clarifying a point or making it vivid, they generally are of limited value as proof. For this purpose it is always more effective to employ comparisons of *like* phenomena—to argue, for example, that a system of one-way traffic on the downtown streets of City X would relieve congestion and promote safety because such a system has had these effects in City Y. Note how a comparison of like phenomena—in this case, two state universities—was used to prove one of the claims advanced in a student speech by George Gruner:

> To show that an active and effective student government would help to reduce disciplinary problems at Iowa, we may refer to the experience of the university I attended before transferring here last fall—a school which, like Iowa, has between 15,000 and 16,000 students and which is a publicly supported state institution.
>
> Prior to reconstituting student government as a vital responsible force, the office of the dean at my former university handled more than 600 disciplinary cases each year. After putting new responsibility and authority into the hands of the students themselves, however, this number was cut by more than half, and the number of merely trivial or nuisance offenses decreased by about two thirds. The dean himself attributed this reduction chiefly to the new sense of pride which a revitalized student government had given the students in their school.[5]

Because it attempts to base a conclusion on a single parallel instance, an analogy used as proof must meet a rigid test: *the instances compared must be closely similar in all essential respects.* Clearly, you could not infer that what worked in a small denominational college also would work in a large state university or that an effect achieved in a select private school also would be achieved in an institution whose student body is more varied. Do the similarities between the items or classes compared outweigh any differences that might be relevant to the conclusion you are drawing? This is the question that always must be asked—and answered—when you attempt to use an analogy as proof for a contention or claim.

Illustration

An illustration is a detailed example in narrative form. It may be used to picture the results that would flow from adopting the proposal you advocate, or to describe in detail conditions as they now exist. In either circumstance, an illustration has two principal characteristics: (1) narrative form—recounting a happening or telling a story; and (2) vividly described details. There are two types of illustrations—*hypothetical* and *factual.* The former describes an imaginary situation; the latter, an actual happening.

Hypothetical Illustration. A hypothetical illustration, although it is an imaginary narrative, must be consistent with the known facts; it must seem probable or likely. In discussing the learning problems of the bilingual child, Mary Neagley of Clarion State College pictured for her audience the pupil whose family speaks little or no English:

> But imagine a child whose English is only a second language. Never spoken at home, this language must be absorbed from the outside—a piecemeal of key phrases; a vocabulary based on acquisition, not comprehension.
>
> Schooling becomes a disadvantage in itself. Forced to use a foreign language, the child can worry about mastery of material covered in class only after comprehending the web of its delivery. He is marked as "slow," unable to comprehend questions directed at him, and too afraid and uncertain to ask. He has been relegated to a position that may very well defy his intellectual capacities. This small, future resource has been dealt the beginnings of its demise.[6]

Factual Illustration. A well-chosen factual illustration is one of the most telling forms of support a speaker can use. Because details are brought into the story, the present or projected situation is made clear and vivid to the listeners; because the incident actually occurred, it frequently has high persuasive value. In a speech on the cost of medical care, Margaret Harrison of Western Kentucky University used this factual illustration to make her point:

> But how much does chronic illness cost in America today? Let me give you a personal example. My mother has rheumatoid arthritis, not an uncommon disease, for most of us as part of the aging process will suffer some stiffening and inflammation of the joints. My mother, however, has

been an arthritic for the last twenty-eight years, and for the past nine has been confined to a wheelchair. During the years '62–'71 she was in and out of the hospital nine separate times and spent a total of thirty-seven weeks between hospital walls. Her hospital bill for that period of time amounted to over $14,200. And that figure does not even begin to include regular visits to her physician, prescribed medication, and physical therapy stretching back over the last twenty-eight years. Now my father is not a rich man, and as a young couple they did not plan on her chronic illness, but he works for a company with an excellent group health insurance plan that pays 80 percent of his medical expenses.

We were lucky. But there seems to be something inherently wrong with a health-care system that can inflict such financial burdens on the consumer. Out of necessity we have become cost-conscious and not care-conscious about our health.[7]

Keep three considerations in mind when choosing a factual illustration to explain or support an idea. First, *is the illustration clearly related to the idea that is to be clarified or proved?* If you have to labor to show its connection, the illustration will be of little use. Second, *is it a fair example?* An audience often is quick to notice unusual circumstances in an illustration; and if you seem to have picked an exceptional case, your description of it will not prove convincing. Third, *is it vivid and impressive in detail?* The primary value of an illustration is the sense of reality it creates. If this quality is absent, the advantage of using an illustration is lost. Be sure, then, that your illustrations meet the tests of relevance, fairness, and vividness of detail.

Specific Instance

A specific instance is an *undeveloped* illustration or example. Instead of describing a situation in detail, you merely refer to it in passing. Such references normally serve one of two purposes: (1) Sometimes, in an effort to make an idea *clear* and *understandable,* you make a passing reference to an event, person, place, or process your audience already is familiar with. Thus Jane Scott of the University of Iowa opened a speech on architecture in this way: "You all are familiar with Old Capitol, the beautiful pillared building you pass each day walking from class to class. It's a perfect example of federal-period Georgian architecture, the subject of my speech this morning."[8] Here, a brief reference to a familiar building enabled the audience to orient itself to the speaker's topic. (2) You can, however, also use specific instances in *proving a proposition.* In this case, instances are often piled one upon the other until you have firmly established the impression you wish to create. Note, for example, how Donna Thomas of Southeast Missouri State University used specific instances in an attempt to get her audience to associate the concept of "revolution" with the concept of "terrorism":

Revolution these days means terror, and not just in Southeast Asia. In Nahariya in Israel last year three members of the Palestinian Fedayeen slipped into an apartment and murdered a thirty-eight-year-old woman and her two children, aged ten and four. In Bet She'an, a dusty little village in the Jordan Valley, Arab terrorists invaded an apartment complex, killed four inhabitants, and wounded nine, including eight children. In America, a Puerto Rican group claimed credit for the bombing of a tavern in New York City in which four people died. And in the Tower of London, a symbol in its own right of terror and injustice, the Irish Republican Army recently planted a plastic bomb which exploded to kill or maim thirty-seven innocent visitors. And in the debris was found . . . a child's foot.[9]

If the names, events, or situations you cite are well known to your listeners, specific instances can aid comprehension or generate support for a claim or contention. On subjects with which the listeners are not familiar, however, or on which there are marked differences of opinion, specific instances usually must be supplemented with more fully developed illustrations.

Statistics

Not all figures are statistics; some are used merely for counting. Statistics are figures that *show relationships among phenomena*—that emphasize largeness or smallness (magnitudes), describe sub-classes or parts (segments), or establish trends. Because statistics reduce great masses of information into generalized categories, they are useful both in *making clear* the nature of a situation and in *substantiating* a potentially disputable claim.*

Magnitudes. We often use statistics to describe in a relatively short space the scope or seriousness of a problem. Statistical description of magnitude, especially when complemented by an analogy, helps an audience grasp the dimensions of a problem clearly. This is what Representative Tom Steed of Oklahoma did in a speech on governmental red tape and paperwork, delivered in the House of Representatives on January 17, 1977:

Government agencies print about 10 billion sheets of paper to be filled out by U.S. businessmen—enough to fill more than 4 million cubic feet. Paperwork stemming from federal, state, and local governments averages about 10 forms for every man, woman, and child in the United States. Official records stored around the country total 11.6 million cubic feet, or an amount 11 times larger than the volume of the Washington Monument. Paperwork generated by Washington alone in one year

---

*For a technical, yet rewarding, introduction to statistical analysis generally, see Frederick Williams, *Reasoning with Statistics* (New York: Holt, Rinehart & Winston, Inc., 1968).

would fill Yankee Stadium from the playing field to the top of the stands 51 times.[10]

Segments. Also helpful, primarily as a descriptive tool, are statistics which isolate the parts into which a problem can be subdivided or which show those aspects of a problem caused by discrete factors. The use of statistics is especially helpful when you are treating highly complex subject matter. A case in point is the topic of international trade, the results of which are usually expressed in complex economic theories and myriad import-export-monetary statistics. By breaking the complicated problems of trade down into smaller and simpler units, a speaker can make those problems understandable to a lay audience. In a speech at the University of Iowa, Rose Fuhrmann sought to dispel a prevalent economic myth—that the *have-not* nations import, whereas the *have* nations only export. Notice not only her use of statistical segments, but also how she translated those segments into more meaningful relationships for her listeners:

> The common vision is that of the poorer nations of the world doing all of the expensive importing of goods, with the richer nations getting richer by carrying out all of the lucrative exporting business. That is not the case at all. In 1971, for example, the United States accounted for 13.9 percent of the world's imports. Further, West Germany was responsible for 10.5 percent of the total; the United Kingdom, 7.3 percent; France, 6.5 percent; Japan, 6.0 percent. In all, almost half of the world's imports went to five of the Western world's largest and most powerful countries—hardly a case of the "haves" doing all of the selling and none of the buying.[11]

Trends. Finally, statistics often are employed to describe a trend across time. Statistical trends indicate where we have been and where we are going. Senator J. William Fulbright, in a speech delivered at Westminster College in Missouri, used a trend in this way to show the growth of inflation and to predict the economic and political disaster that awaits us unless the trend is stopped or reversed.

> The major cause of accelerated inflation is the massive imbalancing of international payments caused by the quadrupling of the price of oil since the October war. The United States—far more fortunate than other countries because we produce nearly two thirds of our own oil requirements—nonetheless will pay an estimated $25 billion for imported oil in 1974, more than triple the $7.5 billion paid in 1973. Meanwhile, the oil reserves of the producing countries will have risen from $15 billion in 1972 to nearly $100 billion in 1974, giving them surplus revenues on the order of $60 billion over and above their total import requirements. With this trend continuing and accelerating, the credit of consuming countries—rich as well as poor—will soon be exhausted, giving rise to economic collapse and political upheaval.[12]

In using statistics to indicate magnitude, divide phenomena into segments, or describe trends, keep in mind the following cautions: (1) *Translate difficult-to-comprehend numbers into more immediately understandable terms.* In a speech on the mounting problem of solid waste, Carl Hall pictured the immensity of 130,000,000 tons of garbage by indicating that trucks loaded with that amount would extend from coast to coast.[13] (2) *Don't be afraid to round off complicated numbers.* "Nearly 400,000" is easier for auditors to comprehend than "396,456"; "over 33 percent" is usually preferable to "33.4 percent" and "over one third" probably is better than either of them. (3) *Whenever possible, use visual materials to clarify complicated statistical trends or summaries.* Hand out a mimeographed sheet of numbers; draw graphs on the chalkboard; prepare a chart in advance. In this way, you can concentrate upon explaining the significance of the numbers, and not spend all of your time merely trying to report them. (4) *Use statistics fairly.* Arguing that professional women's salaries increased 12.4 percent last year may sound impressive to listeners—until they realize that women still are generally paid almost a quarter less than men for equivalent work. In other words, be sure to provide *fair contexts* for your numerical data and comparisons.*

Testimony

When speakers cite verbatim the opinions or conclusions of others, they are using testimony. Sometimes testimony is offered merely to clarify or explain an idea; more often, it is intended to supply support for an arguable claim or contention. Normally, as listeners we are interested in two kinds of testimony—*expert* and *peer testimony.* An expert is someone qualified by virtue of station, training, office, or vision to make observations the rest of us consider as authoritative. A peer is a person like ourselves—someone who, without specific training or knowledge in a given field, observes what is going on in the world and whose opinions and judgments are deemed less expert or authoritative.

Expert Testimony. We usually turn to expert testimony when problems are complicated and creative solutions are demanded. Notice how Omer G. Voss, Executive Vice-President of International Harvester Company, used expert testimony to substantiate his claim that practical methods of farming will enable the world to feed itself:

> Can the world feed itself? Colin Clark, past director of Oxford University's Agricultural Institute, has made this observation: "Confining ourselves to practical farming methods already used by good farmers in different parts of the world, the world's cultivated and pastureable lands

---

*To protect yourself from the unscrupulous use of statistics, read Darrel Huff, *How to Lie with Statistics* (New York: W. W. Norton & Company, Inc., 1954).

> could feed something like ten times the world's population — not at subsistence levels, but in an American style of diet."[14]

This example demonstrates important facets of good expert testimony: *authoritativeness* and *audience acceptability.* More specifically, expert testimony should satisfy the following criteria:

1. The training and experience of the persons quoted should qualify them to express the judgments offered. Expertness is essential.

2. The statements of the authority should be based, whenever possible, on firsthand knowledge.

3. The judgments expressed should not be unduly influenced by personal interest.

4. The hearers should recognize persons quoted as real authorities. If listeners do not automatically accept them as such, they should at least be told why the opinion deserves acceptance.

Peer Testimony.   As listeners we often are interested not only in testimony of experts, but also in the opinions of persons like ourselves. In a democracy, especially, commonness is a virtue in many situations. Notice, for example, how some years ago Roger Woodruff of Illinois State University, when discussing the need for amnesty, went not to a military authority or a political observer, but to the father of a soldier who died in Vietnam:

> And the final statement [after some others] is from Mr. Robert Ranson, father of one of the 50,000 young men who gave their lives in the rice paddies of Vietnam. Mr. Ranson feels that those who lost their sons in Vietnam can view the war with a perspective that is simply not available to the rest of us. And he writes: "As we come to grips with the grim reality of what has gone on in the minds and consciences of those who have left the country, deserted, or gone to jail, it would be most gratifying to me if I felt that I could have contributed in any small measure toward the granting of the broadest kind of general amnesty, one without penalties and conditions."[15]

When citing testimony, avoid especially the temptation to use big names simply because they are well known. Seeking out experts in specific subject matter or peers able to capture citizens' feelings is a much wiser course, and usually will produce more audience acceptance and respect than opinions from movie stars and athletes. Again, as with statistics, take care not to misrepresent the views of your authorities and to use both expert and peer testimony in conjunction with other forms of support. When properly used, testimony — especially if included with summaries of ideas and opinions — can add much to your cause.

Restatement

As a form of support, restatement gains its strength from the power of repetition to clarify or emphasize. Advertisers, masters of restatement, spend millions of dollars repeating the same message or a slight variation of it over and over on television, radio, and billboards, and in newspapers and magazines. Restatement, however, is not mere repetition. For the public speaker especially, it often means *saying the same thing two or more times, but each time in a fresh and different way* in the hope that listeners who do not grasp or respond to the idea in one form will do so in another. By rephrasing a previously stated idea in more familiar terms or more vivid language, frequently you can simplify it, stress its importance in relation to your speech as a whole, or even enhance its acceptability to your listeners. The second of the two quotations with which we opened this book (page 4) demonstrates this principle. In that instance, Professor Waldo Braden, in concluding a speech on what it means to communicate, effectively employed two elements of restatement—simple repetition and careful redefinition—to drive home the idea that communication is a process in which the listener as well as the speaker plays a vital role.

Although restatement as such is not in the strictest sense *proof,* the fact that it can provide you with opportunities for *re-emphasis* and *summation* sometimes endows it with considerable persuasive power. It not only enables you to *review* and *sum up* the evidence of your case quickly, concisely, and climactically, but it also gives you a chance to hit the high points again or to rephrase an argument more convincingly. With restatement, you can selectively *focus* on the real highlights in the big picture, telling your audience specifically what you want it to understand and remember.

Finally, by restating your essential information or key point from time to time, you will be supplying your listeners with the kinds of ongoing, internal signposts or directions needed to ensure their understanding, cooperation, or compliance. Such summaries map the movement and progression of your speech, in effect saying to your audience: "I want to pause here briefly and add up for you what I've been saying up to now." Or, at the end, "This is the 'bottom line' of what I've tried to tell you in this talk."

These, then, are the seven forms of supporting materials. Select them judiciously; use them generously, but discerningly. Do not depend solely upon assertions of your own opinions unless you have unlimited power over audiences, which few of us do. Express your views, by all means; but amplify and develop them by using the materials we have just discussed: restatement, testimony, statistics, specific instances, detailed illustrations, analogies or comparisons, and explanations. *How* you can use such materials in specific situations will be our next concern.

Factors Influencing the Speaker's Choice of Supporting Materials

Being able to identify the various forms of supporting materials and their basic functions is, of course, only a portion of the battle a speaker fights for an audience's mind. Each time you enter a public communication arena, you must make strategic *choices:* What sorts of materials should I select? How should I balance them? How much of any given type should I include? What materials are best adapted to what kinds of propositions or claims? These are the decisions upon which you launch your assault. To make these decisions, you should consider *(a)* your personality as a speaker, *(b)* the function of your speech, *(c)* the expectations of your audience, and *(d)* the demands of the occasion.

Supporting Materials and the Speaker's Personality

In choosing the kinds of supporting materials you will use, begin with *you*—your self—your personality. Because of your background, experiences, and predispositions generally, you probably prefer to use certain kinds of supporting material and not others. Some speakers, for example, shy away from statistics, finding mere numbers meaningless, confusing, and cold. Instead of abstract generalizations based upon numerical quantification, they prefer personalized illustrations, anecdotes, advice from sages, etc. Others find pithy quotations, touching stories, and analogies equally loathsome. "I'll just stick to the facts," they say, "and forget the sentimental garbage."

In terms of the possibilities you encountered in Chapter 5, what are your *valuative orientations?* Are you highly pragmatic or political? You may well have a preference for hard evidence—facts, figures, totals, concrete illustrations, specific instances. Are you theoretically, philosophically, or aesthetically oriented? You may well prefer definitions coupled with analogies, restatements, and hypothetical illustrations. We are citing here only general tendencies, of course, and urging that, above all, you discover your own propensities. We are asking you to recognize the kinds of supporting materials you are most comfortable with. In this, clearly, your first touchstone is your *self.*

Supporting Materials and the Function of the Speech

As you are already well aware, however, you cannot be completely selfish or self-oriented when choosing materials to support the ideas in your speeches. You also have to ask yourself how you conceive of your role in relation to your audience. What are *you* trying to do for *them?* What *service* are you offering? Your purpose as a speaker significantly affects the choices you may need to make among the various kinds of supporting materials. Consider these three detailed examples:

EXAMPLE 1. A SPEECH ON HOMEMADE CHEESE

A. *How-to Explanation* (How to make cheese at home)
    — *explanations,* obviously, are very important (step-by-step description of the process).
    — *analogies* also are useful (literally, to show relationship to other food-preparation processes; figuratively, to communicate the sense of personal creativity felt with any hobby).
B. *Why-to Explanation* (Why to make cheese at home)
    — *statistics* on money saved, number of home cheesemakers, etc., usually add credibility and interest.
    — *testimony* concerning the unique flavors of homemade cheese, the sense of accomplishment, etc., frequently are highly supportive.

EXAMPLE 2. A SPEECH ON A CAREER-PLACEMENT OFFICE

A. *How-to Explanation* (How to use the office)
    — *explanation* of the process, step by step, for using the office is important.
    — *analogy* between the office's processing of your credentials and a production assembly line may clarify ways in which its services can be used.
B. *Why-to Explanation* (Why to use the office)
    — *testimony* from other satisfied users can be highly supportive.
    — *statistics* on the office's placement record can also provide strong support.

EXAMPLE 3. A SPEECH ON CABLE TELEVISION

A. *Explanation of What* (What cable TV is)
    — *explanation* of a typical cable system, from license to neighborhood hookup, is essential.
    — *analogy* with the operation, control, and governance of broadcast television can clarify its technical and political aspects.
B. *Explanation of How* (How cable TV will affect individuals)
    — *explanation* of banking, shopping, checking out library books, and other communicative services can increase understanding.
    — *analogy* with the telephone service can help to clarify effects of cable TV on the public.
C. *Explanation of Why* (Why a community should accept cable TV)
    — *explanation* of its community control and licensing can demonstrate its distinctiveness as a mass medium.
    — *statistics* on the variety of programming available in cable vs. non-cable markets can underscore its artistic, social, and commercial uses.

In these three examples, you can see at least a few of the many possible ways in which your choices of speech materials will be influenced by your role relationship with your audience. You will be guided in these decisions by your *intentions* toward your listeners, by what you wish to *do* for them, by the *service* you hope to provide. These examples also suggest that speakers offering explanations or demonstrations tend to rely upon supporting materials that describe and clarify, such as explanations of what and how, analogies, illustrations, etc. (as in Examples 1A, 2A, 3A, and 3B). In contrast, speakers viewing themselves in a position of arguing or persuading often employ harder forms of support or evidence, such as statistics, testimony, specific instances, etc. (as in Examples 1B, 2B, and 3C). In short, the function of your speech and the role in which you hope to fulfill that function offer you a second touchstone for selecting the most appropriate supporting materials.

Supporting Materials and the Audience's Expectations

Your potential impact upon an audience is often determined by (1) *what it knows about your topic;* (2) *what it knows about you;* and, therefore (3), *what it expects from both.* You need, therefore, to ask yourself: What does this audience know about me? Does it expect me to be an expert on certain subjects? On the basis of my previous speeches, does it expect me to rely heavily upon particular kinds of ideas and supporting materials? Does it expect me to be excessively biased on certain matters? Does it expect me always to be earnest and factual? Amusing or serious? Idealistic or cynical? Facile or groping in my phrasing? Such questions often determine how much an audience will expect from you and the kinds and amounts of supporting materials you will use.

If, for example, you have customarily sprinkled your speeches with sprightly witticisms, amusing analogies, personal anecdotes, and have spoken in a light, breezy style, but suddenly shift to a style that is ponderous and deadly serious and begin to rely heavily upon technical testimony, extended statistics, and abstract generalizations, you upset your listeners' expectations. They will begin to wonder why you have changed and what lies behind your shift. In not behaving as expected, you force your audience to ask questions—not necessarily about *what* you have to say, but about *why* you are saying it as you are. We are not maintaining, certainly, that you should never vary the characteristic content of your speeches or your style in delivering them. You should experiment freely with variations in both. But when you do so, be sure to state your reasons explicitly so that your listeners can change their expectations accordingly.

Supporting Materials and the Demands of the Occasion

In a somewhat narrower and probably more predictable sense, *speech occasions*—like audiences—have certain inherent expectations concerning the selection and use of supporting materials in public communication. A religious revival meeting, for instance, can be expected to produce a considerable amount of testimony from people already converted to a given religious philosophy. A hearing before a congressional subcommittee gathering information can be expected to generate an abundance of statistics, literal analogies, and how-to explanations. The dedication of a monument can be expected to offer much testimony, many figurative analogies, and at least a few anecdotal illustrations. Each of these occasions—like innumerable others—has its own particular rhetorical tradition with accompanying rules which govern at least the general nature and scope of the materials that may appropriately be used to support ideas given voice in that setting.*

As a speaker, of course, you are expected to be aware of these traditions and rules; and you are obliged to assemble and incorporate in your messages—to the best of your ability—those forms of speech materials which are in accord with the demands of such occasions.

Using Supporting Materials: The Central-Idea Speech

Thus far in this chapter we have considered the various forms of supporting materials and suggested some factors which can guide speakers in selecting prudently from among the available options. In this concluding section, we shall try to demonstrate how particular types of materials may be effectively packaged to explain, verify, and otherwise develop the *central idea* of a speech. Frequently, you will find yourself involved in speech situations—classroom presentations, oral reporting, committee meetings, business conferences, etc.—where you want only to make clear one central idea or prove one simple point. In fact, in the earlier speeches you make, you may wish to limit yourself to a single, well-supported point. Later, when you attempt more complex subjects, you will discover that the units of a longer speech are essentially *a succession of such points,* strategically arranged.

Selecting the Central Idea

To organize a central-idea speech is a comparatively simple process. To begin, decide on the exact idea you wish to explain or the point you wish to prove. To be sure that you really have one point—and *only* one point—in mind, frame it in a short, simple sentence. *Example:* "The death penalty is barbarous." (*Not* "The death penalty results in psychological, sociological, and penal inequities.") Focus upon this central idea throughout your entire speech. Stick steadfastly to it as you select and assemble the supporting material best suited to achieving your purpose, whether it be to *explain* or *clarify* it or to *prove* it. Finally, arrange these materials in a sequence or pattern that will be easy for listeners to understand and follow.

---

*For a fuller discussion of ways in which speech occasions or situations call forth fitting responses from speakers, see Lloyd Bitzer, "The Rhetorical Situation," *Philosophy & Rhetoric* 1 (January 1968): pp. 1–14.

Using Supporting Material to Explain an Idea

If the purpose of your speech is to explain an idea, proceed as follows:

1. State the idea or point in a short, simple sentence.
2. Make it clear
   a. by explanation, comparisons, and illustrations;
   b. by using diagrams, pictures, models, or maps.
3. Restate the idea you have explained.

In the clarification (step 2 above), you may present the verbal and nonverbal supporting materials either separately or together. That is, you may tell your listeners and *then* show them; or you may show them *while* you are telling them. The following outline for a central-idea speech illustrates how supporting materials may be assembled to explain an idea and make it clear.

Subject: THE CITY MANAGER AND MUNICIPAL EFFICIENCY

I. *The council-manager form of city government is an efficient way to handle municipal affairs.*
    Statement of central idea.

    A. A city council of four or five members elected by the citizenry to establish policy employs a professionally trained administrator to carry out its directives.
    Explanation as a form of support.

    B. The city manager is responsible for all aspects of administration.
        1. He supervises the day-to-day operations of the various departments of municipal functioning.
    Specific instances.

            a. He sees that ordinances are properly enforced.
            b. He appoints, directs, and—if necessary—removes department heads and other city employees.
        2. He recommends to the council needed programs and improvements.
            a. His intimate knowledge of municipal affairs enables him to spot problems quickly.
            b. His professional training enables him to offer sound proposals.
        3. He maintains channels of communication with all segments of the community.
            a. He listens to complaints from individuals and groups.
    More specific instances.

            b. He delivers speeches and makes other public appearances.
            c. He prepares municipal exhibits for informative purposes.

II. Thomas Harrison Reed, a well-known municipal consultant, has compared the council-manager plan of city government to the organization of a business corporation.

Comparison as a form of support.

    A. The city council functions as a policy-determining board of directors.

    B. The position of the municipal manager as principal administrator is similar to that of the company president.

Literal analogies as forms of support.

III. Professor George Buresh, author of *How Our Cities Are Governed,* declares, "Under the council-manager form of municipal government, the council must answer to the people for policy, and the manager must answer to the council for the implementation of that policy. This fixes responsibility."

Testimony as a form of support.

IV. The "chain of command" in the council-manager form of city government is simple, practical, and directly accountable to the citizenry—as this diagram suggests:

Explanation with visual support.

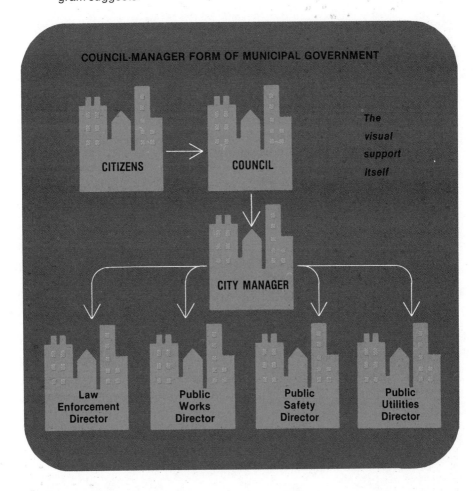

COUNCIL-MANAGER FORM OF MUNICIPAL GOVERNMENT

CITIZENS → COUNCIL

CITY MANAGER

Law Enforcement Director   Public Works Director   Public Safety Director   Public Utilities Director

The visual support itself

V.   The council-manager form of city government is an
    effective plan for administering municipal affairs
    because
      A.   It provides a clear-cut organization.
      B.   It fixes civic responsibility.
      C.   It utilizes a trained administrator.

Restatement of the central idea of the speech — in summary form.

Using Supporting Material to Verify or Prove a Claim

When supporting materials are used to prove a point, they may be organized in either of two ways: (1) the *didactic method* or (2) the *method of implication.*

The Didactic Method.   In using this method, you first state the idea you wish to verify or the proposition you wish to prove, then you present the proof in the form of concrete supporting materials, and finally you restate the idea or proposition as an established conclusion. Specifically, follow these steps:

1.   State your point.
2.   Make it clear by explanation, comparison, or illustration.
3.   Prove it by specific instances, testimony, statistics, or additional factual illustrations.
4.   Restate your point as an established conclusion.

The Method of Implication.   In using this method, you present your facts first, then state the conclusion toward which these facts inevitably lead. You do not bring out the point to be proved until you have made clear the evidence upon which your contention rests. This method, sometimes called the "natural" method of argument, more nearly coincides with the way in which people arrive at conclusions when thinking things through for themselves. For this reason, the method of implication — though sometimes not as direct and as easy to use as the didactic method — may be more persuasive. Because it works by indirection or inference rather than frontal assault, it is almost always the better method to use when speaking to a skeptical or hostile audience. Usually, when using the implicative method, follow these four steps:

1.   Present a comparison or illustration which *implies* the point you wish to make.
2.   Offer additional illustrations, instances, statistics, and testimony which point unmistakably toward this conclusion without actually stating it.
3.   Show specifically how these supporting materials lead inevitably to this conclusion; use explanation if necessary.
4.   Definitely state your point as a conclusion.

The speech outline below is an example of the didactic method. Note that if the initial statement of the central idea were omitted, this organization pattern would illustrate almost equally well the method of implication.

CABLE TELEVISION WILL REVOLUTIONIZE YOUR LIFE

I. Cable television soon will revolutionize your everyday life.

Statement of central idea or claim.

   A. Suppose, on a rainy day a few years from now, you decide to "run" your errands from your living room.

First supporting statement.

      1. You turn on your two-way communication unit, and begin your round of errands:

Hypothetical illustration — developed by a succession of specific instances.

         a. On Channel 37, your bank's computer verifies the amount of a recent withdrawal.

         b. On Channel 26, you ask the telephone company to review last month's long-distance charges.

         c. On Channel 94, a supermarket lets you scan products, prices, and home-delivery hours.

         d. On Channel 5, you study a list of proposed changes in the city charter.

           (1) You can call in for further information.

           (2) You can vote from your own home.

         e. Channel 115 gives you access to resource personnel at the public library.

      2. Thus — with "cable television at your service" — you have accomplished your day's errands with minimum expenditure of time, gas, and parking-meter money.

Restatement of first supporting statement.

II. The vast possibilities of cable TV, once thought of only as dreams, are becoming actualities across the United States.

Second supporting statement.

   A. New York City already has a channel which gives citizens direct access to city officials.

Specific instances.

   B. San Francisco's "public-access channels" already are filled with local talent and ethnic programming.

   C. Ann Arbor, Michigan, has been leasing chan-

nels to private firms and public-utility companies.

III. Cable television soon will be available to virtually
every household in the U.S. at a reasonable cost.

    A. Because the cost is shared by licensee and
householder alike, no one bears an excessive
burden.

        1. Studio facilities for the public-access
channels are made available at cost in
most cable television contracts—normally about $30 per hour.

        2. Monthly rental fees per household sel-
dom exceed $6.

        3. Current installation charges for neces-
sary home equipment range from $15
to $50.

    B. The technical characteristics of cable televi-
sion render it inexpensive.

        1. Some existent telephone lines and
equipment can be used.

        2. The conversion box mounts easily on a
regular television set.

IV. Given actual and potential uses, plus the positive
cost-benefit ratio, cable television will revolutionize
your daily life.

    A. Just as the wheel extended our legs and the
computer our central nervous system, so will
cable television extend our communicative
capabilities.

    B. In the words of Wendy Lee, communication
consultant to new cable-television fran-
chises: "We soon will be a nation wired fully
for sight and sound. We will rid ourselves of
the need for short shopping trips; we will cut
the lines in doctors' offices; and we will put the
consumer and the constituent into the front
offices of his or her corporate suppliers and
political servants. The telephone and the
motor car will become obsolete."

*Third supporting
statement.*

Statistics.

*Explanation com-
bined with specific
instances.*

*Restatement of
central idea or
claim.*

*Analogy or com-
parison.*

*Testimony used to
support restate-
ment and summa-
rize the central
idea of the
speech.*

Not all central-idea speeches require as many different forms of supporting materials as were used in either of the sample outlines in this
section. Most central-idea speeches also are briefer. These samples do,
however, show how you may combine a number of different materials to
achieve a single purpose and to reach a variety of audiences.

Using Supporting Material to Amuse or Entertain

Sometimes in using forms of support to explain an idea or verify a point,
you can strengthen your explanations and enliven your arguments with

a measure of *entertainment* or *humor.* In fact, as we noted briefly in Chapter 4, your major purpose may not be to inform or persuade your listeners, but simply to *amuse* them — to cause them to sit back and enjoy themselves. But whether you intend primarily to amuse or divert your audience or merely to lighten the more serious substance of your speech, you will need to assemble your humorous or entertaining materials around a *central idea* in much the same way as you do when you wish principally to clarify or verify something. You will need to choose illustrations, comparisons, instances, and even testimony and numbers for their clarity and substance as well as for their capability to amuse. Humorous anecdotes, exciting experiences, tales of odd encounters, curious happenings involving unusual people, ironic twists of fate, exaggerated descriptions — all may serve effectively to illuminate your central idea in an entertaining and memorable way. Be careful, however, that the entertainment does not overpower or run away with your speech. If you elect to use jokes or amusing stories, be sure to *connect them meaningfully to your central idea.* See that your tales and personal anecdotes are to the point and that your humor does not divert attention from your explanation or proof — unless, of course, entertainment is your only objective.

When arranging speech materials mainly to entertain, develop a series of illustrations, short quotations or quips, and stories, each following the other in fairly rapid succession and each bearing upon a central theme having some merit in the human scheme of things. As a point of departure at least, consider the following steps:

1. Relate a story or anecdote, present an illustration, or quote an appropriate verse.
2. State the essential idea or point of view implied by your opening remarks.
3. Follow with a series of additional stories, anecdotes, or illustrations that amplify or illuminate your central point. Arrange these supporting materials in order of increasing interest or humor.
4. Close with a striking or novel restatement of the central point you have developed. As in Step 1, you may use a bit of poetry, a striking quotation, or even a brief anecdote to provide the necessary "clincher" and sum up your speech as a whole.

By organizing your materials in this way, you not only will provide your listeners with entertainment, but you will also help them to remember your central idea.

A Sample Speech to Entertain

The speech printed below illustrates the four steps we have described. In addition, it demonstrates how light and humorous materials may be used to develop a potentially useful thought.

A Case for Optimism[16]
Douglas Martin

I'm sure you have heard the verse that runs:

Poem embodying contrast used as opening

'Twixt optimist and pessimist
The difference is droll:
The optimist sees the doughnut,
The pessimist, the hole.

Statement of central idea

The longer I live, the more convinced I am of the truth of this poem. Life, like a doughnut, may seem full, rich, and enjoyable, or it may seem as empty as the hole in the middle. To the pessimist, the optimist seems foolish. But who is foolish—the one who sees the doughnut or the one who sees the hole?

Contrast

Somebody else pointed out the difference between an optimist and a pessimist this way: An optimist looks at an oyster and expects a pearl; a pessimist looks at an oyster and expects ptomaine poisoning. Even if the pessimist is right, which I doubt, he probably won't enjoy himself either before or after he proves it. But the optimist is happy because he always is expecting pearls.

Illustration

Pessimists are easy to recognize. They are the ones who go around asking "What's good about it?" when someone says "Good morning." If they would look around, they would see *something* good, as did the optimistic merchant whose store was robbed. The day after the robbery a sympathetic friend asked about the loss. "Lose much?" he wanted to know. "Some," said the merchant, "but then it would have been worse if the robbers had got in the night before. You see, yesterday I just finished marking everything down 20 percent."

Illustration

There is another story about the happy-go-lucky shoemaker who left the gas heater in his shop turned on overnight and upon arriving in the morning struck a match to light it. There was a terrific explosion, and the shoemaker was blown out through the door almost to the middle of the street. A passerby, who rushed up to help, inquired if he were injured. The shoemaker got up slowly and looked back at the shop, which by now was burning briskly. "No, I ain't hurt," he said, "but I sure got out just in time, didn't I?"

Testimony (pro and con)

Some writers have ridiculed that kind of outlook. You may recall the fun Voltaire made of optimism in *Candide:* "Optimism," he said, "is a mania for maintaining that all is well when things are going badly." A later writer, James Branch Cabell, quipped: "The optimist proclaims that we live in the best of all possible worlds; the pessimist fears this is true." These writers, I suppose, couldn't resist the urge to make light of optimists; but I, for one, refuse to take *them* seriously. I like the remark by Keith Preston, literary critic and journalist: "There's as much bunk among the busters as among the boosters."

Beginning the summary

Optimism, rather than the cynicism of Voltaire, is the philosophy I like to hear preached. There was a little old lady who complained about the weather. "But, Melissa," said her friend, "awful weather is better than no weather." So quit complaining, I say, and start cheering; there is always something to cheer about. And stop expecting the worst. An optimist cleans his glasses before he eats his grapefruit.

Restatement

Give in to optimism; don't fight it. Remember the doughnut. And, as Elbert Hubbard advised:

As you travel on through life, brother,
Whatever be your goal,
Keep your eye upon the doughnut
And not upon the hole.

In the preceding pages we have examined the substantive elements that you as a speaker may employ to explain, clarify, amplify, verify, or prove the central ideas in your messages. In the process we have ventured into some of the rational and affective corners of the human mind. When you have combined your understanding of these matters with those of Chapters 5 and 6, you will have at hand most of the principles and much of the advice needed to make intelligent choices regarding the emotional and substantive demands which a given audience is likely to make upon you, your ideas, and your propositions. You will also have largely completed four of the eight essential steps of the speechmaking process.

Reference Notes

[1] From a speech given at The University of Iowa, winter term, 1977. Reprinted with the permission of Mr. Andrews.

[2] From a speech given at The University of Iowa, fall term, 1976. Reprinted with the permission of Ms. Gilbert.

[3] From "The Threat of Famine" by Henry A. Kissinger, from *Vital Speeches of the Day*, Volume XXXXI, December 1974. Reprinted by permission of Vital Speeches of the Day.

[4] Excerpt from "Can You Trust God?" by Dr. Louis Hadley Evans. Reprinted by permission of the author.

[5] "Let's Revitalize Student Government," delivered in an advanced course in public speaking at The University of Iowa, March 14, 1966.

[6] From "Un Hombre Que Habla Dos Idiomas Vale Por Dos" by Mary Neagley. Reprinted from *Winning Orations* by special arrangement with the Interstate Oratorical Association, Larry Schnoor, Executive Secretary, Mankato State University, Mankato, Minnesota.

[7] From "Medical Care" by Margaret Harrison. Reprinted from *Winning Orations* by special arrangement with the Interstate Oratorical Association, Larry Schnoor, Executive Secretary, Mankato State University, Mankato, Minnesota.

[8] From a speech given at The University of Iowa, fall term, 1976. Reprinted with the permission of Ms. Scott.

⁹From "Of Tea and Terror" by Donna Thomas. Reprinted from *Winning Orations* by special arrangement with the Interstate Oratorical Association, Larry Schnoor, Executive Secretary, Mankato State University, Mankato, Minnesota.

¹⁰Representative Tom Steed. *Congressional Record,* 95th Congress, 1st Session, Volume 123, Part 8. Washington, D.C.: U.S. Government Printing Office, 1977, H379-H380.

¹¹From a speech given at The University of Iowa, winter term, 1977. Reprinted by permission of Ms. Fuhrmann.

¹²From "The Clear and Present Danger" by Senator J. William Fulbright, from *Vital Speeches of the Day,* Volume XXXXI, December 1974. Reprinted by permission of Vital Speeches of the Day.

¹³From "A Heap of Trouble" by Carl Hall. Reprinted from *Winning Orations* by special arrangement with the Interstate Oratorical Association, Larry Schnoor, Executive Secretary, Mankato State University, Mankato, Minnesota. (For the complete text of the speech, see pages 315–318 of this book.)

¹⁴From "Can the World Be Fed?" by Omer G. Voss, from *Vital Speeches of the Day,* Volume XXXXI, December 1974. Reprinted by permission of Vital Speeches of the Day.

¹⁵From "Amnesty" by Roger Woodruff. Reprinted from *Winning Orations* by special arrangement with the Interstate Oratorical Association, Larry Schnoor, Executive Secretary, Mankato State University, Mankato, Minnesota.

¹⁶Based in part on material taken from *Friendly Speeches* (Cleveland: National Reference Library).

Problems and Probes

1. Read three recent public addresses in *Vital Speeches of the Day* or some other suitable source, and tabulate the supporting materials employed by the speakers. Which forms of support are used most frequently? Which least frequently? Considering the subjects with which these speeches deal and the purposes at which they are aimed, try to explain why some forms of supporting material appear more frequently than others. For anthologies of recent speeches, see Carroll C. Arnold, Douglas Ehninger, and John Gerber, *The Speaker's Resource Book,* 2nd ed. (Scott, Foresman, 1966); Glenn Capp, *The Great Society* (Dickenson, 1968); Wil A. Linkugel, R. R. Allen, and Richard L. Johannesen, *Contemporary American Speeches* (Wadsworth, 1972).

2. Review a transcript from the Carter/Ford debates, or listen to a tape of the actual proceedings. What kinds of supporting materials were employed by these Presidential candidates? Did the materials substantiate the claims that were made? Did one candidate have better supporting material than the other? Did this affect the outcome of the debate(s) and your perception of which speaker did the better job of debating?

3. Recheck your Personal Speech Journal to determine whether you have previously listed five general subject-areas about which you would like to speak. If you have not yet entered such a list, do so now. Then, for each of these areas, first frame a specific purpose suitable for a central-idea speech on the subject, and then devise a specific purpose for a longer and somewhat more detailed speech. Prepare these purpose statements in writing, hand them to your instructor, and be able to defend your choice of purposes and explain why each is suitable for central-point development or for a longer speech.

4. Prepare a brief, written description of the circumstances under which you would choose to organize a central-idea or "one-point" speech according to the *didactic* method, and another description of the circumstances under which you would use the method of *implication.* Include among these circumstances the nature of the subject, the attitude of the hypothetical audience, the time available, etc.

Oral Activities and Speaking Assignments

1. Present to the class a five-minute, central-idea speech, the purpose of which is either to explain or clarify a term, concept, process, or to verify or prove a point. Use at least three different forms of supporting material in developing your idea. To formulate an evaluation of the effectiveness of your speech, the instructor and the other students will consider the following: *(a)* adequacy of supporting material; *(b)* appropriateness of supporting material, both as to type and to substance; and *(c)* the insight and skill with which the supporting material is developed.

2. Following the suggestions offered in this chapter, prepare to present in class a two- or three-minute central-point speech to inform, to convince, to actuate, or to entertain your listeners. For a subject, consult entries in your Personal Speech Journal, the list of subject categories at the end of Chapter 4, or both.

 Suggestions for Further Reading

Donald C. Bryant and Karl R. Wallace, *Fundamentals of Public Speaking,* 5th ed. (New York: Appleton-Century-Crofts, 1976), Part IV.

William R. Dresser, "The Impact of Evidence on Decision Making," in *Concepts in Communication,* ed. Jimmie D. Trent et al. (Boston: Allyn & Bacon, Inc., 1973), pp. 159 – 166.

Douglas Ehninger, *Influence, Belief, and Argument* (Glenview, Ill.: Scott, Foresman and Company, 1974), Chapter 5.

Thomas Harte, "The Effects of Evidence in Persuasive Communication," *Central States Speech Journal* 27 (Spring 1976): 42 – 46.

James C. McCroskey, "The Effects of Evidence in Persuasive Communication," *Western Speech* 31 (Summer 1967): 189 – 199.

Selecting Material That Will Hold Attention

In Chapter 2 we examined the components of the listening process, and in Chapter 6 we discussed the various types of appeals a speaker may use to motivate listeners to belief or action. In this chapter, we shall see how both of these concerns are united in the problems of getting and sustaining attention.

The Nature of Attention

Attention is a great deal like electricity: We don't know exactly what it is, but we do know what it does and what conditions bring it about. We also know that it is subject to *constant change* and is, therefore, *unstable* and *impermanent*. Assume, for example, that you are a baseball fan sitting in the bleachers. There are two outs, and the count is three and two. The home-team pitcher settles on the rubber, stretches, and sends a fast ball over the plate. The umpire bawls, "Strike three! Yer out!" Only then do you the spectator lean back, take a long breath, and notice what has been going on about you: the person in the next row who has been thumping you on the back, the half-eaten sack of peanuts you have dropped, the threatening clouds in the sky, the crumpled scorecard at your feet. What has happened? Essentially, in paying attention to the game you have so *focused* your sense-perceptors and so controlled both your internal and external perceptual fields that everything else, every other stimulus, has been forced into the background of your conscious perception. Thus, we may say that attention — as this hypothetical illustration suggests — is "the psychological process of selecting only a portion of the available stimuli to focus upon while ignoring, suppressing, or inhibiting reactions to a host of other stimuli."[1]

Some Interrelated Aspects of Attention

Psychologists suggest that, insofar as human speech transactions are concerned, the perceptual focus we call attention may be looked upon as having three concomitants or interrelated aspects:

1. An adjustment of the body and its sense organs to receive a particular stimulus.
2. A focus upon a stimulus to increase its clearness and vividness in our consciousness.
3. A readiness to respond to stimuli—a set toward action.

During the attention-paying process, bodily posture is adjusted, and the sense organs are "aimed at" the stimulus in order to gather and receive impressions from it more readily. Just as the robin cocks its head to listen for the worm underneath the sod, so people lean forward and turn their eyes and ears toward the object which captures their attention. You have only to call your friend by name, and he will turn toward you in order to attend to your remarks. Similarly, by gaining the attention of your public audience, you increase their capacity to hear what you say because they will have adjusted themselves *physically* to listen.

Of greater importance to you as a speaker, however, is the second characteristic of attention—the fact that when members of an audience attend to or focus upon a stimulus, it becomes clearer and more vivid in their consciousness, while other equally strong stimuli seem to grow weaker or fade out altogether. This explains why as the spectator at the ball game you were unaware of so many of the other things going on at the same time. During every moment of your life innumerable stimuli impinge on your senses. You can hear the wind whistling, the birds calling, or the trucks rumbling; you can feel your clothing pressing against your skin; you can see a hundred different sights moving across your field of vision. Why don't you notice them all? You do not—cannot—notice them all because of the *selective nature* of attention.

Research has shown that three factors are important in determining what you or anyone else attends to: *motivation, learning,* and *expectation.* As we have noted, you are motivated to focus on food when you are hungry, warmth when you are cold, or companionship when you are lonely. When reading a difficult assignment, you are able to attend to it in a way a small child could not because you have *learned* or been *conditioned* to study. When a firecracker is lighted, you await the bang because you *expect* it.[2] In all of these cases, the stimuli from the people and objects you attend to grow in strength and vividness, while other stimuli recede and become less influential. To the extent that you as a speaker can command the attention of your audience—can significantly influence their perceptions through selectivity of stimuli—the ideas you express will make a clearer and more vivid impression on them, while distracting sights and sounds or conflicting ideas will tend to recede into the background of their awareness.

Finally, as we have suggested, a *set toward action* accompanies attention. This involves both the factors of expectation and readiness-adjustment. You have a tendency, while attending to a series of stimuli, to "get set" to do something about them. Thus as a motorist who pays attention to highway-safety signs, you have certain expectations regarding those signs and, therefore, get ready to steer your car around a curve or to stop at an intersection. Similarly, assuming that what you say makes sense and contains the proper motivational appeals, the closer your listeners pay attention to you and your message, the more likely they will be to behave as you suggest. As they listen, particularly if you give them clear and unmistakable "signs" of the mental highway you are traveling, they will get set to think or act as you propose and will be more disposed to do so without wavering or hesitation. In sum *what holds attention tends strongly to determine action.* * Certainly, the most influential speakers are those who most successfully hold the attention of their listeners — a point which we shall develop more fully in Chapter 18.

Voluntary Versus Involuntary Attention

Do not assume, however, that paying attention is entirely a spontaneous and involuntary reaction on the part of the audience. Many times people must force themselves to concentrate on something which in itself does not attract them. Students, for example, who are required to pass a course may compel themselves to focus attention on a textbook assignment in spite of distractions or to listen attentively to a dull classroom lecture. Necessity or some other strong motivation often leads listeners to exert this type of conscious effort in order to focus their minds on stimuli which in themselves are not attention-provoking.

The attention which results from such conscious effort often is referred to as *voluntary* or forced, and is to be distinguished from the *involuntary* or *effortless* attention paid to loud noises, flashing lights, or similar stimuli which command attention in their own right. The very fact that voluntary attention requires conscious effort, however, also makes it tiring to the listeners. To use the phraseology of the psychologists, "It is accompanied by a mass of strain sensations" resulting, ultimately, in fatigue and boredom. As a speaker, you cannot, therefore, depend on voluntary or forced attention alone. Desirable as it is to give your listeners a reason at the start for paying voluntary attention, it is also your task as a communicator to ensure that as soon as possible their attention becomes effortless and involuntary. By choosing a sub-

---

*For a classic discussion of this principle applied specifically to the problems of the public speaker, see James Winans, *Public Speaking* (New York: The Century Company, 1917), pp. 245–248; Lew Sarett and William Trufant Foster, *Basic Principles of Speech* (Boston: Houghton Mifflin Company, 1936); pp. 14–16.

ject that is intrinsically interesting or by using speech material which employs one or more of the factors of attention which we are about to identify, you can make it easier for your audience to listen to you and to focus attention on what you have to say.*

The Factors of Attention

By *factors of attention* we mean certain kinds or qualities of subject matter which because of their intrinsic attractiveness or interest value tend to capture the spontaneous attention of listeners. These factors are: (1) *activity* or *movement*, (2) *reality*, (3) *proximity*, (4) *familiarity*, (5) *novelty*, (6) *suspense*, (7) *conflict*, (8) *humor*, and (9) *the vital*.

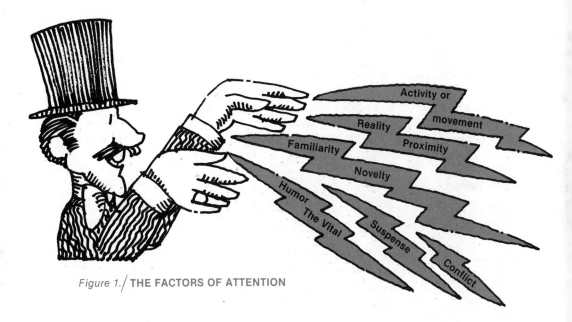

Figure 1./ THE FACTORS OF ATTENTION

Activity or Movement

If you are standing on the sidewalk and two cars of the same make, model, style, and color are in your view, one parked at the curb and the other speeding down the street at seventy miles an hour, which one will

---

*Obviously, interest and attention are closely related. People not only pay attention to what interests them, but—conversely—what they pay attention to over a period of time tends to *become* interesting to them. Frequently a student begins a required course convinced that it is going to be boring. After a while, however, the course begins to seem interesting and may actually arouse the student to the point that he or she continues for many months or years to investigate the subject matter covered. It is of utmost importance in a speech, therefore, to capture the attention of the audience in the first place and to ensure that it gives the speaker's message a fair hearing. When this is done—if the speaker is skillful and the message worthwhile—interest probably will grow as the speech proceeds.

you look at? The *moving* one, of course. Your speech likewise should "move." The more active or animated the ideas and events you talk about, the more intently audiences will listen. Instead of describing the structure of a machine, tell how it works—get the wheels turning, the parts moving, the pistons pounding. Show what happens as you move through the operation step by step. Foreshadow your destination; set up some signposts pointing toward your goal as you advance toward it. Make the movement of your speech clear to your audience by indicating when you are done with one point and ready to advance to the next.

Reality

The earliest words a child learns are the names of *real* objects and *tangible* acts. This interest in reality—in the personal perception of the immediate, the concrete, the actual—persists through life. The proposition 2 + 2 = 4, while true, is in itself so abstract that it holds little interest. Instead of talking abstract theory, therefore, talk in terms of real-life people, events, places, and tangible circumstances. Use pictures, diagrams, and charts. Tell not what happened to "a certain prominent physician of this city," but to Dr. Fred Carver who lives at 418 Paine Street. Make good use of all the forms of support we talked about in Chapter 7, especially examples. Render your descriptions specific and vivid. Remember that individual cases are more real than general classifications. Actual names and places are more fascinating than impersonalized, generalized, or vague allusions.

Proximity

Usually you can command attention by making a direct reference to someone in the audience, to some object near at hand, to some incident that has just occurred, or to the immediate occasion on which the speech is being made. A reference to a remark of the preceding speaker or of the chairperson creates a similar effect. Allude to a member of your audience *by name,* or make that person the central character in a hypothetical illustration. Not only will this awaken anyone who happens to be dozing (heaven forbid!), but it will also tend to increase the attention-level of the rest of the audience. To single out one or more persons in this way establishes your audience *as individuals;* it draws them closer to you and to each other; they are no longer a remote, anonymous mass in which personal identities are lost. As Ruch and Zimbardo point out, "Individuating listeners is one of the most effective means of getting—and holding—attention. When you are talking to a single individual, looking him straight in the eye increases the likelihood that he will look back at you and listen to what you have to say."[3]

Familiarity

Many things are familiar to us because of the frequency with which we meet them in our daily lives. Thus, knives, forks, rain, automobiles, toothbrushes, classes, and a host of other common objects and events are closely built into our experiences. Being so much a part of us, these and other familiar things catch our attention. But, as with old acquaintances, we become bored if we see too much of them and nothing else. In a spoken message, the familiar holds listeners' attention primarily when you introduce it in connection with something unfamiliar or when you point out some fresh or unknown aspect of it. Stories about Lincoln and Washington, for example, usually are interesting because listeners are familiar with their characters and certain of the beliefs, attitudes, and values they represent. Audiences do not, however, like to hear the same old rail-splitter or cherry-tree tales unless they are given a new twist or applied anew to current situations and problems.

Novelty

According to newspaper lore, when a dog bites a man, it's an accident; when a man bites a dog, it's news. While we enjoy renewing acquaintance with familiar objects and scenes, we also are strongly attracted to that which is new or unusual. Hence, the factor of novelty, if judiciously used, can be a potent force in arousing the attention of an audience. In building your speech, give particular consideration to two properties that render something novel: (1) *size* and (2) *contrast*.

Size. Objects that are extremely large or extremely small attract our attention. People often are startled into attention by large numbers, especially if they are much larger than commonly supposed or are figures with which they are not familiar. In an address given at the University of Virginia, Henry A. Grady remarked, "A home that cost three million dollars and a breakfast that cost five thousand are disquieting facts."[4] Notice, however, that size alone is not sufficient; the size must be unusual or startling *in comparison* to what we expect or are already familiar with. Reference to a truck costing six thousand dollars or a bridge worth three million would hardly be striking. The movie *King Kong* would not have drawn huge audiences had not the enormous ape so far outscaled the size of the picture's heroine and object of his amorous advances.

Contrast. At a formal dance, evening clothes pass unnoticed; but let a student come to class so dressed, and immediately attention centers on this fact. The student would have been equally conspicuous had he or she gone to the dance in gym clothes. Consider how much more compelling the facts mentioned by Grady become when he throws them into contrast with others: "Our great wealth has brought us profit and splendor, but status itself is a menace. A home that cost three million dollars and a breakfast that cost five thousand are disquieting facts to the millions who live in a hut and dine on a crust. The fact that a man . . . has an income of twenty million dollars falls strangely on the ears of those who hear it as they sit empty-handed with children crying for bread."[5]

In utilizing the materials of novelty be careful, of course, not to inject elements that are so different or unusual that they are entirely unfamiliar. Your listeners must be able to relate what you say to things they know and — preferably — have some direct experience with. Best results are achieved by the proper combination of the new and the old, of the novel and the familiar. Remember, too, that while novelty may capture attention, it may not hold a listener's interest over a period of time.

Suspense

Much of the fascination of a mystery story arises from uncertainty as to who committed the crime or, if known, whether the culprit will be caught. If the reader were to be told at once who killed the murdered man and how, why, and when the deed was done, probably the rest of the book never would be read. Listeners, like readers, are more attentive when they must mentally predict outcomes having a measure of uncertainty. So plan to hold their attention by introducing elements of suspense into your speech. Point out results, the cause of which must be explained, or call attention to a force the effect of which is uncertain. Keep up suspense in the stories you use to illustrate your ideas. Mention some valuable information that you expect to divulge later, but which first requires an understanding of the point you are now developing. Make sure, however, that the suspenseful situation you are unfolding is important enough to the audience so that the suspense *matters.* Attention is seldom drawn by uncertainties which are trivial.

Conflict

The opposition of forces compels attention — especially if the listeners identify themselves with one of the contending sides. In a sense, conflict is a form of activity; but it is more than that — it is also a clash between competing desires or actions. Often conflict, like suspense, hinges upon uncertainty; but even when there is little doubt of the outcome, the collision of contending forces attracts attention. Football games, election contests, the struggle against the adverse elements of nature and disease — all these have an element of conflict within them, and people become interested when the conflicts are vividly described. A vigorous attack upon some antisocial force — be it gangsterism, graft, or child-neglect — will draw more immediate attention than an objective analysis of it, although the analysis might in the long run prove more effective or enduring. Beware, however, of drawing artificial conflicts or engaging in sham battles. If you set up straw men and knock them down, the reality — and hence the effectiveness — of your message may be largely destroyed.

Humor

Laughter, usually, is a product of enjoyment, and people pay attention to that which they enjoy. Few things, in fact, will hold an audience as well as the speaker's judicious use of humor.* With it, you can help your audience relax from the tension often created by other factors of attention—conflict and suspense, for example—and thus reduce fatigue while still exercising a measure of control over the perceptions of the listeners. In general, you will find that the attention-holding power of humor is stronger if you keep in mind two guidelines: (1) *Be relevant.* As we have previously emphasized, any joke or anecdote you may use should reinforce and in no way detract from the central idea of your speech. (2) *Use good taste.* Avoid humor on occasions where it would be out of place, and refrain from using those types of humor which may offend the sensitivities of your listeners.

The Vital

Finally, audiences pay attention to those things which vitally, directly, and immediately affect their lives or health, their reputations, property, or employment. Life, death, progeny, and the pocketbook are typically vital concerns which usually can be counted on to grab the attention. If you can show an audience that what you say concerns one of the basic needs or motives discussed in Chapter 6, it will nearly always consider your message vital and will listen attentively. All of the other eight factors of attention are, of course, exceedingly important to an effective speech communication transaction; but the close linking of your ideas and speech materials to the vital priorities of your listeners is indispensable. You cannot hope to hold their attention for long if you fail to relate your proposals and appeals to matters vital to their survival, well-being, success, or happiness.

The vital, humor, conflict, suspense, novelty, familiarity, proximity, reality, and activity or movement—these, in sum, are the magnetic "fingers" that beckon an audience's attention. Let us now look for a moment at how these nine attention attractors can serve as your constant guides when you are assembling, sorting out, and presenting ideas and materials for speeches.

Choosing and Using the Factors of Attention

Attention, as we have emphasized, is *unstable* and *impermanent.* Focus tends to come and to go, and your listeners' internal and external perceptual fields are under a steady bombardment from a variety of stimuli. When preparing and presenting a speech, therefore, do not assume that all you need to do is catch the attention of your listeners in the first moments of your discourse. As your message proceeds, your audience's attention will ebb and flow, peak and lag. Consequently, *you must be*

---

*For a discussion of the use of humor to support and enliven your speech materials, see pages 122–123. See also the sample speeches, "A Case for Optimism" (pages 123–125) and "The Comic Spirit and the Public Speaker" (pages 283–288).

concerned throughout your speech — in the opening, closing, and at all points in between — with recapturing your listeners' attention and bringing it back again and again to the ideas you wish to communicate. To accomplish this as a speaker, you have three things going for you: your self or personality, your message, and your audience's expectations.

Attention and the Speaker's Personality

Ideas, after all, do not really speak for themselves. Someone must formulate them, shape them, communicate them. That someone — you — becomes inextricably bound up with those ideas. The reason oral communications often are more effective than written communications is that you, as a human being, give *living embodiment* to the ideas you express. In part, you gain and sustain attention by being visually and aurally an interesting stimulus.

Being interesting as a person, however, does not necessarily require the personality of a charismatic, golden-tongued orator or the grace of a prima ballerina. Rather, it involves your being a stimulus which provides a reasonable amount of activity, movement, proximity, contrast, and vitality. Specifically, to accomplish this:

1. *Use a variety of vocal-delivery patterns.* Vocal variety, in and of itself, is potentially attention-sustaining because it ensures *contrast.* Properly used, your voice mirrors your feelings and convictions, instills emotional coloring, scales the relative importance of your meanings, and underscores the purpose of your message as a whole.*

2. *Use bodily movement purposefully.* Move from one spot to another as you make the transition between major ideas. Use gestures which help emphasize key points and which visualize the size and shape of things you are describing. Being a moving, communicative, visual stimulus is part of what you as a speaker have going for you — use it.

3. *Use your eyes and your facial expressions to communicate ideas and feelings to your audiences.* Look at your audience as *individuals,* not as just a mass of faceless blobs. Smile, frown, or in other ways express facially whatever emotion is appropriate to your speech. In doing this, you will be communicating with people on a person-to-person basis. Listeners, in turn, normally examine you and your face carefully for evidences of sincerity, shared concern, or nervousness. Learn, therefore, to use your face as a flexible and communicative instrument.

In brief, you *as a person* are important in gaining and sustaining an audience's attention because, first of all, people in general are interested in other people and, if given guidance and proper materials, will pay at-

---

*The voice and the body as modes of communication are considered in depth in Chapters 14 and 15 and Appendix B.

tention to what speakers say and do. In choosing and using the factors of attention, therefore, capitalize on this human tendency by using yourself as an effective communicative stimulus.

Attention and Message Characteristics

Listeners are also likely to pay attention when they recognize in your messages an awareness of and sensitivity to their needs. As you assemble your materials, therefore, and construct your speech, strive to build into it the kinds of ideas and techniques that will help your audience to grasp what you are saying and follow your line of thinking. Here are some possibilities:

1. *Build introductions which make what you have to say relevant and interesting to your audience.* If you can demonstrate at the outset that your subject matter affects the audience's beliefs, attitudes, values, or behaviors in some significant way, you have won half the battle. Also, if you can show at the very beginning of your speech that the route you plan to take to your objective is simple and easy to follow, your audience will be more willing to give its attention and follow the route with you.

2. *Organize your ideas in the body of your speech so as to renew attention frequently during the presentation.* As you outline the major and supporting points, be sure to provide stimuli for the periodic reinforcement of your listeners' concentration. Often you can do this by incorporating the following kinds of materials:
    (a) *Interesting, detailed, concrete examples of both oral and visual kinds.* In addition to verbally describing the operation of the eye in a speech on glaucoma, present a blowup of a photograph or an oversized drawing of the eyeball to show how pressure builds up inside it.
    (b) *Figures of speech, pieces of intense or colorful language.* From time to time—but not too often—employ a memorable phrase, an exquisitely balanced sentence, a surprising analogy, etc. Such devices can inject the contrast needed to re-energize your audience's attention.
    (c) *A variety of supporting materials.* Balance them in terms of their rational appeal and their human-interest appeal. Distribute them strategically throughout the speech, remembering that different listeners are susceptible to different forms of material.
    Overall, think of your speech as a body of water with waves on it. Some are high; some are low. And each wave, as it rolls over the audience, renews attention. Be sure, therefore, to build a succession of such waves into your speech.

3. Finally—especially in the conclusion of your speech—*provide summary, recapitulation, or restatement for listeners who have not attended well enough while you were delivering the body of it.* Help

them to catch up, to gain at least an overall vision of what you have been saying. With a quick summation of the high points, you may be able to rectify misunderstood or misinterpreted messages.

Attention and the Audience's Expectations

A third factor strongly influencing the techniques you will use in gaining and sustaining attention for your speech is *audience expectation.* These expectations are created *(a)* by the audience's previous knowledge of or association with you, and *(b)* by cues you give the audience at the beginning and during the speech.

Previous Knowledge.   Based on what they know of Billy Graham, audiences expect the evangelist to call for "times of decision," to repeat the phrase "But the Bible says, . . . ," and to provide them with a smooth-flowing message. This is what they look for—and get. Based on their previous experiences with William F. Buckley, Jr., conservative broadcast commentator, author, and campus lecturer, listeners expect to hear his diverse and abstract vocabulary, his original metaphors, and his biting sarcasm. Knowing this, he doesn't disappoint them. He gives them the cues they anticipate. Such expectations guide audiences' listening and watching, and provide speakers with some useful means of focusing audiences' attention.

Probably by the time you have presented your first or second classroom speech—and almost certainly by the time you have delivered your third or fourth—you, too, will have created a set of listeners' expectations. From what they know of you and the cues you have provided in previous appearances, they can anticipate what you will talk about, what concerns you have, how you will speak to your peers, what your attitude toward them will be. Their previous experience with you will help them to follow your actions more readily, help them decide what to listen for, and—in short—tell them "what to look for" in your messages. As a speaker, therefore, draw upon such audience expectations to guide you as you:

1.   *Make references to the audience's previous associations with you*—within the classroom situation, within the school, and elsewhere. Help it to draw upon the associations and commonality of experiences by which it can better interpret your particular message at this time.
2.   *Seek to focus attention on particularly important points in your speech.* When the nineteenth-century British Prime Minister Benjamin Disraeli reached for his handkerchief, members of Parliament were alerted to the fact that he was about to verbally destroy an opponent. Today's college students soon learn that certain lecturing professors emphasize important ideas by writing them on the board, handing out visually graphic data on dittos, taking off their eyeglasses, or moving in a particular way. These are cues indicat-

ing to the audience that something vital is about to be stated. Whatever *your* usual emphasis patterns, think about them and remind yourself that your audience expects them and that you can therefore use them to gain and hold attention.

Within-Speech Cues. You should also provide your listeners with a continual stream of indicators that will make it easier for them to follow the development of your ideas. With a little thought and practice, you can learn to use effectively such techniques as these:

1. *Forecast at the start the developmental pattern you will use.* Such phrases as "First, I will . . . ; . . . then, I will . . . ; and, finally, I will . . ." help an audience anticipate points of importance.
2. *Employ internal transitions or connective phrases.* "An even more important consideration is . . . ," "Moving now to our next point . . . ," etc., tell an audience to follow you into new and different territory.
3. *Plant signposts in your speech.* Incorporate simple verbal constructions such as "But what I *really* want to do for you is this: . . . ," "If you forget everything else I have said today, remember one absolutely crucial lesson; namely: . . . ," etc. These serve to rank the elements of your speech in the order of their importance. They tell an audience what you think especially merits its attention.
4. *Use repetition or restatement when helpful.* "In other words . . . ," "To put this another way . . . ," "From another point of view . . . ," and the like, indicate to an audience that you are trying to help it understand you, that you care about its comprehension of what you are saying. You can employ such signposts also to restate your main ideas.

Overall, in this chapter we have identified and illustrated the factors of attention and have emphasized with respect to them that your task as a public communicator is twofold: (1) you must *gain* your audience's attention at the outset, and (2) you must *sustain* that attention throughout your speech. In the First Century B.C., the great Roman orator Cicero advanced the view that the key to successful communication was what he called *amplificatio* — so filling an audience's mind with your ideas and propositions that it could be occupied with nothing else at the time. This, essentially, is an approach we have urged in these pages. You can, we have said, work toward the management of an audience's external and internal perceptual fields. You can train yourself to constantly seek means and materials designed to *renew* attention periodically and frequently, thus crowding competing external and internal stimuli out of your listeners' minds. To accomplish this in practical terms, as a public speaker you should *(a) try to make yourself such an effective verbal and visual stimulus that your audience will want to give you its attention; (b)* in preparing your messages — especially in the introductory, transitional, and concluding portions—*build in techniques and materials de-signed to help your audience pay close attention and follow your line of thought with relative ease;* and *(c) generate and sustain your listeners' attention by capitalizing on their expectations of you as a person and as a speaker.* If you can achieve these specific goals, you will significantly increase your chances of transmitting your public messages success-fully.

Reference Notes

[1]Floyd L. Ruch and Philip G. Zimbardo, *Psychology and Life,* 8th Edition (Glenview, Ill.: Scott, Fores-man and Company, 1971), p. 267.

[2]G. A. Miller, *Language and Communication* (New York: McGraw-Hill Book Company, 1951), p. 200; and C. M. Solley and G. Murphy, *Development of the Perceptual World* (New York: Basic Books, Inc., Publishers, 1960), pp. 188, 194–195.

[3]Floyd L. Ruch and Philip G. Zimbardo, *Psychology and Life,* 8th Edition (Glenview, Ill.: Scott, Fores-man and Company, 1971), p. 268.

[4]From an address by Henry W. Grady, presented to the Literary Societies of the University of Vir-ginia, June 25, 1889.

[5]Ibid.

Problems and Probes

1. Using recent issues of *Vital Speeches of the Day* or a contemporary an-thology of speeches, locate an example of each of the nine factors of attention considered in this chapter. Drawing upon these examples, point out those fac-tors which commanded your attention most strongly. Explain how some of the weaker examples might have been enhanced. Find instances where factors were presumably combined to gain the attention of the audience, and describe the combinations which seemed to you to be the most effective. Hand the results of your analysis to your instructor in written form.

2. From the pages of popular magazines and daily newspapers, select five advertisements which seem to you to be particularly attention-catching. Analyze them for the effectiveness with which they employ the factors of attention and the skill with which the copywriters have phrased the advertising message. As a result of this analysis, carefully phrase five different statements which you as a public speaker could use to introduce a speech. Employ a different factor of at-tention in each statement, and remember that the purpose of the statement is twofold: *(a)* to *capture* listener interest and *(b)* to *hold* or *sustain* it.

3. Listen to the commercials given on radio or television, and select five which you believe are probably effective in capturing and holding the attention of listeners or viewers. Summarize in writing the text of these commercial mes-sages; identify the factors of attention employed in them; and, finally, decide which of the attention-getting and attention-holding techniques or devices would be useful to the public speaker.

4. Think back over your experiences of the past three days and select at least five instances in which you paid sustained attention to an object, process, or event: a classroom lecture, a book, a magazine, a television program, a visit to an art museum—for example. To which of these things did you pay attention *effortlessly* or *involuntarily*? To which of them did you have to pay *forced* or *vol-untary* attention? What elements in the involuntary group especially attracted

you? In the voluntary group, what particular elements or factors seemed to work against effortless attention?

Oral Activities and Speaking Assignments

1.   Present a three- or four-minute speech especially designed to gain and hold the attention of your audience. Employ a large number of the attention-getting and attention-holding devices discussed in this chapter. After the speech, survey your audience orally or by means of a written questionnaire to determine which devices were most effective in this regard, and what other things you could have done to increase attention.

2.   After studying your Personal Speech Journal for any useful data you may have on subject choices and preferences, present to the class a speech on a subject that has little or no inherent interest-value for your audience, and strive to make it as interesting and attention-commanding as possible.

3.   Perform the following experiment. After your instructor has placed a small white dot on an otherwise clean chalkboard, you and the other members of the class will sit in silence as you attempt to focus your attention *exclusively* on that dot for one full minute. At the end of that time, discuss the results of the test and what happened while it was taking place. Who, among you, was able to pay attention to nothing but the dot? How many of you were unable to keep your attention from wandering to something else—either tangible or intangible? As a result of the experiment and the ensuing discussion, formulate some useful conclusions concerning the nature of attention and interest and the obligations of the speaker who hopes to attract and sustain them throughout the presentation of his or her message.

Suggestions for Further Reading

J. Anthony Deutsch and D. Deutsch, "Attention: Some Theoretical Considerations," *Psychological Review* LXX (1970): 80–90.

Charles Gruner, Cal Logue, Dwight Freshley, and Richard Huseman, *Speech Communication in Society* (Boston: Allyn & Bacon Inc., 1972), pp. 213–219.

Saundra Hybels and Richard L. Weaver, II, *Speech Communication* (New York: D. Van Nostrand Co., 1974), pp. 88–89 and 165–167.

C. David Mortensen, *Communication: The Study of Human Interaction* (New York: McGraw-Hill Book Company, 1972), pp. 35 and 84–86.

Magdalen D. Vernon, "Perception, Attention, and Consciousness," *Foundations of Communication Theory,* ed. Kenneth K. Sereno and C. David Mortensen (New York: Harper & Row, Publishers, 1970), pp. 137–151.

John Vohs and G. P. Mohrmann, *Audiences Messages Speakers* (New York: Harcourt Brace Jovanovich, Inc., 1975), pp. 209–210.

Adapting the Speech
Structure to the Audience:
The Motivated Sequence

In preceding chapters we considered how to select the basic appeals and support the principal ideas of which your speech consists. It is now time to consider how these materials should be structured or organized so as to form the speech as a whole. In this connection, the most important single thing to remember is that you cannot ram ideas down people's throats. Instead, you must lead their thinking along lines they will follow voluntarily. You must cause them to see for themselves why they need to know, believe, or do as you urge. In short, organizing a speech is fundamentally a psychological process—a process that has its basis in the normal and customary thought patterns of your listeners.

A Psychological Basis for Speech Organization

On first consideration, you might suppose that your listeners' mental processes will vary according to the type of response which you seek— that a response of understanding will differ in substantial ways from a response of belief or of action. The fact of the matter, however, is that the mental processes involved in making various kinds of responses differ not so much in kind as in completeness. The reason for this is that in most cases the responses your listeners make will be motivated by the same factor—a desire to maintain or restore some kind of *consistency* or *balance* among their ideas, beliefs, and values. When they feel a need to know, their natural impulse is to seek information; when they recognize a problem that is important to them, they seek a solution in the form of a reconstituted belief or pattern of action.

Today the desire of the individual to maintain internally a consistency or balance of ideas and attitudes is widely accepted as explaining many aspects of human behavior. In fact, in a recent textbook on persuasion the author goes so far as to state quite flatly: "The job of persuaders is first to create psychological imbalance in persons they seek to persuade, and then to 'close off' undesired rebalancing mechanisms while simultaneously promoting the resolutions they favor."[1]

Many years ago, the philosopher John Dewey drew upon a similar principle to develop a detailed description of the way individuals characteristically proceed when they are confronted with a problem or required to make a difficult choice. *First,* said Dewey, they become aware of a specific lack or disorientation—some situation with which they are, for one reason or another, dissatisfied. *Second,* they examine this difficulty to determine its nature, scope, causes, and implications. *Third,* they search for a new orientation that will solve the problem or satisfy the need. *Fourth,* they compare and evaluate the possible solutions which have occurred to them. And, *fifth,* they select the solution or course of action which, upon the basis of the foregoing reflection, seems most likely to put their minds at rest.[2]

Of course, there is no guarantee that everyone, even in reflective moments, will always think through a problem or arrive at a decision in exactly this fashion. But much observation and testing have made it apparent that, typically, when confronted with a problem or forced to make a choice, most of us do raise questions such as these: Exactly what is the nature of the problem? How serious is it? Are persons other than myself affected? Is an immediate decision called for? What courses of action are open? Which of these courses would be most likely to produce a sound and satisfactory solution? Which would solve the problem most quickly and at least cost and inconvenience to myself and others? Until we are satisfied on these and similar matters, we are reluctant to make a decision ourselves or to support another's proposal.

The Motivated Sequence

As we shall now see, by attending to the kinds of questions we have just noted, speakers may—if they choose—develop a pattern of organization which, with appropriate adaptations, is applicable to all of the basic types of speeches. This pattern is called the *motivated sequence* and derives its name from the fact that *by following the normal processes of human thinking it motivates an audience to respond affirmatively to the speaker's purpose.* (The complete sequence is illustrated on page 151.)

In order to see how this motivated sequence may be applied when the purpose of a speech is to win a response of overt action, let us begin by examining an advertisement which appeared some years ago in *Fortune Magazine.*[3] It is entitled "Motivated Men Made America Great" and describes a service provided by Maritz Inc. The text, in part, appears on the following page.

1 The phonograph, the incandescent light, central electrical power systems, the fluoroscope, moving pictures...these are Thomas A. Edison's best remembered contributions to the well-being of the world. There were thousands more. All testify to the genius of a man who worked best under competitive pressure and once explained his success by saying,*"I can only invent under powerful incentives. No competition means no invention. It's the same with the men I have around me. It's not money they want but a chance for their ambition to grow."*

2 Countries need motivated men. Companies do, too, especially when their success depends on the extra effort of individual salesmen and entire sales organizations.

3 We help fill this need for companies in all industries. Maritz is the only company in the United States engaged exclusively in the business of motivating men to sell. As specialists, we offer complete sales motivation services including basic planning, program promotion, complete administration and thorough *follow-through.* All are offered in conjunction with distinctive merchandise and glamorous travel awards.

4 The combination causes salesmen to work harder, more intelligently, and more successfully. Their increased productivity improves sales and profits for the clients we serve.

5 Your Maritz Account Executive can tell you why salesmen become more productive when rewards for extra achievement are more than monetary. He can also help you plan, announce, and conduct sales motivation programs to meet your company's specific needs. We suggest you contact him. He alone offers you the exclusive services of the leader in the field of sales motivation.

As you will observe, this advertisement contains five distinct steps: (1) your *attention* is caught; (2) you are made to feel a definite *need;* (3) you are shown a way in which this need can be *satisfied;* (4) the benefits of purchasing the Maritz service are *visualized;* and (5) *action* in the form of contacting a representative of Maritz Inc. is called for.

The Five Basic Steps in the Sequence

To each of the steps just noted, let us assign a name indicative of its function: (1) Attention, (2) Need, (3) Satisfaction, (4) Visualization, and (5) Action. With these names in mind, look again at the advertisement, noting how the steps jointly work to "motivate" the reader to action:

1. *Attention.* Using the interest factor of "the familiar," as explained in Chapter 8 (page 132), the writer of the ad attempts to capture your attention by a brief description of Edison's strong motivation to succeed.
2. *Need.* A direct statement asserts that businesses need motivated individuals.
3. *Satisfaction.* Because it specializes in all phases of motivation, the Maritz agency says it is well qualified to meet this need and can, therefore, ensure satisfaction.
4. *Visualization.* Benefits in the form of higher sales and greater profits are pictured.
5. *Action.* The reader is asked to contact a Maritz account executive.

The Motivated Sequence Applied to Speeches to Actuate

Let us now see how the motivated sequence may be used, not in an advertisement, but in a speech designed to secure action from the listeners. Here, in outline form, is a typical example:

FIRE PREVENTION IN THE HOME

Attention Step
 I. If you like parlor tricks, try this:
  A. Place a blotter soaked in turpentine in a jar of oxygen.
  B. The blotter will burst into flames.
 II. If you do not have a jar of oxygen around the house, try this:
  A. Place a well-oiled mop in a storage closet.
  B. In a few days the mop will burst into flames.

Need Step
 I. Few homes are free from dangerous fire hazards.
  A. Attics with piles of damp clothing and paper are combustible.
  B. Storage closets containing cleaning mops and brushes are fire hazards.
  C. Basements often are filled with dangerous piles of trash.
  D. Garages attached to houses are danger spots.

Satisfaction Step

I.   To protect your home from fire requires three things:
- A.   A thorough cleaning out of all combustible materials.
- B.   Careful storage of such hazards as oil mops, paint brushes, etc.
  1.   Clean them before storing.
  2.   Store them in fireproof containers.
- C.   A regular check to see that inflammable trash does not accumulate.

II. Clean-up programs show practical results.
- A.   Clean-up campaigns in Evansville kept insurance rates in a "Class 1" bracket.
- B.   A clean-up campaign in Fort Wayne helped reduce the number of fires.

Visualization Step

I.   You will enjoy the results of such a program.
- A.   You will have neat and attractive surroundings.
- B.   You will be safe from fire.

Action Step

I.   Begin your own clean-up campaign now.

THE MOTIVATED SEQUENCE APPLIED TO SPEECHES TO ACTUATE

Step	Function	Audience Response
1 Attention Step.	Getting attention.	"I want to listen."
2 Need Step.	Showing the need: describing the problem.	"Something needs to be done."
3 Satisfaction Step.	Satisfying the need: presenting the solution.	"This is what to do to satisfy the need."
4 Visualization Step.	Visualizing the results.	"I can see myself enjoying the benefits of such an action."
5 Action Step.	Requesting action or approval.	"I will do this."

The Motivated Sequence Applied to Speeches to Persuade

Thus far we have considered the motivated sequence only as it applies to speeches to actuate. Let us suppose, however, that instead of moving your listeners to overt action, your purpose is merely to influence their beliefs or attitudes — to *persuade* them to adopt your point of view on a matter of mutual interest. In this case, obviously, the fifth or "action" step in the sequence is not called for. Instead, your speech may terminate once you have visualized the advantages or benefits to be derived from adopting the belief or attitude you advocate. Here is an example — in outline form:

LOCAL GOVERNMENT IS IMPORTANT

Attention Step
I. Look first at the person sitting on your right; then at the person sitting on your left.
    A. The chances are neither of them voted in the recent municipal election.
    B. The chances are at least one of them could not even name the candidates.

Need Step
I. Most of us do not realize how important local government is to us.
    A. We are concerned with making a living.
    B. We get our news from the national radio and television networks.
    C. We do not attend meetings of our city's boards or agencies.

Satisfaction Step
I. Our local government is of vital importance to all of us.
    A. It collects and spends a large portion of our tax dollars.
    B. It provides the police, fire, and sanitary services on which our security and health depend.
    C. It is responsible for the schools our children attend.

Visualization Step
I. Today we stand at the fork of the road insofar as our towns and cities are concerned.
    A. Continued apathy will compound their present problems.
        1. They will gradually degenerate into slums.
        2. The benefits of community life will be lost.
    B. Citizen interest will do much to reverse these trends.
        1. The efficiency of local government will be increased.
        2. Our cities will become more pleasant and healthful places in which to live and raise our families.
    C. Which way shall we choose?

**THE MOTIVATED SEQUENCE APPLIED TO
SPEECHES TO PERSUADE** *

	Step	Function	Audience Response
1	Attention Step.	Getting attention.	"I want to listen."
2	Need Step.	Showing the need: describing the problem.	"Some attitude or belief needs to be changed."
3	Satisfaction Step.	Satisfying the need: presenting the solution.	"This is the attitude or belief that should be adopted."
4	Visualization Step.	Visualizing the results.	"This is how things will be when the proposed attitude or belief is endorsed."

The Motivated Sequence Applied to Speeches to Inform

Finally, let us see how the motivated sequence may be applied when your general purpose is neither to actuate nor persuade your audience but to convey to them some information which you think they ought to know. In this case, only three of the five steps would be required. As always, you would need to catch your listeners' *attention* and direct it to the substance of your remarks. In addition, you would need to motivate them by pointing out why they *need* to know what you are about to tell them. And, of course, you would have to *satisfy* this need by supplying the information. Here, however, your speech could terminate since the purpose for which you are presenting it would have been fulfilled. Note how these three steps are applied in an informative speech on how to rescue drowning persons:

ROW — THROW — GO

Attention Step
I. Holiday deaths by drowning are second in number only to automobile accidents.

---

*Although from a purely structural point of view, the speech to persuade is complete once the benefits of believing as the speaker urges have been pointed out, it sometimes is desirable to add by way of conclusion a kind of pseudo-action step in which the audience is asked to retain and apply the belief which the speaker has proposed.

Need Step

I. Every person should know what to do when a call for help is heard.
   - A. This information may help you save a friend.
   - B. This information may help you save a member of your family.

Satisfaction Step

I. Remember three important words when someone is drowning: *row, throw, go.*
   - A. *Row:* Look for a boat.
      1. You can well afford to take a little time to look for a means of rowing to the rescue.
         - a. Look for a boat.
         - b. Look for a canoe.
         - c. Look for a raft.
      2. Rowing to the rescue is always the wisest way.
   - B. *Throw:* Look for a life buoy.
      1. See if you can locate something buoyant to throw to the person in distress.
         - a. Look for a life buoy.
         - b. Look for an inflated inner tube.

THE MOTIVATED SEQUENCE APPLIED TO SPEECHES TO INFORM*

Step	Function	Audience Response
1 Attention Step.	Getting attention.	"I want to listen."
2 Need Step.	Demonstrating the need to know.	"I need information on this subject."
3 Satisfaction Step.	Presenting the information itself.	"The information being presented helps me understand the subject more satisfactorily."

*When giving a speech to inform, a speaker sometimes may wish to add to the three basic steps of attention, need, and satisfaction *(a)* a visualization step in which he or she briefly suggests the pleasure to be gained from having the information presented and *(b)* an action step in which the listeners are asked to study further the matters discussed. These steps, however, are purely optional and not essential to the completion of the speech as a logically coherent unit.

          c.   Look for a board.
          d.   Look for a child's floating toy.
      2.   You can throw an object faster than you can swim.
   C.   *Go:* As a last resort, swim out to the drowning person.
      1.   Approach the victim from the rear.
      2.   If you are grabbed, go underwater.
      3.   Clutch the person's hair.
      4.   Swim for shore.
II.   Remember, when you hear the call for help:
   A.   Look first for something in which to row.
   B.   Look for something buoyant to throw the victim.
   C.   Swim out only as a last resort.

The Structure and Development of the Steps in the Motivated Sequence

Now that we have viewed the motivated sequence as a whole and considered in some detail its application to the three basic types of speeches, let us look more closely at the *individual steps,* noting in particular their internal structuring, the methods of their development, and the kinds of materials that may be used with good effect in each. The five basic steps in the motivated sequence are illustrated in the diagram on page 151.

The Attention Step

As a speaker, your first task, of course, is to *gain attention.* But merely gaining attention is not enough: you must also gain *favorable* attention, and you must direct it toward the major ideas in your speech. Customarily the methods and materials that may be used to attain these ends include the following: *(a)* reference to the subject, *(b)* reference to the occasion, *(c)* personal greeting, *(d)* rhetorical question, *(e)* startling statement, *(f)* quotation, *(g)* humorous anecdote, and *(h)* illustration.* Remember, however, that while the attention step is important, it is only a *means* to an end. Be sure, therefore, that your attention step leads naturally into the ensuing portions of your speech.

The Need Step

Ideally, a good need step should contain four parts or elements:

1. *Statement* — a clear, concise statement or description of the need or problem.
2. *Illustration* — one or more detailed examples which illustrate the need.
3. *Ramification* — additional examples, statistical data, testimony, and other forms of support to show the extent of the need.

---

*These methods and materials will be considered in detail in Chapter 12, "Beginning and Ending the Speech," pp. 189–203.

Figure 1. / THE MOTIVATED
SEQUENCE

1 Attention

Getting
attention

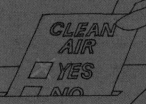

2 Need

Showing
the need:
Describing
the problem

3 Satisfaction

Satisfying
the need:
Presenting
the solution

4 Visualization

Visualizing
the results

5 Action

Requesting
action or
approval

CLEAN
AIR

☐ YES
☐ NO

4. *Pointing*—a convincing demonstration of how the need directly affects the people addressed: their health, happiness, security, or other interests.

When dealing with a simple problem or with one the audience knows a good deal about, you may not find it necessary to use all four of these parts or structural elements. But regardless of whether you use the complete fourfold development, only a part of it, or some other structure, you will find that the need step is one of the most important in your speech. *It is here that you relate your subject to the vital concerns and interests of your audience.*

The Satisfaction Step

The purpose of the satisfaction step, as we have suggested, is to enable your hearers to understand the information you are presenting or to get them to agree that the belief or action you propose is the correct one. The structure of this step differs somewhat, however, depending on whether your major purpose is primarily informative or persuasive. For this reason, the satisfaction step for informative or instructive speeches and the satisfaction step for persuasive and actuative speeches must be considered separately.

The Satisfaction Step in Speeches to Inform.   When your purpose is to inform—to give your audience a clear understanding of some subject— the satisfaction step usually will constitute the bulk of your speech and will present the information that was specified as necessary in the need step. The development of the satisfaction step as used in informative speeches customarily includes:

1. *Initial summary*—briefly state in advance the main ideas or points you intend to cover.
2. *Detailed information*—discuss in order the facts or explanations pertaining to each of these ideas or points.
3. *Final summary*—restate the main points or ideas you have presented, together with any important conclusions you have drawn from them.

The Satisfaction Step in Speeches to Persuade.   When the purpose of your speech is to persuade or to actuate, these four elements are usually included in the satisfaction step:

1. *Statement*—briefly state the attitude, belief, or action you wish the audience to adopt.
2. *Explanation*—make sure your proposal is understood. Diagrams or charts are often useful here.
3. *Theoretical demonstration*—show how this belief or action logically

meets the problem pointed out in the need step.

4. *Practical experience* – give actual examples showing that this proposal has worked effectively or that this belief has been proved correct. Use facts, figures, and the testimony of experts to support your claims.

Here again, probably, you will find that you do not need to include all of these elements or parts in the satisfaction step of every persuasive speech. Nor will it be necessary that they always appear in the same order. For instance, you can sometimes meet objections best by distributing answers strategically throughout the step, at whatever point questions are likely to arise. When developing the satisfaction step in speeches to persuade or to actuate, however, the first four elements — *statement, explanation, theoretical demonstration,* and *practical experience* – offer a convenient and effective sequence, thus: *(a)* Briefly state the attitude, belief, or action you propose. *(b)* Explain it clearly. *(c)* Show how, in theory, it will meet the need. *(d)* Give actual examples of how the proposal or plan is working.

Parallel Development of the Need and Satisfaction Steps. In some speeches of a persuasive nature, the need step may have two or more important aspects. To give each of these aspects sufficient emphasis and to make your discussion clear, you may decide to develop the need and satisfaction steps in a *parallel* order. That is, you first present one aspect of the need and show how your proposal satisfies it; then you follow this same procedure in treating the second aspect, the third aspect, and so on. This method weakens the cumulative effect of the motivated sequence, but the additional clarity often makes up for the loss.

The *normal order* and the *parallel order* for developing the need and satisfaction steps of a speech to actuate are illustrated in the following skeletal outlines:

OUTLINE I: NORMAL ORDER

Attention Step
I. While working on the construction of the new state highway last summer, I witnessed a number of automobile accidents in which the driver was severely injured.
    A. Vivid description of how the accident occurred.
    B. Vivid description of the injuries sustained by the driver.

Need Step
I. In each case the driver was injured either because he or she was driving too fast or failed to wear a seat belt.
    A. The driver was unable to stop in time.
    B. The driver was thrown through the windshield or against the steering post.

Satisfaction Step
I. In order to reduce your chances of serious injury or even death, you must do two things above all others.
    A. You must slow down.
    B. You must wear your seat belt at all times.

Visualization Step
I. You will actually enjoy driving more when you have the assurance these actions bring.

Action Step
I. Resolve right now to do two things when you drive.
    A. Go slower.
    B. Always wear your seat belt.

OUTLINE II: PARALLEL ORDER

Attention Step
I. While working on the construction of the new state highway last summer, I witnessed a number of automobile accidents in which the driver was severely injured.
    A. Vivid description of how the accident occurred.
    B. Vivid description of the injuries sustained by the driver.

Need and Satisfaction Steps (First phase)
I. In some cases the driver was unable to stop in time.
II. To assure yourself a safe stopping distance you must slow down.

Need and Satisfaction Steps (Second phase)
I. In some cases the driver was thrown through the windshield or against the steering post.
II. To guard against such an eventuality, you must wear your seat belt at all times.

Visualization Step
I. You will actually enjoy driving more when you have the assurance these actions bring.

Action Step
I. Resolve right now to do two things when you drive.
    A. Go slower.
    B. Always wear your seat belt.

Whether you use the normal order or the parallel order in the satisfaction step, you will, of course, always need to develop support for your statements by supplying an abundance of illustrations, statistics, quotations, and comparisons.

The Visualization Step

The visualization step, as we have said, is commonly used only in the speeches to persuade or to actuate. (See the chart on page 157.)

The function of the visualization step is *to intensify desire:* to help motivate the listeners to believe, feel, or act. In order to do this, it projects them into the future. Indeed, this step might also be called the "projection" step, for its effectiveness depends in large part upon the vividness with which it pictures the future or potential benefits of believing or acting as the speaker proposes. Accordingly, the visualization step may be developed in one of three ways: (1) by projecting a picture of the future that is *positive,* (2) by projecting a picture that is *negative,* or (3) by projecting first a negative and then a positive picture in order to show *contrast.*

The Positive Method of Developing the Visualization Step. When using the positive method, describe conditions as they will be in the future if the belief you advocate is accepted or the action you propose is carried out. Provide vivid, concrete descriptions. Select some situation which you are quite sure will arise in the future, and in that situation picture your audience actually enjoying the safety, pleasure, pride, etc., which the belief or proposal will produce.

The Negative Method of Developing the Visualization Step. When using the negative method, describe the adverse conditions that will prevail in the future if the belief you advocate is *not* adopted or the solution you propose is *not* carried out. Graphically picture for your audience the danger or unpleasantness which will result. Select the most striking problems or deficiencies you have pointed out in the need step and demonstrate how they will continue unless your recommendations are adopted.

The Contrast Method of Developing the Visualization Step. The method of contrast combines the positive and negative approaches. Use the negative development first, visualizing the *bad* effects that are likely to occur if your listeners fail to follow your advice; then introduce the positive elements, visualizing the *good* effects of believing or doing as you urge. By means of this contrast, both the bad and the good effects are made more striking and intense.

Whichever method you use, however, remember that the visualization step always must stand the test of *reality.* The conditions you picture must seem probable. In addition, you must to the fullest extent possible *put your listeners into the picture.* Use vivid imagery: make them actually see, hear, feel, taste, or smell the things and benefits you describe.* The more real you make the projected situation seem, the stronger will be their reaction.

The following visualization step, in a speech advocating planned and orderly urban growth, illustrates the method of contrast:

---

*See Chapter 13, "The Effects of Language on Communication," especially pp. 214–218 where the usefulness of imagery is considered in detail.

Whether we like it or not, then, as these facts show, nearly all of our towns and cities are going to continue to grow and expand in the years ahead. *How* your town grows, however, is going to be entirely up to you.

As new suburbs are developed and annexed, one of two policies can be followed. First, this growth may be haphazard and unplanned, and may occur without strict zoning ordinances to regulate it. In this case, it is likely that paved streets, if they are present at all, will be cheaply constructed without storm sewers or attention to traffic flow. Houses will be crowded together on tiny lots and will vary widely in value and in architectural style. Filling stations, business establishments, and even light industries—with their odors and noises—may appear in the middle of residential neighborhoods. In short, if you were to buy a home in such an area, it is altogether likely that you would soon be faced with huge bills for new streets and sewers, and that your property, instead of appreciating in value, would decline rapidly in the years ahead. As a home buyer you would be a loser all around—a loser not only because of the poor quality of life you and your family would experience, but a loser, and a big loser, in hard dollars and cents.

On the other hand, if additions to your town are properly planned and zoned, as a home owner you will be assured of clean air and adequate living space, will enjoy a house that increases rather than decreases in value, and will be assured that you are not paying for new streets and sewers a few years after you move in. Isn't it worthwhile requiring that your town annex only subdivisions that have been properly planned and zoned—that it insist on orderly responsible growth? Remember, buying a home is very probably the largest single purchase you will make during the course of your entire life. Remember, too, that a healthy, attractive environment is perhaps the greatest gift you can give to your family.

The Action Step

As the chart on page 157 indicates, only the speech to actuate *always* requires an action step. At times, however, as a speaker you may use something resembling an action step to urge further study of the topic dealt with in an informative speech or to strengthen the belief or attitude urged in a persuasive one.

There are many methods for developing the action step, but most commonly these methods employ one or more of the following devices: *(a)* challenge or appeal, *(b)* summary, *(c)* quotation, *(d)* illustration, *(e)* statement of inducement, *(f)* statement of personal intention—materials which are considered in detail in Chapter 12, pages 197–201.

Whatever method or material you use, be sure to keep the action step *short.* Someone has given the following rule for effective public speaking: "Stand up, speak up, shut up!" Insofar as the action step is concerned, modify this admonition to read: *Clinch your major ideas, finish your speech briskly—and sit down.*

The ways in which the motivated sequence can be adapted to the basic types and the general ends of speech are diagrammed in the following chart.

ADAPTATION OF THE MOTIVATED SEQUENCE TO THE GENERAL ENDS OF SPEECH

General End	To Inform	To Persuade	To Actuate
Reaction Sought	Understanding (Clarity)	Belief (Internal)	Specific Action (Observable)
1 Attention Step	Draw attention to the subject.	Draw attention to the need.	Draw Attention to the need.
2 Need Step	Show why the listeners need a knowledge of the subject; point out what problems this information will help them meet.	Present evidence to prove the existence of a situation which requires that something be decided and upon which the audience must take a position.	Present evidence to prove the existence of a situation which requires action.
3 Satisfaction Step	Present information to give them a satisfactory knowledge of the subject as an aid in the solution of these problems; begin and end this presentation with a summary of the main points presented. (Normal end of the speech.)	Get the audience to believe that your position on this question is the right one to take, by using evidence and motivational appeals.	Propose the specific action required to meet this situation; get the audience to believe in it by presenting evidence and motivational appeals (as in the speech to persuade).
4 Visualization Step	Sometimes: briefly suggest pleasure to be gained from this knowledge.	Briefly stimulate a favorable response by projecting this belief into imaginary operation. (Normal end of the speech.)	Picture the results which such action or the failure to take it will bring; use vivid description (as in the speech to persuade).
5 Action Step	Sometimes: urge further study of the subject.	Sometimes: arouse determination to retain this belief (as a guide to future action).	Urge the audience to take definite action proposed.

The full motivated sequence, then, consists of five steps which correspond to the natural thought processes by which people usually come to understand, to believe, or to act. Our purpose in this chapter has been to explain the psychological principles upon which this motivational structuring is based and to suggest why each of its steps is important in winning a response from a listener. By this, we do not mean to imply that the motivated sequence is the only method of structuring a speech or that all speeches of every type always must be built in this way. In fact, in the chapter that follows we examine a number of alternate plans of speech organization. The motivated sequence does, however, provide an especially effective and widely applicable structure for speeches designed to inform, persuade, or actuate; and when you are called upon to present such speeches, we recommend that you always consider it as one of your prime organizational options.

A Sample Speech Utilizing the Motivated Sequence

The following speech to actuate provides a practical example of the motivated sequence in its fully developed, five-step form. It was prepared by Ms. Jan Bjorklund of Mankato State College, Mankato, Minnesota, and was presented in one of the annual contests sponsored by the Interstate Oratorical Association.

As you read the speech, note how Ms. Bjorklund (1) calls *attention* to her subject by piquing the curiosity of her hearers; (2) points out—with statistics, specific instances, authoritative testimony, and comparisons—the crucial *need* to bring venereal disease under control; (3) demonstrates—by offering a three-way solution—that this need can be *satisfied;* (4) briefly *visualizes* the results of carrying out the proposed solution; and (5) concludes with an appeal for direct and immediate *action* in the form of a concerted drive against the disease.

"Nice People"[4]
Jan Bjorklund

[1. ATTENTION STEP]

What I am about to say, I have said before; so have many others in many other ways. And that's about it. A great deal has been *said,* but very little has been *done;* so this problem remains a problem. For this reason, I'd like to emphasize the words and the meaning of this speech, hoping that you will react from an understanding of these words.

[2. NEED STEP]

An epidemic of contagious disease is threatening the United States at this very minute: one so massive that a new case occurs every 15 seconds, for a total of 7,500 a day.[1]

All age levels are being victimized by this disease, but most selectively young people, ages 16 to 30. This epidemic is capable of spreading undetected inside the bodies of over 700,000 women, allowing them to continue a normal life, causing them no discomfort, no disability, no pain, while robbing them of their ability to bear children.[2]

All the while this disease continues to strike, to spread, and to slay, the means to cure it not only exist, but are relatively inexpensive, relatively simple to administer, and painless to the receiver.

Isn't it strange that our nation, one of the healthiest in the world, should allow such a disease to continue, to multiply into an uncontrollable epidemic? One would think that the halls of government would be echoing with the debate and discussion of possible courses of action to eradicate this festering blight. Yes, one could think that—until realizing this is not the case, due to the small and medically irrelevant fact that the disease in question is *venereal* disease.

In 1936, the Surgeon General of the United States Public Health Service, Thomas Parran, stated that the great impediment to the solution of the VD problem was that "nice" people don't have it.[3] Since then, the basis for this statement has disappeared. Oh, Freaks have it, and Blacks, and Jesus People, and urban disadvantaged, and poverty-stricken, and people on welfare: *they* all have it, all right! It's been called "their" disease. But is it theirs alone?

Berkeley, California, is a "nice" place to live. Within the city's limits, we find the University of California and many of its prominent faculty and students. Last year, 2,000 cases of gonorrhea were reportedly found there, too.[4]

Houston, Texas, is a "nice" place, too. Nice enough to attract attention and become the headquarters for our national space program. Last year it also attracted 1,266 cases of gonorrhea for every 100,000 inhabitants.[5] Atlanta, Georgia, the cultural and commercial capital of the South, also leads the nation in the reported number of cases of gonorrhea. Last year it reported 2,510 cases for every 100,000 inhabitants.[6]

These are only the *reported* cases, estimated to be 25 percent of all cases, for only 1 out of every 4 cases is ever reported.[7]

This would mean that of the 100,000 inhabitants of Berkeley, California, approximately 8,000 contracted VD; that would be 1 out of 12!

This ratio isn't so crucial, though, when you compare it to that in some San Francisco high schools where a student has 1 chance in 5 of contracting syphilis or gonorrhea before he graduates.[8]

Why? People neglect to get the proper treatment; or when they do, they don't name all their contacts, so the disease continues to spread.

According to *Today's Health* magazine, of the 4 out of 5 cases that are treated by private physicians, only 1 out of 9 is reported.[9] And of the many, many that go by unreported, I'd guess that 90 percent involve nice people.

Syphilis and gonorrhea are infectious diseases outranked in incidence only by the common cold.[10]

. . . .

Venereal disease is especially rampant among young people. As reported in *Newsweek,* January 24, 1972, at least 1 of every 5 persons with gonorrhea is below the age of 20.[12] Last year, over 5,000 cases were found among children between the ages of 10 and 14. Another 2,000 cases were found among children below the age of 9. Dr. Walter Smartt, Chief of the Los Angeles County Venereal Disease Control Division, states that the probability of a person acquiring VD before he reaches the age of 25 is about 50 percent. This would mean that of the number of us here in this room, one half of us have already or shortly will come in contact with VD. Where does that put you? Or me? It's always easy to say it can only happen to someone else, to the other person, but there is only one guarantee that it can't strike me or you.

And that one guarantee is abstinence. But in this day and age, that's hardly a likely possibility. We wouldn't think of stopping tuberculosis by stopping breathing, so how could we think of stopping venereal disease by stopping sex?

[3. SATISFACTION STEP]

What is the solution? A number of suggestions have been made.

First of all, in the opinion of many experts, syphilis could be brought under control by case-finding. However, in the last few years the number of case-finders has been reduced. The federal government is not supporting this effort.

Secondly, there is a deplorable inadequacy in both teaching and courses of instruction concerning VD. We need an educational effort at the earliest feasible age group. Looking at the ages of the patients coming into the clinics, we see we almost have to beat puberty.

Another possibility has been suggested by Dr. John Knox of Houston's Baylor College of Medicine. He predicts that a vaccine for syphilis could easily be developed in 5 years, but at the rate the government is putting out money, it will probably take 105 years.[13] A vaccine for gonorrhea, on the other hand, seems almost impossible at this point. There is a crying need for more research.

[4. VISUALIZATION STEP]

I thought for sure that such a complex problem would require a complicated cure. However, I became aware of my mistaken thinking during a visit with my college physician, Dr. Hankerson. He informed me that syphilis and gonorrhea can be brought under control and cured by simple treatments of penicillin or similar antibiotics. If every American would have a regular checkup, and receive treatment if necessary, by 1973 we could begin to send venereal disease the way of typhoid, measles, polio, and the bubonic plague. If each of us would begin with a regular checkup, now.

[5. ACTION STEP]

As you can see, it is a complex problem, and no one solution can completely eliminate it. What we need is a concerted drive that will encompass case-finding, support for an educational effort, and the search for a vaccine, along with the use of penicillin and other similar antibiotics.

But even if this does happen, the effort cannot be successful, for venereal disease will continue to spread as long as it is thought of as dirty and shameful. Dr. McKenzie-Pollock, former director of the American Social Health Association, made the following statement: "Once the public is aware and notified that syphilis and gonorrhea are serious factors in our everyday lives right now, the rest will follow."[14]

Very well, consider yourself *notified* . . . or are you one of those "nice people"?

Reference Notes (for the Speech)

[1]*VD Fact Sheet—1971, U.S. Department of Health, Education, and Welfare, Public Health Service, page 9.* [2]*Today's Health, April 1971, page 16.* [3]*Today's Health, April 1971, page 16.* [4]*VD Statistical Letter, DHEW, February 1972, page 11.* [5]*Ibid., page 4.* [6]Newsweek, *January 24, 1972, page 46.* [7]*Minneapolis Tribune, Wednesday, April 5, 1972, page 2A.* [8]Newsweek, *January 24, 1972, page 46.* [9]*Today's Health, April 1971, page 69.* [10]*Sex and the Yale Student, Student Committee on Human Sexuality, 1970, page 51.* [12]*Ibid., page 46.* [13]*Ibid., page 49.* [14]*Today's Health, April 1971, page 69.*

Reference Notes

[1]Herbert W. Simons, *Persuasion: Understanding, Practice, and Analysis* (Reading, Mass.: Addison-Wesley Publishing Company, Inc., 1976), p. 17.

[2]John Dewey, "Analysis of Reflective Thinking," *How We Think* (Boston, Mass.: D. C. Heath & Company, 1910), p. 72.

[3]"Motivated Men Made America Great," from *Fortune Magazine* (March 1966). Reprinted by permission of Maritz Inc.

[4]"Nice People" by Jan Bjorklund. Reprinted from *Winning Orations* by special arrangement with the Interstate Oratorical Association, Larry Schnoor, Executive Secretary, Mankato State University, Mankato, Minnesota.

Problems and Probes

1. Examine the following list of suggested proposals or statements of belief for persuasive and actuative speeches, and choose one that is of special interest to you personally. Or, if that is not feasible, devise one of your own liking and ask your instructor to approve it.

Strict gun-control laws should be enacted.
Legalize marijuana.
Go to church every Sunday.
Exercise to benefit your heart.
All college students should take at least three years of science (or mathematics, foreign language, etc.).
We should have a national repertory theater.
Good books are a permanent source of satisfaction and pleasure.
Solve the problem of race relations.
Improve the quality of television programs.

We can conquer urban blight.
Give a fair deal to the farmer.
We should have a national system of health insurance.
Reform college teaching.

Assuming that the members of your class will be your audience for a speech on this topic or thesis, devise an appropriate *specific purpose* for a speech either to persuade or to actuate. Set this purpose down in writing. Then prepare a five-sentence plan or structure designed to elicit the response you desire — *one carefully written sentence for each step in the motivated sequence.* Develop a strong need step directly related to the interests and desires of your prospective listeners. Show through careful reasoning and vivid examples how your proposal or idea will satisfy this need. Use the positive, negative, or contrast method to build the visualization step. Close with a direct appeal for belief or action relative to your specific purpose.

2. Using the motivated sequence as a pattern, construct an outline for a speech urging support of a proposed reform in college life or in municipal, state, or national affairs. For this speech, prepare *three different visualization steps:* one using the positive method, one the negative method, and one the method of contrast. Also prepare *three different action steps:* one using inducement, one using a statement of personal intention, and one using one of the four other possibilities listed on page 156. Which type of visualization step and which action step appear to be most effective for this particular speech? Why?

3. Find in *Vital Speeches of the Day* or elsewhere a speech to inform developed according to the steps in the motivated sequence. In writing, analyze the speech structurally, pointing out where each step begins and noting its method of development. Look in particular at the conclusion of the speech. Does the speaker suggest the pleasure or advantages to be gained from a study of the subject or urge further attention to it? That is, does he or she add to the three basic steps (attention, need, satisfaction) an optional visualization and/or action step? If not, how is the speech terminated?

4. Find in *Vital Speeches of the Day* or elsewhere a speech to persuade or to actuate that is *not* developed according to the steps in the motivated sequence. Without altering in any material way the ideas presented, rewrite the speech so that it conforms to the motivated sequence.

5. Defend (orally or in writing, as your instructor may require) the *logical* validity and the *psychological* effectiveness of the motivated sequence. That is, point out why — both logically and psychologically — the attention step must *begin* the sequence, why need must *precede* satisfaction, why action appropriately *follows* visualization, etc. Would any other ordering of these five steps have equal logical and psychological validity?

Oral Activities and Speaking Assignments

1. After your instructor has divided the class into small groups of four, five, or six members, meet with your group and discuss your plans for a six-minute persuasive or actuative speech. As a basis for the discussion, each member of the group will read aloud the proposal or belief selected in Problem 1 (page 161), the statement of the specific purpose evolved for it, and the five-sentence, motivated-sequence plan or structure designed to influence audience belief in and/or acceptance of the idea or proposal. Other members of the group will then respond to these matters analytically, suggesting clarifications, improvements, etc. Afterward, revise or reconstruct your speech plan, making it as effective as you possibly can.

2. Present to the class as a whole the six-minute persuasive or actuative speech evolved from your work with Problem 1 and the small group discussion generated in Oral Activity 1 on the preceding page.

Suggestions for Further Reading

Winston L. Brembeck and William S. Howell, *Persuasion: A Means of Social Influence,* 2nd ed. (Englewood Cliffs, N.J.: Prentice-Hall, Inc., 1976), Chapter 6, "Attitudes and Attitude Change: Theory and Practice."

John Dewey, *How We Think* (Boston: D. C. Heath & Company, 1910).

Joseph T. Plummer, "A Theoretical View of Advertising Communication," *The Journal of Communication* 21 (December 1971): 315–325. Reprinted in Ronald L. Applbaum, Owen O. Jenson, and Richard Carroll, *Speech Communication: A Basic Anthology* (New York: The Macmillan Company, 1975), pp. 268–276.

Thomas M. Scheidel, *Speech Communication and Human Interaction,* 2nd ed. (Glenview, Ill.: Scott, Foresman and Company, 1976), Chapter 8, "Bases of Decision Making."

Otis Walter, *Speaking Intelligently* (New York: The Macmillan Company, 1976), Chapter 5, "Solutions."

Adapting the Speech Structure to the Audience: Alternative Patterns of Organization

In the preceding chapter, we considered in some detail the so-called *motivated sequence,* a pattern of speech organization based on the thought processes listeners naturally follow when called upon to receive new information or to consider how a problem may be solved. Moreover, we showed how this pattern may be adapted so as to fit each of the three basic types of speeches: speeches to inform, to persuade, and to actuate. Because of its versatility the *motivated sequence* provides the speaker with an option that should always be carefully considered.

There may be occasions, however, on which it seems best to organize your speech in some other way. Therefore, in this chapter we present a number of alternative patterns for structuring the substance or body of a speech and suggest some of the factors that should guide you in choosing among them.*

Optional Patterns: Criteria and Types

If a speech, whatever its type or purpose, is to communicate your thoughts effectively, it must satisfy at least three general criteria: (1) *The plan of the speech as a whole must be easy for the audience to grasp and remember.* If listeners have difficulty seeing how your ideas fit together or if the ideas are joined in ways that do not immediately make

---

*For information on developing the introduction and conclusion of a speech, see Chapter 12, "Beginning and Ending the Speech," pp. 189–203. The structure of the central-idea speech was discussed in Chapter 7, "Supporting the Major Ideas," pp. 117–123.

sense, attention will be distracted from the matters you wish considered and will be focused instead on untangling your remarks. (2)*The pattern must provide for a full and balanced coverage of the subject under consideration.* If you ignore or slight essential aspects of the topic, not only will the audience's understanding of the subject be incomplete, but you will be open to the charge of having presented an unfair or biased discussion. (3) *The speech must move forward steadily toward a complete and satisfying termination.* If you repeatedly backtrack to mention again points made earlier or if after a time the speech begins to run down or ramble, whatever punch it may have carried earlier will be lost; and the members of your audience, instead of listening as they should, will be impatient for it to end.

Holding these criteria in mind, let us consider some of the organizational options other than the motivated sequence. These options may be viewed as falling into four major types: (1) *sequential patterns,* (2) *causal patterns,* (3) *topical patterns,* and (4) *special patterns.*

Sequential Patterns

Sequential patterns have as their defining characteristic the fact that they adhere to the order in which events actually occurred or trace the physical relationships existing among the parts of a whole. In the first case, the sequence is called *chronological;* in the second case, *spatial.*

Chronological Sequence. When employing the chronological sequence, you begin at a certain period or date and move forward — or backward — in a systematic way. For example, you might describe last year's weather by considering conditions as they existed in the spring, summer, fall, and winter, respectively; methods for refining petroleum, by tracing the development of the refining process from the earliest attempts down to the present time; the manufacture of an automobile, by following the assembly-line process from beginning to end. Here is an example of an outline for a speech developed according to the *chronological* or *time* sequence:

THE EARLY HISTORY OF PHOTOGRAPHY

I.   In 1839 the French painter Daguerre introduced the daguerreotype.
II. In 1851 the wet-plate process was discovered by Frederick Archer.
III. The modern era of dry-plate photography began in 1878.
IV. Roll-film first came on the market in 1883.

Spatial Sequence. In the spatial sequence the major points of a speech are arranged in terms of their *physical proximity* to one another. Comparative densities of population, for instance, may be discussed by referring in order to contiguous areas of the country; the plans for a building may be considered floor by floor; the layout of a new suburb may be explained by proceeding from east to west or north to south. Different aspects of a problem also may sometimes be arranged according to this *spatial* or *geographical* method. For example:

OUR SUMMER DROUGHT

I.   The Dakotas and Minnesota are worst hit by the present drought.
II. Iowa and Missouri also are suffering crop losses.
III. Illinois and Indiana are little affected.

Causal Patterns

As their name implies, causal patterns of speech organization move either (1) from an analysis of present causes to a consideration of future effects, or (2) from a description of present conditions to an analysis of the causes which appear to have produced them. When employing the cause-effect arrangement, you might, for instance, first point out that a community's zoning ordinances are outdated or ineffective, and then predict that as a result of this situation fast-food chain establishments and gas stations will soon invade prime residential areas. Or, reasoning in the other direction, you could argue that the continued spread of fast-food chain establishments and gas stations into prime residential areas is the result of outmoded or ineffective zoning ordinances. Compare the following outlines:

PRODUCTION COSTS

I.   Each year the cost of producing manufactured goods increases.
    A.   Labor costs go up.
    B.   Raw materials cost more.
    C.   Plant improvements become more expensive.
II. The effect is a steady increase in consumer prices.

- - - - -

I.   Over the past decade consumer prices have increased steadily.
II. This has been caused by three factors:
    A.   Higher cost of labor.
    B.   Higher cost of raw materials.
    C.   Higher cost of plant improvements.

Topical Patterns

Speeches on familiar topics sometimes may best be organized in terms of subject-matter divisions which over a period of time have become more or less standardized. For example, financial reports customarily are divided into assets and liabilities. Discussions of government usually focus on legislative, executive, and judicial functions. Policies characteristically are considered in terms of advantages and disadvantages. A speech on the superiority of democratic institutions might employ the *topical* pattern in this way:

DEMOCRATIC INSTITUTIONS ARE BEST

I.   They guarantee freedom to the individual.
II. They respond to the will of the majority.
III. They regard all persons as equal.

The types of speech organization thus far discussed, though by no means unmindful of the audience, are shaped principally by the nature of the subject matter that you as a speaker wish to communicate. Some subjects, such as the historical development of a nation or region, or a person's rise from obscurity to prominence, lend themselves more or less readily to the chronological pattern. Subjects of a geographical nature — discussions of the world's stock of natural resources or of its chronic famine areas — fit more easily into the spatial structure. Still other matters — the reasons for the success of a given economic policy or an account of recent rule changes in football — call, respectively, for the causal or special topical plan.

Special Patterns

At times, however, rather than employing any of these subject-oriented speech structures, you may decide that, for psychological or rhetorical reasons, it would be better to impose some special or more strongly audience-oriented pattern upon your material. Many such special patterns are possible and have been successfully employed by resourceful speakers. Four of them, however, are generally useful enough to warrant special mention here. We shall call them (1) familiarity-acceptance order, (2) inquiry order, (3) question-answer order, and (4) elimination order.

Familiarity-Acceptance Order.   When using this order in giving an informative-type speech, you work from the familiar to the unfamiliar — from that which the audience already knows or understands to that which is new or strange. Similarly, if your aim is to persuade or to actuate, you take as a base the facts or values the listeners already accept, and you seek to show how the beliefs or actions being urged follow logically from them.

Relating new or unfamiliar material to what is already known or understood has long been recognized by teachers as one of the most effective methods of classroom instruction. Indeed, it has often been argued that all of our knowledge is derived "analogically" in the sense that we learn not by adding unrelated bits of information or understanding to things previously known, but by comparing or contrasting the new with the old. Provided you appraise the audience's existing state of knowledge correctly and do not move on to new matters too rapidly, an informative speech structured on this principle usually has a better-than-average chance of success.

Persuasive speeches which use as their starting point facts or values the audience already accepts and then demonstrate how the matters to be established follow from them often are especially suited to doubting or hostile audiences. Of course, your reasoning must be valid and the conclusion advanced must not exceed the evidence; but when you meet these standards, the claim which the speech seeks to make good can be denied only if the listener is willing to be recognized as inconsistent. Here is an example of an outline of a persuasive-type speech employing the pattern just described:

VOTE FOR MARY JONES FOR GOVERNOR

I.   We all agree, I am sure, that experience, ability, and integrity are prime requisites for a holder of high public office.
II. Mary Jones has these qualities.
    A.   She is experienced.
        1.   She has served two terms as mayor of one of our largest cities.
        2.   She has been in the State Senate for twelve years.
    B.   She has ability.
        1.   She has successfully reorganized the cumbersome administrative machinery of our city government.
        2.   She has become a recognized leader in the Senate.
    C.   She has integrity.
        1.   She has never been suspected of any sort of corruption.
        2.   Her word is as good as her bond.
III. Because Mary Jones clearly has the qualities we demand of the holder of high public office, she deserves our support in her bid to be elected governor of this state.

Inquiry Order.   When using inquiry order in a speech, you retrace step by step the way in which you yourself acquired the knowledge or arrived at the proposal which you are now communicating to the audience. You may, for example, inform listeners how to grow prize-winning dahlias by describing how the success and failure of your own experiments with various kinds of seeds, fertilizers, and garden locations eventually led to the recommendations now being offered. Or, if the purpose of your speech is to persuade or to actuate, you may recount how you first became aware of the existence of a problem or evil and then searched for its causes and weighed possible solutions until the one now being advocated emerged as superior to all of the others.

An arrangement of this kind, many speakers believe, has a double advantage. First, it enables listeners to judge more accurately the worth of the information or policy being presented; and, second, because all facts and possibilities are laid out for critical examination, it results in a more complete understanding or a firmer conviction than that produced by other methods.

Question-Answer Order. When following question-answer order in a speech, you attempt to determine in advance the questions most likely to arise in the listeners' minds concerning the subject being explained or the proposal being advanced, and then you deal with these questions according to a strategically advantageous plan. Often, for example, upon first hearing of a new development in medical science, people will immediately want to know how it relates to their own health problems or to the needs of their loved ones; or upon first being told of a pending piece of legislation, they will wonder how it will affect their taxes or whether it will curb their freedom of decision and action. By skillfully structuring your material so as to address these questions early in the speech, you will be assured of a high degree of audience interest and will pave the way for the remainder of the material to be presented.

Elimination Order. Whereas the sequential, causal, and topical patterns of organization are applicable to both informative- and persuasive-type speeches, elimination order fits more naturally speeches designed to influence belief or secure action.

In this order, you first survey with the listeners all of the available solutions to a recognized problem or all of the courses of action which could reasonably be pursued in a given situation. Then, proceeding in a systematic order, you show that all of the possibilities except one would be unworkable, excessively costly, or in some other way impracticable or undesirable. By these means, you lead the audience, in effect, to agree with the belief or behavior you advocate.

If elimination order is to be used effectively, two requirements are important. First, the possibilities you survey must be all-inclusive. If one or more options are overlooked, the logic of the process will be defective; and the listeners will not be obliged to accept the conclusion you desire. And, second, the possibilities must be mutually exclusive; for, unless this is the case, one or more of the characteristics which render a rejected possibility impracticable or undesirable also may be present in the preferred point of view. Consider this example:

RELIEVING TRAFFIC CONGESTION

    I.   There are really only three ways in which the congested traffic in our business district could be relieved.
          A.   We could ban automobiles from the area.
          B.   We could widen the streets.
          C.   We could get more people to ride the buses.

II. Banning automobiles would be impracticable.
  A. The citizens would object strongly.
  B. The city would lose the revenue from existing parking lots.
III. Widening the streets would be impracticable.
  A. The cost would be prohibitive.
  B. The inconvenience to the business community would be great.
IV. Therefore, the only acceptable solution is to get more people to ride the buses.
  A. Bus service could be more frequent.
  B. Our present buses could be overhauled and new ones purchased.
    1. The federal government would supply some of the necessary funds.
    2. A modest increase in fares would help offset the cost.

Arranging the Subpoints in the Structure

After you have selected a pattern of organization and arranged the major ideas of your speech accordingly, you must determine how to organize the subpoints and supporting materials that fall under them. Unless you do this thoughtfully, with due attention to the principles of proper subordination and coordination, you will lose much of the effectiveness of your speech. Here are five standard ways in which the subpoints within a speech may be systematically arranged:

Parts of a Whole

If a major idea concerns an object or a process which consists of a series of component parts, the subpoints may treat those parts in order. For example, you may describe a golf club by discussing the grip, the shaft, and the head. Or you may cite the number of churches in England, Scotland, Ireland, and Wales as subtotals of the aggregate number of churches in the British Isles.

Lists of Qualities or Functions

If the main point suggests the purpose of some mechanism, organization, or procedure, the subpoints may list the specific functions it performs. Thus timbre, pitch, and loudness are qualities under which the nature of sound may be discussed; or the purpose of a police department may be made clear by citing its various responsibilities or functions.

Series of Causes or Results

If you use the cause-effect sequence to arrange your major ideas, you will often find that neither cause nor effect is single. Each of the several causes or results may then constitute a subpoint. Even when another type of sequence is used for the major ideas, a list of causes and results often forms the sub-items under these points. The causes of highway accidents, for instance, might be listed as excessive speed, poor roads, and improperly maintained vehicles. The results of a balanced diet could be given as greater comfort, better health, and longer life.

Items of Logical Proof

In a speech to persuade or to actuate, the subpoints often provide logical proof for the idea they support. When this is the case, you should be able to connect the major idea and subpoints with the word "because" (the major idea is true *because* subpoints a, b, c, etc., are true); and, conversely, you should be able to use the word "therefore" when reasoning from the subpoints to the major head (the subpoints are true; *therefore* the main point is true). Here is an example of this type of subordination: Strikes are wasteful because *(a)* workers lose their wages; *(b)* employers lose their profits; and *(c)* consumers lose the products they might otherwise have had.

Illustrative Examples

Many times the main point consists of a generalized statement for which the subpoints provide a series of specific illustrative examples. This method may be used both in exposition and in argument, the examples constituting clarification or proof, respectively. Thus, the general statement that fluoride helps reduce tooth decay might have as its subpoints a series of examples citing the experience of those cities which have added fluoride to their drinking water.

You may decide to use one of the foregoing sequences for the items under one major idea and a different sequence for those under another, but do not shift from one sequence to another *within* the same coordinate series since this is likely to confuse your listeners. Above all, be sure that you do employ some kind of systematic order; don't throw items together haphazardly just because they are subordinate points. The following outline illustrates how the spatial and chronological sequences may be combined in ordering the main and subordinate points of a speech:

INDUSTRIAL DEVELOPMENT IN THE UNITED STATES

I. New England
    A. The first industries.
    B. Expansion following the War Between the States.
    C. Present conditions.
    D. Future prospects.

II. The South
   A. The first industries, etc. *(Developed chronologically as above.)*
III. The Middle West
   A. . . . etc. *(Developed as above.)*

Problems and Probes

1. Select from *Vital Speeches of the Day* or some other suitable source four speeches for close organizational analysis. Comment critically on the order in which the speaker's major ideas were arranged in view of the subject dealt with and the audience addressed. Study also the arrangement of the subpoints which fell under the major ideas. Were they presented in a systematic, orderly fashion? Can you describe the patterns of organization which they followed? Give each of the speeches you study a letter grade (A, B, C, D, etc.) on organization, and be prepared to defend your evaluation of it. If some of your classmates studied the same speeches, see how closely your evaluations agree with theirs.

2. Write a short paper on "How *Not* to Organize a Speech." Draw your material not only from the principles and suggestions offered in this chapter, but also from your own observations of speakers, past and present. Circulate this paper in class, using it and the papers of your classmates to determine which faults are mentioned most frequently and which of your classmates comes up with the longest list. (By thus concentrating on the "don't's," the "do's" of speech organization will receive what some psychologists term negative reinforcement.)

Oral Activities and Speaking Assignments

1. Prepare a five- to seven-minute speech on a subject of your choice for presentation in class. After you've delivered it, and without receiving critical comments from your instructor or classmates, write and give to the instructor a short paper titled "If I Had It to Do Over." In this paper, either defend the pattern of organization you employed in arranging the major heads and developing the subpoints; or suggest how, after the experience of actually presenting your material to an audience, you see now where you could make improvements. See if your instructor and the other members of the class agree with your critical perceptions of your own work.

2. With the whole class participating, hold a general discussion in which you consider how each of the following topics might be most effectively arranged for a short speech to be delivered to your speech class:

Why many small businesses fail.
Developments in automotive engineering.
The "hot spots" of world politics.
Digging for diamonds.
Eat wisely and live long.
How the world looks to your dog.
The "new math."
Bridge for the beginner.
Appreciating contemporary art.
The metric system.
Making out your income tax return.

Suggestions for Further Reading

Ernest G. Bormann and Nancy C. Bormann, *Speech Communication: A Comprehensive Approach,* 2nd ed. (New York: Harper & Row, Publishers, 1977), Chapter 7, "How to Organize a Public Speech."

Jon Eisenson and Paul H. Boase, *Basic Speech,* 3rd ed. (New York: The Macmillan Company, 1975), Chapter 17, "Synthesis and Organization."

James Gibson, *Speech Organization: A Programmed Approach* (New York: Holt, Rinehart & Winston, Inc., 1971).

Thomas M. Scheidel, *Speech Communication and Human Interaction,* 2nd ed. (Glenview, Ill.: Scott, Foresman and Company, 1976), Chapter 13, "Speech Planning and Preparation."

Rudolph F. Verderber, *The Challenge of Effective Speaking,* 3rd ed. (Belmont, Calif.: Wadsworth Publishing Company, Inc., 1976), Chapter 4, "Organizing Speech Materials."

11

Outlining the Speech

When the major ideas of your speech have been selected and its basic pattern of organization determined, you are ready to begin making an outline. A carefully developed outline serves a number of essential functions. First, it lays out before you the entire structure of your speech so that you can see whether you have *(a)* fitted the parts together smoothly, *(b)* given each idea the emphasis it deserves, and *(c)* covered all important aspects of the subject. Second, it enables you to check on the adequacy and variety of your supporting materials. If you have failed to substantiate any of your leading ideas or have used only one or two forms of support throughout, your outline will reveal these deficiencies. Third, and finally, an outline will help you fix firmly in mind the ideas you wish to communicate and the order in which you plan to present them. As we emphasized in Chapter 3—where we considered the speechmaking process as a whole—by reading through your outline repeatedly, you can memorize the pattern or "geography" of your speech, with its principal headings and developmental materials, so that as you stand before your listeners you will recall how the speech "looks" as well as what it says. A visual map of this kind can be a valuable aid to memory.

Requirements of Good Outline Form

The amount of detail and type of arrangement you use in an outline will depend on the simplicity or complexity of your subject, the nature of the speaking situation, and your previous experience in speech composition. Any good outline, however, should meet four basic requirements:

174

1. *Each item in the outline should contain only one unit of information.* This is essential to the very nature of outlining. If two or three items or statements are run together under one symbol, the relationships they bear to one another and to other items in the outline will not stand out clearly. Compare these examples:

Wrong

I. The United States should not intervene militarily in the internal affairs of Third-World nations, because such interventions result in massive losses of revenue and the death of innocent persons, impair our own prestige in the world, and because this practice could be stopped by placing additional restrictions on the President and restoring to Congress the authority to conduct our foreign affairs.

Right

I. The United States should not intervene militarily in the internal affairs of Third-World nations.
    A. Military interventions harm the United States.
        1. They result in massive losses of revenue.
        2. They result in the death of innocent persons.
        3. They impair our prestige in the world.
    B. Military interventions can be stopped.
        1. Additional restrictions can be placed on the President.
        2. The authority of Congress to conduct our foreign affairs can be restored.

2. *The items in the outline should be properly subordinated.* Because a subordinate idea is a subdivision of the larger heading under which it falls, it should rank *below* that heading in scope and importance. It should also directly support or amplify the statement made in the superior heading.

Wrong

I. "Crime in the streets" is a constantly growing problem.
    A. Serious offenses are becoming more common.
    B. Present means of combatting crime are ineffective.
II. The number of juvenile crimes has increased drastically.
    A. Police departments are understaffed.
III. Many police officers are poorly trained.

Right

I. "Crime in the streets" is a constantly growing problem.
    A. Serious offenses are becoming more common.
    B. The number of juvenile crimes has increased drastically.
II. Present means of combatting crime are ineffective.
    A. Police departments are understaffed.
    B. Many police officers are poorly trained.

3. *The logical relation of the items in an outline should be shown by proper indentation.* The greater the importance or scope of a statement, the nearer it should be placed to the left-hand margin. If a statement takes up more than one line, the second line should be indented the same as the beginning of the first.

Wrong

I.   The sale and use of marijuana should not be legalized.
     A.   Studies show that legalization would result in a far greater number of
persons using the substance.
     B.   Smoking marijuana results in serious and irreversible physical damage.
          1.   After a time it begins to destroy the smoker's brain cells.
          2.   In many cases it creates serious psychological problems.

Wrong

I.   The sale and use of marijuana should not be legalized.
A.   Studies show that legalization would result in a far greater number of per-
     sons using the substance.
B.   Smoking marijuana results in serious and irreversible physical damage.
1.   After a time it begins to destroy the smoker's brain cells.
2.   In many cases it creates serious psychological problems.

Right

I.   The sale and use of marijuana should not be legalized.
     A.   Studies show that legalization would result in a far greater number of
          persons using the substance.
     B.   Smoking marijuana results in serious and irreversible physical
          damage.
          1.   After a time it begins to destroy the smoker's brain cells.
          2.   In many cases it creates serious psychological problems.

4. *A consistent set of symbols should be used.* One such set is exemplified in the outlines printed in this chapter. But whether you use this set or some other, be consistent; do not change systems in the middle of an outline. Unless items of the same scope or importance have the same type of symbol *throughout,* the mental "map" you have of your speech will be confused, and the chances of a smooth and orderly presentation impaired. The following examples demonstrate the wrong and the right usage of this set of symbols.

Wrong

I.   Our penal system should be reformed.
     II.   Many of our prisons are inadequate.
          A.   They fail to meet basic structural and safety standards.
               1.   They lack the facilities for effective rehabilitation programs.

  A. The persons who manage our prisons are ill equipped.
      I. All too often they have had little or no formal training for their jobs.
          1. Low rates of pay result in frequent job turnovers.

Right

I. Our penal system should be reformed.
    A. Many of our prisons are inadequate.
        1. They fail to meet basic structural and safety standards.
        2. They lack facilities for effective rehabilitation programs.
    B. The persons who manage our prisons are ill equipped.
        1. All too often they have had little or no formal training for their jobs.
        2. Low rates of pay result in frequent job turnovers.

Types of Outlines

There are two principal types of outlines, each of which fulfills a different purpose—the *full-content* outline and the *key-word* outline. The former helps make the process of speech preparation more systematic and thorough; the latter serves as an aid to memory in the early stages of oral practice.

The Full-Content Outline

As its name implies, a full-content outline represents the complete factual content of the speech in outline form. Whether you use the traditional divisions of the speech (introduction, body, conclusion) or the steps in the motivated sequence (attention, need, satisfaction, visualization, action), each major component is set off in a separate section. In each of these sections, the principal ideas are stated; and under them—properly indented and marked with the correct symbols—is put all the material used to amplify and support them. *Each major idea and all of the minor ones are written down in complete sentences* so that their full meaning and their relation to other points are made completely clear. Often, after each piece of evidence or supporting material, the source from which it was obtained is indicated, or these sources are combined in a bibliography at the end of the outline. Thus, when the outline has been completed, simply by reading it you or any other person can derive a clear, comprehensive picture of the speech as a whole. The only thing lacking is the specific wording to be used in presenting the speech and the visible and audible aspects of your delivery. The purpose of this type of outline is obvious. By bringing together all the material you have gathered and by stating it completely and in detail, you ensure thoroughness in the preparation of your speech. (The outline on pages 178–179 is a full-content outline.)

    To prepare a full-content outline requires much effort. It cannot be written offhand even by a person who has had a great deal of experience; the beginner should allow plenty of time for developing one. If you go about the task systematically, however, you can keep the time to a minimum.

The Key-Word Outline

The key-word outline has the same indentation and the same symbols as the full-content outline, but it boils down each statement to a key word, phrase, or—at most—a brief sentence that can be more easily remembered. By reading a key-word outline through several times from beginning to end, you will be able to fix the ideas of your speech firmly in mind and to recall them readily as you stand before the audience. Thus, it is an excellent aid to memory in the oral practice of your speech. Of course, to ensure accuracy you may want to read specific quotations or figures from notecards.

Steps in Preparing an Outline

An outline, like the speech it represents, should be developed gradually through a series of stages. While these stages may vary somewhat, depending on the work habits of the speaker, certain steps always should be included:

STEPS IN PREPARING A GOOD OUTLINE

I. Select the subject and determine the general purpose of your speech.
    A. Limit the subject to fit the available time and to ensure the unity and coherence of your remarks.
    B. Phrase your specific purpose in terms of the exact response you seek from your listeners.
II. Develop a rough draft of your outline.
    A. List the main ideas you wish to cover.
    B. Arrange these main ideas according to the steps in the motivated sequence (attention, need, satisfaction, etc.) or according to one of the alternate patterns of organization (i.e., chronological sequence, spatial sequence, etc.) described in Chapter 10.
    C. Insert and arrange the subordinate ideas that fall under each main point.
    D. Fill in the supporting materials to be used in amplifying or proving your ideas.
    E. Check your rough draft to be sure it covers the subject adequately and carries out your specific purpose.
    F. If you are dissatisfied, revise your rough draft or start over.
III. Put the outline into final form.
    A. Write out the main ideas as complete sentences.
        1. State the main ideas concisely, vividly, and—insofar as possible—in parallel phraseology.
            a. In a speech on different types of taxes, for example, your major points or heads might be worded as follows:

    (1) The amount you earn dictates your income tax.

    (2) The amount you own controls your property tax.

    (3) The amount you buy determines your sales tax.

  2. State the major heads so that they address directly the needs and interests of your listeners. (Instead of saying "Chemical research has helped improve medical treatment," say "Modern chemistry helps the doctor keep you well," etc.)

 B. Write out the subordinate ideas either as complete sentences or as key phrases.

  1. Be sure they are subordinate to the main idea they are intended to develop.

  2. Be sure they are coordinate to the other items in their series.

 C. Fill in the supporting materials.

  1. Be sure they are pertinent.

  2. Be sure they are adequate.

  3. Be sure to include a variety of types of support.

 D. Recheck the entire outline.

  1. It should represent good outline form.

  2. It should adequately cover the subject.

  3. It should carry out your speech purpose.

In order to see how this process may be followed in a specific situation, let us apply the principles we have just discussed to the selection and limitation of a speech subject, the development of a rough draft, and the preparation of an outline in final form.

Selecting the Subject and Determining the Purpose

Suppose your instructor has asked you to prepare a ten- to twelve-minute persuasive-type speech on a subject of current importance. Because of a prolonged and serious illness which has recently occurred in your family, you are very much aware of how drastically the costs of medical care have increased over the past few years. Therefore, you decide to talk about the need for a comprehensive system of medical care available to all persons. Moreover, because costs threaten to shoot up still more rapidly in the future, you believe that immediate action is called for. Your broad subject area, then, is

COMPREHENSIVE MEDICAL CARE

and the general purpose of your speech is to move your listeners to

ACTION.

In the ten or twelve minutes you have at your disposal, however, you obviously will not be able to consider all of the proposals which have been advanced to solve the problem. Consequently, your first task is to narrow your topic. After considering various options, it seems to you that the best of the plans you have read about is that in which groups of private physicians band together to provide prepaid comprehensive medical care to their patients. Therefore, you decide to offer this plan as your remedy, and you choose as your specific purpose getting your listeners to go on record as endorsing it.

Developing the Rough Draft of the Outline

During the time you have been selecting your subject and determining your purpose you also have begun to think about some of the major ideas you want to be sure to include in your speech. Now you set these points down on paper to see how they may be modified and fitted into a coherent pattern. Initially, your list might look something like this:

—Under the present fee-for-service system of delivering medical care, many persons delay seeing a doctor until it is too late.
—Physicians practicing alone often are so overburdened that they cannot keep up with developments in medical science.
—At present, medical manpower is badly maldistributed, with rural and ghetto areas suffering most.
—Systems of medical delivery similar to the one proposed have worked well in England and the United States.
—Private insurance plans seldom provide for catastrophic illnesses.

This list covers a number of things you want to be sure to include, but the order is random, and you realize that your present stock of information on the subject is inadequate. Consequently, you begin to gather additional data;* and as you find ideas and facts you wish to include, you distribute them under the appropriate heads—in the case of the motivated sequence plan of development: attention, need, satisfaction, visualization, and action. You also begin to distinguish between main ideas and subordinate ones, and to group these into appropriate units. Finally, you sketch in the necessary supporting materials in the form of statistics, comparisons, specific instances, etc.

At this point, examine your rough draft carefully to be sure (1) that you have included all the ideas you want to cover, (2) that you have not unbalanced your discussion by expanding unimportant items too greatly or skimping on important ones, (3) that in ordering your ideas you have followed the principles of systematic arrangement and subordination, and (4) that you have assembled a sufficient amount of pertinent and varied supporting material. When you are satisfied on these matters, you are ready to cast your outline into final form.

Putting the Outline into Final Form

This task consists, in part, of examining what you have already done and of adjusting the details. Sometimes you may want to combine or rearrange certain of the points as they appear in your rough draft, or per-

---

*Sources of speech information and procedures for recording data are discussed in Appendix A.

haps you will even decide to drop several of them. In addition, you will now need to restate all of the major ideas in your outline as complete sentences—sentences that convey your meaning clearly and exactly— and to see that your outline meets the requirements listed on pages 174–177. To do this, begin by working on the main points, rephrasing each until it is clear and vivid. Then, taking each main point in turn, work on the subordinate ideas that fall under it, striving for proper subordination and coordination. Finally, make certain that the supporting materials are set forth in the most economical and effective way.

The Technical Plot: Testing Your Outline

In analyzing the completed outline to discover possible gaps or weaknesses, it frequently is helpful to work out a *technical plot* of your speech. To make such a plot, lay the completed outline beside a blank sheet of paper; and on this sheet, set down opposite each unit a statement of the materials or devices used in developing it. Where you have used statistics in the outline, write the word *statistics* in the technical plot, together with a brief statement of their function. In like manner, indicate all of the forms of support, attention factors, motive appeals, and methods of development you have employed.

Used as a testing device, a technical plot can help you determine whether your speech is structurally sound, whether there is adequate supporting material, whether you have overused one or two forms of support, and whether the appeals you plan are adapted to the audience and occasion. Many speeches, of course, do not need to be tested this thoroughly; and experienced speakers often can make an adequate analysis without drafting a complete technical plot. For the beginner, however, there is no more effective way of checking the structure of a speech and testing the methods used to develop it.

The following example shows the complete outline for the speech on comprehensive medical care drawn up in final form and with an accompanying technical plot. For illustrative purposes, all items in the outline are stated as complete sentences. Such completeness of detail may be desirable if the occasion is an especially important one or if you sometimes have difficulty framing thoughts extemporaneously. Usually, however, as we have said, it is sufficient to write out only the main ideas as complete sentences and to state the subordinate ideas and supporting materials as key phrases.

COMPREHENSIVE MEDICAL CARE

FULL-CONTENT OUTLINE   TECHNICAL PLOT

Attention Step

I. Did you know that under the present fee-for-service
system many Americans die each year because they

Startling statements of fact

FULL-CONTENT OUTLINE   TECHNICAL PLOT

Attention Step (continued)

are too poor to receive medical care or because the
care they receive is inferior or delayed?

  A.   Senator Edward Kennedy reports that millions   *Specific instances*
       of persons are priced out of the medical-care   *in support of state-*
       market.   *ment*

  B.   Often doctors are too busy to make thorough
       diagnoses or to supervise the therapies they
       prescribe.

  C.   Many people in lower income brackets delay
       seeking needed care.

      1.   They do not visit their doctor until after
          a serious condition has developed.

      2.   Treatment may be postponed so long
          that it is not effective when given.

  D.   These facts are increasingly becoming a reali-
       ty for more and more Americans.

II.   There is no question that each of you is affected by   *Statement relating*
this problem.   *subject to listeners*

  A.   Economists warn that medical costs will
       continue to rise sharply.

  B.   Responsible critics believe that the fee-for-
       service system will continue to provide less
       than the best kind of medical care.

  C.   As costs rise, more and more persons will de-
       lay seeking the help they need.

III.   These deficiencies in our present system can be   *Transition to Need*
repaired only through a comprehensive program of   *Step*
medical care available to all citizens.

Need Step

I.   Any program of comprehensive medical care must   *Criteria for a*
meet three criteria.   *sound medical*

  A.   The system must deliver services to large   *program*
       numbers of people.

  B.   The system must be efficient.

  C.   The system must have built-in quality con-
       trols.

II.   In the past, these criteria have been ignored.   *General statement*

  A.   Present medical-delivery systems have failed   *of need*
       to provide services to a great many people.

      1.   Sometimes individuals must wait days   *Supporting expla-*
          or weeks for an appointment with their   *nation and statis-*
          doctor.   *tics*

      2.   Often doctors are so overworked that
          they refuse to take new patients.

      3.   Many Americans find themselves in a
          dilemma.

a. Either they go without care because it is too expensive.
b. Or they receive medical care at the risk of financial bankruptcy.
    (1) Last year alone, over two million persons went without needed care.
    (2) Over the last few years, several hundred thousand families have been forced into bankruptcy.

B. The present system of delivering medical services is inefficient.
    1. There is a serious maldistribution of medical manpower.
        a. Rural areas have a shortage of doctors.
            (1) Studies show that several hundred rural communities have been without a doctor for many years.
            (2) Rural communities lack the economic base necessary to attract skilled physicians.
        b. Our "inner cities" also have a serious shortage of doctors.
            (1) Doctors in these areas often have difficulty in collecting their fees.
            (2) The dangers of inner-city life discourage doctors from practicing there.
    2. Planning to correct the present maldistribution is difficult under our existing system.
        a. There is no central planning agency.
        b. There is no authority to implement recommendations offered by students of the problem.

C. Our present medical system lacks built-in quality controls.
    1. When doctors practice privately, thorough peer review is difficult.
        a. County medical associations are not effective policing bodies.
        b. Consultation with specialists often is difficult.
    2. Because quality control is lacking, mistakes are made.

Barriers to efficient medical care

Effects of poor quality controls

FULL-CONTENT OUTLINE   TECHNICAL PLOT

Need Step (continued)

    a. Many patients are hospitalized needlessly.
        (1) This places a further burden on our already overcrowded hospitals.
        (2) It consumes time and attention that should be devoted to the seriously ill.
    b. There are documented records of thousands of patients who suffered and died needlessly because of the poor quality of care.

D. Existing government and private insurance programs cannot solve these problems.
    1. Government programs have serious deficiencies.
        a. The services they provide are not comprehensive in scope.
        b. These programs are understaffed and underfinanced.
    2. Private programs also have weaknesses.
        a. Many persons cannot afford them.
        b. They do not cover catastrophic illnesses.

Existing alternatives inadequate

III. It is high time that we institute a medical-delivery system that meets the three criteria described.

Statement summarizing Need Step

Satisfaction Step

I. A twofold program of comprehensive medical care should be implemented as soon as possible.
    A. A national system of prepaid group-medical practices should be phased in over a five-year period.
    B. Within each practice group a rigorous program of peer review should be instituted.

Program required to solve need

II. Such a program would meet the three requisites of a sound medical-delivery system.
    A. Prepaid group-medical practices can provide greater access to medical services.
    1. By eliminating the fee-for-service system, the cost of medical care would be reduced.
    2. The Kaiser Permanente program attests to the reduced costs unique to a prepaid system.

First criterion considered

Support by explanation

a. The Kaiser program charged people a standard yearly fee for all medical services, regardless of type or amount.

b. These fees were scaled according to an individual's ability to pay.

c. This system eliminated the cost preclusions that occur under the fee-for-service plan.

Support by example

B. Prepaid group practices can raise the efficiency of medical services.

  1. Organizing doctors into groups increases the amount and the efficiency of medical care.

    a. Under the Kaiser program 20 percent more service was provided.

    b. Studies show that group practices are 40 percent more efficient.

Second criterion considered

Support by explanation and statistics

C. Prepaid group practices can improve the quality of medical care.

  1. Under the group system, other doctors are readily available for consultation.

  2. When doctors work under scrutiny, the quality of care is enhanced.

    a. Studies show that when doctors practice in groups there is more innovation and updating.

    b. Under the Kaiser program there was a significant reduction in the number of unnecessary operations.

Third criterion considered

III. Programs comparable to the prepaid group system have obtained encouraging results.

A. A similar program was established in England.

  1. Doctors cooperated willingly.

  2. Access to medical care improved.

  3. Serious maldistribution and shortages of personnel were avoided.

  4. The overall quality of care was enhanced.

Practicability (workability) of system advocated

Support by example

B. American studies also show the feasibility of this system.

  1. Investigations conducted by the U.S. Senate show that the cost of phasing in such a program would be minimal.

  2. Experts contend that within a ten-year period, prepaid systems of group practice would be nationwide.

Support by expert testimony and recent studies

FULL-CONTENT OUTLINE   TECHNICAL PLOT

Satisfaction Step (continued)

   3. Doctors and medical economists agree that such a system makes medical care more accessible.

Visualization Step

I. Unless it is drastically overhauled, our present method of delivering medical care will continue to deteriorate.

   A. More and more Americans will be priced out of the medical-care market.

     1. Even persons with substantial incomes will be affected.

     2. You and your family could suffer.

   B. The efficiency of the system will continue to decline.

   C. More unnecessary operations and other services will be performed.

     1. These will increase costs.

     2. These will result in needless deaths and suffering.

II. Only by establishing a system of comprehensive medical care along the lines indicated can these undesirable developments be averted.

Negative development of Visualization Step

Appeal to fear

Appeals to security and well-being

Action Step

I. A comprehensive program of medical care for all demands the full cooperation of every citizen.

   A. We can begin right here in our own town by instituting one or more prepaid group practices.

     1. Such groups already exist in some cities.

     2. Doctors who now practice in partnerships would be approached.

   B. We must act *today*, not later.

     1. The problem exists here and now.

     2. Each year it grows more serious.

II. Indicate your interest by signing your name on the sheet I am circulating.

   A. You will derive the satisfaction of helping bring more and better medical care to present and future members of this community.

   B. Remember that the life you save may be your own.

Program of action recommended

Practicability of action shown

Need for prompt action stressed

Specific, overt action called for

Appeals to self-preservation and future benefits

Bibliography (for the preceding Outline)

Rashi Fein, *The Doctor Shortage* (Washington, D.C.: Brookings Institute, 1968).

Victor R. Fuchs, ed., *Essays in Economies of Health and Medical Care* (New York: Columbia University Press, 1972).

Alex Gerber, *The Gerber Report* (New York: D. McKay Co., 1971).

Edward M. Kennedy, *In Critical Condition* (New York: Simon & Schuster, Inc., 1972).

Anne R. Somers, ed., *The Kaiser-Permanente Medical Care Program* (New York: Commonwealth, 1972).

Seminar on the National Issues of Health Care in Washington, D.C., 1976 (New York: Public Relations Society of America, 1976).

See also *The National Health Care Hearings of the 90th Congress* (Both Senate and House of Representatives).

Problems and Probes

1.   As a means of developing skill in outlining, select three speeches of different lengths and types from a recent issue of *Vital Speeches of the Day* or some other likely source. Prepare a full-content outline of two of those speeches and a key-word outline of the third. Append to each a technical plot on which you indicate the forms of support, attention factors, and motive appeals which the speaker employed.

2.   Select a subject with which you are familiar. Prepare an outline for a persuasive-type speech on this subject, demonstrating your understanding of *(a)* the rules of subordination, *(b)* the use of number-letter symbols, and *(c)* the indentation of minor ideas and supporting materials.

3.   For a speech entitled "Make Reading Your Hobby," rearrange the following points and subpoints in proper outline form:
Low-cost rental libraries are numerous.
ǀ Reading is enjoyable.
It may lead to advancement in one's job.
Books contain exciting tales of love and adventure.
Many paperback books cost only 95¢ to $1.95.
People who read books are most successful socially.
ǀ Reading is profitable.
One meets many interesting characters in books.
Nearly every town has a free public library.
Through books, one's understanding of human beings and the world is increased.
The new and stimulating ideas found in books bring pleasure.
ǀ Reading is inexpensive.

Oral Activity and Speaking Assignment

1.   Prepare a five- to seven-minute speech on a subject of your choice. As a part of your preparation, draw up a detailed outline of this speech and also a complete technical plot in accordance with the sample form provided in this chapter. Hand your speech outline and technical plot to your instructor at least one week before you are scheduled to present the speech in class. The instructor will check these materials and return them to you with suggestions for possible improvement. Following these suggestions, carefully rewrite both the outline and the technical plot, and hand the improved versions back to your instructor just before you begin your actual presentation of the speech.

Suggestions for Further Reading

Donald C. Bryant and Karl R. Wallace, *Fundamentals of Public Speaking,* 5th ed. (Englewood Cliffs, N.J.: Prentice-Hall, Inc., 1976), Chapter 15, "Rhetorical Synthesis: The Brief and the Outline."

Jon Eisenson and Paul H. Boase, *Basic Speech,* 3rd ed. (New York: The Macmillan Company, 1975), pp. 379–385, "Outlining the Speech."

Gerald M. Phillips and J. Jerome Zolten, *Structuring Speech. A How-to-Do-It Book About Public Speaking* (Indianapolis: The Bobbs-Merrill Company, Inc., 1976), Chapter 5, "Structuring: Putting It Together."

Otis M. Walter, *Speaking Intelligently: Communication for Problem Solving* (New York: The Macmillan Company, 1976), pp. 239–243, "Outlining."

John F. Wilson and Carroll C. Arnold, *Dimensions of Public Communication,* (Boston: Allyn & Bacon, Inc., 1974), Chapter 8, "Disposition: Organizing Materials."

12

Beginning and Ending
the Speech

All too often speakers devote much labor to preparing the body of a speech, but pay little or no attention to its introduction or conclusion. They prefer, apparently, to leave these vital parts to the inspiration of the moment. Unfortunately, the needed inspiration is not always forthcoming; and, as a result, they introduce their otherwise carefully planned remarks in a haphazard, fumbling fashion to an audience that quickly grows bewildered or bored. Or they bring an otherwise polished speech to a weak, ineffectual close because they have not prepared a clear and satisfying conclusion.

As we have repeatedly emphasized in these pages, to communicate successfully, the overriding thrust of your speechmaking effort should be devoted to choosing and developing the major ideas you want your listeners to carry away with them. Obviously, these ideas must be worked out in some detail before you can intelligently determine how best to *lead into them* and how to *tie them together* most tellingly at the end. But it is folly to leave the opening and closing of your message to mere chance. In an effective speech, *each* part or division—beginning, body, and conclusion—has a vital role to play. If it is to play that role well, each must be the product of thoughtful planning and preparation.

How you choose to open and close a speech depends, usually, on five interrelated factors:

The subject—the central idea or ideas you wish to communicate.
The purpose—the reason or objective you have in speaking.
The listeners—the people whose acceptance and/or understanding you seek.
The occasion—some occasions—memorial services, dedicatory exer-

cises, Fourth-of-July celebrations, and the like—call for more or less standard introductions and conclusions.

Your own special aptitudes or skills as a speaker—if, for example, you use humor effectively, you may give special consideration to beginning or closing some, but not all, of your speeches with an amusing story or reference.

To choose wisely in terms of these factors and make them work for you, you will, however, first need to know some of the standard methods or devices for beginning and ending a speech. In this chapter, we shall examine and exemplify these methods.

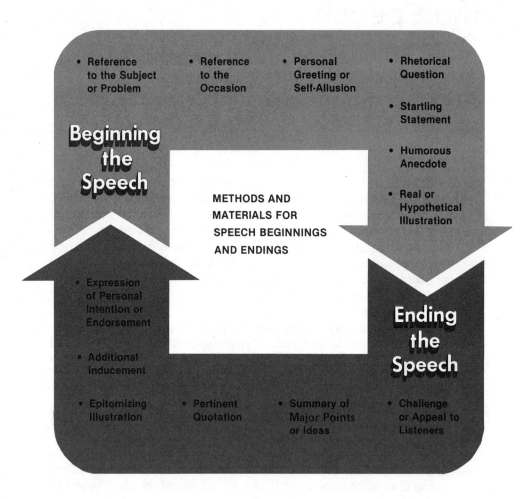

- Reference to the Subject or Problem
- Reference to the Occasion
- Personal Greeting or Self-Allusion
- Rhetorical Question
- Startling Statement
- Humorous Anecdote
- Real or Hypothetical Illustration

Beginning the Speech

METHODS AND MATERIALS FOR SPEECH BEGINNINGS AND ENDINGS

- Expression of Personal Intention or Endorsement
- Additional Inducement

Ending the Speech

- Epitomizing Illustration
- Pertinent Quotation
- Summary of Major Points or Ideas
- Challenge or Appeal to Listeners

Beginning the Speech: Methods and Materials

As we emphasized in Chapter 8, you must sustain your audience's attention *throughout* the entire course of your speech. At the beginning, however, your principal task is to *capture* that attention. Nowhere is there a greater need for such factors as novelty, reality, activity, or the vital. But merely to gain attention is not enough: your introduction also must earn the good will and respect of those with whom you wish to communicate. In many situations your reputation or the chairperson's introduction will create a favorable attitude toward you; and when this is the case, you need only be sure to start your speech in a confident and tactful manner. When, however, you are unknown to your listeners or are confronted by suspicion or skepticism, you must immediately take steps to overcome this handicap.

Another important function of the introduction is to make clear the specific topic you wish to discuss and to lead your hearers easily and naturally into an examination of it. A good introduction, therefore, has three goals: *to win attention, to gain good will and respect,* and *to prepare your audience for the ideas you are about to present.* To attain these results speakers frequently use one or more of the following methods:

1. Refer to the subject or problem.
2. Refer to the occasion.
3. Extend a personal greeting or make a personal allusion.
4. Ask a rhetorical question.
5. Make a startling statement of fact or opinion.
6. Use an apt quotation.
7. Relate a humorous anecdote relevant to a topical point.
8. Cite a real or hypothetical illustration.

Reference to the Subject or Problem

When your audience already is interested in the problem or subject you are to discuss, often it is enough merely to state the topic succinctly and then plunge at once into your first main point. The speed and directness of this approach suggest an eagerness to present your ideas and to press for understanding or belief. For example, a speaker recently began a talk to college seniors with this brief and forthright statement: "I'm going to talk to you tonight about jobs: how to get them and how to keep them." In an address to the World Food Conference in Rome in November, 1974, Secretary of State Kissinger also opened with a direct reference to the subject:

> We meet to address man's most fundamental need. The threat of famine, the fact of hunger have haunted men and nations throughout history. Our presence here is recognition that this eternal problem has now taken on unprecedented scale and urgency and that it can only be dealt with by concerted worldwide action.[1]

Although a reference to the subject is a good way to begin a speech when the audience is friendly or already interested in the subject, if listeners are skeptical, such a beginning lacks the elements of *common ground* and *ingratiation* upon which acceptance often depends. When used in the latter situation, therefore, it should be combined with material specifically designed to arouse interest. How this may be done is illustrated by the opening of a speech delivered by Father Theodore M. Hesburgh, President of the University of Notre Dame:

> I wish to address you this evening on the subject of science and man. It is a fair assumption that the majority of this audience knows much more about science and technology than I do. This being so, one might wonder why I do not drop the first part of my title of science and man. This is why: I shall not pretend to make any startling revelations in the field of science and technology; but I do want to consider this twin reality in conjunction with man and his actual world. What I have to say may not be popular, but then I never have found this to be a good reason for not saying something that should be said. Anyway, most statements that are popular and safe are also generally dull. This you should be spared.[2]

Reference to the Occasion

Sometimes you may begin your speech by referring to the occasion which prompts its delivery. Here is an example from a campaign speech which Jimmy Carter presented at the Iowa State Fair in Des Moines on August 26, 1976:

> I'm glad to be here today, especially to be with you at your Iowa State Fair — in a state which is No. 1 in corn, No. 1 in hogs, and which produces one-sixth of the nation's soybeans and about 10 percent of all U.S. food.[3]

Personal Greeting or Self-Allusion

At times, a warm personal salutation from the speaker or a pleasurably recalled earlier association with the audience or the scene serves as an excellent starting point. This is particularly the case if the speaker occupies a high-status position and has considerable prestige in the eyes of the audience. President Gerald Ford took advantage of this situation in opening his remarks before the House of Representatives on August 21, 1974:

> *Mr. Speaker and my former colleagues of the House of Representatives:* You do not know how much it means to me to come back and see all of you and to be so warmly welcomed. It makes one's political life a great, great experience to know that, after all of the disagreements we have had and all of the problems we have worked on, there are friends such as you. It is a thing that in my opinion makes politics worthwhile. I am proud of politics, and I am most grateful for my friends.[4]

The way in which a personal reference may be used in an introduction to gain a hearing from a suspicious or skeptical audience is shown by

Anson Mount, Manager of Public Affairs for *Playboy* magazine, in a talk presented to the Christian Life Commission of the Southern Baptist Convention:

> I am sure we are all aware of the seeming incongruity of a representative of *Playboy* magazine speaking to an assemblage of representatives of the Southern Baptist Convention. I was intrigued by the invitation when it came last fall, though I was not surprised. I am grateful for your genuine and warm hospitality, and I am flattered (though again not surprised) by the implication that I would have something to say that could have meaning to you people. Both *Playboy* and the Baptists have indeed been considering many of the same issues and ethical problems; and even if we have not arrived at the same conclusions, I am impressed and gratified by your openness and willingness to listen to our views.[5]

A personal reference or self-allusion should, of course, be modest and sincere. If it is otherwise, it may gain the attention of the audience, but is unlikely to establish rapport and good will. Beware, however, of being *overly* modest or apologetic. Avoid saying, "I don't know why your organization picked me out to talk on this subject when others could do it so much better," or "The person who was scheduled to address you couldn't come, and so at the last minute I agreed to speak, but I haven't had much time to prepare." To introduce yourself and your message with self-denigrating allusions of this sort tends to defeat your basic communicative purpose by suggesting that neither you nor your message is worthy of attention. Be cordial, sincere, and modest, but not apologetic.

In the three types of speech openings we have just analyzed—reference to the subject or problem, reference to the occasion, and personal greeting or self-allusion—you probably noticed that the establishing of *common ground* is a predominating concern. In the remarks offered, the speaker attempts to tie his or her experience or interests to those of the hearers. This thread of common ground runs throughout the fabric of all effective speech communication, and can be a powerful force in winning a favorable response to your message.

Rhetorical Question

To ask a rhetorical question—a question to which no immediate and direct answer is sought—is another effective means of introducing the central ideas of a speech. One or more such questions, especially if they are well phrased and strike swiftly and cleanly at the core of your subject, will prompt hearers to seek an answer in their own minds and stimulate them to think about the matters you wish to deal with.

In beginning his discussion of fire hazards in campus buildings, a student pointedly asked: "What would you do if a fire should break out downstairs while I am talking and the stairway collapsed before you could get out?" Rhetorical questions of this kind are especially effective if they impinge on some immediate interest of the listener or deal with a problem of widespread concern. Indeed, if you are following the need-satisfaction or problem-solution approach by posing a series of rhetorical questions, you may lead your audience to formulating an answer or series of answers by which they themselves will arrive at the solution you advocate.

Here is how Dave Wallace, a cadet at the Air Force Academy, effectively used a series of rhetorical questions to introduce a speech advocating a no-fault divorce law:

> The beginning of the end for an American marriage; a minor tragedy? Perhaps it's not so minor. In 1973, 913,000 couples—one in every four marriages in this country—came uncoupled. An American tragedy, or a realization of the truth about certain kinds of marriages? What's so sacred about an institution which does nothing but make you miserable? Why do we keep antiquated divorce laws on the books which do nothing but prolong the agony?[6]

Startling Statement

Another method of opening a speech consists of jarring the audience into attention by a startling statement of fact or opinion. An example of this type of introduction is provided in a student speech by Connie Eads, titled "Subliminal Persuasion: Mental Rape":

> Man's most precious possession is his mind. Our ability to reason is what distinguishes us from lower forms of life. We look down on those who have lost their ability to reason: call them crazy, loony, retards. Today, in our country, our powers of reasoning have been undermined; our minds have been raped. Everyone of us has been victimized and manipulated by the use of subliminal or subconscious stimuli directed into our unconscious minds by the mass merchandisers of the media.[7]

Whether you use a startling statement as the sole method of beginning a speech or combine it with one or more other methods, keep in mind that to rivet your listeners' attention, you will have to phrase your assertions with special care and as strikingly as possible. In both the phrasing and the selecting of ideas to be presented, however, you must be careful to avoid obvious sensationalism—shock solely for the sake of shock. Nor should you use materials which, because they are questionable factually, overexaggerated, or in poor taste, impair the listeners' respect for your integrity and good judgment. The objective is to invite and attract their *favorable* attention, not to alienate them.

Pertinent Quotation

If properly chosen and presented, a quotation may be an excellent means of introducing a speech. Here, however, the qualities of simplicity and succinctness are highly desirable. Observe, for example, the way

Pat Mealey, a student at Carroll College, used a quotation to open a speech criticizing the federal Food and Drug Administration:

> George Washington once said: "Government is not eloquence, it is not reason, it is force. Like fire, it is a dangerous servant and a fearful master." We always hear stories of how destructive a bureaucratic government, responsible to no one, can be. An all-powerful, self-perpetuating bureaucracy becomes locked in its own red tape; and unless it is carefully watched, it ceases to serve.
>
> Let's take a look at a case in point involving the Food and Drug Administration. . . .[8]

Humorous Anecdote

Another often-used — and often-abused — way to begin a speech is to tell a funny story or relate a humorous experience. A word of caution is in order here, however: be sure that the story or experience you recount will amuse the audience and that you can tell it well. If your opening falls flat (and an unfunny or irrelevant story may do just that), your speech will be off to a poor start. If the story has no apparent connection with the circumstance or context of the message, at the very least your audience will be perplexed; if your story is off-color and offends their sensibilities, you will have alienated them at the outset. It is imperative, therefore, that an introductory anecdote be relevant and appropriate to your *subject,* your *purpose,* and your *audience.* A joke or a story that is unrelated to these important concerns wastes valuable time and channels the attention and thoughts of your listeners in the wrong direction.

Exercise care, too, in the *manner* in which you tell the story or recount the experience. The speaker who "*tries* to be funny" rarely is. Few people enjoy listening to a smart aleck. Tell your tale simply and clearly, letting a quiet sense of humor and enthusiasm shine through. Take the general attitude: "I myself enjoyed the humor and good fun of this joke, and I'm hoping you will share a measure of that enjoyment with me." Above all, if you insist on laughing at your own jokes, at least give the audience a chance to laugh first.

Businessman Allan D. Schuster used these words to introduce a speech to the American Life Insurance Association in San Francisco on November 18, 1974:

> Thank you for the fine introduction, Don (Jondahl). That was the *second-best* introduction I've ever had. The best was once when the program chairman was missing, and I had to introduce myself.[9]

And this how John A. Howard, President of Rockford College, used humor in the form of an anecdote to lead into the ideas he wished to present at a convocation of the student body:

> Two caterpillars were crawling across a lawn one day when a handsome butterfly flew overhead. One caterpillar was heard to remark to the other,

"Some folks may think that's the way to live, but you couldn't get me up in one of those flimsy things for a million dollars."

This morning I want to share with you some thoughts about liberal arts education which appears to be carrying on very much like the grumpy caterpillar just quoted. The potential is there, but the creature, seemingly ignorant of its potential, is somewhat obtuse in its thinking and earthbound in its performance.[10]

Real or Hypothetical Illustration

Still another method of starting a speech is to use a vivid narrative which illustrates the central point or thrust of your message. Especially useful in this connection are *real-life* incidents and stories taken from history, literature, or the daily newspapers. Equally valuable for this purpose — but sometimes more difficult to evolve — are *hypothetical* illustrations: imagined happenings or events that closely parallel actual ones. Fables and parables may be included in this category. Again, as in the case of a startling statement, quotation, or anecdote, be sure that the illustration you use is *interesting in itself* and *that it connects closely with the central idea of the speech* that is to follow.

In introducing a speech on the large number of needless surgical operations that are performed each year, John Marquette of Georgetown College used this illustration:

Forty-seven years ago one of my aunts who was then five years old was suffering from severe inflammation of the left eye with partial loss of sight. My grandparents consulted a leading ophthalmologist in Cincinnati, Ohio. His diagnosis was that the eye was badly infected and would have to be removed within two weeks or otherwise jeopardize the right eye. Shocked by such a radical report, my grandmother insisted that they get a second doctor's opinion. The second ophthalmologist reached the same diagnosis, but recommended medication and close care of the infection rather than surgery. Within six months the child's eye was free from infection, and she had been spared the physical and emotional anguish of having her eye needlessly removed. Thanks to two wise and cautious parents, the second opinion was sought, and my aunt can see clearly today despite the inept and hasty judgment of the first doctor.

This happened forty-seven years ago, but the problem of needless surgery still exists.[11]

An example of a hypothetical or fictitious illustration is provided by Eric Lund in a speech titled "Against Triage."

I would like you to use your imaginations for a few moments. I would like you to imagine that you are on a ship at sea with five hundred other passengers. Suddenly the ship begins to sink and you all crowd onto the lifeboats. But the lifeboats can hold only three hundred of you. But you crowd on anyway; and since they are so overcrowded, they begin to swamp and sink. It becomes apparent that some of you must jump overboard if the rest are to live. Or else you will all die, together. Not a very pretty picture, is it? Yet according to Garret Hardin, a University of California biology professor, this is what is happening in our world-food situation. He and other noted authorities on the subject of world famine and population growth have come to the conclusion that some countries must die if the rest are to live. This choice between who will live and who will die has been given the name *triage,* derived from the French verb, *trier,* meaning to sort. The concept of triage was first used extensively during World War I as a means of separating the medical patients into their respective tents. Those patients that would live without much help were put into one tent; those who would die, no matter what, were put into another; and those that would live, but only with immediate medical attention, were given priority. In the next few minutes I hope to ask and answer two very important questions involving triage: How does it function? And what can be done to prevent it?[12]

Actual and hypothetical illustrations, relevant anecdotes, pertinent quotations, startling statements, rhetorical questions, personal greetings or self-allusions, and references to the subject or occasion — these, then, are all useful ways of beginning a speech. Sometimes one method may be used alone; at other times, two or more of them will work more effectively in combination. Observe how Professor Lester Thonssen brought together an illustration, a personal reference, and a reference to the occasion in opening a commencement address at Huron College:

In his essay on "The Anthropology of Manners," Edward T. Hall, Jr., tells of a tribesman who came to a prearranged spot in Kabul, the capital of Afghanistan, to meet his brother. But he couldn't find him. So he left, giving instructions to the local merchants where he might be reached if his brother showed up. Exactly a year later, there was his brother. It seems that the brothers had agreed to meet in Kabul on a certain day of a certain month at a particular place, but they failed to specify the year.

My plans have been like those of the tribesman. Often I've agreed to meet friends on a return to the campus at commencement time, but the year was never definitely set. Now thirty-two years after graduation — a disturbingly grim statistic — I'm honored and privileged to keep an appointment on this important occasion in the life of a fine institution.[13]

Whatever method or methods you use to begin a speech, however, you must not only gain attention but also lead the minds of your listeners easily and naturally into your subject. Remember, too, that you must gain their good will and respect for you as a person.

Ending the Speech: Methods and Materials

The principal function of any method used to end a speech is to focus the thought and feeling of the hearers on the central theme developed during the course of the talk. Clarity, conciseness, and a sense of completeness characterize an effective conclusion. If your speech has but one idea, that idea must be restated at the end in a manner that will make your meaning clear and forceful. If your speech is more complex, its important points must be brought together in a condensed and unified form that sums up or embodies unmistakably their overall significance, or suggests the action or belief which you are urging.

In addition to bringing the substance of the speech into final focus, a good ending should leave the audience in the proper state of mind. If you expect your listeners to express vigorous enthusiasm, you must stimulate that feeling by the way you close. If you want them to reflect thoughtfully on what you have said, your conclusion should encourage a calm, judicious attitude. Decide whether the response you seek requires a mood of serious determination or good-humored levity, of warm sympathy or cold anger, of objective deliberation or vigorous action. Then plan to conclude your speech in such a way as to generate that mood or create that frame of mind.

Finally, remember that the end of a speech should convey a sense of *completeness* and *finality.* Few things annoy an audience as much as to think the speaker has finished, only to have him or her go on again. Avoid false endings. Tie the threads together so that the pattern of your speech is brought to completion; deliver your concluding sentence with finality—and then stop. If you bring the central theme into sharp focus, create the proper mood, and close with decisiveness, you probably will have gone far toward gaining the purpose for which you speak.

To achieve these effects when ending a speech, speakers frequently employ one or more of the following methods:

1.   Issue a challenge or an appeal to the listeners.
2.   Summarize major points or ideas.
3.   Provide an appropriate quotation.
4.   Epitomize with a thematic illustration.
5.   Offer an additional inducement for accepting or acting upon the proposal advocated.
6.   Express their own intention or endorsement.

Challenge or Appeal to Listeners

When using this method, appeal openly for belief or action, or remind your listeners of their responsibilities in achieving a desirable goal. Such an appeal should be vivid and compelling, and should contain a suggestion of the principal ideas or arguments you have presented. On May 20, 1975, Robert E. Thomas, President of MAPCO, in concluding a speech on the energy crisis, used such an appeal:

> Collectively, we are on a collision course with economic disaster. Unless some drastic changes occur, unless Congressmen from the heavy oil-consuming states in particular stop playing games, our country is headed for lower business activity, lower standards of living, lower employment, and other unpleasant consequences.

It is so sad and so completely unnecessary. We do have vast quantities of energy; we have the manpower, talent, expertise, and money—in short, we have the foundation for energy independence in our time—provided—and this proviso is a must—clear-cut guidelines are established by the Congress, and Congress ceases its political vendetta directed at destroying our energy companies. Only if you and other concerned citizens become aroused, only if you and other concerned citizens across this great land of ours maintain steady pressure on your Congressmen and Senators, can we hope to accomplish such a result. Many connected with energy are belatedly doing their best—but we badly need the help of every concerned American.[14]

Summary of Major Points or Ideas

A summary conclusion reviews the main ideas that have been presented and draws whatever inferences may be implicit in the speech as a whole. In a speech to inform, a summary ending is nearly always appropriate because it restates and helps impress upon the listeners the points you especially want remembered. In a speech to persuade, a summary conclusion provides a final opportunity to reiterate your principal arguments and appeals.

As part of his conclusion to a speech delivered at Aquinas Junior College in Nashville, Tennessee, and titled "What the Future Demands," Guilford Dudley, Jr., an insurance executive, used this summary:

> Let me try to wrap all that I have said to you into a tight little ball before we get into the discussion period. . . .
>
> We have accented the need for a profound understanding of the impact of accelerating change and global shrinkage. . . .
>
> We have discussed not so much a reorientation of our values as a need to reorient the roles of the various parts of our society in working toward the common goals.
>
> We have noted that our vision must encompass the fact that our goals are no longer fixed by physical limitation, though our achievements may be limited by our lack of will.
>
> And, finally, we have stated that the profile of tomorrow's business executive must include raw courage.
>
> We have spoken of very basic things, like the need to be multilingual. We have moved into philosophical discussions in our awareness that more and more daily problems and challenges present themselves in moral terms.[15]

Pertinent Quotation

A quotation, either in poetry or prose, may be used to end a speech if it bears directly on the central idea you have been trying to communicate, or if it strongly suggests the attitude or action you wish your listeners to take. A few lines of poetry, for instance, may provide in figurative, climactic language the theme or essence of your message. A few words of quoted prose may encapsulate your speech purpose and lend color and authority to your conclusion. Lisa Hartman used this method in concluding a speech on television titled "Hope for the Medium":

> Television can never begin anew. We cannot erase what has happened to our medium in the last three decades. The effects of television are too well-rooted in the foundations of this nation and of nations abroad. We can only hope that through the processes of adaptation and change, television will evolve into a source of enlightenment for the 20th Century. In the words of the late Edward R. Murrow: "This instrument can teach; it can illuminate; yes, it can even inspire. But it can do so only to the extent that humans are determined to use it to those ends. Otherwise, it is merely lights and wires in a box."[16]

Epitomizing Illustration

Just as an illustration epitomizing your leading ideas may be used to open a speech, so may an illustration — real or hypothetical — be used to close it. A speech-ending illustration should be both *inclusive* and *conclusive:* inclusive of the main focus or thrust of your speech, conclusive in tone and impact. Dr. Samuel B. Gould, former president of the Educational Broadcasting Corporation, concluded a speech to the students and faculty of Hunter College in this way:

> Whatever the career and whatever the task, it deserves what is best and finest in us. . . . B. J. Chute, the writer, tells a wonderful story about a small child who watched a sculptor working on a slab of marble. Day after day, the child watched and the sculptor worked. And then, at last, there came a day when the child drew his breath and looked at the sculptor in amazement and said, "But how did you know there was a lion in there?"
>
> To know there is a lion in one's mind, and finally to produce it — that is success. That is the flavor for our daily bread, the closest we shall ever come to human happiness.[17]

Additional Inducement

Sometimes a speech may be concluded by quickly reviewing the most important ideas presented in the body of the talk and then supplying one or two additional reasons for accepting the belief or taking the action proposed. A speech urging the importance of an annual medical checkup might, for example, be concluded as follows:

> All in all, then, you will find an annual checkup by a competent physician to be a wise investment, no matter what your age or how well you may feel at the moment. As I have pointed out, in their early stages a number of potentially serious diseases have no symptoms of which the victim is in any way aware. Many other ills if caught in time can be eliminated or brought under control. Finally, the time and money a good checkup will

cost you are only a tiny fraction of the time and expense a serious illness entails.

Here, as in other aspects of life, be guided by the old but still pertinent adage, "A stitch in time saves nine." Remember that even though you may be foolish enough to take chances with your own well-being, you owe it to your loved ones and to those dependent on you to take no chances with the most precious of all things — your own good health. Make an appointment for a checkup today!

Expression of Personal Intention or Endorsement

A statement of personal feeling or of intention to act as your speech recommends is another common way of concluding a talk. This method is particularly valuable when your prestige with the audience is high, but may also be employed with good effect in other circumstances. Perhaps the most famous example of this method of closing a speech is the declaration attributed to Patrick Henry: ". . . As for me, give me liberty or give me death!" In concluding the Des Moines address to a farm audience cited earlier in this chapter, Jimmy Carter also took occasion to express his personal feelings and intentions:

> I believe in hard work. I believe that the best government is the one closest to the people.
>
> And I believe in a close-knit family.
>
> These things have got to be preserved. They are the values that have lived on the farm, and which our government needs to rediscover. They are the values I will carry with me into the White House if I am elected.
>
> I want to improve the quality of life of our rural people. I live on the outskirts of a little town of only 683 people. I don't care if 100 years from now it still has less than 1,000 population. But it's important to me that my children and your children have as good an education and as high an income, and the same right to shape their own destiny as children who live in the largest or wealthiest community in our nation.
>
> We have a long way to go. We can restore the precious things we've lost, the things which remain strong in rural America. Then all of us can be sure again that we still live in the greatest country on earth.[18]

In sum, then, the methods and materials which you use to open and close your speech should be chosen with due attention to (1) your subject, (2) your purpose, (3) your listeners, (4) the nature of the occasion, and (5) your own special aptitudes or skills as a speaker. Always, however, you should carefully plan in advance the kind of introduction and conclusion you will employ and would do well to consider as options the methods we have here described. To trust the vital beginning and concluding words of your speech to chance is to risk the failure of an otherwise sound and well-developed message.

Reference Notes

[1]From "The Threat of Famine" by Henry A. Kissinger, from *Vital Speeches of the Day*, Volume XXXXI. December 1974. Reprinted by permission of Vital Speeches of the Day.

[2]Excerpt from a speech by Father Theodore M. Hesburgh from *Representative American Speeches: 1962–1963*, published by the H. W. Wilson Company. Reprinted by permission of the author.

[3]From a speech at Iowa State Fair by President James E. Carter, August 26, 1976.

[4]Excerpt from speech before House of Representatives on August 21, 1974, by President Gerald Ford, from *Public Papers of the President*. Washington, D.C.: U.S. Government Printing Office, 1975, p. 39.

[5]Excerpt from a speech by Anson Mount from *Contemporary American Speeches*, 3rd Edition, by Wil A. Linkugel, R. R. Allen, and Richard Johannesen. © 1973 by Wadsworth Publishing Company, Inc., Belmont, California 94002. Reprinted by permission of the author and the Christian Life Commission.

[6]From "No-Fault Divorce" by Dave Wallace. Reprinted from *Winning Orations* by special arrangement with the Interstate Oratorical Association, Larry Schnoor, Executive Secretary, Mankato State College, Mankato, Minnesota.

[7]From "Subliminal Persuasion: Mental Rape" by Connie Eads. Reprinted from *Winning Orations* by special arrangement with the Interstate Oratorical Association, Larry Schnoor, Executive Secretary, Mankato State College, Mankato, Minnesota.

[8]From "FDA—The Folly of the Drug Administration" by Pat Mealey. Reprinted from *Winning Orations* by special arrangement with the Interstate Oratorical Association, Larry Schnoor, Executive Secretary, Mankato State College, Mankato, Minnesota.

[9]From "Real Estate" by Allan D. Schuster, from *Vital Speeches of the Day*, Volume XXXXI, December 1974. Reprinted by permission of Vital Speeches of the Day.

[10]From "The Apprehension of Human Dignity" by John A. Howard, from *Vital Speeches of the Day*, Volume XXXXI, November 1974. Reprinted by permission of Vital Speeches of the Day.

[11]From "Are You Willing to Take the Risk?" by John Marquette. Reprinted from *Winning Orations* by special arrangement with the Interstate Oratorical Association, Larry Schnoor, Executive Secretary, Mankato State College, Mankato, Minnesota.

[12]From "Against Triage" by Eric Lund. Reprinted from *Winning Orations* by special arrangement with the Interstate Oratorical Association, Larry Schnoor, Executive Secretary, Mankato State College, Mankato, Minnesota.

[13]Excerpt from "The Anthropology of Manners" by Lester Thonssen, from *Representative American Speeches, 1958–1959*, ed. by Lester Thonssen (Bronx, N.Y.: The H. W. Wilson Company, 1959), pp. 132–133. Reprinted by permission of the author.

[14]From "Can We Solve the Energy Crisis?" by Robert E. Thomas, from *Vital Speeches of the Day*, Volume XXXXI, July 1975. Reprinted by permission of Vital Speeches of the Day.

[15]From "What the Future Demands" by Guilford Dudley, Jr., from *Vital Speeches of the Day*, Volume XXIV, April 1968. Reprinted by permission of Vital Speeches of the Day.

[16]From "Hope for the Medium" by Lisa Hartman. Reprinted from *Winning Orations* by special arrangement with the Interstate Oratorical Association, Larry Schnoor, Executive Secretary, Mankato State College, Mankato, Minnesota.

[17]Excerpt from "A Flavor for Our Daily Bread" by Samuel B. Gould. Reprinted by permission.

[18]From a speech at Iowa State Fair by President James E. Carter, August 26, 1976.

Problems and Probes

1. Select twelve or fifteen speeches from recent issues of *Vital Speeches of the Day, Representative American Speeches,* or one of the sources suggested in the Problems and Probes of earlier chapters. Following the methods described in this chapter, classify the various ways in which these speeches begin and end. Are certain types of beginnings and endings used more frequently than others? Do some types seem to be more common in speeches to inform and others more common in speeches to persuade? What types appear most frequently in speeches delivered on special occasions—anniversaries, dedications, farewells, etc.?

2.   Select at least eight of the beginnings and endings cataloged in Problem/Probe 1. Evaluate these in terms of their suitability to *(a)* the speaker's purpose, *(b)* the subject matter of the speech, and *(c)* the nature and attitude of the audience (insofar as you are able to determine them). Which of the beginnings and endings could have been improved? How?

 ## Oral Activities and Speaking Assignments

1.   Participate in a class discussion concerning introductions and conclusions to public speeches. The discussion might be structured as follows: One student leads off by suggesting a topic for a possible speech to this class. A second student then suggests an appropriate type of introduction and conclusion, justifying those choices. A third student, in turn, challenges that selection, proposing alternative introductions and/or conclusions. Continue this discussion until everyone has proposed and defended the different types of introductions and conclusions that would be appropriate for the speech topics discussed.

2.   Select a subject toward which the members of your speech class probably will hold one of the attitudes described in Chapter 18, pages 304–308: Favorable, but not aroused; apathetic; interested, but undecided; hostile to any change; etc. Prepare and present a five-minute speech on a subject of interest to the members of your class. Conclude it with an ending designed to leave the audience *(a)* thoughtful or reflective, *(b)* emotionally aroused or excited, or *(c)* determined to take the action you propose. At the conclusion of your presentation, take a quick survey of your listeners to determine how well you fulfilled your purpose.

 ## Suggestions for Further Reading

Aristotle, *Rhetoric,* 1414b – 1415a, "The Proem or Introduction"; and 1419b – 1420b, "The Epilogue."

Donald C. Bryant and Karl R. Wallace, *Fundamentals of Public Speaking,* 5th ed. (Englewood Cliffs, N.J.: Prentice-Hall, Inc., 1976), pp. 277 – 287, "Introductions" and "Conclusions."

Jon Eisenson and Paul H. Boase, *Basic Speech,* 3rd ed. (New York: The Macmillan Company, 1975), pp. 364 – 373, "The Introduction" and "The Conclusion."

Leon Fletcher, *How to Design and Deliver a Speech* (New York: Chandler Publishing Company, 1973), Chapter 11, "Designing the Introduction" and Chapter 12, "Designing the Conclusion."

Larry A. Samovar and Jack Mills, *Oral Communication. Message and Response,* 3rd ed. (Dubuque, Iowa: Wm. C. Brown Company, Publishers, 1976), pp. 116 – 126, "Preparing the Introduction" and "Preparing the Conclusion."

Part 3

PUBLIC DISTANCE
(12 feet or more)

SOCIAL DISTANCE
(4 to 12 feet)

PERSONAL DISTANCE
(1½ to 4 feet)

INTIMATE DISTANCE
(up to 1½ feet)

"the fuzz"

Public Communication:
Modes of Communicating Meaning

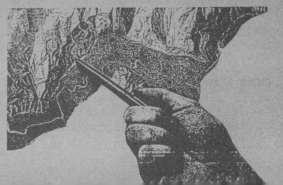

13

The Effects of Language on Communication

In the chapters of Part Two we examined the process of public speech-making, stressing the preparation and organization of messages and the need to adapt them carefully to the audiences for whom they are intended. Here in Part Three we turn our attention to *the modes of encoding and decoding messages.* These modes—language, bodily behaviors, vocal behaviors, and visual reinforcement—are the means by which public speakers most frequently and effectively communicate important dimensions of themselves, their ideas, feelings, attitudes, and values to their listeners. We begin with *language.*

At several junctures in this book we have referred to the "problems of language," that is, to the choices which you as a speaker must make when you encode your ideas and feelings *in words.* There are at least three good reasons why such choices demand your careful attention: First, language is used to reveal your *self* and your communicative intentions as a speaker. Second, language is used to communicate the *meaning* or sense of your messages. Third, language is used to communicate your *feelings* and *values*—to show how you feel about the subject you are discussing and the audience you are addressing. These, essentially, are the three most important *functions* of language in communication.

Using Language to Reveal the Self

Many of the ways in which you habitually use language are deeply engrained in your subconscious, for the core of your language reflects the innermost structure of your *self* and your view of the world. Actually, however, because your self consists of many *different* "selves," each of which manifests itself at various times in various ways, there are some aspects of your language usage which you can consciously change from speech to speech, from setting to setting. Such adaptation is possible because, in a special and limited sense at least, each of your "selves" has its own voice and its own vocabulary. Three of the most important of these adaptations concern your use of: (1) the "is" verb and modal verbs, (2) qualifiers, and (3) active and passive verbs.

"Is" and Modal Verbs

Is and other forms of the verb *to be* are among the commonest in our culture. The way you use these verbs can reveal a good deal about your dogmatism and aggressiveness and also about how you view the world in relation to your listeners.

In their observation of language behavior, the general semanticists have identified these four prevalent uses of the word *is:*

1. *Auxiliary verb,* as in "He is running."
2. *Verb of existence,* as in "He is [exists] in this room."
3. *Verb of identity,* as in "He is [can be identified as] a communist."
4. *Verb of predication/attribution,* as in "An apple is round" (i.e., " 'roundness' is an attribute of an 'apple' ").*

The semanticists have been especially concerned about the *is of identity* and the *is of attribution* because of the widespread tendency to use them assertively to denote permanence. When we use the *is* of identity, as in "He is a communist," we often are tempted to think that we have categorized someone completely and finally. Even in using the *is of predication,* we can be lured into assuming that a person, event, or thing has certain attributes forever and ever.

The danger is not simply that we often forget that persons, events, or things change through time and in different settings, but that as oral communicators we tend to transmit a sense of dogmatism and assertiveness when we make unusually heavy use of the "ises" of identity and attribution. Now, there certainly is nothing wrong with strong, assertive communication when that is the kind you intend. But when you are in fact more tentative, more judicious, in your judgments, be careful to use *qualifiers* ("seems," "perhaps," "probably," etc.) and specific *narrowers* and *modifiers* ("His *political* philosophy is communistic," "He is *acting like* [not *is*] an idiot," etc.). In sum, control your "ises."

The same advice, for the same sorts of reasons, applies to your use of

---

*For an introduction to the field of General Semantics and a more detailed analysis of these four "ises," see Irving J. Lee, *Language Habits in Human Affairs* (New York: Harper & Brothers, 1941), especially Chapter 11.

modal verbs, that is, verbs which indicate various degrees of force or determination. Consider the following sequence of sentences:

"You could do that."   "You should do that."
"You can do that."   "You must do that."
"You might do that."   "You will do that."
"You may do that."   "You shall do that!"

In this sequence we have varied only the modal verb in each instance, but look at the differences in perceptible force: *Could* implies tentativeness; *can* means you have the capacity to do something, but no one is telling you what to do; *might* is a soft, unsure prediction; *may* indicates permission, but not advice; *should* admonishes or offers advice; *will* makes a strong prediction; and *shall* gives an order. Thus, the simple choice of a modal verb can give an audience different impressions of your dogmatism and aggressiveness. You will find it literally impossible, of course, to think about every single modal — just as you cannot possibly stop to think as you use every *is.* But you can try, nevertheless, to phrase your key ideas with some careful attention to the possible effects of the modals that you choose.*

Qualifiers

The kinds and numbers of qualifiers you employ in your language also reveal something significant about both you as a person and also about the materials you present. For example, a qualifier may reveal (1) the limits you place upon the strength of a claim or the worth of an idea ("That is *probably* true") or , more often, (2) on the degree of your self-assurance ("I *think* that is *probably* true").

Notice in the first instance that the *probably* is used in conjunction with a third-person, so-called impersonal construction ("That is . . ."), or it could be used also with a passive construction ("It could be said that . . ."). When you attach a qualifier to such statements, you are indicating to your listeners that something is only generally or occasionally true; that is, the qualification arises from your perception of the *outside* world. In the second instance, the *probably* is used with the first-person singular ("I think that is *probably* true"); or it could be used also with the first-person plural ("We might now assert that . . ."); that is, the qualification arises from the perception of your *self* as being uncertain and, therefore, unwilling to risk a personal judgment. In other words, as a speaker you can attach qualifiers either to your *subject matter* (implying that there is not yet enough evidence to warrant an out-and-out assertion) or to your *self* as the maker of a claim (implying

---

*To pursue this subject, see especially Julian Boyd and J. P. Thorne, "The Semantics of Modal Verbs," *Journal of Linguistics* 5 (1969), p. 62.

your internal uncertainty or restraint). Especially in highly controversial situations either type of tentativeness is no vice.*

Active and Passive Verbs

As a speaker you also reveal your *self* to your listeners by your use of active verbs and passive verbs. From your previous study of English grammar, you will recall that declarative sentences may be cast in either active or passive voice. As examples, "He hit the ball," "I think two points stand out," "The tree shades the park" are *active* constructions. "The ball was hit by him," "Two important points can be considered," "The park is shaded by the tree" are *passive* constructions.

The active construction normally emphasizes (1) the *agent* ("He," "I," and "tree" in our examples), and also stresses (2) dynamic *action* or *interaction* ("hit," "stand out," "shades"). Active verbs, therefore, tend to dominate your messages when you are urging your listeners to do something, when you wish to visualize conflict, action, or an effect, and when you want to communicate to your audience that you are a change-seeking speaker.

The passive construction usually emphasizes (1) the *object* (the *ball* that was hit, the *points* that can be considered, the *park* that is shaded), and typically focuses on (2) *static patterns or relationships.* Passive verbs, therefore, tend to dominate your messages when you advise your listeners to think about an idea or an object or to contemplate a concept, when you wish to provide overall descriptions, and when you want to communicate to your audience that you are a thoughtful, objective speaker assessing the world as it *is* rather than as it *ought to be.*

Thus, your preponderant use of either active-voice or passive-voice verbs helps to reveal to audiences still more about you, your view of your *self,* and of the world. In practical terms, as a speaker you should not use either active or passive constructions exclusively; for neither is, as a rule, to be preferred over the other. Rather, as you think over those aspects of your self that you want to reveal to your audience in a given situation, you will need to make some *conscious* decisions as to which of the two types will probably "work best" in achieving your communicative purpose, which of the two will probably contribute more to the effect you desire to create, and—therefore—which one should be your preferred construction-pattern in these circumstances.

In the statements which follow, notice how the speaker—in confronting some of the decisions we have described—has elected to lay out specific options as a basis for making her choices:

> International war strains both foreign relationships and domestic economies. On the foreign front, it disrupts the exchange of goods, cultural

---

*For a discussion of both modal verbs and qualifiers, see Stephen E. Toulmin, *The Uses of Argument* (Cambridge: Cambridge University Press, 1964), esp. Chapters 1 and 2.

affairs, and shared development, while on the domestic front, it diverts funds from consumer goods to war matériel; it accelerates the growth of already powerful special interests; and it threatens to destroy the social usefulness of young adults.

Or:

Both foreign relationships and domestic economies are affected by international war. The exchange of goods, cultural affairs, and shared development are disrupted on the foreign front, while consumer goods are replaced by war matériel; already powerful special interests are allowed to grow; and the social usefulness of young adults is threatened on the domestic front.

The first of these two examples, as you can readily see, is the more active; the second is more passively put, lending a feeling of judiciousness and possibly a greater objectivity. The choice that the speaker would ultimately make between them will depend to a discernible degree upon the self-image she wants to project to her audience.

Using Language to Communicate Meaning

A second function of oral language is to help the audience understand as precisely as possible the sense or meaning of your message. Here we are concerned, not with what language reveals about you as a speaker, but with language selection as it increases listeners' *comprehension* (the capacity to understand and "make sense" of what you say) and *retention* (the capability to recall or retrieve and reassemble thoughts, concepts, and information after a period of time). These have been the concerns of rhetorical theorists and practitioners in both ancient and modern times; and the virtues of appropriate language selection as reflected in *accuracy, simplicity, reiteration,* and *coherence* are now widely recognized.

Accuracy

Precise meaning can be expressed only if words are carefully chosen. The man who tells the hardware clerk that he has "broken the hickey on his hootenanny and needs a thing'ma-jig to fix it" expresses his meaning vaguely. But his vagueness is only a little greater than that of the orator who proclaims that "we must follow along the path of true Americanism." The probable sentiment obviously is to be admired, but just what does this statement mean? Remember that words are only symbols which *stand for* meanings, and your listener may attach to a symbol a meaning quite different from the one you intend. *Democracy,* for example, does not mean the same thing to a citizen of the United States that it does to a citizen of the Soviet Union. An *expensive* meal to a college student may appear quite moderate in price to a wealthy celebrant.

A mode of travel that was fast in 1878 seems painfully slow a century later. The English language is rich in subtle variations of meanings. For example, among the synonyms for the verb *shine* are *glow, glitter, glisten, gleam, flare, blaze, glare, shimmer, glimmer, flicker, sparkle, flash,* and *beam.* To ensure the accuracy of your meanings, make sure that you select precise words, offer definitions, and—where necessary—add specific details.

Simplicity

No matter how accurately a word or phrase may express a speaker's meaning, it is useless if the audience cannot understand it. For this reason, your expression not only must be exact, but it must also be clear and simple. "Speak," said Lincoln, "so that the most lowly can understand you, and the rest will have no difficulty." This rule is as valid today as when Lincoln uttered it. Say *"learn"* rather than *"ascertain,"* *"after-*

dinner speech" rather than *"postprandial* address," *"large"* rather than *"elephantine."* Choose a longer or less familiar word only if it will improve accuracy or heighten emotional effect. In particular, choose words that are concise and concrete over those that are longer and more abstract. Billy Sunday, the famous evangelist, put the point well:

> If a man were to take a piece of meat and smell it and look disgusted, and his little boy were to say, "What's the matter with it, Pop?" and he were to say, "It is undergoing a process of decomposition in the formation of new chemical compounds," the boy would be all in. But if the father were to say, "It's rotten," then the boy would understand and hold his nose. "Rotten" is a good Anglo-Saxon word and you do not have to go to the dictionary to find out what it means.[1]

In sum, to ensure simplicity, use short words, specific words, words with meanings that are immediately obvious.

Reiteration

Were accuracy and simplicity the only resources of the oral communicator wishing to convey meanings clearly, messages probably would resemble the famous bulletin of World War II: "Sighted sub, sank same." But because you are working with your listeners face-to-face, in oral and not written language, a third stylistic factor becomes important: reiteration. Reiteration, as we are using the term, is intentional repetition, especially of two kinds: (1) *rephrasing* of ideas or concepts in more than one set of words or sentences, and (2) *re-examination* of ideas or concepts from more than one point of view. Because in oral communication words literally disappear into the atmosphere as soon as you utter them, as an oral communicator you do not have the writer's advantages when transmitting ideas to others. Instead, you must rely heavily upon the linguistic techniques of rephrasing and re-examination.

Rephrasing.   The effect of skillful rephrasing in clarifying a message and making it more specific can be seen in the following passage from John F. Kennedy's inaugural address:

> Let the word go forth from this time and place, to friend and foe alike, that the torch has been passed to a new generation of Americans — born in this century, tempered by war, disciplined by a hard and bitter peace, proud of our ancient heritage — and unwilling to witness or permit the slow undoing of those human rights to which this nation has always been committed, and to which we are committed today at home and around the world.
>
> Let every nation know, whether it wishes us well or ill, that we shall pay any price, bear any burden, meet any hardship, support any friend, oppose any foe to assure the survival and the success of liberty.[2]

Re-examination. Re-examining an idea from a number of perspectives can be achieved usually through a reformulation of its constituent elements or a redefinition of the basic concept. You can see this principle of re-examination at work in the following excerpt from a student speech. Note how the speaker defines and redefines "political image" in a variety of ways, thereby providing metaphorical, psychological, and sociological perspectives:

> A "politician's image" is really a set of characteristics attributed to that politician by an electorate [*formal definition*]. A political image, like any image which comes off a mirror, is made up of actions and ideas which reflect the audience's concerns [*metaphorical definition*]. An image is composed of bits and pieces of information and feelings which an audience brings to a politician [*psychological definition*], and therefore it represents judgments made by the electorate on the bases of a great many different verbal and nonverbal acts a politician has engaged in [*sociological definition*]. Therefore, if you think of a political image only in terms of manipulation, you are looking only at the mirror. Step back and examine the beholder, too, and you will find ways of discovering what a "good" image is for a politician in 1976.

If carefully handled, reiteration in the form of rephrasing or re-examination is a linguistic tactic which you may employ to clarify ideas and help your listeners remember them more readily. Be careful, however, of mindless repetition—too many restatements, especially restatements of ideas already clear to any alert member of your audience.

Coherence

An audience listening to an oral presentation has no visible paragraphs or written punctuation marks to guide interpretation and understanding. Instead, you must make relationships between ideas clear by *signposts* in the form of carefully worded phrases and sentences inserted at appropriate points. You must ensure *coherence* both in your speech as a whole and also in the individual ideas of which it consists.

Use summaries to make sure that your audience is able to see the overall structure of your speech. Especially helpful are *preliminary summaries* ("Today I am going to talk about three aspects . . .") and *final summaries* ("I have discussed three aspects . . ."). Also, as a general rule, you will need to set up additional signposts as you go along to help *connect* your ideas and to effect *transitions* from one to another. The following are typical:

> In the first place . . . The second point is . . .
> In addition to . . . notice that . . .
> Now look at it from a different angle . . .
> This last point raises a question . . .

You must keep these three things in mind in order to understand the importance of the fourth . . .
What was the result? . . .
Turning now . . .

Expand this list, especially to include phrasings adapted to your own speaking style; and use them to make easy, smooth transitions from point to point.

To ensure coherence *within* successive ideas or points of your speech and to establish relationships between specific ideas or concepts within a single point, you will need to employ more subtle kinds of directives or signposts. Often you will want to make your audience aware of whether two ideas are *similar or different, parallel or hierarchical, coordinated or subordinated.* This requires that you use such connectives as these:

Not only . . . but also . . . [*parallel*]
More important than these . . . [*hierarchical*]
In contrast . . . [*different*]
Similar to this . . . [*similar*]
One must consider X, Y, and Z . . . [*coordinated*]
On the next level is . . . [*subordinated*]

Precision in choice and use of such connectives communicates to an audience a kind of structural picture of the idea you are expounding. It allows them to "map," to configure, your idea.

Using Language to Communicate Feelings and Values

The third major function which a speaker's linguistic choices serve is to provide the audience with cues concerning his or her feelings, attitudes, and values. A given idea can be phrased in a variety of words, all of which have the same *denotative* meaning, but each of which *connotatively* conveys a positive or negative valuation or a sense of the perspective from which the speaker is viewing that idea. While there are numerous ways in which these affective dimensions of language usage can be approached, we shall concentrate upon only three of them: *imagery, intensity,* and *ideological metaphor.*

Imagery

We receive our impressions of and feelings about the world around us through our senses of sight, smell, hearing, taste, and touch. In order to get listeners to experience the object or state of affairs you are describing, you must, therefore, appeal to their senses. But you cannot punch them in the nose, scatter exotic perfume for them to smell, or urge them to taste foods which are not present. The only senses through which you as a speaker can reach them *directly* are the visual and the auditory:

They can see you, your movements, and your facial expressions; and they can hear what you say. However, you can *indirectly* stimulate all of the senses by using language that has the power to produce imagined sensations in listeners, or which causes them to recall images they have previously experienced. As listeners thus recall or re-create an image of a person, place, object, or idea in their minds, they tend to associate attitudes, feelings, or values with it — a tendency we noted in Chapter 5.

The language of imagery falls into seven classes, or types, each related to the particular sensation or feeling it seeks to evoke. The seven types of imagery are:

1. Visual *(sight)*
2. Auditory *(hearing)*
3. Gustatory *(taste)*
4. Olfactory *(smell)*
5. Tactual *(touch)*
6. Kinesthetic *(muscle strain)*
7. Organic *(internal sensations)*

Visual Imagery. Try to make your audience actually "see" the objects or situations you are describing. Mention size, shape, color, movement, and the relative position of one part or element to another. Notice how C. P. Snow uses visual imagery in this description, both to engage our sense of humanitarianism and also to communicate his feeling that we should help people in the underdeveloped countries "live as long as we do and eat enough." He says:

> We are sitting like people in a smart and cozy restaurant and we are eating comfortably, looking out of the window into the streets. Down on the pavement are people who are looking up at us, people who by chance have different colored skins from ours, and are rather hungry. Do you wonder that they don't like us all that much? Do you wonder that we sometimes feel ashamed of ourselves, as we look out through that plate glass?[3]

Auditory Imagery. Make the audience hear not only what you say, but also the sounds which you are describing. In the following example, Tom Wolfe vividly describes the opening of a stock-car race in order to tap our sense of excitement:

> Then the entire crowd, about 4,000, started chanting a countdown, "Ten, nine, eight, seven, six, five, four, three, two," but it was impossible to hear the rest, because right after "two" half the crowd went into a strange whinnying wail. The starter's flag went up, and the 25 cars took off, roaring into second gear with no mufflers, all headed toward that same point in the center of the infield, converging nose on nose.
>
> The effect was exactly what one expects that many simultaneous crashes to produce: the unmistakable tympany of automobiles colliding and cheap-gauge sheet metal buckling.[4]

Sounds vary not only in loudness, pitch, and rhythm, but also in quality. By calling attention to these details, you can create a more vivid auditory image and communicate your feeling about it.

Gustatory Imagery.   Help your audience imagine the taste of what you are describing. Mention its saltiness, sweetness, sourness, or its spicy flavor. Observe how Charles Lamb in his "Dissertation Upon Roast Pig" describes that delicacy in language that not only stimulates the taste buds, but also appeals to our aesthetic values:

> There is no flavor comparable, I will contend, to that of the crisp, tawny, well-watched, not over-roasted, *crackling,* as it is well called—the very teeth are invited to their share of the pleasure at this banquet in overcoming the coy, brittle resistance . . . the tender blossoming of fat . . . the lean, not lean, but a kind of animal manna—or, rather, fat and lean . . . so blended and running into each other, that both together make but one ambrosian result . . . too ravishing for mortal taste.[5]

Olfactory Imagery.   Help your audience smell the odors connected with the situation you describe. Do this not only by mentioning the odor itself, but also by describing the object that has the odor or by comparing it with more familiar ones, as shown in this example:

> As he opened the door of the old apothecary's shop, he breathed the odor of medicines, musty, perhaps, and pungent from too close confinement in so small a place, but free from the sickening smell of stale candy and cheap perfume.

Such associations also allow your audience to make positive or negative judgments about the experience.

Tactual Imagery.   Tactual imagery is based upon the various types of sensations that we receive through physical contact with an object or substance. Particularly it gives us sensations of *texture* and *shape, pressure,* and *heat* and *cold*—sensations which, in turn, cause listeners to feel pleasure, pain, discomfort, disgust, etc.

—*Texture and Shape.* Enable your audience to feel how rough or smooth, dry or wet, slimy or sticky a thing is.
—*Pressure.* Phrase appropriate portions of your speech in such a way that your auditors will sense the pressure of physical force upon their bodies: The weight of a heavy trunk borne upon their backs, the pinching of shoes that are too tight, the incessant drive of the high wind on their faces.
—*Heat and Cold.* These sensations are aroused by what is sometimes called "thermal" imagery.

The following passage by Loren Eiseley well illustrates the use of tactual imagery:

I thought of all this, standing quietly in the water, feeling the sand shifting away under my toes. Then I lay back in the floating position that left my face to the sky, and shoved off. The sky wheeled over me. For an instant, as I bobbed into the main channel, I had the sensation of sliding down the vast tilted face of the continent. It was then that I felt the cold needles of the alpine springs at my fingertips and the warmth of the Gulf pulling me southward. Moving with me, leaving its taste upon my mouth and spouting under me in dancing springs of sand, was the immense body of the continent itself, flowing like the river was flowing, grain by grain, mountain by mountain, down to the sea.[6]

Kinesthetic Imagery. Kinesthetic imagery is useful in describing or picturing sensations of muscle strain and movement. If appropriate to the content of your speech, word passages in such a way that your listeners may feel for themselves the stretching and tightening of their tendons, the creaking in their joints. The following passage illustrates this type of language imagery:

He climbed two thousand feet above the black sea, and without a moment for thought of failure and death, he brought his forewings tightly in to his body, left only the narrow swept daggers of his wingtips extended into the wind, and fell into a vertical dive.

The wind was a monster roar at his head. Seventy miles per hour, ninety, a hundred and twenty and faster still. The wing-strain now at a hundred and forty miles per hour wasn't nearly as hard as it had been before at seventy, and with the faintest twist of his wingtips he eased out of the dive and shot above the waves, a gray cannonball under the moon.[7]

Organic Imagery. Hunger, dizziness, nausea—these are a few of the feelings organic imagery calls up. There are times when an image is not complete without the inclusion of specific details likely to evoke these inner feelings in listeners. Be careful, however, not to offend your audience by making the picture too revolting. Develop the sensitivity required to measure the detail necessary for re-creating vividness without making the resultant image so gruesome that it becomes either disgusting or grotesque. Observe how H. G. Wells has made use of organic imagery to create a desired effect:

That climb seemed interminable to me. With the last twenty or thirty feet of it a deadly nausea came upon me. I had the greatest difficulty in keeping my hold. The last few yards was a frightful struggle against this faintness. Several times my head swam, and I felt all the sensations of falling. At last, however, I got over the well-mouth somehow and staggered out of the ruin into the blinding sunlight.[8]

A somewhat different kind of organic imagery is used by Tom Wolfe in this passage:

All the faces come popping in clots out of the Seventh Avenue local, past the King Size Ice Cream machine, and the turnstiles start whacking away as if the world were breaking up on the reefs. Four steps past the turnstiles everybody is already backed up haunch to paunch for the climb up the ramp and the stairs to the surface, a great funnel of flesh, wool, felt, leather, rubber and steaming alumicron, with the blood squeezing through everybody's old sclerotic arteries in hopped-up spurts from too much coffee and the effort of surfacing from the subway at the rush hour.[9]

In sum, while we may customarily think of imagery as a poetic device, it can also be employed by oral communicators to fill out details and to arouse or engage the feelings of audiences — an engagement which, in turn, provides bases for positive or negative attitudinal and valuative judgments.

Language Intensity

As noted earlier, any given concept probably can be identified with several different word-labels. As a speaker, your choice of a label often is determined by the way you feel about the object to which you attach it and the strength or *intensity* of that feeling. That is, by the chosen word or phrase you communicate your *attitude* toward it. Consider, for example, the following "attitudinally weighted" terms:

RELATIVELY POSITIVE
- "men in blue"
- "safety officials"
- "officers of the law"

RELATIVELY NEUTRAL
- "traffic officials"
- "police personnel"
- "cops"

RELATIVELY NEGATIVE
- "the brass"
- "the fuzz"
- "pigs"

These nine terms are roughly rank-ordered according to their intensity, ranging from the highly positive "men in blue" to the highly negative "pigs." For some examples of attitudinally weighted statements having highly positive, relatively neutral, or highly negative language intensity, examine the chart on the next page.

It is out of such language choices that you make apparent to your listeners the particular intensity of the attitudinal language you are using. Some of these decisions in this regard are, of course, out of your precise control because of the limitations on your experience and vocabulary. And only on rare occasions can you hope to choose each word in an entire speech with perfect care, for such an exercise very likely would produce stilted or artificial oral discourse. Yet, the key ideas you

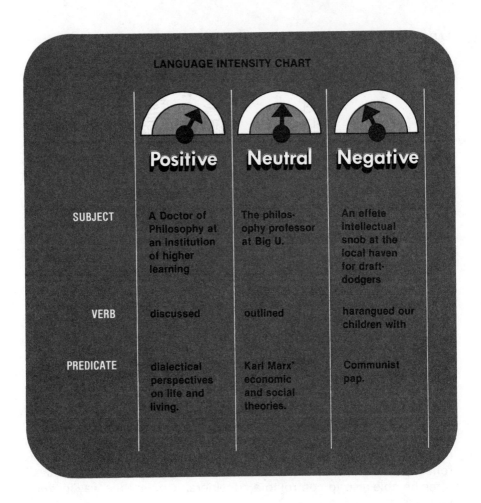

	Positive	**Neutral**	**Negative**
SUBJECT	A Doctor of Philosophy at an institution of higher learning	The philosophy professor at Big U.	An effete intellectual snob at the local haven for draft-dodgers
VERB	discussed	outlined	harangued our children with
PREDICATE	dialectical perspectives on life and living.	Karl Marx' economic and social theories.	Communist pap.

LANGUAGE INTENSITY CHART

develop do deserve careful attention to the intensity of the language with which you express them. Equally deserving of careful thought is the material you wish to quote from others.

How intense should your language be? Professor John Waite Bowers has suggested a useful rule of thumb: Let your language be, roughly, one step more intense than the position or attitude of your audience.* If your audience seems generally neutral toward your idea or proposal, make your key pieces of language slightly positive or slightly negative in the degree of intensity you employ. If your audience already is committed, say, to your positive position on reform, then you can afford to make your language quite intense. That is, on a one-to-seven scale, if your audience is at "four," aim at "three" or "five"; whereas if it is al-

---

*John Waite Bowers, "Language and Argument," in *Perspectives on Argumentation,* ed. Gerald R. Miller and Thomas R. Nilsen (Glenview, Ill.: Scott, Foresman and Company, 1966), esp. pp. 168–172.

LANGUAGE REVEALS ATTITUDES.

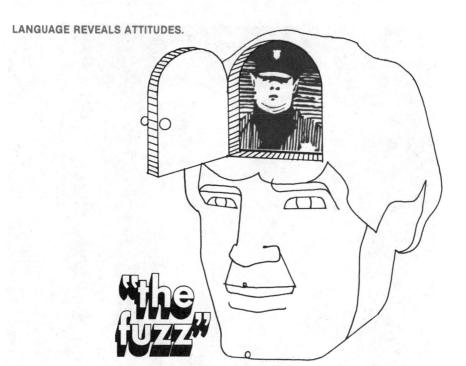

"the fuzz"

ready at "five," push it to "six." In sum, as you select precise wording for important ideas in your speeches, make a careful effort to employ different degrees of intensity. By this means, you will be able not only to reflect your own attitudes more accurately and judiciously, but you will often be able also to control to a considerable extent the way in which your audience will respond.

Ideological Metaphor

Finally, your selection of an oral vocabulary can reveal — intentionally or inadvertently — your philosophy or ideology. By *ideology* we mean a *set* of ideas, an inclusive or comprehensive *system* of attitudes and values — your habitual world-views or overriding outlooks on life. *Ideological language* is made up of words which sometimes reveal, sometimes disguise, such "sets" or "systems," but which you may or may not wish to describe explicitly.

Sometimes, of course, you may elect to speak about your pragmatic, political, sociological, psychological, philosophical-theological, or aesthetic valuative orientations — those we examined in Chapter 5. For example, you may urge listeners to give to the United Way Fund drive for humanitarian (sociological) or practical (pragmatic) reasons. But more often, probably, for reasons that are both sound and practical, you do not openly discuss your value system or ideology with your audience. But even if you try consciously to conceal it, the audience can, nevertheless, sense what those underlying values are simply because of the words you choose. Inescapably, your choice of words reflects your ideological inclinations.

The more comprehensive a set of ideas or a system of values, the more abstract the terminology must be to describe or refer to it. That is why *metaphors* are useful and recurring elements in ideological language. In education, for instance, the phrase "Back to Basics" surfaced in many discussions of the disciplines in the mid-1970s. It referred— metaphorically—to a complex set of propositions: Basic, concrete skills are more important than esoteric, abstract perspectives on knowledge. Hard-core learning, usable in many contexts, is preferable to fragmented-by-situation education. The "Old Math" is better than "New Math." Reading is more important than other symbol-usage, etc.

These and similar terminologies involve much more than mere metaphors, of course; they represent full-fledged *systems of thought.* They are shorthand terms for complete philosophies or orientations. Inherently, they provide ways of looking at problems, methods of seeking solutions—and the *language* for speaking about both. Each time you address a controversial topic, one wherein you take a position and urge others to think about and possibly adopt it, consciously or subconsciously you select a vocabulary which reflects a certain ideological framework. How many times, for instance, have you heard or uttered these or similar phrases:

The feminist perspective on . . .

The humane thing to do is . . .

If you want to play hard ball . . .

For my money . . .

If you're hung up [psychologically frustrated] on . . .

The beauty of it all is . . .

All of these expressions contain implicit but nonetheless potent value orientations; all of them express ideologies. As a student of communication, learn to monitor carefully your own word choices and the word choices of others. Try to become increasingly aware of unstated value systems. Examine proposals and claims in the light of implicit and explicit ideologies.

Language, as we have emphasized throughout this chapter, must be an all-pervasive concern of the effective oral communicator. Some two hundred years ago, the French critic Count Buffon observed: "The style is the man himself." *Your* language "style," certainly, reveals much about you, your concern for accurate and coherent meaning, your feelings about the feelings and attitudes of your listeners, and the hopes that you have for your messages. As you prepare your speeches, therefore, think through those linguistic choices carefully. Language is not only one of the most prevalent modes of public communication; often it can also be one of the most potent.

Reference Notes

[1]Quoted in J. R. Pelsma, *Essentials of Style* (New York: Crowell, Collier and Macmillan, Inc., 1924), p. 193.

[2]From *Public Papers of the Presidents of the United States: John F. Kennedy.* Washington, D.C.: U.S. Government Printing Office, 1961.

[3]From "The Moral Un-Neutrality of Science," *Representative American Speeches, 1960–1961,* ed. Lester Thonssen (New York: The H. W. Wilson Company, 1961), p. 53.

[4]Reprinted with the permission of Farrar, Straus & Giroux, Inc., and International Creative Management, from *The Kandy-Kolored Tangerine-Flake Streamline Baby* by Tom Wolfe, Copyright © 1963, 1964, 1965 by Thomas K. Wolfe, Jr., Copyright © 1963, 1964, 1965 by New York Herald Tribune, Inc.

[5]Charles Lamb, "A Dissertation Upon Roast Pig." *The Complete Works and Letters of Charles Lamb* (New York: Modern Library, Inc., 1935), pp. 110–111.

[6]From *The Immense Journey* by Loren Eiseley. Copyright © 1957 by Loren Eiseley. Reprinted by permission of Random House, Inc.

[7]Reprinted with permission of Macmillan Publishing Co., Inc., and Turnstone Press Ltd. from *Jonathan Livingston Seagull* by Richard Bach. Copyright © 1970 by Richard D. Bach.

[8]H. G. Wells, "The Time Machine," *The Complete Short Stories of H. G. Wells* (London: Ernest Benn Limited, 1927), p. 59.

[9]Reprinted with the permission of Farrar, Straus & Giroux, Inc., and International Creative Management, from *The Kandy-Kolored Tangerine-Flake Streamline Baby* by Tom Wolfe, Copyright © 1963, 1964, 1965 by Thomas K. Wolfe, Jr., Copyright © 1963, 1964, 1965 by New York Herald Tribune, Inc.

Problems and Probes

1.   Make a list of ten neutral words or expressions. Then for each word in this list find *(a)* an attitudinally weighted synonym which would cause listeners to react favorably toward the object or idea mentioned, and *(b)* an evaluative synonym which would cause them to react unfavorably toward the same object or idea. (Example: *neutral word*—"old"; *complimentary synonym*—"mellow"; *uncomplimentary synonym*—"senile.")

2.   What connective phrase might you use to join *(a)* a major idea with a subordinate one, *(b)* a less important idea with a more important one, *(c)* two ideas of equal importance, *(d)* ideas comparable in meaning, and *(e)* ideas that stand in contrast or opposition?

3.   Using varied and vivid imagery, prepare a written description of one of the following:
Sailboats on a lake at sunset
Goldfish swimming about in a bowl
Traffic at a busy intersection
Sitting in the bleachers at a football game in 15° weather
The hors d'oeuvre table at an expensive restaurant
The city dump
A symphony concert

4.   Read at least one speech by two or three well-known public speakers (Edmund Burke, Daniel Webster, Abraham Lincoln, Martin Luther King, Jr., etc.). Compare the wording in these speeches, giving special attention to *(a)* accuracy of word choice, *(b)* simplicity, *(c)* appropriateness, *(d)* imagery, and *(e)* use of evaluative language.

5.   Study the following groups of words and decide whether the individual words or phrases are *(a)* appropriate for any speech situation, *(b)* appropriate

for informal speech situations, *(c)* appropriate for formal situations. Be prepared to defend your decisions regarding these terms:

    hoggish, greedy, gluttonous

    drunk, intoxicated, soused, inebriated, tight, blotto, pie-eyed

    falsehood, whopper, lie, fib, misrepresentation, untruth

    crabby, ill-tempered, cross, quarrelsome, grouchy

    savory, appetizing, delicious, tasty, scrumptious

    laughable, funny, amusing, ludicrous, hilarious, killing

    a capricious elderly man, a queer old duck, a nutty old character, an eccentric old man, a strange old fellow, a crazy old geezer

 ## Oral Activities and Speaking Assignments

1.   Describe orally, in class, a personal experience or an event you have recently witnessed—for example, a traffic accident, the crucial moment in a basketball game, a memorable meal, big city noises. Employ vivid imagery in an effort to stimulate your listeners to relive this experience or event with you.

2.   Write a four- to six-minute speech to be presented from manuscript. Revise the manuscript several times to be sure that *(a)* the words and expressions you choose are accurate, simple, and appropriate; *(b)* wherever possible, you have employed live and vivid imagery; *(c)* you have used attitudinally weighted words skillfully, but ethically; and *(d)* your connective phrases are clear and graceful.

 ## Suggestions for Further Reading

Kenneth Boulding, "Introduction to 'The Image,'" *Dimensions in Communication: Readings,* ed. James H. Campbell and Hal W. Hepler (Belmont, Calif.: Wadsworth Publishing Company, Inc., 1970), pp. 26–35.

Abne M. Eisenberg, *Living Communication* (Englewood Cliffs, N.J.: Prentice-Hall Inc., 1975), pp. 149–180.

Saundra Hybels and Richard Weaver, II, *Speech Communication* (New York: D. Van Nostrand Co., 1974), pp. 113–138.

Wendell Johnson and Dorothy Moeller, *Living With Change: The Semantics of Coping* (New York: Harper & Row, Publishers, 1972).

Dan P. Millar and Frank E. Millar, *Messages and Myths; Understanding Interpersonal Communication* (Port Washington, N.Y.: Alfred Publishing Co., Inc., 1976), esp. Chapter 6.

Bardin H. Nelson, "Seven Principles of Image Formation," *Dimensions of Communication,* ed. Lee Richardson (New York: Appleton-Century-Crofts, 1969), pp. 53–60.

Using the Body to Communicate

In a story that has come down through the centuries, the Greek orator Demosthenes, when asked for the most important ingredient of effective public speaking, replied, "Delivery." When asked for the second and third most important ingredients, his answer remained the same. *Delivery,* as we have been using the term in this textbook, refers to the manner in which a speaker presents a message to others, including the use of the voice and of gestural actions.

In the nineteenth century, great attention was devoted to delivery skills. The minutest adjustments of gesture, body, and voice were thought to communicate subtle shifts of meaning and feeling. Elaborate systems were developed for coordinating meaning- and feeling-states with physical and vocal shifts, and the "refinements" of delivery behaviors came to constitute a kind of rule-governed, universal language or code. Students of public speaking spent many hours working with instructors or before mirrors, trying to perfect the tiniest movements of the hands or body. Because of these and other extremes to which the study of "delivery" went, *elocution* — as it then was called — fell into a period of neglect and disgrace at the beginning of this century.

Within the last thirty years or so, however, we have witnessed a renewed interest in the subject among scholars, teachers, and students of oral communication. Once we discarded the innumerable "rules" for delivery which the elocutionists followed and began to explore anew the kinds of meanings and feelings which are communicated *nonverbally,* we found that the nineteenth-century teachers were on the right track. They merely had jumped too quickly to the setting forth of innumerable *do's* and *don't's.* In this chapter, therefore, you will not find a list of predetermined rules or directions. Rather, you will find discussions of those aspects of your physical behavior which affect the reception of your message by an audience. You also will find some help in deciding how to handle yourself in the speaking situation.

Delivery and Nonverbal Message Systems

If it is true (as we suggested in Chapter 13) that your *words* communicate your thoughts or ideas, it is equally true that your *non-words* often communicate your feelings and attitudes. In support of this view, sociologist Erving J. Goffman says that your words "give," but your body "gives off"—that is, reflects most accurately your *feelings* toward yourself, your message, your audience, and your situation.[1] Extending and reinforcing this notion of the verbal/nonverbal duality of delivery is communications scholar Dale G. Leathers, who notes: "Feelings and emotions are more accurately exchanged by nonverbal than verbal means. . . . The nonverbal portion of communication conveys meanings and intentions that are relatively free of deception, distortion, and confusion."[2] In view of such statements, it seems sensible to conclude that delivery represents a system of communicative cues, a kind of "language" every bit as important to communication as are words. Let us, therefore, look at some of the *nonverbal message systems* which make up and facilitate delivery, especially the four primary ones: proxemics, facial expression, arm-and-hand gestures, and bodily movement.*

Proxemics

One of the most important but perhaps least recognized of the message systems which make up delivery is proxemics, or the use of space by human beings. Effective delivery calls for an awareness of two of its components:

1. *Physical space*—the "geographical" arrangement of a communication area or room, including the boundaries or walls which surround it and the objects, barriers, etc., within it.
2. *Distance*—the extent or degree of separation between persons communicating with one another within the physical space.[3]

Each of these components of proxemics has a bearing on how you communicate publicly. Most public speaking situations include an audience seated or standing at a distance from a podium, table, or raised platform, with a speaker facing the audience. Objects in the physical space—the podium, table, platform—tend to set the speaker apart from

---

*The nonverbal message systems of touch *(haptics)*, smell *(aromatics)*, and costume or mode of dress *(fashion)*, even though they may significantly affect some communication transactions, seem to us more pertinent to interpersonal than to public communication—the principal concern of this book.

the audience. This "setting apart," we must remember, is *both physical and psychological.* Physically and psychologically, the objects stand in the way of open and free communicative exchange. This particularly is the case in public speaking, where one of the persons (the speaker) is doing most, if not all, of the talking. The speaker who wishes to avoid such barriers can of course move from behind the podium or change positions on the platform. However, the limitations of the proxemic message-delivery system cannot be completely overcome because, even though the speaker has changed the spatial relationship, there remains both a physical and psychological *distance* between speaker and listeners. As a public communicator, usually you should try to get as close to your listeners as possible; but because of what Edward T. Hall calls the individual's "personal space bubble,"[4] you should never get inside what they regard as their own personal field or territory.

Figure 1./ CLASSIFICATION OF INTER-HUMAN DISTANCE

INTIMATE DISTANCE
(up to 1½ feet)

PERSONAL DISTANCE
(1½ to 4 feet)

SOCIAL DISTANCE
(4 to 12 feet)

PUBLIC DISTANCE
(12 feet or more)

Hall has provided much information on the distance component of proxemic message systems and its effect on communicative behaviors. Specifically, he has divided inter-human distances into four segments: *intimate distance* — up to 1½ feet apart; *personal distance* — 1½ to 4 feet; *social distance* — 4 to 12 feet; and *public distance* — 12 feet or more. On the basis of these distinctions he has carefully noted how people's eye contact, tone of voice, and ability to touch and observe, change from one distance to another.[5]

For our purposes, the most important of Hall's findings are those having to do with the characteristics of *public distance* — particularly as it affects communicating over an expanse of 25 feet or more. To communicate with people that far away, you obviously cannot rely upon your normal speaking voice, minute changes in posture or muscle tone, etc. Instead, you must *compensate* for the distance by relying more heavily upon relatively large gestures, gross shifts from place to place, and increased vocal energy. Perhaps this urgent necessity to communicate *more in the large,* with bigger-than-usual movements, is one of the things which makes public speaking such a strange experience to some. Once understood and knowledgeably applied, however, the proxemics of nonverbal message systems can greatly enhance your delivery.

Facial Expression

Your face is another important nonverbal message-delivery system. On the one hand, working largely independently of words, your face can communicate messages of its own. That is, it can express such emotions as surprise, fear, excitement, and anger. Also, your face can communicate messages *about* your messages — clues that tell your listeners how they are to *interpret* what you are saying.[6]

More specifically, for you as a public speaker, facial expressions function as message-delivery systems in three useful ways. First, they communicate much about yourself or your own feelings. What Paul Ekman and Wallace V. Friesen call *affect displays* are given to an audience via your face.[7] That is, an audience "reads" your face to see how you *feel.* Second, facial details provide connotative cues to *interpretation* — answers to such questions as: Are you being ironic or satirical? How angry are you? Are you sure about some conclusion you have stated, or haven't you really put yourself on the line with the assertion? Do you like this audience, or are you afraid of it? As a nonverbal message-delivery system, your face provides audiences with partial answers to these questions of interpretation. And, third, the "display" elements of your face — your eyes especially — establish a *visual bonding* between you and your listeners. The speaker who looks down at the podium instead of at listeners, who reads excessively from notes or manuscript, or who delivers a speech to the back wall has severed visual bonding — that ever important eye-to-eye contact which our culture has come to expect if a speaker is to be deemed "earnest," "sincere," "forthright,"

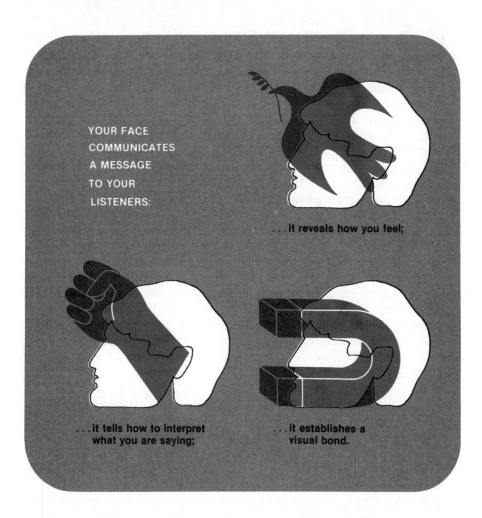

YOUR FACE
COMMUNICATES
A MESSAGE
TO YOUR
LISTENERS:

. . . it reveals how you feel;

. . . it tells how to interpret
what you are saying;

. . . it establishes a
visual bond.

"self-assured," etc.[8] In the familiar adage "The eyes have it," there is more than a modicum of cultural truth.

Of course, you cannot control your face completely—which is probably why people search it so carefully for both "meaning" and "feelings"—but you can attempt to make sure that your facial messages do not belie your verbal messages. In practical terms this means that when you are uttering angry words, your facial message-delivery system will also be communicating anger; when you are uttering key assertions or points that members of your audience may consider controversial or at odds with their belief-attitude-value systems, your eyes will be seeking out theirs for feedback indicating disagreement, rejection, or contempt.

Gesture

Gestural communication involves *purposeful movements* of the head, shoulders, arms, hands, or some other part of the body (as distinguished from movements of the *whole* body). Fidgeting with your jacket buttons or aimlessly rearranging notecards on the podium are not gestures because they are *not* purposeful, and they detract from rather than support or illustrate the ideas you are expressing. The public speaker commonly employs three kinds of gestures:

1. *Conventional gestures*—signs or symbols which have specific meanings assigned to them by convention or custom. The raised-hand "stop" gesture of the policeman directing traffic, the hand-and-finger language of deaf-mutes, the arm signals of football referees are examples of conventional gestures.
2. *Descriptive gestures*—signs or symbols which depict or describe more or less directly the idea to be communicated. Speakers, for example, often describe the size, shape, or location of an object by movements of hands and arms. They may extend an upraised arm to indicate the height of a stranger. They may make hand-and-finger

motions to help describe what a punch press looks like and to demonstrate the successive steps in its manipulation.

3. *Affective gestures* — movements of the hands and arms, often in combination with the rest of the body, which represent feeling-states or emotions. Thus, speakers may throw up their arms when disgusted, pound the podium when angry, or point a threatening finger when issuing a warning. In using affective gestures, speakers are in a sense trying to transmit, even "transplant," their own feelings and emotional states to their listeners.[9]

As should be obvious from the foregoing, gestural communication functions in three important ways for the speaker: (1) *Pictorialization.* Gestures can be used to "draw pictures" for your audience, especially to indicate sizes, shapes, and relationships between, as well as the motions of, objects. Such pictures, of course, depend primarily upon what we have called descriptive gestures. (2) *Condensation.* Gestures, particularly conventional gestures, may take the place of words in many instances. They may function as shorthand terms for things it would take many words to describe fully. (3) *Affect display.* And, finally, gestures often work in concert with facial expressions to communicate your state of mind to the audience. Affective gestures are especially important in this regard because an audience usually scans not only your face but also the rest of your body for cues concerning how your message is to be interpreted.

Bodily Movements and Stance

How you move and stand provides still other important message-delivery systems. Basically, these are of two kinds:

1. *Bodily movements* — the shifts which you make from one spot to another during the delivery of a speech.
2. *Postural adjustments* — the relative relaxation or rigidity of the body, as well as your overall posture or stance (erect, slightly bent forward or backward, or full-scale slumping).

Here again, we are concerned with *purposive movement,* and not nervous hobbyhorsing from one foot to another, the foot shufflings that betray excessive tension, or the twistings of the trunk that untrained speakers often use to burn up extra energy.

Purposive bodily movements can, in a very real sense, communicate propositions about yourself to an audience. The speaker who stands stiffly and erectly may, without uttering a word, be saying either *(a)* "This is a formal occasion" or *(b)* "I am tense, even afraid, of this audience." The speaker who leans forward, physically reaching out to the audience, is saying silently but eloquently: "I am interested in you. I want you to understand and accept my ideas." A head cocked to the right or left, drawn slightly back and with an appropriate facial expression, communicates incredulity. Sitting casually on the front edge of a table and assuming a relaxed posture communicates informality and a readiness to engage in a dialogue with the listeners.

Bodily movements and postural adjustments function also to *regulate communication.* As a public speaker you may, for instance, move from one end of a table to the other to indicate a change in topic; or you may accomplish the same purpose simply by changing your posture. At other times, you may move toward your audience when making an especially important point. In each case, you are using your body to signal to your audience that you are making or are about to make a change or transition in the subject matter of your speech, or are dealing with a matter of special concern.

Posture and bodily movement, therefore, are far more than matters of "standing straight," "looking your audience in the eye," and "avoiding random movements" of your body in order to "look poised on the platform." They are important aspects of *communication,* matters that provide you with one of your most potent message-delivery systems for "telling" an audience what your ideas are and how they ought to be taken or interpreted.

Choosing Among the Available Techniques of Nonverbal Communication

Obviously, as a speaker you cannot completely control *everything* that you "say" with your body. The place you will stand when facing your audience often is largely dictated by the physical arrangement of the room. Some of your facial expressions, your hand-and-arm gestures, your bodily movements, and even your posture may be so ingrained — so habituated — by previous experience and social conditioning that they are to a greater or lesser extent out of your control.

Equally obvious, however, should be the fact that you *can* control many aspects of your "body language." While you should never pre-plan your gestures and other movements, you can gain skill in orchestrating them and can develop a sensitivity to the messages you are communicating verbally. In short, you can consciously make *some* decisions about how you will use your body to communicate.

Start with Your Self

In making decisions about how you will communicate nonverbally, begin by studying your *self.* Know what kind of person you are — whether, for example, you are basically quiet and reticent or excitable and extroverted; whether you are prone to vigorous physical activity or like to "take things easy and relax"; whether you talk easily and well on your feet or prefer to sit while communicating. In short, you must decide who you are, what you are, and what works best for you. Consciously copying another person's mannerisms and behaviors will work for you only if you really are like that person.

Whatever your overall behavioral pattern, however, work on your own mind and motivation, "psyching yourself up" for the moment of public communication. Find ways of stimulating yourself — for if you do not, an audience will notice and judge you as apathetic, indifferent, or listless. Some speakers prepare by convincing themselves that public speaking is a challenge to be met and surmounted. Others remind themselves how important their ideas are, telling themselves that those ideas are worth more than any amount of personal fear or insecurity they may experience. Choose the mode of self-motivation that is best for *you.* And remember that we all need to psyche ourselves up even if we make our living speaking day after day. As you do this, however, avoid excessive bodily tension. *Find some means of relaxing yourself to the extent that you are able to function as a physically free and mobile human being.* Bodily freedom and facial relaxation will help ensure that your non-verbal messages, while vigorous and animated, are consonant with your verbal ones.

Adjust Proxemic Relationships

Insofar as possible, arrange the physical setting to make it comfortable for you and your listeners. If you feel more at home behind a podium, plan to have it placed accordingly. If you want your whole body to be visible to the audience, yet feel the need to have notes at eye level, stand beside the podium and arrange your notecards upon it. If you want to relax your body (and are sure you can compensate for the resulting loss of bodily action by increasing your vocal volume) sit behind a table or desk. If you feel free physically and want to be wholly "open" to your audience, stand in front of a table or desk. Consider all the possibilities. Then *plan a proxemic relationship with your audience which reflects your own needs and attitudes toward your subject and your listeners.*

A second proxemic consideration has to do with the amount of distance between you and the persons you are addressing. As a general rule, *the farther you are from an audience, the more of your physical being you should expose to it.* The speaker who crouches behind a podium in an auditorium of three hundred people soon loses contact with them. The farther away your audience is, the harder you must work to project your words, and the broader your physical movements must be. Review in your own mind large lecture classes you have attended, sermons you have heard in large churches, or political rallies you have attended. Recall the behaviors of speakers who worked effectively in such situations, choosing and adapting those that might also work for you.

Third, insofar as practical, *adapt the physical setting to your communicative needs and desires.* If you are going to use such visual aids as a chalkboard, flipchart, working model, or process diagram, remove the tables, chairs, and other objects which cut off the listeners' view and therefore impair their understanding of your message.

Adapt Your Delivery to the Situation

Adapting your delivery to the needs of the speaking situation involves a series of interlocking decisions on your part. You must think through not only your own capabilities and the limitations of the physical setting, but also *(a)* the nature of your topic and purpose, *(b)* the kinds of feelings you are interested in communicating to the audience, and *(c)* the audience's expectations of you and your message. Let us begin by considering the audience — its needs and its size.

Adapt the size of your gestures and the amount of your bodily movement to the size of the audience. Keeping in mind what Edward Hall noted about *public distance* in communication, you should realize that subtle changes of facial expression or small movements of the fingers cannot be communicated clearly when you are twenty-five or thirty feet away from your listeners. Although a great many of the auditoriums in this country have a raised platform and a slanted floor to allow a speaker to be seen more clearly, you should, nevertheless, adjust by making your body movements and gestures larger.

Second, in order to assess your listeners' responses to your message and to discern whether you are fulfilling their expectations, *continuously scan your audience from side to side and from front to back, looking specific individuals directly in the eyes.* This does not mean, of course, that your own head is to be in a constant state of motion; "continuously" does not imply rhythmical, non-stop bobbing. Rather, it implies that you must be aware — and must let an audience know you are aware — of the entire group of human beings in front of you. Take them all into your field of vision periodically; establish firm visual bonds with most of them occasionally. Such bonding does two things for you: *(a)* It keeps you and your message audience-centered; that is, it does something beneficial for *you* psychologically. And *(b)* it keeps an audience looking back at you. Remind yourself of what it is like to be in an audience where a speaker does not look at you: You are tempted to look away, to let your attention wander. If the speaker looks directly at you occasionally, however, you return the look, if for no other reason than to avoid embarrassment. The visual bonding that results from close eye contact is good for both you and for your listeners and facilitates the communicative transaction.

Third, *use your body to communicate your feelings about what you are saying.* When you are angry, do not be afraid to gesture vigorously. When you are expressing tenderness, let that message come across your face. In other words, when you are communicating publicly, employ the same affective responses you do when you are talking to another individual on a one-to-one basis.

Physical Actions . . .

especially when they are definite, definitive, and purposive . . . may "speak" at least as loudly as words. Often, in fact, they are referred to as "body language" and may communicate meaning independently of spoken language. Much more often, probably, the speaker uses physical movements of the body to reinforce, extend, sustain, and enhance the utterance of public messages.

Gestures . . .

particularly those of the face, fingers, hands, and arms . . . are among the speaker's most useful communicative tools, for they facilitate the projection of ideas and feelings. Serving as signs or symbols, they communicate both conventional and descriptive meanings, as well as the ongoing feelings and emotional states of the user, and potentially are the most powerful of the nonverbal message-delivery systems.

Fourth, *use your body to regulate the pace of your presentation and to control transitions.* Many speakers change positions or shift their bodies as they move from the introductions of speeches to their main points. They increase the amount of nonverbal movement when they speak more rapidly; they tend to decrease their bodily and gestural action when they are verbally slowing down to emphasize particular ideas. Because arbitrarily pre-planning all such movements never works, we do not recommend it; but we do urge you to give careful thought to pacing and regulating by nonverbal means those portions of your speech that could well benefit from such considerations.

Finally, *use your full repertoire of descriptive and conventional gestures while talking publicly.* You probably do this in everyday conversation without even thinking about it; so recreate that same set of mind when addressing an audience. Here, physical readiness is the key concern. Keep your hands and arms free and loose enough so that you can call them easily, quickly, and *naturally* into action when you need them. Let them hang comfortably at your sides, relaxed, but in readiness. Occasionally, rest them on the lectern. Then, as you unfold the ideas of your speech, use descriptive gestures to indicate size, shape, or relationship, making sure the gestures are large enough to be seen in the back row. Use conventional gestures also to give visual dimension to your spoken ideas. Keep in mind, of course, that there are no "right" *types* of gestures, just as there are no "right" *number* of gestures that you ought to use. As you prepare your speech, and especially as you practice it orally, however, think carefully through your purpose, your topic, and your plan of development — all the while thinking of the kinds of bodily and gestural actions that would most appropriately and effectively contribute to your delivery of it.

Although much more could be said about using your body to communicate, and more advice obviously could be generated, we have tried to provide at least a basis on which you can build. What happens from here on is up to you. You must engage in careful, systematic self-analysis and study, examining your own and other speakers' use of nonverbal communication systems as means for transmitting messages to an audience. Capture a vision of your communicative behaviors as *others* see them, utilizing videotapes, diagnoses from instructors, and feedback from friends. Armed with this enlarged understanding of your speaking behavior, you will be better prepared to form necessary personal decisions on ways to make your body work better for you. Above all, *keep at it.* It takes much practice to ensure that your visual and verbal messages are congruent, and that you are using your total *self* with maximum effectiveness to transmit messages in situations where words alone may fail. One of the principal strengths of oral communication is that a living, breathing, and active human being encases the intellectual and emotional message being transmitted to other living, reacting human beings. Use that strength well.

Reference Notes

[1]Erving Goffman, *The Presentation of Self in Everyday Life* (New York: Doubleday & Company, Inc., 1959), pp. 2–4.

[2]Dale G. Leathers, *Nonverbal Communication Systems* (Boston, Mass.: Allyn & Bacon, Inc., 1976), pp. 4–5.

[3]For a fuller discussion of each of these components, see Leathers, pp. 52–59.

[4]Edward T. Hall, *The Hidden Dimension* (New York: Doubleday & Company, Inc., 1969), pp. 119–120.

[5]Hall introduces these discussions of distance in his *The Hidden Dimension* (New York: Doubleday & Company, Inc., 1969), Chapter X, "Distances in Man."

[6]An excellent review of research on facial communication can be found in Leathers, Chapter 2. Those wishing a larger treatment should see Paul Ekman, Wallace V. Friesen, and P. Ellsworth, *Emotion in the Human Face: Guidelines for Research and an Integration of Findings* (New York: Pergamon Press, Inc., 1972).

[7]Paul Ekman and Wallace V. Friesen, "The Repertoire of Nonverbal Behavior—Categories, Usage and Coding," *Semiotica* 1 (1969): 49–98.

[8]For a difficult but rewarding essay on the management of demeanor, see Erving Goffman, *Interaction Ritual; Essays on Face-to-Face Behavior* (New York: Doubleday & Company, Inc., 1967), "On Face-Work," pp. 5–46.

[9]For a useful system for classifying gestures, see "Hand Movements" by Paul Ekman and Wallace V. Friesen, *Journal of Communication* 22 (December 1972): 360.

Problems and Probes

1.   It has been estimated that words account for 7 percent, vocal elements 38 percent, and facial expression 55 percent of the emotional impact of an oral message. Defend or attack that assertion on the basis of your own experience with communication. In what speech communication situations—interpersonal, public, mass-media—would you expect these percentages to be largely valid? In what situations would you question them? Further, how might the percentages have to be adjusted when discussing descriptive information rather than matters of emotional impact? Why?

2.   Listen to some speaker on the campus or in your community, and write a brief report on your observations regarding his or her platform behaviors. Before you attend, make a short outline of the suggestions and warnings contained in this chapter, and use it as a checklist against which to compare the speaker's physical behavior. Your commentary on both strong and weak qualities in the speaker's physical contact with the audience can be centered on two important questions: *(a)* Did the speaker's use of proxemics, facial details, gesture, posture, and bodily movement reinforce or detract from the emotional impact of his or her verbal message? *(b)* Did the speaker's use of those aspects of delivery reinforce or detract from your comprehension of the message? Observe particularly patterns of emphasis, body tension, gestures which depicted qualities or shape, and—in general—movement which seemed to draw in or repel an audience.

3.   "Body language" is a term often used to describe much of what is considered in this chapter. Drawing upon the "Suggestions for Further Reading" (page 238), enlarge your understanding of this subject, and prepare a short report upon some aspect of nonverbal message systems for your instructor, your journal, or your class.

4.   As a class, take the Facial Meaning Sensitivity Test reprinted on pages 26–32 in Dale Leather's book, *Nonverbal Communication Systems* (see "Suggestions for Further Reading"). What do the results of that test tell you

about the validity of generalizations concerning our culture's ability to "read" facial expressions?

Oral Activities and Speaking Assignments

1.   Using descriptive, conventional, and affective gestures, try to communicate to the other members of your class the following ideas silently—by means of physical actions alone:
a.   "Get out of here!"
b.   "Why, Thomas (or Mary)! I haven't seen you in ages!"
c.   "I'd like to get to know you better."
d.   "Come on! Give her a chance to explain."
e.   "Every penny I had is gone."
f.   "Let's get out of here."
g.   "If we're going to get what we want, we'll have to fight for it."

2.   Divide the class into teams and play "charades." (Those needing rules for classroom games should read David Zauner, "Charades as a Teaching Device," *Speech Teacher* 20 [November 1971]: 302.) A game of charades not only will loosen you up physically, but also should help sensitize you to the variety of small but perceptible cues—both descriptive and conventional gestures—you "read" when interpreting messages.

3.   Make a two- or three-minute speech explaining to the class how to do something: driving a golf ball, bowling, performing a sleight-of-hand trick, cutting out a shirt, tieing some difficult knots, or playing a musical instrument. Use movement and gestures to help make your ideas clear. Do not use the chalkboard or previously prepared diagrams.

4.   Prepare and present a short speech describing some exciting event you have witnessed—an automobile accident, a political or campus rally, a sporting event. Use movement and gestures to render the details clear and vivid. That is, the audience should be able to "see" and "feel" the event as you seek to integrate words/ideas and movements/actions for maximum impact. Successful completion of this assignment should demonstrate to you your ability to employ all of the available message systems.

Suggestions for Further Reading

Paul Ekman, W. V. Friesen, and P. Ellsworth, *Emotion in the Human Face: Guidelines for Research and an Integration of Findings* (New York: Pergamon Press, Inc., 1972).
Edward T. Hall, *The Hidden Dimension* (New York: Doubleday & Company, Inc., 1969).
Randall P. Harrison, *Beyond Words: An Introduction to Nonverbal Communication* (Englewood Cliffs, N.J.: Prentice-Hall, Inc., 1974).
Mark L. Knapp, *Nonverbal Communication in Human Interaction* (New York: Holt, Rinehart & Winston, Inc., 1972).
Dale G. Leathers, *Nonverbal Communication Systems* (Boston: Allyn & Bacon, Inc., 1976).
Albert Mehrabian, *Nonverbal Communication* (Chicago: Aldine-Atherton, Inc., 1972).
Rhetorica Ad Herennium, III. 26–27, "Physical Movement."

15

Using the Voice
to Communicate

Reflect for a moment, and you will realize that you have more than one way of speaking. You speak one way to your parents, another to your dear old Aunt Matilda, another to your college instructors, and still another to the person you encounter by chance in a local cafe. You talk one way when despondent, another when overjoyed, another when reticent, and still another when confidently assertive. Add to these possibilities all of the potential *combinations* of your vocal characteristics, and you will find that you have more ways of communicating orally— more *vocal styles*—than you could ever hope to catalog. One of your tasks as a public communicator, therefore, is to select from this large repertoire of oral communication styles those most consistent with your habitual modes of expressing yourself and which, at the same time, best fit the demands of the particular situation in which you will be speaking publicly.

"Using the voice," as we view it in this chapter, is a complex *physiological-psychological process*. On the one hand, vocal communication—as Figure 1 suggests—involves a speaker's producing a stream of sounds which is taken in aurally by a listener. Persons interested in the *physiological* aspects of oral communication often concern themselves with the actual production of these sounds and with their intelligibility or understandability. They, therefore, ask such questions as:

NOTE: Users of previous editions of this textbook will find intact the customary and more fully developed considerations of the voice-producing and articulatory mechanisms, the basic vocal characteristics, and a wealth of oral practice materials in Appendix B, "Making Your Speaking Voice More Effective," pages 409–431.

1. Does the speaker or hearer have physiological problems in produc-
    ing and receiving speech sounds?
2. Are the speaker's vocal cues loud enough to be heard?
3. Is the communicator speaking too loudly or too softly?
4. Are there enough pauses or "breaks" in the stream of sound to
    maximize comprehension by the hearer?
5. Is the speaker articulating sharply enough to allow for discrimina-
    tion between similar words (for instance, "hair" and "heir," "slob-
    ber" and "slaughter")?
6. Does the speaker's vocal variety—emphasis and stress pattern,
    changes in pitch and duration—aid auditors' comprehension?

For the most part, answers to these questions involve measurement and
interpretation of the physiological production and reception of sound.
As such, they are the concerns of *speech scientists*—audiologists,
speech pathologists, voice therapists, etc. They are also highly important concerns of the student of speech communication who desires to
understand the workings of the speech mechanism in order to make it
more flexible and effective through exercise and practice.

On the other hand, vocal communication and the voice have important *psychological* dimensions which cannot be ignored. In recent
years, researchers have concentrated their study on the *effects* which
various vocal characteristics have upon listeners in a variety of situations. Through their research they are finding that to a significant extent
listeners judge a speaker's *background* (age, sex, race, education, geographical origin, etc.), *personality, emotional state, stock of information,* and *degree of authority* on how they perceive his or her vocal delivery.[1] Persons interested in the *psychological* aspects of oral communication are interested in answering such questions as:

1. In what ways do such vocal cues as loudness, stress patterns, pitch
    variation, tempo, and the like affect an audience's judgment of a
    speaker's background, personality, emotional state, etc.?
2. How do members of this culture *expect* a doctor, a professor, a
    mechanic, a president, etc., to "sound"? That is, what kind of and
    how much "vocal stereotyping" is likely to be at work in a given
    communication transaction?
3. To what degree do regional or ethnic dialects control an audience's
    perception of expertness and authority?

Answers to such questions involve an exploration, not so much into the
ways in which vocal sounds are produced and absorbed, but rather of
the impact or effects they are likely to have upon receivers' perceptions
and judgments. Those who seek answers to such questions are often
termed "paralinguists." A *paralinguist,* to be more specific, is a person
interested in the way in which *vocal sounds* interact with *words* to produce *meaning.*

Because in this chapter we wish you to understand how vocal communication "works" as one of the modes of oral transmission of meaning, we shall be writing — for the most part — from the perspective of the paralinguists. As a result, we shall touch upon the physiological aspects of the human voice *only* to define a few terms. Those interested in making their voice a more flexible instrument of communication will find material and exercises for that purpose in Appendix B, "Making Your Speaking Voice More Effective," pages 409–431. In the main, we will focus here upon the four major psychological aspects of paralinguistic communication systems — *intelligibility, variety, rhythm,* and *quality* — and some of the resultant problems and decisions you must face.*

VOCAL CHARACTERISTICS

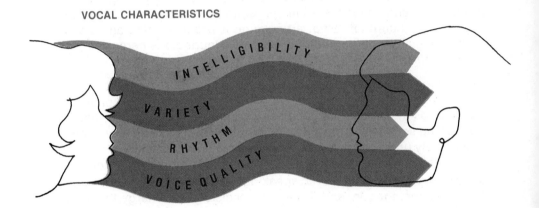

Paralanguage and Voice

Your voice is made up of a series of communication *sub-systems* which shape the stream of sound you emit in accordance with "rules" you learned as an infant. Even before you were one year old, you were taught by parents and siblings that some sounds could get you food and clothing, that others could give you attention and love. Later, you learned how to express your feelings of loneliness, anger, joy, and sorrow. As you matured, you learned more complex vocal patterns: how to "throw a fit," how to pause "dramatically" before stomping out of a room, how to insinuate a desire without actually expressing it, how to slow down to

---

*All attempts to classify or categorize the elements and aspects of vocal-sound production *paralinguistically* involve arbitrary decisions — decisions which vary according to the purposes of the persons conducting the research. For alternatives to the classification employed here, see: David Crystal, *Prosodic Systems and Intonation in English* (Cambridge: University Press, 1959); David Crystal and Derek Davy, *Investigating English Style* (Bloomington: Indiana University Press, 1969); Kenneth L. Pike, *The Intonation of American English* (Ann Arbor: University of Michigan Press, 1945); and Howard R. Martin and Kenneth L. Pike, "Analysis of the Vocal Performance of a Poem: A Classification of Intonational Features," *Language and Style* 7 (1974): 209–218.

make certain words emphatic, etc. You learned, in short, how to make yourself understood emotionally and intellectually. Conversely, of course, you learned — usually for the good, but sometimes for ill — how to interpret the vocal characteristics of others; often indirectly, you were taught to understand the voices of authority, stereotypical reactions to geographical and ethnic dialects, etc. Let us begin by considering the four important paralinguistic communication systems that we have already cited — the *vocal cues* your culture deems important in those judgmental processes.

Intelligibility. Perhaps, when you first think of voice or speech, you recall your parents' admonition to "speak clearly" or a deaf aunt's injunction to "speak up." Two of the crucial aspects of intelligibility are *articulation* and *loudness* — both physiological concerns. The social-psychological counterpart of articulation is *pronunciation* and *dialect,* and the social-psychological counterpart of loudness is *perceived loudness* or *volume.*

Articulation. Technically, articulation refers to the shaping, joining, or separating of sounds produced by the vocal mechanism. (See pages 243 and 410–411.) Good articulation has a great deal to do with the distinctness of the sounds you produce and is chiefly the job of the jaw, tongue, and lips. By using them with skill and energy you can segregate or individuate the sounds *(phonemes)* which comprise the verbal "letters" of a language. Especially in public speaking, you should use your articulators — the lips, tongue, and jaw — with precision and energy to cut and mold the phonemes or sounds because problems of intelligibility are magnified when you are addressing an audience at some distance from you. Poor articulation, then, in and of itself can create unintelligibility.

Pronunciation and Dialect. Beyond the physiological problems of poor articulation are the *psychological* problems involving pronunciation and dialect. First, if you fail to pronounce your words acceptably, your listeners may not quickly and easily grasp the meaning or significance of what you say. It was not for nothing that teachers in elementary and secondary schools drilled you on the use of diacritical or phonetic marks in dictionaries. In fact, many peculiarities of pronunciation are noticed by some listeners; and not only will they distract an audience's attention, but may also discredit your knowledge and authority.

Second, your intelligibility may be impaired by obtrusive *regional pronunciations* or *dialect.* A dialect, as you may know, is "a variety of language that is used by one group of persons and has features of vocabulary, grammar, and pronunciation distinguishing it from other varieties used by other groups."[2] Thus, your pronunciation of words, together with the ways in which you arrange them grammatically or syntactically, helps determine your dialect: an English or German "accent," a white Southern or black Northern dialect, a Detroit vernacular, a New England "twang," etc. Any given dialect has its own "rules" for

Figure 1./ THE PRODUCTION AND RECEPTION OF HUMAN SOUND.

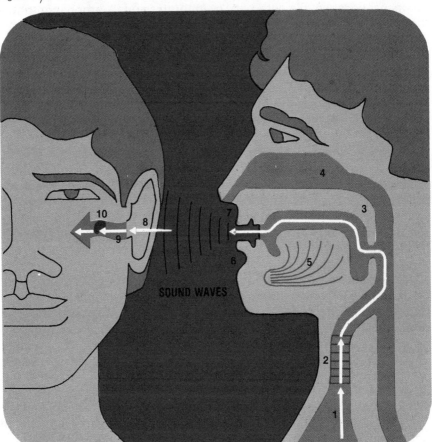

(1) A *stream of air* is sent from the lungs through the trachea to (2) the *vocal folds* ("voice box"), which in turn vibrate at various pitches, depending upon tension in the muscles. As the sound proceeds up the throat, it is shaped by (3) the *palate* and given resonance or additional tones by (4) the *nasal and sinus regions.* The sounds or phonemes which make up our language are formed primarily by (5) the *tongue,* (6) *jaw placement,* and (7) the *lips.* The formed sound, in "waves," travels through the air to an ear. It enters (8) the *outer ear* (concha), moves through (9) the *auditory canal* (external meatus), and strikes (10) the *tympanum* (eardrum). The eardrum "translates" the sound waves once more to physical vibrations, which, through the bones of the middle ear, send the vibrations via nerves to the brain.

pronunciation which, in turn, may be quite different from the "rules" of another dialect. Thus, when a Midwestern American ear tries to interpret the sounds emitted by a cockney English mouth, non-communicative confusion may result.

Unfortunately, dialects and regional pronunciations may produce not only misunderstandings between speakers and listeners, but often they may also produce *negative judgments* — judgments which may seriously affect some auditors' perceptions of the speaker's credibility, education, reliability, responsibility, and capabilities for leadership.[3] This happens because dialects and even professional jargon contribute heavily to what paralinguists call "vocal stereotypes."[4] For example, patients expect their doctors to "sound" like doctors, and even judge medical expertise on that basis.[5] Because such vocal stereotyping can affect human relationships and speech transactions, it is an important factor in public communication. It raises a problem and identifies an area in which you as a public speaker must make some personal decisions — a matter which we will consider in more detail later.

Loudness. "Loudness," as we use the term here, refers to the amount of energy or pressure a sound exerts on your eardrum. The amount of that pressure is affected by *(a)* the energy level of the sound produced by the speaker, *(b)* the distance the sound has to travel from speaker to listener, and *(c)* the amount of noise through which the sound must go. Thus, the farther away your listeners are, the louder you must talk to reach them; less obviously, the closer you are to an audience, the less the loudness required.

For a number of reasons too complicated for us to review here, your loudness level *as perceived by listeners* — the *psychological* dimension of volume — is affected by a number of factors: the heaviness of the air in the room, the pitch at which you are speaking, the fatigue your audience is feeling, periodic increases or decreases in loudness, etc. For example, if you have been speaking at a moderate loudness level of, say, 50–60 decibels and then move up 70 decibels on a particular sentence, that degree of change will not stand out greatly. However, if you have been speaking at a low level of, say, 30–40 decibels, an increase to 70 decibels would stand out markedly and would call attention to itself — and to the idea expressed in the sentence. (Note that we are using the term "decibel" only to suggest *comparative* loudness levels. Actually, it is a highly technical term used by acoustic experts and voice scientists to mean "a unit for expressing the relative intensity of sounds on a scale from zero for the average least perceptible sound to about 130 for the average pain level."[6] Thus, the decibel is usually considered to be the smallest degree of difference in sound detectable by the human ear.)

The psychological variable of perceived loudness is related also to human motivation. If a jackhammer is running outside your window at, say, 80 decibels, an audience *genuinely interested* in the subject matter of your speech will force itself to focus on your oral message even if you are speaking at a loudness of only 50 decibels. Obviously, your hearers will tire in time and may "drop out," but the fact remains that motivation can affect an audience's reception of variations in the loudness with which you speak.

And, finally, one of the most important psychological variables of perceived loudness is *contrast.* A "steady" voice — one maintaining the same loudness level (as well as the same pitch, same rate, etc.) throughout — usually causes an audience to "tune out." Hence, the degree of loudness with which you speak, whether it be 25 decibels or 85 decibels, is not nearly as important to your intelligibility as *variety* in your loudness. When perceptibly increased *or* decreased, loudness adds emphasis and therefore helps to make your message more intelligible.

Variety. Whereas variety in loudness is important in determining the intelligibility of your message, other aspects of variety—*pitch, extent or duration of sounds, rate,* and *pauses or intrusions*—are of great importance in controlling the degree of audience interest you are able to generate and sustain and the subtle shades of attitude and feeling you can communicate.

Pitch. Physically, pitch is a matter of vibrations or "waves" produced in air or other media by an energy source. The greater the number of vibrations produced in a given time, the *higher* the pitch; the fewer the number, the *lower* the pitch. As all stereo buffs know, the human ear can hear wide variations in pitch (measured in waves or cycles per second or *cps*), and those variations are important to the perception of sound by listeners.

As a public speaker you should concern yourself with three aspects of pitch: (1) *pitch level*—whether it is high or low or in between; (2) *pitch range*—nearly everyone, for example, can easily span an octave, and many people have voices flexible enough to vary more than two octaves without strain; and (3) *pitch variation*—how often you change the pitch level of your voice. Psychologically, all of these affect an audience's perception of your personality and emotional state. Characteristically, for instance, a low-pitched voice is associated with pleasantness, serenity, or sadness; a high-pitched voice is frequently associated with fear, surprise, or anger. A narrow pitch range tends to be monotonous and usually communicates boredom or a lack of involvement, whereas an extremely wide-ranging pitch indicates enthusiasm, excitement, or—sometimes—fear. Extreme variations, in which the pitch "slides" rapidly up and down the scale, create impressions of happiness, surprise, and activity.[7] These indicators are, of course, suggestive rather than arbitrary, but should at least be taken into account when you are trying to analyze the effect of your voice upon others. Developing pitch levels is a matter we will explore more fully in Appendix B. (See page 420.)

Duration. By duration we mean the extent or amount of time you devote to the production of particular sounds within the syllables you utter. But merely slowing down is not enough. How well you are understood depends also upon "quantity" or—as we have termed it—duration. Talking at a moderate rate *while prolonging the sounds uttered* improves intelligibility markedly.[8] If you spend very little time producing each sound, the overall effect is an enunciation that is "clipped," as in the dialogue in bad movies about stereotyped Germans, who usually speak in overly clipped English. If you spend a comparatively long time forming each sound, the result is an enunciation that is "drawled" or "rounded," as in equally bad movies about stereotyped hillbillies.

Duration of speech sounds is important psychologically because (1) almost every speaker has habitual patterns of duration which make up his or her regional or ethnic dialect, and (2) variations in syllable or sound duration indicate variations in mood or emotional state. For example, research has shown that a communicator who speeds up the speaking rate and decreases syllable duration is likely to be thought happy, surprised, or excited; a speaker who slows the rate and increases syllable duration is likely to be thought sad, disgusted, fearful, or bored.[9] In short, duration ought to *vary* with the thrust of your words: a "clipped" vocal delivery makes sense when you are communicating excited or angry thoughts, but it is hardly the voice of love.

Rate.   Another important means by which you can control audience interest through offering vocal variety is *rate*—the speed at which you speak. Most persons speak an average of 120 to 180 words per minute, but they do not maintain that rate uniformly. In normal speech, the speed of utterance corresponds to the thought-content of the message or the feeling of the speaker. The emotional character and intellectual weight of your subject matter affect variations in rate. Also, as a rule, your vocal rate should vary with the size of your audience and the nature of the surroundings. In a large auditorium, for instance, where sound reverberates, you should speak more slowly than in interpersonal exchanges where you are only three or four feet from your listener. In general, by maintaining variety in your vocal rate you aid your listeners' comprehension, communicate your feelings or emotional states more clearly, and give emphasis to ideas that deserve emphasis.

Pauses and Intrusions.   This aspect of vocal rate involves *(a)* the silences and *(b)* the extraneous vocal noises you build into your utterances. *Pauses* are intervals of silence between or within words, phrases, or sentences. *Intrusions,* sometimes called vocalized pauses, include the "uhs," "ums," "ahs," and similar meaningless noises with which we so often fill our speech. These vocalized intrusions obviously serve no useful purpose in sustained public discourse, for they transmit to an audience only a sense of the speaker's unsureness, hesitancy, possible lack of preparation or conviction, and fear—at least the fear of being literally "speech*less*."

Silent pauses, in contrast, may be either positive or negative in their effect, depending upon their frequency, duration, and placement within the flow of spoken sounds. Such pauses *punctuate thought* by separating groups of spoken words into meaningful units. The silent pause placed immediately before a key idea or the climax of a story creates suspense; placed immediately after a major point or key idea, it adds emphasis. Introduced at the proper moment, a dramatic pause may express your feeling more forcefully than words. Clearly, silence can be a highly effective communicative tool *if* used intelligently and sparingly and if not embarrassingly prolonged.[10]

Rhythm. A third significant system of vocal cues involves rhythm. This has to do with the regularity or irregularity with which sounds, syllables, and words are accented, both in smaller units of expression (for example, the sentence) and in larger ones (across an entire speech, for instance). Ordinarily, the term *stress* or *accent* is used in referring to the smaller units, and *tempo* or *emphasis* in referring to the larger ones. Both aspects of rhythm not only add grace and aesthetic appeal to a speech, but also aid comprehension and strengthen the total effect of a message.

Stress. By stress we refer to those points in a sentence where, principally through increased vocal energy (loudness) and intonation (pitch), you utter a sound or word more forcefully or "hit" it harder than normal. By emphasizing vocally the important or key words in your discourse, you are able to communicate meanings more clearly and accurately. If you regularly stress syllables—as in "MA-ry HAD a LIT-tle LAMB"—you are employing a *rhythmical* pattern in your speaking. If you irregularly accent words—for example, the first, fourth, fifth, and eleventh words in a sentence—you are using an *arrhythmical* or *non-rhythmical* pattern. Both rhythmical and arrhythmical stress patterns are useful to public speakers.

Consider, for example, the accent-and-stress pattern in these words of the Revolutionary War propagandist Thomas Paine: "THESE are the TIMES *(pause)* that TRY *(pause)* men's SOULS." When you read that statement aloud, evenly spacing the emphasized words *these, times, try,* and *souls,* not only can you sense a kind of muffled drumbeat that helps to communicate the solemnity and seriousness of the crisis, but you see also how stress may be used to facilitate comprehension and heighten listeners' feelings.

Arrhythmical or non-rhythmical stress, too, can be important in helping an audience comprehend what you are saying. Consider the simple statement: "The book was on the table." By stressing any one of the words in that sentence, you can change the meaning of the whole. Thus:

1. THE book was on the table. (A specific book both you and I think was there.)
2. The BOOK was on the table. (It was the book, and not something else, which was there.)
3. The book WAS on the table. (But now it is somewhere else.)
4. The book was ON the table. (Not under it.)
5. The book was on THE table. (On the table both you and I know is a particular one.)
6. The book was on the TABLE. (And not on, say, the piano.)

So, by using vocal stress carefully you can almost certainly communicate your intended meanings with greater clarity and accuracy, thereby increasing the likelihood that your message will be received and interpreted as you wish it to be.

Tempo. A second aspect of rhythm has to do with longer patterns of emphasis in messages. Tempo involves a sense of change in *(a)* rhythm patterns over a time interval and *(b)* changes in rate from one section of a message to another. If you listen to classical music, for example, you are aware that the first section or movement has one tempo pattern, that in the second section or movement the tempo changes (perhaps to an *andante* tempo), and that it finishes in a third (perhaps *allegretto*). These changes in tempo parallel changes in the mood of the music. Similarly, in a public speech, you can employ rhythm and rate patterns to assist your audience's sensing of verbal tempo across several sentences. Consider how these two factors have been combined and orchestrated in the following passage from Franklin D. Roosevelt's declaration of war against Japan in 1941:

LAST NIGHT the Japanese forces attacked HONG KONG.

LAST NIGHT the Japanese forces attacked GUAM.

LAST NIGHT the Japanese forces attacked the PHILIPPINE ISLANDS.

LAST NIGHT the Japanese attacked WAKE ISLAND.

THIS MORNING the Japanese attacked MIDWAY ISLAND.[11]

By maintaining a regular *stress pattern,* by speaking at a slow and deliberate *rate* befitting the seriousness and solemnity of the occasion, and by using a *language pattern* in which all five statements were of similar length and parallel construction, Roosevelt achieved a *rhythmic effect* which contributed much to the vocal grace and aesthetic appeal, as well as the listeners' comprehension, of his message.

Tempo and vocal stress are also important aspects of rhythm *across a whole discourse*—throughout an entire speech. For example, as we have frequently emphasized, one of your goals as a speaker is always to make one, two, or three central ideas indelibly important to your listeners. That is, among all the things you say in a speech, some of them are *most* important; others, next-most-important, etc. Thus, vocally you may move rather rapidly through a series of details—say, a long descriptive passage, a quotation, background examples, etc.—then slow down, and add particular vocal stress to the key idea, for instance, "THAT is what we are talking about today: AMERICA'S (slight pause) MISSION." Again, by controlling the tempo of your speech by means of stress, rate, and linguistic patterns, you can affect to an important extent the audience's comprehension of your message while, at the same time, accurately reflecting your emotional state.

Voice Quality. Finally, the listeners' initial judgment of a speaker's voice often centers on its *quality*—the fullness or thinness of its tone, whether or not it is harsh, husky; mellow, nasal, breathy, resonant, etc. On the psychological basis of voice quality they also make judgments about a speaker's attitude or state of mind: they characterize the speaker as being angry, happy, confident, fearful, sad, sincere, insincere, etc.

Fundamental to an audience's reaction to your voice quality are what G. L. Trager calls *emotional characterizers*—laughing, crying, whispering, yelling, moaning, whining, spitting, groaning, belching, marked inhaling or exhaling, etc.[12] Physiologically, such "characterizers" are produced by highly complex adjustments of your vocal mechanism: lips, jaw, tongue, hard and soft palates, throat, vocal folds, etc. (For a fuller consideration of the physiological basis of voice quality, see Appendix B, pages 413–414.) Psychologically, what is important about emotional characterizers is that they combine in various ways with the words you speak to communicate different shades of meaning to a listener. Consider, for a moment, a few of the many ways you can say the simple sentence:

"Tom's going for pizza tonight with Jane."

First, say it as though you were only *reporting the fact* to a mutual friend. Now say it as though *you can't believe* Tom is going with Jane.

Or, again, as though it is *impossible* Jane would go with Tom. Then indicate that you wish *you were going* instead of Tom or Jane. Next, say it as though you cannot believe Tom is *actually spending money* on pizza (when he could be purchasing something less expensive). Finally, say it as though you are *expressing doubts* about Tom's motive—indicate that you think he is after more than pizza on this trip.

As you said that sentence over and over, you not only varied your pitch and loudness, but you probably also made some strange and complicated changes in your emotional characterizers. Such changes are important determiners of how a message should be taken or interpreted by listeners.

In brief, the characterizing aspects of voice, or what David Crystal defines as "a single impression of a voice existing throughout the whole of a normal utterance,"[13] are of prime importance in determining the overall or general impression you make upon an audience. While, of course,

VOCAL CHARACTERISTICS AND THEIR COMMUNICATIVE EFFECTS*

VOCAL CHARACTERISTICS	Ability to be Heard	Ability to be Understood	Ability to Communicate Your Purpose	Ability to Communicate Your Feelings	Ability to Communicate Your Background
INTELLIGIBILITY					
Articulation and Pronunciation/Dialect		•••	•	•	•••
Volume/Loudness Level	•••	•		••	
VARIETY					
Pitch	•	•••	••	•••	••
Duration		••		•••	••
Rate	•	•••	••	•••	•••
Pauses/Intrusions	•	••	•••	•••	
RHYTHM					
Stress	••	•••	••	•••	••
Tempo	•••	•••		•••	••

*On this chart, one dot (•) indicates mildly important, two indicates relatively important, and three dots indicate the characteristic is very important in its effect upon the reception of your oral message. These judgments are based on the research reported in the footnotes to this chapter.

you cannot completely control your emotional characterizers, you can be alert to the effects they are likely to produce in listeners and try to make meaningful adjustments in your voice quality consistent with the demands of your spoken messages—as you have just done in repeating the simple statement about Tom, Jane, and pizza. We are not urging, of course, that you experiment over and over again with every sentence in a speech so as to achieve a "proper" emotional overtone. We are emphasizing, however, that key ideas—and more especially, key evaluations and expressions of your attitudes—will be interpreted more accurately by an audience if you give consideration to such characterizers. In sum, keep your repertoire of voice qualities in the forefront of your mind as you decide whether to yell at, cry with, sneer at, plead with, harp upon, or humble yourself before an audience.

Thus far in this chapter we have considered four important paralinguistic communication systems—*intelligibility, variety, rhythm,* and *quality*—and their respective sub-systems of vocal cues which are given off by speakers and by which listeners attribute meanings to the sounds accompanying oral, verbal language. Together, they significantly influence audiences' perceptions of you as a person, of your message, and of its emotional overtones. Some of the communicative effects of the vocal characteristics we have examined are briefly summarized in the table on page 250.

Problems of Paralinguistic Communication

Now that we have looked at vocal characteristics individually, let us look for a moment at some of the problems that are likely to arise when you use them in actual communicative transactions. Two areas in particular require consideration: (1) *normalcy* and (2) *vocal style.*

The Problem of Normalcy

Vocal Production and Normalcy. It is one thing to know the aspects of voice that make up the paralinguistic cues you emit every time you open your mouth, but quite another to choose ways of effectively adapting your normal speaking voice when you stand up to face an audience. On the one hand, certainly, it is desirable for you to employ your normal voice at all times. It communicates quite well, probably, the nuances of meanings and feelings you wish to produce in your hearers. On the other hand, however, your normal speaking voice may not suffice to meet the physical and psychological demands of many communicative contexts. It may not be loud enough. The careless, mumbling delivery you use in everyday conversation may not work in a larger setting. You may not have learned as yet how to cope with the fact that public speaking requires a greater control of articulation and tempo than does one-to-one talk. Perhaps, your voice qualities—especially as you grow nervous and tense when talking to a large group—tend to become un-necessarily formal and somewhat distorted. You must, therefore, strive to *strike a balance between your normal, everyday speech habits and the special demands which public speaking places upon your voice.* In Appendix B (pages 409–431) we will consider specific ways in which you can effect these improvements in your speaking voice. You must learn to use particular voice qualities, achieve intelligibility, ensure variety and rhythm, and make the necessary adaptations as these re-quirements vary from situation to situation and from one public speech transaction to the next.

Dialect and Normalcy. If you are a public speaker with a regional dialect or an ethnic background which is characterized by either a special syn-tax or unique pronunciation, what should you do about it? On the one hand, you have to be true to yourself and your roots; on the other, you have an obligation to accommodate audiences who are taking their valuable time to listen to you. Only *you* can decide. Only you can choose, for example, whether to maintain your personal dialect or ac-cent, to adapt to Midwestern standards of American speech, or to mix in some way the native and the standard syntax and pronunciation—the kind of balanced blend, say, achieved by the late Martin Luther King, Jr.[14] In final analysis, after careful self-examination, you must choose the dialect—or the degree of it—which you believe will work best for you and which will fulfill best the expectations of your audience. Then be ready to accept the consequences of that choice, whatever they may be.

The Problem of Vocal Style

As we noted at the outset of this chapter, as a communicator you have at your disposal a large repertoire of vocal styles—ways of talking which you vary according to the people you are with, the situation you are in, your purpose in speaking, etc. Normally you make choices, whether consciously or sub-consciously, among those vocal styles, expressing yourself in a variety of ways on a variety of occasions. By now it should be apparent that sometimes it is important for you to sort through your vocal options *consciously* and *explicitly.* In deciding upon which of your many styles to employ in a given circumstance, you must carefully consider all of the factors which affect your speech and its delivery—your purpose, the setting, the traditions, and the mechanical devices required.

Purpose and Vocal Style. Basically, the way you use your voice should vary with the purpose for which you are speaking. Suppose, for exam-ple, that in giving an informative speech, Speaker X realizes that she will be presenting factual data and ideas with which her listeners are proba-bly unfamiliar. Being sensitive to their need to grasp these data, and concerned that she project an image of herself as an explainer or purvey-or of factual information, she recognizes the need to use what might be called an informative vocal style. In terms of the vocal characteristics we have discussed—*intelligibility, variety, rhythm,* and *voice quality*—how might such a style sound? Taking into account the infinite number of possibilities, the fact that no two speakers would ever have identical notions of what an informative style ought to be, and the hypothetical nature of our example, let us try, nevertheless, to form a composite picture of the vocal behaviors Speaker X might conceivably exhibit and the related concerns she might have. As we observe her presentation, specifically she might:

Voice Quality — (1) Employ a relatively matter-of-fact emotional characterizer.

Intelligibility — (1) Articulate precisely so that unfamiliar words or ideas can be understood; (2) use standard, community-based pronunciations, especially of technical terms, because some listeners may be hearing these words for the first time; (3) avoid extreme dialect to ensure maximum communication of information.* Maintain moderate volume, neither extremely loud nor extremely soft.

Vocal Variety — (1) Sustain a normal pitch range and level, avoiding distracting extremes; (2) keep enough pitch variation, however, to maximize intelligibility and minimize monotones; (3) maintain a moderate rate, slowing down especially at points where the material is unfamiliar, but important; (4) pause after key ideas, checking audience feedback to make sure that her information is getting through to her listeners.

Rhythm — (1) Stress words which express key concepts, and vary the tempo enough to attract and hold her audience's attention.

Now, for the sake of contrast, let us suppose that Speaker X is aiming not at the intellectual and emotional detachment of a so-called informative speech, but rather at the reforming fervor of one bent on righting a wrong. In achieving what she considers an appropriate persuasive style, what vocal behaviors might she conceivably exhibit, and what related concerns might she have? As we observe her presentation this time, she might:

Voice Quality — (1) Employ a wide assortment of emotional characterizers which reflect the emotional states through which she and (she hopes) her audience are progressing, as she pleads, condemns, cajoles, exhorts, etc.

Intelligibility — (1) Articulate carefully to compensate for the fact that emotional fervor tends to make articulation somewhat hurried and possibly less distinct; (2) give careful attention to pronunciation of key words, especially those expressing highly positive and highly negative concepts, because her sense of urgency can cause her to rush or blur such pronunciations; use—within rather strict limits—

---

*She would avoid dialect if speaking to a mixed or heterogeneous audience. If her listeners consisted primarily of individuals who speak a dialect, then she would use it, of course. For an interesting study of a speaker who easily shifted back and forth between black dialect and white English, see Robert L. Scott and Wayne Brockriede, *The Rhetoric of Black Power* (New York: Harper & Row, Publishers, 1969), pp. 84–132.

somewhat altered pronunciations to heighten emotional effect;* (3) utilize only as much dialect as is appropriate to herself as a concerned person and to her audience as concerned listeners; (4) employ loudness levels that range from shouts to whispers if and when they are appropriate to her topic, her audience, and the occasion.

Variety — (1) Vary her pitch, giving it higher tops and bottoms than in her informative speech; (2) employ a greater pitch variation when excited; (3) take vocal duration into careful account, "clipping" words and phrases she feels she can afford to hurry by, but sustaining the appropriate syllables within words expressing key ideas; (4) allow for considerable variation in her rate of speaking, being careful only to avoid a rate so rapid and excited that it reduces listeners' comprehension; (5) typically avoid "uhs," "ums," and other vocal intrusions, even though this is difficult when the speaker is highly emotional; and (6) employ pauses strategically to heighten message impact.

Rhythm — (1) Seek to maintain, in conjunction with her phrasing of key ideas, an appropriate stress pattern, occasionally employing highly rhythmical patterns when trying to carry her audience along with her to an emotional pinnacle; (2) vary her tempo considerably throughout the speech, in harmony with the emotional characterizers she is employing.

We are not recommending, certainly, that you try to imitate or reproduce any of the behaviors we have described. We have presented these hypothetical contrasts *only* to start you thinking carefully about vocal communication styles which are appropriate to you and to emphasize that whatever your communicative purpose, you must vary your vocal style accordingly.

Physical Setting and Vocal Style. In public communication especially, you must adapt your voice to meet the demands of the physical setting. Earlier, you will recall, we noted Hall's conception of *public distance* as measuring twelve feet or more between speaker and listeners; and when you project your voice through that much space, you are compelled to change to a significant degree certain of its characteristics and qualities. Specifically, to be heard distinctly without using electronic amplification, you will have to increase your vocal intensity or loudness while, at the same time, exercising careful articulatory control. You will need to pay close attention to pitch and pitch variation, and usually slow your speaking rate. In other words, when you are speaking publicly to large numbers of listeners at some distance from you, very often you have to enlarge — even exaggerate — the vocal adjustments you make.

Formality, Tradition, Electronic Devices, and Vocal Style. Your style of utterance should vary also to accommodate the degree of formality you perceive in a situation, the specific traditions surrounding the particular

---

*If you have listened to recordings of Winston Churchill's World War II speeches, for example, you were quickly aware that he did not pronounce "Nazi" as did most other speakers. Rather, he said "Naz-z-z-i," with a snarl in his voice, as if indicating his hatred of them.

communicative transactions, and the presence or absence of electronic amplification. When you are faced with delivering a *formal* speech—one requiring more than ordinary attention to dignity of physical appearance and bearing, precise wording, and extended discourse—you will be acutely aware of attendant social pressures with which you must cope. This awareness should, of course, be reflected in the vocal adjustments you make: You will probably employ slower rate, more measured rhythms, careful pitch variations, and certainly more careful articulatory control. In contrast, when you are delivering an *informal* speech, very likely you will feel freer to use "street talk," speak at an accelerated rate, and pay less attention to smooth-flowing rhythms and articulation. In matters of vocal formality, it makes a difference, for instance, whether you are addressing the monthly lecture meeting of the Daughters of the American Revolution or haranguing a group of college students gathered around "The Speakers' Soapbox" near a campus crosswalk.

Furthermore, as a speaker you will sometimes face situations where *traditions* or long-standing *customs* dictate, in part, how you are expected to behave vocally. Clergymen, for example, soon discover that congregations expect formal address to take traditional vocal patterns; preachers, priests, and rabbis are expected to sound like preachers, priests, and rabbis. Similarly, people hold stereotyped images of what college professors, professional athletes, presidents of ladies' clubs, presidents of Toastmaster Clubs, board chairmen, etc., traditionally sound like. Therefore, when you are called upon to speak in situations where precedents and customs exert a significant influence, you must decide in what respects and to what degree you will adapt your characteristic vocal behaviors to accommodate the demands thus imposed.

And, finally, as a public speaker, be prepared to find yourself from time to time in situations requiring you to use a microphone, bullhorn, or some other mechanism for enlarging and transmitting your voice *electronically.* One comparatively simple way to approach such devices and adapt your vocal behaviors to them is to speak as you do when using the telephone: slow down your rate, articulate somewhat more carefully and precisely than you ordinarily do, and pay close attention to your vocal resonance. Even though these vocal adjustments may at first sound unnatural or strange to your ears, they can help you cope with the demands of electronic amplification.

Reference Notes

[1]Much of this research on judgments people make about your voice is summarized in and comes from Mark L. Knapp, *Nonverbal Communication in Human Interaction* (New York: Holt, Rinehart & Winston, Inc., 1972), especially Chapter 6; Randall P. Harrison, *Beyond Words: An Introduction to Nonverbal Communication* (Englewood Cliffs, N.J.: Prentice-Hall, Inc., 1974), Chapter 6; and Dale G. Leathers, *Nonverbal Communication Systems* (Boston: Allyn & Bacon, Inc., 1976), Chapter 6.

[2]By permission. From *Webster's Third New International Dictionary,* copyright © 1976 by G. & C. Merriam Co., publishers of the Merriam-Webster dictionaries.

[3]In support of these ideas, see Mark L. Knapp, *Nonverbal Communication in Human Interaction* (New York: Holt, Rinehart & Winston, Inc., 1972), pp. 155–158.

[4]Recent studies of vocal stereotyping may be found in W. E. Lambert, H. Frankel, and G. R. Tucker, "Judging Personality Through Speech: A French-Canadian Example," *Journal of Communication* 16 (1966): 312–313; David W. Addington, "The Relationship of Selected Vocal Characteristics to Personality Perception," *Speech Monographs* 35 (1968): 492–503; W. J. Weaver and R. J. Anderson, "Voice and Personality Interrelationships," *Southern Speech Communication Journal* 38 (1973): 275–278; and B. L. Brown, W. J. Strong, and A. C. Rencher, "The Effects of Simultaneous Manipulations of Rate, Mean Fundamental Frequency, and Variance of Fundamental Frequency on Ratings of Personality from Speech," *Journal of the Acoustical Society of America* 55 (1974): 313–318. (The last study is particularly interesting because it offers advice on ways of altering vocal stereotypes.)

[5]See Susan Milmoe et al., "The Doctor's Voice: Postdictor of Successful Referral of Alcoholic Patients," *Journal of Abnormal Psychology* 72 (1967): 78–84.

[6]By permission. From *Webster's New Collegiate Dictionary,* copyright © 1977 by G. & C. Merriam Co., publishers of the Merriam-Webster dictionaries.

[7]From "Acoustic Concomitants of Emotional Dimensions: Judging Affect From Synthesized Tone Sequences," by Klaus R. Scherer, presented at Eastern Psychological Association meeting, Boston, April 1972. Reprinted in *Nonverbal Communication; Readings with Commentary,* ed. Shirley Weitz. Reprinted by permission of the author.

[8]From "Effects of Duration and Articulation Changes on Intelligibility, Word Reception, and Listener Preference," by Gilbert C. Tolhurst, *Journal of Speech and Hearing Disorders* XXII, September 1957. Reprinted by permission of the American Speech and Hearing Association and Dr. Gilbert C. Tolhurst.

[9]From "Acoustic Concomitants of Emotional Dimensions: Judging Affect from Synthesized Tone Sequences," by Klaus R. Scherer, presented at Eastern Psychological Association meeting, Boston, April 1972. Reprinted in *Nonverbal Communication; Readings with Commentary,* ed. Shirley Weitz. Reprinted by permission of the author.

[10]For further study of pauses and intrusions, see F. G. Lounsbury, "Pausal, Juncture, and Hesitation Phenomena," *Journal of Abnormal Social Psychology* 49 (1954): 99; and Stanislav Kasl and George Mahl, "The Relationship of Disturbances and Hesitations in Spontaneous Speech to Anxiety," *Journal of Personality and Social Psychology* 1 (1965): 425–433.

[11]Franklin D. Roosevelt. *Congressional Record,* 77th Congress, 1st Session, Volume 87, Part 9, December 8, 1941, pp. 9504–9505.

[12]For an analysis of emotional or vocal characterizers, see George L. Trager, "Paralanguage: A First Approximation," *Studies in Linguistics* 13 (1958):1–13.

[13]David Crystal, *Prosodic Systems and Intonation in English* (Cambridge: University Press, 1959), p. 123.

[14]For a review of black dialect and its attendant communicative effects, see R. W. Fasold and W. Wolfam, "Some Linguistic Features of Negro Dialect," in *Teaching Standard English in the Inner City,* ed. R. W. Fasold and R. W. Shuy (Washington, D.C.: Center for Applied Linguistics, 1970), pp. 41–86.

Problems and Probes

1.   To verify Edward T. Hall's conception of *intimate* distance, *personal* distance, *social* distance, and *public* distance *(a)* read the appropriate section of Hall's book, *The Hidden Dimension* (New York: Doubleday & Company, Inc., 1966); *(b)* then—in conducting your own investigation—purposely place yourself at the specified distances from others and carry on conversations, noting carefully the changing characteristics of voice quality, loudness, syllable duration, distinctness of articulation, vocal stress, variety, rate, force, and pitch; *(c)* finally, chart several of these characteristics and compare your conclusions with those of Hall.

2.   Listen to a successful speaker addressing a crowd—someone who, because of the extended distance involved, must project his or her voice to a large audience without a microphone. Chart the vocal characteristics listed in Problem 1 above. Then answer these questions: *(a)* What kinds of sentence structures are spoken easily by someone forced to project vocally? *(b)* What kinds of sentence structures are apparently difficult for listeners to understand in such

circumstances? *(c)* Can you discern relationships between vocal quality, loudness, rate, pitch, etc., and the physical behavior of the speaker? Identify these relationships. *(d)* In general, describe some of the relationships among vocal, physical, and verbal characteristics of successful, large-scale, public communication.

3.   Are you sensitive to variations in vocal dialects? Do you associate personality types, intelligence, communication mannerisms, etc., with a British accent, a German accent, an Oriental accent — or with a Georgia accent, a Texas accent, a Bronx accent, a Minnesota-Scandinavian accent? Why? Bad movies? Limited experiences? Or do you think members of these cultures and subcultures *actually* think and, therefore, speak differently? How can you be sure?

The power of vocal stereotyping cannot be underestimated. Explore such stereotyping by reading and by making personal contacts with members of various subcultures or cultures other than your own. Take careful, objective notes on what the resulting face-to-face interviews and dialogues reveal.

 Suggestions for Further Reading

D. W. Addington, "The Relationship of Selected Vocal Characteristics to Personality Perception," *Speech Monographs* 35 (1968): 492–503.

Bert E. Bradley, *Fundamentals of Speech Communication: The Credibility of Ideas* (Dubuque, Iowa: Wm. C. Brown Company, Publishers, 1974), "Pronunciation" and "Attitude Toward a Non-Standard Dialect," pp. 244–249.

Joseph A. DeVito, Jill Giattino, and T. D. Schon, *Articulation and Voice: Effective Communication* (Indianapolis: The Bobbs-Merrill Company, Inc., 1975).

Donald H. Ecroyd, Murray M. Halfond, and Carol C. Towne, *Voice and Articulation: A Handbook* (Glenview, Ill.: Scott, Foresman and Company, 1966), esp. Chapters 3–7 and 9.

Randall P. Harrison, *Beyond Words: An Introduction to Nonverbal Communication* (Englewood Cliffs, N.J.: Prentice-Hall, Inc., 1974), Chapter 6.

Robert G. King and Eleanor M. DiMichael, *Improving Articulation and Voice* (New York: The Macmillan Company, 1966), esp. Chapters 2, 5, 6, and 8.

16

Using Visual Materials in Communication

In the mid-1960s, when Marshall McLuhan asserted that American culture was returning to a tribal state, he was recognizing the power of electronic, visual communication to integrate diverse peoples and ideas.[1] Humanity, we can safely assume, invented visual art long before it concocted the arbitrary system of signs we call language; and human beings, we are discovering through careful observation, become visually literate before they can be deemed verbally literate.

Visual communication, indeed, is fast becoming a well-developed and important area of scholarly and practical study. The Gestalt psychologists in the 1930s and 1940s offered us our first theories concerning how people learn to perceive and interpret visual media; and the growth of the visual-media industries (film, television, and photographic reproduction) spurred studies of psychological and social conditions which maximize visual learning and information-intake.[2] Such ongoing research is of vital importance to a world in which computers can reproduce information spatially and in which copying machines put faithful duplicates of originals in the hands of consumers almost instantly. Today the average person cannot escape the bombardment of visual messages—films, television, billboards, tee-shirts, bumper stickers, handouts, mass-mailed advertising circulars, buttons, store-window displays, business signs, etc.—that comes at us constantly.

The study of visual communication is especially important to the public speaker because it relates to oral communication in two significant ways. (1) As we noted in Chapter 14, the human body itself is a visual message, one which is "read" by an information-seeking audience; and (2) as a speaker you are frequently faced with questions concerning the use of so-called visual aids or visual supporting materials: Should I employ visual aids? If so, what kind? How big? When should I introduce a picture, a bar graph, or a working model? Should I look at the chalk-board or the audience? These are eminently practical questions about everyday speechmaking. Systematic research has not offered answers to all such questions, but it is far enough along to help you as a public communicator make some important decisions.

In this chapter, we first will consider briefly how you learn to recognize and "read" four commonly used visual-message systems: shape, size, color, and complexity. Then we will examine two key functions of visual support—aiding comprehension and memory and increasing persuasiveness. Third, we will identify several useful types of visuals. And, finally, we will suggest some factors to consider when choosing among the several types of visual aids.

"Reading" Visual Symbols and Patterns

The phrase *visual literacy* refers to the idea that all people have been taught, in varying degrees, to "read" visual symbols and visualized configurations or patterns. Thus, you have learned that smoke is a visual sign for fire. You have learned that—for your generation at least—a raised arm with the second and third fingers extended from a clenched fist means "Victory!" And you have learned that inverted yellow-hued clouds riding a southwest wind on a hot muggy day in southern Illinois portend a tornado. Some such patterns you learn through *personal experience,* as when children learn to identify friendly and unfriendly dogs by watching their tails, shoulders, teeth, and eyes. Other patterns you acquire from *institutions* and *instruction,* as when you were taught the meaning of certain conventional gestures by your family or friends and certain religious symbols by a church or synagogue. Overall, in a few short years you learned to discriminate among visual objects that differ only in the slightest detail, as when you distinguish among almost identical shades of red or between lines which are perfectly parallel and those which are slightly angular. And, of course, you may even be one of those rare people who have sharpened their visual acuity to a point where they are hypersensitively literate—for example, the experts who spot painting forgeries, or the standards-control inspectors who can see the tiniest ripple in an assembly-line paint job at five feet. Why are we able to make such subtle discriminations? Because what we are really perceiving are several discrete or separate *visual-message systems,* including *shape, size, color,* and *complexity.*

Shape. You not only have been taught to identify certain shapes, forms, and configurations as significant to your life, but also your basic perceptual equipment seems designed to allow you to finish out or "complete" partial shapes and figures. A standard section on drivers' tests, for example, includes a number of geometric figures—a circle, a hexagon, a square, a wedge—which you know from road experience represent different highway warnings or directions. Psychologically, you *complete* shapes only partially formed, either by adding missing portions or items or by associating an incomplete shape with a complete object.[3]

Size. As a child, you probably were confused by the fact that objects at a distance appeared smaller than objects nearby. You soon learned, however, to estimate distance and adjust your perspectives accordingly, just as you learned to judge loudness, odors, etc. Now you are able to *focus* your perceptual equipment. Through a highly complex process of physiological adjustment and psychological training, you can perceive almost invisibly small objects (such as pins) and distinguish them from among a host of larger objects (such as the chairs, coffee table, and lamps in a room).

Color. As we have noted, you also are able to discriminate among a great variety of colors, hues, and shades. A farmer, by noting the color of a field of wheat, can judge the appropriate time to harvest it. A clothes designer makes decisions on hues based on the subtlest of differences. Homeowners determine when to water their lawns, often unconsciously, by observing the color of the grass. As a matter of fact, people even go so far as to react *attitudinally* to colors. Motivational consumer research in the 1950s, for example, demonstrated that detergents packaged in yellow boxes were deemed more harsh and acidic than the same soaps offered in blue boxes. And it is not for naught that we sing of "amber waves of grain" and "purple mountain majesties," or that we talk about the "red badge of courage," "true-blue friends," "yellow journalism," etc.[4]

Complexity. Finally, as you grow up, you are taught to process visual messages that have varying degrees of complexity. A child of four has a great deal of difficulty verbally describing pictures that contain a number of objects, abstract line drawings, etc., whereas a child of eight or nine can do this with relative ease. You learn to scan visual objects and to rank elements in them hierarchically in order to determine what is most important, next-most important, etc. Most significantly, perhaps, you learn to make judgments about *figure-ground relationships.* That is, you learn to identify the central figure or point of focus in a visual presentation. The makers of television commercials are among our culture's most careful students of figure-ground relationships. It makes a difference, for example, whether an oil company shows its derricks against the background of the North Sea (ruggedness, exploration, adventure) or against a bird sanctuary and bayou swamp (serenity, preservation, reverence); whether soda pop is being consumed on the family porch (hominess, day-to-day existence) or in a group of eighteen-year-olds having fun (excitement, peer approval).

In other words, we are learning much about the associations people make with shapes, sizes, colors, and varying degrees of complexity.

This research has had considerable impact upon advertising, the preparation of materials for school-age children, and the like. It also can be put to practical use by public speakers in their day-to-day presentations. Before we can explore such applications, however, we must first understand the functions of visual materials in public communication settings.

The Functions of Visual Materials

Visual materials serve the speaker in two important ways: (1) they aid listener comprehension and memory; (2) they add persuasive impact to a message.

Comprehension and Memory.   Well-executed visuals can aid significantly your auditors' comprehension of your message. If a picture is worth a thousand words, then it is useful principally because it adds important information that is more easily understood visually than aurally. Visual research has demonstrated that bar graphs, especially, make statistical information more accessible to an audience, that simple (as opposed to complicated) drawings enhance recall, and that charts and even "human interest" visuals (especially photographs) help an audience retain data.[5]

Persuasiveness.   A growing body of literature supports the notion that visual aids, in addition to enhancing comprehension and memory, may actually heighten the persuasive effects of speeches. Undeniably, a speaker's credibility—the audience's perception of the speaker's good sense, trustworthiness, and dynamism—is positively affected by appropriate visuals. Moreover, certain types of messages—especially those which can be supported by facts, figures, and examples—are strengthened by visual support.[6]

Types of Visual Support

Here, briefly, are some kinds of visual materials the public speaker may use to support and enhance the ideas in a message:

The object itself (for example, a metronome or a CB radio) has strong, immediate impact and intensity.

Models, either small-scale models of large objects (a model racing car) or large-scale models of small objects (a model of the structure of a molecule) often have the added advantage of showing the operation of a device or apparatus, as well as its basic design.

Slides require projection equipment, and the fact that they must be shown in a darkened room obscures the speaker, but they usually add interest and promote understanding.

Movies require more equipment than slides, but have the advantage of showing action.

TYPES OF VISUAL SUPPORTING MATERIALS

1. OBJECT

2. MODELS

3. SLIDES

4. MOVIES

5. MAPS

6. CHALKBOARD DRAWINGS

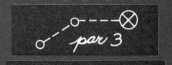

7. GRAPHS

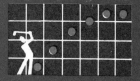

8. DIAGRAMS

9. CHARTS OR TABLES

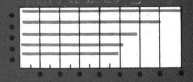

10. HANDOUTS

Maps should be large enough to be seen easily and should emphasize those details which relate to the point being made.

Chalkboard drawings should be prepared before the audience assembles, but kept covered until the speaker is ready to refer to them. Be sure the chalk marks are heavy enough to be seen by the entire group.

Graphs take several different forms. *Bar* graphs show the relationship of two sets of figures. *Line* graphs show two or more variable facts. *Pie* graphs show percentages by a circle divided proportionately. *Pictorial* graphs show relative amounts by size or number of symbols.

Diagrams can, of course, vary considerably in their complexity. *Cutaway* diagrams of an object display its inner workings as well as its external aspects. Diagrams which allow for a *three-dimensional* view are especially helpful.

Organization charts or *tables of organization* illustrate the parts and structure of a business, bureau, or agency. (See page 119.)

Mimeographed, dittoed, xeroxed, or *printed information* can be handed out to an audience and used to communicate statistical information, give suggestions to be followed up later (for instance, addresses to write to), or provide full descriptions of the steps in a complex process.

For illustrations of some of these types of nonverbal supporting materials, see pages 262 and 268–269.

The Selection and Use of Visual Materials

Given the fact, then, that as a resourceful speaker you can employ a number of different types of visuals, you must make careful choices from among them. These choices usually should be based on three factors: (1) *your own personality and purposes,* (2) *the communicative potential of each type of visual material,* and (3) *the nature of the audience and the occasion.*

Start with Your Self

Visual materials may contribute in important ways to your audience's perception of you as a person—your concerns, your values, your feelings, and your ideas. A speech on scrimshawing, with examples of objects that you have carved from whalebones, not only tells an audience that you have certain skills and hobbies, but also indicates your attitudes toward the preservation of folk culture. The bar graphs you utilize in a speech on inflation not only demonstrate support for your proposition, but also represent your attitudes toward concrete, summary data. Visual aids, especially those you prepare in color and detail, communicate both your forethought (you cared enough for your audience to make something for them) and, perhaps, a measure of your ingenuity and flair for the artistic. Because visual supporting materials are presented as a *part* of the total communication process, you reveal much about yourself by what you show an audience. They "express" *you* while, at the same time, helping to express and support your ideas.

Consider the Communicative Potential of Various Visual Materials

Keep in mind, of course, that each type of visual material has certain potentials for communicating particular kinds of information, and that each type interacts with your *spoken* presentation as well as your audience's state of mind. In preparing speech materials of this kind, remember that visuals primarily pictorial or photographic in nature have the potential for making an audience *feel* the way you do. Aids such as slides, movies, sketches, and photographs often may be used effectively to accompany travelogs or reports of personal experiences because they illustrate or reproduce in others the kinds of *feelings* you experienced in another place, situation, or time.

Visuals containing descriptive or verbal materials, on the other hand, can help an audience to *think* the way you do. In contrast to pictorial materials, such aids as cutaways, models, diagrams, charts, and dittoed summaries of statistical data frequently add *rational support* to propositions you are attempting to defend. The nature of your topic and your communicative purpose, therefore, play a large role in determining the kinds of visuals you ought to employ in a given circumstance. A speech informing listeners of your experiences in Indonesia should probably be accompanied by slides or films and even some household artifacts. A speech to persuade your listeners that the United States ought to sever all association with the Southeast Asia Treaty Organization probably should be supported by maps, charts, and chalkboard drawings.

In sum, as you make your decisions about the visual elements you will use to support and illustrate your speech, *choose only those objects and materials which are relevant to your speech topic and communicative purpose.* In other words, be sure that your visual materials will work *for,* and not *against,* you. Some visuals, if not selected carefully, may distract, frustrate, or actually anger an audience. You can guard against such negative and unintended effects by the following means:

1. *Painstakingly prepare all of your visual aids well in advance of your speech.* Exercise considerable care in conceptualizing them, using familiar shapes (for example, the pie) and contrasting colors (red on white, blue on yellow, etc.), and making sure that the image, concept, steps, or other constituent elements—the things you really wish to emphasize—are immediately and strikingly visible.

2. *Keep charts, diagrams, and other graphic aids clear and simple.* Research has demonstrated that plain bar graphs—probably because they offer not only numbers but also a visualization of numbers through the use of "bars"—are the single most effective method for displaying

statistical comparisons.[7] To restate a point we emphasized earlier, make sure that the central element or "figure" — the essential information you want your audience to focus upon — stands out clearly from the background of your chart, diagram, or other visual depiction. This is most easily done by cutting away interesting, but extraneous, information and by displaying the information in bars, pies, and pictures.

3. *Make your visuals — especially those with materials which must be read or scrutinized closely — large enough to be seen clearly and easily.* Listeners — especially those in the back rows — get frustrated when, in the middle of the speech, they suddenly notice that they are having to lean forward and squint in order to see a detail on a sketch or diagram. Make your figures and lettering large enough so that, as John Hancock noted in connection with the Declaration of Independence in 1776, they "can be seen by the King of England without his glasses."

4. *In preparing to present visually the details of an object, device, or process, decide well in advance whether or not to bring in the object or device itself or a model of it.* This is especially pertinent to the so-called "demonstration" speech. For instance, if you have practiced a particular craft or mastered a certain skill and wish to communicate the details or steps in the creative process, you probably will want to show a working sample or product of that process. This can be effective; but when you elect to do it, keep in mind throughout the demonstration speech that the *object* or *process model* is communicating at the same time and very possibly as much as you are. It is telling the audience: "Here's what it is." "Here's why it's worth your while," etc. Take pains to ensure, therefore, that everyone in your audience can clearly see the object or device — perhaps even handle it. This latter possibility gives rise to a fifth precaution.

5. *Be prepared to compensate orally for any distraction your visual aid may inadvertently create among your audience.* If you do pass around a sample of your work — a purse you have beaded or a shirt you have embroidered — remember that an actual object or a detailed model is a complex, potent visual stimulus. This makes it a "message-maker" in its own right; and in a very real sense, you must compete with it for the listeners' attention. Very carefully tell your audience what aspects of it to examine closely, and which ones they may ignore. If, despite your precautions, the actual object or full-scale model is likely to prove unavoidably distracting, build enough reiteration into your speech to make reasonably certain your hearers can follow your train of thought even while they are studying the object and passing it around. As added insurance, you might also provide a schematic diagram or sketch of it on the chalkboard, visually reinforcing the verbal message you are trying to communicate.

6. *When using slides, films, overhead projectors, or videotapes, be prepared to make the verbal and physical adjustments necessary to*

coordinate the visual materials with the spoken materials. When employing such visual aids, you often darken the room, thereby compelling your audience to concentrate upon a source of light: the "silver screen" in the case of slides and films, the 21-inch screen in the case of a TV set. At such times, you—the *oral* communicator—must compete with the *machine* or *electronic* communicator. If, as often happens, your audience begins to concentrate harder upon the flow of light than upon the flow of words, you defeat your own purpose. Therefore, when using projected materials as visual support, either *(a)* talk more loudly and move more vigorously when communicating simultaneously with the machine, or *(b)* refuse to compete with it at all. That is, show the film or the slides either *before* or *after* you comment on their contents. Whatever strategy you use, however, make sure that the projected visual materials are well integrated into the rest of your presentation.

7. *Hand to your listeners a dittoed or xeroxed copy of those materials you wish them to think back on or carry away from your speech.* If, for example, you are making recommendations to a student council, you may provide copies of a proposal for the council's subsequent action. Or, if you are reporting in a speech the results of a survey, the most pertinent statistics will be more easily comprehended (and remembered later) if you give each listener a duplicate copy. Few people can recall the "seven warning signs" for cancer, but they could keep a list of them in a handy place if you presented each member of your audience with a notecard on which such a list appears. Remember that we are referring here only to speech material that is legitimately a *visual aid.* Obviously, you will not put everything you have to say on a ditto. Select only those elements or items bearing upon the information you have introduced in your speech, especially those having future or lasting value.

While more could be said about choosing and using the various types of visual media to which we have referred, the foregoing suggestions should at least enable you—with some pre-speech thought and planning—to take good advantage of their communicative potential. In any event, it should be apparent that by judicious selection, preparation, and handling of diagrams, charts, models, slides, and similar graphic aids, the conscientious speaker can increase listeners' comprehension.

Consider the Audience and the Occasion

In choosing the types and contents of the visual supporting materials you will use, your common sense will tell you that you must also take into consideration the *status* of the subject in the minds of your audience. Ask yourself: Do I need to bring a map of the United States to an audience of American college students when discussing the westward movement of population in this country? As I argue that our school needs to expand its transportation services, need I show a picture of a campus bus to students who ride them? Or, if I'm going to discuss offensive and defensive formations employed by a football team, should I or should I not bring in a "play book" showing such formations? And, can I really expect an audience to understand the administrative structure of the federal bureaucracy without an organizational chart?

How much an audience *already knows, needs to know,* and *expects to find out* about you and your subject are clearly determinants which must weigh heavily when you are faced with a choice as to the types and numbers of visual supports you will use in a speech. How readily that audience can comprehend *aurally* what you have to say is another. Granted, it is not always easy to assess any of these conditions or capabilities. It may be exceedingly difficult, in fact, to decide how much an audience of college freshmen and sophomores knows about school or governmental structures; and, certainly, you cannot judge easily how well acquainted a Rotary Club audience is with football plays. That being the case, probably the next-best thing you can do is to reinforce your speculations by "asking around" among your probable listeners well ahead of the time you are scheduled to deliver your speech. In other words, before making any final decisions about visual supporting materials, *do as much audience research and analysis as you possibly can.*

As a part of your advance planning for the use of visuals, also take into thoughtful account the nature of the *occasion* or the uniqueness of the *circumstances* in which you will be speaking. You will find that certain kinds of occasions seemingly cry out for certain types of graphic supporting materials. The corporate executive who presents a projective report to the board of directors without a dittoed or printed handout and without diagrams and pictures probably would be drummed out of the firm. The military adviser who calls for governmental expenditure for new weapons without offering simultaneously pictures or drawings of the proposed weapons and printed technical data on their operations is not likely to be viewed as a convincing advocate. At half-time, an athletic coach without a chalkboard may succeed only in confusing team members—not helping them. And the encyclopedia sales representative almost certainly will sell nothing without showing sample volumes. In classroom settings, students who give demonstration speeches without visuals frequently feel inadequate, even helpless—especially when they realize that most of the other speakers are well fortified with such supports. In short, if you are to speak in a situation which literally demands certain kinds of visual media, plan ahead and adapt your message to take full advantage of them. If the speech occasion does not appear to require visual supports, analyze it further for possibilities anyway. Use your imagination. Be innovative. *Do not overlook opportunities to make your speech more meaningful, more exciting, and more attention-holding in the eyes of your listeners.*

Future research on the effects of visual communicative efforts undoubtedly will expand this set of admonitions on the use of visual aids. In time, we will learn much more about visual literacy, about ways in

Visual Support . . .

may be given to meanings and messages through the media of films, slides, overhead projections, actual objects under consideration, models or miniatures of machines and processes, maps, graphs, flipcharts, chalkboards, and dittoed handouts. When carefully evolved, clearly and simply developed, and skillfully handled, they serve well to enliven and enrich speeches and add both informative and persuasive impact.

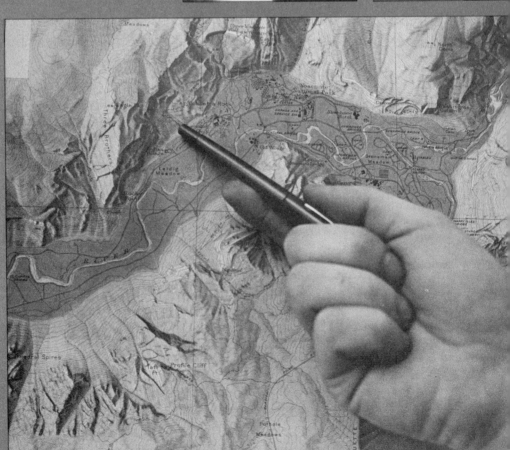

which people "read" objects, sketches, diagrams, and drawings. For the present, in a basic speech communication course you can at least practice integrating visual and verbal communication carefully and smoothly. You can gain experience using a flipchart with ease, writing legibly on a chalkboard, and drawing a graph which helps rather than hinders the transmitting of messages. With practice, you will discover that the visual mode, like the other modes of communicating meaning, can become a useful—even exciting—part of your public speech-making. Making your words, your voice, your bodily movement, and your visual materials *all communicate the same message* to an audience may well provide you with one of the most potent challenges you will encounter in the basic college speech communication course.

Reference Notes

[1]Marshall McLuhan, *Understanding Media: The Extensions of Man* (New York: McGraw-Hill Book Company, 1965).

[2]The general theories of Gestalt psychology are reviewed understandably in Ernest R. Hilgard, *Theories of Learning* (New York: Appleton-Century-Crofts, 1956). Their applications in areas of visual communication can be found, among many other places, in Rudolph Arnheim, *Visual Thinking* (Berkeley: University of California Press, 1969); John M. Kennedy, *A Psychology of Picture Perception* (San Francisco: Jossey-Bass, Inc., Publishers, 1974); Sol Worth, "Pictures Can't Say Ain't," *Versus* 12 (December 1975): 85–108; and Leonard Zusne, *Visual Perception of Form* (New York: Academic Press, Inc., 1976).

[3]The principle of perceptual completion is discussed in Hilgard.

[4]See F. M. Dwyer, "Exploratory Studies in the Effectiveness of Visual Illustrations," *AV Communication Review* 18 (1970): 235–40; G. D. Feliciano, R. D. Powers, and B. E. Kearle, "The Presentation of Statistical Information," *AV Communication Review* 11 (1963): 32–39; and William J. Seiler, "The Effects of Visual Materials on Attitudes, Credibility, and Retention," *Speech Monographs* 38 (November 1971): 331–34.

[5]See Seiler's article (note 4).

[6]See Feliciano et al. (note 4), as well as M. D. Vernon, "Presenting Information in Diagrams," *AV Communication Review* 1 (1953): 147–58; and L. V. Peterson and Wilbur Schramm, "How Accurately Are Different Kinds of Graphs Read?" *AV Communication Review* 2 (1955): 178–89.

[7]Ibid.

Problems and Probes

1.   Recall a number of the courses you have taken in high school and college, and thoughtfully review them in your mind. What uses did the instructors make of visual aids in presenting the subject matter of these courses? Were such materials effectively used? Did the instructors take full advantage of the possibilities afforded by such supporting materials? Prepare a brief, written description of several instances in which the instructors might have expanded or improved the visual presentation of the materials.

2.   Visual supporting materials capture appropriate moods, clarify potentially complex subjects, and sometimes even carry the thrust of a persuasive message. Examine magazine advertisements and "how-to-do-it" articles in periodicals; look at store windows and special displays in museums and libraries; and observe slide-projection lectures in some of your other college classes. Then *(a)* using the *types* considered in this chapter, classify the nonverbal supporting

materials you have encountered; *(b)* assess the *purposes* these materials serve—clarification, persuasion, attention-focusing, mood-setting, and others you may wish to cite; *(c)* evaluate the *effectiveness* with which each of the materials you have examined is doing its job; and, finally *(d),* prepare a report, a paper, or an entry in your journal on the results of your experiences and observations.

3. The question of *figure-ground relationships* is one of the most important faced by the oral communicator when preparing visuals. To explore such relationships in your communicative world: *(a)* Examine magazine advertisements to see ways in which writers and artists isolate figures through techniques of shape, color, size, and detail, and the ways in which they use backgrounds to add feelings and associations to the central figure. *(b)* Study television commercials with these same concerns in mind. *(c)* Then write a brief description of a series of visuals you conceivably could incorporate into your next speech, and specify the characteristics you might try to build into each visual aid in order to make maximum use of figure-ground relationships. (If you desire additional help in the exploration of magazines especially, see Stephen Baker, *Visual Persuasion* [New York: McGraw-Hill, 1961.])

Oral Activities and Speaking Assignments

1. Present to the class a five-minute, central-idea speech, the purpose of which is to explain or clarify a term, concept, process, plan, or proposal. Use several of the forms of *verbal* supporting material suggested in Chapter 7; and employ at least one chart, diagram, map, picture, or other *visual* support.

2. Using as a basis the series of visual aids you evolved in Problem/Probe 3 above, present a short oral report in which you describe a speech you will give and the ways in which you plan to incorporate the visual materials and coordinate them with the verbal materials. If you can, bring in some rough-draft examples of the visuals for the purpose of illustrating your intentions.

3. Participate in a class discussion on the topic "Proper and Improper Uses of the Chalkboard." Consider how some of your current and former teachers have used it. The following questions may be useful in guiding the group's considerations: What communicative functions are best served by the chalkboard? What communicative functions could be better served by slides, overhead projectors, or dittoed handouts? Are there special problems with the use of visuals when audience members are taking notes while listening?

Suggestions for Further Reading

Rudolph Arnheim, *Visual Thinking* (Berkeley: University of California Press, 1969).

Doris A. Dondis, *A Primer of Visual Literacy* (Cambridge, Mass.: The M. I. T. Press, 1973).

George F. Horn, *Visual Communication: Bulletin Boards, Exhibits, Visual Aids* (Worcester, Mass.: Davis Publications, Inc., 1973).

Walter A. Wittich and Charles F. Schuller, *Audio-Visual Materials: Their Nature and Use,* 2nd ed. (New York: Harper & Row, Publishers, 1957).

Sol Worth, "Pictures Can't Say Ain't," *Versus* 12 (December 1975): 85–108.

Leonard Zusne, *Visual Perception of Form* (New York: Academic Press, Inc., 1976).

Part 4

Inform Actuate

WEBSTER'S UNABRIDGED DICTIONARY
A LIBRARY IN ITSELF

Public Communication:
Basic Types

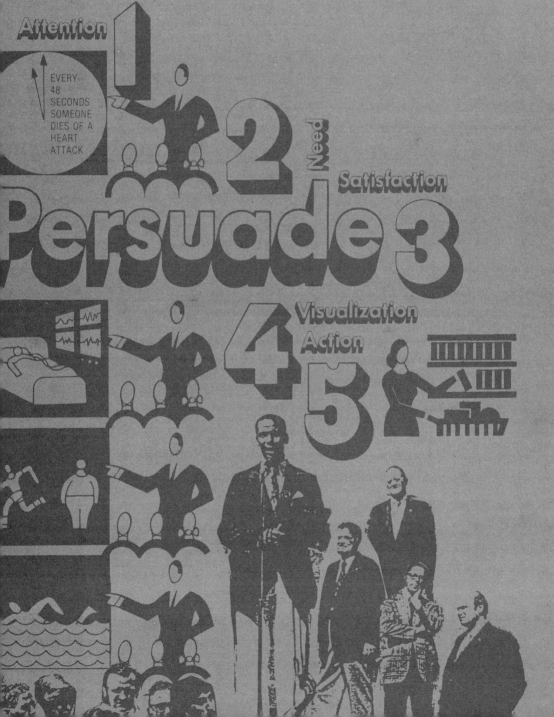

17

The Speech to Inform

Informative speeches take many forms. Three forms occur so frequently, however, that they merit special mention: (1) *Oral reports:* scientific reports, committee reports, executive reports, and similar informational accounts. Experts who engage in research projects announce their findings. Committees carry on inquiries and report their results to the parent organization. Teachers, representatives of fraternal groups, and businessmen and women attend conventions and then share what they have learned with others.* (2) *Oral instructions:* class instructions, job instructions, and instructions for special group efforts. Teachers instruct students in ways of preparing assignments and performing experiments. Supervisors tell their subordinates how a task should be carried out. Leaders explain to volunteer workers their duties in a fund-raising drive or a citywide cleanup campaign. For convenience, such instructions often are given to a group of persons rather than to single individuals and, even when written, may need to be accompanied by oral explanations. (3) *Informative lectures:* public lectures; class lectures; and lectures at meetings, study conferences, and institutes. People often are invited to share information or knowledge with groups interested in receiving it. Many informative speeches are given each week before civic luncheon clubs and study groups. Instructors present lectures daily on every college campus; and visiting speakers appear before church groups, conventions, and business and professional institutes.

Whatever form your speech takes, however, your purpose remains the

---

*"Techniques for Making Oral Reports" are examined in detail in Chapter 20, pages 341–343.

same: to help the audience grasp and remember important data and ideas about your subject. Hence, you should not view an informative speech as an opportunity to parade your knowledge; nor should you try to see how much ground you can cover in a given period of time. Rather, you should concentrate on securing understanding and on presenting materials in such a way that they will remain firmly planted in the listeners' minds.

Content of the Speech to Inform

To help insure that the materials you present will be understood and remembered, when planning the content of a speech to inform adhere to the following guidelines:

Keep the Leading Ideas Few in Number.   If masses of data are thrown at people too rapidly, they soon become bewildered; or, catching only an occasional point here and there, they acquire an imperfect understanding of the subject. For this reason, it is important—especially when discussing a new or difficult topic—not to attempt to deal with too many major ideas or to pass over any of them too rapidly. Select those facts and concepts which are most essential to an understanding of the topic you are presenting or the procedure you are describing. Then, through the use of appropriate forms of supporting material, hold each of them before the audience until you are reasonably sure it has been absorbed.

Define All Strange or Ambiguous Terms.   In many situations, how well an audience understands a subject will depend upon whether it is able to grasp the meaning of certain key terms. Therefore, whenever such a term is either strange or ambiguous, stop to define it before you proceed. For this purpose, one or more of the methods of definition described below may prove helpful:

Dictionary Definition. Put the term or concept to be defined into a general class or category and then carefully distinguish it from the other members of this class. ("An apple is a *fruit* that is *red* and *round* and *hard* and *juicy*." "Man is a *rational* animal.")

Etymology. Clarify meaning by telling the history of a word—tracing the source from which it derived. ("*Propel* comes from the Latin prefix *pro* meaning *forward* and the verb *pellere* meaning *to drive*. Therefore, a *propeller* is an instrument which drives something forward.")

Negation. Clarify the meaning of a term or concept by telling what *it is not*. ("By *socialism* I do not mean *communism,* which believes in the common ownership of all property. Instead, I mean . . .")

Example. Clarify by mentioning an actual example or instance of what you have in mind. ("You all have seen the Methodist church on Maple Street. That is what I mean by English Gothic architecture.")

Use in a Context. Clarify the meaning of a term or concept by actually using it in a sentence. ("*Hopping* is a slang term for *very* or *exceedingly.* For instance, if I say, 'He was *hopping* mad,' I mean that he was angry indeed.")

Pace the Rate at Which Information Is Presented.   If you pass over a point too rapidly, your listeners often will fail to grasp it or to appreciate its significance. On the other hand, if you dwell on a point too long, your speech will drag, and attention will wander. Learn to pace your presentation of information in such a way that your speech keeps moving forward at the rate best calculated to ensure comprehension, but avoid boredom.

Make Transitions Clear.   As you pass from one aspect of your subject to another, make clear to your listeners where you are going and how your new point relates to the preceding one. Say, "So much, then, for how a combine works and the uses it serves. Let us next consider whether it is a good investment for the small farmer." Or, say: "Therefore, before World War I, courses in public speaking seldom were taught in American colleges. As we shall now see, however, shortly after that war they began to appear in large numbers."

Use Concrete Data—Don't Be Abstract.   A good speech to inform must be meaty—that is, packed with facts, figures, explanations, and examples. When presenting these data, however, *do not sacrifice clarity in your concern for accuracy of detail.* Many laws or theories, for example, have exceptions. As a rule, these laws or theories should first be stated in general terms, saving a discussion of the exceptions for later. Statistics, too, usually should be presented in round numbers; and explanations and examples should not be so extensively qualified that their central point is lost in a mass of details. Be honest and fair in what you say, but also keep in mind the problem of getting your material understood and remembered by your listeners.

Connect the Unknown with the Known.   As we pointed out in Chapter 10 (pages 167–168), new material usually is learned more readily when it is related to something the listeners already know or understand. If, for example, you are speaking to a group of nurses on new procedures for treating terminally ill patients, you might compare and contrast these procedures with existing practices. A college president speaking to a manufacturers' convention on the problems involved in educating students presented his ideas under the heads of *raw materials, casting, machining, polishing,* and *assembling.*

Inject Interest-Arousing Material.   In most instances, you will find that there is a limit to the cold facts and figures an audience is able or willing to absorb. Therefore, from time to time you must inject into an informative speech some material designed to rekindle interest and revive attention. Review the *factors of attention* described in Chapter 8 (pages 131–135), and keep them constantly in mind as you plan and present your speech.

Organization of the Speech to Inform

As we explained in Chapter 9, one effective way to organize a speech to inform is to employ the first three steps in *the motivated sequence:* attention, need, and satisfaction. When following this pattern, develop your speech as follows:

Attention Step

Since the persons who gather to receive information usually contract in advance to accept what they are told, you seldom will need to spend much time establishing your own credibility or conciliating skeptical or hostile listeners. Often, however, you will need to capture your audience's attention and direct it to the subject you are going to discuss. For this purpose, you may employ a startling statement, a striking quotation, a humorous anecdote, or any of the other methods of focusing attention in the beginning of a speech, as described in Chapter 12 (pages 190–197).

Need Step

Although it generally should be short, the need step in a speech to inform is exceedingly important. Even experienced speakers sometimes fail because they assume that their listeners are waiting to seize the "pearls of knowledge" their speeches contain. Unfortunately, this is not always the case. Unless you are certain of their interest in advance, show your listeners *why* the information you are about to present is important to them — why it is something they need to know or even to act upon. If you can suggest how your speech will help them get a better job, save money, or enhance their position in the community, they usually will be willing to listen.

In developing the need step of an informative speech to an audience that is encountering the subject for the first time or is not already interested in it, include these four elements:

1. *Statement.* Point out the importance of your subject and the listeners' need to be better informed concerning it.

2. *Illustration.* Present one or more stories or examples which illustrate the importance of the need or demonstrate its significance and timeliness.

3. *Reinforcement.* Provide as many additional facts, figures, or quotations as are required to make the need convincing and impressive.

THE MOTIVATED SEQUENCE

APPLIED TO SPEECHES

To Inform

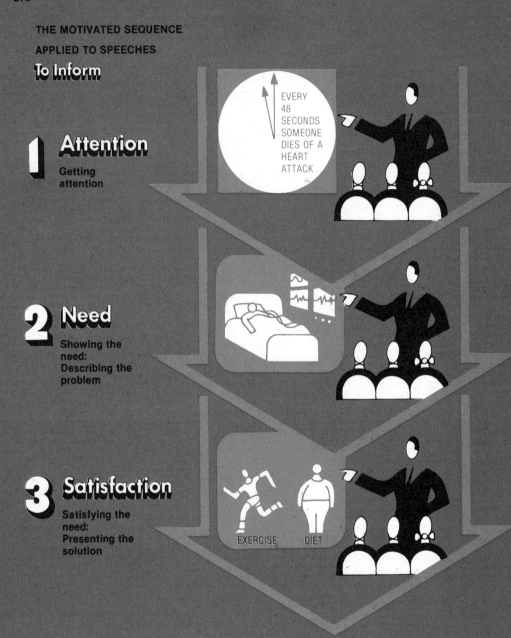

1 Attention

Getting
attention

EVERY
48
SECONDS
SOMEONE
DIES OF A
HEART
ATTACK

2 Need

Showing the
need:
Describing the
problem

3 Satisfaction

Satisfying the
need:
Presenting the
solution

EXERCISE   DIET

The above illustration suggests how the first three steps of the motivated sequence
might be used to structure an informative speech on the general subject, "The Care
and Protection of Your Heart." Using the same subject, you could of course effectively
structure a speech to *persuade* by using the first four steps, and a speech to *actuate*
by using all five. (See pages 294 and 322.) Variations for each type of speech would
be significantly influenced by the intended audience, the speaker's general and
specific purpose, the choice and emphasis of supporting materials, the physical-
psychological setting, and the style and tone of the presentation.

4. *Pointing.* Show how your subject directly relates to the interests, well-being, or success of your hearers. Say, in effect: "This information vitally concerns *you* because . . ."

There will be times, of course, when the information in your speech is not of a practical or workaday variety—something which does not directly affect the health, happiness, or prosperity of your listeners. When this is the case, you may be able to use the element of suspense or curiosity in building your need step. A noted chemist, for example, began a lecture by telling of an unusual murder case. He made his audience wonder who the guilty man was and then proceeded to show how, through certain chemical tests, the man was identified and convicted.

Satisfaction Step: The Information Itself

Having captured the attention of your listeners and shown them why they *need* the information you are about to present, you are ready to offer the information itself. This is done in the satisfaction step—the step in which you answer or satisfy the need you have created. Because this step usually constitutes the bulk of a speech to inform, it often is helpful to develop it in three phases: an *initial summary,* the *detailed presentation of the information,* and a *closing summary.*

1. *The Initial Summary.* As its name suggests, the initial summary consists of a brief enumeration of the main points you expect to cover. Its purpose is to help your listeners grasp the plan of your speech as a whole, as well as to see the relationship one idea bears to another. For example, if you were going to explain athletic activities as they exist on your campus, you might begin your satisfaction step in this way:

> In order to give you an idea of athletic activities on our campus, I shall discuss, first, the intercollegiate sports; second, our intramural program; and third, the courses offered in the Department of Physical Education.

Note also how such a preview or initial summary was used by Whitney J. Oates, chairman of the Council of Humanities at Princeton University, in an address on "Philosophy as the Center of Liberal Education":

> I propose first to sketch briefly the role of philosophy, as I see it, in history, in literature and the arts, the social sciences and the natural sciences—in other words, those subjects which constitute, broadly speaking, the traditional content of liberal education. And I shall conclude with a discussion of other ways in which philosophy reveals its significance in the intellectual life.[1]

The order in which you list the main points in your initial summary obviously should follow the same sequence you intend to use in your detailed discussion; otherwise, you will confuse your listeners by setting up a guidepost which points in a direction different from the road you actually will take. Properly developed, however, an initial summary will help your audience follow your discussion and will help them see the relation of each point to the whole.

2. *The detailed information.* The detailed information you wish to impart is presented next, covering in order the main points enumerated in your initial summary. Explanations, facts, comparisons, and other forms of supporting material should be grouped around each main point in a systematic fashion and, when possible, amplified and illustrated by maps, pictures, tables, demonstrations, or other visible or audible aids to understanding. Here is how some of the standard sequences described in Chapter 10 (pages 164–170) may be used to organize the main points of your detailed information:

TIME SEQUENCE: FLIGHTS IN SPACE

  I. The first space flight was made on April 12, 1961, by Major Yuri Gagarin of the Soviet Air Force.
 II. On May 5, 1961, Alan Shepard became the first American to enter space.
III. Astronauts Neil Armstrong and Edwin Aldrin set foot on the moon on July 20, 1969.
 IV. The final flight of the $25 billion Apollo Project occurred on December 11-14, 1972, when Astronauts Eugene Cernan and Jack Schmitt explored the mountainous side of the moon.

SPACE SEQUENCE: PRINCIPAL AMERICAN DIALECTS

  I. Eastern dialect is heard chiefly in New England.
 II. Southern dialect is heard in former Confederate states.
III. General American dialect is common west and north of these two areas.

CAUSE-EFFECT SEQUENCE: AIR POLLUTION

  I. Motor vehicles, industrial plants, and home incinerators discharge large amounts of waste material into the atmosphere.

 II. This discharge has created a serious air-pollution problem in most of our cities.

OR

EFFECT-CAUSE SEQUENCE: AIR POLLUTION

  I. Most of our major cities face a serious problem of air pollution.
 II. Important causes of this problem are the vapors discharged from motor vehicles, industrial plants, and home incinerators.

SPECIAL TOPICAL SEQUENCE: SOURCES OF VITAMINS

I. Vitamin A is found in butter, fortified margarine, and vegetable oils.
II. B-complex vitamins come from bread, flour, and cereals.
III. Vitamin C is supplied by citrus fruits, tomatoes, and raw cabbage.

Regardless of the subject or specific purpose of an informative speech, or how it may be treated in the satisfaction step, let us stress once again that its main objective is to ensure a clear and thorough understanding on the part of your audience. The detailed information, therefore, must be clearly organized and fully amplified with concrete and specific supporting material.

3. *The closing summary.* In your closing summary, review the information you have presented and tie it together in such a way as to give your audience a unified picture. This may be done by restating your main points and reviewing any important conclusions or implications which have grown out of your discussion. The closing summary is similar to the initial one, but is usually somewhat longer. Notice the difference between this closing summary and the initial summary (see page 279) for the speech on athletic activities:

> From what I have said, you can readily see that the three main divisions of our athletic system are closely related to one another. The intercollegiate sports serve as the stimulus for developing superior skill as well as a source of revenue for financing the rest of the program. Our intramural system extends the facilities for physical recreation to a large part of our student body—three thousand last year. And our physical education classes not only serve in training men and women to become the coaches of the future, but also act in systematically building up the physical endurance of the student body as a whole and in giving corrective work to those who have physical defects. The work of these three divisions is well organized and complete.

Concluding the Informative Speech

When you have presented your information and created an understanding of it, you will have attained your purpose. Ordinarily, therefore, the closing summary as given at the end of the satisfaction step concludes an informative speech. There are times, however, when you may wish to urge your listeners to pay additional attention to the subject you have been discussing—that is, when you want to actuate as well as simply inform. In such cases, add to the summary a few words suggesting that your listeners apply what they have learned, or recommend books and articles in which they can find a further consideration of the matter. Then close quickly with a sentence of appreciation for their attention or a few remarks aimed at motivating the behavior or study you recommend.

Special Patterns for Special Purposes

The organizational pattern we have described in the preceding pages is well suited to most speeches of an informative nature, and usually may be followed with only minor adaptations to the subject being discussed. However, when you are reporting on a specific piece of research you have done, or when instructing an audience how to carry out a step-by-step procedure or perform a complicated manual task, more specialized patterns of organization often are helpful. The following are examples:

Research Reports.   Research reports should, as a rule, begin with a clear statement of the hypothesis to be tested or the problem to be investigated; next, give a brief review of previous research on the subject; follow this with an explanation of the materials used, the apparatus employed, or the literary or historical sources investigated; then describe the procedure followed in carrying out the study; and finally, summarize the data or results obtained. For *other types of reports* — such as those resulting from committee discussions, financial operations, travel, or direct observation — adapt the foregoing steps as follows: first, state the nature or scope of the subject to be covered; second, review the sources from which material was gathered (discussion, observation, written records, etc.); and, third, set forth the salient points discovered as a result of the inquiry.

Giving Instructions.   When the purpose of an informative speech is to *give instructions,* it usually contains: first, an overall statement of the nature and purpose of the operation to be performed; and, second, an explanation of each step in that operation *in the order in which it is to be taken.* The discussion of each step also may include the reason for it, the materials or tools or special information required, and the precautions to be observed. Finally, when giving instructions, you may find it useful to pause after explaining each step in the process, so as to invite questions or to test the listeners' understanding in some appropriate way.

A Sample Speech to Inform

On October 9, 1974, Dr. George P. Rice, Professor of Speech at Butler University and a practicing attorney, presented the following lecture to a student audience assembled on the Indianapolis campus of Purdue University. Notice in particular the way in which the speaker employs the first three steps in the motivated sequence: *Attention, Need,* and *Satisfaction.* Appropriately, in an informative-type speech, the Visualization and Action steps are omitted; and Dr. Rice closes with a brief summary and an apt quotation.

   In the Attention step, free speech is defined, the conditions essential to its existence are mentioned, and the audience's attention is focused on the subject by differentiating speaking to *entertain* from speaking designed to inform or persuade. A brief Need step points out that speaking to entertain has been largely neglected, and that some knowledge of it would be of use to business and professional persons. The Satisfaction step then surveys in reasonable detail the sources, functions, tests, and types of *humor,* suggests certain precautions to be observed in its use, and reviews relevant research findings.

Throughout his speech, Dr. Rice presents a wealth of pertinent examples, many of which are highly entertaining in their own right, and hence illustrate well the use that humor may have in developing informative material. Not only is the subject well adapted to an audience of college students, but the wide range of ancient and modern authors cited by the speaker give his remarks an air of authority. The style of the presentation is clear and attractive, and ideas are advanced at a pace which enables the speaker to cover much ground without hurrying.

"The Comic Spirit and the Public Speaker"[2]

George P. Rice

[*Attention Step*]

Free legal speech has been defined as any oral communication which does not invade the protected rights of others. Its origins are found in Athens during the Golden Age where, by 450 B.C., the role of freedom of utterance in a democratic society had been clearly established. Its use in the *ekklesia* (deliberative assembly) or the *dicastery* (courts of law) was predicated upon not only the right but the duty of every qualified male citizen to express his views and to vote on matters of public interest. The rules to govern effective public speaking evolved slowly, but by 355 B.C. Aristotle had produced his treatise on the art of rhetoric which he defined as ". . . the faculty of discovering in the particular case what are the available means of persuasion." He further explained the kinds of speaking, their purposes, the nature of ethical, logical, and pathetic proof, and the parts of the speech and the function performed by each. In the course of time, the Romans made their contributions through the works of Cicero, Quintilian, and the "unknown" Longinus. The influence of these men and their works has been commanding from their publication to the present. /1

Now the effective use of free speech, as demonstrated by the polities of Athens, Rome, France, England, and the United States among others, has shown that certain necessary conditions must exist in order for speech to function for the public benefit: (1) there must be freedom of speech; (2) there must be important issues to discuss and engage public attention; (3) eminent speakers of ability must be available to present the merits and facts of all sides of a controversy; (4) the audience which hears and judges their arguments must be intelligent and educated so that truth may triumph in the marketplace of public opinion; and (5) the language used by such speakers as the medium for communication must be highly developed in its grammar, diction, and sounds. /2

Basically, all oral communication is for one or the other of three purposes (or a combination of them): to entertain, to inform, or to persuade. Of these, the persuasive speech with conviction as its end is by common consent the most important and makes the greatest demands upon the skill of the spokesman. The capable critic judges the man on the rostrum by his integrity, his knowledge, his rhetorical skills, and his self-confidence. The speeches themselves, of course, are given substance by the use of various forms of "speech supports," including anecdote, definition, quotation of authority, example, generalization, statistics, and illustrations. /3

[*Need Step*]

It is the thesis of this discourse that the evocation of the comic spirit for speech purposes is a much-neglected but vitally important aspect of public address both by the classical and the modern theorists. Literature on the subject is scant. Hence, this survey of the nature and functions of humor and wit with some definitions and examples may advantage the business or professional man called upon to address his fellows. /4

[*Satisfaction Step*]

The fundamental object of the speaker who arouses the comic spirit is to produce enjoyment not only in his audience, but in himself. Some of his effects will be gained by the tasteful and timely use of humor. Humor has been defined as the quality of being funny. It embraces what is amusing or comical. Whim and caprice are its near companions. They combine to produce an assembly of incongruities as these become manifest from the revelation of character and situation. Hence, humor *per se* is genial, mellow, and kind. Upon occasion, however, it relies upon the rhetoric of invective and irony for effect. Wit, another component of the comic spirit, is purely intellectual and usually spontaneous. The quick and clever expression of an apt idea is its essence. The revelation of wit by brief, diverting, or caustic observation touches upon the hearer's sensitivity to create instant laughter in contrast to the smiles which humor provokes. Skilled use of the figure of comparison is one characteristic of the witty talker. Laughter, of course, is the physiological reaction to display of the comic spirit. /5

It is the merest commonplace that much more is known about tragedy than comedy. This may perhaps be due to the fact that most of Aristotle's treatise on comedy was lost, hence no foundation was available for later writers to build upon. Nevertheless, parts of Aristotle and studies by Fielding, Meredith, and Bergson repay a cruise of the timber in the search* for the prevailing theories. From these and other sources one may infer that comedy, like every other fine or useful art, has its own qualities and capacities for the production of specific intended effects. There is a tendency to agree that pleasure is derived from humor by the perception of a defect or ugliness that is neither painful nor injurious,

---

*A figurative way of saying that an examination of the relevant works of these writers would reveal some of the prevailing theories of humor.

but which awakens one's sense of disproportion of character or situation. The effect is a release of tensions accumulated in the hearer who is amused by heightened awareness of what is ludicrous or ridiculous in human affairs. /6

He who would hunt the comic spirit in its native habitat must explore the works of Aristophanes and Menander among the Greeks; Plautus and Terence among the Romans; Boccaccio and Goldoni among the Italians; Rabelais and Molière among the French; Lessing, Goethe, and Heine among the Germans; Shakespeare, Congreve, and Sheridan among the English; and Irving and Twain among Americans. The literary vehicles for the conveyance of the comic spirit are many and varied: plays, poems, epigrams, fables, essays, dialogues, parodies, anecdotes, short stories, maxims, conversations, graffiti, figures of speech, and even individual words. These writings reveal the vital function performed by wit and humor in keeping a cultivated society in good political and mental health. Conversely, it may be claimed that their absence—or worse, their appearance in vulgar form—suggests the decay and decline of a nation. /7

At this point it is in order to remark upon the duality of the nature of man. He is in part mind and intelligence, and these are supple and free. But this spiritual-intellectual aspect is housed in a physical body with specific earthy demands and subordinate to the mechanized routines of his daily life. These two elements, as William Wordsworth has said, are in conflict one with the other much of the time. As man strives to adjust these two aspects of his being with the demands of a technological environment, tensions build up. When they reach a certain duration and intensity, his nature seeks relief. Thus, when the spiritual-intellectual element perceives a demonstration of the absurdities, the affectations, the vanities, the vices, the imperfections, and the pretensions of mankind, collectively or individually, the comic spirit functions and is aroused by what is amusing, ludicrous, or awakens the observer's sense of superiority. Smiles and laughter result, producing the panacea so greatly needed for relief. The chief result, then, is a purgation of tensions, comparable to that of pity and fear resulting from witnessing a great tragedy as described in *The Poetics* of Aristotle. /8

How does one recognize the presence of an activated comic spirit? By such traits as these:

1. It is a living spirit, its abode the mind of man.
2. It is intellectual in its nature, appealing to the imagination as does good poetry, rather than to the emotions.
3. It cannot occur in isolation.
4. It can be expressed by non-human agents when these are personified.
5. It is revealed by gestures, attitudes, and bodily movements as in pantomime.
6. It may originate in an action and be expressed in language.
7. It will be callous on occasion since one of its aims is reformation.
8. It appears to best advantage in a sophisticated society such as that of ancient Athens or the France of Louis XIV, and only such a society can sustain it. /9

Some insight into the psychological and social functions of the comic spirit has been obtained. It includes:

1. Exposure and correction of the foibles and prejudices which afflict society by holding them up for inspection and ridicule.
2. Preservation of the proper balance between the spiritual-intellectual and the physiological components of human nature.
3. Creation of a more democratic spirit in society at large.
4. Provision for proportion and perspective in human judgment.
5. Establishment of a bond of fellowship with the great minds, causes, and societies of past and present.
6. Avoidance of hostility toward religions, races, and political credos, save where these are corrupt.
7. Prevention of laughter that is perverse, cruel, or untasteful. /10

How can one tell when the wit and humor of his talk have blended with the rest of it for successful achievement of his aims? Answers to questions such as these help provide the standard: Did the speaker himself enjoy the experience? Was there evidence from the audience by the various forms of feedback (such as laughter, smiles, concentrated attention) that the design was fulfilled? Did the speech move easily from point to point? Was the material used appropriate to the speaker, his message, the audience, and the occasion? Was the comic element properly subordinated, and did it advance the primary purpose of the speech? /11

Certain precautions in the use of humor and wit must be taken; for the nature of laughter is such, the philosophers tell one, that it represents a descent in terms of emotional values and loses its effect if continued too long or applied to improper purposes. The audience must be analyzed in advance—size, age, sex, race, religion, education, financial status, and political views—so that what is presented will not strain its limits of tolerance or affront its collective values. At all times the boundaries of decorum and decency must be preserved. /12

Max Eastman's "Ten Commandments"[3] for use of humor are instructive:

1. Be interesting.
2. Exhibit personal emotional control at all times.
3. Be easy and effortless.
4. Make careful distinction between the practical joke and the portrayal of the ludicrous.
5. Be plausible.
6. Be sudden.
7. Be neat.
8. Be careful with timing.
9. Be sure to give a good measure of serious satisfaction.
10. Be alert to redeem all serious disappointments. /13

The anecdote is a favorite vehicle of humor for the public speaker. Chairmen employ it to introduce him, and he in turn uses it to establish rapport with his audience and interest in his message. For maximum good effect it must be brief, polished, pointed, and relevant. For example, a gentleman in the U.S. Department of State once gave a talk on Russo-American diplomacy to an audience of business and professional men.

When he finished, the floor was open for questions from the audience. These were numerous and incisive. When the period ended, the chairman thanked the speaker, concluding: "I hope, Sir, there were no embarrassing questions asked of you in the light of the delicacy of your subject." Came the spontaneous reply: "Have no fears on that score, Mr. Chairman. There is no such thing as an embarrassing question. *There are only embarrassing answers!"* /14

Graffiti, the archaeologists say, are as old at least as Pompeii and Herculaneum. Here are some contemporary examples:

1. Abbie Hoffman is revolting.
2. Sigmund Freud was symbol-minded.
3. Jack the Ripper was a scream.
4. Save cigarette coupons and get a free cancer.
5. Dr. Jekyll isn't himself today.
6. Oscar Wilde was prematurely gay.
7. Frankenstein was a man of parts.
8. Lizzie Borden really knew how to hurt a guy.
9. College is a fountain of knowledge where many go to drink.
10. Any rich man will tell you that poverty is no disgrace. /15

Almost everyone takes pleasure in hearing the unexpected turn of phrase derived from the use of conventional expressions with surprise endings. An incomparable harvest of these may be gleaned from the comedies and reported conversations of Oscar Wilde who, along with Dr. Samuel Johnson and the Reverend Sidney Smith, ranks highest among brilliant talkers.

. . . .

Early evidence of wit in Wilde is found in a book review he published shortly after coming down from Oxford in 1878. Two women had combined to write a book, and the reviewer expressed his opinion of this literary abortion in the first line of his review: "It has taken two people to write this book, and even to read it requires assistance." /16

The poetry of Samuel Taylor Coleridge provides an excellent example of definition of epigram: "What is an Epigram? A dwarfish whole; its body brevity and wit its soul." /17

Puns and plays on words are popular vehicles for wit and humor. (A pun is a play on words of the same sound but with different meaning.) For example, "Too often we seek justice for just us." And there is the celebrated characterization of the Earl of Chesterfield by Sam Johnson: "This man I had thought a Lord among wits; but, I find, he is only a wit among Lords." A newspaper once listed births, marriages, and deaths under these captions: "Hatched, matched, and detached." A witty pastor once pasted this notice on his church bulletin board: "Come in and have your faith lifted." And there was the actress who, after a boring party, commented, "It was a fête worse than death." /18

Exaggeration and absurdity are favorite weapons of speakers who prefer the flick of the rapier to the whack of the barrel stave. Benjamin Disraeli was once asked to distinguish between "misfortune" and "calamity" and said: "If William Gladstone fell into the Thames, it would be a misfortune. But if someone dragged him out, it would be a calamity!" Bernard Shaw one day received an invitation to tea with a noblewoman celebrated for stalking famous men. The card read: "Lady X will be at home Tuesday between four and six o'clock." Shaw returned the card with these words upon it: "Mr. Bernard Shaw likewise." Finally, there is the famous epitaph written by John Dryden: "Here lies my wife: here let her lie! Now she's at rest, and so am I!" /19

Can the comic spirit, once invoked, persuade on the basis of its own intrinsic merits? Or must it be used as adjunct to other rhetorical devices? A few studies have been published, based upon research, which permit these conclusions:

1. It may be that wit and humor serve their purpose best when used to crystallize or make more vivid a truth already partially perceived by the audience.
2. But if, in fact, wit and humor gain reaction by artistic condensation of what is already perceived as truth, it may be that they should be used to reinforce and strengthen existing attitudes or values arrived at, rather than be employed in an attempt to change them.
3. Because humor is unrelated to persuasive purpose, it can hardly be expected to produce conviction in the audience by itself alone. /20

In the area of law, where the speaker has had some experience, it would appear that judges and lawyers think that humor has little place for the prosecution in criminal causes, whereas its use by counsel for the defense is sometimes effective with a jury. The judges, protected by the sanctity of the Bench, have a wider latitude, as evidenced by the Indiana judge who gave a divorced husband rights of visitation with his dog who was placed in the wife's custody. /21

[*Summary*]

In sum, the persuasive speech pervaded by the comic spirit is subject to the same rules governing selection of material, structuring organization, and guiding its presentation to an audience. Its function, though subordinate, is to create good rapport between speaker and listener, to provide relaxing interludes in substantial matter, and to create empathy not only with the speaker but with other members of the audience. /22

[*Closing Quotation*]

If the speaker masters and combines all of the rhetorical weapons available and cultivates the comic spirit in its various phases, the result may be an address to measure by the standard composed so carefully by Richard Murphy: "A speech as a literary form, then, is a prose composition of varying length, fashioned for a specific or generic audience, usually but not necessarily spoken and listened to, written or recorded in some way on brain, paper, or tape for permanence, in which are interrelated author, reading or listening audience, theme, and occasion; it has ethical appeal and universality, moving force and fluency; its design is artistic, and its purpose is to direct the reader or listener to a conclusion selected by the composer."[4] /23

Reference Notes

¹*Liberal Education,* ed. F. L. Wormald (Washington, D.C.), *Bulletin of the Association of American Colleges* (May 1964): 213

²"The Comic Spirit and the Public Speaker: Some Basic Rhetorical Concepts," by George P. Rice, from *Vital Speeches of the Day,* XXXXI (November 1, 1974). Reprinted by permission of Vital Speeches of the Day.

³From *The Emjoyment of Laughter* by Max Eastman. Copyright © 1936, 1963, by Max Eastman. Reprinted by permission of Simon & Schuster, a Division of Gulf & Western Corporation.

⁴From "The Speech as Literary Genre," by Richard Murphy from *Quarterly Journal of Speech,* 46, April 1958, p. 119. Reprinted by permission of Speech Communication Association.

Problems and Probes

1.   Make a study of one particular type of informative speaking — the classroom lecture, the expository sermon, the oral report, the informative radio or television speech, etc. After reading or listening to a number of speeches of this type, prepare a paper in which you comment on the special problems of organization or presentation which seemed to be present. In the speeches you studied and analyzed, how were these problems solved?

2.   In a concise written report, indicate and defend the type of arrangement (chronological sequence, spatial sequence, etc.) you think would be most suitable for an informative speech on at least five of the subjects listed below. (See the types of speech structure discussed in Chapter 10, 164–170.)

The campus parking situation
Recent developments in the women's rights movement
Indian jewelry of the Southwest
Saving our environment
How the stock market works
Censorship of the arts
Wonder drugs of the 1970s
The fraternity tradition
Space stations: Living in a weightless world
What life will be like in 1990

3.   Select a principle of physics, chemistry, biology, or a similar science and describe how you might explain this principle to: *(a)* a farmer, *(b)* an automobile repairman, *(c)* a twelve-year-old newsboy, *(d)* a blind person, *(e)* a well-educated adult who is just learning to speak English. See how inventive you can be in making the principle clear without resorting to highly technical language.

Oral Activities and Speaking Assignments

1.   Select five terms or concepts that are likely to be strange to your classmates and, using one or more of the methods of definition described on pages 275–276, orally make their meaning or significance clear to a classroom audience. Be prepared to explain why in each case you used the method or methods you did.

2.   Present to the class a three- or four-minute speech in which you describe how something looks, or explain a relatively complex operation or procedure. Instead of using gestures or visual aids to assist in making your description or explanation, *depend on language alone.* At the conclusion of your speech, see how accurately selected members of your audience can verbally re-create the appearance of the object you have described or the procedure you have explained. The following are possibilities to work with:

A play in football (or some other sport)
The appearance of your living room at home
The layout of some city
Women's or men's styles of a bygone day
How to knit
The proper way to serve in tennis
Holds in wrestling
A rotary automobile engine
The anatomy of the finger

3.   Prepare a speech to inform for delivery in class. Using one of the topics suggested below or a similar one drawn from your Personal Speech Journal and approved by your instructor, select and narrow the area of the subject to be covered, develop whatever visual aids may be appropriate, and settle upon the order or pattern you will be following in setting forth the information. Take special pains to make clear why the audience needs to know the material you are presenting. Suggested topics:

Contemporary American writers (artists, musicians)
The physical effects of marijuana
How to become a better listener
The agencies of the United Nations
A first lesson in aircraft-recognition
Changing perspectives in American foreign policy
Planning a freeway or toll-free highway system
How to read lips
The romance of archaeology
Exercising to lose weight
How television programs are rated

 ## Suggestions for Further Reading

Charles R. Gruner, Cal M. Logue, Dwight L. Freshley, and Richard Huseman, *Speech Communication in Society* (Boston: Allyn & Bacon, Inc., 1972), Chapter 10, "The Informative Speech."
Kenneth G. Hance, David C. Ralph, and Milton J. Wiksell, *Principles of Speaking,* 3rd ed. (Belmont, Calif.: Wadsworth Publishing Company, Inc., 1975), Chapter 16, "Speaking to Inform."
Bernard P. McCabe, Jr., and Coleman C. Bender, *Speaking Is a Practical Matter,* 2nd ed. (Boston: Holbrook Press, Inc., 1973), Part IV, "Speaking to Inform."
Thomas H. Olbricht, *Informative Speaking* (Glenview, Ill.: Scott, Foresman and Company, 1968).
Loren Reid, *Speaking Well,* 2nd ed. (New York: McGraw-Hill Book Company, 1972), Part III, "Interesting and Informing."
Raymond S. Ross, *Speech Communication: Fundamentals and Practice,* 4th ed. (Englewood Cliffs, N.J.: Prentice-Hall, Inc., 1977), Chapter 9, "Presenting Information."

18

The Speech to Persuade

We live today in a complex society. No longer can one person working alone accomplish a task of any magnitude. Others also must be convinced that the task is worthwhile and agree to lend their support and encouragement. In the preceding chapter we explained how a speaker may organize and present ideas when seeking to increase the knowledge or understanding of the listeners. In this chapter we shall explain how to organize and present ideas when your purpose is to persuade — that is, to induce your listeners to believe the claim or proposition you are advancing or to win their support for the policy you propose.

Although your ultimate aim in speaking is to win acceptance of your point of view, in order to achieve this goal, you must, as a rule, keep two subsidiary or intermediary purposes in mind: *(a)* to provide your listeners with a motive for believing or acting — show them how the endorsement of your claim or proposition will, for example, remove an existing evil or contribute in some way to their happiness, power, profit, or pride; and *(b)* to convince them of the factual correctness, moral soundness, or inherent practicability of the claim or proposition you advance.

Analyzing the Claim

The first step in constructing a successful speech to persuade is to get clearly in mind the nature of the claim or proposal you wish to establish. Basically, there are three kinds of claims which you may either advocate or oppose. They are called claims of *fact*, claims of *value,* and claims of *policy.*

Claims of Fact

If you were attempting to persuade your listeners that "the routine of assembly-line work causes mental depression" or that "price controls on raw agricultural products result in food shortages," you would in each case be presenting a factual claim — asserting that a given state of affairs exists or that something is indeed the case. When confronted with a claim of this sort, two questions are likely to arise in the mind of a thoughtful listener:

1. *By what criteria or standards of judgment should the truth or accuracy of this claim be measured?* If you were asked to determine a person's height, you would immediately look for a yardstick or other measuring instrument. Listeners likewise look for a standard when judging the appropriateness of a factual claim. In the first of the examples given above, before agreeing that assembly-line workers do experience "mental depression," the members of your audience would almost certainly want to know what you as a speaker mean by that term. In the second example, they would, no doubt, demand a definition of "shortages." Does it mean "the disappearance, for all practical purposes, of a given kind of food" or merely "less of that food than everyone might perhaps desire"? Against what standard, precisely, is the accuracy of the claim to be judged?

2. *Do the facts of the situation fit the criteria as thus set forth?* Is it a fact that all, or at least a reasonable majority of, assembly-line workers experience those feelings or symptoms which you have previously defined as constituting "mental depression"? Does the amount of produce and other raw agricultural products presently on supermarket shelves fall within the limits set by your definition of "shortages"? If you can first get your listeners to agree to certain standards or measurements for judgment and then present evidence to show that a given state of affairs meets these standards, you will, in most instances, be well on your way toward winning their belief.

Claims of Value

When, instead of asserting that something is or is not so, you assert that something is good or bad, desirable or undesirable, justified or unjustified, you are advancing a claim of value — a claim concerning the intrinsic *worth* of the belief or action in question. Here, as in the case of claims of fact, it is always appropriate to ask: (1) *By what standards or criteria is something of this nature to be judged?* (2) *How well does the item in question measure up to the standards specified?* We may, for example, assert that the quality of a college is to be measured by the distinction of its faculty, the excellence of its physical plant, the success of its graduates in securing positions, and the reputation it enjoys among the general public; and then proceed to show that because the college we are concerned with meets each of these tests, it is indeed a good one.

Claims of Policy

A claim of policy recommends a course of action for which you seek the audience's approval. Typical examples are: "Federal expenditures for pollution control *should be* substantially increased"; "The student senate *should have* the authority to expel students who cheat"; "Fines for overtime parking in city lots *should be* increased from $1.00 to $2.00." In each instance, you are asking your audience to endorse a proposed "policy" or course of action. When analyzing a policy claim, four subsidiary questions are relevant:

1. *Is there a need for such a policy or course of action?* If your listeners do not believe that a change is called for, they are not likely to approve your proposal.

2. *Is the proposal practicable?* Can we afford the expense it would entail? Would it really solve the problem or remove the evil it is designed to correct? Does such a policy stand a reasonable chance of being adopted? If you cannot show that your proposal meets these and similar tests, you can hardly expect it to be endorsed.

3. *Are the benefits your proposal will bring greater than the disadvantages it will entail?* People are reluctant to approve a proposal that promises to create conditions worse than the ones it is designed to correct. Burning a barn to the ground may be a highly efficient way to get rid of rats, but it is hardly a desirable one. The benefits and disadvantages that will accrue from a plan of action always must be carefully weighed along with considerations of its basic workability.

4. *Is the offered proposal superior to any other plan or policy?* Listeners are hesitant to approve a policy if they have reason to believe that an alternative course of action is more practicable or more beneficial.

Organization of the Speech to Persuade

With the claim you wish to establish clearly in mind, you are ready to gather material* and to consider how your speech should be organized. The motivated sequence, as outlined in Chapter 9, provides an organizational pattern which may be followed, whether your aim is to win belief in a claim of fact, a claim of value, or a claim of policy. Let us see how it may be applied in each case, beginning with a claim of fact.

Seeking Belief or Disbelief in a Claim of Fact

Before constructing a speech designed to persuade an audience of the truth or accuracy of a factual claim, make sure that the claim in question cannot be settled by other more direct and expedient means. Often differences concerning matters of fact may be resolved by personal obser-

---

*For suggestions on finding and recording speech materials, see Appendix A (pp. 397–407).

THE MOTIVATED SEQUENCE
APPLIED TO SPEECHES

To Persuade

1 Attention

Getting
attention

2 Need

Showing the
need:
Describing the
problem

3 Satisfaction

Satisfying the
need:
Presenting the
solution

4 Visualization

Visualizing
the results

vation, by looking in a reliable reference source, or by conducting a controlled experiment. It would, for example, be absurd to give a speech aimed at proving that it is or is not raining outside, that the distance between Cleveland and Chicago is approximately three hundred miles, or that the fruit in a given basket is contaminated. The first of these questions can be settled simply by looking out the window, the second by consulting a road map, the third by making appropriate tests.

But now consider these questions: "Is China gaining on us in the missile race?" "Are the OPEC nations likely to continue to increase the price of oil?" "Is Jones guilty of murder as charged?" Although these questions, too, raise issues of a factual nature, for one reason or another satisfactory answers cannot be arrived at by observation, by checking reference works, or by conducting an experiment. While data gathered from such sources may contribute in a major way to the judgment that is made, in the end we must rely upon our own informed opinion—we must reason from the best facts available to what appears to be the correct conclusion. It is on questions of this second type that speeches in support of factual claims become necessary and may appropriately be made.

Although departures sometimes are required by the nature of the subject or by the situation in which you find yourself, generally in a speech presented in support of a factual claim you may employ the steps in the motivated sequence in the following way:

1. Secure the *attention* and *interest* of the listeners.
2. State clearly the claim you are advancing and show why a judgment of its truth or validity is *needed.* Do this either by pointing out *(a)* why the matter at hand concerns the listeners personally or *(b)* why it concerns the community, state, nation, or world of which they are a part.
3. *Satisfy* the need developed in the preceding step by advancing what you believe to be the correct judgment and offering facts and reasoning in support of your view.
4. *Visualize* for your listeners what they will gain by accepting the judgment you recommend or the evils or dangers they will incur by rejecting it.

   If appropriate to the subject and the audience, appeal for *action*— for acceptance of your proposal and adherence to it. These steps (with emphasis only upon the first four of them) are illustrated in the following skeleton outline:

OUR STUDENT GOVERNMENT

I. State University has one of the oldest and most widely imitated systems of student government in the entire nation.   *Attention*

   A.   It was founded in 1883, when student govern-
       ment was almost entirely unknown.
   B.   Many of the leaders of our state and nation
       gained their first practical administrative ex-
       perience as campus officers.

II. Has our student government, once a free and power-   *Statement of*
     ful institution, become a mere tool of the dean of   *Question*
     men and the university administration?

I. This is a question of vital importance to each of us.   *Need*
   A.   The prestige of the university is at stake.
   B.   Our freedom as students to govern ourselves
       and conduct our own affairs is endangered.

I. In recent years the dean of men and other adminis-   *Satisfaction:*
     trative officers of the university have encroached   *Statement of*
     upon the rights and powers of our student govern-   *Claim*
     ment to an alarming extent.
   A.   All actions of the Student Senate must now   *Supporting Evi-*
       have administrative approval.   *dence*
   B.   The budgets of student organizations must be
       approved and their accounts audited by the
       university treasurer's office.
   C.   The election of class officers is conducted
       under the supervision of the dean.

I. Unless we are all aware of these serious encroach-   *Visualization:*
     ments upon our traditional rights as students and   *Warning of Future*
     consider steps to oppose or counteract them, further   *Evils*
     encroachments will amost certainly occur.

I. Make these facts known to your fellow students.   *Action (Optional)*

II. Resolve that student government will once again be
     a strong and vital force on this campus.

If your purpose is to oppose a factual claim advanced by another (in
this case, to prove that the administration has not infringed upon student rights and privileges), proceed in the same way, except to offer a
negative rather than an affirmative claim at the beginning of the satisfaction step and present facts and reasoning that justify this stand.

Seeking Belief or Disbelief in a Claim of Value

Whereas claims of fact assert that something is so, claims of value, you
will recall, assert that something is good or bad, desirable or undesirable, justified or unjustified. Typical claims of value are: "Quotas on the
export of agricultural products are unfair to the farmer." "Big-time athletics are detrimental to the best interests of college students." "Harry
Truman was one of our greatest Presidents."

When advancing a valuative claim, with a view to persuading your listeners to agree with your estimate of a person, practice, institution, or theory, you may adapt the basic pattern of the motivated sequence as follows:

1. Capture the audience's *attention* and *interest.*
2. Make clear that an estimate concerning the worth of the person, practice, or institution is *needed.* Do this by showing either *(a)* why such an estimate is important to your listeners personally or *(b)* why it is important to the community, state, nation, or world of which they are a part. With the need made clear, set forth the criteria on which an appropriate estimate must rest.
3. *Satisfy* the need developed in the preceding step by advancing what you believe to be the correct estimate and by showing how this estimate meets the criteria specified.
4. *Visualize* the advantages that will accrue from agreeing with the estimate you offer or the evils and dangers that will follow from endorsing an alternative.
   If appropriate to the subject and the audience, appeal for *action* — for acceptance of the proposed estimate and a determination to gain it.

Each of these basic steps is present in the following speech outline:

THE VALUES OF INTERCOLLEGIATE DEBATING

I. In recent years intercollegiate debating has come under strong attack from many quarters.   *Attention*
   A. Philosophers and social scientists charge that debate is a poor way to get at the truth concerning a disputable matter.
   B. Educators charge that debate teaches the student to approach a problem with an "either-or" attitude, thus causing him or her to develop habits of contentiousness and dogmatism rather than of fact-centered objectivity.

I. How we evaluate debate is important to each of us for at least two reasons: *Need: Evaluation Necessary*
   A. As students, we help support the debate program on this campus because a portion of our activity fee is allocated to the Debate Society.
   B. As citizens in a democratic society, we are concerned because the method of decision making employed in intercollegiate debating is essentially the same as that employed in the courtroom and the legislative assembly.
II. As is true of any extracurricular activity, there are two important criteria by which debate may be evaluated: *Criteria*

      A. Does it develop abilities and traits of mind that will aid the student in his or her course work?
      B. Does it develop abilities and traits of mind that will be of value in later life?

I. The experience of many years has shown that debate is valuable in both respects.   *Satisfaction: Evaluation Provided*
      A. Debate helps students do better work in their courses.
           1. It teaches them to study a subject thoroughly and systematically.
           2. It teaches them to analyze complex ideas quickly and logically.
           3. It teaches them to speak and write clearly and convincingly.
      B. Training in debate is of value later in life.
           1. It teaches courtesy and fair play.
           2. It develops self-confidence and poise.

I. Picture serious students of debate in the classroom and in their post-college careers.   *Visualization*
      A. As students, they will know how to study, analyze, and present material.
      B. As business or professional persons, they will be better able to meet arguments and to express their views in a fair and effective manner.

II. Remember these facts whenever you hear the value of intercollegiate debating questioned.   *Restatement and Summary*
      A. The contribution debate training makes to business or professional success has been eloquently affirmed by many thousands of prominent men and women who were themselves debaters in college.
      B. We should encourage and support this worthwhile activity in every way we can.

    A speech opposing a claim of value (for instance, a speech intended to prove that debating does not provide desirable and useful training) may be developed according to the same general pattern. In this case, however, instead of showing that debate meets the criteria outlined in the need step, you would show that it fails to meet them. The visualization step then might assert that college debate experience is not merely useless to a person in business or professional life, but actually harmful.

Seeking Belief in a Claim of Policy

When your purpose is to induce your listeners to endorse a claim of policy, you may use the steps in the motivated sequence as follows: (1) secure *attention;* (2) assert that because of existing deficiences or evils there is a *need* for some action; (3) provide *satisfaction* for this need by presenting a remedy which will remove the evils or deficiencies; (4) *visualize* the benefits to be obtained from believing or acting as you propose; and — if appropriate and desirable — (5) request *action* in the form of an endorsement of the proposal you advance.

Opposing Endorsement of a Claim of Policy

When opposing a policy (for example, taking cars away from freshmen), also try to (1) capture attention; but then proceed by denying any or all contentions embodied in steps 2, 3, and 4 above. Thus you may argue: (2) There is no need for such a policy; things are perfectly all right as they are. (3) The proposal is not practicable; it could not be made to work. (4) Instead of bringing benefits or advantages, the proposed policy would actually introduce new and worse evils; it would be unfair, difficult to administer, etc.

Sometimes all three of these contentions may be combined when developing a speech in which you oppose a policy. On other occasions you will find that only one or two of them apply, and your speech will be limited accordingly. Proof beyond reasonable doubt on any of the three, however, will cause an earnest listener to reject a proposal because, obviously, no one wants to adopt a policy that is not needed or is impracticable, or productive of new problems and evils. Proof beyond reasonable doubt on all three contentions usually constitutes the strongest possible case that can be made against a proposed change.

Here is a skeleton outline of the main points of a speech in which a policy is opposed on the grounds that it is unneeded, impracticable, and undesirable. For purposes of simplification, the attention step and supporting material have been omitted.

THE PROPOSED TURNPIKE

I. The turnpike from Ashton to Waterton, proposed by the Governor's Committee on Highways, is not needed. *Not Needed*
   A. The existing highway connecting the two cities is only three years old and is in excellent condition.
   B. Automobile traffic between Ashton and Waterton, instead of increasing, has actually decreased 6 percent during the last decade.
II. Even if the proposed turnpike were needed, it could not be built at this time. *Impracticable*
   A. State funds for road construction are at an all-time low.
   B. Borrowing for road construction is difficult and costly in the present bond market.
III. Finally, even if such a turnpike were both needed and possible, its construction would be undesirable. *Undesirable*

    A. It would impose a serious hardship on owners of motels, filling stations, restaurants, and other businesses along the present highway.
    B. The suggested route would spoil the Ashton State Park.

Content of the Speech to Persuade

Authoritative Facts and Figures

When speaking to persuade, take special pains to avoid generalities and abstractions. Pack your speech with specific facts and figures that touch on the experience of your listeners. Incidents that are recent, common, or striking generally carry strong conviction; statistics, when drawn from authoritative sources and clearly presented, endow appeals with compelling force. As a first consideration, then, when your purpose is to influence the beliefs or attitudes of your listeners, assemble a strong factual foundation upon which your claims may rest. Review the forms of supporting material described in Chapter 7, and use them in abundance.

Sound Reasoning

Although facts and figures furnish an essential base, your speech will seldom carry strong conviction unless you relate them to your claim by clear and cogent reasoning. A brief review of the forms of reasoning most commonly used in persuasive speaking is, therefore, important.

Reasoning from Sign.   When we use an observable mark or symptom as proof for the existence of a given state of affairs, we are said to be reasoning from *sign.* A flag seen at half-mast is a sign that someone of importance has died; a rash and fever are signs that a child has measles; burnt fields with scrawny crops are a sign that a given region has experienced drought conditions.

    Signs traditionally have been classified as either *infallible or fallible.* An infallible sign is a sure or certain indication of the existence of a given state or condition; a fallible sign signifies probability or likelihood rather than certainty. Ice on the pond, for example, is an infallible sign that the temperature is 32°F or below; a large diamond ring on a lady's finger is a fallible sign that she is wealthy. When testing the reliability of a judgment or conclusion based upon a sign, therefore, always ask: *Is the mark or symptom taken as a sign fallible or infallible?* As a sign approaches the level of infallibility, its power to influence belief in the existence of a given state of affairs increases; to the extent that it is fallible, its force is correspondingly diminished.

Reasoning from Cause.   When something happens, we assume that it had a cause; and when we see a force in operation, we realize that it will produce an effect. The rate of violent crime goes up, and we hasten to lay the blame on drugs, bad housing, public apathy, or inept public officials. We hear that the star on our football team is in the hospital with a broken ankle, and we immediately become apprehensive about the results of Saturday's game. We reason from known effects to inferred causes, and from known causes to inferred effects. There is perhaps no other form of reasoning so often used by speakers, nor is there any form of reasoning which is more likely to contain flaws. Always test causal reasoning for soundness by asking:

1. *Has a result been mistaken for a cause?* When two phenomena occur simultaneously, it sometimes is difficult to tell which is the cause and which the effect. Do higher wages cause higher prices, or is the reverse true?
2. *Is the cause strong enough to produce the result?* A small pebble on the track will not derail a passenger train, but a large boulder will. Be careful that you don't mistake a pebble for a boulder.
3. *Has anything prevented the cause from operating?* If a gun is not loaded, pulling the trigger will not make it shoot. Be certain that nothing has prevented the free operation of the cause which you assume has produced a given situation.
4. *Could any other cause have led to the same result?* Note that at the beginning of the section, four different, possible causes were listed to account for the increase in violent crime. Each one of these causes is cited—by some persons—as the sole cause. Be sure that you diagnose a situation correctly; don't put the blame on the wrong cause or all the blame on a single cause if the blame should be divided among several causes.
5. *Is there actually a connection between the assumed cause and the alleged effect?* Sometimes people assume that merely because one thing happens after another, the two are causally connected. Developing a pain in your back shortly after you have eaten strawberries does not mean, however, that the pain was caused by the strawberries. Do not mistake a coincidence for a true cause-effect relationship.

Reasoning from Random Instances. This form of reasoning consists of drawing a general conclusion about a given class of persons or objects after studying several members of that class selected at random. For instance, if you wished to determine whether the peaches in a basket are ripe, you might examine three or four of them or may even dig down to test those on the bottom. If the sample thus examined meets your approval, you reason that all of the peaches will be of the same nature, and, therefore, purchase them with confidence. Reasoning in this way from a random sample to a general conclusion plays an important role in much of our thinking, not only in daily life but also in conducting scientific experiments and polling public reactions to persons or events. In order to be sound, however, three tests must be successfully met:

1. *Is the sample large enough to support the conclusion arrived at?* One robin does not make a spring, nor can only two or three examples prove that a broad or general claim is true.
2. *Are the instances fairly chosen?* To show that something is true of such large cities as New York, Chicago, and Los Angeles does not prove that it also is true of all or most of the nation's cities and towns.
3. *Are there any outstanding exceptions to the generalizations offered?* One well-known instance which differs from the general conclusion you urge may cause doubt unless you can show that in this case unusual or atypical circumstances were at work.

Reasoning from Parallel Case.   Whereas in reasoning from random instances we draw a general conclusion about most or all of the members of a given class, in reasoning from a parallel case we compare one object or item with another to which it is closely similar. Suppose, for instance, you wished to prove that a certain method of teaching French would enable students to learn that language more easily and quickly. You might take as the basis for your proof a method of teaching Spanish which already is recognized by your listeners to be highly effective in these respects, and then reason that because the two languages are very much alike in all essential regards, the method of instruction used for Spanish would also ease and hasten the learning of French. Or you might contend that because a police crackdown on drunk driving significantly reduced the number of traffic accidents in City A, it would have the same effect in neighboring City B.

As we pointed out when discussing comparison as a form of support in Chapter 7 (pages 105–107), since in reasoning of this kind the claim or conclusion rests on a single piece of evidence, it is crucial that the matters compared be closely analogous. In testing proof by parallel case, therefore, these two questions are relevant:

1. *Do the points of similarity between the objects or items being compared outweigh the points of difference?* No two things or situations are ever exactly alike in every possible detail; but unless the matter you employ as fact or evidence and the matter concerning which you advance your claim are more alike than different, clearly your reasoning will be deficient.
2. *Are the characteristics singled out for comparison relevant to the point to be proved?* Two things may be alike in many respects, but have little or no bearing on the claim you are trying to establish. The police in City A and City B, for instance, may both wear blue uniforms, drive Ford cars, and have a policemen's ball once a year. These similarities, however, are not relevant to your purpose. On the

other hand, such matters as the level of morale, the type of training, the size of the forces, and the methods of patroling streets do bear upon the question of whether the sort of crackdown that was successful in City A also would succeed in City B. It is to such essential or crucial items of comparison that you must direct attention when reasoning from one case to another.

Reasoning from Axiom. This form of reasoning consists of applying an accepted rule or principle to a specific situation. For example, it is generally conceded that by buying in large quantities you may get merchandise more cheaply than by buying in small lots. When you argue that discount stores save money because they purchase goods in large quantities, you are, therefore, merely applying this general rule to a specific instance. Reasoning from axiom may be tested as follows:

1. *Is the axiom, or rule, true?* For many years people believed the world was flat, or that prices responded automatically to changes in supply and demand. Before applying an axiom, make sure of its validity. Remember also that no matter how true a principle may be, you cannot base an argument upon it unless you can first convince your audience of its truth.
2. *Does the axiom apply to the situation in question?* A rule that is itself true or valid may be improperly applied. For instance, to argue, on the basis of the above-mentioned principle, that discount stores buy goods more cheaply than individual merchants is warranted; but to argue on this same basis that the customer can always buy goods from discount stores at lower prices is not valid. Additional proof would be required to establish this further contention.

Strong Motivational Appeals

A third characteristic of an effective speech to persuade is strong motivation. Unless your listeners are able to see how the claims or proposals you present are related to them and are likely to satisfy one or more of their basic needs or wants, they will not be disposed to listen for long to the facts and reasoning you set forth. The major points in your speech should, therefore, meet a double requirement. First, they should be securely grounded in facts and sound reasoning; and, second, they should, in some way, be addressed to one or more of the motive appeals described in Chapter 6. In this respect, each of your major points may be thought of as an arrow. The motive appeal, like the sharp-pointed arrowhead, pierces a vulnerable spot in your listeners' armor; the facts and reasoning, like the shaft of the arrow, drive the arrowhead home.

Attention-Commanding Material

Fourth, it is important to recognize that if you are to influence the beliefs and attitudes of others, you first must succeed in holding their attention.

Not only will ideas and appeals that are unattended fall on sterile ground, but there are good reasons for holding that what we attend to contributes in an important way to what we believe or how we behave. More than half a century ago the distinguished Harvard psychologist and philosopher, William James, wrote:

> What holds attention determines action. . . . It seems as if we ought to look for the secret of an idea's impulsiveness . . . in *the urgency with which it is able to compel attention and dominate in consciousness.* Let it once so dominate, let no other ideas succeed in displacing it, and whatever motor effects belong to it by nature will inevitably occur.[1]

Since James' day, students of persuasion have recognized the validity of this principle and often have made it a central part of their teaching.* What blocks or inhibits a response, such writers maintain, is "thinking of ideas to the contrary." If, as a public speaker, you can cause an idea to dominate the consciousness of your audience so fully that competing ideas or courses of action are closed out, there is a strong likelihood that the response which you desire will be forthcoming.

When presenting a persuasive speech, therefore, keep in mind the *factors of attention* as explained in Chapter 8 (pages 131 – 135). See to it also that your vocal delivery is animated and that you reinforce your points with appropriate gestures and movements. In speaking to persuade, holding the listeners' attention at a high peak is more than half the battle.

Persuasive Strategies and Techniques

As we have repeatedly emphasized throughout this book, any successful speech, whatever its purpose, must be adapted to the interest and level of understanding of the listeners. However, when your purpose is to persuade, you face a special problem in adaptation. In addition to presenting material that is interesting and comprehensible, you also must adapt your speech to the attitude or mental frame of the audience. Therefore, as a final step in our study of speaking to persuade, let us consider some of the attitudes an audience may display toward your claim or proposal, and the adaptations you should make to each.

When Your Audience Is Not Aware That a Problem Exists

Sometimes your listeners are not aware that a problem exists or that a decision is called for. When this is the case, you may utilize the steps of the motivated sequence as follows:

---

*See, for example, James Winans, *Public Speaking,* rev. ed. (New York: The Century Co., 1917), pp. 191 – 195; Lew Sarett and William Trufant Foster, *Basic Principles of Speech* (Boston: Houghton Mifflin Company, 1936), pp. 14 – 16; Robert T. Oliver, *The Psychology of Effective Speech,* 2nd ed. (New York: Longmans, Green and Co., 1957), pp. 116 – 117; Wayne C. Minnick, *The Art of Persuasion* (Boston: Houghton Mifflin Company, 1957), pp. 39 – 47; Jon Eisenson, J. Jeffery Auer, and John V. Irwin, *The Psychology of Communication* (New York: Appleton-Century-Crofts, 1963), pp. 289 – 291; Thomas M. Scheidel, *Persuasive Speaking* (Glenview, Ill.: Scott, Foresman and Company, 1967), pp. 65 – 69.

Attention Step. Arouse audience interest with a factual illustration, an apt quotation, or with a few startling facts or figures. Be careful, however, not to present material so new or dramatic that it tends to call your own credibility into question. Since the listeners are not aware of the existence of the problem you are going to describe to them, it is important that they recognize you to be a reasonable person and not an alarmist or someone who has been influenced by unfounded tales or rumors.

Need Step. Present an abundance of facts, figures, and quotations designed to show that the problem you are presenting actually does exist. Point out its scope and seriousness; show what segments of the population are affected. Mention in particular how the situation as it now exists directly touches upon the security, happiness, or well being of your listeners.

Satisfaction, Visualization, and Action Steps. With the existence, seriousness, and relevance of the problem thus established, develop the satisfaction, visualization, and (if appropriate) the action step according to the suggestions outlined in Chapter 9. During this development, however, take every reasonable opportunity to introduce more factual material designed to show that the problem does exist, and refer to it again as you summarize your arguments and make your closing appeal for belief or action.

When Your Audience Is Apathetic

In contrast to the audience just discussed, an apathetic audience is aware that a problem exists but is indifferent to it. They say, "What's it to me?" "I should worry about this? That's up to George." Obviously, with such persons your main objective is to make them realize that the matter at hand *does* affect them — that they must assume a direct responsibility for arriving at a proper decision. Proceed step by step, as follows:

Attention Step. Overcome apathy and inertia by touching briefly some matter that is related to your listeners' self-interest. Present one or two striking facts or figures, and use vivid phraseology to show them how their health, happiness, security, chances for advancement, and other personal concerns are directly involved.

Need Step. With interest thus aroused, proceed to demonstrate fully and systematically how the question under discussion affects each individual present. Relate the problem to them by showing: *(a)* its direct and immediate effect upon them; *(b)* its effects on their families, friends, business interests, or the social and professional groups to which they belong; *(c)* its probable future effects upon their children. In showing these effects, employ the strongest possible evidence — specific instances and illustrations, striking statistics, authoritative testimony — and emphasize little-known or startling facts and conditions.

Satisfaction Step. In building the satisfaction step, emphasize again how the proposal or solution you offer bears directly upon the concerns of the listeners themselves, and on those of their families and associates. That is, continue to show in this step, as well as in the need step, that continued apathy concerning the matter is not justified.

Visualization and Action Steps. Visualize vividly the benefits the audience will gain by endorsing your view or the evils they will suffer by continuing to ignore it. Then, upon the basis of this visualization, appeal either for study of the problem or for some kind of action concerning it.

When Your Audience Is Interested but Undecided

Some audiences are conscious that a problem exists or a decision is called for, but they are uncertain as to the belief they should adopt or the course of action they should pursue. In such cases, where your primary proposal is to get the listeners to agree that your claim is correct or that your proposal is the best one possible, try the following steps:

Attention Step. Since the audience already is interested in the question to be decided, the attention step may be brief. Often it merely consists of a direct reference to the subject. At other times, it may be a short example or story. When using this second method, however, take care to center your listeners' attention on the heart of the matter rather than on side issues or irrelevant details. Focus their thinking on fundamentals by excluding all but the central issue under consideration.

Need Step. Review briefly the background out of which the need for a decision has grown. Summarize its historical development if this will help your listeners understand the situation more clearly. Also, describe in a few words the situation as it now exists, and show why an immediate decision is imperative. Finally, set forth the standards or criteria which a sound decision must meet.

Satisfaction Step. This will usually be the most important, and probably the longest, part of your speech. State your claim, or outline the plan of action you wish adopted, and define any vague or ambiguous terms. Show specifically how what you recommend will satisfy the criteria outlined in the need step. Proceed to demonstrate the advantages to be gained by accepting your proposition and why it is superior to any possible alternative. Prove each of your contentions with an abundance of facts, figures, testimony, and examples.

Visualization Step. Make this step rather brief in relation to the rest of the speech. Be vivid and persuasive, but don't exaggerate. Project the audience into the future by painting a realistic picture of the desirable conditions which will be brought about by approving your claim or supporting your proposal — or the evils that will result from a failure to do so.

Action Step. Restate in clear and forceful language your request for belief in or for endorsement of the plan you advocate. Recapitulate briefly the principal arguments and appeals presented earlier in the speech.

When Your Audience Is Hostile

Sometimes audiences are conscious that a problem exists or that a question must be decided, but are hostile to the particular policy or plan of action you wish them to accept. Often this opposition is based either on a fear that some undesirable result will accompany the proposed action or on a positive preference for an alternative belief or policy. Sometimes the hostility is a reflection of deeply ingrained prejudices. In any case, where your goal must be to overcome existing objections and promote the acceptance of your ideas, adapt the motivated sequence as follows:

Attention Step. Since you know there will be hostility toward your proposition, you must try, first of all, to conciliate your audience and win a hearing. Approach your subject indirectly and gradually. Take special pains to concede whatever you can to your listeners' point of view; establish common ground by emphasizing areas of agreement; minimize or explain away differences. Proceed bit by bit, beginning with those ideas that are least likely to arouse strong opposition and moving a step at a time toward more controversial matters. Make the members of your audience feel that you are genuinely interested in achieving the same results they are.

Need Step. Attain agreement on some basic principle or belief, and use this principle as the criterion by which to measure the soundness of the proposition you advance. Otherwise, develop this step as you would for an audience that is interested but undecided.

Satisfaction Step. Show specifically how your proposed policy or plan of action meets the criteria the audience has endorsed in the preceding step. Offer strong and extensive proof of the superiority of your claim to the proposition or proposal which they favor. Otherwise, develop this step as you would if you were addressing an undecided audience.

Visualization and Action Steps. If you have been successful thus far, your listeners should be in the same frame of mind as the audience that is interested in the question but undecided about what to think or do. The development of your speech from this point on, therefore, may follow the pattern outlined for that type of audience, but should place special emphasis on the visualization, or benefits, step.

Finally, in planning a persuasive speech for an audience that is essentially hostile, remember that there will be times when you will find it helpful to develop the need and satisfaction steps in parallel order — a procedure we explained in Chapter 9 (pages 153 – 154). When this developmental order is used, each aspect of the need is discussed individually, together with the particular part of the policy or proposal which will satisfy it. The division of points may often be made according to the criteria advanced as a basis for judgment. Thus, you might first consider the "cost" criterion — that is, the desirability of adopting a proposal that will prove as economical as possible — and then show how your proposition meets this test. Next, you might present certain social or cultural criteria and demonstrate that your proposal satisfies each of these also. Finally, you might indicate the desirability of having a plan that is flexible enough to meet changing conditions and show that your proposal has this quality. In this way, you may develop your complete case in appropriate, parallel segments.

Real-life audiences, obviously, are seldom as clear-cut and uniform in their attitudes as the foregoing suggestions would seem to imply. But if you can determine the attitudes, beliefs, and values of the majority or of the more influential members of an audience, you can usually develop an effective persuasive speech by following one of the four plans we have just outlined or by employing variations or combinations of them. Whatever method of organization you choose to follow, however, *be sure to keep in mind the attitude of your listeners toward your proposition or policy.* Always speak from the point of view of the people who are sitting before you.

A Sample Speech to Persuade

Persuasive speeches advancing claims of policy are often set in a problem-solution framework, which forms the core (*need* and *satisfaction* steps) of the motivated sequence. Professor Waldo W. Braden, Chairman of the Department of Speech at Louisiana State University, uses a problem-solution pattern effectively in the following keynote-type speech, "Has TV Made the Public Speaker Obsolete?"

Following an attention-getting introduction, Professor Braden carefully forecasts the stages in which he will develop the *problem* section of his address: first, "a little theoretical background" on the implications of freedom of speech; next, a look at political campaigning in *pre-television* days; and, finally, a review of *contemporary* campaign practices in terms of radio and television. In the development of these successive stages, the speaker sets up five possible solutions — all of which he promptly rejects (by his use of the "this-or-nothing" technique) in favor of a solution he really *prefers:* a search for an informed and interested public. Especially note how the speaker justifies his proposed solution both logically and psychologically: *logically* by his development of the problem, *psychologically* by taking into careful account the predispositions and motives of his listeners.

"Has TV Made the Public Speaker Obsolete ?"[2]

Waldo W. Braden

[*Attention Step*].

I was somewhat surprised when I was invited to speak at this luncheon today because, as you know, I am not a broadcaster or a teacher of radio and television or a member of the Council for Better Broadcasts. Perhaps the explanation of my invitation is that I go to football games with the local arrangements chairman, Clinton Bradford. I am the former teacher of your gracious president, Martha Kennedy, and I directed the doctoral dissertation of Mrs. Kennedy's husband. /1

I have one little claim that permits me to attend this meeting. In 1969, John Pennybacker and I assembled for Random House the little book entitled *Broadcasting and the Public Interest.* On the team, John upheld the Industry, and I argued for the Consumer. During our eighteen months of collaboration, we frequently engaged in vigorous and sometimes stormy debate. I must admit that I sometimes baited my young colleague by repeating Ferry's statement to the effect that mass communication delights in "the shoddy, the tasteless, the mind-dulling, the useless." But at those moments when the Devil egged me on, I always stirred John to give most eloquent rebuttals. Of course, I overstated my case. I do hope that today I will not be repossessed; but if I am, perhaps you will need to call an exorcist to rid me of my evil thoughts. I assure you that I am an avid and enthusiastic viewer of television. I thoroughly enjoy football games, Ironsides, and all kinds of entertainment. /2

Many of [us] . . . like millions of [other] Americans, think ourselves lucky to live in a television age in which the average home set operates as much as seven hours per day, and the average male watcher like myself may devote as much as 3,000 days or nine years of his life to viewing football games and other excitement on the magic tube. Recently, a select list of prominent Americans from many fields was asked to rate eighteen powerful institutions according to their influence; they placed television at the top, above the White House, the Supreme Court, and the newspapers. But it is my belief, as I shall attempt to make clear, that the gains and benefits of television have also brought some questionable results, particularly in the political forum. Some have suggested that without our knowing it television controls our lives even in a political sense and has made the world into a global village. Many of our attitudes and feelings are shaped by television. /3

What I am saying was recently confirmed by a published interview with Alistair Cooke, chief U.S. correspondent for *The Guardian,* one of England's most distinguished newspapers. . . . When asked "What effect is television having on American society and the generation formed by this new experience?" he replied: "We are all getting more information now than we can cope with. I think that's the reason for the sort of low-key hysteria—Thoreau's 'quiet desperation'—that a lot of us live in. The images overwhelm our ability to make judgments or handle our government and our lives because we are so continuously aware of the disruption that's going on everywhere." /4

[Problem (Need) Step]

Let me tell you the route I intend to follow in this speech which I probably should have entitled, "The First Amendment, Public Decision Making, and Television," . . . First, I intend to sketch a little theoretical background involving the implications of the First Amendment to the Constitution. Second, I intend to do a flashback and discuss how the political speaker faced the voters in pre-television days. Third, I shall consider how and why television has altered the role of the speaker and politician. /5

Let me start with a little background. Why did the Founders think it was necessary to include a Bill of Rights in the Constitution? Why did they lead off that Bill of Rights with the First Amendment which reads in part "Congress shall make no law . . . abridging the freedom of speech, or of the press; or of the rights of the people peaceably to assemble, and to petition the government for a redress of grievances." That declaration did not suddenly appear in the Constitution of the United States. Our English forebears had long experience with denial of their rights and had due cause to hold such freedom precious and important. /6

Why did a statement concerning freedom of speech and press lead off the Bill of Rights? Why was the First Amendment given priority over the next seven amendments which protected property rights? /7

In my opinion, Madison and others recognized that the free exchange of ideas, the give-and-take of debate, the posing of questions for office-seekers to answer was at the very heart of the democratic process or a government controlled by the citizens. It has frequently been said that "ours is a government by talk," which is another way to say oral decision making. If free government is to operate, the citizen must have free access to many kinds of opinions and arguments, varied points of view — that is, if the voter is to choose intelligently among the alternatives. Judge Learned Hand said, "Right conclusions are more likely to be gathered out of a multitude of tongues than through any kind of authoritative selection." /8

We operate on the premise that the collective opinions arrived at openly and without fear are likely to give us the most satisfactory decisions. They may not always be the *best* or the *right* ones, but from the point of view of the majority they are the least objectionable. /9

Today I am talking about the role of public debate. How does the campaigner — the discusser, the debater, the interviewer — fit into this picture? Oral communicators, with the reporters, keep the citizenry informed, healthy, and capable of making reasonable and desirable judgments. /10

Now let me turn to my flashback and discuss the speaker's role in pre-television days. In the old days, the politician — the policy maker, the leader — had to go directly to the voters. He might go by riverboat, or in rugged country he might walk or go by horseback, or in later times by train. Moving about among the voters was within the reach of any aspiring politician who was vigorous and eager. He did not need a big bank roll; he needed energy and courage. The office-seeker made extensive speaking tours, sometimes even traveling with his opponent and on a given day sharing the platform, or as they said, "dividing time." A good example of this confrontation was the Lincoln and Douglas campaign of 1858. They carried their canvass into the nine congressional districts in Illinois; after speaking in the first two, they agreed to seven public engagements from Freeport, Illinois, to Little Egypt and back again. They made long speeches, asked each other searching and difficult questions, and employed shrewd and sometimes tricky strategies. What these two frontier lawyers did was not unusual, for it happened all over the place in Louisiana, Indiana, Tennessee, Ohio, and even Texas. /11

What did these face-to-face encounters contribute to the voter? Of course, the voter could hear the candidate and observe him under pressure. He could note how the candidate handled hostile questions and damaging arguments. The brave and vocal listener might actually get into the act by putting a question to a speaker or by sneaking in a little refutation. At least he met the office-seeker face to face, shook hands with him, rubbed shoulders with fellow party members, challenged the opposition, and even engaged in a little physical violence when arguments seemed inadequate. /12

At these hustings an office-seeker could not hide behind a ghost-writer or avoid the queries of his fellow citizens. In full view, a speaker had to adjust his arguments to local conditions, had to cope with the unexpected, the unforeseen, and the embarrassing. There was no way to edit or cover up a faulty pronouncement or change a bad impression. An answer given to significant questions—like the one Lincoln addressed to Douglas at Freeport—stood. And Douglas' answer cost him the presidency in 1860. /13

I am not saying that these face-to-face forays were free of nonsense and theatrical displays and did not sometimes mislead or pander to baser motives. At times, rationality lost out to flag raisings, parades, fireworks, and barbecues. Yes, these were the Log Cabin campaigns; the Davy Crocketts with coonskin caps and the ignorant Zach Taylors and some politicians got by with front-porch campaigns, letting their surrogates speak for them. But there is one significant difference. In the face-to-face encounters, the listener actually participated. He might get drunk, do silly things, but he was involved. He was there! He did not sprawl at home in his easy chair with a can of beer in hand and view a *show* carefully written, edited, rehearsed, and planned in some far-off New York office by a sleek public relations man. When he made a fool of himself, he had only himself to blame. /14

Now let us turn to the present. Let us consider how television has altered the role of the speaker and politician. /15

The consumer—the voter—the average citizen—no longer has an opportunity to judge a speaker by old means and in the old ways, and many persons who have significant ideas or who aspire to represent us will never be able to gain a hearing with significant numbers of voters. The would-be politician—in a hurry to move up the ladder—will not take time to go to Dry Prong or Waterproof to speak to the citizens because it is too slow, and he knows that he won't be able to pull the voters away from Gunsmoke or Ironsides. More likely, he will employ a public relations firm, buy time on the local radio or, still better, on the local television. Newton N. Minow and his colleagues, in their new book *Presidential Television,* observe:

> Television's most significant political characteristic probably is its ability to present an image of a politician — providing an indication of his character and personality. An aspiring political leader today is likely to rise faster and further if he "comes across" well on television. . . . It is not unusual for politicians at all levels to hire television advisers, speech therapists, makeup artists, or other professionals to put on the leader's television image. /16

What puts television and, to a lesser extent, radio beyond the reach of many persons who might make great contributions? Let me mention three inherent factors: (1) It is expensive; (2) it is technically complex to operate; and (3) it lends itself to manipulation out of the view of listeners. /17

With this audience, I need not dwell long on these three characteristics. /18

First, TV is so expensive that it is beyond the reach of many who might seek office or contribute to our political life. In 1970, during an off-presidential election, candidates spent $158 million on political broadcasts. In that campaign the three candidates for the governorship of New York spent more than $2 million on television and radio broadcasts. Nelson Rockefeller reportedly used $6 million and utilized a staff of 370 full-time employees. A one half-minute spot announcement on the leading Baton Rouge TV stations costs as much as $150 to $300 at prime time and $50 for poorest time (probably at 1:30 in the morning). To present a fifteen-minute speech on the leading channel in Baton Rouge at 7:30 P.M. costs as much as $300 to $500. To broadcast a half-hour speech over Louisiana TV networks might cost $25,000 or $30,000. It is estimated that a half-hour program broadcast simultaneously on three national networks at prime time would cost $250,000 or one million dollars for four such shows. /19

Robert Bendiner, in the *New York Times,* notes that "to get elected to high public office today, a candidate must either be a man in the top tax brackets himself or, more serious, a man unhealthily dependent on those who are and have axes to grind." Certainly the high cost of campaign advertising can allow a heavily financed candidate to dominate the most important means of communication, adding credence to the cynics' view that politics is but a rich man's game. /20

My second point is that television is beyond the reach of many persons because it is technically complex to operate. The Great Debates of 1960 between John F. Kennedy and Richard M. Nixon dramatically illustrated this statement. As the debates progressed, it became evident that program format, camera position, lens openings, temperature of the studio, lighting, makeup, dress, and the positions of the debaters were most important. In fact, much to his dismay, Richard Nixon soon discovered that a free form of debate involved many uncontrolled elements which could be embarrassing. In 1968, he took no chances. He assembled a large staff of experts—writers, producers, directors, cameramen, coachers, and makeup men—to make sure that he presented an attractive image to the viewing public. In 1972, he took even fewer risks—expressing himself as little as possible before the cameras. Both Nixon and McGovern found the thirty- and sixty-second, short spot announcements to their liking. What can a political candidate tell of significance in a half minute? /21

My third reservation about television is that it lends itself to manipulation out of view of the listener. The most dramatic demonstration we have had of editing in recent years was the CBS special, "The Selling of the Pentagon." In the name of producing an interesting show, the producer and his helpers lifted material out of context, rearranged interviews, and actually included some footage that had been filmed on another subject at another time. /22

When you view a speaker—or the product, as they say in the Industry—what do you actually know about what you are seeing? Is he reading what someone else has written? How much has he rehearsed? Has the film been edited? By that I mean, have embarrassing or awkward portions been deleted? Is the camera actually revealing the real man or what the director or public relations man wants you to see? Are you seeing the real personality or an image created by clever advertising men? /23

Is it any wonder that we live in an age characterized by what the Quaker philosopher Elton Trueblood calls "deep sickness"? Let me quote Alistair Cooke again. When he was asked, "Are Americans becoming more cynical as they view television and the extravagant promises it proclaims?" he answered, "Yes . . . this is an open society, and whether you like it or not, it does encourage cynicism. It makes demands on the maturity and judgments of the individual that are more severe than any he ever had to meet when he had only the press to ponder." /24

Many of you have perhaps wondered why I entitled my speech "Has TV Made the Public Speaker Obsolete?" Quite obviously, in a TV age only those with great resources or great power can gain access to effective use of this powerful means of communication. /25

Minow and his colleagues argue that: "The drafters of the American Constitution strove diligently to prevent the power of the President from becoming a monopoly, but our inability to manage television has allowed the medium to be converted into an electronic throne." They argue convincingly that through the prestige of his office the President has an unfair advantage over all of his competitors. However, this analysis does not go far enough. Not only has the President made television into "an electronic throne," but also anyone with adequate financial support can buy time. Because it is expensive, technical, and capable of being manipulated, television is a tool at the disposal of the rich, the Establishment, the labor union, the pressure group—in fact, any faction that has great resources. It is not a medium generally at the disposal of the man, the minority groups, the have-nots, the intellectuals, and at times even the opposition party with financial problems. /26

At the present time, we have a tussle going on between the President and the TV industry. The President has the clout to command free time, and the networks dare not deny him his national audience. But let us change the characters in the drama. Suppose it were a struggle matching big television versus a man of limited resources or perhaps a minority leader or the leader of an unpopular group. Then how would scenes be played? Remember when poor, misguided Agnew dared to make a speech about the networks in Des Moines, Iowa? As a result, day after day on news programs, on talk shows, in television editorials, the whole thrust of the TV industry was turned on the Vice President. Now, suppose Agnew had been a little American. The manipulation of television has changed the balance so that the First Amendment no longer works the way it was intended to. /27

What has television done to the speaker or office-seeker? /28

On the positive side, if he has the resources or power, it provides him a great audience — that is, if he can put on a good show. /29

On the negative side, if he is a little American, he can't even get into the game. But if he does sell himself to a bankroll, it may make out of him an image, an actor, and often a puppet of those who pay the bills. /30

It is likely to cause him to put his message in broad, sweeping generalizations designed to offend no group, but to soothe a significant percentage of the viewers. Remember, ratings or the percentage of the market are more important than ideas or sound advice. /31

What about the consumer? It is possible that we may elect a profile, a voice, a smile, an image who may be ignorant, immoral, and unwise. /32

[Solution (Satisfaction) Step]

The time has come for me to resolve the difficulties that I have gotten myself into in this speech. /33

At this moment there are several things that I could do. /34

First, I could stop. Many of you would no doubt think that wise. But that would be the coward's way out, and cowards die many deaths, but the valiant die but once. /35

Second, I could advocate the abolition of the First Amendment. Although I would not find support for that proposition here, there are persons in this country that would favor that drastic course of action. /36

Third, I could advocate the return to the "Good Ole Days," and some of you probably have concluded that that is what I would like. But the "Good Ole Days" never really existed. Besides, who wants to wear a coonskin cap! /37

Fourth, I could advocate the elimination of speaking. You know that I would never favor that. /38

Fifth, I could advocate the abolition of the networks. But I do not see how I could give up Ironsides, Lawrence Welk, Lucy, and Matt Dillon — even if I do have to see them six times on reruns. /39

No, there must be a better solution to the problem that I have presented to you today. /40

We must have an alert citizenry trained to evaluate what they see on television and [who] have the courage to demand that what is "cheap and shoddy" be taken off the air and to demand that the industry use the air waves fairly. When licenses are renewed, they must attend the hearings and speak. /41

We must have a strong Federal Communication Commission which will resist pressure from all directions. It must not be under the control of President Nixon or NBC or Walter Cronkite. [The] FCC must not be a slave of any pressure group or business group. /42

I would hope that the Federal Communication Commission will always make its first concern the protection of the consumer. I am hopeful that more persons like Nicholas Johnson will be appointed to the Commission. /43

[Visualization Step]

I commend the Council for Better Broadcasts because its program starts educating viewers and citizens at the right time and in the right way. The persons who participate in your surveys and programs will be the influential citizens of tomorrow, and it may be that a member of your group will sometime have an opportunity to serve on the Federal Communication Commission or some other federal communication agency. /44

One further word. The confrontation between speaker and voters must not be replaced. It must not be replaced if the First Amendment is to be meaningful. We must force the advocate to face the voters in a variety of situations giving them ample opportunity to express themselves in questions and rebuttal. /45

The First Amendment was intended more for the protection of the consumer than it was the communicator. Newspapers and television talk about their rights under the Constitution. But, I think, even more important are the rights that the consumer has to full and complete information, access to all points of view, and opportunity to make up his mind without coercion or force and without being lulled into inactivity by a public relations man. /46

It is highly appropriate that I remind you of two planks of the preamble of the Constitution of your organization. They read:

> . . . Recognizes that the Public Interest in the area of TV must be defined and protected by the public itself;
> . . . Recognizes that, since all broadcasting is done in the public domain, listeners and viewers have rights, privileges, and duties. /47

A Persuasive Speech for Analysis

Study the following speech to persuade by Carl Hall, a student at Trevecca Nazarene College. Determine where each of the steps in the motivated sequence begins: Attention, Need, Satisfaction, and Visualization. Analyze the speaker's use of supporting materials and motivational appeals. Evaluate the appropriateness and effectiveness of the introduction and conclusion to the speech. Decide whether—in general—the style of the speech is suitable to its subject and purpose. Consider whether the speaker's arguments and appeals convince you of the seriousness of the problem and the soundness of the solution he proposes. If you are convinced, ascertain some specific reasons; if you are not persuaded, note specifically those aspects of the speech which contributed to this result. Suggest at least two ways of improving the speech.

"A Heap of Trouble"[3]

Carl Hall

What I am about to tell you is a bunch of garbage. /1

"In the beginning, Man created the plastic bag and the tin and aluminum can and the cellophane wrapper and the paper plate and the disposable bottle. And Man said this was good because Man could then take his automobile and buy all his food in one place, and Man could save that which was good to eat in the refrigerator and throw away that which had no further use. And soon the earth was covered with plastic bags and tin and aluminum cans and paper plates and disposable bottles, and there was nowhere to sit down or walk. And Man shook his head and cried, "Look at this awful mess."[4] These words, written by Art Buchwald in 1970, are not as humorous today as they were a few years ago. /2

Ever since Eve ate the first apple, man has been plagued with the problem of what to do with the core. For a while, sweeping it under the rug seemed to be the answer, but soon the rug became lumpy and smelly. Then we thought maybe we could wash it down the sink, but soon the sink became clogged. And when there was not a rug or a sink handy, we just threw it alongside of the highway. /3

Now it seems that everywhere we look there is garbage, and it just keeps on coming. Fifty years ago the average American threw away every day a little over two and a half pounds of garbage. Today each of us will create six pounds of trash, and — it is projected by the Environmental Protection Agency — by 1980, considering all of our waste, our country will have to dispose of fifty pounds of refuse per person per day. /4

That sounds like quite a mess, doesn't it? But wait until you start adding your mess and my mess together. Last year we as a nation threw away one hundred and thirty million tons of garbage. This is enough trash to fill enough garbage trucks lined bumper-to-bumper to stretch from New York to Los Angeles, three abreast. /5

When I read that statement, I asked the same question you are probably asking yourself right now. Where did we put all of it? Our city dumps gobbled up over eighty-four percent of it, but most all of our dumps have stopped gobbling and have started to nibble. It is projected that in the next five years half of America's dumps will have reached their capacity. The other sixteen percent of last year's garbage was either dumped in our waterways or scattered along our highways. /6

A survey was taken of a typical one-mile stretch of two-lane highways in Kansas. The collection revealed 770 paper cups, 730 empty cigarette packs, 590 beer cans, 130 soft-drink bottles, 120 beer bottles, 110 whiskey bottles, and 90 beer cartons. But we don't have to go to Kansas to witness the failure of our one-billion-dollar-a-year "Keep America Beautiful" campaign. /7

Why has this campaign failed, and why is garbage becoming the problem it is today? The answer to this question can be traced back in history to every affluent civilization since the world began . . . WASTEFULNESS. Today we are treating our world as though we have a spare in the trunk. /8

Every year Americans throw away eight million television sets, a large portion of which are in working order or in need of inexpensive repairs. Because we now can afford newer models, seven million automobiles are junked each year; and because we don't want to be bothered with returnable containers, in the last decade our production of disposable bottles and cans has doubled. And if the present rate continues, in two years the only place we'll be able to find a returnable container will be in a museum. /9

It is this wasteful attitude that has made garbage collection the fifth-largest industry and made garbage our nation's grossest national product. This year we Americans will spend four and a half billion dollars for refuse collection. This sum is exceeded only by our expenditures for schools, roads, and national defense. Our wastefulness is costing us dearly. If you live in Philadelphia, it costs you forty million dollars a year. If you're from New York City, the price is one hundred and fifty million dollars a year. For every newspaper copy the *New York Times* puts out it costs the city a dime to dispose of it, and — for each edition — one hundred and fifty acres of forest. New York's former Environmental Protection Administrator, Merril Eisenbud, warns that the city could become buried under the seven million tons of refuse that it now generates annually if something drastic is not done quickly. During the garbage strike of 1968, New York was literally digging out from under 100,000 tons of trash after only a few days. /10

The 1970 strike by sanitation workers in the nation's capital shut down the District of Columbia's four incinerators and dirtied the city's streets and alleyways with appalling speed. /11

Dozens of other walkouts by underpaid municipal trash collectors in other communities have brought right to the doorsteps of millions of Americans the cold, hard fact that waste management is a terribly serious daily concern. /12

The question then arises: Will we wait to deal with this great social problem until it reaches the crisis stage as we did with our nation's energy situation? Or can you and I realize the urgency of our condition? The answer will be left up to us. /13

There is an answer to our impending crisis if we will commit ourselves to it. Conservation and utilization are the keys that can keep the lid on our nation's garbage can locked, and the garbage inside. /14

Recycling is a term that is familiar to all of us, but few have realized its great value. Maybe Senator Edmund Muskie, chairman of the pollution sub-committee of the Senate Committee on Public Works, caught a glimpse of its importance when he said, "If future generations of Americans are to inherit adequate economical supplies of our natural resources, we must move now to find ways of reusing solid waste." /15

Former Secretary of the Interior, Stewart Udall, posed a probing question when he asked: "Why do we continue to dip into our natural-resource reserves when we might be turning our choking wastes into wealth?" But what *is* this wealth Secretary Udall was talking about? Beer and soft drinks in returnable, reusable containers can be used as many as twenty times. Dr. Douglas Bynum, a research professor at Texas A & M, has developed a technique for building better and cheaper roads by using ground-up glass, plastic containers, and rubber tires. In addition to ridding our country of seventy-five million discarded tires annually, this method would cut roadbuilding costs by as much as one fifth. To help eliminate the seventy million automobiles we discard each year, they can be shredded and used in concrete building blocks. But perhaps the most promising use of trash is its conversion into energy which could enable us to kill two birds with one rotten apple. In cities such as St. Louis and Baltimore, experimental conversion plants are already in use converting garbage to electricity with satisfactory results. /16

With further development the potential is unlimited. Figures revealed in May of this year showed that within the one hundred and thirty million tons of garbage we threw away last year, there was enough unused energy to light the nation for a year. /17

. . . And then Man wiped his tears, rolled up his sleeves, and picked up the plastic bags, the tin and aluminum cans, the paper plates and disposable bottles and used them over again and again in as many ways as he could think of. Slowly, the earth began to be uncluttered, and Man said, "It is better." /18

Our world is already in a heap of trouble, but let's not end up in a heap of trash. /19

Reference Notes

[1]William James, *Psychology: Briefer Course* (New York: Holt, Rinehart & Winston, Inc., 1892), p. 448.

[2]"Has TV Made the Public Speaker Obsolete?" by Waldo W. Braden, from *Vital Speeches of the Day,* Volume XXXX, June 1974. Reprinted by permission of Vital Speeches of the Day.

[3]"A Heap of Trouble" by Carl Hall. Reprinted from *Winning Orations* by special arrangement with the Interstate Oratorical Association, Larry Schnoor, Executive Secretary, Mankato State University, Mankato, Minnesota.

[4]From The Washington Post, April 21, 1970. Reprinted by permission of Art Buchwald.

 Problems and Probes

1.   Make a list of ten of your personal beliefs or convictions. Which items in this list would you say constitute claims of fact? which claims of value? and which claims of policy? Explain your choices.

2.   Find in some suitable source three speeches to persuade: one on a claim of fact, one on a claim of value, and one on a claim of policy. Outline these speeches and compare their structures with the patterns of development recommended on pages 293–300. If any of the speeches depart radically from these structures, give reasons why this may be the case.

3.   Find several newspaper editorials or speeches which employ one or more of the forms of reasoning described on pages 300–303. In each instance, apply the appropriate test to determine how sound the reasoning is.

4.   On pages 298–299, we considered a number of techniques that are especially useful when the speaker's purpose is to urge acceptance of a policy or program for action. Find a number of persuasive speeches of this type and see if you can identify examples of the techniques in question. If so, describe how they were used and evaluate their effectiveness.

5.   With your instructor's aid, locate a speech presented to an audience exhibiting one of the attitudes discussed on pages 304–308 (interested, but undecided, etc.). Attempt to determine the means the speaker employed to adapt his or her arguments and appeals to this type of audience. How well would you say the speaker succeeded in doing this?

Oral Activities and Speaking Assignments

1.   Conduct a class discussion on the ethics of persuasion, and consider these questions, among others: What methods and appeals should always be avoided? Are there any circumstances in which a person not only has the right, but also has the obligation to undertake to persuade others by any means at his or her disposal?

2.   Build and present to the class a six-minute persuasive speech designed to win acceptance for a claim of fact, value, or policy. Follow carefully the steps in the motivated sequence appropriate to the type of speech chosen. Make sure that you have an abundance of appropriate facts and data, that your reasoning is sound, and that your major ideas are cast in a form that will motivate your listeners. In developing your remarks, keep in mind the probable attitude of the audience toward your claim or proposal, and make such adaptations as may be necessary. For suggestions concerning subjects, consult the subject categories in Chapter 4, pages 64–65.

Suggestions for Further Reading

Erwin P. Bettinghaus, *Persuasive Communication,* 2nd ed. (New York: Holt, Rinehart & Winston, Inc., 1973).

Winston L. Brembeck and William S. Howell, *Persuasion: A Means of Social Influence,* 2nd ed. (Englewood Cliffs, N.J.: Prentice-Hall, Inc., 1976).

Douglas Ehninger, *Influence, Belief, and Argument* (Glenview, Ill.: Scott, Foresman and Company, 1974), Chapter 6, "Relating the Evidence to the Claim: Warrant"; and Chapter 7, "Patterns of Proof."

Kenneth G. Hance, David C. Ralph, and Milton J. Wiksell, *Principles of Speaking,* 3rd ed. (Belmont, Calif.: Wadsworth Publishing Company, Inc., 1975), Chapter 15, "Speaking to Advocate."

Bernard McCabe, Jr., and Coleman C. Bender, *Speaking Is a Practical Matter,* 2nd ed. (Boston: Holbrook Press, Inc., 1973), Part V, "Speech of Persuasion."

Herbert W. Simons, *Persuasion: Understanding, Practice, and Analysis* (Reading, Mass.: Addison-Wesley Publishing Company, 1976).

The Speech to Actuate

Any situation in which it is appropriate to call for immediate action, rather than mental resolution or the intention to act at some indefinite time in the future, provides a suitable occasion for a speech to actuate. Hence such speeches frequently are given in deliberative or legislative bodies by persons who wish other members to vote for a motion they have introduced or to support a program they favor. Sales talks, speeches asking for contributions, lawyers' pleas before juries, and evangelistic sermons are other common examples of this type of address. In short, whenever the speaker seeks some kind of *immediate* and *overt* behavior from the listeners, a speech to actuate is called for.

But while the purpose of a speech to actuate is to elicit observable behavior from an audience, as a public speaker your request for action usually will fall on deaf ears unless your listeners recognize the need and practicability of the proposal and are moved to act upon it. Therefore, two secondary or intermediate purposes of a speech to actuate are (1) to *convince* and (2) to *motivate* the audience. In cases where the behavior requested must continue over a period of days or weeks, it is especially important that you make clear the need and practicability of the action you are advocating. The determination and enthusiasm which your listeners feel as you conclude your speech may dissipate rapidly when they come out on the cold street corner where they have agreed to hand out literature or when they encounter the rebuffs of the first persons they ask to contribute money or buy tickets. In all types of persuasive speaking, you have the obligation to support your recommendations with sound evidence and valid arguments. In a speech to actuate, however, such support is more than a question of ethics; it is indispensable for attaining the action sought.

In addition to solid proof and strong motivation, a successful speech to actuate usually calls for a dynamic manner of delivery. This does not mean that you need to shout, pound the table, or use sweeping gestures. It does mean, however, that your delivery must be animated and must mirror an inner intensity of belief and feeling. You cannot stir an audience to action unless your own commitment to the cause is evident. Be honestly enthusiastic; pattern your vocal and physical delivery on the model of a well-informed and responsible individual who is genuinely aroused. A delivery of this type can contribute significantly toward moving people to action.

Organization of the Speech to Actuate

When organizing a speech to actuate, adapt the five basic steps in the motivated sequence as follows:*

Attention Step

Although your attention step may be short, it is extremely important. If you are to motivate people to act, everything in your speech, from the very first words to the very last, must drive strongly and steadily at generating the behavior you desire. Moreover, what you say as you begin should contribute directly toward clarifying the action you propose. Do not waste time by telling a funny story that has only a marginal bearing on your purpose, or by reading a quotation which—though timely and interesting—might point the audience in a different direction. Be brief, but be direct and forceful. From the very first moment, begin to build toward the specific action you wish your hearers to take.

Need Step

If the audience already is aware of the need for the action you recommend, review that need briefly, perhaps adding one or two illustrations which show its urgent nature, and remind your listeners of significant ways in which it affects them. When, on the other hand, the audience is unaware of the need or does not recognize its full scope and importance, develop the need step at some length and with strong emphasis. Follow the pattern described in Chapter 9 in our discussion of the motivated sequence:

1. *Statement.* State clearly the specific need or problem which requires action.
2. *Illustration.* Give one or two examples which further clarify this need.

---

*These steps are discussed in detail in Chapter 9, pp. 142–163. Also see illustration on the next page.

THE MOTIVATED SEQUENCE
APPLIED TO SPEECHES

To Actuate

1 Attention

Getting
attention

2 Need

Showing the
need:
Describing the
problem

3 Satisfaction

Satisfying the
need:
Presenting the
solution

EXERCISE   DIET

4 Visualization

Visualizing
the results

5 Action

Requesting action
or approval

LOW-FAT-FOODS

3. *Reinforcement.* Employ as many forms of support as may be required to make this need convincing and impressive.
4. *Pointing.* Show how your listeners are involved — how their health, security, happiness, etc., are directly affected.

Satisfaction Step

Combine solid proof of the practicability of your proposal with strong motivation for doing as you recommend. Show that the action you are urging actually will produce the improvement you claim or remove the evils you decry. Support your contention by showing that similar actions have had these results in the past, or are now having these results in other states or communities. Give facts and figures. Take full advantage of the motive appeals described in Chapter 6. Show how the action you advocate will be easy to perform, or relatively cheap, or will bring favorable recognition to the person or group performing it. Fit your appeals to the listeners you are addressing. If security is their dominant motive, show how your proposal will provide that security. If they value self-enhancement or freedom of action, emphasize how your plan can help them attain and strengthen that value. Be ethical, of course, in your use of motivational appeals, and always aim at people's nobler desires rather than their baser drives. But, within these limits, *motivate your audience as strongly as you can.* Logical arguments can produce the conviction that sustains action once it is under way; strong motivation, however, is needed to arouse people from their apathy and prompt them to action in the first place.

Visualization Step

Use the positive or joint rather than the negative method for developing the visualization step, as explained on pages 154–156. If you tell an audience how bad things will be if they do not act as you urge, that description may crystallize negative or inhibitory ideas in their minds. On the other hand, a positive description of benefits, especially when projected in vivid and compelling language, clarifies the goal toward which the proposed action is directed and is itself a strong motivating factor.

Action Step

The action step should continue the strong motivation which you launched in the satisfaction and visualization steps, and should review the arguments which prove your proposed action necessary and practicable. *In addition, the action step should contain a clear and sufficiently detailed statement of exactly what you want the listeners to do or exactly where they should go to do it.* All too often speakers get their audiences aroused and determined to act, but fail to give them precise directions for carrying out the action. Sometimes the listeners do not know exactly where to go to vote, or the hours at which the polling places will be open. They may not know where to send their contributions or how to address the envelope. They are sometimes left with only a vague impression concerning the corner on which the mass rally is to be held or the hour at which they are to assemble.

Even with the best of intentions, most individuals are remiss about initiating the inquiries which will bring them the needed information. They tend to say, "Yes, I must find that address, but I am so busy today that I will wait until tomorrow." The trouble is that one "tomorrow" follows another, and the matter continues to drift. To help ensure action, then, make such inquiries unnecessary. Before concluding your speech, state fully and explicity—repeating information you have given earlier if necessary—exactly what you want done, and exactly where, when, and how to do it. Remember: *what, where, when, how*—and *now*. When your hearers are armed with this information, they are much more likely to act as you wish.

As the foregoing discussion suggests, in structure the speech to actuate is closely related to the speech to persuade, differing only in that it attempts to translate belief or feeling into immediate, overt *behavior*. In content also, these two types of speeches are similar. When moving listeners to action, ideas must be expressed in language that is vivid as well as clear. Be ever alert for an opportunity to cast the central message of your speech into an appropriate slogan or catchphrase such as "No taxation without representation," "The life you save may be your own," "All that we have to fear is fear itself." Such phrases must, of course, be short and easily remembered, and you should plan to repeat them several times during the course of your speech.

Combining Organization and Content: A Sample Outline for a Speech to Actuate

The following outline is based upon a speech which United States Senator John Culver presented before the Chicago Council on Foreign Relations.[1] Observe that each of the steps in the motivated sequence appropriate to an actuative speech is fully represented. Note also the liberal use of examples and statistics, and the strong motivation present in the closing appeal for action.

WORLD TRADE IN WEAPONS MUST CEASE

Attention Step
  I. Suppose a proposal were made that the United States go into the international heroin business.
      A. Such a proposal sounds outlandish.
      B. It would, however, "have some things going for it."
          1. It would stimulate industry and provide employment.

2. It would be beneficial to our balance of payments.
3. It would give us influence of sorts in some quarters.
4. It could be argued that if we didn't produce and sell heroin, someone else would.

II. Today the United States and its allies are heavily involved in another deadly traffic, that of arms and military equipment.
   A. This traffic has produced more death and suffering than all of the drugs produced since the beginning of time.
   B. It is escalating rapidly.
   C. It sometimes is justified by arguments similar to those I have cited for the heroin business.

Need Step

I. World trade in arms and military equipment has reached gigantic proportions.
   A. Trade in conventional weapons has soared to $18 billion annually.
      1. Developed and developing nations are laying in arsenals of the most sophisticated weapons they can obtain.
      2. United States arms sales to other countries amount to about one half of what we produce for our own use—$10 billion a year.
      3. The aerospace industry of the United Kingdom ships nearly one third of its annual production abroad.
      4. The Soviet Union accounts for nearly one fourth of the world's arms transfers.
         a. It sends to the less-developed countries twice as much in weapons as in economic assistance.
         b. It has helped to equip the pro-Soviet faction in Angola and elsewhere.

II. Arms exports from the United States are so large that they can no longer be monitored as the law directs.
   A. The executive branch has not always weighed the political, economic, and security factors involved in weapons sales.
      1. President Nixon decided on his own that Iran should get virtually any conventional weapons it desired.
      2. President Ford openly bypassed the normal decision-making process when he permitted the delivery of certain highly advanced weapons to Israel.
   B. Control by Congress is ineffective.
      1. Until 1974, Congress had practically no voice in arms sales.
      2. Recently, Congress faced the impossible task of reviewing forty-three separate sales proposals in the final hectic month before adjournment.

III. The benefits allegedly derived from foreign arms sales are by no means assured.
   A. In some countries the improved internal security resulting from arms purchases has led to increasingly repressive regimes.
   B. Savings from reduced unit costs of weapons produced in greater quantity, according to findings by the Congressional Budget Office, have been the exception rather than the rule.
   C. A "worst-case analysis" has shown that if we completely eliminated

foreign military sales, by 1981 there would be only three-tenths of a percent difference in the unemployment rate.

IV. The problems arising from foreign arms sales are already seriously jeopardizing our national defense.
    A. The defense-readiness of our own forces has suffered.
        1. The Army claims an overall deficiency of 61 percent in tanks.
        2. We are transferring some of our most advanced technology to other countries.
        3. Many countries to which we are selling arms are unable to absorb, utilize, and maintain the new equipment.
            a. Large quantities of uncrated weapons are stacked up on the docks of Persian Gulf countries.
            b. United States technicians complain that they cannot train adequate numbers of local personnel to operate and maintain the sophisticated weapons.
    B. Our arms merchants have been thoughtlessly arming potential adversaries.
        1. We have armed both Greece and Turkey.
        2. We have sold weapons to both Pakistan and India.
        3. We have given Israel $4.4 billion worth of military assistance since 1973, but have given the Persian Gulf states four times as much.
    C. The oil-rich states of the Middle East can afford weapons which the underdeveloped nations of Africa cannot.

V. One year ago, one hundred members of Congress joined me in urging Secretary of State Kissinger to sponsor an international conference on arms control.
    A. The Secretary ordered a full-scale review of possible limitations on weapons sales.
    B. The resulting report gave little hope that any initiative toward such a conference would come from our government.

Satisfaction Step

I. In the face of the foregoing situation, I have suggested that a step-by-step approach be taken to control international arms sales.
    A. This approach could be limited to the Middle East and Africa.
    B. It could be broadened to include other areas as well.
II. First, we should consult with our Canadian and Western European friends.
    A. We should explore mutual needs and interests.
    B. We should link discussion of arms sales to discussions on standardizing weapons among the NATO nations.
III. Second, we should seek to eliminate bribery and corruption in arms sales.
    A. Tentative guidelines are now being worked out by the Organization for Economic Cooperation and Development.
    B. Appropriate agencies of the United Nations also could attack the problem.
IV. Third, we should reduce the export of highly complex technology systems.
    A. We have been successful in restricting the transfer of computer know-how to Eastern European nations.
    B. We can be equally successful in devising feasible agreements on limiting arms sales to Third-World nations.

Visualization Step

I. Successful cooperation among our Canadian and Western allies would pave the way for future bargaining with the Soviet Union, China, and Eastern Europe.

Action Step

I. We must make the effort, difficult though it may be.
   A. The world looks to the United States for moral leadership and deceleration of the arms race.
   B. It is our responsibility to initiate action before it is too late and the momentum is irreversible.

A Sample Speech to Actuate

On Monday, April 18, 1977, President Carter delivered the following speech over the country's major radio and television networks as a way of "kicking off" a week-long campaign designed to sell his administration's energy program to the American people. This program, described by *Newsweek* magazine as a "complete and controversial" energy policy that could dramatically alter our present way of life, called for some of the sternest and most far-reaching sacrifices ever asked of the nation in time of peace, and was specifically intended to jolt people out of the notion that energy will always be cheap and abundant.

With polls showing that only about half of the public believed the energy crunch to be serious, the President's strategy was to take his case to the public with this speech before presenting his formal proposals to Congress on the following day. Later in the week, with a well-advertised press conference on the energy problem, he concluded this organized effort to sell his program.

As you read the speech, observe not only how President Carter made use of each of the five steps in the motivated sequence appropriate to a speech to actuate, but also how he combined facts and figures with a variety of motivational appeals in order to communicate to his listeners a strong sense of urgency and the need to take drastic measures to meet a most serious problem.

"Energy Address to the Nation"[2]
Jimmy Carter

Attention Step

(Startling statements show seriousness and urgency of the problem.)

Tonight I want to have an unpleasant talk with you about a problem unprecedented in our history. With the exception of preventing war, this is the greatest challenge our country will face during our lifetimes. The energy crisis has not yet overwhelmed us, but it will if we do not act quickly. /1

It is a problem we will not solve in the next few years, and it is likely to get progressively worse through the rest of this century. /2

We must not be selfish or timid if we hope to have a decent world for our children and grandchildren. /3

We simply must balance our demand for energy with our rapidly shrinking resources. By acting now we can control our future instead of letting the future control us. /4

Two days from now, I will present my energy proposals to the Congress. Its members will be my partners, and they have already given me a great deal of valuable advice. /5

Many of these proposals will be unpopular. Some will cause you inconveniences and sacrifices. /6

(Consequences of isolation or delay strongly stressed.) The most important thing about these proposals is that the alternative may be a national catastrophe. Further delay can affect our strength and our power as a nation. /7

Our decision about energy will test the character of the American people and the ability of the President and the Congress to govern. This difficult effort will be the "moral equivalent of war"—except that we will be uniting our efforts to build and not destroy. /8

Need Step

I know that some of you may doubt that we face real energy shortages. The 1973 gasoline lines are gone, and our homes are warm again. /9

But our energy problem is worse tonight than it was in 1973 or a few weeks ago in the dead of winter. It is worse because more waste has occurred, and more time has passed by without our planning for the future. /10

And it will get worse every day until we act. /11

(Nature of problem explained and supported with facts and figures.) The oil and natural gas we rely on for 75 percent of our energy are running out. In spite of increased effort, domestic production has been dropping steadily at about 6 percent a year. Imports have doubled in the last five years. Our nation's independence of economic and political action is becoming increasingly constrained. Unless profound changes are made to lower oil consumption, we now believe that early in the 1980s the world will be demanding more oil than it can produce. /12

The world now uses about 60 million barrels of oil a day, and demand increases each year about 5 percent. This means that just to stay even we need the production of a new Texas every year, an Alaskan North Slope every nine months, or a new Saudi Arabia every three years. Obviously this cannot continue. /13

We must look back into history to understand our energy problem. /14

Twice in the last several hundred years there has been a transition in the way people use energy. /15

The first was about 200 years ago, away from wood—which had provided about 90 percent of all fuel—to coal, which was more efficient. This change became the basis of the Industrial Revolution. /16

The second change took place in this century, with the growing use of oil and natural gas. They were more convenient and cheaper than coal, and the supply seemed to be almost without limit. They made possible the age of automobile and airplane travel. Nearly everyone who is alive today grew up during this age, and we have never known anything different. /17

Because we are now running out of gas and oil, we must prepare quickly for a third change: to strict conservation and to the use of coal and permanent renewable energy sources, like solar power. /18

The world has not prepared for the future. During the 1950s, people used twice as much oil as during the 1940s. During the 1960s, we used twice as much as during the 1950s. /19

And in each of those decades, more oil was consumed than in all of mankind's previous history. /20

World consumption of oil is still going up. If it were possible to keep it rising during the 1970s and 1980s by 5 percent a year as it has in the past, we could use up all the reserves of oil in the world by the end of the next decade. /21

(Counteracts audience's possible doubts with additional explanation.)

I know that many of you have suspected that some supplies of oil and gas are being withheld. You may be right, but suspicions about the oil companies cannot change the fact that we are running out of petroleum. /22

All of us have heard about the large oil fields on Alaska's North Slope. In a few years when the North Slope is producing fully, its total output will be just about equal to two years' increase in our nation's energy demand. /23

Each new inventory of world oil reserves has been more disturbing than the last. World oil production can probably keep going up for another six or eight years. But sometime in the 1980s it can't go up much more. /24

Demand will overtake production. We have no choice about that. /25

But we do have a choice about how we will spend the next few years. Each American uses the energy equivalent of 60 barrels of oil per person each year. Ours is the most wasteful nation on earth. We waste more energy than we import. With about the same standard of living, we use twice as much energy per person as do other countries like Germany, Japan, and Sweden. /26

One choice is to continue doing what we have been doing before. We can drift along for a few more years. /27

(Projects problem into immediate future to show consequences of further delay.)

Our consumption of oil would keep going up every year. Our cars would continue to be too large and inefficient. Three-quarters of them would continue to carry only one person—the driver—while our public transportation system continues to decline. We can delay insulating our houses, and they will continue to lose about 50 percent of their heat in waste. /28

We can continue using scarce oil and natural gas to generate electricity, and continue wasting two thirds of their fuel value in the process. /29

If we do not act, then, by 1985, we will be using 33 percent more energy than we do today. /30

We can't substantially increase our domestic production, so we would need to import twice as much oil as we do now. Supplies will be uncertain. The cost will keep going up. Six years ago, we paid $3.7 billion for imported oil. Last year we spent $36 billion—nearly ten times as much—and this year we may spend $45 billion. /31

Unless we act, we will spend more than $550 billion for imported oil by 1985—more than $2,500 for every man, woman, and child in America. Along with that money, we will continue losing Americans' jobs and becoming increasingly vulnerable to supply interruptions. /32

Now we have a choice. /33

(Uses fear appeals to motivate listeners.)

But if we wait, we will live in fear of embargoes. We could endanger our freedom as a sovereign nation to act in foreign affairs. /34

Within ten years we would not be able to import enough oil—from any country, at any acceptable price. /35

If we wait, and do not act, then our factories will not be able to keep our people on the job with reduced fuel. /36

Too few of our utilities will have switched to coal, our most abundant energy source. /37

We will not be ready to keep our transportation system running with smaller, more efficient cars and a better network of buses, trains, and public transportation. /38

We will feel mounting pressure to plunder the environment. We will have a crash program to build more nuclear plants, strip-mine and burn more coal, and drill more off-shore wells than we will need if we begin to conserve now. /39

Inflation will soar, production will go down, people will lose their jobs. /40

Intense competition will build up among nations, and among the different regions within our own country. /41

If we fail to act soon, we will face an economic, social, and political crisis that will threaten our free institutions. /42

But we still have another choice. We can begin to prepare right now. We can decide to act while there is time. /43

That is the concept of the energy policy we will present on Wednesday. /44

Satisfaction Step

(Begins point-by-point explanation of the administration's energy plan.)

Our national energy plan is based on ten fundamental principles. /45

The first principle is that we can have an effective and comprehensive energy policy only if the government takes responsibility for it and if the people understand the seriousness of the challenge and are willing to make sacrifices. /46

The second principle is that healthy economic growth must continue. Only by saving energy can we maintain our standard of living and keep our people at work. An effective conservation program will create hundreds of thousands of new jobs. /47

The third principle is that we must protect the environment. Our energy problems have the same cause as our environmental problems—wasteful use of resources. Conservation helps us solve both at once. /48

The fourth principle is that we must reduce our vulnerability to potentially devastating embargoes. We can protect ourselves from uncertain supplies by reducing our demand for oil, making the most of our abundant resources such as coal, and developing a strategic petroleum reserve. /49

The fifth principle is that we must be fair. Our solutions must ask equal sacrifices from every region, every class of people, every interest group. Industry will have to do its part to conserve, just as consumers will. The energy producers deserve fair treatment, but we will not let the oil companies profiteer. /50

The sixth principle, and the cornerstone of our policy, is to reduce demand through conservation. Our emphasis on conservation is a clear difference between this plan and others which merely encouraged crash-production efforts. Conservation is the quickest, cheapest, most practical source of energy. Conservation is the only way we can buy a barrel of oil for a few dollars. It costs about $13 to waste it. /51

The seventh principle is that prices should generally reflect the true replacement costs of energy. We are only cheating ourselves if we make energy artificially cheap. /52

The eighth principle is that government policies must be predictable and certain. Both consumers and producers need policies they can count on so they can plan ahead. This is one reason I am working with the Congress to create a new Department of Energy, to replace more than fifty agencies that now have control over energy. /53

The ninth principle is that we must conserve the fuels that are scarcest and make the most of those that are more plentiful. We can't continue to use oil and gas for 75 percent of our consumption when they make up only 7 percent of our domestic reserves. We need to shift to plentiful coal while taking care to protect the environment, and to apply stricter safety standards to nuclear energy. /54

The tenth principle is that we must start now to develop the new, unconventional sources of energy we will rely on in the next century. /55

These ten principles have guided the development of the policy I [will] describe to you and the Congress on Wednesday. /56

Visualization Step

(Goals visualize the effects of the proposed program.)

Our energy plan will also include a number of specific goals, to measure our progress toward a stable energy system. /57

These are the goals we set for 1985:
- Reduce the annual growth rate in our energy demand to less than 2 percent. /58
- Reduce gasoline consumption by 10 percent below its current level. /59
- Cut in half the portion of U.S. oil which is imported — from a potential level of 16 million barrels to 6 million barrels a day. /60
- Establish a strategic petroleum reserve of one billion barrels, more than six-months' supply. /61
- Increase our coal production by about two thirds, to more than one billion tons a year. /62
- Insulate 90 percent of American homes and all new buildings. /63
- Use solar energy in more than 2.5 million houses. /64

We will monitor our progress toward these goals year by year. Our plan will call for stricter conservation measures if we fall behind. /65

I can't tell you that these measures will be easy, nor will they be popular. But I think most of you realize that a policy which does not ask for changes or sacrifices would not be an effective policy. /66

This plan is essential to protect our jobs, our environment, our standard of living, and our future. /67

Action Step

(Makes direct appeal for listeners' support.)
(Challenges listeners.)

Whether this plan truly makes a difference will be decided not here in Washington, but in every town and every factory, in every home, and on every highway and every farm. /68

I believe this can be a positive challenge. There is something especially American in the kinds of changes we have to make. We have been proud, through our history, of being efficient people. /69

(Appeals to pride.) We have been proud of our ingenuity, our skill at answering questions. We need efficiency and ingenuity more than ever. /70

We have been proud of our leadership in the world. Now we have a chance again to give the world a positive example. /71

And we have been proud of our vision of the future. We have always wanted to give our children and grandchildren a world richer in possibilities than we've had. They are the ones we must provide for now. They are the ones who will suffer most if we don't act. /72

I've given you some of the principles of the plan. /73

(Calls for sacrifices.) I am sure each of you will find something you don't like about the specifics of our proposal. It will demand that we make sacrifices and changes in our lives. To some degree, the sacrifices will be painful — but so is any meaningful sacrifice. It will lead to some higher costs, and to some greater inconveniences for everyone. /74

(Assures listeners that sacrifices will be gradual and fair to all.) But the sacrifices will be gradual, realistic, and necessary. Above all, they will be fair. No one will gain an unfair advantage through this plan. No one will be asked to bear an unfair burden. We will monitor the accuracy of data from the oil and natural gas companies, so that we will know their true production, supplies, reserves, and profits. /75

The citizens who insist on driving large, unnecessarily powerful cars must expect to pay more for that luxury. /76

We can be sure that all the special interest groups in the country will attack the part of this plan that affects them directly. They will say that sacrifice is fine, as long as other people do it, but that their sacrifice is unreasonable, or unfair, or harmful to the country. If they succeed, then the burden on the ordinary citizen, who is not organized into an interest group, would be crushing. /77

There should be only one test for this program — whether it will help our country. /78

(Again challenges listeners in closing.) Other generations of Americans have faced and mastered great challenges. I have faith that meeting this challenge will make our own lives even richer. If you will join me so that we can work together with patriotism and courage, we will again prove that our great nation can lead the world into an age of peace, independence, and freedom. /79

Reference Notes

[1] Outline from speech to the Chicago Council on Foreign Relations by Senator John C. Culver. Reprinted by permission.

[2] President James E. Carter. "Energy Address to the Nation," delivered April 18, 1977.

Problems and Probes

1.   Radio and television commercials, as well as advertisements in newspapers and magazines, are of course aimed at actuating listeners or readers. Compare the actuative methods and strategies used by the mass media with those recommended in this chapter for the public speaker. Identify some actuative methods used by television and newspapers which you think would not be effective in speeches.

2.   Would you agree or disagree with this statement: "Those attempts to actuate which are guided by high ethical and moral standards are, in the end, always more persuasive than those which are not"? Explain your answer.

3.   What motive appeals would you employ if you were attempting to induce an audience of college students to take the following actions: *(a)* contribute to the campus charity drive, *(b)* enroll in the ROTC program, *(c)* study harder, *(d)* give up their automobiles, *(e)* have an annual physical examination, *(f)* learn to speak Russian, and *(g)* drop out of college?

4.   Comment on this statement: "Most people act out of desire rather than reason; they only use reason to justify to themselves what they want to do anyway." Use the remark to formulate at least three useful principles for speeches to actuate.

5.   Devise a slogan or catchphrase which you might use in a speech to actuate your hearers to respond positively to each of the following proposals:

Work for student representation on city boards and commissions.
Participate actively in clean-up, paint-up week.
Devote Saturday morning to working with handicapped children.
Take a rapid-reading course.

Oral Activity and Speaking Assignment

1.   Present a five-minute speech to actuate, the purpose of which is to move the members of your speech class to sign a petition requesting the alteration of an unpopular rule or the correction of an undesirable situation on the campus or in your community. Select a rule or situation which actually exists—not an imaginary or fictional one. Show your listeners why they should be concerned; explain why a petition of this kind has a good chance of influencing the authorities in charge; point out the advantages to be gained from acting as you recommend, etc. Use carefully reasoned arguments, strong motivation, and vivid and compelling language. Your delivery should conform to the suggestions offered in this chapter. At the close of your speech, pass the petition among the members of the class for signatures. You might, for example, urge your audience to sign a petition requesting one of the following changes:

Graduating seniors should be excused from final examinations.
The student government should be given complete control over "activity fees."
Campus food service should be improved.
All curfew restrictions for men and women should be lifted.
Parking meters should be installed on X Street.
Advertising sound trucks should be prohibited in the area of the campus.
The college should establish a cooperative bookstore (or grocery, or gasoline station).
Landlords renting to students should conform strictly to anti-discrimination laws.

The community should enter at once upon a plan of environmental protection.

 Suggestions for Further Reading

Saundra Hybels and Richard L. Weaver, II, *Speech Communication* (New York: D. Van Nostrand and Co., 1974), Chapter 6, "The Power of Communication."

Charles U. Larson, *Persuasion: Reception and Responsibility* (Belmont, Calif.: Wadsworth Publishing Company, Inc., 1973), Chapter 7, "The Persuasive Campaign or Movement."

Herbert W. Simons, *Persuasion: Understanding, Practice, and Analysis* (Reading, Mass.: Addision-Wesley Publishing Company, Inc., 1976), Chapter 13, "Persuasion in Social Conflicts."

Rudolph F. Verderber, *The Challenge of Effective Speaking,* 3rd ed. (Belmont Calif.: Wadsworth Publishing Company, Inc., 1976), Chapter 15, "Motivating Audiences: Speeches to Actuate."

Otis M. Walter, *Speaking Intelligently* (New York: The Macmillan Company, 1976), Chapter 8, "Motivation by Group Behavior: Group Determinism."

Part 5

REPORT

OPEN FORUM

PANEL DISCUSSION

Public Communication:
Special Types

20

Group and Conference Presentations

From the chapters of Part Four, you have no doubt correctly concluded that speeches to inform, to persuade, and to actuate are the three types of one-to-many communication that you will most often be called upon to make. Many situations and circumstances, however, require *special* types of public oral presentations and speeches. Here, in Part Five, we shall examine three categories of these special types, beginning with *group and conference presentations,* followed by *speeches of argument,* and concluding with *speeches for special occasions.*

The world of business literally runs on group and conference presentations. On monthly, quarterly, semiannual, or annual schedules, members of business teams exchange data on sales, production, and growth; analyze those data in small groups; and make recommendations for adjustment and change so as to better meet the organization's goals. Research-and-development teams constantly discuss new ideas to increase efficiency, to expand the business into new territories, and to evaluate experimental programs and procedures. The board of directors prepares and often orally presents annual reports for the stockholders and the public. And business persons, gathered together locally (for example, in the Chamber of Commerce) or nationally (for example, in the National Association of Manufacturers), exchange information on business conditions, and lobby for advantages on the local, state, regional, and national levels.

Group and conference presentations also are found in realms of private and public deliberation. Your college or university undoubtedly has a great number of committees—on personnel, resource allocation, promotion, the library system, curriculum policies, and the like—which

meet periodically to review important matters and make recommendations for continuance or change. Similarly, private groups and clubs—
coin enthusiasts, stamp collectors, transcendental meditation practitioners, etc.—regularly listen to updates on matters of interest, hear
reports from members, or enter upon campaigns for community action
and involvement. And, of course, government—particularly in the legislative and executive branches—depends upon committees and sub-
committees, and open and closed meetings of concerned persons to
formulate legislation and to discuss methods for making administration
more efficient. The old saw has it that a camel is a "horse built by a
committee"; but, problems notwithstanding, we are a culture dominat-
ed by group decisions.

In this chapter, therefore, we shall review several types of group and
conference presentations because they require that you as a communicator operate somewhat differently than you do in other communication
settings. We then will review some of the communicative techniques
especially valuable when you are *making reports* and *participating in
panels, public discussions, and conferences.* Our focus will be upon
public presentations made by a uniquely qualified individual or a small
group of individuals to or on behalf of a larger group of individuals.

Types of Presentations

Group presentations characteristically occur in situations in which
some person has previously assembled or evaluated information,
framed questions, or developed solutions to problems with a view to
presenting these findings or arguing for a point of view *in a small group*
(three to twelve or fifteen persons) or as a member of a small group
before a public audience. A *group presentation,* therefore, differs from a
group discussion in that it is the product of an individual rather than a
cooperative process, and in that an individual has been chosen to speak
because he or she has special expertise to be shared with people who
want information, opinions, or recommendations. On the other hand, a
group presentation differs from a regular public speech in that the audience nearly always is smaller and more specialized, and, in the case of
multiple speakers, the session is usually focused or problem-centered.
(See "Communicating in Small Groups," page 447, for a detailed treatment of small-group discussion.) Group presentations most commonly
take one of four forms: (1) the *report session,* (2) the *panel discussion,*
(3) the *symposium,* and (4) the *open forum.*

The Report Session.   When a group is too large, the subject matter too
complicated, or the situation too pressing to allow for the leisurely contemplation of a problem, many organizations call upon experts or staff
researchers to prepare special reports on various aspects of the problem or on proposed solutions. Thus, as we noted earlier, a business firm
may ask some of its members to assemble statistics relative to employ-

ment, sales, or costs; a congressional committee may call in outside experts to offer testimony; a club may ask its secretary to report on patterns or trends in its finances over a specified period. The "report session," in short, is distinguished by its reliance upon certain members who are specifically asked to provide information and guidance for the others.

The Panel Discussion.   When a group is too large to engage in effective round-table discussion or its members are not well enough informed to make such discussion profitable, a panel of individuals — from three to five, usually — may be selected to discuss the topic for the benefit of the others, who then become an audience. The discussants on this special panel are chosen either because they are particularly well informed on the subject and can supply the information needed for understanding or action, or because they represent divergent views on the matter at issue. The members of the panel, under the direction of a leader, discuss the subject among themselves. Following this interchange, they frequently invite questions and comments from the audience.

The Symposium.   A third type of audience-oriented discussion is the symposium. In this format, several persons — again from three to five, usually — present short speeches, each focusing on a different facet of the subject or offering a different solution to the problem under consideration. Especially valuable when recognized experts with well-defined points of view or areas of competence are available as speakers, the symposium is the discussion procedure commonly employed at large-scale conferences and conventions.

Various modifications of the panel and the symposium are possible, and sometimes the two formats may be successfully combined. As we have just suggested, frequently the set speeches of the symposium are followed by an informal interchange among the speakers. Then the meeting is "thrown open" to audience questions, comments, and reactions. The essential characteristic of both the panel and the symposium, however, is that a few persons discuss a subject or problem while many persons listen.

The Open Forum.   As it is generally planned and conducted, the open forum consists of a single, relatively long speech or lecture followed by a period in which — under the direction of the speaker or a chairperson — the listeners raise questions or make statements of their own. In one important respect, however, the open forum differs from the usual persuasive public speaking situation: Instead of the speaker's trying to influence the direction and outcome of the listeners' thinking — winning from them a carefully predetermined response — he or she plans remarks with the specific purpose of stimulating the audience to ask questions and make comments from the floor. The aim of an open-forum speech, in short, is to cause the listeners to think and respond rather than simply to be informed or persuaded. As a result, the success of a speech made in this situation is to be measured not by products sold or votes won, but rather by the extent and vigor of the discussion it generates.

Techniques for Making Oral Reports

Making reports to small groups or even to large ones does not differ substantially from delivering a successful informative speech. But because the report-making session takes place before a group of concerned individuals who are expecting useful information which they have specifically called for and probably are going to use practically, as a reporter you should be aware of certain strictures. Above all, you should be conscious of your role as an *expert* — the *source* of predigested information for an assemblage of people who, in turn, will act upon it. That role carries with it tremendous responsibilities. It demands that you prepare with special care and that you present your material with the utmost clarity and balance. The success of a business firm, the government's legislative program, or your club's future—all may depend upon your reporting abilities. Therefore, keep the following guidelines in mind as you prepare and deliver your report:

The information you present must be researched with great care. While you may be asked only to present a series of statistical generalizations in a short, five-minute report, your research must be extensive and solid. You must assemble your material "cleanly," without bias or any major deficiencies. The quarterly report for a business which relies only upon material gathered from one of the territories in which it operates may not only be partial, but also skewed. Furthermore, even though you may be asked only to report the bare facts or "bottom lines" of your information, in a question-and-answer session you could be asked to expand upon what you say—to supply the figures on which you based your statistical conclusions. So, bring all of your information along even if you have only a short time for your actual presentation.

When making recommendations rather than merely reporting information, be sure to include a complete rationale for the advice you present. Suppose, for example, that you have been called upon by your student-government council to recommend ways in which certain developmental monies should be spent. First, you will need to gather information on certain needs: Does this campus require additional buses (and should you, therefore, recommend further subsidy for public transportation)? Could it use more student-sponsored scholarships? Might it profit from a "careers week" in which recruiters from various businesses, industries, and other endeavors put on special seminars for interested students? To make recommendations on these needs, you must have financial information on the costs incurred in filling each demand. Second, you will need to assemble data on student interest, based upon interviews and patterns of usage observed in the past. Third, in order to make sound recommendations, you then will have to rank-order the options open to the group. Fourth, you will need to build a rationale for your rank-ordering, including answers to such questions as: What student needs will each course of action meet? Why do you consider one need more pressing than the other? Why should student government, and not some other college or university agency, act to meet that need? Were student government to act on a specific need, what other kinds of university, community, and/or governmental supports would be forthcoming over the short and long term?

Answers to such questions would in each case provide the rationale for a decision. This is important for two reasons: (1) Such a rationale enhances your *image or credibility* because it demonstrates your ability to think through and rationally solve problems. Unless your credibility is strong, your recommendations have little chance for action. (2) More importantly, if your rationale is a good one, it probably will be adopted by the audience as a whole; for the audience, in turn, has constituencies—the student body, specific organizations represented on the government council, etc.—to which it must answer when it takes action. In other words, by not only making recommendations but also offering reasons, you allow your auditors to meet objections, to urge the action, etc., in the important second step of persuasion—the appeal to secondary audiences.

Make full use of visual aids when making reports. Because reports often have to be short and to the point and yet contain a great amount of information, the reporter must decide how to present a maximum amount of useful material in the shortest period of time. The advice on the employment of visual aids presented in Chapter 16 is germane. Use each aid to its maximum advantage. Were you to give the speech to the student-government council mentioned earlier, for example, you might (1) offer statistical data on a mimeographed handout, with summaries in the form of bar or pie graphs; (2) audiotape and replay sample student interviews; (3) employ a brief slide show to help the audience visualize either the problems or the solutions (for example, slides of "career days" at other schools); (4) exhibit a flipchart with diagrams of proposed bus routes, a floor plan for a ballroom setup for a career-days fair, or an organizational chart delineating the sources of scholarship monies currently available on campus; or (5) hand out a dittoed sheet containing the wording of a motion you would introduce to make official your recommendations. Under these circumstances, you could limit your remarks to those aspects of the report best enhanced by your voice—the rationales or persuasive appeals. The employment of such visual aids, therefore, would help to keep you within the assigned time limit and would make full use of both the verbal and the visual communication channels.

Whatever you do, stay within the boundaries of your report-making charge. As a reporter, you are a conduit—a pipeline between the audience and some subject of interest. You therefore must be highly sensitive to the audience's expectations: Were you charged with gathering information only? Or were you told what kind of information to bring in? Did your instructions say to assemble recommendations for action? Were you to include financial and impact analyses along with those recommendations? Most reporters are given a charge—a duty to perform. If you depart too far from that charge—if you make recommendations when you are expected only to gather information, *or* if you only gather information when you have been asked to make recommendations— you are likely to create ill will among your listeners. When this occurs, your work often will be for naught; you will have failed as a reporter. So, clarify the boundaries within which you are operating; when given a task, ask for relevant instructions. In that way, as you discharge your duties, you probably will satisfy the group and, consequently, will also increase (or at least not decrease) your own credibility and status.

Group and Conference Presentations . . .

typically employ *open forums, symposiums, panel discussions,* or oral *report sessions.* Nearly always, the purpose and format are audience-oriented and well "advertised" in advance. In some, the initial communication at least is largely one-to-many; in others, it is mainly "several-to-many." Characteristically, all such presentations seek in one way or another an immediate or nearly immediate vocal response from and a personal involvement of audience members.

Techniques for Participating in Panels and Conferences

While the techniques you employ as a conference or panel speaker do not vary substantially from those used for any other type of speech, remember always that you are participating as a member of a *group* who is centering its remarks, information, and opinions upon a specific topic or problem. You, therefore, have an obligation to function as *part of a team,* to do what you can to coordinate your communicative behaviors with the efforts of others in order to give your audience a full range of viewpoints and options. Thus, in an important sense, in group and conference presentations you must sacrifice part of your individual freedom and latitude for the greater good of all.

With this important caution in mind, we can proceed to discuss how you should prepare for a panel presentation and to mention four "commandments" for maintaining the free and open atmosphere essential to development and growth in a panel setting.

Essentials for the Individual Participant.   If a discussion for whatever purpose is to be successful, you must have a *thorough knowledge of the subject being considered.* Unless this is the case, misinformation rather than solid facts will be exchanged, and a decision will be made on the basis of incomplete or incorrect data. A second essential is an *acquaintance with the other members of the group.* The more you know about each other, the better you will be able to understand why certain persons take the positions they do, and why at a particular point the discussion may cease to be productive. Third, you must pay *close attention to the discussion* as it proceeds. Unless you listen carefully to what is going on, you will lose track of where the discussion is, double back to repeat points already covered, or entertain mistaken ideas concerning the views of the other discussants. Finally, *meaningful contributions to the discussion itself* are imperative. A person who remains silent may learn much, but silence does not enhance the knowledge of others or help to solve the problems faced by the group. A good discussion participant has the ability to present ideas clearly and tactfully and knows how to interject them at the most strategic time.

These four essentials, of course, have numerous ramifications and specific applications; and as you gain experience in the discussion process, you should note them and use them to put together a more detailed "profile" of the effective discussant. (See also page 449.)

Preparation for Panels and Conferences.   Because in panels and conferences you are one of a team of communicators, it is important that you take others into account as you prepare your remarks. This taking-into-account involves considerations which you do not have to face in other speaking situations. First, *you have to fit your comments into a general theme.* If, say, the theme of your panel is "The State of American Culture at the Beginning of Its Third Century," not only will you be expected to mention "American," "culture," "two hundred years," and the like, but probably you will also be expected to say something about where society has been over those two hundred years, where you think it is today, and how you see it evolving. The theme, in other words, goes far toward dictating how you will treat your subject, and perhaps even forces you to approach it in a particular way. Also, *remember that you may be responsible for covering only a portion of a topic or theme.* In most symposia and panels, the speakers divide the topic into parts, to avoid duplication and to provide an audience with a variety of viewpoints. For example, if you are discussing the state of American culture, you might be asked to discuss education, while others will examine social relations, the state of science and technology, leisure time, etc., thus dividing the theme *topically.* Or, alternatively, you might be asked to discuss *problems* (depersonalization, the "plastic" world, the limits of the work force) while other participants examine *solutions* (individual, corporate, ethical, political). Part of your preparation, therefore, involves coordinating your communicative efforts with those of others.

The more you know about the subject under discussion, the better. Don't rely on obsolete information, however; make sure your facts are up-to-date. The broader and readier the knowledge at your command, the better able you will be to take part in the discussion no matter how it may develop or what course it may follow. Although many persons believe they do not need to prepare as carefully for a group discussion as for a public speech, the truth of the matter is just the opposite. In communication of this kind, you cannot arbitrarily narrow the subject or determine the specific purpose in advance; nor can you be sure of the exact direction the group will take. To be ready for any eventuality, therefore, you must have a flexibility born of broad knowledge. For each aspect of the subject or implication of the problem you think may possibly be discussed, make the following analysis:

First, review the facts you already know. Go over the information you have acquired through previous reading.or personal experience and organize it in your mind. Prepare as if you were going to present a speech on every phase of the matter. You will then be better qualified to discuss any part of it almost spontaneously.

Second, bring your knowledge up-to-date. Find out if recent changes have affected the situation. Fit the newly acquired information into what you already know.

Third, determine a tentative point of view on each of the important issues. Make up your mind what your attitude will be. Do you think that Hemingway was a greater writer than Faulkner? If so, exactly how and why? What three or four steps might be taken to attract new members into your club? On what medical or health-related grounds should cigarette-smoking be declared illegal? Stake out a tentative position on each question or issue that is likely to come before the group, and have clearly in mind the facts and reasons that support your view. Be ready to state and substantiate this opinion at whatever point in the discussion seems most appropriate, but also be willing to change your mind if information or points of view provided by other discussants show you to be wrong.

Fourth—and finally—to the best of your ability anticipate the effect of your ideas or proposals on other members of the group or the organization of which the group is a part. For instance, what you propose may possibly cause someone to lose money or to retract a promise that has been made. Forethought concerning such eventualities will enable you to understand opposition to your view if it arises and to make a valid and intelligent adjustment. The more thoroughly you organize your facts and relate them to the subject and to the people involved, the more effective and influential your contributions to the discussion will be.

Participation in Panels and Conferences. Your style and vocal tone will, of course, vary according to the nature and purpose of the discussion as a whole, the degree of formality that is being observed, and your frame of mind as you approach the task. In general, however, *speak in a direct, friendly, conversational style.* As the interaction proceeds, differences of opinion are likely to arise, tensions may increase, and some conflict may surface. You will need, therefore, to be sensitive to these changes and to make necessary adjustments in the way you voice your ideas and reactions.

Present your point of view clearly, succinctly, and fairly. Participation in a panel or conference should always be guided by one underlying aim: to help the group think objectively and creatively in analyzing the subject or solving the problem at hand. To this end, you should organize your contributions not in the way best calculated to win other people to your point of view, but rather in the fashion that will best *stimulate them to think for themselves.* Therefore, instead of stating your conclusion first and then supplying the arguments in favor of it, let your contribution recount how and why you came to think as you do. Begin by stating the nature of the problem as you see it; outline the various hypotheses or solutions that occurred to you as you were thinking about it; tell why you rejected certain solutions; and only after all this, state your own opinion and explain the reasons that support it. In this way, you give other members of the group a chance to check the accuracy and completeness of your thinking on the matter and to point out any deficiencies or fallacies that may not have occurred to you. At the same time, you will also be making your contribution in the most objective and rational manner possible.

Maintain attitudes of sincerity, open-mindedness, and objectivity. Above all, remember that a serious discussion is not a showplace for prima donnas or an arena for verbal combatants. When you have something to say, say it modestly and sincerely, and always maintain an open, objective attitude. Accept criticism with dignity and treat disagreement with an open mind. Your primary purpose is not to get your own view accepted, but to work out with the other members of the group the best possible choice or decision that all of you together can devise, and as a team to present a variety of viewpoints to the audience.

We are indeed a culture run by group decisions, conferences, conventions, and committees. Even if many of the panels and committees you attend seem less formal than some which have been described in this chapter, they nevertheless provide arenas for public communication, most of which take the form of "mini" speeches. In making more or less formal, more or less prepared remarks in panels and other group settings, you will be exercising the communicative skills with which this book is concerned. Sometimes you will work in an impromptu fashion; at other times, you will be expected to speak from a carefully prepared outline. Whatever the form of the discourse, however, it will demand that you consider all of the communication decisions stressed in earlier chapters. A committee may well look like a camel to outsiders; but it can, nevertheless, lead to an interdependence in thinking, a communal sharing in action, and a lively and even entertaining exchange in human communication.

Problems and Probes

1.   Assume that you are to act as chairperson on one of the following occasions (or on some similar occasion): a school assembly celebrating a successful football season; a student-government awards banquet; a one-day orientation session for prospective students from nearby high schools; a student-faculty mass meeting called to protest a regulation issued by the dean's office.
In your role as chairperson, *(a)* plan a suitable program of speeches, entertainment, etc.; *(b)* allocate the amount of time to be devoted to each item on the program; *(c)* outline suitable speeches of introduction for the featured speakers; *(d)* prepare publicity releases for the local newspapers and electronic media; *(e)* suggest how you might arrange for press coverage, etc. Work out a complete plan, one that you might show to a steering committee or a faculty sponsor.

2.   List several specific situations other than radio or television broadcasts in which a *panel discussion* might be the most appropriate form of communication to use. List other non-broadcasting situations in which the *symposium* probably would be more suitable. And, finally, list a number of non-broadcasting situations in which the *open forum* would be appropriate. What considerations of audience, materials, type of public controversy, etc., were most important in your determinations?

3. Assume that, as part of a mythical National Student Week, you have been asked to arrange on your campus a panel, symposium, open forum, or workshop to which all students and faculty members will be invited. Select a subject that you think would be of interest to such an audience. Indicate whom you would ask to participate, and how you might instruct them for their preparations. Where and when would you hold the meeting? How long would it last? What would be the audience's role? In carrying out your charge and in answering the additional questions, be prepared to defend your choices and answers.

4.   Select and watch one of the weekly television discussion shows on which persons from government, business, or the professions are questioned by a person or a panel ("Meet the Press," "Face the Nation," "Issues and Answers," "Firing Line," etc.). To what extent do the formats and procedures used on

these shows adhere to principles of communication outlined in this chapter? Do you think any of the departures you see make the sessions more or less effective means for capturing and maintaining public interest? Also note the extent to which a moderator (if there was one) controlled the direction and emphases of questioning.

5.   Interview an executive of a local business or industry of some size, and explore with that person the extent to which oral reports are used in the business. Attempt to find out *(a)* the kinds of reports made orally, *(b)* the frequency of such reports and report sessions of various kinds, and *(c)* the executive's perceptions of what the qualities of good reports are. You may also wish to discover what kinds of materials and problems are treated in written media, and what kinds in oral media.

 Oral Activities and Speaking Assignments

1.   From a list of topics found in this book or prepared by your instructor, select a subject treating communication phenomena which interest you, and prepare a five-minute oral report on them for your class. Make use of readings suggested in footnotes and in chapter-end materials, as well as additional articles and books known to your instructor. Carefully decide how you ought to use visual aids in preparing and presenting the material, and work hard to make sure your speech achieves clarity, informativeness, and interest.

2.   Divide the class into four-person teams. Each team will select a topic around which public messages will be constructed. Each will then select an appropriate format—a report session, a panel discussion, a symposium, or a public discussion—and have members of the team construct speeches. Each team will be given a half or a whole period to present the speeches to the class, with one of the team members acting as moderator. In the teams, make sure that you provide a variety in viewpoints or sub-topics and that you orient the audience to what it should expect.

 Suggestions for Further Reading

Roy M. Berko, Andrew D. Wolvin, and Darlyn R. Wolvin, *Communicating: A Social and Career Focus* (Boston: Houghton Mifflin Company, 1977), Chapter 9, "Small-Group Communication."

Cal Downs, David M. Berg, and Wil Linkugel, *The Organizational Communicator* (New York: Harper & Row, Publishers, 1977).

Bernard P. McCabe, Jr., and Coleman C. Bender, *Speaking Is a Practical Matter,* 3rd ed. (Boston: Holbrook Press, Inc., 1976), Chapter 6, "Small Group Communication."

S. Bernard Rosenblatt, T. Richard Cheatam, and James T. Watt, *Communication in Business* (Englewood Cliffs, N. J.: Prentice-Hall, Inc., 1977).

21

Public Argumentation and Advocacy

Argument, considered by many to be the lifeblood of democratic institutions, is a species of communication wherein a speaker—using reason-giving discourse—seeks adherence to a particular claim in opposition to a claim or claims advanced by others. In earlier chapters we have already examined some of the substance and strategies of argument. Arguments must be adapted to the audiences we analyzed in Chapter 5, must utilize the motive appeals identified in Chapter 6, must employ the forms of support suggested in Chapter 7, must be structured as are most other speeches, and must rely upon the logical appeals described in Chapter 18. Argument, in fact, often is treated in public-speaking textbooks merely as a kind of reasoned persuasion.

When you move beyond these concerns, however, and into the *forms* of discourse, you soon discover why arguments can be of special significance in the life of the oral communicator. You soon discover why some people are afraid of arguing ("I want to discuss this with you, not argue about it") and why others relish an argumentative encounter ("Now *that* was a good fight"). Arguments represent a special type of communicative transaction in all cultures; and in our culture, many of the most important decisions—in legislatures, in courtrooms, in club meetings, and in corporate board meetings—are made via argumentation. In this chapter, we shall examine the communication principles that make argument unique, note those occasions requiring argument, examine the overall structure of the process, and review briefly two of the specific kinds of speeches arguers often have to make.

Argument as a "Species" of Communication

In the final analysis, what makes argument special is not the fact that it is a *fight,* which it is; not that ordinarily you are *attacked,* which you are; and not even that it is perfectly *logical,* which frequently it is not. Rather, what distinguishes argument from other communicative forms is the fact that it is *rule-governed.* That is, when you decide to argue with others, rather than merely offer information or attempt to persuade them that you are right and they are wrong, *you are committing yourself to communicating according to certain rules,* especially *(a) social conventions* and *(b) technical regulations.*

Social Conventions

In this and most other societies, there are tacit yet potent *conventions* or habitual *expectations* which govern argument. That is, when you decide to argue with another person, you are making, generally, commitments to four standards of judgment or four of these conventions:

1. Convention of Bilaterality. Argument is explicitly bilateral: it requires at least two persons or two competing messages.* The arguer, implicitly or explicitly, is saying that he or she is presenting a message which can be examined and evaluated by others. Now, the seller of toothpaste seldom invites this kind of critical examination of the product; Proctor and Gamble is in the business of persuasion, not argumentation. A U.S. senator, in contrast, assumes a party label and pits a proposed solution to some social problem against solutions proposed by others, thus specifically calling for counter-analysis or counter-argument. The arguer invites not mere reflection or acceptance, but reasoned inquiry in return.

2. Convention of Self-Risk. By at least implicitly calling for a critique of your ideas and propositions from others, you assume certain risks, of course. There is always the risk of failure, naturally; but you face that risk any time you open your mouth. More importantly, in argument there is the risk of being proven *wrong.* For example, when you argue that a federal system of welfare is preferable to a state- or local-based system of relief, you face the possibility that your opponent will convince *you* that local control creates fewer problems and more benefits than does federal control. The bright light of public scrutiny often can expose your own as well as your opponent's weaknesses and shortcomings. That

---

*We say "two persons" here, but remember that you can also argue *intrapersonally* — with yourself. You split your personality, so to speak, into two *personae* or *selfs* when you debate in your own mind what to do on Saturday night or how best to approach an instructor you wish to raise a grade. For a discussion of these and other conventions governing argument, see Douglas Ehninger, "Debate as Method: Limitations and Values," *The Speech Teacher* 15 (September 1966): 180–185.

risk is potent enough, indeed, to make many people afraid of arguing publicly.

3. The Fairness Doctrine. Arguers also commit themselves to some version of what the radio and television industry calls the "fairness" doctrine. The fairness doctrine of the Federal Communication Commission maintains that all competing voices ought to be given equal access to the airways to express their viewpoints. Similarly, arguers say, in effect, "You may use as much time as I have (or as much time as you need) to criticize my claims and reasons." This is why, for example, most legislative bodies are reluctant to cut off debate by invoking closure rules even in the face of political filibustering. Our legislative bodies are committed to the fairness doctrine: the idea that debate (argument) ought to be as extended and as complete as possible in order to guarantee that all considerations be aired, considered, and defended.

4. Commitment to Rationality. Arguers commit themselves to rationality, to a willingness to proceed logically. That is, when you argue, you are at least implicitly saying, "Not only do I believe X, but I have *reasons* for doing so." When you argue, for instance, that nonreturnable bottles should be banned by state law, someone else has the right to say "No" (the convention of bilaterality) and the right to assert a contrary proposition (the fairness doctrine). But—in addition—all parties to the argument have a right to ask,"*Why* do you believe that?" (the convention of rationality). As an arguer, you are committed to *giving reasons,* reasons that you think support your claim and ought to be accepted by unsure or doubtful listeners. Argument, therefore, is a rational form of communication, not in the sense that speakers often use syllogisms or other strictly logical structures, but in the sense that all arguers believe they have good reasons for the acceptance of their claims. They are obligated to provide those reasons; they cannot get away with saying, "Oh, I don't know—I just feel that is true." When reasons are given, if they are relevant to the claim being advanced and if they are acceptable to the audience hearing the claim defended, then the arguer will have met the commitment to rationality.

Technical Rules

In some cases, arguers are committed not only to generalized conventions or accepted bases of argument, but also to arguing in accordance with particular formalized procedures or unusual technical strictures. At a monthly meeting of a hobby club, for example, you may well find that you are expected to offer motions and amendments according to *Robert's Rules of Order.** In many formal meetings, Robert's or some other

---

*Henry M. Robert, *Robert's Rules of Order Newly Revised,* ed. Sarah Corbin Robert, Henry M. Robert III, James W. Cleary, and William J. Evans (Glenview, Ill.: Scott, Foresman and Company, 1970).

set of parliamentary procedures are used. Parliamentary procedures are technical rules. They limit *what* you can say (some motions are "out of order"), *how* you can say it (you may not be allowed to defend an idea unless your motion is seconded), and even *when* you can say it (everything you say must be germane to the motion under consideration). The essential details of parliamentary procedure for handling motions are shown in the chart on pages 360–361. Argumentation in legislatures and courtrooms is governed by such specifically defined rules, as it is in many clubs and other decision-making organizations.

In other settings and contexts, arguers are expected to follow somewhat different, but analogous, technical rules. The social scientist who has made a study, say, of the effect of source credibility upon the persuasiveness of messages must report the results in a specific way. The "scientific method" is, in effect, a set of rules—rules of procedure, statistical rules for proper measurement, and rules of inference: what we can infer about the whole society as the result of a limited experiment carried out on a small portion of that society. The social scientist who—in writing a report of his findings—does not carefully define, scrupulously measure, and statistically compare data, and who then draws broad conclusions about the universe from a limited study, will not be published. The argument, as social scientists view their work, would not be "proper," and the report would be rejected. Various academic and business disciplines thus lay out their own rules for arguing, rules which must be followed if you are going to engage in argument in a given profession or field.*

Occasions Requiring Argument

We have already alluded to a few of the occasions on which speakers argue; but because of the variety of rules which can apply in communicative contexts, we need to review these occasions more systematically. Typical public and non-public occasions for oral arguments include:

Political assemblies—the House of Representatives and the Senate; student-government councils; student organizations devoted primarily to political action; county, regional, state, and national political party conventions; the social and political action caucuses of labor unions.

Business meetings of organizations and clubs—board meetings of corporations and businesses; the monthly meetings of book clubs, investors' clubs, etc.; quarterly or annual meetings of church or synagogue congregations.

Formal meetings of other organizations—parent-teacher organizations' action and finance sessions; decision-making sessions in YMCA and

---

*The idea that particular disciplines have their own "rules" is illustrated clearly in Richard D. Rieke and Malcolm O. Sillars, *Argumentation and the Decision Making Process* (New York: John Wiley & Sons, Inc., 1975), Chaps. 11–13.

YWCA meetings; college and university faculty meetings devoted to policy-making.

Problem-solving discussions—nonparliamentary business and industrial meetings where ideas are openly explored before anyone is committed to particular plans; many congressional committee hearings; community forums; radio and television call-in programs.

Classrooms—in-class discussions of readings, lectures, and outside-of-class events deserving commentary; student-to-student discussion groups; student-teacher exchanges; and recitations.

Informal social gatherings—"bull sessions" in dormitory rooms; cocktail party chatter; conversations along the street; gatherings in restaurants, bars, and college food centers; employer-employee, husband-wife, and parent-child exchanges.

The Structure of Argument

In Chapter 18 we gave careful attention to the *materials* of argument: claims of fact, value, and policy; the structure of speeches seeking belief or disbelief in claims; speeches opposing endorsement of claims; and reasoning from sign, cause, specific instances, parallel case, and axiom. What we need to stress here is the notion that because argument involves at least two speeches, and often many more, this type of communication transaction demands the *orchestration* of materials: appeals, speeches, and general analytical techniques. This is because as an arguer you have an explicit opponent and occasionally a chance for a second speech in defense of your claim (or one which can be given by someone else defending your claim). You must, therefore, think in terms of *multiple messages.* More specifically, as an arguer you have to consider (1) constructing your case, (2) reacting critically to the attacks made upon it, and then (3) defending or rebuilding your case in the face of attack.*

Constructing Your Case

This is your first concern when you begin to think about arguing. Assume, for example, that you are urging that your student-government council expend money to mount a summer orientation program for incoming freshmen. You know that in a speech of this type you must (1) gain attention, (2) develop the specific need as well as criteria for judging its seriousness, (3) provide satisfaction by demonstrating that the need meets the criteria, (4) visualize the advantages to be gained by acceptance of your analysis, and (5) appeal for direct action. As you think about this skeletal outline in terms of your speech proposing a

---

*For further reading centering on these three "messages," see Nicholas Capaldi, *The Art of Deception* (Buffalo, N.Y.: Prometheus Books, 1971).

summer orientation program, notice that you have these prominent problems to overcome through argument:

A. You must be able to demonstrate that your proposal comes within the purview of student-government activites. That is, you must meet *general criteria* applicable to all student-government projects. If you cannot do this, your opponent(s) can argue that the proposed program, even if it is a good one, ought to be financed by the institution's various departments, by a dean's office, or by the registrar's office.
B. You must grapple with the issue of *practicality* that we talked about in Chapter 18. That is, you must demonstrate that this project *can* be made to work and that a significant number of students will benefit from it.
C. And, in these days of tightening college and university budgets, *feasibility* likewise is an important issue. If the student government spends money on this project, then other projects will either be narrowed or eliminated.

Thus, a mere inspection of the topic and the demands of this type of speech indicate those points of analysis on which you must argue especially well. Given these three problems, consider how you may proceed practically to solve them. Specifically:

Where can you find supporting materials relative to the general criteria by which student-based projects ought to be judged? In a student-government constitution? In the precedents set by actions the student council has taken in the past? In campaign statements made by specific members of the council? In other words, the general criteria probably can be supported by various kinds of *testimony*—from documents, from "history," and from individuals.

How can you demonstrate the practicality of something which your school has never attempted? From examination of other orientation programs at your school (e.g., the one for foreign students)? From examination of summer orientation programs at other schools similar to yours? From statements of support made by students who wish they had had a better orientation? In other words, practicality is probably best demonstrated by arguments from *parallel cases* (both inside and outside your school) and by *illustrations.*

How can you answer the feasibility question? Are sources of money available? Can the personnel needed to run the operation be assembled in time? Will the deans' and registrar's offices cooperate? In other words, you will have to show that your plan will meet the *causes* of the problem (freshmen disorientation), that it has the support of the school's administration *(testimony),* and that it will work—a claim you will be prepared to substantiate by *illustrations, examples,* and perhaps *analogies* which compare the testimony of students who have had and have not had a summer orientation program. And, again, you may have to appeal to your listeners on the basis of this project's virtues in *comparison* with those of other student-government projects.

Thus, it does seem possible to construct a reasonable case to secure initial belief in your claim of policy once you have determined in your own mind where your proposal is likely to raise the most questions. Of course, you still have to assemble the actual materials—the pieces of testimony, the parallel cases, the commitments from administrators, etc. But that is to be done only after you have settled upon your primary strategies.

Reacting Critically to Attacks

As you construct your case, of course, you must be sensitive to points on which you might be attacked. For instance, if you are arguing for the summer orientation program mentioned earlier, some opponents may counter your argument by maintaining that your school constitution is so vague as to make reasoning axiomatically from it impossible. Others may counter by insisting that there really are no cases parallel to the situation in your school. Some will wince when you propose cooperating with the administration. And still others will have pet projects of their own which, they will point out, are threatened by your proposed expenditure. Thus, even before you actually present what might be called your "constructive case," you will need to be aware of some potential objections and vulnerabilities.

Do not, however, build defensive reactions into your initial argument. If you are a speaker who attempts to anticipate and answer all possible objections before they are lodged, you are in double danger: (1) You may appear paranoid and thereby cause listeners to say, "Boy, if she is this unsure, then maybe the proposal isn't any good." (2) Worse, you may actually suggest negative aspects of your proposal others had not thought of! You may, in other words, actually fuel discontent by proposing counter-arguments.

As a rule, therefore, you should set forth your initial case directly and simply, and then sit back and await the counter-arguments presented by others. You may even want to work from a so-called "flow chart"—a sheet of paper which enumerates your principal arguments down the left-hand side, with space along the right-hand side for recording objections. In that way, you can identify where you are being questioned, note carefully how the attacks affect your overall analysis, and think specifically in terms of answers.

In sum, reacting critically to attacks on your arguments involves (*a*) a careful recording of counter-arguments so as to be fair, and (*b*) a decision on how to answer germane objections. You have to be cool and dispassionate enough to do both.

Rebuilding Your Case

Having isolated and considered possible counter-arguments, your next task is to answer those arguments so as to rebuild your initial case. This rebuilding requires *rebuttal* and *reestablishment.*

Rebuttal.   Your first rebuilding task is to rebut counter-arguments. In our example, this would mean answering to the satisfaction of your audience the objection to precedent-setting and strengthening the literal analogy between the foreign-student orientation program and the one you propose. To rebut the counter-argument concerning precedents, you might, for example, indicate this is an exceptional case and hence is not precedent-setting in any meaningful way. You could show that student government already contributes to other programs shared co-operatively with the administration (the student-elections program and student-faculty committee assignments), and/or could cite additional precedents in student-government history (student-government contri-butions to the foreign-student orientation program when it was original-ly set up). And to meet the objection to your analogy, you could show that disorientation is troublesome whether it occurs in foreign or do-mestic students—that there may be differences in *degree* but not in *kind;* and thus you defend your analogy as a good one.

Whatever tack you take, you should be careful to handle the rebuttal fairly and clearly. "Fairly" involves stating the objection in words closely approximating those of the objector, so that everyone feels you have understood and are answering the central thrust of the attack. "Clearly" demands that you carefully explain and make evident the nature of your reaction to the objection, that you assemble whatever evidence you need to provide the necessary answers, and that—once you have done these things—you indicate why you think you have answered the objec-tion properly. A rebuttal, therefore, involves three steps: (1) counter-assertion, (2) evidence, and (3) an indication of the argumentative sig-nificance of your answer.

Reestablishment.   In most instances, however, you cannot be content merely to answer opponents' objections. You also should take the extra step of reestablishing your case as a whole. That is, you should first point out what portions of your argument have *not* been attacked and indicate their importance. Then you should introduce more evidence in support of your reconstructed case—further testimony, additional par-allel cases, etc.—to bolster your argument as a whole. To return to our earlier example, you might indicate that no one has questioned the fea-sibility of your plan—a strong point in its favor—and then add further cases of schools which are using summer orientation successfully.

Overall, then, by fairly rebutting objections and by conscientiously reestablishing your whole case, you will add further rational and psychological strength to your claim, increasing your own credibility and your chances for the success of your argument. As you can see, the *structure* of argumentation, therefore, involves both careful selection and also scrupulous ordering of materials, attentive listening to and careful contemplation of objections, and the successful reconstruction of your case in light of the counter-arguments. Mastery of these techniques should enable you to communicate effectively through argument.

Special Forms of Parliamentary Argument

The model for arguing we have just described can be used in almost any everyday setting where the rules of parliamentary procedure are not strictly applied. When you argue in more formal parliamentary settings, however, you are often required to adhere to specific rules and procedures—as detailed in the chart, "Parliamentary Procedure for Handling Motions," pages 360–361. These, in turn, govern the special types of argumentative speeches that you give.* Here we consider only two of these special types: the speech proposing a motion and the speech summarizing the main issues in a controversy.

The Speech Proposing a Motion

When offering a motion, you are delivering essentially an actuative speech as described in Chapter 19. The difference is that the action you wish your listeners to take is specified in a formal motion: "I move that we endorse John Doe as a candidate for the office of Student Body President"; "I move we spend $500 on new office equipment"; "I move that we pledge ourselves to work on the campus muscular dystrophy campaign." A motion, in other words, usually specifies an action or goal based on a particular belief or attitude to which it sometimes commits the group as a whole, or in terms of which it sometimes makes demands upon individuals within the group. Whatever the specific motion called for, however, a speech proposing a motion normally follows an altered version of the motivated sequence, modified more or less along these lines:

1. Attention Step. Because the motion itself, of course, calls attention to a problem, as the mover you seldom develop a full attention step, except perhaps to indicate that certain events or certain problems have called for examination.

2. Need Step. The need step can be either preceded by the action step (for the motion, after all, specifies the action to be taken), or it can follow immediately upon the attention step in its usual manner. Whichever

---

*One of these special types—the speech to nominate—we will examine in Chapter 22 because it is rooted in speeches of introduction and tribute. Another type—the speech of opposition to a policy —we have already treated in Chapter 18, pages 299–300.

PARLIAMENTARY PROCEDURE FOR HANDLING MOTIONS

Classification of motions	Types of motions and their purposes	Order of handling	Must be seconded	Can be discussed	Can be amended	Vote required [1]	Can be re-considered
Main motion	(To present a proposal to the assembly)	Cannot be made while any other motion is pending	Yes	Yes	Yes	Majority	Yes
Subsidiary motions [2]	To postpone indefinitely (to kill a motion)	Has precedence over above motion	Yes	Yes	No	Majority	Affirmative vote only
	To amend (to modify a motion)	Has precedence over above motions	Yes	When motion is debatable	Yes	Majority	Yes
	To refer (a motion) to committee	Has precedence over above motions	Yes	Yes	Yes	Majority	Until committee takes up subject
	To postpone (discussion of a motion) to a certain time	Has precedence over above motions	Yes	Yes	Yes	Majority	Yes
	To limit discussion (of a motion)	Has precedence over above motions	Yes	No	Yes	Two-thirds	Yes
	Previous question (to take a vote on the pending motion)	Has precedence over above motions	Yes	No	No	Two-thirds	No
	To table (to lay a motion aside until later)	Has precedence over above motions	Yes	No	No	Majority	No
Incidental motions [3]	To suspend the rules (to change the order of business temporarily)	Has precedence over a pending motion when its purpose relates to the motion	Yes	No	No	Two-thirds	No
	To close nominations [4]	[4]	Yes	No	Yes	Two-thirds	No
	To request leave to withdraw or modify a motion [5]	Has precedence over motion to which it pertains and other motions applied to it	No	No	No	Majority [5]	Negative vote only
	To rise to a point of order (to enforce the rules) [6]	Has precedence over pending motion out of which it arises	No	No	No	Chair decides [7]	No
	To appeal from the decision of the chair (to reverse chair's ruling) [6]	Is in order only when made immediately after chair announces ruling	Yes	When ruling was on debatable motion	No	Majority [1]	Yes
	To divide the question (to consider a motion by parts)	Has precedence over motion to which it pertains and motion to postpone indefinitely	[8]	No	Yes	Majority [8]	No

						Two-thirds	Negative vote only
Privileged motions	To object to consideration of a question	In order only when a main motion is first introduced	No	No	No	Chair decides	No
	To divide the assembly (to take a standing vote)	Has precedence after question has been put	No	No	No	No vote required	No
	To call for the orders of the day (to keep meeting to order of business) [6, 9]	Has precedence over above motions	No	No	No		No
	To raise a question of privilege (to point out noise, etc.) [6]	Has precedence over above motions	No	No	No	Chair decides [7]	No
	To recess [10]	Has precedence over above motions	Yes	No [10]	Yes	Majority	No
	To adjourn [11]	Has precedence over above motions	Yes	No [11]	No [11]	Majority	No
	To fix the time to which to adjourn (to set next meeting time) [12]	Has precedence over above motions	Yes	No [12]	Yes	Majority	Yes
Unclassified motions	To take from the table (to bring up tabled motion for consideration)	Cannot be made while another motion is pending	Yes	No	No	Majority	No
	To reconsider (to reverse vote on previously decided motion) [13]	Can be made while another motion is pending [13]	Yes	When motion to be reconsidered is debatable	No	Majority	No
	To rescind (to repeal decision on a motion) [14]	Cannot be made while another motion is pending	Yes	Yes	Yes	Majority or two-thirds [14]	Negative vote only

1. A tied vote is always lost except on an appeal from the decision of the chair. The vote is taken on the ruling, not the appeal; and a tie sustains the ruling.
2. Subsidiary motions are applied to a motion before the assembly for the purpose of disposing of it properly.
3. Incidental motions are incidental to the conduct of business. Most of them arise out of a pending motion and must be decided before the pending motion is decided.
4. The chair opens nominations with "Nominations are now in order." A member may move to close nominations, or the chair may declare nominations closed if there is no response to his/her inquiry, "Are there any further nominations?"
5. When the motion is before the assembly, the mover requests permission to withdraw or modify it, and if there is no objection from anyone, the chair announces that the motion is withdrawn or modified. If anyone objects, the chair puts the request to a vote.
6. A member may interrupt a speaker to rise to a point of order or or of appeal, to call for orders of the day, or to raise a question of privilege.
7. Chair's ruling stands unless appealed and reversed.
8. If propositions or resolutions relate to independent subjects, they must be divided on the request of a single member. The request to divide the question may be made when another member has the floor. If they relate to the same subject but each part can stand alone, they may be divided only on a regular motion and vote.

9. The regular order of business may be changed by a motion to suspend the rules.
10. The motion to recess is not privileged if made at a time when no other motion is pending. When not privileged, it can be discussed. When privileged, it cannot be discussed, but can be amended as to length of recess.
11. The motion to adjourn is not privileged if qualified or if adoption would dissolve the assembly. When not privileged, it can be discussed and amended.
12. The motion to fix the time to which to adjourn is not privileged if no other motion is pending or if the assembly has scheduled another meeting on the same or following day. When not privileged, it can be discussed.
13. A motion to reconsider may be made only by one who voted on the prevailing side. It must be made during the meeting at which the vote to be reconsidered was taken, or on the succeeding day of the same session. If reconsideration is moved while another motion is pending, discussion on it is delayed until discussion is completed on the pending motion; then it has precedence over all new motions of equal rank.
14. It is impossible to rescind any action that has been taken as a result of a motion, but the unexecuted part may be rescinded. Adoption of the motion to rescind requires only a majority vote when notice is given at a previous meeting; it requires a two-thirds vote when no notice is given and the motion to rescind is voted on immediately.

order you follow, be sure you construct the need step so as to focus attention upon criteria for judgment and upon illustrations, statistics, analogies, etc., which show that the situation to which the motion pertains is deserving of group action.

3. Satisfaction Step.   In this step, you should explain precisely how the action called for in your motion *(a)* is consistent with the criteria you have suggested, and *(b)* alleviates the problems which, you argue, exist.

4. Visualization Step.   Especially if your motion calls for a specific action requiring expenditures of money, individual commitments to certain tasks by your listeners, etc., you will need to concentrate upon visualizing the results of the motion. Visualization may involve specifying who will sit on a certain committee and how that committee will proceed. Or you might visualize for your audience a chronology which individual members of the group might follow to carry out your motion. In any case, if your motion calls for action, the visualization step is of utmost importance.

5. Action Step.   Actually, because the motion expresses the desired action, you need to do little with the action step in this type of speech. You might, as we suggested earlier, even move it up to follow the attention step. If you do, the modified, step-by-step structure of the speech will look like this:
   (1) Attention step *(the call for a motion).*
   (2) Action step *(the motion).*
   (3) Need step *(why the motion is justified).*
   (4) Satisfaction step *(how the motion meets the need).*
   (5) Visualization step *(how the motion will be implemented).*

The Speech Summarizing an Argument

Not only does formal, parliamentary argument require motions and counter-motions, amendments, and votes, but also—as an extended argument runs its course—it usually requires that someone take the lead in summarizing the contentions advanced by one side or the other. After all have had their say, someone must pull together all of the speeches favoring and all of those opposing a particular motion. Arguments grow heated, often are deflected into discussions of relatively minor issues, and in general can become filled with irrelevancies. The speech summarizing a particular side of the problem is, therefore, highly important in capturing the few wavering votes which can spell victory or defeat. In such a speech, the framework of the motivated sequence may be employed as follows:

1. Attention Step.   Argument, in and of itself, is a good generator and holder of attention. For this reason, in a speech summarizing an argument you need not devote much, if any, time to this initial step. If you decide to include it, keep it short, and focus the audience's attention upon the few pivotal arguments which form the center of the dispute. Note, for example, the text of the speech "In Support of the Equal Rights Amendment" by Congresswoman Shirley Chisholm, pages 364–368.

2. Need Step. Similarly, in a summary speech of this type, the need step seldom is fully developed. After all, the criteria have already been advanced and the needs articulated quite completely in earlier portions of the argument. You need only, therefore, highlight those criteria and needs. Occasionally, you may have to bring in some additional evidence, but you certainly should not be building the full case in this step.

3. Satisfaction Step. At this point, we move into the heart of a good summary speech. There probably are still some doubts among your listeners as to the positive benefits of the main motion. People, even at the end of a protracted debate, may need to be convinced that a particular course of action not only will solve a problem, but also that it will solve it efficiently and without raising new problems. Again, refer to the sample speech on pages 364–368, and observe how Congresswoman Chisholm emphasizes the benefits of ERA in legal and economic sectors to show that the amendment will solve a great variety of discrimination problems.

4. Visualization Step. In a speech summarizing an argument, as in other types of speeches, a strong visualization step should grow out of the satisfaction step. Notice how, in this step, Ms. Chisholm—even as she discusses particular needs and arenas where proposed legislation would apply—pictures what the country will look like when ERA is ratified. She visualizes the passing of sex prejudice and the implementation of the Founding Fathers' hopes for America. By thus tieing together potential satisfaction and visualization of that potential, she points firmly to the need to pass the proposed constitutional amendment.

5. Action Step. Often, the speech which sums up all of the arguments advanced during the course of a debate may conclude most naturally with one last, urgent call for action. Therefore, in your summarizing speech, do not routinely rehash all that has gone before. Rather, try to distill the debate, to isolate the key arguments and drive them home. Then make a powerful and persuasive call for immediate action. This step is, as a rule, best handled by a public communicator who is skilled in the analysis of issues and audiences and who is gifted with at least a modest amount of vision. At this point in your speech development, you should be such a communicator.

As you conclude your study of this chapter, you are probably aware that good arguments are rare. Few people, really, are ready for the social conventions of bilaterality, self-risk, the fairness doctrine, and the commitment to rationality which govern argumentative discourse and which can seem restrictive at times. Both as speakers and as audiences, however, we cannot afford impatience. Democratic countries like ours are unalterably committed to argument as a way of making social-political decisions. Even though the testing of ideas in the public marketplace can at times be a slow and frustrating process, it offers the best hope for ensuring openness, equal voice, and general satisfaction with the resulting decisions. Persist and be diligent, therefore, in your efforts to gain proficiency in argumentative communication. Study the chart of parliamentary motions (pages 360–361) to better understand the dynamics of formal argument. Critically analyze the argumentative speeches of others. As you acquire the skills of public advocacy, you will become an increasingly productive, contributing member of the groups in which you speak and of the society in which you live.

A Sample Speech Summarizing an Argument

In the House of Representatives on August 10, 1970, the debate over the Equal Rights Amendment (ERA) had gone on for about three hours when Congresswoman Shirley Chisholm rose to speak. As you study her remarks, note particularly how she summarizes the dispute around three central issues: (1) the positive legal effects of the ERA, (2) the positive economic benefits of it, and (3) the inadequacy of current legislation for ensuring the political and economic rights of women. In these issues she sums up the argument from the viewpoint of the ERA advocates. She also attempts to answer the arguments of the opposition, in particular, those of Representative Emmanuel Celler of New York.

"In Support of the Equal Rights Amendment"[2]
Shirley Chisholm

[*Generalized Need*] Mr. Speaker, House Joint Resolution 264, before us today, which provides for equality under the law for both men and women, represents one of the most clear-cut opportunities we are likely to have to declare our faith in the principles that shaped our Constitution. *(Constitutional remedy is needed.)* It provides a legal basis for attack on the most subtle, most pervasive, and most institutionalized form of prejudice that exists. Discrimination against women, solely on the basis of their sex, is so widespread that it seems to many persons normal, natural, and right. Legal expression of prejudice on the grounds of religious or political belief has become a minor problem in our society. Prejudice on the basis of race is, at least, under systematic attack. There is reason for optimism that it will start to die with the present older generation. It is time we act to assure full equality of opportunity to those citizens who, although in a majority, suffer the restrictions that are more commonly imposed on minorities, to women. / 1

(Answer to the "real-solution" argument of Celler analogy.) The argument that this amendment will not solve the problem of sex discrimination is not relevant. If the argument were used against a civil rights bill —

as it has been used in the past – the prejudice that lies behind it would be embarrassing. Of course, laws will not eliminate prejudice from the hearts of human beings. But that is no reason to allow prejudice to continue to be enshrined in our laws – to perpetuate injustice through inaction. / 2

[*Positive Legal Effects*] The amendment is necessary to clarify countless ambiguities and inconsistencies in our legal system. For instance, the Constitution guarantees due process of law, in the fifth and fourteenth amendments. But the applicability of due process to sex distinctions is not clear. *(Series of specific instances.)* Women are excluded from some state colleges and universities. In some states, restrictions are placed on a married woman who engages in an independent business. Women may not be chosen for some juries. Women even receive heavier criminal penalties than men who commit the same crime. / 3

What would the legal effects of the equal rights amendment really be? The equal rights amendment would govern only the relationship between the state and its citizens – not relationships between private citizens. / 4

The amendment would be largely self-executing, that is, any federal or state laws in conflict would be ineffective one year after date of ratification without further action by the Congress or state legislatures. / 5

(Refutation of the "confusion" argument.) Opponents of the amendment claim its ratification would throw the law into a state of confusion and would result in much litigation to establish its meaning. This objection overlooks the influence of legislative history in determining intent and the recent activities of many groups preparing for legislative changes in this direction. / 6

State labor laws applying only to women, such as those limiting hours of work and weights to be lifted, would become inoperative unless the legislature amended them to apply to men. As of early 1970 most states would have some laws that would be affected. However, changes are being made so rapidly as a result of the Title VII of the Civil Rights Act of 1964, it is likely that by the time the equal rights amendment would become effective, no conflicting state laws would remain. / 7

(Refutation of "usefulness" argument.) In any event, there has for years been great controversy as to the usefulness to women of these state labor laws. There has never been any doubt that they worked a hardship on women who need or want to work overtime and on women who need or want better paying jobs, and there has been no persuasive evidence as to how many women benefit from the archaic policy of the laws. After the Delaware hours law was repealed in 1966, there were no complaints from women to any of the state agencies that might have been approached. / 8

Jury service laws not making women equally liable for jury service would have to be revised. / 9

(Extended examples of legal applicability.) The selective service law would have to include women, but women would not be required to serve in the Armed Forces where they are not fitted any more than men

are required to serve. Military service, while a great responsibility, is not without benefits, particularly for young men with limited education or training. Since October 1966, 246,000 young men who did not meet the normal mental or physical requirements have been given opportunities for training and correcting physical problems. This opportunity is not open to their sisters. Only girls who have completed high school and meet high standards on the education test can volunteer. Ratification of the amendment would not permit application of higher standards to women. / 10

Survivorship benefits would be available to husbands of female workers on the same basis as to wives of male workers. The Social Security Act and the civil service and military service retirement acts are in conflict. / 11

Public schools and universities could not be limited to one sex and could not apply different admission standards to men and women. Laws requiring longer prison sentences for women than men would be invalid, and equal opportunities for rehabilitation and vocational training would have to be provided in public correctional institutions. /12

Different ages of majority based on sex would have to be harmonized. / 13

Federal, state, and other governmental bodies would be obligated to follow nondiscriminatory practices in all aspects of employment, including public school teachers and state university and college faculties. / 14

[*Positive Economic Effects*] What would be the economic effects of the equal rights amendment? Direct economic effects would be minor. If any labor laws applying only to women still remained, their amendment or repeal would provide opportunity for women in better-paying jobs in manufacturing. More opportunities in public vocational and graduate schools for women would also tend to open up opportunities in better jobs for women. / 15

Indirect effects could be much greater. The focusing of public attention on the gross legal, economic, and social discrimination against women by hearings and debates in the federal and state legislatures would result in changes in attitude of parents, educators, and employers that would bring about substantial economic changes in the long run. / 16

(Present discriminations unfair to both sexes.) Sex prejudice cuts both ways. Men are oppressed by requirements of the Selective Service Act, by enforced legal guardianship of minors, and by alimony laws. Each sex, I believe, should be liable when necessary to serve and defend this country. / 17

Each has a responsibility for the support of children. / 18

There are objections raised to wiping out laws protecting women workers. No one would condone exploitation. But what does sex have to do with it? Working conditions and hours that are harmful to women are harmful to men; wages that are unfair for women are unfair for men. Laws setting employment limitations on the basis of sex are irrational, and the proof of this is their inconsistency from state to state. The physical characteristics of men and women are not fixed, but cover two wide spans that have a great deal of overlap. It is obvious, I think, that a robust woman would be more fit for physical labor than a weak man. The choice of occupation would be determined by individual capabilities, and the rewards for equal work should be equal. / 19

(Internal summary of legal and economic arguments.) This is what it comes down to: artificial distinctions between persons must be wiped out of the law. Legal discrimination between the sexes is, in almost every instance, founded on outmoded views of society and the prescientific beliefs about psychology and physiology. It is time to sweep away these relics of the past and set future generations free of them. / 20

(Inadequacies of existent laws.) Federal agencies and institutions responsible for the enforcement of equal opportunity laws need the authority of Constitutional amendment. The 1964 Civil Rights Act and the 1963 Equal Pay Act are not enough; they are limited in their coverage — for instance, one excludes teachers, and the other leaves out administrative and professional women. The Equal Employment Opportunity Commission has not proven to be an adequate device, with its powers limited to investigation, conciliation, and recommendation to the Justice Department. In its cases involving sexual discrimination, it has failed in more than one half. The Justice Department has been even less effective. It has intervened in only one case involving discrimination on the basis of sex, and this was on a procedural point. In a second case, in which both sexual and racial discrimination were alleged, the racial bias charge was given far greater weight. / 21

[*Summation of the Need for a New Law*] Evidence of discrimination on the basis of sex should hardly have to be cited here. It is in the Labor Department's employment and salary figures for anyone who is still in doubt. Its elimination will involve so many changes in our state and federal laws that, without the authority and impetus of this proposed amendment, it will perhaps take another 194 years. *(The "time is now" argument.)* We cannot be parties to continuing a delay. The time is clearly now to put this House on record for the fullest expression of that equality of opportunity which our Founding Fathers professed. / 22

They professed it, but they did not assure it to their daughters, as they tried to do for their sons. / 23

(The "we must start somewhere" argument.) The Constitution they wrote was designed to protect the rights of white male citizens. As there were no black Founding Fathers, there were no founding mothers — a great pity, on both counts. It is not too late to complete the work they left undone. Today, here, we should start to do so. / 24

[*Conclusion of Appeal for Action*] In closing I would like to make one point. Social and psychological effects will be initially more important than legal or economic results. As Leo Kanowitz has pointed out:

> *(Quotation for an additional, broader inducement to action.)* Rules of law that treat of the sexes per se inevitably produce far-reaching effects upon social, psychological, and economic aspects of male-

female relations beyond the limited confines of legislative chambers and courtrooms. As long as organized legal systems, at once the most respected and most feared of social institutions, continue to differentiate sharply, in treatment or in words, between men and women on the basis of irrelevant and artificially created distinctions, the likelihood of men and women coming to regard one another primarily as fellow human beings and only secondarily as representatives of another sex will continue to be remote. When men and women are prevented from recognizing one another's essential humanity by sexual prejudices, nourished by legal as well as social institutions, society as a whole remains less than it could otherwise become. / 25

Reference Notes

[1] Adapted from *Robert's Rules of Order, Newly Revised,* ed. Sarah Corbin Robert, Henry M. Robert III, James W. Cleary, and William J. Evans (Glenview, Ill.: Scott, Foresman and Company, 1970).

[2] Originally printed in the *Congressional Record,* 91st Congress, 2nd Session, Volume 116, Part 21, pp. 28028–28029, August 10, 1970.

Problems and Probes

1. Think through two or three of the informal arguments you have engaged in during the last few days: in the student union; in classroom discussions; in exchanges with an instructor, a close friend, or your roommate. *(a)* In any of them, did you present a relatively sustained speech? *(b)* What kinds of arguments and reasons for accepting those arguments did you offer as the disagreement progressed? *(c)* Did you or any of the other arguers become angry? If so, who handled it—and how? *(d)* Looking back, recall whether you or any others invoked conventions of self-risk ("How can you stubbornly hold that view?"), the fairness doctrine ("Come on! Give me a chance to explain!"), or a commitment to rationality ("That's the dumbest reason I ever heard! Don't you have any better reasons than that?"). Prepare a short paper summarizing the foregoing analysis and, in addition, clearly distinguish informal arguments of this type from the more formal ones we have considered in this chapter. Hand your written analysis to the instructor, and be prepared to discuss your ideas if called upon to do so.

2. Using as a basis a disputatious in-class discussion in which you have recently participated, analyze it in terms of the types of claims advanced by the various members of the class. Did any of the arguers try to specify criteria for judgment of the issues? How was the dispute resolved? Did the instructor choose to drop the matter? Or did he or she "pull rank" to influence the outcome or make the argument go in a certain direction? In general, did the form of the argument follow any of the patterns suggested here? Why or why not?

3. Interview a business executive or an active faculty member at your school to discover ways in which these people argue. *(a)* Through what kinds of structures do their ideas get examined: Official agenda? Committees? At-large discussion sessions? *(b)* How are ideas to be presented? What kinds of evidence— verbal and visual—are expected? *(c)* What business or university, political, and communicative factors seem to influence the outcome of a proposal to change business or university procedures?

Oral Activities and Speaking Assignments

1.   Prepare a twelve-minute argumentative exchange on a topic involving you and one other member of the class. Dividing the available time equally, one of you will advocate a claim; the other will oppose it. Adopt any format you both feel comfortable with. You may choose: *(a)* a Lincoln-Douglas format — the first person speaks four minutes; the second, six; and then the first person returns for a two-minute rejoinder; *(b)* an issue format — you both agree on, say, three key issues, and then each one of you speaks for two minutes on each issue; *(c)* a debate format — each speaker talks twice alternatively, four minutes in a constructive speech, two minutes in rebuttal; and *(d)* a heckling format — each of you has six minutes, but during the middle four minutes of each speech, the audience or your opponent may ask you questions.

2.   Turn the class into a parliamentary assembly; decide on a motion or resolution to be argued; and then schedule a day or two for a full debate. An interesting format is the one devised for the public television program, "The Advocates," in which as many as twenty-two speakers can be involved in the argumentative procedure. This format forces participants into particular argumentative roles: advocate, witness, direct examiner, cross-examiner, summarizer. It also allows each speaker to be part of a team; what you do affects not only yourself but also other speakers on your side of the argument. In all, it can lead to exciting public argumentation. [For guidance in the use of this format, see John D. May, ed., *American Problems: What Should Be Done? Debates from "The Advocates"* (Palo Alto, Calif.: National Press Books, 1973).]

Suggestions for Further Reading

C. William Colburn, *Strategies for Educational Debate* (Boston: Holbrook Press, Inc., 1972).

Douglas Ehninger, *Influence, Belief, and Argument: An Introduction to Responsible Persuasion* (Glenview, Ill.: Scott, Foresman and Company, 1974).

Richard D. Rieke and Malcolm O. Sillars, *Argumentation and the Decision Making Process* (New York: John Wiley & Sons, Inc., 1975).

22

Speeches on Special Occasions

Throughout this book we have emphasized that situational demands and audience expectations must be taken into account by any speaker addressing any audience at any time. Such demands and expectations exert an even greater force upon the maker of *special-occasion* speeches because the speaker is required to be especially sensitive to the uniqueness of the circumstances, highly selective in terms of appropriate materials, and ever alert as to whether he or she is "saying the right thing" and saying it in the way best calculated to accord with the audience's expectations and emotional state. For example, even if you have never spoken at a funeral, you are aware that the situation demands that the bereaved be comforted and the deceased be praised. And even if you have not heretofore been called upon to make a speech of introduction, you know that characteristically such speeches consist of an attention-catching statement, at least a brief review of the accomplishments of the person being introduced, a note on the timeliness or importance of the topic to be discussed by that person, and a bit of rhetorical flourish: "It is, therefore, with great pleasure that I . . . ."

While there are innumerable such occasions which could be considered in this chapter, we shall limit ourselves to some representative, commonly recurring types: speeches of introduction, speeches of tribute, speeches of nomination, speeches of exoneration or self-justification, and speeches of good will. We shall consider each of these special types of speeches briefly, noting in each case the *purpose* toward which the speech is directed, the *manner* in which it usually is delivered, the kinds of *ideas* it contains, the principles by which it is *organized*, as well as how certain aspects of the motivated sequence may be applied.

Speeches of Introduction

Speeches of introduction usually are given by the person who arranged the program or by the chairperson or president of the group to be addressed. Sometimes, however, they are presented by another person who, because of personal association or professional interests, is especially well acquainted with the featured speaker.

Purpose and Manner of Speaking. The *purpose* of a speech of introduction is, of course, to create in the audience a desire to hear the speaker you are introducing. Everything else must be subordinated to this aim. Do not make a speech yourself or air your own views on the subject. You are only the speaker's *advance agent;* your job is to sell him or her to the audience. This task carries a two-fold responsibility: (1) You must arouse the listeners' curiosity about the speaker and/or subject, thus making it easier for the speaker to get the attention of the audience. (2) You must do all that you reasonably can to generate audience respect for the speaker, thereby increasing the likelihood that listeners will respond favorably to the message that is presented.

When giving a speech of introduction, your *manner of speaking* should be suited to the nature of the occasion, your familiarity with the speaker, and the speaker's prestige. If you were introducing a justice of the United States Supreme Court, for instance, it would hardly be appropriate to poke fun at him. Nor would this approach be tactful if the speaker were a stranger to you, or the occasion serious and dignified. On the other hand, if you are presenting an old friend to a group of associates on an informal occasion, a solemn and dignified manner would be equally out of place.

Formulating the Content of the Speech of Introduction. The better known and more respected a speaker is, the shorter your introduction can be. The less well known he or she is, the more you will need to arouse interest in the subject or build up the speaker's prestige. In general, however, observe these principles:

Talk about the speaker. Who is he? What is her position in business, education, sports, or government? What experiences has he had that qualify him to speak on the announced subject? Build up the speaker's identity, tell what he knows or what she has done, but do not praise his or her ability as a speaker. Let speakers *demonstrate* their skills.

Emphasize the importance of the speaker's subject. For example, in introducing a speaker who is going to talk about the oil industry, you might say: "All of us drive automobiles in which we use the products made from petroleum. A knowledge of the way these products are manufactured and marketed is, therefore, certain to be valuable to our understanding and perhaps to our pocketbooks."

Stress the appropriateness of the subject or of the speaker. If your town is considering a program of renewal and revitalization, a speech by a city planner is likely to be timely and well received. If an organization is marking an anniversary, the founder may be one of the speakers. Reference to the positions these persons hold is obviously in order and serves to relate the speaker more closely to the audience.

Organizing the Speech of Introduction.   In a long and formal speech of introduction, you may wish to employ all five steps in the motivated sequence. Usually, however, one of the following abbreviated forms will suffice: Create attention and arouse interest by plunging directly into the (1) *need step,* in which you state the importance of the subject to the audience; follow with the (2) *satisfaction step*, in which you state in sharply abbreviated form why the speaker is qualified to speak on this subject; then close with an (3) *action step*, in which the actual presentation of the speaker is made.

Sometimes who the speaker is may be more important than the subject he or she is going to discuss. In such instances, create attention by beginning with the (1) *satisfaction step,* in which you state the facts about the speaker, especially facts that are not ordinarily known or those that are of particular significance to the occasion; then proceed to the (2) *action step,* in which you present the speaker and make a brief announcement of the subject. When time is short or the speaker is so well known that extreme brevity is desirable, gain attention by your salutation, ''Ladies and Gentlemen,'' ''Members of the Izaak Walton League,'' etc.; then move at once to the *action step:* a brief announcement of the speaker's name, position, and subject. Under all circumstances, remember that the four primary virtues of a speech of introduction are *tact, brevity, sincerity,* and *enthusiasm.*

Speeches of Tribute

As a speaker you may be called upon to pay tribute to another person's qualities or achievements. Such occasions range from the awarding of a trophy after an athletic contest to delivering a eulogy at a memorial service. Sometimes tributes are paid to an entire group or class of people — for example, teachers, soldiers, or mothers — rather than to an individual. Frequently, awards are presented to groups or to individuals for outstanding or meritorious service. In such cases, public tribute often is paid, and the presentation calls for appropriate remarks from a speaker. The following typically require a speech of tribute:

Farewells.   In general, speeches of farewell fall into one of three subcategories: (1) When people retire or leave one organization to join another or when persons who are admired leave the community where they have lived, the enterprise in which they have worked, or the office they have held, public appreciation of their fellowship and accomplishments may be expressed by associates or colleagues in speeches befitting the circumstances. (2) Or the individual who is departing may use

the occasion to present a farewell address in which she voices her grati-
tude for the opportunities, consideration, and warmth afforded her by
co-workers and, perhaps, calls upon them to carry on the traditions and
long-range goals which characterize the office or the enterprise. In both
of these situations, of course, verbal tributes are being paid. What distinguishes them, bascially, is whether the retiree or departing one is
speaking or is being *spoken about.* (3) More rarely, when individuals —
because of disagreements, policy-differences, organizational stresses,
etc. — decide to resign or sever important or long-standing associations
with a business or governmental unit, in messages of farewell they may
elect to present publicly the basis of the disagreement and the factors
prompting the resignation and departure. Used thus, the farewell
speech becomes, in part at least, a speech of self-defense or *apologia* —
a form we shall examine in some detail on pages 381 – 384.

Memorial Services. Services to pay public honor to the dead usually
include a speech of tribute or *eulogy.* Ceremonies of this kind may hon-
or a famous person (or persons) and be held years after his or her death.
Witness, for example, the many speeches paying tribute to Abraham
Lincoln. More often, however, a eulogy honors someone personally
known to the audience and only recently deceased.

At other times, a memorial — particularly to a famous person — honors
certain of the qualities that person stands for. In that case, the speaker
uses the memorial to renew and reinforce the audience's adherence to
certain ideals, compelling it to think about problems facing humanity
in general. The following brief, but vividly phrased, remarks eulogize
Wernher von Braun, renowned scientist and space pioneer. The guiding
genius behind Germany's "buzz bomb" and rocket weaponry in World
War II, von Braun came to this country when hostilities ended, became
an American citizen, and was a major directing force behind the U.S.
space program, which ultimately landed the first men on the moon.
Written and presented by Eric Sevareid on *CBS Evening News,* June 17,
1977, the commentary pays tribute to von Braun's dream while at the
same time recognizing the country's pressing technological and social
problems. In a number of respects, it is an excellent example of a eulogy.

"Eulogy for Wernher von Braun"[1]

Eric Sevareid

A generation ago, the Allied military, using the old-fashioned airplane,
did their best to kill the German, his associates, and their new-fashioned
rockets, which were killing the people in London. Yesterday, Wernher
von Braun, American citizen, died peacefully in George Washington's
hometown of Alexandria, Virginia. /1

Without this man, Hitler would not have held out as long as he did; without him, Americans would not have got to the moon as soon as they did. /2

Counting up the moral balance sheet for this man's life would be a difficult exercise. The same could be said for the Wright brothers. Perhaps the exercise is meaningless. Airplanes would have come anyway from someone, somewhere, and so would modern rockets. And what was done with these instruments would have been equally beyond the control of the individuals who first made them work. /3

There's always a dream to begin with, and the dream is always benign. Charles Lindbergh, as a young man, saw the airplane, not only as an instrument to liberate man from the plodding earth, but as a force for peacefully uniting the human race through faster communication and the common adventure. Now its benefits are measured against its role in returning warfare to the savagery of the Middle Ages, burning whole cities with their occupants. /4

And rockets are now the easiest instrument for sending the ultimate atomic weapon against any spot on the globe. They've also put men into space; and von Braun, like Lindbergh with the upper atmosphere, saw goodness in that. He said once, when men manning an orbital station can view our planet as a planet among planets, on that day fratricidal war will be banished from the star on which we live. /5

Lindbergh was wrong about aircraft in the atmosphere; there's no reason to believe that von Braun was right about spacecraft in space. /6

Everything in space, von Braun said, obeys the laws of physics. If you know these laws and obey them, space will treat you kindly. The difficulty is that man brings the laws of his own nature into space. The issue is how man treats man. The problem does not lie in outer space, but where it's always been: on terra firma in inner man. /7.

Dedications. Buildings, monuments, parks, etc., may be constructed or set aside to honor a worthy cause or to commemorate a person, a group, a significant movement, an historic event, or the like. At their dedication, the speaker says something appropriate about the purpose to be served by whatever it is that is being set aside and about the personage(s), event, or occasion thus commemorated.

The following remarks were made by Mr. Harold Haydon at the unveiling of "Nuclear Energy," a bronze sculpture created by Henry Moore and placed on the campus of the University of Chicago to commemorate the achievement of Enrico Fermi and his associates in releasing the first self-sustaining nuclear chain reaction at Stagg Field on December 2, 1942. The unveiling took place during the commemoration of the twenty-fifth anniversay of that event. Mr. Haydon is Associate Professor of Art at the University, Director of the Midway Studios, and art critic for the *Chicago Sun-Times.* By combining specific references to the sculptor and his work with more general observations concerning the function of art and humankind's hopes and fears in a nuclear age, Mr. Haydon produced a dignified and thoughtful address, well suited to the demands of the occasion.

"The Testimony of Sculpture"[2]
Harold Haydon

Since very ancient times men have set up a marker, or designated some stone or tree, to hold the memory of a deed or happening far longer than any man's lifetime. Some of these memorial objects have lived longer than man's collective memory, so that we now ponder the meaning of a monument, or wonder whether some great stone is a record of human action, or whether instead it is only a natural object. / 1

There is something that makes us want a solid presence, a substantial form, to be the tangible touchstone of the mind, designed and made to endure as witness or record, as if we mistrusted that seemingly frail yet amazingly tough skein of words and symbols that serves memory and which, despite being mere ink blots and punch-holes, nonetheless succeeds in preserving the long human tradition, firmer than any stone, tougher than any metal. / 2

We still choose stone or metal to be our tangible reminders, and for these solid, enduring forms we turn to the men who are carvers of stone and moulders of metal, for it is they who have given lasting form to our myths through the centuries. / 3

One of these men is here today, a great one, and he has given his skill and the sure touch of his mind and eye to create for this nation, this city, and this university a marker that may stand here for centuries, even for a millennium, as a mute yet eloquent testament to a turning point in time when man took charge of a new material world hitherto beyond his capability. /4

As this bronze monument remembers an event and commemorates an achievement, it has something unique to say about the spiritual meaning of the achievement, for it is the special power of art to convey feeling and stir profound emotion, to touch us in ways that are beyond the reach of reason. /5

Nuclear energy, for which the sculpture is named, is a magnet for conflicting emotions, some of which inevitably will attach to the bronze form; it will harbor or repel emotion according to the states of mind of those who view the sculpture. In its brooding presence some will feel the joy and sorrow of recollection, some may dread the uncertain future, and yet others will thrill to the thought of magnificent achievements that lie ahead. The test of the sculpture's greatness as a human document, the test of any work of art, will be its capacity to evoke a response and the quality of that response. / 6

One thing most certain is that this sculpture by Henry Moore is not an inert object. It is a live thing, and somewhat strange like every excellent beauty, to be known to us only in time and never completely. Its whole meaning can be known only to the ever-receding future, as each succeeding generation reinterprets according to its own vision and experience. / 7

By being here in a public place the sculpture "Nuclear Energy" becomes a part of Chicago, and the sculptor an honored citizen, known not just to artists and collectors of art, but to everyone who pauses here in the presence of the monument, because the artist is inextricably part of what he has created, immortal through his art. /8

With this happy conjunction today of art and science, of great artist and great occasion, we may hope to reach across the generations, across the centuries, speaking through enduring sculpture of our time, our hopes, and fears, perhaps more eloquently than we know. Some works of art have meaning for all mankind and so defy time, persisting through all hazards; the monument to the atomic age should be one of these. / 9

Purpose and Manner of Speaking for the Tribute Speech. The *purpose* of a speech of tribute is, of course, to create in those who hear it a sense of appreciation for the traits or accomplishments of the person or group to whom tribute is paid. If you cause your audience to realize the essential worth or importance of that person or group, you will have succeeded. But you may go further than this. You may, by honoring a person, arouse deeper devotion to the cause he or she represents. Did he give distinguished service to his community? Then strive to enhance the audience's civic pride and sense of service. Was she a friend to youth? Then try to arouse the feeling that working to provide opportunities for young people deserves the audience's support. Create a desire in your listeners to emulate the person or persons honored. Make them want to develop the same virtues, to demonstrate a like devotion.

When making a speech of tribute, suit the *manner* of speaking to the circumstances. A farewell banquet usually blends an atmosphere of merriment with a spirit of sincere regret. Dignity and formality are, on the whole, characteristic of memorial services, the unveiling of monuments, and similar dedicatory ceremonies. Regardless of the general tone of the occasion, however, in a speech of tribute avoid high-sounding phrases, bombastic oratory, and obvious "oiliness." These hollow elements will quickly dampen or destroy its effect. A simple, honest expression of admiration presented in clear and unadorned language is best.

Formulating the Content of Speeches of Tribute. Frequently, in a speech of tribute a speaker attempts to itemize all the accomplishments of the honored person or group. This weakens the impact because, in trying to cover everything, it emphasizes nothing. Plan, instead, to focus your remarks, as follows:

Stress dominant traits. If you are paying tribute to a person, select a few aspects of her personality which are especially likeable or praiseworthy, and relate incidents from her life or work to illustrate these distinguishing qualities.

Mention only outstanding achievements. Pick out only a few of the person's or group's most notable accomplishments. Tell about them in detail to show how important they were. Let your speech say, "Here is what this person (or group) has done; see how such actions have contributed to the well-being of our business or community."

Give special emphasis to the influence of the person or group. Show the effect that the behavior of the person or group has had on others. Many times, the importance of people's lives can be demonstrated not so much by any traits or material accomplishments as by the influence they exerted on associates.

Organizing the Speech of Tribute. Ordinarily you will have little difficulty in getting people to listen to a speech of tribute. The audience probably already knows and admires the person or group about whom you are to speak, and listeners are curious to learn what you are going to say concerning the individual or individuals being honored. Consider employing the steps of the motivated sequence somewhat as follows:

Attention step. Your task, first of all, is to *direct* the attention of the audience toward those characteristics or accomplishments which you consider most important. There are three commonly used ways to do this: (1) Make a straightforward, sincere statement of these commendable traits or achievements or of the influence they have had upon others. (2) Relate one or more instances which vividly illustrate your point. (3) Relate an incident which shows the problems faced by your subject, thus leading directly into the need step.

Need step. The speech of tribute contains no real need step in the sense of demonstrating a problem confronting the audience. The tribute subsequently paid in the satisfaction step may be heightened, however, by emphasizing obstacles overcome or difficulties faced by the person or group being honored. This serves to bring into focus the traits or achievements which you wish to commend. A slightly different method is to point out not the personal problems of the persons to whom tribute is paid, but the problems of the organization which it was their official responsibility to meet or—in a still larger sense—the problems of society which their accomplishments helped solve. Thus an account of the extent and seriousness of the pollution problem in a large city might precede a tribute to the women and men who developed and enforced an effective pollution-control plan.

Satisfaction step. The lengthiest part of a speech of tribute usually will be the satisfaction step, for it is here that the tribute is actually paid. Relate a few incidents which show how the problems, personal or public, which you have outlined in the need step were met and surmounted. In doing this, be sure to demonstrate at least one of the following: (1) how certain admirable traits—vision, courage, and tenacity, for example—made it possible to deal successfully with these problems; (2) how

378

Special Occasions . . .

Patriotic gatherings, graduation ceremonies, service-club meetings, the presentation and acceptance of awards, the honoring of public heroes and high attainments, political acceptances or concessions, inaugurations, funerals . . . typically generate very specific expectations in audiences. The public speaker is thus obliged to analyze the ritualistic requisites—the "occasional" demands—and meet them.

remarkable the achievements were in the face of the obstacles encountered; (3) how great the influence of the achievement was on others.

Visualization step. In the preceding step, you will have enumerated the traits or achievements of the person (or group) being honored. In the visualization step, then, try to bring all of these together so as to create a vivid composite picture of the person and his or her accomplishments. It will help you to achieve this if you: *(a) Introduce an apt quotation.* Try to discover a bit of poetry or a literary passage which fits the person or group to whom you are paying tribute, and introduce it here. *(b) Draw a word picture of a world (community, business, or profession) inhabited by such persons.* Suggest how much better things would be if more people had similar qualities. *(c) Suggest the loss which the absence of the individual or group will bring.* Show vividly how much he, she, or they will be missed. Be specific: "It's going to seem mighty strange to walk into Barbara's office and not find her there ready to listen, ready to advise, ready to help."

Action step. Frequently, no action step is used in a speech of tribute. When it is, it will vary with the occasion somewhat as follows: *Eulogy*—suggest that the best tribute the audience can pay the person being honored is to live as that person did or to carry on what he or she has started. *Dedication*—suggest the appropriateness of dedicating this monument, building, or plaque, to such a person or group, and express the hope that it will inspire others to emulate their accomplishments. *Farewell*—extend to the departing person or persons the best wishes of those you represent, and express a determination to carry on what they have begun. Or, if you yourself are saying farewell, call upon those who remain to carry on what you and your associates have started.

By adapting the foregoing principles and procedures to the particular situation in which you find yourself, you should be able to devise a useful framework upon which to build a speech of tribute. To complete your speech, however, you will need to fill out this plan with vivid illustrative materials and appropriate motivational appeals.

Speeches of Nomination

The speech to nominate contains elements found in both speeches of introduction and speeches of tribute. Here, too, your main *purpose* is to review the accomplishments of some person whom you admire. This review, however, instead of standing as an end in itself (tribute) or of creating a desire to hear the person (introduction), is made to contribute to an actuative goal—obtaining the listeners' endorsement of the person as a nominee for an elective office.

In a speech of nomination, your *manner of speaking* generally will be less formal and dignified than when you are giving a speech of tribute. It should, however, be businesslike and energetic. In general, the content of the speech will follow the pattern of a speech of tribute; but the illustrations and supporting materials should be chosen with the intent of showing the nominee's qualifications for the office in question. Although the speech to nominate has certain special requirements, fundamentally it is a speech to actuate. Organize it, therefore, as follows:

In the *attention step,* announce that you arise to place a name in nomination. In the *need step,* point out the qualifications needed for success in the office; enumerate the problems that must be met, the personal qualities that are called for. In the *satisfaction step,* name the person you are nominating, and show that he or she has these qualifications. Point to the individual's training, experience, success in similar positions, etc. In the *visualization step,* picture briefly the accomplishments which may be expected if your nominee is endorsed and elected. Finally, in the *action step,* formally place the name in nomination and urge audience endorsement and support. Sometimes the naming of the nominee is part of the attention step. This is a good practice if the audience is favorably disposed toward the person being nominated. However, if there is some doubt about their attitude, wait until the satisfaction step to reveal the name. In this way, by first showing the particular fitness of the person you may avoid unnecessary hostility.

Not all nominations, of course, need to be supported by a long speech. Frequently, especially in small groups and clubs, the person nominated is well known to the audience, and his or her qualifications are already appreciated. Under such circumstances, all that is required is the simple statement: "Mr. Chairman, given her obvious and well-known services to our club in the past, I nominate Marilyn Cannell for the office of treasurer."

Speeches of Self-Justification

At times, individuals may encounter situations which force them to speak in defense of themselves. Historical and contemporary examples abound. In early America, a criminal about to be executed was offered a chance to speak to the crowd assembled to witness his demise.* In a modern-day courtroom trial, the defendant nearly always is given an opportunity to address the court and speak in his or her own behalf. Politicians often feel called upon to justify or explain their actions. Recent examples occurred during the 1976 presidential campaign, when Gerald Ford had to explain a reference to the "independence" of Poland, and Jimmy Carter had to justify and explain remarks he had made in a *Playboy* magazine interview. Also, as we noted earlier, individuals may use a farewell or resignation speech to present their side of the dispute which prompted their dismissal or resignation, as did Spiro Agnew in 1973 and Richard Nixon in 1974. In fact, almost anyone in almost any public office may occasionally need to justify an action or explain a

---

*For a discussion of this fascinating occasion out of our country's past, see Bower Aly, "The Gallow's Speech: A Lost Genre," *Southern Speech Journal* 34 (Spring 1969): 204–213.

statement. Club treasurers sometimes have to explain extraordinary expenditures; city mayors must justify a show of force by their police departments during times of stress; and organizational presidents at least annually are required to account for ways they have implemented programs. Especially in cultures where decision making and resource management are relatively open, speeches of self-justification and self-exoneration abound.

Purpose and Manner of Speaking for Speeches of Self-Justification. The general purpose of a speech of self-justification is to convince those who hear it that the speaker's actions or beliefs are not illegal, imprudent, or immoral. The specific purpose of such a speech, however, varies with the nature of the charges leveled against the speaker. If persons are accused of serious crimes, for example, they may wish to flatly deny charges of wrongdoing. If they cannot be denied, speakers may believe the best course is to explain why they acted as they did, on the assumption that explanation will allow them to escape condemnation. Finally, speakers may attempt to go even beyond explanation, seeking instead full and complete justification in an appeal to the culture's basic beliefs or principles. By appealing to either *circumstances* or *principles,* therefore, public communicators seeking self-justification may have as their specific purposes *denial, explanation,* or *transcendence* (the moving beyond).*

Whatever the specific purpose, the speech of self-justification is an intensely personal message. The situation that precipitated the speech usually causes the audience to adopt an unfavorable—or at least a wait-and-see—attitude toward you as a person. Regardless of your specific purpose, try to make the audience view your actions from *your* perspective. Above all, do not speak in a manner that will alienate them even more. You should avoid formality and adopt as much of a conversational style of speaking as possible. Do not convey to the audience the sense that you are disinterested or aloof. Instead, make them feel you are speaking to each of them on a person-to-person level. Your style should also express sincere feelings and emotions, but carefully avoid blatant and contrived emotional outbursts.

Formulating the Content and Organizing Speeches of Self-Justification. Usually, your audience will have some notion of the charges leveled against you, or at least will be aware there is some controversy surrounding your motives and actions. Consequently, they will be curious to learn what you are going to say regarding them. While the specific

---

*Ware and Linkugel argue that there are always, in some combination, four main strategies in a speech of self-justification: *denial, bolstering* (bringing in new facts and considerations), *explanation,* and *transcendence* (moving from the specific to a more general issue). For an analysis of self-justification, together with a solid list of illustrative speeches, see B. L. Ware and Wil A. Linkugel, "They Spoke in Defense of Themselves: On the General Criticism of Apologia," *Quarterly Journal of Speech* 59 (October 1973): 273–283.

purpose of your speech will tend to dictate its content, most speeches of self-justification can be organized effectively in accordance with the motivated sequence, thus:

Attention step. In the first step, state why it is important that you speak in defense of yourself at this time and what your specific purpose is. This statement should be followed, normally, by an initial summary detailing how you intend to deal with the charges or questions. If you intend to deny them, for example, tell the audience that you are going to review counter-arguments and then refute them. If you intend to explain or justify your actions, you should suggest that you are going to answer questions by showing that your actions were precipitated by a set of circumstances beyond your control or by principles they all live by.

Need step. In this section, proceed to detail the charges of which you are accused. If your specific purpose is merely to deny them, you then can move on to the satisfaction step. If, however, you choose not to deny directly, then you should also include in this step a detailed discussion of the set of circumstances which prompted you to act as you did. You may treat the circumstances in one of two ways: First, accentuate the *novelty* or *uniqueness* of the circumstances, as Senator Ted Kennedy did when discussing the drowning of Mary Jo Kopechne at Chappaquiddick.* In other words, you could attempt to make the audience realize that highly unusual circumstances called for equally unusual actions to remedy them. Indian Premier Indira Gandhi attempted, for example, to justify her assumption of dictatorial powers in 1975 by stating that circumstances (rampant corruption, economic crises, subversive activities, etc.) were threatening to destroy the country's social-political structure. Or, second, you may elect to emphasize the *common* or *conventional* aspects of the circumstances, letting the audience know that others face similar problems and that your actions did not deviate from the norm. This is essentially what Spiro Agnew did by claiming that he had acted no differently than any other politician who allows fund-raising and contract-dispensing activities to overlap. This strategy also is practiced often by club presidents and other officers, as when they appeal to the organization's constitution, which allows them certain discretionary powers.

Satisfaction step. You now are ready either to deny the charges or explain your actions in light of the circumstances and principles which prompted them. If the circumstances were unique and could have created a problem, try to demonstrate how your actions helped to avert an even larger crisis, as did Gandhi, stressing that there was no other way to act. When the circumstances are conventional or common, assert that your actions have not differed from the ways others have acted, as did Douglas MacArthur when he discussed ways generals have to think

---

*For a discussion of Kennedy's speech, read David A. Ling, "A Pentadic Analysis of Senator Edward Kennedy's Address 'To the People of Massachusetts,' July 25, 1969," *Central States Speech Journal* 21 (Summer 1970): 81–86.

in wartime. Support these contentions with actual examples, vivid enough to give satisfaction.

Visualization step. Having convinced the audience that you either did not commit the alleged offense or were justified in doing what you did, you must now strive to create a positive and convincing picture of yourself as one who has been wrongfully accused. You must create understanding and sympathy for yourself. Often you can accomplish this by reminding the audience of the good things you have done for the society or the organization. Be careful only that you do not offer a lengthy, self-conscious biography, one which raises further suspicions rather than understanding. If your review of past accomplishments is handled tactfully, you not only will add to your *ethos* or credibility, but also will imply that you are at least as good a person as are your accusers.

Action step. In the action step, you should simply call for positive judgment. You should review the main points of your speech as well as the reasons why you chose to speak. Do not threaten the audience, but make them aware of the responsibility they have to judge you fairly in light of *all* the evidence. Thank them for giving you the opportunity to speak, and indicate that you will abide by their decision, whatever it is.

Speeches of self-justification or exoneration, as you can see from the foregoing review, probably are among the most difficult types of addresses to prepare because the communicator constantly must balance appeals to circumstances and to principles, to the audience's good judgment and the speaker's special self-interest, to the critics' rights to question, and to the accused's right to respond. In addition, the decisions surrounding evidence, emotional or motive appeals, and self-reference demand a kind of delicacy seldom required in most speaking situations. When they are made well, however, they produce some of the most satisfying discourses you will ever prepare.

Speeches to Create Good Will

The final type of speech we will discuss is the speech to create good will. While *ostensibly* the purpose of this special type of speech is to inform an audience about a product, service, operation, or procedure, *actually* it is to enhance the listeners' appreciation of a particular institution, practice, or profession—to make the audience more favorably disposed toward it. Thus, the good-will speech is also a mixed or hybrid type. Basically, it is informative, but—at the same time—has a strong, underlying persuasive purpose.

Typical Situations Requiring Speeches for Good Will.   There are numerous situations in which good-will speeches are appropriate, but the three which follow may be considered typical:

Luncheon meetings of civic and service clubs. Gatherings of this kind, being semisocial in nature and having a built-in atmosphere of congeniality, offer excellent opportunities for presenting speeches of good will. Members of such groups — prominent men and women from many walks of life — are interested in civic affairs and in the workings of other people's businesses or professions.

Educational programs. School authorities, as well as leaders of clubs and religious organizations, often arrange educational programs for their patrons and members. At such meetings, speakers are asked to talk about the occupations in which they are engaged and to explain to the young people in the audience the opportunities offered and the training required in their respective fields. By use of illustrations and tactful references, a speaker may — while providing the desired information — also create good will for his or her company or profession.

Special demonstration programs. Special programs are frequently presented by government agencies, university extension departments, and business organizations. For example, a wholesale food company may send a representative to a meeting of nutritionists to explain the food values present in various kinds of canned meat or fish products, and to demonstrate new ways of preparing or serving them. Although such a speech would be primarily informative, the speaker could win good will indirectly by showing that his or her company desires to increase customer satisfaction with its products and services.

Manner of Speaking in the Speech for Good Will.   Three qualities — modesty, tolerance, and good humor — characterize the manner of speaking appropriate for good-will speeches. Although you will be talking about your business or vocation and trying to make it seem important to the audience, you should never boast or brag. In giving a speech of this type, let the facts speak for themselves. Moreover, show a tolerant attitude toward others, especially competitors. The airline representative, for instance, who violently attacks trucking companies and bus lines is likely to gain ill will rather than good. Finally, exercise good humor. The good-will speech is not for the zealot or the crusader. Take the task more genially. Don't try to force acceptance of your ideas; instead, show so much enthusiasm and good feeling that your listeners will respond spontaneously and favorably to the information you are providing.

Formulating the Content of the Speech for Good Will.   In selecting materials for a good-will speech, keep these suggestions in mind: *Present novel and interesting facts about your subject.* Make your listeners feel that you are giving them an inside look into your company or organization. Avoid talking about what they already know; concentrate on new developments and on facts or services that are not generally known. *Show a relationship between your subject and the lives of the members of your audience.* Make your listeners see the importance of your organization or profession to their personal safety, success, or happiness. Finally, *offer a definite service.* This offer may take the form of an invitation to the audience to visit your office or shop, to help them with their problems, or even an expression of your willingness to answer questions or send brochures.

Organizing the Speech for Good Will. The materials we have just described may be organized into a well-rounded speech of good will in accordance with the following steps:

Attention step. The purpose of the beginning of your speech will be to establish a friendly feeling and to arouse the audience's curiosity about your profession or the institution you represent. You may gain the first of these objectives by a tactful compliment to the group or a reference to the occasion that has brought you together. Follow this with one or two unusual facts or illustrations concerning the enterprise you represent. For instance: "Before we began manufacturing television parts, the Lash Electric Company confined its business to the making of clock radios that would never wear out. We succeeded so well that we almost went bankrupt! That was only fifteen years ago. Today our export trade alone is over one hundred times as large as our total annual domestic business was in those earlier days. It may interest you to know how this change took place." In brief, you must find some way to arouse your listeners' curiosity about your organization.

Need step. Point out certain problems facing your audience—problems with which the institution, profession, or agency you represent is vitally concerned. For example, if you represent a radio or television station, show the relationship of good communications to the social and economic health of the community. By so doing, you will establish common ground with your audience. Ordinarily the need step will be brief and will consist largely of suggestions developed with only an occasional illustration. However, if you intend to propose that your listeners join in acting to meet a common problem, the need step will require fuller development.

Satisfaction step. The meat of a good-will speech will be in the satisfaction step. Here is the place to tell your audience about your institution, profession, or business and to explain what it is or what it does. You can do this in at least three ways: (1) *Relate interesting events in its history.* Pick events which will demonstrate its humanity, its reliability, and its importance to the community, to the country, or to the world of nations. (2) *Explain how your organization or profession operates.* Pick out those things that are unusual or that may contain beneficial suggestions for your audience. This method often helps impress upon your listeners the size and efficiency of your operation or enterprise. (3) *Describe the services your organization renders.* Explain its products; point out how widely they are used; discuss the policies by which management is guided—especially those which you think your audience will agree with or admire. Tell what your firm or profession has done for the community: people employed, purchases made locally, assistance with community projects, improvements in health, education, or public safety. Do not boast, but make sure that your listeners realize the value of your work *to them.*

Visualization step. Your object here is to crystalize the good will that the presentation of information in the satisfaction step initially has created. Do this by looking to the future. Make a rapid survey of the points you have covered or combine them in a single story or illustration. Or, to approach this step from the opposite direction, picture for your listeners the loss that would result if the organization or profession you represent should leave the community or cease to exist. Be careful, however, not to leave the impression that there is any real danger that this will occur.

Action step. Here, you make your offer of service to the audience — for example, invite the group to visit your office or plant, or point out the willingness of your organization to assist in some common enterprise. As is true of every type of speech, the content and organization of the speech for good will sometimes need to be especially adapted to meet the demands of the subject or occasion. You should, however, never lose sight of the central purpose for which you speak: to show your audience that the work which you do or the service which you perform is of value to them — that in some way it makes their lives happier, more productive, interesting, or secure.

The following is an example of a good-will speech which was presented to the Economic Club of Detroit on March 14, 1977, by Arthur Ochs Sulzberger, president and publisher of the *New York Times.* In this address, Mr. Sulzberger combines information about the press with subtle appeals skillfully designed to alter his listeners' attitudes toward it. In particular, note how he identifies the interests of the press with those of business in general and also how he argues that, on the whole, "tension" between business and the press is a good, rather than a bad, thing. By these and similar means, Mr. Sulzberger is able to clear up common misunderstandings and to show the relationship between business and the press in a fresh and more favorable light, thus communicating the good will he intends.

"Business and the Press: Is the Press Anti-Business?"[3]

Arthur Ochs Sulzberger

It's good to be here in Detroit, the home of the "Big Two" — *The Detroit News* and the *Detroit Free Press.* About a year ago, I was looking through a newspaper, and I came across a story that gave me my topic for today: Is the press anti-business? /1

The story that triggered that question in my mind was a report of the dreary 1975 earnings of The New York Times Company. /2

Happily, I can address that question today in a more objective frame of mind. The 1976 figures, as reported in the paper, show circulation, advertising, and earnings on a satisfying march upward. The article about it looked decidedly pro-business. In fact, I cannot recall a morning on which I read the *Wall Street Journal* with greater pleasure. /3

Is the press anti-business? That question breeds another: How can the press be anti-business when the press is business, and often big business at that? After all, like many of you in the room today, we, too, face boards of directors, union leaders, the EEOC, the S.E.C., and stockholders. It's hard to remember a *Times* annual meeting which Evelyn Y. Davis missed. /4

But the fact that the press is often big business itself does not really enable us to duck the question: Are we anti-business? A great many businessmen suggest that a new tone is creeping into journalism. They find that the big corporation *too* is often portrayed as the villain, and the consumer movement the hero; that bad news is reported with glee, and good corporate news is relayed grudgingly; that the profit motive is *derogated* by writers who seem to prefer more government control and, at best, have little or no training in the world of finance. Too often they feel the deadline conflicts with accuracy, and the deadline too often wins. It is argued that a general public distrust of institutions is being *focused* by the media into a lack of confidence in all American business enterprise. /5

Let me pass along a tip on how to detect bias in any speaker on this subject. If he talks about "the media," he's against us; if he talks about "the press," he's for us. I speak to you today as a member of the press. /6

Let me grant this at the outset: press coverage of business has changed and is still changing. A more analytical—a more skeptical, sometimes more critical—approach is being taken. And this is not only true with business reporting. Government, education, the courts, and the press itself are subject to this new scrutiny. /7

The printing of handouts—or "editing with a shovel"—is on the decline, and that's good. /8

But why, journalists are asked, don't we play up the good news? Why does the corporate bribe or the drop in earnings get the big headline—while the advance in technology or the rise in earnings gets buried? /9

One answer, of course, is in the nature of news: we give more space to a plane crash than to a report on the thousands of safe landings made every day. I would never suggest that "good news is no news," but I would suggest that bad news is often big news. /10

Another answer is in the changing nature of the news business. In every field, editors are emphasizing two basic questions: One is *How?* How will this affect the reader's life? And newspapers respond with more service columns, more pieces on personal investing, and more columns on the significance of business news on readers' lives. The other is *Why?* Why did they abandon the merger? Why did they fire the boss? Readers, investors, and creditors all want these answers. And as business becomes more complex, more international, answers to these questions become increasingly important. /11

On this point, I should add that not all reporting of good news is necessarily welcome to businessmen. For example, when the Bell Telephone System became the first corporation in history to earn one billion dollars in a single quarter, we thought the achievement ought to be recognized, and displayed the story on the front page. But a New Jersey public-service commissioner saw it there, and rejected a rate increase on the ground that profits were too high. Bell System executives might well think it would be wiser in the future to hide their light under a bushel. So, I don't think "Why don't you play up the good news?" is a valid question. That's not our function. Our job is to give the reader accurate information he can use about what is important and what interests him. That is also an important goal of business. /12

Let's get to basics. Fifty years ago, an American president could say, with much justification, that "the business of America is business." We've gone beyond that. The business of America is freedom. /13

For the journalist, that means the freedom to get to the root of the truth, the freedom to criticize, the freedom to goad and stimulate every institution in our society, including our own. /14

For businessmen, that means the freedom to compete fairly, on the basis of value and service. And it means the freedom to defend themselves against unfair charges by pressure groups, to assert the principle of the profit motive, and to fight off excessive or stultifying government regulation. /15

For the consumer of your product and mine, it means the freedom to hold our claims to account, the freedom to complain like hell and get attention paid to those complaints, and the freedom to choose a competitor if we fail them. /16

Let me, then, practice what I preach about the new coverage of business news. Here are a few ideas we can use in our business lives. /17

First: *Get out front.* Teamwork may be great, and the organization spirit is commendable, but business news is made by people. Individuals. Human beings. Business leadership ought to include some public leadership — but the trouble is, the public perception of business leaders is all too often that of the *bland* leading the *bland.* Oh, there are some exceptions, and Detroit is home to some of them. Yet, in a recent poll, 93 percent of the people interviewed could identify Walter Cronkite; 79 percent, Henry Kissinger; 66 percent, George Meany; but when they were asked about Thomas Murphy and John de Butts, they wondered if the pollsters were putting them on. Less than 3 percent could identify the heads of General Motors and AT&T. /18

Why are there so few business heroes? Is the press trying to hide the identity of businessmen, or are businessmen worried about becoming celebrities? It is true that with public renown comes vulnerability, both personal and corporate; many businessmen choose, out of modesty or caution, to stay out of the limelight. A faceless official spokesman often becomes the voice of the company. /19

Even publishers should show their faces now and then. I think it's a fine thing when somebody comes up to me after a speech and says, "You're doing a great job with your newspaper, Mr. Chandler." /20

Next, *stop talking the inside lingo of business.* Whenever businessmen get together, they bemoan the fact that business is "failing to communicate," whatever that means. One reason may be that they're talking a specialized language that the public is not about to take the time to learn. /21

That language barrier concerns us at *The Times.* Occasionally, we hear the charge that newspaper and television reporters are poorly prepared to talk to business people about financial subjects. And it is true that the subject matter is becoming more complex, involving nuclear safety, or tanker technology, changes in accounting rules, and the like. From our side, we're hiring more reporters with formal educations in business subjects—*not* so much to talk the language of businessmen, but to interpret these complex subjects for the lay reader. /22

Third: *Go looking for complaints.* That sounds strange, I know—most of us have all the complaints we can handle. But I was reading a *U.S. News and World Report* survey of some 5,000 heads of households. The biggest problem business had was credibility: most people say they do not believe what business claims about its products. That's troublesome, but the same survey turned up this hopeful note: of the one-fourth of the people who had made a complaint to a manufacturer about a product in the past year, nearly half of them said they were satisfied in the way those complaints were handled. /23

Think about that: one of the biggest pluses American business has going for it is the satisfaction of the customer who complains, and whose complaints are heard. And it's better that *they* complain to the businessman than to write to their Congressman. /24

We deal with gripes in the newspaper business all the time. One of the best-read sections of every paper is the "Letters to the Editor," and the best letters are the ones that slam us all over the page. *The Times* also has a "corrections" corner, originally because we thought that was the responsible thing to do, but now it is turning into a well-read feature. Why? Because nobody's perfect—customers and readers understand that, and react well to efforts to improve. /25

And, finally—*do some complaining yourself.* Fight for your rights—everyone else is, and business has just as much a right to be heard as any other force in our society. /26

Just about every survey about public perceptions of business shows that the strongest anti-business feeling is on the college campus. That's a big challenge, and it invites a kind of sensitive confrontation. Businessmen, especially young businessmen, should assume that burden; it cannot be solved only by taking an ad in the college newspaper. To combat anti-business feeling at its source, businessmen have to arrange to tie into college activities, participate in seminars, and have honest answers to student questions about environmental and human concerns. Nor is there any need to be on the defensive; we know that the market system outperforms any other, and it includes the irreplaceable element of personal freedom. That's not something to apologize for; that's something to proudly assert. /27

I think you'll find more places in which to make that kind of affirmation. Many newspapers are adopting op-ed [opinion-education] pages, seeking expressions of outside opinion. /28

On *The Times,* one of our most popular Sunday features is a page of outside opinion labeled "Point of View," where businessmen and academics and government officials blaze away on everything from energy policy to capital shortages. / 29

More than ever, across the spectrum of our lives, that element of controversy is a vital part of the news. News is not only what happens, but what people think has happened, and what values they attach to what *has,* or *has not,* taken place. Business is a prime part of that creative controversy; so is journalism. Sometimes it hurts; most of the time it's fairly exciting and quite constructive. / 30

My point is this: It is not so much a matter of the *press* being anti-business, which I have to admit it *sometimes* is. Nor is it a matter of *business* being anti-press, which you will have to admit it *usually* is. That tension between press and business—in a relationship not quite so adversary as that which exists between press and government—is the healthy tension in a land of separated and balancing centers of power. / 31

Is the press anti-business? The answer is no. Is the press anti-dullness, anti-stuffiness, anti-corporate secrecy? The answer is yes. / 32

Is a probing, skeptical, searching press coverage good for business? I think so. You may not agree completely. You might look at modern business news coverage the way John Wanamaker looked at advertising: half of it is wasted, he felt, but he never knew which half. / 33

Business and journalism share certain great values: we are both pro-opportunity; we are both pro-consumer; we are both pro-profit; and we are both pro-freedom. /34

We are looking at each other now with new eyes, in a kind of institutional mid-life crisis. And I think we're both going to come through it stronger than ever. / 35

Speeches of introduction, tribute, nomination, self-justification, and good will represent but five of the many *speeches for special occasions.* In all of them, certain communicative decisions are, to some degree, dictated by the occasion and by audience expectations. Yet, as should be clear by now, in each you face a set of unique challenges—substantive, emotive, and stylistic challenges of the first order. At the same time, you will find that these occasions provide you with some of your most rewarding efforts at public communication.

Reference Notes

[1]Copyright 1977 by CBS, Inc. Reprinted by permission of Harold Matson Co., Inc.

[2]"The Testimony of Sculpture," by Harold Haydon. Copyright © 1968, *The University of Chicago Magazine.* Reprinted with permission from *The University of Chicago Magazine.*

[3]"Business and the Press: Is the Press Anti-Business?" by Arthur Ochs Sulzberger, from *Vital Speeches of the Day,* Volume XXXXIII, May 1977. Reprinted by permission of Vital Speeches of the Day.

Problems and Probes

1.   This chapter has argued that good-will speeches usually are informative speeches with underlying persuasive purposes. Describe various circumstances under which you think the informative elements should predominate in this type of speech, and then describe other circumstances in which the persuasive elements should be emphasized. In the second case, at what point would you say that the speech becomes openly persuasive in purpose? Or, if you prefer to work with advertisements, scan magazines to find so-called public service ads—ones which emphasize what a company is doing to help society with its problems or to promote social-cultural-aesthetic values. Then ask yourself similar questions about these advertisements.

2.   In this chapter we have discussed speeches of introduction and tribute, but we have ignored the *responses* which speakers make to them. After you have been introduced, given an award, and received a tribute, what should you say? Knowing what you do about speeches of introduction and tribute, what kinds of materials might you include as attention, satisfaction, and visualization steps? (Those wishing to read about speeches of this type should see Eugene E. White's book mentioned in "Suggestions for Further Reading.")

3.   Similarly, you can ask, how should I respond to a speech of nomination? To what degree should I as the responder attempt to balance thanks and positive statements on my own behalf? For a careful, content analysis of political speeches of nomination-acceptance, see Marshall S. Smith with Philip J. Stone and Evelyn N. Glenn, "A Content Analysis of Twenty Presidential Nomination Acceptance Speeches," in *The General Inquirer: A Computer Approach to Content Analysis,* ed. Philip J. Stone et al. (Cambridge, Mass.: M.I.T. Press, 1966), pp. 359–400.

4.   Keynote speeches at political conventions are another interesting type of occasional speechmaking. Read Edwin Miles' article, "The Keynote Speech at National Nominating Conventions," *Quarterly Journal of Speech* 46 (1960): 26–31. Then, find a recent keynote speech, in *Vital Speeches of the Day,* in summaries of national party conventions, or in *The New York Times,* and determine if its characteristics are similar to those which Miles identified. Also consider such questions as these: Has keynote speaking changed markedly with nationwide television coverage? Has the lack of strong party unity in recent years affected such speeches? Why are keynote speeches generally delivered by young, rising politicians? As you see it, what is the full range of general and specific purposes served by the keynote speech? (Part of the answer to this question can be found in Craig R. Smith, "The Republican Keynote Address of 1968: Adaptive Rhetoric for a Multiple Audience," *Western Speech* 39 [Winter 1975]: 32–39.)

Oral Activities and Speaking Assignments

1.   Your instructor will prepare a list of special-occasion, impromptu speech topics, such as: "Student X is a visitor from a neighboring school. Introduce the

student to this class." "You are Student X. Respond to this introduction." "Dedicate your speech-critique forms to the state historical archives." "You have just been named Outstanding Classroom Speaker for this term. Accept the award." "You are a representative of a Speech-Writers-for-Hire firm. Sell your services to other members of the class while you are explaining how your company works." "Nominate a class member for Student Senate." You will have between five and ten minutes in which to prepare, and then will deliver the speech on the topic assigned or drawn. Be ready to discuss the techniques you employed in putting the speech together.

2.   Prepare for delivery in class a five-minute good-will speech on behalf of a campus organization (or some national organization such as the Boy Scouts or the YWCA) to which you belong. Select new and/or little-known facts to present; pay particular attention to maintaining interest; keep your arguments and appeals indirect; and show tact and restraint in your speaking manner. Be prepared to answer questions after your speech is completed.

3.   Prepare a five-minute speech paying tribute to:
A man or woman important in national or world history.
A group of volunteers who participated in a successful (or unsuccessful) charity drive.
Someone in your home community or college who, though never famous, contributed in a significant way to the success, well-being, or happiness of many others.
A group of scientists who have just completed an important project.
An outstanding athlete or team which has received state or national recognition.
Founders of an organization for civic betterment.
An especially talented student in your class.

 ## Suggestions for Further Reading

Lloyd Bitzer, "The Rhetorical Situation," *Philosophy & Rhetoric* 1 (Winter 1968): 1–14.
Guy R. Lyle and Kevin Guinagh, *I Am Happy to Present: A Book of Introductions* (Bronx, N. Y.: The H. W. Wilson Company, 1953).
Rudolph F. Verderber, *The Challenge of Effective Speaking,* 3rd ed. (Belmont, Calif.: Wadsworth Publishing Company, Inc., 1976), Chapter 18, "Speeches for Special Occasions."
B. L. Ware and Wil A. Linkugel, "They Spoke in Defense of Themselves: On the General Criticism of Apologia," *Quarterly Journal of Speech* 59 (October 1973): 273–283.
Eugene E. White, *Practical Public Speaking,* 2nd ed. (New York: The Macmillan Company, 1964), Chapter 15, "Speeches of Special Types."

Appendix

Finding and Recording Speech Materials

Making Your Speaking Voice More Effective

Evaluating and Criticizing the Speeches of Others

Communicating in Small Groups

Finding and Recording Speech Materials

For most speeches, you will need to find out more about your subject than you already know; and you will need to record this information and to classify it. In this section we shall describe the sources from which speech materials are commonly drawn and suggest a practical method for recording and filing them.

Gathering Information

Personal Experience

A good way to begin your search for speech materials is to jot down on a piece of paper everything you already know about your subject as a result of personal experience or observation. As we emphasized in Chapter 4, you always speak best about the people, ideas, and events that you know best; and you know best those things you have actually seen, heard, touched, tasted, smelled, or done. Even when materials of this kind cannot appropriately be cited in your message, they will sharpen your perspective or provide insights into the subject—something which almost invariably makes for greater clarity and vividness of expression. Whenever possible, make personal experience and observation your first "port of call" when searching for speech materials.

At times, however, you will be called upon to speak about matters which fall entirely outside the range of your own experience or observation. When this is the case, there are several sources of information open to you: interviews with experts, letters and questionnaires, publications of all kinds, and radio and television broadcasts. Let us consider how each of these sources can be used to best advantage in accumulating substantive materials for your speeches.

Interviews

Beginning speakers often fail to recognize that vast amounts of useful and authoritative information may be gathered merely by asking questions of the right persons. If, for example, you expect to talk about interplanetary navigation, what better-informed and more convenient source of information could there be than a member of your college's astronomy department? Or if you are to discuss a problem in national or international affairs, why not talk first with a trained political scientist? Nearly all faculty members are willing to talk with you on questions pertaining to their special fields of interest. In your town or community also you usually will find one or more experts on nearly any topic you choose to speak about. Of course, you must avoid being bothersome or pushy in approaching these persons, and you must respect their time and schedules. But brief interviews, properly arranged and scheduled, frequently can yield invaluable factual data; and, even more important, they can be a source of authoritative interpretations and opinions.

Generally, a well-managed information-seeking interview entails seven separate but related tasks:

1. Selecting the informant.
2. Obtaining the informant's cooperation.
3. Learning about the informant.
4. Developing a plan or procedure.
5. Formulating specific questions and tactics.
6. Conducting the interview.
7. Interpreting and evaluating the results.

1. Selecting the Informant. Although selecting the informant—the person from whom information is to be sought—may at first appear to be a simple matter, this is not always the case. If, for example, your subject is a controversial one and you intend to interview only one informant, you must try to choose someone who will approach the subject with reasonable objectivity and be able to give you all relevant points of view concerning it. If you plan to gather the necessary information from a large number of individuals, you should select them at random or should choose those most likely to represent all prevailing shades of opinion. In every instance, pick your informant or informants with care. Remember that the data you gather will be no more reliable than the persons with whom you talk.

2. Obtaining the Informant's Cooperation. If you wish to interview a busy or important individual, usually you will have better results if you get in touch with that person in advance. Write or telephone for an appointment, stating your purpose and explaining why you think he or she can supply you with the information you desire. Promise to keep the source's identity confidential if that is desired; and if you would like to tape all or a part of the conversation, be sure to get permission. Promise also that, if requested, you will let the interviewed person check over any direct quotations you plan to use.

3. Learning About the Informant. Between the time you obtain permission to conduct an interview and the time the interview actually takes place, find out as much as you can about the person you will be talking with. What is his current position? What positions or jobs has she previously held? What books or articles has he written? Has she been interviewed on this same subject or similar ones before? What opinions has he expressed on the subject? Information gained from these questions will help you frame more pertinent and penetrating questions and will also help you interpret and evaluate the responses you receive.

4. Developing a Plan or Procedure. An interview, like any other important speech transaction, requires planning and preparation. To enter upon it unprepared will in most instances waste the time of your informant and greatly reduce the profit that you yourself derive. Before you make specific plans for an interview, therefore, fix clearly in your mind the precise purpose you wish to achieve as a result of the encounter.

5. *Formulating Specific Questions and Tactics.* What is it that you want to know? Do you wish to learn more about the early history and development of the subject? About its economic or social aspects? Or about its moral and ethical implications? Are you interested in digging out new facts, or do you want to learn your informant's interpretation of facts you already know? One of the least productive ways to approach an expert on any matter is to ask what he or she knows or thinks about a subject. Formulate in advance the principal questions you wish to raise and determine at least tentatively the order in which they might best be introduced. In doing this, see to it that your questions are clear, specific, and to the point. Plan to begin the interview with questions that are likely to arouse the interest of the informant and stimulate him or her to start talking freely. Save for the end questions that probe into difficult or controversial matters.

6. *Conducting the Interview.* In conducting the interview itself, bear in mind the following "do's" and "don't's":

DO *Be on Time.* When a busy person does you the courtesy of agreeing to an interview, the least you can do is to appear at the appointed time. Remember that in supplying information you desire, the interviewee is helping you; you are not helping him or her.

DO *Restate Your Purpose.* Even though you already have told the informant your purpose in a prior letter or phone call, take a minute or two at the outset to restate your purpose and intentions and also to make clear why you think he or she can be of help. This will strengthen the focus of the interview and direct the informant's attention to the areas you are more interested in exploring.

DO *Observe Not Only "What" the Informant Says, but Also "How" He or She Says It.* In all communication transactions, as we have emphasized, the tone of voice or inflectional pattern with which the informant makes a response may be highly revealing of an attitude on a given point—whether he or she regards it as important or unimportant, desirable or undesirable, etc. During an interview, changes in facial expression and bodily posture provide similar cues that should be taken into account when interpreting an informant's comments.

DO *Move the Interview Ahead at a Lively Pace.* Don't rush the informant; but on the other hand, don't let the conversation drag or die. When one question has been answered to your satisfaction, move on to the next without a long and awkward pause or undue shuffling of notes and papers. Maintain a businesslike manner at all times, avoiding side issues or wandering into matters totally unrelated to the topic you are exploring.

DO Respect Your Informant's Time. When you have concluded the last of the questions you wish to ask, terminate the interview, thank the informant, and depart. To prolong the interaction unduly is to run the needless risk of sinking into trivial matters or retreading ground you already have covered.

DO Make a Record of What Transpired. Either during the course of the interview or immediately thereafter, when everything is still fresh in your mind, make a record of what the informant said.

DON'T

DON'T Request an Interview Until You Already Know a Good Deal About the Subject. The more you know about a subject, the more intelligent and provocative your questions will be and the better you will be able to evaluate your informant's responses. As a rule, an interview should not be scheduled until you already are well along with your other research into a topic. It never should be used as a way of avoiding a thorough examination of printed sources or of gathering information by firsthand observation.

DON'T Parade Your Own Knowledge of the Subject. Your purpose in requesting an interview is to *get* information from the respondent, not to give it. Demonstrate your knowledge of the subject by asking intelligent questions, but do not use the encounter as an excuse for showing off your own brilliance.

DON'T Reveal Your Doubts or Disagreements in Point of View. If your informant says something with which you disagree or which you believe to be factually wrong, keep your feelings to yourself. Do not frown, shake your head, or look skeptical. Above all, do not argue about the matter. Remember that your purpose is to get your informant's view of the subject—not to expound or defend your own. You can discount a dubious opinion or check up on a doubted fact later. During the interview itself, maintain a courteous and attentive attitude.

7. *Interpreting and Evaluating the Results.*   The final step in a productive information-seeking interview consists of interpreting and evaluating what you have been told. To make the necessary interpretations and evaluations you may have to draw inferences and conclusions from data supplied by the informant. Sometimes you may find it necessary to decide how certain statements are to be classified or categorized—the general heading under which they properly fall. In any event, do not consider your task complete until you have reviewed in your own mind all the informant has said and determined its meaning and worth as you understand them.

Letters and Questionnaires

If you find it impossible to talk with an expert directly, you can sometimes obtain the information you need through correspondence. When using this method, however, be sure that you make clear exactly what information you want and why you want it. Moreover, be reasonable in your request. Do not expect a busy individual to spend hours or days gathering facts for you. Above all, do not ask for information that you yourself could find if you were willing to search for it. Write to an expert only after you have exhausted the other resources available to you.

When there is controversy on some point and you want to get a cross section of the varying opinions, you may send a questionnaire to a number of people and compare their answers. This method is valuable, but has been somewhat overused. As a result many people merely discard a questionnaire, particularly a long one. Therefore, make your questions as easy to answer as possible, and keep the list of questions brief. Always enclose a stamped, self-addressed envelope for the reply. If you can find out an individual's name, address him or her personally instead of mailing your questionnaire to a general address.

Printed Materials

Even where the substance of your speech may come from questionnaires, interviews, or through personal experience, it often will have to be supplemented by *printed* data contained in newspapers, magazines, and books.

Newspapers. Newspapers obviously are a useful source of information about events of current interest. Moreover, their feature stories and accounts of unusual happenings provide a storehouse of interesting illustrations and examples. You must be careful, of course, not to accept as true everything printed in a newspaper, for the haste with which news sometimes must be gathered makes complete accuracy difficult. Your school or city library undoubtedly keeps on file copies of one or two highly reliable papers such as *The New York Times, The Observer,* or the *Christian Science Monitor,* and probably also provides a selection from among the leading newspapers of your state or region. If your library has *The New York Times,* it is likely to have the published index to the paper. By using this resource, you can locate accounts of people and events from 1913 to the present. Another useful and well-indexed source of information on current happenings is *Facts on File,* issued weekly since 1940.

Magazines. An average-sized university library subscribes annually to hundreds of magazines and periodicals. Among those of general interest, some — such as *Time, Newsweek,* and *U.S. News and World Report* — summarize weekly events. *The Atlantic* and *Harper's* are representative of a group of monthly publications which cover a wide range of subjects of both passing and permanent importance. Such magazines as *The Nation, Vital Speeches of the Day, Fortune,* and *The New Republic* contain comment on current political, social, and economic questions. Discussions of popular scientific interest appear in *Popular Science, Scientific American,* and *Popular Mechanics.* For other specialized areas, there are such magazines as *Sports Illustrated, Field and Stream, Saturday Review, Better Homes and Gardens, Today's Health, National Geographic Magazine,* and *American Heritage.*

This list is, of course, merely suggestive of the wide range of materials to be found in periodicals. When you are looking for a specific kind of information, use the *Readers' Guide to Periodical Literature,* which indexes most of the magazines you will want to refer to in preparing a speech. Look in this index under various topical headings that are related to your subject. Similar indexes also are available for technical journals and publications.

Professional and trade journals. Nearly every profession, industry, trade, and academic field has one or more specialized journals. Such publications include: *Annals of the American Academy of Political and Social Science, Ameri-*

can *Economist, Quarterly Journal of Communication, Journal of the American Medical Association, Journal of Afro-American Studies, AFL-CIO American Federationist, Trade and Industry, Coal Age, Educational Theatre Journal,* and others. These journals contain a great deal of detailed and specialized information in their respective fields.

Yearbooks and encyclopedias. The most reliable source of comprehensive data is the *Statistical Abstract of the United States,* which covers a wide variety of subjects ranging from weather records and birth rates to steel production and population figures. It is published by the federal government and is available in most libraries. Also useful as sources of facts and figures are the *World Almanac, The People's Almanac,* and – as previously mentioned – *Facts on File.* Encyclopedias such as the *Encyclopaedia Britannica* and *Americana Encyclopedia,* which attempt to cover the entire field of human knowledge in a score of volumes, are valuable chiefly as an initial reference source or for information on subjects which you do not need to explore deeply. Refer to them for important scientific, geographical, literary, or historical facts, and also for bibliographies of authoritative books on a subject.

Documents and reports. Various government agencies – state, national, and international – as well as many independent organizations publish reports on special subjects. Among government publications, those most frequently consulted by speakers are the reports of Congressional committees or those of the United States Department of Labor or of Commerce. Reports on agricultural problems, business, government, engineering, and scientific experimentation are issued by many state universities. Such endowed organizations as the Carnegie, Rockefeller, and Ford Foundations, and such groups as the Foreign Policy Association, the League of Women Voters, and the United States Chamber of Commerce also publish reports and pamphlets.

Books on special subjects. There are few subjects suitable for a speech upon which someone has not written a book. As a guide to these books, use the subject-matter headings in the card catalog of your library.

Collections of quotations. A wide range of quotations useful for illustrating an idea or supporting a point may be found in such works as Bartlett's *Familiar Quotations,* H. L. Mencken's *A New Dictionary of Quotations on Historical Principles from Ancient and Modern Sources,* Arthur Richmond's *Modern Quotations for Ready Reference,* George Seldes' *The Great Quotations,* and Burton Stevenson's *The Home Book of Quotations.*

Biographies. The *Dictionary of National Biography* (deceased Britishers), the *Dictionary of American Biography* (deceased Americans), *Who's Who* (living Britishers), *Who's Who in America, Current Biography,* and similar collections contain biographical sketches especially useful in locating facts about famous people and in finding the qualifications of authorities whose testimony you may wish to quote.

Radio and Television Broadcasts

Lectures, discussions, and the formal public addresses of leaders in business and government frequently are broadcast over radio or television; and many of these talks later are mimeographed or printed by the stations or by the organizations that sponsor them. Usually, copies may be obtained on request. If no manuscript is available and you are taking notes as you hear the broadcast, listen with particular care in order to get an exact record of the speaker's words or meaning. Just as you must quote items from printed sources accurately and honestly, so you are obligated to respect the remarks someone has made on a radio or television broadcast and to give that person full credit.

Obviously, you will not have to investigate all of the foregoing sources for every speech you make. Usually, however, a well-conducted search turns up materials that will make your speech more authoritative and interesting than it otherwise would be. Learn how to skim rapidly through a mass of information to pick out the important facts and ideas. This skill is valuable not only in preparing speeches, but also in every type of work where extensive research is required.

Recording Information

Have you ever begun to tell a story only to find that the essential details have slipped your mind entirely? Or have you ever tried in vain to recall an important date or name? Since it is impossible to remember everything you read or hear, you must have some method for recording potential speech materials. Moreover, it is important that you *record immediately* any data which you think may later prove useful. All too often, to recover a fact or idea after a period of days or weeks, you must engage in a long and laborious search, and sometimes you lose the desired data forever.

Some speakers prefer to keep their notes in notebooks, but for most research purposes notebooks are not as efficient as cards. Use the kind of cards that will best suit your inclination and purpose (4″ × 6″ is recommended), and carry a few of them in your pocket or briefcase for use whenever you encounter an idea you wish to preserve. If your handwriting is difficult to read after it has "cooled," plan to transfer your notes to a card by means of a typewriter. In some instances, too, you may want to make a xerox copy of the information and paste the appropriate portion of it on a notecard (see illustration, page 404). Keep your completed cards in a classified file where they will be easy to sort and rearrange when you begin to organize your speech. Often statistics or quotations which you wish to present to your audience verbatim may be read directly and unobtrusively from the card itself. In preparing notecards observe the following rules:

Place in the upper left-hand corner a subject heading which accurately labels the material recorded on the card. Such a heading will greatly facilitate the process of organizing and selecting ideas when you begin to put your speech into final form.

Note in the upper right-hand corner of the card the part or section of your speech in which the information probably will be used. Will it help to develop the necessary background or illustrate the problem with which you are concerned? Will it prove the soundness of the solution you propose? Will it point to certain benefits or advantages to be gained from acting according to your recommendations? If it is not possible to decide on the proper classificatory label during the early stages of your speech preparation, momentarily leave the space blank, and fill it in later.

Put only one fact or idea, or a few closely related facts or ideas, on each card. Unless you follow this rule, you will not be able to sort and classify the data properly, or to have at hand the specific information needed to develop a particular part of your speech.

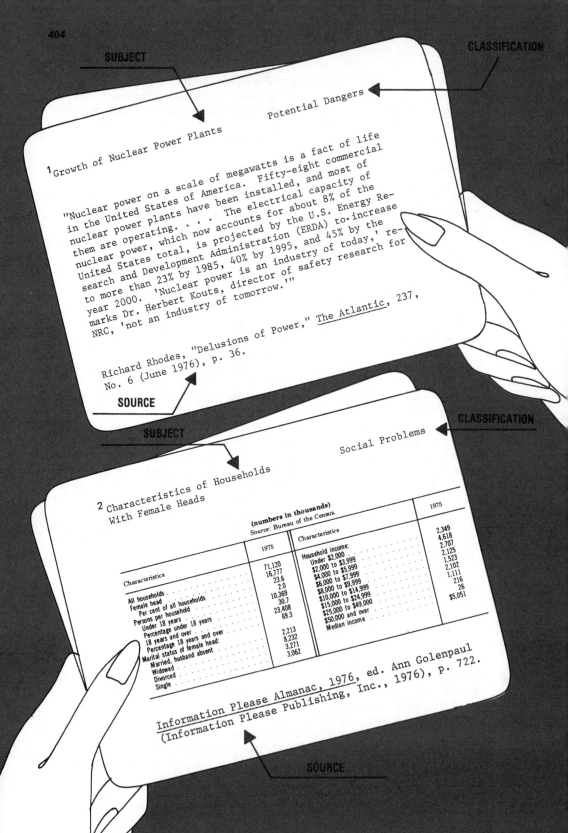

Indicate verbatim quotations by quotation marks. If the note consists in whole or in part of a direct quotation, indicate this fact by using quotation marks. (See illustration, page 404.) Use direct quotations when they are sufficiently brief or when they state facts or ideas so clearly or forcefully that you probably will want to reproduce the original wording in your speech. Condense or paraphrase longer or less important statements; but in doing so, be sure to preserve the author's meaning.

Note at the bottom of the card the exact source from which the information is drawn. This point cannot be stressed too strongly. Often you will want to re-check a note for accuracy or completeness, or you may be called upon to verify the facts or figures you cite. For both of these reasons it is important that you have an exact record of the source from which you have drawn the information. (See illustration, page 404.)

Classifying Information

When you first begin to gather material, a simple *topical* method of classification usually is satisfactory. Group your notecards together according to the apparent similarity of the headings which you have placed in the upper left corner. As the number of cards increases, however, you probably will need a more systematic method. Here are a few possibilities:

Chronological method. You may classify your material on the basis of the time to which it refers—by years, by months, or by its relation to some fixed event.

Causal method. This method divides material relating to the apparent causes of a phenomenon from material relating to its probable effects.

Problem-solution method. Here the facts about a *problem* are put into one group, and the descriptions of the various *solutions* and the evidence which supports them are put into another.

Geographical method. When this method is used, the material is divided according to the communities, cities, counties, countries, states, or other localities to which it refers.

Begin by classifying your notes according to one of these methods or a method equally appropriate to your purpose. Then as the cards in any category become bulky or unwieldy, subdivide that class. The value of classifying your material as you gather it is twofold: *First, you can see at a glance the kinds of information you lack and, in this way, can make your further investigations more purposeful. Second, the structuring of the material into a speech is made much simpler if it is in some reasonable order before the actual organizing process begins.* If you follow a systematic method of filing your speech materials as you collect them over a period of time, you will have a steadily growing mass of available information for future use—not merely for one speech, but for *many*.

In sum, the gathering, recording, and classifying of data usually comprise no small part of the total task of speech preparation. Therefore, you will do well to begin your research early enough so that you have plenty of time to find the information you need and to organize it in the way that will be of maximum use to you as you plan and outline your speech.

Reference Notes

¹Richard Rhodes. "Delusions of Power." *The Atlantic Monthly,* June, 1976.

²"Characteristics of Households with Female Heads," from *Information Please Almanac,* edited by Ann Golenpaul, Copyright © 1976. Reprinted by permission of Information Please Publishing, Inc.

Problems and Probes

1. Visit your college library and list the following:
   a. Five yearbooks or compilations of statistical data.
   b. Four encyclopedias, with some indication of the kind of information in which each specializes.
   c. Three technical or scholarly journals relating to your present or proposed major in college.
   d. Two indexes to periodical literature other than the *Readers' Guide.*
   e. Five biographical dictionaries.
   f. Two standard atlases of the world.
   g. Two reference works that list books in print.

2. Examine carefully selected cards in the card catalog of your library, and answer the following questions:
   a. How many times is each book listed in the catalog, and *how* is it listed?
   b. What information about the author is given on the catalog card?
   c. What information does the card give you about the book itself?

3. Without the help of a reference librarian, answer the following questions and name the sources in which you found the answers:
   a. How many miles of interstate highways have been completed in the United States to date?
   b. What was the size of the American expeditionary force in Europe during World War I? During World War II?
   c. Where did the governor of your state attend college?
   d. How many hits were collected by the baseball team that won the World Series in 1976?
   e. How did the senators from your state vote on the last defense budget passed by Congress?
   f. Who were the authors of *All the President's Men?* Who was the publisher? How many copies have been sold to date? Have the authors written other books also? If so, what are their titles and when were they published?
   g. Name some articles on Africa that were published during the first four months of 1977.
   h. How much does your state government contribute to the support of the schools in your community?
   i. Give the authors and titles of five recent books on corporation finance.

4. Select a subject of some substance and scope on which you would like to give a classroom speech in the future.
   a. Jot down in proper note form all the pertinent information you already have on this subject.
   b. Indicate the firsthand observations you can make concerning it.
   c. List persons whom you could interview on the subject, and decide what questions you would ask each one.
   d. Devise a sample questionnaire on the subject and indicate the groups or individuals to whom it might be sent.
   e. Prepare a bibliography of printed materials on the subject, including *(a)* five references taken from an index to periodicals, and *(b)* five books found in the card catalog of your library.

5. Read selected articles or books on a subject of your choice; and, following the samples shown in the illustrations on page 404, prepare five or six notecards, at least one of which presents *statistics,* one a *direct quotation,* one an *indirect quotation,* and one *an illustration* or *example.*

6. On slips of paper write three questions beginning, "Where would you go to find out about _____?" Put these questions in a hat with those submitted by your classmates and take turns drawing them out and answering them.

7. Evaluate radio and television newscasts and public service programs as sources of speech materials, and be prepared to answer the following questions: What advantages do they have over printed sources? What disadvantages? What special rules or cautions should be observed when gathering materials from these sources?

Oral Activities and Speaking Assignments

1. Practice gathering speech materials through interviews. Use the following procedure: Select five or six persons in your speech class who because of work experience, travel, their majors in school, hobbies, or other personal involvement have acquired a considerable amount of knowledge concerning a certain subject. After your instructor has paired you with one of these individuals, *interview* him or her, following the suggestions set forth in this chapter. Make sure that you have a series of questions planned in advance, that you interpret correctly the information you are given, that you record it accurately, and that you subsequently verify with the informant any statements which you might want to quote verbatim. Let another member of the class "listen in" on this interview and evaluate it critically.

2. Prepare and present a five-minute speech on any subject that you believe will be of interest to your classmates. (Check the analyses you have made earlier in your personal speech journal, and also review Chapter 5, "Analyzing the Audience and Occasion.") In this speech, use some material gathered from personal experience, some based on interviews, and some derived from printed sources. In addition to the usual outline, hand to your instructor a dozen properly prepared notecards on which you have recorded the material gathered in interviews and from printed sources.

Suggestions for Further Reading

Pearl Aldrich, *Research Papers: A Beginner's Manual* (Cambridge, Mass.: Winthrop Publishers, 1976).

Jean Key Gates, *Guide to the Use of Books and Libraries,* 3rd ed. (New York: McGraw-Hill Book Company, 1974).

Raymond L. Gordon, *Interviewing: Strategy, Techniques, and Tactics* (Homewood, Ill.: Dorsey Press, 1969), Chapter 4, "Interviewing Strategy"; Chapter 5, "Techniques in Interviewing"; and Chapter 6, "Tactics in the Interview."

James D. Lester, *Writing Research Papers,* 2nd ed. (Glenview, Ill.: Scott, Foresman and Company, 1976).

Alden Todd, *Finding Facts Fast* (New York: William Morrow & Co., Inc., 1972).

Barbara Walters, *How to Talk to Practically Anybody About Practically Anything* (New York: Dell Publishing Company, Inc., 1970).

Making Your Speaking Voice More Effective

In Chapter 15, you will recall, our emphasis was primarily upon the *psychological* aspects and implications of vocal communication. Here, our concerns center upon the *physiological* nature of the human voice as an instrument of communication and upon some of the practical means by which you may improve its effectiveness.

Good vocal behavior is *habitual.* Any vocal skill, before it can be natural and effective with listeners, must become so much a habit that it will work for you without conscious effort when you begin to speak, and will continue to do so throughout the utterance of your message. To make practice knowledgeable and worthwhile, you should understand first the *mechanics* of voice production, the *characteristics* of a good speaking voice, and the *methods* by which these characteristics may be developed or improved. In this appendix, therefore, we will *(a)* describe in simple terms the nature of the vocal mechanism, *(b)* consider the essential characteristics of voice quality, intelligibility, and variety, and *(c)* provide some exercises and practice materials for each. These exercises, together with the directions and guidance of your instructor, will—we believe—help you move purposefully toward a goal of developing a flexible and serviceable speaking voice.

The Mechanics of Speaking

In the strictest sense, there is no such thing as a "speech mechanism." We shall use the term, however, to include those parts of the body which—though seemingly designed by nature primarily for other functions—are used in producing the sounds of the human voice. These parts we shall consider in combination as a single "instrument of speech," having a *voice-producing mechanism* and an *articulatory mechanism.* (See illustrations on pages 410–411 and 243.)

NOTE: In Appendix B we necessarily employ some of the key terminology utilized in Chapter 15, "Using the Voice to Communicate" (pp. 239–257), where we considered primarily the *psychological* aspects of the voice and its *effects upon listeners.* Since, among other things, we attempt now to explore in somewhat greater depth and detail certain of the ideas and concepts introduced in those earlier pages, some of what we say here should be viewed as essentially an *extension,* an *elaboration,* or—in a few instances—an intentionally close *approximation* of information touched upon only briefly in previous mentions.

THE VOCAL MECHANISM
(anatomy involved in speech)

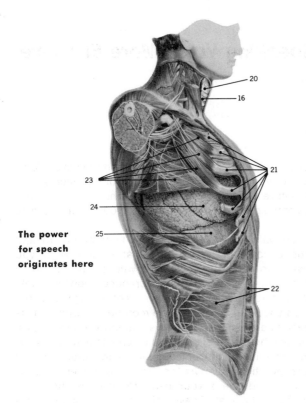

The power
for speech
originates here

1. Sinuses
2. Nasal cavity
3. Hard palate
4. Upper lip
5. Upper teeth
6. Tongue
7. Lower lip
8. Lower teeth
9. Lower jaw
10. Soft palate
11. Base of the tongue
12. Epiglottis
13. Thyroid cartilage
14. Vocal fold
15. Cricoid cartilage
16. Trachea (windpipe)
17. Esophagus
18. Pharynx (throat)
19. Vertebrae
20. Larynx
21. Rib bones (numbers
    6, 7, and 8 cut away)
22. Abdominal muscles
23. Chest muscles
24. Lungs
25. Diaphragm
26. Base of epiglottis
27. Glottis
28. Arytenoid cartilage

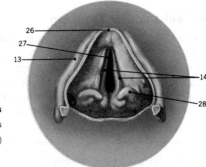

The vocal folds
(laryngoscopic view of the vocal folds
in relaxed position at normal breathing)

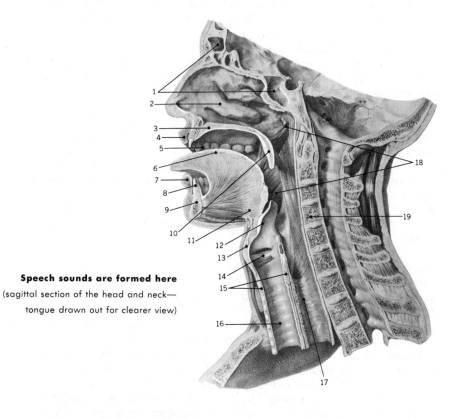

1
2
3
4
5
6
7
8
9
10
11
12
13
14
15
16
17
18
19

Speech sounds are formed here
(sagittal section of the head and neck—
tongue drawn out for clearer view)

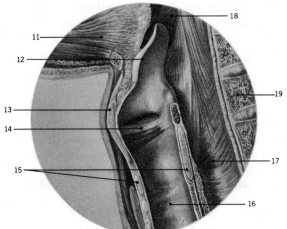

18
11
12
19
13
14
17
15
16

**Detail showing
structure of the larynx**

The Voice-Producing Mechanism

The Motor. The "motor" of the speech mechanism is essentially a pump for compressing air. It consists of *(a)* the *lungs,* which contain spaces for the air; *(b)* the *bronchial tubes,* which converge into the windpipe or *trachea,* out of which the compressed air is released; *(c)* the *ribs* and other bones, cartilages, and tissues which serve to hold the motor in place and give leverage for the application of power; and *(d)* the *muscles,* which alternately expand and contract the area occupied by the lungs, thus allowing air to enter and then compressing it for expulsion.

This human air pump works in two ways: Certain muscles draw the ribs down and in when you exhale, so as to squeeze the lungs like the motion of a bellows, while others — the strong abdominal muscles — squeeze in below to exert pressure up against the bottom of the lungs like the motion of a piston. This double action is also exerted when you inhale: One set of muscles pulls the ribs up and out to expand the horizontal space, while the diaphragm — a layer of muscles and flat tendon tissue — expands the vertical space by lowering the floor of the chest cavity. This two-way expansion creates a suction, so that air rushes into the lungs.

The Vibrator. The air compressed in the lungs during exhalation is directed through the trachea into the *larynx* or "voice box," which contains the main vibrating unit. The larynx is situated at the upper end of the trachea and is attached above and below by muscles which shift it up and down. The larynx itself consists of a group of small cartilages, the relative positions of which can be changed by a number of small muscles which are delicately intertwined.

Within the larynx, stretched between the cartilages, are the *vocal folds.* The folds are the tendonous inner or facing edges of two muscles. When sound is to be produced, they come together until there is only a tiny slit between them. The compressed air from the lungs, pushing against and between the vocal folds, causes a vibration which results in sound. The pitch of this sound — its highness or lowness on the scale — depends on the muscles which control the tension and length of the folds. While the muscles which manipulate the movement and functioning of the larynx cannot be controlled individually, you can operate the laryngeal muscles as a group to control pitch.

The Resonators. The sound produced in the larynx by the vibration of the vocal folds is thin and weak. It is resonated by a group of air chambers in the throat and head. The principal resonators of the human voice are the upper part (the *vestibule*) of the larynx, the *throat (pharynx),* the *nasal cavities,* and the *mouth.* These resonators act much as do the resonating parts of a musical instrument: they amplify the sound; and they modify its quality, making it rich and mellow or harsh or whining. Moreover, the changes in the size and shape of some of these chambers result in the different tone qualities that constitute the vowel sounds.*

The Articulatory Mechanism

The *tongue, lips, teeth, jaw,* and the *hard* and *soft palates* act — as we have noted — as modifying agents or "shapers" of speech sounds. By moving them, you

---

*By definition, vowels are resonant speech tones produced by the vibration of the vocal folds, amplified in the pharyngeal and oral resonators, and not significantly obstructed by the modifiers.

modify the size and shape of the mouth and, therefore, the quality of the tone. Another important function of these modifiers is the formation of consonant sounds—the stops, hisses, and other interruptions in the steady flow of vowel sounds that serve to make words out of what would otherwise be mere vocal tones. Precision and sharpness of articulation come from the proper use of these modifiers.

Characteristics of a Good Speaking Voice

A good speaking voice is reasonably pleasant to listen to, communicates your ideas easily and clearly, and is capable of expressing the fine shades of feeling and emotion which reveal your attitude toward yourself, your subject, and your listeners. Within a *physiological* framework, we refer to these properties as (1) *quality,* (2) *intelligibility,* and (3) *variety.* As you proceed to consider these properties or characteristics individually, bear in mind that later on in this appendix each serves also as the basis for a number of *specific exercises* and *practice materials* designed to help you develop or improve your speaking voice.

Voice Quality

The basic component of a good voice is a pleasing quality. Quality is sometimes referred to as "timbre" or "tone color." It is, as we pointed out in Chapter 15, the overall impression which the voice makes upon a listener as being harsh, mellow, nasal, thin, or resonant. Depending upon the size, shape, and state of health of the vocal mechanism, everyone has what for him or her is a best or optimum quality. This quality results when a proper balance is preserved between oral and nasal resonance, and when excessive muscular tension and breathiness are avoided. Let us review a few of the more common types of poor voice quality and consider what may be done to remedy them.

Thin, weak voices do not "carry well" because they are faint and lack body. A number of causes may combine to produce this quality: the muscles of the tongue and palate may be so inactive that inadequate use is made of the resonating cavities; the pitch level may be too high—even a falsetto—so that the lower resonances are not used (something like this happens when you tune out the lower partials on your radio or hi-fi set); or the power given to the voice by the breathing muscles may be inadequate. Of these causes, the latter two are the most common. If your voice is thin, try lowering your pitch and at the same time talk a little louder. Open your mouth wider, especially on the vowel sounds *ah, oh,* and *aw,* in order to increase the size of the oral cavity and improve its resonating effect. For practice, say *bound* as if projecting the word deep in your chest and bouncing it upon the back wall of the room.

Huskiness and *harshness* may result either from tension in the throat or from the pressure of too much air against the vocal folds. An irritated or diseased condition of the throat sometimes creates the same effect. Barring a pathological condition, the huskiness often can be lessened or eliminated by proper breathing and relaxation. Let the neck muscles become slack; then say a word like *one, bun,* or *run* very quietly, prolonging it until it becomes almost a singing tone. Work at this until the tone is clear and free of all breathiness. If you have trouble, use less breath. When the tone seems clear, gradually increase the volume until you can produce a strong tone without tension or huskiness.

Nasality, contrary to popular notion, is more often the result of too little nasal resonance, rather than too much; that is, the nasal passages are not sufficiently open. Say *button* or *mutton*. Notice what happens to your soft palate. Did you feel it tighten up just before the production of the *t* sound and then relax to allow the *n* sound to be emitted through the nose? For consonant sounds such as *t* and *p*, the palate has to close tight; but if this tension is continued during the production of vowel sounds, a flat quality is likely to result.

To correct this difficulty, begin by working on those sounds which must be produced through the nose—*m-m-m-m* and *n-n-n-n*. Hum these sounds, prolonging them until you can feel the vibration in your nose. At the same time, keeping the lips closed, drop the jaw somewhat and let the sound reverberate in the mouth cavity. When you feel a "ringing" sensation in both mouth and nose, open your lips and let the *m* become an *ah,* thus: *m-m-m-m-m-a-ah.* You should feel some vibration in the mouth and nose; continue until you do so. Once you recognize the sensation of nasal resonance, try the same exercise with other vowel sounds: *m-m-m-m-m-o-o-oh, n-n-n-n-n-ee-ee-ee,* etc.

As we have previously pointed out, changes in quality are, of course, closely related to your emotions as a speaker and your state of mind. Ideally, your voice should change to accord with and to reflect your feelings. Never attempt to vary the quality of your voice artificially, or you will almost certainly lose the direct, conversational speech pattern that ensures maximum contact with your audience. Feel deeply, and let your voice respond freely to your thoughts and feelings, with the subtle and varied shadings which will carry conviction to your listeners. Overall, in order to develop a more pleasing voice quality, learn to control your breathing and to relax your throat. Let your voice then respond naturally to the ideas and moods you wish to communicate. Using the exercises on pages 422–431, practice under the supervision of your instructor and with special concern for your own individual problems.

Intelligibility

Although a pleasing quality is basic to effective vocal delivery, it does not in itself guarantee good speech. To communicate your ideas and feelings meaningfully to others, your speech must be easily *intelligible.* As we observed in Chapter 15, the intelligibility or understandability of your voice normally depends upon five separate but related factors: (1) the overall level of loudness at which you speak; (2) the duration of sounds within the syllables you utter; (3) the distinctness with which you articulate words and syllables; (4) the standard of pronunciation you observe; and (5) the vocal stress you give to a syllable, word, or phrase.

Loudness Level. Probably the most important single factor in intelligibility is the loudness level* at which you speak as related to the *distance* between you and your listeners and the amount of *noise* that is present. When projecting your voice over extended distances, you probably make the necessary loudness-adjustments unconsciously. But often, probably, you tend to forget that a corresponding adjustment is required when the listeners are only a few feet away. You must realize also that your own voice will always sound louder to you than

---

*The term *loudness* here is used synonymously with *intensity* because the former term is clearer to most people. Technically, of course, loudness is not strictly synonymous with intensity.

to your listeners because your own ears are closer to your mouth than theirs are. These are matters the psychological implications of which were discussed in Chapter 15.

In addition to distance, the amount of *surrounding noise* with which you must compete has an effect on the required loudness level. Even in normal circumstances some noise always is present. For example, the noise level of rustling leaves in the quiet solitude of a country lane (10 decibels) is louder than a whisper six feet away. The noise in empty theaters averages 25 decibels, but with a "quiet" audience it rises to 42. In the average factory, a constant noise of about 80 decibels is characteristic. This is just about the same level as very loud speaking at a close range.

How can you determine the proper strength of voice to use in order to achieve sufficient loudness for the distance and noise conditions of a particular speech situation? While apparatus is available to measure the intensity of sounds with considerable accuracy, you probably do not have access to it and would not want to carry it around with you if you did. You can, however, always use your eyes to see if your auditors appear to be hearing you; or, even better, you can *ask* them. Get your instructor's advice on this point. Ask your friends to report on the loudness of your voice as you talk in rooms of various sizes and under varying noise conditions. Learn to gauge the volume you must use in order to be heard.

Syllable Duration. The second factor that affects intelligibility involves the "holding" or prolonging of a sound within syllables. To be well understood by your listeners depends in large part on *quantity,* or the duration of sound within a syllable; and *pause,* the silent interval between sounds. Bear in mind that both quantity and pause, in addition to being the essential components of syllable duration, are also the key components of speaking *rate,* which contributes significantly to vocal variety—a topic we will develop in detail in a later section of this appendix. At this point, we want only to emphasize that the *intelligibility* of your speech—how much of it your listeners hear—depends more on syllable duration than on the overall rate at which you speak. A slow staccato utterance, for example, is not much more intelligible than a faster staccato utterance. However, if you speak at a moderate rate while at the same time giving careful attention to appropriate duration of syllables, you can greatly enhance your chances of being understood.[1]

This does not mean that everything you say should be spoken in a slow drawl. It does mean that a rapid "machine-gun" utterance often is hard to understand and should, therefore, be avoided. When the momentum of a fast-moving narrative is more important to your purpose than exact listener comprehension of every word you say, naturally you will want to speak with more speed. But when you want to be sure your listeners understand precisely what you are saying on some important point, take time to dwell on every significant word long enough to be sure it will be heard and understood. This, of course, requires *practice*— practice in prolonging syllables without losing the rhythm and emphasis of your sentences. Be careful, though, not to overdo this manner of speaking when neither noise nor distance requires you to do so.

Distinctness of Articulation. Besides increasing the loudness of utterance and giving individual syllables greater duration, you may improve the intelligibility of your speech by exercising greater care in articulation. Good articulation, we have said, requires that you be able to manipulate with skill and energy the muscles which control the lower jaw, the tongue, and the lips. Some Oriental people move their jaws very little in speaking; in their language, so much of the meaning is conveyed by variation in pitch that scarcely any jaw movement is necessary. In English, however, failure to open the jaws adequately while speaking is a serious fault because meaning is largely conveyed by consonant sounds, and these cannot be made effectively unless the tongue is given enough room to move vigorously. Even vowel sounds are likely to be muffled if the jaws are kept immobile.

The tongue has more to do with the distinct formation of speech sounds than does any other organ. Even when the jaws are opened adequately, the sounds produced cannot be sharp if the tongue lies idle or moves sluggishly. All the vowels depend partly on the position of the tongue for their distinctive qualities. Try saying "ee, ay, ah, aw, oor" and notice how the tongue changes its position. A great many consonant sounds, such as *d, th, ch, g,* and *k,* also depend upon the active movement of the tongue.

The lips, too, are important to distinct speech. If they are allowed to become lazy, the result will be a mumbled articulation, particularly of sounds such as *p, b, m,* and *f,* which depend chiefly on lip position. Of course, when talking directly into a microphone, you should avoid violent and explosive utterance of consonant sounds. However, in ordinary speaking—and especially in public speaking—use your lips decisively to shape and to articulate the sounds.

When you speak on unfamiliar subjects requiring the use of terms—particularly technical terms—which are strange to your listeners, talk more slowly, prolong your syllables, and articulate your words more carefully. Whenever possible, try also to choose words that cannot be mistaken or misinterpreted in context. In particular, be careful about using similar-sounding words close together in statements where the meaning of the first word may influence the meaning of the second. Learn to think of words in terms of the way they *sound* because—in the final analysis—what counts is what listeners *think* they hear.

Acceptable Pronunciation. A fourth factor that contributes to the intelligibility of vocal utterance is adherence to an accepted standard of pronunciation. To pronounce a word is to produce the specific speech sounds of which it is composed, "including articulation, vowel formation, accent, and inflection, often with reference to some standard of correctness and acceptability."[2] As a guide to determining how specific speech sounds are put together in a word and are supposed to "sound," consult a good dictionary and learn its system of diacritical markings—if you haven't already done so. Standards of pronunciation differ, of course, sometimes making it difficult to know what is acceptable. For most words, a dictionary provides a helpful beginning; but dictionaries do not always agree with one another and—worse—can quickly become outdated. They should not, therefore, be followed slavishly. Moreover, most dictionaries do not take sufficient notice of *regional differences* in dialect. A native of Louisiana pronounces words differently from a person who lives in Montana, and the speech of a Chicagoan is easily distinguished from that of a Bostonian. The standard of an up-to-date dictionary, *modified to agree with the generally accepted usage in your community,* should, therefore, be the basis of your pronunciation.

A common fault of pronunciation is to misplace the accent in words—to say "genu-*ine*," "*de*-vice," "the-*ay*-ter," "pre-*fer*-able," instead of the more accepted forms, "*gen*-uine," "de-*vice*," "*the*-ater," "*pref*-erable." Other errors arise from the omission of sounds (as in the pronunciation "guh' mnt" for *government*), from the addition of sounds ("athalete" for *athlete*), and from the substitution of sounds ("git" for *get*). Furthermore, the way words are spelled is not always a safe guide to pronunciation, for English words contain many silent letters (of*t*en, i*s*land, mor*t*gage), and many words containing the same combinations of letters require different pronunciations (b*ough*, r*ough*, thr*ough*; call*ed*, shout*ed*, gasp*ed*). In addition, the formality of the occasion exerts considerable influence. Many omissions acceptable in social conversation, informal interviews, or business conferences become objectionable in formal, public address.

Overall, do not be so labored and precise as to call attention to your pronunciation rather than to your ideas, but do not take this as an excuse for careless speech. Avoid equally pronunciation that is too pedantic and that which is too provincial. Use your ears: listen to your own pronunciations and compare them with those of other people in your community or walk of life. If reactions or feedback from listeners suggest that your pronunciation of a particular word is faulty or unusual, make a note of it, look it up in two or three different dictionaries, and also check it with your instructors. Make it a practice to record in your Personal Speech Journal or a small notebook a list of the words you mispronounce, and practice their acceptable pronunciation frequently.

Vocal Stress. Fifth, and finally, the intelligibility of a word or phrase—as you may remember from Chapter 15—often depends on how it is stressed. Consider the word *content,* and note the change of meaning produced by shifting the stress from one syllable to the other. The rules of stress, however, are by no means inflexible when words are used in connected speech. Emphasis and contrast often require the shifting of stress for the sake of greater clarity of meaning. For example, notice what you do to the accent in the word *proceed* when you use it in this sentence: "I said to proceed, not to recede." Many words change considerably in sound when they are stressed; especially is this true of short words such as pronouns, articles, and prepositions. For example, if you are speaking in a casual context, you might say, "I gave 'er th' money." But if you stress the third word, or the fourth one, you will say, "I gave *her* th' money," or "I gave 'er *the* money." In short, the requirements of contrast and emphasis, as well as the conventional rules of accent, influence the placing of stress in words.

Variety

Although your speech may be easily intelligible, it may yet be dull and monotonous to listen to. Moreover, it may fail to communicate to the audience the full measure of thought and feeling you wish to transmit. This may happen if your voice is not flexible enough to express the fine shades of attitude or emotion upon which accurate and pleasing expression depend.[3]

How may you *vary* your voice so as to make it more lively or colorful and, at the same time, communicate your feelings and attitudes more precisely? How can you make important ideas stand out *vocally* from those that are less significant? Some answers to these questions can be found in a consideration of the "fundamentals" of *rate, force, pitch,* and *emphasis.*

Rate. Appropriately adapted to the subject and tone of your discourse, your speaking rate can be a strong contributor to variety. If you are an enthusiastic and reasonably poised speaker who is in command of your material and of the speaking situation, you can vary your rate of speech, using the variation to express the intensity of your convictions and the range of your feelings—an idea we discussed briefly in Chapter 15. You can tell a story, lay out facts, or summarize arguments at a lively pace; but you can also present your main ideas and more difficult concepts slowly and emphatically so that their importance may be fully grasped by listeners.

As we have previously noted, two factors determine your speaking rate—the same factors that affect syllable duration: (1) *quantity*, or the length of time used in the actual utterance of a sound within a word; and (2) *pause*, or the cessation of sound between words. If you say "ni-i-ine fo-o-o-our three-ee-ee," you are using long quantity. If you say "nine four three," you are using short quantity. Similarly, you may say "nine . . . four . . . three," using long pauses; or "nine/four/three," using short pauses. The longer the quantity or pause or both, the slower the overall rate; the shorter the quantity or pause or both, the faster the rate.

Quantity. Quantity is usually associated with the mood or sentiment expressed. If you were to say "Four score and seven years ago, our fathers brought forth on this continent a new nation . . ." with sharp staccato quantity, the result would be absurd. Such serious and dignified sentiments customarily call forth sustained tones. On the other hand, imagine the result of delivering the following play-by-play account of a basketball game in a slow drawl: "Jones passes to Schmidt . . . he's dribbling down the floor . . . back to Jones . . . back again to Schmidt . . . over to Lee . . . and it's in. Another basket for . . ." Like the pace of the game itself, such a description needs snap; short quantity provides it.

A good way to develop sensitivity to quantity values is to practice reading aloud prose or poetry selections in which a particular mood or sentiment prevails or in which there is a definite shift from one mood to another. A number of prose passages near the close of this section (see especially pages 429–431) are useful for this purpose. Notice when studying them that vowel sounds are usually longer than consonant sounds, and that some consonant and vowel sounds are longer than others. The word *roll,* for example, contains sounds that are intrinsically longer than those in *hit.* Many words suggest their meaning by the quantity or duration of the sounds they contain. Compare *flit* with *soar, skip* with *roam, dart* with *stroll.*

Pause. In addition to varying syllable duration and the rate of utterance to achieve changes in thought or mood, the skilled speaker knows how to use pauses effectively to *provide emphasis* and *punctuate thought.* Just as commas, semicolons, and periods separate written words into thought groups, so pauses of different lengths separate spoken words into meaningful units. In using pauses for such separation, of course, be sure that your pauses come *between* thought units and not in the middle of them. Moreover, when reading a speech aloud, remember that oral and written punctuation differ; not every comma calls for a pause, nor does the absence of punctuation always mean that no pause is required. In extemporaneous speaking, pauses tend to fall naturally between thought groups. Here, as in the speech that is read aloud, be careful to set off one idea from another clearly and definitely, thereby providing both oral punctuation and desired emphasis.

Many speakers are afraid to pause. Fearful that they will forget what they want to say or that silence will focus attention on them personally, they rush on with a stream of words or vaguely vocalize the pause with an "and . . . er . . . uh . . ." These random and meaningless syllables draw attention away from the ideas you wish to express, are annoying to listeners, and contribute nothing positive to vocal variety. Remember that a pause seldom seems as long to the hearer as it does to the speaker. So do not be afraid to pause whenever a break in utterance will help clarify an idea or emphasize an important point. And when you do pause, stop completely. Do not fill the gap with intrusive, meaningless vocalizations. The ability to pause *purposefully* is still another indication of your poise and self-control as a speaker.

Vocal Force. Basic to vocal force is adequate breath supply and control. As we have already noted in connection with intelligibility, as a speaker you have the responsibility to use sufficient vocal force or energy—to talk loudly enough to be heard easily. You must maintain the force needed to communicate your ideas and remarks with confidence and vigor. Talking too softly suggests that you are not sure of yourself or that you do not believe deeply in what you are saying. On the other hand, continuous shouting wears out your audience and dissipates attention. With force, as with rate, *variety* should be the rule that guides you; and, in order to ensure variety in your speaking, you must employ *differing amounts* of vocal force.

Variations in the force or energy of speech have as their primary purpose the adding of emphasis. Gaining and sustaining listener attention is a secondary— but almost equally important—objective. By increasing the loudness of a word or phrase or by pointedly reducing its loudness, you may make an idea stand out as if it had been underscored. By changing the degree of vocal force you use, you can also effectively reawaken lagging interest in your speech. Usually, a drowsy audience will sit up quickly and pay closer attention if you suddenly project an important word or phrase with sharply increased energy. Remember, however, that the effect of variety is produced not so much by the force itself as by the *change in the degree* of force you employ; a sudden reduction may be quite as effective as a sharp increase.

While you are practicing to develop variety in vocal force or energy, take care not to alter the pitch and quality of your voice. The natural tendency for most speakers is to raise their pitch when they try to increase their loudness. This happens because the nerves which control the speaking mechanism tend to diffuse their impulses to all of the muscles involved, and the resulting general tension—especially in the area of the vocal folds—is likely to produce a higher pitch, as well as more force. Sometimes this tension is so great that it simultaneously creates a harsh quality.

Practice should enable you to overcome this tendency. Just as you have learned to wiggle one finger without moving the others or to wink one eye without the other, so you can learn to apply force by contracting the breathing muscles without tightening the muscles of the throat and thus unnecessarily raising the pitch of your voice. A good way to begin is by repeating a sentence such as "That is absolutely *true!*" Hit the last word in the sentence with a greater degree of vocal energy, and—at the same time—lower your pitch. When you are able to do this, say the entire sentence louder, and LOUDER, and *LOUDER,* until you can shout it without allowing your pitch to go up, too. As you practice, sustain the tone; use a long quantity, and try to maintain a full resonance. By learning to control the force of your voice, you will do much to inject desired variety while simultaneously making your speaking more emphatic and conveying to your audience an impression of power in reserve.

Pitch. Nothing reflects the animation and vivacity of speech so much as effective pitch variation. Just as singers' voices differ, some being soprano or tenor and others contralto or bass, so do people in general vary in the normal pitch level at which they speak. Except when you are impersonating a character to embellish a story or an anecdote, it is best to speak in your normal pitch range — somewhere, probably, between one and two octaves. Otherwise, there is danger of straining your voice. Fortunately, you will find that within this normal range you have considerable latitude. So take advantage of the possibilities it affords. Avoid hitting only one pitch level and staying there.

Ideally, your *habitual pitch level* — the level at which you customarily speak — should be in the lower half of your *natural* range. In particular, be careful when you are applying increasing degrees of force not to let your voice get out of control, going to a higher and higher key until it cracks under the strain. If you feel tension, pause for a moment and lower your pitch. At times, of course, you will be excited, and your voice naturally will rise to a high key to match your emotion. Remember, however, that a somewhat restrained emotion makes a more favorable impression on listeners than does emotion which has gone completely out of control.

Steps and Slides. In connected speech, pitch is changed in two ways: by steps and by slides. Suppose, for example, that someone has made a statement with which you agree and you answer by saying, "You're exactly right!" The chances are that you will say it something like this:

Notice that a complete break in pitch level occurs between the first and second syllables of the word *exactly.* This abrupt change in pitch is what we mean by a *step.* On the word *right,* however, a more gradual pitch inflection accompanies the production of the sound. Such a continuous change of pitch within a syllable is a *slide.* Both steps and slides may go upward or downward, depending on the meaning intended. Slides also may be double, the pitch going up and then down or vice versa, as when one says:

to express the meaning, "I didn't realize that!"

In general, an upward step or slide suggests interrogation, indecision, uncertainty, doubt, or suspense, whereas a downward inflection suggests firmness, determination, certainty, finality, or confidence. Thus if you were to say, "What shall we do about it? Just this . . . ," a rising inflection in the question would create suspense; a downward inflection of the last phrase would indicate the certainty with which you were presenting your answer. A double inflection, as indicated by the example above, suggests a subtle conflict or contradiction of meaning, and is frequently used to express irony or sarcasm, or to suggest innuendo. Steps and slides are primarily useful in communicating thought content rather than expressing emotional tone or color. By mastering their use, you will be able to make your meaning clearer and more precise.

All this does not mean that when you are about to speak to another individual or a group of individuals you should say to yourself: "This sentence requires an upward inflection," or "I shall use a *step* between these two words and a *slide* on that one." Such concentration on the mechanics of utterance would destroy communicative contact with your listeners. Rather, in private and in class exercises, practice reading aloud selected passages which require extensive pitch inflection and which encourage the habit of flexibility to grow in your speaking. Then, when you speak to others, your voice will tend to respond more or less appropriately and spontaneously to the ideas and moods you wish to convey.

Intonation Patterns. In all kinds of speech the rhythm and swing of phrase and sentence weave themselves into a continuous pattern of changing pitch. As the individual's thought or mood changes, the intonation pattern changes also. The use of an unvaried intonation pattern, however, is just as deadly as staying at one pitch level all of the time. Beware, therefore, of seesawing back and forth in a singsong voice. Avoid also the tendency of many inexperienced speakers to end nearly every sentence with an upward inflection. Assertions, when inflected in this way, sound more like questions; and you may sound doubtful even though you feel certain. A downward inflection at the close of each sentence is almost as bad, for it suggests an intolerance or dogmatism to which most listeners react unfavorably. If you can develop *variety of pitch inflection,* your melody pattern normally will adjust itself to the thought and mood you intend to express. Be careful, however, not to get into a vocal rut, unconsciously using the same pattern for everything you say.

Emphasis. Obviously, all forms of vocal variety help provide emphasis. Any change in rate, force, or pitch serves to make the word, phrase, or sentence in which the change occurs stand out from what precedes or follows it. This is true regardless of the direction of the change. Whether the rate or force is increased or decreased, whether the pitch is raised or lowered, emphasis will result. And the greater the amount of change or the more suddenly it is effected, the more emphatic will the statement be. In addition, emphasis is increased by pause and contrast: a pause allows the audience to "get set" for or to think over an important idea; contrast makes the idea seem more important than it otherwise would be.

Two warnings, however, should be noted: (1) Avoid *over*-emphasis. (2) Avoid *continuous* emphasis. If you emphasize a point beyond its true value or importance, your audience will lose faith in your judgment. If you attempt to emphasize everything, nothing will stand out. Be judicious. Pick out the ideas that are really important, and give them the emphasis they deserve.

In this section we have considered principally the physiological origination and characteristics of a good speaking voice. We have recommended some means of improving the *quality* of your voice. We have suggested how—through careful management of the factors of loudness level, syllable duration, articulation, pronunciation, and stress—you can make your speech more *intelligible.* In addition, we have pointed out the importance of having a voice that is varied as well as clear, and have shown how you can achieve *vocal variety* by the judicious use of rate, force, pitch, and emphasis. Do not assume that you will be able to master in a day or a week all of the vocal skills we have described. Take time to review, to understand, and to apply to your own vocal mechanisms those principles and procedures that seem to you pertinent and potentially profitable.

The Importance of Practice

To make your voice work more effectively for you, institute a carefully thought-out program, establishing regular and persistent *practice* sessions aimed at achieving a specific vocal objective or set of objectives. Enlist your instructor's assistance and guidance. Such a program should employ at least two approaches: (1) *voice exercises* on which you work and drill chiefly on your own time outside of class, but for which you may wish to arrange occasional "progress-checks" or "accountability" sessions with your instructor; and (2) *in-class speech work* in which you use your voice to participate frequently—every day if possible—in informal group discussions, formal speechmaking, and other kinds of oral presentations and vocal activities.

In the ensuing section of this appendix, "Exercises for Voice Practice," you will find a number of vocal activities, specific drills, and practice procedures designed to assist you in improving the quality, intelligibility, and variety of your voice. Your instructor, very probably, will have additional practice and voice-improvement materials to supplement those offered here. There are also a number of excellent voice-exercise and drill books available, a few of which are listed in "Suggestions for Further Readings" on page 431.

Exercises for Voice Practice

Voice Quality

1. *To Improve Control of Breathing:*
   A. Practice expelling the air from your lungs in short, sharp gasps; place your hand on your abdomen to make sure there is a sharp inward contraction of the muscle wall synchronous with the chest contraction on each outgoing puff.
      (1) Then vocalize the puffs, saying hep!—hep!—hep! with a good deal of force.
      (2) In the same way, say "bah, bay, bee, bo, boo" with staccato accents and considerable vigor.
   B. Fill your lungs, then exhale *as slowly as possible* until the lungs are empty. Time yourself to see how long you can continue exhaling without a break. (Note that the object here is not to see how much air you can get into the lungs, but how slowly you can let it out.)
      (1) Filling your lungs each time, vocalize the outgoing breath stream first with a long, continuous hum; second, with an

oo sound; and then with other vowel sounds. Be careful not to let the sound become "breathy"; keep the tone clear.

(2) Place a lighted candle just in front of your mouth, and repeat the series outlined above. The flame should just barely flicker.

2. **To Induce Relaxation of the Throat and Jaw:**   Repeat the following sequence several times in succession:

   A.   Keeping your eyes closed and your neck and jaw muscles as relaxed as possible, raise your head easily to an upright position, and then yawn with your mouth open as wide as possible.

   B.   While your mouth is thus open, inhale deeply and exhale quietly two or three times, then intone "a-a-a-a-h" very quietly.

   C.   Say "m-m-a-a-a-h" several times slowly, each time nodding your head forward gently and without tension.

3. **To Improve the Quality of the Vocal Tone:**   Intone the following words quietly at first, then louder and louder; try to give them a ringing quality; put your fingertips on your nose and cheekbones to see if you can feel a vibration there.

one	ring	plain	tone	tong
rain	home	nine	mine	alone
lean	moan	soon	fine	moon

4. **To Improve the Clarity and Resonance of the Vocal Tone:**   Read aloud the following passages in tones as clear and resonant as you can produce. Be sure that you open your mouth wide enough and that you use only enough air to make the tones vibrate. Do not force the tone. If you notice any tension in your throat or harshness in your voice, repeat the exercises until the tension and harshness disappear.

from THE RIME OF THE ANCIENT MARINER

> Alone, alone, all, all alone,
> Alone on a wide, wide sea!
> And never a saint took pity on
> My soul in agony.

> *Samuel T. Coleridge*

from THE RAINY DAY

> The day is cold, and dark, and dreary;
> It rains, and the wind is never weary;
> The vine still clings to the mouldering wall,
> But at every gust the dead leaves fall,
> And the day is dark and dreary.

> *Henry W. Longfellow*

5. **To Further Improve Tonal Quality and Resonance:**   The selected passages which follow are intended for further practice in improving voice

quality. One of them is included because of the emotional tone it portrays, the other because of the vocal control it requires. Both, however, call for a clear, resonant quality. Study them first for their meaning; try to understand fully what the author is saying. Then absorb the feeling; allow yourself to follow the author's mood. Finally, read the passage aloud, putting as much meaning and feeling into your reading as you can.

from THE MAN WITH THE HOE[4]

> Bowed by the weight of centuries he leans
> Upon his hoe and gazes on the ground,
> The emptiness of ages in his face,
> And on his back the burden of the world.
> Who made him dead to rapture and despair,
> A thing that grieves not and that never hopes,
> Stolid and stunned, a brother to the ox?
> Who loosened and let down this brutal jaw?
> Whose was the hand that slanted back this brow?
> Whose breath blew out the light within this brain?

Edwin Markham

from APOSTROPHE TO THE OCEAN

> Roll on, thou deep and dark blue Ocean, roll!
> Ten thousand fleets sweep over thee in vain;
> Man marks the earth with ruin — his control
> Stops with the shore; — upon the watery plain
> The wrecks are all thy deed, nor doth remain
> A shadow on man's ravage, save his own,
> When for a moment, like a drop of rain,
> He sinks into thy depths with bubbling groan,
> Without a grave, unknelled, uncoffined, and unknown.

George Gordon, Lord Byron

Intelligibility

6. ***To Test the Intelligibility of Your Speech:*** Following are ten lists of sixteen words each which may be used in class to test whether your speech is intelligible to others.[5] Your scores will not be as accurate as if the test were conducted under scientifically controlled conditions, but they will provide a measure of the relative intelligibility of your speech as compared with your classmates' and will show you what happens under various conditions. Proceed with the test as follows: Read silently the list of words which is assigned to you. Stand in a corner of the classroom with your back to the class. Read the first four words aloud; then pause long enough for your classmates to write down the four words before going ahead to the next group of four words. Continue in this manner until you have read the complete list. To determine your score, count the total number of words understood correctly by all listeners. Divide this total by the number which is the

product of the number of listeners times sixteen (the number of words spoken). The result will be your percentage of intelligibility on this test.

A. Three, flap, switch, will————resume, cold, pilot, wind————chase, blue, search, flight————mine, area, cleared, left.

B. Iron, fire, task, try————up, six, seven, wait————slip, turn, read, clear————blue, this, even, is.

C. Nan, flak, timer, two————course, black, when, leave————raise, clear, tree, seven————search, strike, there, cover.

D. List, service, ten, foul————wire, last, wish, truce————power, one, ease, will————teach, hobby, trill, wind.

E. Flight, spray, blind, base————ground, fog, ceiling, flame————target, flare, gear, low————slow, course, code, scout.

F. Tall, plot, find, deep————climb, fall, each, believe————wing, strip, clean, field————when, chase, search, select.

G. Climb, switch, over, when————this, turn, gear, spray————black, flare, is, free————runway, three, off, red.

H. Thing, touch, marker, sleeve————find, top, leave, winter————skip, free, have, beach————meet, aid, send, lash.

I. Try, over, six, craft————green, victor, yellow, out————trim, X ray, ramp, up————speed, like, believe, sender.

J. Dim, trip, fire, marker————wave, green, rudder, field————climb, to, plot, middle————speed, like, straight, lower.

7. *To Develop an Adequate Degree of Loudness and Syllable Duration:* Practice saying the words in the above lists with a voice loud enough:

A. to be barely understood (score below 50%) in a quiet classroom.
B. to be perfectly understood in a quiet classroom.
C. to be understood in a quiet classroom with your listeners' ears plugged with cotton (to simulate distance).
D. to be understood above the noise of two, three, or four other students who are all reading aloud from different pages of the textbook.

8. *To Develop Skill in Varying Loudness Levels:* Prepare sentences requiring precise communication of the component words, and practice saying them with the loudness and syllable duration required for:

A. a small group in a small room.
B. a class in a fairly large lecture room.
C. an audience in your college auditorium.
D. a crowd in your football stadium.

Here are a few sample sentences to use:

"Just ten minutes from now, go in single file to room 316."
"In 1985, the population of Panama may be one and two fifths what it was in 1948."
"Hemstitching can be done by machine operation, using strong thread."
"Oranges, nuts, vegetables, and cotton are raised on the Kingston ranch."

9. *To Increase Distinctness of Articulation:* Stretch the muscles of articulation as follows:

A. Stretch the mouth in as wide a grin as possible; open the mouth as wide as possible; pucker the lips and protrude them as far as possible.
B. Stretch out the tongue as far as possible; try to touch the tip of the nose and the chin with the tongue tip; beginning at the front teeth, run the tip of the tongue back, touching the palate as far back as the tongue will go.

10. **To Improve Articulation of Consonant Sounds:** With vigorous accent on the consonant sounds, repeat "pah, tah, kah" several times. Then vary the order, emphasizing first *pah,* then *tah,* then *kah.* In the same way, practice the series "ap, at, ak" and "apa, ata, aka." Work out additional combinations of this kind, using different combinations of consonants and vowels.

11. **To Develop Vocal Precision with the Tongue:** Make a list of as many tongue twisters as you can find and practice saying them rapidly and precisely. Here are a few short examples to start on:

A. She sells seashells on the seashore.
B. National Shropshire Sheep Association.
C. "Are you copper-bottoming them, my man?" "No, I'm aluminuming 'em, mum."
D. He sawed six long, slim, sleek, slender saplings.
E. Dick twirled the stick athwart the path.
F. Rubber baby-buggy bumpers.
G. B - A, Ba; B - E, Be;
    B - I, Bi; Ba Be Bi;
    B - O, Bo; Ba Be Bi Bo;
    B - U, Bu; Ba Be Bi Bo Bu!
H. Twenty Scots in assorted tartans went to Trenton.
I. Winds were eastward for the Easter weekend.

12. **To Increase Precision of Tongue, Jaw, and Lip Action:** Read the following passages in a distinct and lively manner, moving the tongue, jaw, and lips with energy:

from THE CATARACT OF LODORE

"How does the water
Come down to Lodore?"
My little boy asked me
Thus once on a time;
And moreover he tasked me
To tell him in rhyme.

. . . .

The cataract strong
Then plunges along,
Striking and raging,
As if a war waging
Its caverns and rocks among;

Rising and leaping,
Sinking and creeping,
Swelling and sweeping,
Showering and springing,
Flying and flinging,
Writhing and ringing,
Eddying and whisking,
Spouting and frisking,
Turning and twisting,
Around and around . . .

And rushing and flushing and brushing and gushing,
And flapping and rapping and clapping and slapping,
And curling and whirling and purling and twirling,
And thumping and plumping and bumping and jumping;
And dashing and flashing and splashing and clashing;
And so never ending, but always descending,
Sounds and motion for ever and ever are blending,
All at once and all o'er, with a mighty uproar—;
And this way the Water comes down at Lodore.

Robert Southey

13. ***To Develop an Awareness of Acceptable Pronunciation:*** Make a list
of words which you may have heard pronounced in more than one way.
Look them up in a dictionary, and come to class prepared to defend your
agreement or disagreement with the pronunciation indicated there. Here
are a few words on which to start:

abdomen	data	grievous	research
acclimated	deficit	humble	roof
advertisement	drowned	idea	route
alias	forehead	indict	theater
bona fide	gauge	inquiry	thresh
creek	gesture	recess	vagary

14. ***To Develop Skill in Adapting Vocally to Audience Size and Noise Levels:***
Try to understand the significance of the following passages before you
start practicing them. Then begin by reading them as you would before a
small, quiet audience; next, as you would need to do if the audience were
large or there were considerable noise-interference. Remember, however,
that exaggerated precision, loudness, syllable duration, etc., beyond the
amount clearly required for easy intelligibility in the actual situation will
sound artificial to your listeners and is not good speech.

from THE WAR SONG OF THE SARACENS[6]

We are they who come faster than fate: we are they who ride early or late:
We storm at your ivory gate: Pale Kings of the Sunset, beware!
Not on silk nor in samet we lie, not in curtained solemnity die
Among women who chatter and cry, and children who mumble a prayer.

But we sleep by the ropes of the camp, and we rise with a shout, and we tramp
With the sun or the moon for a lamp, and the spray of the wind in our hair.

James Elroy Flecker

from THE SEA AROUND US[7]

For the sea as a whole, the alternation of day and night, the passage of the
seasons, the procession of the years, are lost in its vastness, obliterated in its
own changeless eternity. But the surface waters are different. The face of the
sea is always changing. Crossed by colors, lights, and moving shadows,
sparkling in the sun, mysterious in the twilight, its aspects and its moods vary
hour by hour. The surface waters move with the tides, stir to the breath of the
winds, and rise and fall to the endless, hurrying forms of the waves. Most of
all, they change with the advance of the seasons. Spring moves over the tem-
perate lands of our Northern Hemisphere in a tide of new life, of pushing
green shoots and unfolding buds, all its mysteries and meanings symbolized
in the northward migration of the birds, the awakening of sluggish amphibian
life as the chorus of frogs rises again from the wet lands, the different sound
of the wind which stirs the young leaves where a month ago it rattled the bare
branches. These things we associate with the land, and it is easy to suppose
that at sea there could be no such feeling of advancing spring. But the signs
are there, and seen with understanding eye, they bring the same magical
sense of awakening.

Rachel L. Carson

Variety

15. **To Develop Facility in Using Vocal Stress:**   While repeating the alphabet
    or counting from one to twenty, stress alternate letters or numbers; then
    change by stressing every third letter or number; and, finally, change back
    to stressing alternate letters or numbers.

16. **To Develop Facility in Pitch Variation:**   While repeating the alphabet or
    counting from one to twenty, begin at the lowest pitch you can comfortably
    reach, then raise the pitch steadily until you reach the highest comfortable
    pitch. Reverse the process. Shift back and forth suddenly from high to low
    to middle, etc.

17. **To Develop Flexibility in Vocal Manipulation:**   Again, while repeating the
    alphabet or counting from one to twenty, perform the following vocal exer-
    cises—trying throughout, of course, to maintain good vocal quality and
    distinctness of utterance:
    A.   Beginning very *slowly,* steadily increase the speaking rate until you
         are speaking as rapidly as possible; then, beginning *rapidly,* reverse
         the process.
    B.   Begin very softly and increase the loudness level or volume until you
         are nearly shouting; then reverse the process. Next, practice shifting
         from one extreme to the other, occasionally changing to a moderate
         degree of loudness.

C. Keeping the loudess level constant, shift from an explosive application of vocal force combined with a rapid-fire, staccato utterance to a firm, smooth-flowing utterance.

18. ***To Vary the Rate of Utterance:*** Say the following sentences in the manner indicated:
    A. "There goes the last one."
       (1) Use long quantity, expressing regret.
       (2) Use short quantity, expressing excitement.
       (3) Use moderate quantity, merely stating a fact.
    B. "The winners are John, Henry, and Bill."
       (1) Insert a long pause after *are* for suspense; then give the names rapidly.
       (2) Insert a pause before each name, as if picking it out.
       (3) Say the whole sentence rapidly in a matter-of-fact way.

19. ***To Vary the Vocal Force:*** In the manner suggested, vary the force or energy for the following sentences:
    A. "I hate you! I hate you!"
       (1) Increase the degree of force with each repetition, making the last almost a shout.
       (2) Say the second *hate* louder than the first, and the last one *sotto voce.*
       (3) Shout the first statement; then let the force diminish as if echoing the mood.
    B. "What kind of thing is this?"
       (1) Repeat the question, stressing a different word each time. Try not to raise the pitch, but to emphasize by force alone.
    C. "I have told you a hundred times, and the answer is still the same."
       (1) Make the statement a straightforward assertion, using sustained force.
       (2) Speak the sentence with a sudden explosion of force, as though you were uncontrollably angry.
       (3) Speak the sentence with deep, but controlled, emotion; apply force gradually and firmly.

20. ***To Develop Skill in Varying Vocal Pitch:*** Practice varying the pitch with which you say the sentences below, following the directions given:

    A. "I certainly feel fine today—that is, except for my sunburn. Now don't slap me on the back! Ouch! Stop it! Please!"
       (1) Begin confidently in a low key, successively raising the pitch level until the "Please" is uttered near the top of your pitch range. Repeat the material several times, trying to begin the pitch of your voice lower each time.

21. ***To Vary Pitch, Rate, and Loudness Level in Order to Communicate Meaning Clearly:*** Practice reading aloud a variety of sentences from prose and poetry that require emphasis and contrast to make the meaning clear. Vary the pitch, rate, and vocal energy in different ways until you feel you have

the best possible interpretation of the meaning. Here are a few examples with which to start your practice:

    A. "One of the most striking differences between a cat and a lie is that a cat has only nine lives." — *Mark Twain*

    B. "So, Naturalists observe, a flea
Has smaller fleas that on him prey;
And these have smaller still to bite 'em;
And so proceed ad infinitum." — *Jonathan Swift*

    C. "I have waited with patience to hear what arguments might be urged against the bill; but I have waited in vain: The truth is, there is no argument that can weigh against it." — *Lord Mansfield*

    D. "Gentlemen may cry, peace, peace! — but there is no peace. The war has actually begun! I know not what course others may take; but, as for me, give me liberty, or give me death!" — *Patrick Henry*

    E. "There is no mistake; there has been no mistake; and there shall be no mistake." — *Duke of Wellington*

    F. "Let us cultivate a true spirit of union and harmony . . . let us act under a settled conviction, and an habitual feeling, that these twenty-four States are one country. . . . Let our object be, OUR COUNTRY, OUR WHOLE COUNTRY, AND NOTHING BUT OUR COUNTRY." — *Daniel Webster*

22. ***To Increase Vocal Variety Through Heightened Feelings:*** Clip a paragraph from a newspaper story describing an exciting event, and read it with appropriate vocal variety. Or memorize a section of one of the speeches printed in this book, and present it in such a way as to make the meaning clear and the feeling behind it dynamic. As still another possibility, find an argumentative editorial or magazine article with which you strongly agree or disagree. In your own words, attack or defend the point of view presented. Do this with all of the emphasis, contrast, and vocal variety of which you are capable.

23. ***To Communicate Mood and Meaning Through Vocal Variety:*** Using the following passage, or another which you prefer, study it carefully to understand its full meaning and dominant mood. Then read it aloud so as to make its meaning entirely clear and its feeling contagious to your listeners. Practice it enough in private so that when you present it to an audience, you will not have to be consciously concerned with your voice, but can concentrate exclusively on communicating feelings and ideas.

from A LETTER TO THE CORINTHIANS (1 *Corinthians,* 13)

Though I speak with the tongues of men and of angels, and have not charity, I am become as sounding brass, or a tinkling cymbal. And though I have the gift of prophecy, and understand all mysteries, and all knowledge; and though I have all faith, so that I could remove mountains, and have not charity, I am nothing. And though I bestow all my goods to feed the poor, and though I give my body to be burned, and have not charity, it profiteth me nothing. Charity suffereth long, and is kind; charity envieth not; charity vaunteth not itself, is not puffed up, doth not behave itself unseemly, seeketh not her own, is not easily provoked, thinketh no evil; rejoiceth not in iniquity, but rejoiceth in truth; beareth all things, believeth all things, hopeth all things, endureth all things. Charity never faileth: but whether there be prophecies, they shall fail; whether there be tongues, they shall cease; whether there be knowledge, it shall vanish away. For we know in part, and we prophesy in part. But when that which is perfect is come, then that which is in part shall be done away. . . . And now abideth faith, hope, and charity, these three; but the greatest of these is charity.

Paul, the Apostle

Reference Notes

[1]From "Effects of Duration and Articulation Changes on Intelligibility, Word Reception, and Listener Preference," by Gilbert C. Tolhurst, *Journal of Speech and Hearing Disorders,* XXII, September 1957. Reprinted by permission of the American Speech and Hearing Association and Dr. Gilbert C. Tolhurst.

[2]*The Random House Dictionary of the English Language* (New York: Random House, Inc., 1966), p. 1152.

[3]See Donald Dew and Harry Hollien, "The Effect of Inflection on Vowel Intelligibility," *Speech Monographs* 35 (June 1968): 175–180; Charles F. Diehl, Richard C. White, and Paul H. Satz, "Pitch Change and Comprehension," *Speech Monographs* XXVIII (March 1961): 65–68; Stafford H. Thomas, "Effects of Monotonous Delivery on Intelligibility," *Speech Monographs* XXXVI (June 1969): 110–113.

[4]Copyright by the author.

[5]From a test used by Gayland L. Draegert in an experiment reported in *Speech Monographs* XIII: 50–53. Reprinted by permission of the Speech Communication Association.

[6]"The War Song of the Saracens," from *Collected Poems* by James Elroy Flecker. Published by Martin Secker & Warburg Limited.

[7]Rachel Carson, *The Sea Around Us,* Oxford University Press, 1961, pp. 28–29.

Suggestions for Further Reading

Joseph A. DeVito, Jill Giattino, and T. D. Schon, *Articulation and Voice: Effective Communication* (Indianapolis: The Bobbs-Merrill Co., Inc., 1975).

Donald H. Ecroyd, Murray M. Halfond, and Carol C. Towne, *Voice and Articulation: A Handbook* (Glenview, Ill.: Scott, Foresman and Company, 1966), esp. Chapters 3–7 and 9.

Jon Eisenson, *Voice and Diction: A Program for Improvement,* 3rd edition (New York: The Macmillan Company, 1977).

Hilda B. Fisher, *Improving Voice and Articulation* (Boston: Houghton Mifflin Company, 1966).

Robert G. King and Eleanor M. DiMichael, *Improving Articulation and Voice* (New York: The Macmillan Company, 1966).

Evaluating and Criticizing
the Speeches of Others

The bulk of this book has been concerned with making you a more skillful producer of oral messages. Except for some comments on listening for evaluation, in Chapter 2, however, we have not explicitly treated the problem of analyzing and evaluating the messages of others.*

Because during your lifetime you will spend more hours listening than talking, it seems appropriate to conclude this book with a look at *communication analysis and criticism.* Since it would take a whole course to treat this subject in the large, here we will review only a few of the fundamentals of criticism. The advice given, however, in conjunction with further reading in suggested sources, should suffice at least to make more effective your evaluation of the speeches you hear and read.

The Functions of Rhetorical Evaluation

After every important Presidential speech, the newspapers and television commentaries are filled with reports and reviews, brief descriptions of what the President said, an accounting for what (if that is important) he did *not* say, and general evaluations of his effectiveness: What will our allies think? Will the American people accept his program? Did he appear comfortable or ill at ease, under strain or confident? Similarly, when a labor leader at an AFL-CIO convention thunders out challenges to politicians and the American public, questions are immediately raised: Is this person really "the voice of labor"? Will he or she be supported by the rank and file? How many members of Congress will say "How high?" when this speaker says "Jump"?

In these reviews and reports of communicative events, therefore, we begin to see elemental speech criticism. From these examples, it should be clear that by "criticism" we do not mean only incredulous carping on the state of a critic's glands, although that certainly is one popular use of the term. We use the word criticism, rather, to refer to a *descriptive-evaluative process of analysis,* one which *(a)* starts from clearly defined purposes or designs, *(b)* systematically

---

*For advice on analyzing and evaluating student speeches presented in the classroom, see the *Instructor's Manual* available for this book.

describes an event from a particular point of view, and *(c)* only then makes a judgment (good/bad, beautiful/ugly, effective/ineffective, useful/useless, ethi-cal/unethical, etc.). Even casual journalistic reports of important oral messages often reveal such purposes, methodical description, and judgment. But the pro-fessional rhetorical or communication critic works somewhat more carefully, more systematically, than the journalist. It is the work or *art* of that critic with which we are concerned. Like any other critic, the rhetorical critic purposively describes and evaluates—but, normally, for comparatively specific ends. Three of the most important of these ends we will review here, namely: (1) to account for the *effects* of communication, (2) to explore the *critical dimensions* of com-munication, and (3) to evaluate the *ethics* of communication.

To Account for the Effects of Communication

Perhaps the most common end of rhetorical analysis is to account for the ef-fects of a message or speaker upon an audience. Almost anyone, with sense and a bit of energy, can *describe many of these effects.* When attempting to assess the effects of a Presidential discourse, for example, you can:
—note the amount of applause and its timing;
—read newspaper accounts and commentary on it the next day;
—check public-opinion polls, especially those assessing "how the President is doing" and those dealing with the particular subject matter of the speech;
—notice how much it is quoted and referred to weeks, months, or even years after it was delivered;
—examine votes in Congress and election results potentially affected by the speech;
—read memoirs, diaries, and books treating the event, the speech, and the speaker;
—read the President's own accounts of the discourse.*

But mere description of effects is not criticism. You can do that, after all, with-out even looking at the speech. The important phrase, therefore, is *accounting for.* Rhetorical analysts discussing the effects of a discourse take that extra step—delving into the speaking process to see if they can find out what pro-duced those effects. That is no easy task, yet it is the central one. The following are examples of where you might look in the communication process to find elements which can account for a message's reception by the audience:

1. *The Situation.* Did the situation make certain demands which the speaker had to meet? A series of events, the traditions of discourse surrounding the occasion (that is, the expectations we have about inaugurals or sermons), or even the date of the speech (it is one thing for a Presidential aspirant to make promises every four years in October, but quite another for the elected per-son to make them in January)—all can provide the critics with clues to situa-tional demands.
2. *The Speaker.* Did the speaker have the authority or credibility to affect the audience, almost regardless of what he or she said? Some speakers have such reputations or carry so much charisma that they can influence an audi-ence with the sheer power and dynamism of their words and presence. The rhetorical critic is interested in such phenomena and seeks to find specific

---

*For an example of how skilled critics search out the effects of a controversial speech of this kind, see Paul Arntson and Craig R. Smith, "The Seventh of March Address (Daniel Webster): A Mediating Influence," *Southern Speech Communication* 40 (Spring 1975): 288–301.

word-patterns and speech behaviors which account for listeners' reactions to these factors.*

3. *The Arguments.* Did the speaker's message strike responsive chords in the audience? Were the motive appeals those to which this audience was susceptible? Why? Were the beliefs, attitudes, values, and ideological orientations advanced by the speaker likely to have made impressions on this audience? Why? Were the supporting materials—and specific combinations of the various types—useful in helping an audience comprehend and accept the overall message? Why? (These "whys" usually have to be answered by assessing the temperament of the times, the dominant ideologies in the culture, and the facts of the situation, as well as the internal and external characteristics of audiences discussed in Chapter 5.)

4. *Uses of Modes of Communication.* Were the linguistic, paralinguistic, bodily, and visual codes of communication used effectively? In other words, as a critic you must look at more than the words on a printed page. Oral communication always needs to be explained as completely as possible, either from videotapes or films, or—if necessary—newspaper descriptions of the speaker and the occasion.

5. *Audience Susceptibility.* In general, why was *this* audience susceptible to *this* message delivered by *this* speaker in *this* setting at *this* time? The critic seeking to explain the effects of a speech ultimately has to answer that single, all-important question.

A solid analysis of communication effects, therefore, demands a careful integration of "who did what to whom, when, and to what effect."** It demands thoughtful assessment—the hard work of deciding which among all of the elements of the speaking process were responsible for particular aspects of audience reaction. The "whys" you must supply in this connection are especially hard to come up with, but often the critic can find support for his or her judgment in various forms of scientific research.[1]

An example to illustrate this point is in order. Two teams of rhetorical analysts—Andrew A. King and Floyd D. Anderson, and Richard D. Raum and James S. Measell—were interested in techniques presumably used by Richard Nixon, Spiro Agnew, and George Wallace to *polarize* public opinion and divide voting groups in order to win elections in the '60s. King and Anderson examined with considerable care the speeches of Nixon and Agnew between 1968 and 1970, while Raum and Measell looked at Wallace's speeches between 1964 and 1972. Neither team felt that a mere listing of argumentative and linguistic techniques was enough, for the listing did not provide them with answers to the question, "Why did these techniques work?" Both teams, therefore, read the social-psychological literature on the concept of *polarization.* King and Anderson then used this research to shed light on ways words can be used to affirm a group's identity (in this case, that of the silent majority), and on methods for isolating or negating the voting power of an opponent. The concept of polarization seemed to them to explain why those tactics supposedly created two different political power blocs or "societies" in the late '60s.

---

*For a discussion of ways to talk critically about *charisma,* see George P. Boss, "Essential Attributes of the Concept of Charisma," *Southern Speech Communication Journal* 41 (Spring 1976): 300–313.

**For a detailed discussion of the kinds of information which can be produced by "effects studies" (also called historical studies), see Bruce E. Gronbeck, "Rhetorical History and Rhetorical Criticism: A Distinction," *The Speech Teacher* 24 (November 1975): 309–320.

Raum and Measell, however, went further. They not only examined tactics and psychological dimensions of polarization, but also looked at the concept as they deemed it to occur in specific situations. George Wallace's effectiveness, they concluded, lay in the kinds of people he appealed to, in his vocabulary which charged his audiences emotionally, and in the ways in which Wallace made himself a social redeemer who could save the country from the "enemy."[2]

Here, then, the rhetorical critic and the social scientist worked hand in hand to help us better understand the world of oral persuasion. The rhetorical critic dug into real speeches in real situations delivered by real speakers, while the social scientist offered findings from laboratory studies which helped explain what happened in these real speeches.

To Explore the Critical Dimensions of Communication
So far, we have been discussing the work of rhetorical analysts who are concerned principally with accounting for the actual effects of speeches—vote shifts, changes in attitude or behavior, acknowledgment of a speaker's rhetorical expertise, etc. Not all critics, however, have those kinds of concerns. A speech, after all, is many things on many different levels; hence, it is possible to talk about a number of different *critical perspectives.* A critical perspective is, in language we already have used, a human design or purpose. It is the reason-for-being of a piece of criticism, the particular viewpoint a critic is interested in bringing to bear on a discourse. Just as *you* can be looked at in a number of different ways—as a student, as a son or daughter, as an employee, as a lover—so, too, can a speech be examined from different vantages, depending upon the observer's purposes or designs. For example, speeches have been viewed critically in the following ways:

1. *Pedagogically.* You can use the speech as a model, as a way of examining public communicators who have made judicious rhetorical choices. You can learn how to speak well, in part, by looking at and listening to other speakers.

2. *Culturally.* Or you can examine a discourse to acquire a better understanding of "the times." For example, you may look at speeches from the Revolutionary War period or from the nineteenth century to better understand *how* our ancestors thought, *how* the great American values were spread through the society, and *how* we as a nation came to be what we are.

3. *Linguistically.* Because human beings are symbol-using animals—because we are distinguished from other animals by the complexity of our symbol systems—it makes sense to be particularly interested in the *language* used in public discourses. Some critics look at oral language to better comprehend the communicative *force* of words—how some words plead, others persuade, still others threaten, etc. Some critics are concerned with *condensation symbols*—the process by which certain words (for example, "communist" in the '50s, "hippie" in the '60s, "polluter" in the '70s) acquire a broad range of ideologically positive or negative connotations. Other critics are especially interested in *metaphors*—in ways we describe experiences vicariously with words ("He's an absolute *pig*") or, in the case of *archetypal metaphors,* ways by which we can capture the essence of humanity by appealing figuratively to the great common human experiences (light and dark metaphors, birth and death metaphors, sexual metaphors, etc.). Whatever approach linguistic critics take, however, they ultimately pursue notions which illuminate what it means to communicate as a symbol-using human being.

4. *Generically.* In this decade especially, we have seen a great number of critics addressing the problem of classifying speeches into types or genres. For example, in this book we generally have classified speeches into three basic types—speeches to inform, to persuade, and to actuate—and we have done this because we think you are most interested in grouping communicative techniques by the ways in which they help you accomplish certain *purposes.* Other critics classify speeches by *situation* or *location*—for instance, the rhetoric of international conflict, the rhetoric of the used-car lot, the political-convention keynote address, etc.—in order to illumine the ways in which the location or expectations created by the occasion determine what must be said. Others argue that speeches are best categorized by *topic* because certain recurrent themes congregate around recurrent human problems. Hence, they write about the rhetoric of war and peace, the rhetoric of women's liberation, of reform or revolution, etc. Whatever approach critics employ in the process of classification, however, they all generally have a singular goal: To categorize speeches in order to find *families of discourses* which have enough in common to help us understand dominant modes of thought or modes of expression typical of an age, a problem, or a set of speakers.*

Pedagogical, cultural, linguistic, and generic critics, therefore, all examine specific aspects of discourses, features they think deserve special attention. They make this examination in order to learn what these aspects tell us about communication practice *(pedagogy),* the condition of humanity *(culture),* the potentials of language codes *(linguistics),* or the dominant species of discourse *(genres).*

To Evaluate the Ethics of Communication

In an age of governmental credibility gaps, charges of corporate irresponsibility, situational ethics, and the rise of minorities who challenge the prevailing social and ethical systems of the United States, a host of ethical questions have come to concern speech analysts: Can we still speak of the democratic ideal as *the* ethical standard for speakers in this country? What are the communicative responsibilities which attend the exercise of corporate, governmental, and personal power? For example, President Nixon's speech on November 3, 1969, in which he talked about the "silent majority," his quest for peace, and three alternatives for ending the war in Vietnam—escalation, withdrawal, or gradual de-escalation—naturally aroused considerable controversy. One critic, Forbes Hill, found no special ethical problems in the speech because the President's appeals to the majority of Americans were consistent with the country's values at that time. Another, Robert P. Newman, assuming the "democratic ideal" as his standard, decried the speech because he claimed that it violated the individual's right to know fully all that a government plans and does. A third critic, Karlyn K.

---

*Literature for these "families of discourse" abounds. For samples of cultural studies, for instance, see Ernest Wrage, "The Little World of Barry Goldwater," *Western Speech* 27 (Fall 1963): 207–215; and Theodore Balgooyen, "A Study of Conflicting Values: American Plains Indian Orators vs. the U.S. Commissioners of Indian Affairs," *Western Speech* 24 (Spring 1962): 76–83. For an example of linguistic analysis—especially as it involves condensation symbols—look at Doris Graber, *Verbal Behavior and Politics* (Urbana: University of Illinois Press, 1976), especially Chapter 7. Additional examples of families of discourse are included in the "Checklist" at the close of this appendix, pp. 444–445.

Campbell, argued that the standards initially set for evaluating the alternatives were violated later in the speech. And Philip Wander and Steven Jenkins accused the President of lying.[3] Thus, each critic assumed a particular ethical posture, and from that posture proceeded to evaluate the speech in accordance with his or her own views and biases.

The Basic Requisites for Critical Analysis

No matter what end or purpose critics seek, they face a series of common problems. To solve these problems satisfactorily and produce valid rhetorical criticism, they must recognize (1) the need for a *coherent vocabulary* with which to talk about speeches and think analytically, (2) the desirability of *careful observation,* and (3) the necessity of having a *plan for writing* the actual criticism in a form readers can follow and understand.

A Coherent Vocabulary for Rhetorical Concepts

Perhaps the most difficult task a fledgling critic faces is that of settling upon a rhetorical vocabulary. The journalist may get by with saying "First she said this, then she said that, and finally she noted . . . ," but the rhetorical critic cannot do that because he or she is engaged in a more systematic, coherent pursuit of specialized knowledge *about* communication, not merely knowledge of the event itself. While there are almost as many critical vocabularies as there are individual critics, we will isolate only three which have been employed often enough to make them fairly familiar to readers and teachers. Each of these vocabularies is also different enough from the others to illustrate the variety of potentially useful concepts.

Textbook Vocabulary. Some critics tend to use a vocabulary very much like the one built into this and other textbooks. This vocabulary, as you are well aware by now, is based on an elemental communication model, one which sees certain *speakers* sending particular *messages* to target *audiences* in some *situation.* Such a vocabulary is especially useful when (1) you want to describe the entire speech or communication process, or (2) you are seeking fact-based generalizations about communication principles.

Burkean Vocabulary. One popular alternative to textbook concepts is the critical vocabulary developed by the literary and social critic Kenneth Burke. Burke has written so profusely and creatively over a fifty-year period that he can no longer be thought of as limiting himself to one single, unified set of concepts. Nevertheless, it is possible to isolate from various portions of his writings a few key words or terms of particular utility in rhetorical criticism.[4] Basically, he has been interested in describing communicative transactions on at least three levels—the grammatical or descriptive level (which he calls "chart" or "charting"), the rhetorical or analytical level (which he terms "prayer" or "praying"), and the symbolic or poetic level (which he names "dream" or "dreaming"). That is, Burke believes critics must carefully describe *situations,* creatively analyze *strategies,* and then symbolically comment upon the *dramas* of human communication—especially the pool of symbols a culture has for guaranteeing its continuance and its ability to deal with conflict and offenders. These are the essential terms and key concepts of Burke's critical vocabulary, as laid out more specifically on page 439.

BURKE'S CRITICAL VOCABULARY

Grammatical or Descriptive Analysis ("Chart"): The Pentad

Agent—who performed an act

Agency—how it was performed (words, behaviors)

Act—what was done or said

Scene—where and for whom the act was done

Purpose—the end sought by the agent and other actors

Rhetorical Analysis ("Prayer"): Strategies

The Strategies of Ideas—scapegoating, victimage, purification, and other ritualistic procedures for uniting societies around enemies and ideals

The Strategies of Identification—methods for finding common ground on which you and I can "fit together" consubstantially

The Strategies of Form—the arousal and satisfaction of audience's expectations through the use of traditional organizational patterns (logical, progressive, etc.)

The Strategies of Language—the discovery of common symbols which evoke proper responses in audiences

The Strategies of Mimesis or Imitation—the use of bodily, paralinguistic, and visual modes which evoke desired responses in audiences

Poetic or Symbolic Analysis ("Dream"): Cultural Symbols

Metaphors—terms which embody attitudes or motives

Dialectical Terms—words which evoke visions of opposites, as "democracy" and "totalitarianism," "belief" and "faith," "good" and "evil," etc.

Myths—idealized patterns of acting together

Burke, you will note, thus calls for a *dramaturgical* approach to the study of communication. To him, we are all actors acting out certain roles or social routines because, if we do, others will act or respond appropriately through complementary roles in our divisive society. We can then achieve *consubstantiality,* or a feeling of oneness with others.

Space does not permit a longer explication of Burke's vocabulary, but even this brief look should be enough to suggest its potential usefulness. It is especially valuable for critics wanting to explore certain linguistic or symbolic dimensions of communicating, in that it urges us to recognize that individuals are inherently separated from each other and to come to grips with the idea that only through communicative transactions—ritualistic transactions—can we achieve the common identity necessary for social survival and cultural cohesion.

BITZER'S CRITICAL VOCABULARY

The Rhetorical Situation

—arising from imperfections in society and calling forth rhetorical discourse from specific speakers or writers

Exigencies—events, people, and happenings which demand that someone speak

Audience Expectations—thoughts about who should speak, what beliefs-attitudes-values should be suggested, what groups should be addressed, etc.

Constraints—rules or laws governing the process of communication in certain settings, the customs or boundaries of social propriety

Fittingness—the degree to which the speech eliminates the exigencies, meets expectations, and operates within the constraints

Bitzer's Vocabulary. Rhetorical critics, as we noted above, often want to look at the communication process as a whole, giving equal emphasis to speaker, message, situation, and audience. At other times, they find it more useful to look at discourse from the vantage of one particular element in the transaction. Such was the concern of Lloyd Bitzer when he wrote an important article about "The Rhetorical Situation."[5] In this article, Bitzer argued that very often the *situation* almost literally dictates what kinds of things must be said, to whom they must be said, and in what forms the messages must come. More specifically, he maintained that situations are marked by *exigencies* (events, peoples, or happenings which call forth discourse from someone), by *audience expectations* (thoughts of who should say what to whom, when, and where), and by *constraints* (the limits of choices speakers can make—for instance, the rules governing Congressional debate, the boundaries of social propriety, the availability or unavailability of certain audiences, etc.). If a speaker in a situation removes the exigencies, meets the expectations, and abides by the constraints, the speech will be a *fitting response.** Thus the critical emphasis is upon *the primacy of situation.*

Bitzer's approach to rhetorical analysis and the vocabulary he uses are especially useful when—as a critic—you are studying the speeches of persons who act as representative spokesmen for a particular group: heads of government, Congressional politicians, leaders of churches, labor unions, and the like. Such speakers, because they are representatives, face many pressures—more, certainly, than most of us do. They sometimes must speak when they would rather be silent (for instance, the President who must talk about an embarrassing international incident or the labor leader who must condemn governmental actions and programs when unemployment rises). The pressures upon such persons are intensified by the fact that they are not speaking for themselves as indi-

---

*For a study clearly illustrating Bitzer's method of analysis, see Allen M. Rubin and Rebecca R. Rubin, "An Examination of the Constituent Elements in Presenting an Occurring Rhetorical Situation," *Central States Journal* 26 (Summer 1975): 133–141.

viduals, but rather for groups or institutions. Hence, no matter where they stand personally, their public utterances must always be consistent with the organization's goals, reinforce its viewpoints, and voice its concerns. They may even be pressured by the forces inherent in certain occasions—by what custom dictates *must* be said in inaugurals, in Labor Day speeches, in Easter sermons, and the like. In short, when speakers are constrained by situationally imposed roles, Bitzer's approach helps us examine how these constraints affect the way such people talk publicly. To guide and help you to formulate an analysis of this kind, the essential terms and key concepts of Bitzer's critical vocabulary are provided on page 440.

These critical vocabularies—those of the textbooks, Burke, and Bitzer—are but three of the many available. The textbook vocabulary, as we have said, views the communicative transaction as a whole and, therefore, is able to "work on" a complete communicative event. The Burkean vocabulary shows what a critic with narrower concerns for particular dimensions of communication may look for. And the Bitzer vocabulary demonstrates what happens when the critic uses one element of the communication model—situation, in this case—to examine the whole process. Some of the readings cited in the "Checklist" on pages 444–445 suggest additional alternatives. Whatever the approach and vocabulary you choose, however, you should attempt to solve the problem of description by adopting some relatively coherent system of concepts.

Careful Observation

The second task you must grapple with as a critic is that of deciding *what* to look at and *how*. In part, of course, this problem is solved by your selection of a vocabulary. If, for example, you employ a textbook vocabulary, you know you will have to isolate motive appeals, look for an arrangement pattern, see if you can find out how the speaker delivered the message, etc. Yet, the vocabulary does not, as a rule, exhaust your task of looking. Often, you must expand it to include searches for information both *inside* and *outside* the speech text itself.

Outside Observation. Very often you have to look for relevant information about the speech, the speaker, the audience, and the situation *outside* the actual text of what was said. As we have already suggested, if you are interested in the effects of the speech, for example, you probably will want to check public-opinion polls, memoirs, diaries, the results of subsequent voting on the issue or issues, newspaper and magazine reactions, etc. If you are working from the textbook vocabulary, you probably will need to see what the audience knew about the speaker beforehand (prior reputation), what kind of people made up the audience present, and what kind of ratings were given to radio or television broadcasts of the speech. Or, if you are doing a cultural analysis of the speech, you will have to read whatever you can find on the cultural values and mores of the era in which the speech was delivered. You cannot, for example, do a study of Daniel Webster as a typical ceremonial orator of the 1830s or 1840s without having a solid grasp of what Americans were doing and thinking about during that so-called early national period. Webster's political generalizations, metaphors, and sweeping vision of the Republic make little sense unless you are acquainted with political-economic expansion, the settling of the Midwest and West, the growing fight between states' righters and nationalists, the problem of slavery, and other key cultural battles which characterized the period. To do

A PLAN FOR WRITING SPEECH CRITICISM

I.
INTRODUCTION

A. As a "starter" for your paper, introduce a quotation, a description of events, a statement of communication principles, or whatever will indicate your approach to the speech or your point of view about it.

B. Make *a statement of questions or propositions*—the point or points you wish to develop or establish in the paper.

C. Make a *statement of procedures*—how you propose to go about answering the questions or proving the propositions.

II.
BODY

A. After you have thus described the basic speech material or the situation with which you are dealing, take each step of your critical analysis one point at a time, looking, for example,

—at *agent/agency/act/scene/purpose* if you are using Burke's critical approach, or

—at *exigencies/audience expectations/ constraints/fittingness* if you are using Bitzer's critical techniques, making sure in this latter approach that you have carefully described the situation around which you are building your analysis.

B. As you offer the subpoints or propositions, liberally illustrate them with quotations from the speech or speeches you are analyzing— quotations which serve as evidence for your point of view or argument. Also quote from other critical observers to further support your position if you wish.

III.
CONCLUSIONS

A. In your *summary,* pull the argument of your paper together by indicating how the subpoints fit together to present a valid and interesting picture of public communication.

B. Draw *implications,* commenting briefly upon what can be learned from your analysis and this speech (or set of speeches) about communication generally. That is, you say—in effect—that this is a case study of something having larger implications.

many kinds of critical studies of speeches, therefore, you must spend time in the library—with newspapers, magazines, history books, and biographies.

Inside Observation. As a critic, you also will have to live with the speech for a while. Often, an initial reading of it produces either a "So what?" or a "What can I say?" reaction. You should read it time and again, each time subjectively projecting yourself into the situation, into the frame of mind of the speaker and the audience. You probably should even read the speech aloud (if you do not have a recording or videotape of it), trying to capture emphases, rhythms, and sounds. Part of *inside* observation, then, is a process of "getting the feel" of the speech.

The other part is discovering the key points on which it turns. Certain statements or phrases in great speeches became memorable because they were *pivotal.* They summarized or encapsulated an important idea, attitude, or sentiment. As you read over, say, Cicero's "First Oration Against Cataline," you are impressed by the initial series of eight rhetorical questions, which immediately put the Roman audience into an abusive frame of mind. You may be similarly impressed by the way Queen Elizabeth I used *I* and *we* in her speeches in order to make her dominance over Parliament eminently clear; by British Prime Minister David Lloyd George's preoccupation with light-dark archetypal metaphors, which elevate his discourse. Contemporary speeches, too—those published in *Vital Speeches of the Day,* for example—have certain elements in common: a heavy reliance upon particular forms of support, especially statistics; quotations from authorities; and explanations.

In other words, looking *inside* speeches intently forces your critical apparatus to operate. Your mind begins to catch points of dominance and memorability—aspects of discourse which *you* find noteworthy and even fascinating. When those insights are coupled with research you have done on the *outside*—in newspapers, magazines, books, etc.—you soon find that *you have something critical to say* about a particular speech or group of speeches.

A Plan for Writing Speech Criticism

Once you have something to say about a speech, you probably will feel impelled to say it in writing. How? You need a plan for your evaluation, for putting your critical essay on paper. While there really are no universal rules for performing this task, there are, nevertheless, a few useful and generally accepted procedures which you may follow. These are suggested in "A Plan for Writing Speech Criticism," which is outlined on page 442.

In sum, with a coherent vocabulary for thinking about public communication, with patient and thoughtful observation, and with a plan for reporting your reactions, you should be able to produce useful and stimulating evaluations and analyses of speeches. You should be able now to get inside rhetorical transactions systematically and to criticize more objectively and expertly the speeches of others. Ultimately, your practice in communication criticism will help you better understand the ways by which public discourse affects the beliefs, attitudes, values, and behaviors of yourself and your society.

In this short appendix, we have been able to describe only *briefly* a few critical frameworks or approaches and to allude to a limited number of actual speeches and speaking events. With the hope that you will desire to read further and also to find public speeches amenable to particular types of analyses, we are including the following "Checklist" of suggestions:

A CHECKLIST OF CRITICAL ARTICLES
AND SPEECHES FOR ANALYSIS

GENERAL READINGS ON RHETORICAL CRITICISM

Carroll C. Arnold, *Criticism of Oral Rhetoric* (Columbus, Ohio: Charles E. Merrill Publishing Company, 1974), especially Chapter 1.

Robert Cathcart, "The Nature of Criticism," *Post Communication: Criticism and Evaluation* (Indianapolis, Ind.: The Bobbs-Merrill Company, Inc., 1965).

Marie Hochmuth, "The Criticism of Rhetoric," in *History and Criticism of American Public Address,* ed. Marie Hochmuth (New York: Longman, Green and Co., 1955), Vol. III.

Lester Thonssen and A. Craig Baird, *Speech Criticism: The Development of Standards for Rhetorical Appraisal* (New York: The Ronald Press Company, 1948).

Donald E. Williams, "The Rhetorical Critic: His *Raison D'Etre,*" *Southern Speech Communication Journal* 37 (Winter 1970): 50–69.

EFFECTS ANALYSIS

Specific Readings on Effects Analysis

Donald M. Dedmon, "The Functions of Discourse in the Hawaiian Statehood Debates," *Speech Monographs* 33 (March 1966): 30–39.

J. J. McKay, "George C. Wallace: Southern Spokesman with a Northern Audience," *Central States Speech Journal* 19 (Fall 1968): 202–207.

John W. Rathbun, "The Problem of Judgment and Effect in Historical Criticism: A Proposed Solution," *Western Speech* 33 (Summer 1969): 149–159.

Forest L. Whan, "Stephen A. Douglas," in *History and Criticism of American Public Address,* ed. William Norwood Brigance (New York: Russell & Russell, 1960), Vol. II, pp. 777–827.

Sample Speeches to Study for Effects Analysis

Henry W. Grady's "The New South" speech of 1886 (use of humor to soften a doubting audience)

Billy James Hargis' "Christ Was a Reactionary" speech, 1967 (the principles of demogoguery)

Ronald Reagan's "Election Eve Address to the Nation," 1976 (principles of refutation)

CRITICAL PERSPECTIVES

Readings on Specific Critical Perspectives

Burkean: Bruce E. Gronbeck, "John Morley and the Irish Question: Chart-Prayer-Dream," *Speech Monographs* 40 (November 1973): 287–295.

Generic: Kathleen Jamieson, "Antecedent Genre as Rhetorical Constraint," *Quarterly Journal of Speech* 61 (December 1975): 406–415.

Burkean: David Ling, "A Pentadic Analysis of Senator Edward Kennedy's Address to the People of Massachusetts, July 25, 1969," *Central States Speech Journal* 21 (Summer 1970): 81–86.

Linguistic: Michael Osborn, "Archetypal Metaphor in Rhetoric: The Light-Dark Family," *Quarterly Journal of Speech* 53 (April 1967): 115–126.

Generic: B. L. Ware and Wil A. Linkugel, "They Spoke in Defense of Themselves: On the General Criticism of Apologia," *Quarterly Journal of Speech* 59 (October 1973): 273–283.

Linguistic: Richard Weaver, "Ultimate Terms in Contemporary Rhetoric," in *Language Is Sermonic,* ed. Richard L. Johannesen et al. (Baton Rouge: Louisiana State University Press, 1970).

Cultural: Gary C. Woodward, "Mystifications in the Rhetoric of Cultural Dominance and Colonial Control," *Central States Speech Journal* 26 (Winter 1975): 298–303.

Cultural: Ernest J. Wrage, "Public Address: A Study in Social and Intellectual History," *Quarterly Journal of Speech* 33 (December 1947): 451–457.

Sample Speeches to Study for Specific Critical Perspectives

For Burkean Perspectives:

Speeches presented in the Women's Rights Convention in Seneca Falls, New York, in 1848—especially the speeches of Elizabeth Cady Stanton and Lucretia Mott, addressing women's roles in society.

Richard Nixon's 1960 campaign speeches—illustrating a variety of identification strategies.

For Generic Perspectives:

Political convention speeches—for instance, Barbara Jordan's keynote address at the 1976 Democratic Convention.

Inaugural addresses of the Presidents.

Presidential declarations of war.

For Cultural Perspectives:

The United Nations' Debate over the Arab-Israeli War of 1967—to see a wide variety of culture-based arguments.

Speeches of American Indians—to note differences in speech forms and cultural values.

For Linguistic Perspectives:

Martin Luther King, Jr.'s "I Have a Dream" speech of 1963—for an analysis of metaphors.

Abraham Lincoln's "Gettysburg Address" of 1863—for an analysis of archetypal metaphors.

ETHICAL EVALUATION

Specific Readings on Aspects of Ethical Evaluation

Anthony Hillbruner, "The Moral Imperative of Criticism," *Southern Speech Communication Journal* 40 (Spring 1975): 228–247.

Edward Rogge, "Evaluating the Ethics of a Speaker in a Democracy," *Quarterly Journal of Speech* 45 (December 1959): 419–425.

Sample Speeches to Study for Ethical Evaluation

Winston Churchill's speeches on the progress of World War II, 1940–1944—for manipulation of wartime information.

Senator Joseph McCarthy's speeches attacking communists in America, 1951–1954—for strategies of innuendo.

Reference Notes

[1] On the relationships between rhetorical criticism and the social sciences, see John W. Bowers, "The Pre-Scientific Function of Rhetorical Criticism," in *Essays on Rhetorical Criticism,* ed. Thomas R. Nilsen (New York: Random House, Inc., 1968), pp. 126–145.

[2] Andrew A. King and Floyd D. Anderson, "Nixon, Agnew, and the 'Silent Majority': A Case Study in the Rhetoric of Polarization," *Western Speech* 35 (Fall 1971):243–255; Richard D. Raum and James S. Measell, "Wallace and His Ways: A Study of the Rhetorical Genre of Polarization," *Central States Speech Journal* 25 (Spring 1974): 28–35.

[3] Forbes I. Hill, "Conventional Wisdom—Traditional Form: The President's Message of November 3, 1969," *Quarterly Journal of Speech* 58 (December 1972): 373–386; Robert P. Newman, "Under the Veneer: Nixon's Vietnam Speech of November 3, 1969," *Quarterly Journal of Speech* 56 (December 1970): 432–434; Karlyn Kohrs Campbell, "Richard M. Nixon," *Critiques of Contemporary Rhetoric* (Belmont, Calif.: Wadsworth Publishing Co., 1972), pp. 50–57; and Philip Wander and Steven Jenkins, "Rhetoric, Society, and the Critical Response," *Quarterly Journal of Speech* 58 (December 1972): 373–386.

[4] The key notions from Kenneth Burke explained here are taken primarily from *A Grammar of Motives* and *A Rhetoric of Motives* (orig. pub. 1945, 1950, separately; New York: The World Publishing Company, 1962). A fuller overview can be found in Marie H. Nichols, "Kenneth Burke: Rhetorical and Critical Theory," *Rhetoric and Criticism* (Baton Rouge: Louisiana State University Press, 1963), pp. 79–92, and another is in Bernard L. Brock, "Rhetorical Criticism: A Burkean Approach," in *Methods of Rhetorical Criticism: A Twentieth-Century Perspective;* ed. Robert L. Scott and Bernard L. Brock (New York: Harper & Row, Publishers, 1972), pp. 315–326.

[5] From "The Rhetorical Situation," by Lloyd F. Bitzer, from *Philosophy and Rhetoric* I, Winter 1968, pp. 1–14.

Communicating in Small Groups

Although *public* communication has consistently been our focus in this book, as we pointed out in Chapter 1 (pages 15–16), there are a number of *other* forms of communication which play an important part in your life and in which, therefore, you should gain proficiency. One of these is *small group communication,* our principal concern in these pages.

In Chapter 20 (pages 338–350), where we discussed briefly the "panel" or small group discussion as a special type of public presentation, we noted that group discussion *as such* is the product of a *cooperative process* rather than that of a single individual. It is a product generated *by* the group *for* the group— not for an audience of listeners or observers. As we use the term here, *group discussion is the cooperative and relatively systematic process in which a small group of persons (typically three to twelve or fifteen) exchange and evaluate ideas in order to understand a subject or solve a problem.* Our objective in this section is to take a second and somewhat more analytical look at the characteristics and dynamics of this cooperative, systematic process and to explain more fully some of the specific procedures and techniques which facilitate this form of communication. We hope to *supplement* and *extend* the information introduced only briefly in Chapter 20.

Increasingly the functions of government, business, industry, and education are carried on by small groups of people meeting as committees, boards, or councils. Politicians, legislators, corporate executives, teachers, ministers, social workers, hardhats, community-action leaders—indeed, persons from all walks of life utilize small group communication to explore subjects, identify problems, and initiate constructive courses of action. As a result, the need to become a skilled communicator in the small group situation is more important today than at any earlier period in history.

From your previous experience with communicating in groups—in the classroom and in social, religious, and campus organizations—you undoubtedly have discovered that merely having a number of people talk over a matter does not always produce the desired result. Sometimes an intelligent or experienced individual can grasp a situation or solve a problem more efficiently when working alone. On the other hand, a collective judgment is often superior to an individual one: a group is more likely than an individual to take into account all aspects of a question; a group decision is more democratic than an individual decision; and, since people tend to support decisions which they have helped frame, a group decision is more likely to produce permanent and satisfying results.*

The efficiency and productivity of group communication, as of any cooperative activity, can be increased if the participants plan for the session in advance and are familiar with methods of participation and leadership. Our purpose here is to explain the principles upon which successful discussion rests.

Type of Group Communication

The two most common types of group communication are (1) *learning discussions* and (2) *decision-making discussions.*

Learning Discussions

In a learning discussion, the participants exchange information and ideas in order to increase their understanding of a subject. As a rule, this type of group communication is not very rigidly structured. A recognized expert may give a speech or lecture in order to introduce the subject, but the participants devote most of their time to an informal exchange of facts and ideas. Their purpose is to learn from one another.

A common type of learning discussion takes place in the college classroom. Another occurs when men and women in the same business or profession talk about their experiences, review recent developments, or consider publications of common interest. In addition, members of social clubs, religious organizations, and civic groups often conduct learning discussions on matters of mutual concern. Essentially, then, this type of group communication serves an information-enhancing or fact-finding function.

Decision-Making Discussions

In a decision-making discussion, the aim is to arrive at an agreement concerning a future policy or course of action. The president of an organization calls a meeting of the executive committee or board of directors so that the group may hear reports and determine policies. The business manager of a student dramatic organization gathers the group's officers to establish the budget for the next play or to work out a ticket-selling campaign. The rules committee of a women's self-government association meets to revise the regulations governing women students. In these instances and countless others, small group communication is used to make decisions and to evolve policies.

Essentials for Effective Communication in Groups

Group communication, to be productive, places certain demands upon *(a)* the group as a whole, *(b)* the individual participant or discussant, and *(c)* the leader of the group. Each of these components should bring to the discussion process

---

*On the relationship between group consensus and subsequent behavior of the discussants, as well as on the group communication process in general, see especially Warren G. Bennis et al., *Interpersonal Dynamics: Essays and Readings in Human Interaction,* rev. ed. (Homewood, Ill.: Dorsey Press, 1968); Dorwin Cartwright and Alvin Zander, eds., *Group Dynamics: Research and Theory,* 2nd ed. (New York: Harper & Row, Publishers, 1960); Robert S. Cathcart and Larry A. Samovar, eds., *Small Group Communication* (Dubuque, Iowa: Wm. C. Brown Company, Publishers, 1970); Joseph Luft, *Group Processes: An Introduction to Group Dynamics* (Palo Alto, Calif.: National Press Books, 1970).

a number of essential qualities and should assume particular responsibilities for its success.

Essentials for the Group as a Whole

The first essential for profitable group communication is *order.* This does not imply great formality; indeed, formality is often undesirable. It does imply, however, that only one person talk at a time, that members be courteous, and that they keep their remarks relevant. A second essential is *cooperation.* If one person monopolizes the discussion, it usually will get nowhere. Participants must be willing to share the speaking time and to listen to views at variance with their own. A third essential, in group decision-making particularly, is a *willingness to compromise.* There are times, of course, when compromise is not desirable; but reasonable concessions hurt no one and sometimes are the only way of reaching an agreement. Finally, the group should have a *feeling of accomplishment.* Unless the members believe they are getting somewhere, their interest and enthusiasm will soon diminish. For this reason, a commonly understood objective should be set and the field for discussion appropriately limited. Moreover, the topic should be phrased as a question and made as specific and impartial as possible. "What of our youth?" for example, is too vague and would probably result in a rambling exchange of generalities; but "Why do teen-agers often rebel against parental authority?" is more specific and would give the group a definite problem to consider.

Essentials for the Participant

In Chapter 20, we discussed briefly the qualities necessary for a participant in group communication. This seems a fitting juncture at which to review and enlarge that discussion by noting that to be genuinely effective each individual's participation should reflect to a significant degree:
1. A thorough grasp of the subject.
2. Pertinent insights into backgrounds of other members of the group.
3. An ability to think clearly, alertly, and quickly.
4. Skills in listening and paying attention.
5. An ability to devise, introduce, clarify, and support new ideas.
6. A capacity for accepting criticism of one's own ideas.
7. An ability to analyze, evaluate, and relate others' views.
8. An ability to agree with good ideas at variance with one's own.
9. Skill in tactful disagreement when indicated or required.
10. Skill in phrasing and asking questions.
11. A willingness to move continuously toward the group's major goal.
12. An ability to summarize points or group progress.
13. A willingness to share leadership responsibilities when need arises.
14. An ability to differentiate significant information and superfluous details.
15. Patience.

Essentials for the Leader

If a discussion is to prove fruitful, the leader of the group must be alert, quick-witted, and clear-thinking — able to perceive basic issues, to recognize significant ideas, to sense the direction an interchange is taking, to note common elements in diverse points of view, and to strip controversial matters of unnecessary complexity. Moreover, a good discussion leader must be capable of the *effective expression* needed to state the results of the group's analyses clearly and briefly, or to make an essential point stand out from the others.*

Another important quality of a discussion leader is *impartiality.* The leader must make sure that minority views are allowed expression and must phrase questions and comments fairly. In this way, a spirit of cooperation and conciliation will be promoted among participants who may differ from one another vigorously. Discussion groups are no different from other groups in preferring leaders who are fair. There is no place for a leader who takes sides in a personal argument or who openly favors some of the members at the expense of others. To help ensure that all may participate in a democratic, representative way — especially if the discussion is a formal, decision-making one — the leader should have a working knowledge of parliamentary procedure and the commonly employed motions. For a table of such motions, review pages 360–361.

Finally, a discussion leader should have an *encouraging or permissive attitude* toward the participants. There are times, especially at the beginning of a discussion, when people are hesitant to speak out. Provocative questions may stimulate them to participate, but even more helpful is a leader whose manner conveys confidence that the members of the group have important things to say about an important subject.

Preparing for Group Communication

General Preparation

As we pointed out in Chapter 20, preparing for group communication is, in many ways, a greater challenge than preparing for a public speech. Because the direction of the discourse is beyond your exclusive control, your preparation must be broadly based and highly flexible. How should you prepare to participate in a discussion or to lead one? As we have already suggested, two fundamental steps are required: (1) you must investigate the subject or problem to be considered, and (2) you must analyze the group which is to consider it.

Investigation of the Subject. On pages 347–348 we suggested four guidelines to help you prepare for communicating in an audience-oriented discussion. These are equally applicable in preparing to participate in a small group discussion, whether its purpose is to seek information or to solve a problem. To refresh your memory, these guidelines can be summarized as follows:

Carefully think through each facet of the subject to be discussed. First, review what you already know about it. Go over the information you have acquired and the judgments you have formed, and organize these materials in note or outline form. Approach the subject as though you were going to present two speeches, one for and one against each phase of it; you then will be familiar with more of its angles and issues.

Second, gather additional material; supplement what you know by reading

---

*We are aware of the distinction sometimes drawn between the "appointed" or "nominal" group leader and the so-called "real" or "emergent" leader — the person who, because of superior knowledge, prestige, or insight, is most influential in moving the discussion forward and determining the direction it will take. However, we still prefer the term *leader* rather than *chairperson* to describe the individual who presides, because it seems to reflect more accurately the duties he or she is expected to perform.

widely and, whenever possible, by observing conditions and consulting experts. Bring your knowledge up to date. Correlate this new information with the opinions you already hold.

Third, if the discussion has decision-making as its purpose, formulate a *tentative* point of view on the question. Decide what your position will be. Are you in favor of limiting membership in the club or of increasing its size? Is $150,000 too much to spend for a new clubhouse? Do you believe dues should be paid annually or monthly? Work out your position on the overall question for discussion and on each of the more specific questions that may arise. Also have clearly in mind the evidence and reasoning needed to support your views. But keep your thinking tentative; be willing to change your mind if additional facts disclosed during the discussion prove you wrong.

Finally, examine the effect your point of view may have on the other members of the group or on the general public. If you do this, you will be better prepared to deal with any objections which may arise. Possibly someone will oppose a solution you support on the ground that it would cause her to lose money or to retract a promise; forethought not only will prepare you for her opposition, but also may suggest another, more workable solution. If an audience will be present to hear the discussion and to participate in a question-and-answer period, or if radio and television audiences will hear you, do not forget to take into account their probable knowledge of and attitude toward the subject.

Analysis of the Group. Even though you are thoroughly familiar with the subject matter to be discussed, you will be handicapped unless you understand the nature of the group and the objectives at which it aims. Have the members come together merely to investigate, or do they have power to make decisions? What resources are at their command? Of what larger unit is the group a part? If you are a member of the student council, for example, you should understand not only the functions of the council but also its relation to the policies and traditions of your college or university. As a part of your analysis, investigate also the individuals who compose the group. In this way you will come to know that Mr. X usually exaggerates or has an ax to grind and that his comments, therefore, must be taken with a grain of salt, but that Ms. W is thoughtful and well informed, and usually makes comments that bear serious consideration. In addition, you should understand something of the social structure of the group— who the natural leaders and followers are and in what relation the members stand to one another. Answer as well as you can the following questions: What is the official position of each member? What are each individual's personal traits? What knowledge does each one have of the questions that will be raised? What attitude will each one have toward the ideas or proposals you intend to introduce?

Developing the Discussion Plan

When people are communicating in groups, there is a possibility that much time may be lost by needless repetition or by aimless wandering from point to point. A carefully developed discussion plan will guard against this danger.

Ideally, the entire group should cooperate in framing the plan the discussion is to follow; but if this is impossible, the leader must take the responsibility for formulating it. In the pages immediately following, we shall consider separate plans for learning discussions and decision-making discussions. Although the plans outlined can be used in most situations, at times modifications may be required because of peculiarities in the composition of the group or because in a decision-making discussion the problem already has received considerable attention, either by individuals or by the group in earlier meetings.

A Plan for Learning Discussions

Sometimes a learning discussion concerns a book or parts of it, or is based upon a study outline or syllabus prepared by an authority in a given field. In such cases, the discussion generally should follow the organizational pattern used in this resource. The ideas in the book or outline, however, should be related to the experience of individuals in the group; and an effort should be made to give proper emphasis to the more important facts and principles. When the group finds that previously prepared outlines are out of date or incomplete, the leader and/or the other participants should modify them so as to bring the missing information or points of view into the group's considerations.

When learning discussions are not based upon a book or outline, the leader and/or the group must formulate their own plan. The first step in this process is to *phrase the subject for discussion as a question.* Usually the question is framed before the actual discussion begins. If not, the leader and the members of the group must work it out together. Ordinarily, it is phrased as a question of fact or of value. (See page 292.) Questions of fact, such as "What are the essentials for effective discussion?" or "What is our community doing to combat the increasing crime rate?" seek an addition to or a clarification of knowledge within the group; questions of value, such as "Is civil disobedience ever justified as a form of social protest?" or "Is our Middle Eastern policy effective?" seek judgments, appraisals, or preferences. The following suggestions should help you develop a satisfactory discussion plan for both types of questions.

Introduction. The introduction consists of a statement of the discussion question by the leader, together with one or two examples showing its importance or its relation to individuals in the group.

Analysis. In this step the group explores the nature and meaning of the question and narrows the scope of the discussion to those phases which seem most important. These considerations are pertinent:

1. Into what major topical divisions may this question conveniently be divided? (See pages 165–171 for some suggestions.)
2. To which of these phases should the discussion be confined?
   a. Which phases are of the greatest interest and importance to the group?
   b. On which phases are the members of the group already so well informed that detailed discussion would be pointless?

At this point the leader summarizes for the group, listing in a logical sequence the particular aspects of the question that have been chosen for discussion. (Suggestions on pages 165–171 also apply here.)

Investigation. In the investigative phase of the discussion, the members focus on the topics they have chosen in the preceding step. Under *each topic,* they may consider the following questions:

1. What terms need definition? How should these terms be defined?

2. What factual material needs to be introduced as background for the discussion (historical, social, geographic, etc.)?
3. What personal experiences of members of the group might illuminate and clarify the discussion?
4. What basic principles or causal relationships can be inferred from consideration of this information and these experiences?
5. Upon which facts or principles is there general agreement and upon which points is information still lacking or conflicting?

Final Summary. At the close of the discussion, the leader briefly restates (1) the reasons which have been given for considering the question important and (2) the essential points which have been brought out under each of the main topics. His or her summary need not be exhaustive; its purpose is merely to review the more important points in a way that will cause them to be remembered and that will make clear their relationship to each other and to the general subject.

A Plan for Decision-Making Discussions

As we stated earlier, the principal function of a decision-making discussion is to consider a problem with the aim of reaching a consensus on what to do and how to do it. If, as in the case of an executive committee, the group meets regularly, the members may not know prior to the meeting what will be discussed. More frequently, however, the members know in advance the problem to be considered. At times, a serious difficulty or conflict of interests may be the very reason for calling the group together.

Decision-making discussions characteristically raise questions of policy. (See page 293.) Examples of such questions are "What can be done to give students a more effective voice in the affairs of our college?" and "How can our company meet the competition from foreign imports?"* As you will see in the following suggested procedure, answering such questions also requires answering subsidiary questions of fact and of value.

The steps in the ensuing plan for decision-making discussions are adapted from John Dewey's analysis of how we think when we are confronted with a problem.[1] Although presented here in some detail, this plan is only one of several possible ways of deciding upon a course of action and, therefore, is intended to be suggestive rather than prescriptive. Any plan that is developed, however, probably should follow—in general—a problem-solution order. Moreover, steps in the plan always should be stated as a series of questions.

Defining the Problem. After introductory remarks by the leader touching on the purpose of the discussion and its importance, the group should consider:

1. How can the problem for discussion be phrased as a question? (*Note:* Usually the question has been phrased before the discussion begins. If not, it should be phrased at this time.)

---

*Not all discussions of this kind deal with problems or policies over which the group has immediate control. For example, a decision-making group may discuss "Should we de-emphasize intercollegiate athletics?" or "What can the government do to ensure a stable food supply at reasonable prices?" The systematic investigation of these subjects, however, requires substantially the same steps as for matters over which the group has direct control. The only difference is that instead of asking, "What shall we *do*?" the group, in effect, asks, "What shall we *recommend* to those in authority?" or "What *would* we do if we ourselves were in positions of authority?"

2. What terms need defining?
   a. What do the terms in the question mean?
   b. What other terms or concepts should be defined?

Analyzing the Problem. This step involves evaluating the problem's scope and importance, discovering its causes, singling out the specific conditions that need correction, and setting up the basic requirements of an effective solution. The following sequence of questions is suggested for this step:

1. What evidence is there that an unsatisfactory situation exists?
   a. In what ways have members of the group been aware of the problem, how have they been affected by it, or how are they likely to be affected?
   b. What other persons or groups does the situation affect, and in what ways are they affected?
   c. Is the situation likely to improve itself, or will it become worse if nothing is done about it?
   d. Is the problem sufficiently serious to warrant discussion and action at this time? (If not, further discussion is pointless.)
2. What are the causes of this unsatisfactory situation?
   a. Are they primarily financial, political, social, or what?
   b. To what extent is the situation the result of misunderstandings or emotional conflicts between individuals or groups?
3. What specific aspects of the present situation must be corrected? What demands must be met, what desires satisfied?
   a. What evils does everyone in the group wish corrected?
   b. What additional evils does a majority in the group wish corrected?
   c. What desirable elements in the present situation must be retained?
4. In light of the answers to Questions 1, 2, and 3 above, by what criteria should any proposed plan or remedy be judged? (See page 292.)
   a. What must the plan do?
   b. What must the plan avoid?
   c. What restrictions of time, money, etc., must be considered?
5. In addition to the above criteria, what supplementary qualities of a plan are desirable, though not essential?

At this stage the leader summarizes the points agreed upon thus far. Particularly important is a clear statement of the agreements reached on Questions 4 and 5, since the requirements there set forth provide the standards against which proposed remedies are judged. Moreover, agreement regarding criteria tends to make further discussion more objective and to minimize disagreements based upon personal prejudices.

Suggesting Solutions. In this step, every possible solution is presented. The group asks:

1. What are the various ways in which the difficulty could be solved?(If the group is meeting to discuss the merits of a previously proposed plan, it asks: What are the alternatives to the proposed plan?)
   a. What is the exact nature of each proposed solution? What cost, actions, or changes does it entail or imply?
   b. How may the various solutions best be grouped for initial consideration? It is helpful to list all solutions, preferably on a chalkboard.

Evaluating the Proposed Solutions. When the discussants have presented all possible solutions which have occurred to them, they examine and compare these solutions in an attempt to agree on a mutually satisfactory plan. The following questions may be asked:

1. What elements are common to all the proposed solutions and are therefore probably desirable?
2. How do the solutions differ?
3. How do the various solutions meet the criteria set up in Questions 4 and 5 of the analysis step? (This question may be answered either by considering each plan or type of plan separately in the light of the criteria agreed upon, or by considering each criterion separately to determine which solution best satisfies it.)
4. Which solutions should be eliminated and which ones retained for further consideration?
5. Which solution or combination of solutions should finally be approved?
   a. Which objectionable features of the approved solution or solutions should be eliminated or modified?
   b. If a number of solutions are approved, how may the best features of all the approved solutions be combined in a single superior plan?

As soon as agreement is reached on these matters, the leader sums up the principal features of the accepted plan. In groups which have no authority to act, this statement normally concludes the discussion.

Deciding How to Put the Approved Solution into Operation. When a group has the power to put its solution into operation, the following additional questions are pertinent:

1. What persons or committees should be responsible for taking action?
2. When and where should the solution go into effect?
3. What official action, what appropriation of money, etc., is necessary? (*Note:* If several divergent methods of putting the solution into effect are suggested, the group may need to evaluate these methods briefly in order to decide on the most satisfactory one.)

When these matters have been determined, the leader briefly restates the action agreed upon to be sure it is clear and fully acceptable to the group.

Adapting the Decision-Making Plan to the Question

The discussion plan suggested above covers the process of decision making from an initial analysis of existing conditions to the implementing of the action chosen. This entire process, however, is not always required in a discussion. As Harrison S. Elliott points out in his book, *The Process of Group Thinking,* "A group may face a question in any one of five stages: (1) a baffling or confused situation; (2) a problem definitely defined; (3) alternatives specifically suggested; (4) a single definite proposal; (5) ways and means of carrying out a conclusion."[2] How much of the five-step decision-making process needs to be included in the discussion plan depends, then, upon the stage at which the question comes before the group. The participants can then limit their outline so as to pick up the discussion at that stage without needless backtracking and time-consuming reconsideration of points already settled. The leader should, of course, study the entire outline in order to make the necessary adaptation in the event that something presumably settled, turns out, actually, still to be in doubt or in dispute. A thorough understanding of the basic stages of the process can help you determine the most appropriate and efficient starting point.

For example, a discussion requiring only the final three steps of the process occurred some years ago in a large university. Three student organizations had made plans to produce musical comedies on the campus during the same week. Obviously, three such shows would conflict with one another, but none of the organizations wanted to give up its plan entirely. All thought that the best solution would be for the three groups to combine their efforts in a joint production; but they realized that the differences in membership requirements, financial policies, and skills required of the participants would make this difficult. Therefore, a preliminary meeting was held in which representatives of the student organizations and representatives of the faculty decided that a joint plan, to be acceptable, must provide for (1) skilled professional direction; (2) opportunity for all students, regardless of organization membership, to try out for roles or to work on the stage crew; (3) equal representation of the three student groups on the managing board; and (4) provision for an adequate financial guarantee.

A second discussion then was scheduled. In preparation for it, the chairperson obtained from members of the joint committee several definite and detailed proposals. She had typewritten copies of these proposals (with the names of the authors omitted) placed before each member at the beginning of the meeting. In opening the discussion, the chairperson restated the four general requirements listed above and secured their confirmation by the group. From this point on, the discussion focused upon the typewritten proposals. The group found that the three plans had a number of common features; they ironed out the differences; they added some details and dropped others; they found a revised plan to be acceptable and adopted it; and they made provisions to put it into operation. Thus, beginning with the suggestion and evaluation of solutions, this second discussion followed almost exactly the procedure indicated in the preceding section of this appendix. The definition and analysis steps, however, were omitted, since these matters had already been settled before the discussion began. Similar abridgments of the five-step discussion plan can often be made, depending upon the stage at which the question comes before the group.

Adapting the Discussion Plan to the Occasion

When circumstances indicate that a procedure other than those suggested here would lead to more rapid progress and more fruitful results, do not hesitate to devise a different type of discussion plan. In the beginning, however, you will be wise to follow rather closely the procedures described; later, when these procedures are firmly in mind, adaptations and modifications may be made as the need arises. Reliable guides for making the necessary adaptations are the good sense and experience of the leader and the group.

Participating in Discussion

One of the principal differences between a public speech and a discussion is that in a speech one person does all the talking, whereas in a discussion everybody contributes. During the greater part of the time, however, a participant in group communication is a listener rather than a speaker. For this reason, you should know how to evaluate the ideas advanced by others, as well as how and when to advance your own.

Evaluating the Contributions of Others

In evaluating a speaker's remarks you should pay close attention to the evidence and reasoning upon which his or her judgments rest. The same rule applies in discussion. When a participant makes a seemingly important contribution, test it by asking yourself the following questions:

1. *Is the speaker expressing an authoritative opinion?* Is this participant qualified by training and experience to speak as an expert on the topic under consideration?
2. *Is the speaker's statement based on firsthand knowledge?* Has the participant actually observed the evidence or merely reported someone else's findings?
3. *Are the speaker's sources of information reliable?* What are the origins of the information being presented? Is there sufficient explanation of where and how it was obtained?
4. *Is the speaker's opinion unprejudiced, or is it influenced by personal interest?* Does this participant have a position to uphold or an ax to grind? Does this individual stand to profit personally from some decision the group may reach?
5. *Is the speaker stating his or her views frankly?* Is this participant revealing all the known data, or concealing items that are unfavorable to his or her cause?
6. *Are the facts or opinions presented by the speaker consistent with human experience?* Do they sound plausible? Could they reasonably be true?
7. *Are the facts or opinions presented by the speaker consistent with one another?* Are they consistent with the reports made by reputable authorities?
8. *What weight will other members of the group give to the speaker's opinion?* Is this participant's prestige so great that the group will agree with her in the face of conflicting evidence? Is he so little respected that he will not be believed unless someone else supports his opinion?

If, while comments are being offered, you ask questions of this kind, you can evaluate the discussants' ideas more easily and accurately. In addition, you will be better able to estimate the group's reaction to contributions you may make.*

Making Contributions

Although you cannot be a good discussant unless you are a good listener, neither can you be a good discussant if you fail to advance constructive ideas, useful information, and sound judgments. As we pointed out earlier, the best listeners in the world, if they *only* listen, contribute little toward understanding or solving the problem confronting the group. When and how, therefore, should you enter into the discussion? How should your contributions be phrased and presented?

There is no simple answer to the question "When should I talk and when should I keep quiet?" Usually, you should speak out when you are asked a direct question, when you have a worthwhile idea to offer, or when you can correct or clarify the remark of another person. More important than any specific

---

*For a fuller discussion of the principles of good listening as they apply in all types of speech situations, review Chapter 2, pp. 21–35.

rules or cautions, however, is the general reminder that discussion is *a coopera-tive process.* You should neither monopolize the conversation nor consistently remain silent. Speak when you believe you can be of definite help to the group, but also give the other discussants a full and fair opportunity to express their views. Usually, the most interesting and profitable discussions are those in which all members of the group participate more or less equally.

When you speak, then, keep in mind the cooperative nature of the discussion process. Advance your ideas tentatively and present the evidence and reasoning upon which they rest. Speak to the point, indicating clearly that you understand the particular issue under consideration. Show by your manner as well as your words that you are more interested in helping the group attain its objective than in impressing your ideas on the others; try to accept criticism and treat dis-agreement objectively; be tactful and courteous; keep your voice and manner calm. Holding fast to these guidelines in the heat of an animated discussion may not always be easy, but at least try to develop the habit of participating with these suggestions in mind.

Leading the Discussion

A discussion leader, in addition to having all the skills and attributes of a good participant, should have other abilities as well. One who would lead a group toward a productive speech transaction of this kind should know how to get discussion started and keep it stimulated, how to prevent it from wandering, how to bring out the essential and pertinent facts, how to draw out silent mem-bers and keep overtalkative ones in check, how to resolve conflicts, and how to summarize and interpret group progress. No wonder good discussion leaders are rare.*

Starting the Discussion and Evoking Response

To get the discussion started, the leader may follow the suggestion made ear-lier — briefly stating the question to be discussed and stressing its importance, especially as it relates to the participants. These introductory remarks should be made with vigor and earnestness, suggesting the vital nature of the subject. They should be expressed in concrete terms supported by specific instances, but they should not be so long that they seem to exhaust the subject. Moreover, they should lead into a series of provocative questions designed to draw mem-bers of the group into the discussion. If such questions fail to produce a re-sponse, the leader may call on certain individuals by name, asking them to relate their experiences or to express their opinions. Or the group leader may go to the chalkboard and start a list. Such a list could include various aspects of the sub-ject or causes of the problem, terms needing definition, proposed courses of action — anything which calls for enumeration or classification. People who hesitate to begin a discussion are often ready to add to a list.

Still another method of evoking response is to start by bringing out one or more extreme points of view on the question. The leader can state these views, or — better — can call on members of the group who hold them. Nothing spurs

---

*The problems of group leadership are discussed in detail in Michael Burgoon, Judee K. Heston, and James McCroskey, *Small Group Communication: A Functional Approach* (New York: Holt, Rinehart & Winston, Inc., 1974), Chapter 10, "Leadership in the Small Group," pp. 143–156.

participants into active discussion so quickly as a statement with which they disagree. The danger of this method is, of course, that it may provoke a verbal battle which consumes too much time or stirs up personal animosity. Usually, the problem which brought the group together is sufficiently provocative to start the exchange; but if the discussion lags at the beginning or hits a "dead spot" later, the foregoing methods may be helpful in energizing or renewing it.

Directing the Discussion

The tendency of a group to stray from central issues can be greatly diminished if the leader outlines on a chalkboard the points that require consideration. When people see what needs to be taken up and in what order, they are likely to focus their attention on these matters. Unless a participant suggests that an important item has been omitted from the outline and asks that it be included, the leader can direct attention to the prearranged points, one after another, and thus keep the discussion progressing steadily. Using the outline on the chalkboard as a skeletal plan, many leaders like to fill in the details as they are introduced, thus providing the group with a visual record of its progress. If, in spite of this planning, the discussion takes an irrelevant turn—if a participant reverts to something already decided, jumps ahead to a point not yet in order, or introduces a seemingly extraneous idea—the leader usually needs only to draw attention to the matter currently before the group. Of course, common sense and fairness must be the constant guides for this kind of leadership. Sometimes the discussion strays because the fault is in the outline, and the participant who moves away from it may be making an important contribution.

Bringing Out the Facts

If the leader follows the preceding suggestions, the information needed to solve the problem or cover the subject usually will be brought out. If the participants are fair-minded and well informed and if the discussion plan includes all the necessary steps, no special effort beyond that already indicated will be required. Unfortunately, discussions do not always proceed perfectly, and the leader sometimes must make sure that important facts are not ignored and that opinions are not mistaken for factual evidence.

When something important apparently has been overlooked, the person directing the discussion may tactfully inquire, "Has anyone noticed that . . .?" and proceed to add the missing fact. Or the leader may say, "Mr. Smith called my attention yesterday to the fact that . . . . Has anyone else noticed this to be true?" It is generally better, however, to ask a participant a specific question designed to bring out the needed information. Similarly, if there is a tendency to dwell on one point of view to the exclusion of an equally important one, the leader may call attention to the oversight by suggesting, "Perhaps we should ask Paul to express his ideas on this" or "I have heard this other point of view expressed, too . . . . What do you think of it, Barbara?"

Although a discussion leader should never directly accuse another member of the group of twisting facts or making unsupported statements, false declarations or doubtful assertions by a participant should not be allowed to pass unchallenged. Ideally, other members of the group should inquire into a speaker's data and claims; but if no one else does, the leader may handle the matter tactfully by asking for further details or for the evidence on which the statement is based. For example, the individual who is directing the discussion may say, "I wonder if you would tell us, Mike, what has led you to this conclusion?" or "Is that a statement of your own opinion, Mary, or have you observed it to be true in practice?" By skillful questioning, a good discussion leader can direct attention to all aspects of a question, see that the important facts are carefully considered, and put the group on guard against unsupported assertions. Whenever possible, however, the person charged with the group leadership should draw the necessary facts and ideas from the other participants, and should never dominate the discussion unduly.

Ensuring Equal Participation

At times, one or two persons in the group may begin to monopolize the conversation. Not infrequently such individuals have a great deal to contribute, but there is also a very strong possibility that they will repeat themselves or expand obvious points needlessly. When this occurs, the leader may avoid recognizing a talkative participant by not looking directly at him or her. Or the leader may call upon other individuals, by name if necessary, asking them questions which will move the discussion forward and away from the overworked point or the overtalkative person. In extreme cases, the leader may find it necessary to suggest in a tactful manner that if the discussion is to be profitable, all members must have an opportunity to participate; or the group or its leader may even have to invoke a limit on the number of times any one discussant can speak. If the time for the close of the discussion is drawing near, sometimes a statement of that fact will spur into action members who hitherto have remained silent. Remember that while the leader does not have the right to tell the group what to think, he or she does have the obligation to maintain an atmosphere in which all members can think most productively; and such an atmosphere will not be possible unless all feel that they have an equal chance to participate.

In larger and more formal situations, as we noted earlier, the leader will find it particularly advantageous to have a practicing knowledge of "Parliamentary Procedure for Handling Motions." These motions, as summarized in the chart on pages 360–361, can do much to imbue the proceedings with a general sense of fairness and stability.

Resolving Conflict

One of the most difficult tasks of the leader in group decision-making is resolving conflict. Although discussion is a cooperative process, progress toward the understanding or solution of a problem can seldom be made unless alternative ideas are examined. If everyone immediately agreed with each new opinion as soon as it was advanced, there would be no point in arranging to discuss the matter. On the other hand, irrational or heated conflict, with the undesirable attitudes it engenders, stifles discussion and renders reflective choices and sound judgments difficult.

Because rational disagreement is essential, but emotional or personalized contention is harmful, the leader must walk a middle path. When there is danger that the conflict is becoming destructive, someone must take steps to curb it. In particular, the leader must be able to distinguish between disagreement based on honest differences in interpretation of facts and contentiousness based on irrational desires and prejudices. When the conflict centers in the interpretation of facts, the difference may be resolved by a careful retracing of the reasoning upon which the competing interpretations rest. When the conflict becomes irrational, especially if the interchange becomes overheated, the leader should urge participants to introduce only the facts and reasoning upon which a rational decision may be based. At times, the person directing the discussion may suggest that the group delay consideration of the disputed point until other, less controversial matters have been settled; or, when the circumstances seem to justify such action, the leader may even urge that the group adjourn and resume the discussion at a later date when all participants have had a chance to cool off.

Advice about the handling of conflict necessarily must be general and incomplete. It is impossible to foresee and provide against all of the situations in which destructive dispute may arise. Chiefly through experience, the leader increasingly learns how to deal with certain kinds of cases; through imagination and resourcefulness, he or she invents conflict-resolving techniques as the need arises. But always, the leader must be alert to the possibility of harmful contention, watchful for its emergence, and ready to curb it before it gets out of hand.

Summarizing Progress Periodically

Throughout, the leader should note the points upon which most members of the group agree and should restate these points in brief summaries at appropriate times during the course of the discussion. This directs attention to matters not yet covered or which remain to be settled. These ongoing summaries also instill a sense of accomplishment and motivate the group to proceed toward a conclusion.

In addition to making internal summaries, at the close of the discussion the leader should make a final summary, reviewing the ground covered and—in a decision-making discussion—emphasizing the points of agreement without overlooking any important minority view. If some matters remain unsettled, these should be noted, especially if there is to be a later meeting. The tone of this final summary should be objective, but should give full weight to the progress or accomplishments of the group.

A Sample Small Group Discussion

The discussion which follows embodies the principles of group communication examined in Chapter 20 with reference to public group presentations and in this section of the appendix with reference to learning groups or problem-solving groups. Actually, this discussion is both a problem-solving transaction and a public panel discussion. It is a problem-solving transaction because it is the product of a cooperative rather than an individual process; it is a public panel discussion because it was prepared with an audience in mind.

It was conducted as part of an annual contest in which colleges and universities across the country submitted twenty-five-minute audiotapes of undergraduate students participating in a consideration of a previously announced question. Judges listened to and evaluated these tapescripts in terms of the following criteria: (1) solid content and perceptive analysis of the question, (2) use of public panel-discussion techniques, and (3) interest-value to a reasonably intelligent adult audience. The panelists in this discussion, students at Kent State University, coached by Dr. Linda Irwin Moore and under the general direction of Dr. Carl M. Moore, were declared the winners of the 1974 competition held in conjunction with the Central States Speech Association Convention in Milwaukee, on April 5, 1974.

If you read the tapescript carefully, you will discover a well-ordered, exploration-and-solution process. The participants adequately oriented their unseen audience to the problem, narrowed the subject in accordance with the prescribed time limits, then approached it systematically, and completed each stage of the problem-solving process before moving on to the next (after the manner suggested on pages 453–455). You will notice that each of the panelists had carried out extensive research on the topic and was prepared to substantiate each point with statistics, examples, details, and the other forms of support. Note particularly the attention paid to definitions, to typical examples, and to generalizations; examine the blending of illustrative, statistical, and testimonial evidence. Note also how the leader/moderator opens the discussion, calls for each stage, summarizes agreed-upon conclusions, and pushes the group more deeply into the problem when she thinks they need more proof for positions taken. Observe, too, how the panelists interact, calling each other by name, controlling carefully their disagreements (to keep the group from drifting off into useless bickering), and supporting each other when desirable.

As you read through this discussion, bear in mind two things: (1) The panelists had to keep within a strict time limit; and, therefore, some stages—particularly the evaluation and summary—had to be treated briefly. (2) This transcription attempts to reproduce the audiotape faithfully; only vocalized pauses, a few "false starts," and the like have been cut. What you are encountering here is "oral," not "written," grammar and syntax at work; do not expect "proper" sentences or polished expression.

How Can the Government Best Protect the American Consumer?[3]

Panelists: Judy Andino *(moderator)*
Gary Pandora
Karen Brown
Jerry Pursley

INTRODUCTION AND BACKGROUND

Judy: "Consumption is the sole end and purpose of all production. And the interest of the producer ought to be attended to so far as it may be necessary for promoting that of the consumer. The maxim is so perfectly self-evident that it would be absurd to attempt to prove it. But in the mercantile system the interest of the consumer is almost constantly sacrificed to that of the producer." Adam Smith noted this paradox of ethics in his book, *The Wealth of Nations;* and it is this issue—consumer protection—that we will consider today in answering the question, "How can the government best protect the American consumer?" I'm Judy Andino, a senior, and I will act as moderator this evening. Joining in the discussion are these panel members: Gary Pandora, a junior; Karen Brown, a senior; and Jerry Pursley, a senior. /1

In considering the topic-question, this panel has agreed on some definitions of terms. "Consumer" is defined as any person who buys and uses food, clothing, and other services. "Government" is defined as "the federal government." Because of the limited time span provided to treat the stated topic-question, we have imposed a limit on the aspect of governmental consumer protection we shall be discussing this evening. Coupled with the time limitation involved, however, is our concern for emphasis on a universal consumptive product, and thus we chose *food.* But, then, perhaps our audience would be interested in hearing our specific rationale for selecting food. /2

Jerry: One of the reasons for choosing the food industry is because it is the single largest industry in the United States; it's a $125 billion-a-year industry, and that makes it over six times as large as General Motors, America's largest industrial corporation. /3

Karen: I think, in addition, Jerry, that there is something that Judy hinted at, and that's the idea that food is such a basic commodity. Regardless of what else the consumer may or may not have, he has to have food. /4

STAGE ONE:

DEFINING THE PROBLEM

Judy: Well, food is definitely important to the average American consumer, but that leaves me with the question, "What are the problems with food?" /5

Jerry: Well, we saw basically three problems with food—that of food *prices,* food *shortages,* and food *quality.* And we came here tonight prepared to discuss all three of those. But due to limitations of time, I suggest that we limit our analysis to that of *food quality.* /6

Gary: I would agree, Jerry. I believe that the quantity of food and food prices are certainly of vital importance to the consumer; but, essentially based on that, we're talking about the quality of food. And, if we haven't got good quality of food, then we're going to be in a lot of trouble. /7

Karen: I think we can all agree, then, that because of the time and the importance of food quality, we may as well just limit ourselves to that. /8

Judy: All right, then, if we are going to do that—to limit ourselves to quality alone—what do we mean by the term "quality," and what problems does the American consumer meet in food quality? /9

Gary: It's very difficult to give a specific definition of quality food or nutritional food. Generally, what is accepted is the recommended daily allowance, or the RDA. Now, this was established by the Food Nutrition Board of the National Research Council and the National Academy of Sciences. And the problem with the RDA is that, first of all, many nutritionists around the country say that it is too low; standards are not sufficient for what people need. And, second, the RDA is based on healthy people—healthy people being those who currently meet the standards of this low RDA. The problem, again, is that many people in this country do not meet even those low standards. /10

Jerry: What you're saying, Gary, is pointed up in two surveys conducted by the Department of Agriculture, one in 1955, and the other in 1965. The Department of Agriculture found in their surveys that half of the people surveyed in 1955 had appallingly inadequate diets; and then in 1965, just ten years later, they found that had increased to two-thirds of those surveyed. And those people were deficient in protein, calcium, vitamins A and C, and all the other nutrients considered, except iron. I think it's important to point out that in the survey, they didn't survey the poor people, the people from the ghetto. This was a survey conducted in *urban* America, in the small urban areas and in rural areas. /11

Karen: Well, it seems to me, Jerry—and Gary, too—what both of you are getting at is that we have a problem as far as nutrients go in our specific diets, but that there are so many people involved that I don't think that we could ever hope to examine all their diets, or regulate their diets, or whatever. So maybe we ought to take a look instead at the quality of food that is available to the American consumer—food that he can choose to put into his diet if he wants to. /12

STAGE TWO

ANALYZING THE PROBLEM

Judy: If you are suggesting, then, that there is a declining value in food that comes to the consumer, I'd like to have some evidence. I'd like to know what are some specific examples. /13

Jerry: Well, I'd like to point out that the trend that I mentioned was noted by the Department of Agriculture, and has been verified by the American Medical Association and the National Academy of Science. They have gone on record to indicate their concern about the diminished nutritive content of American foodstuffs, and they point out that problems in current methods used in food production, processing, storage, and the distribution of American foods are some of the primary problems in this area. /14

Karen: I think it's really interesting, Jerry, that they mention processing and refinement as a problem with food, because there are a couple of examples I noticed when we were doing our research. And one of them deals with a very basic food commodity, and that's *bread.* During the processing of bread—the refinement or roller milling or whatever term you want to use—bread loses about 98% of its manganese value, about 80% of its iron value, about 80% of thiamine nutrients that are available to it, and about 75% of the niacin. The list goes on down through the rest of the nutrients that could be gotten by the consumer through bread. /15

Jerry: Well, I hate to sound discouraging, but I wonder how many of you had your breakfast this morning? When you had your breakfast, how many of you had breakfast cereals? /16

Karen: I did. /17

Judy: Me, too. /18

Jerry: Well, I have some sad news for you, then. /19

All: Oh? /20

Jerry: A Georgia University study revealed that cereal *boxes,* if taken with milk and raisins, are as nutritious as all but the most sophisticated cereals. So probably you would have been better off eating the boxes. /21

Karen: Oh? /22

Jerry: Yet, the Food and Drug Administration has avoided the development of a standard on the cereals simply for that reason. They don't want to give breakfast cereals the respectability of being called a food. /23

Karen: Jerry, when I pulled out my cereal this morning, my Rice Krispies, on the box there is a label on the side that lists the kinds of vitamins and nutrients that are in that specific cereal. Is that label false? /24

Jerry: The listing on the cereal boxes is accurate, but it's accurate when the cereal is eaten *with milk and sugar.* /25

Gary: Jerry, I might take issue with that because refined white sugar retains not one milligram of vitamins or minerals. I think in discussing refined flour or cereals or breads, it has been illustrated historically on at least two occasions that unrefined breads or cereals actually improved health. These occurred in World War I and in World War II. During that period in England and in Denmark, both of those countries did not refine their cereals or their breadstuffs. As a result, health improved. Also, I might add that when we talk of breadstuffs, this can be expanded to cereals as well as macaronies, spaghetti, noodles, crackers, cookies, pastries, cakes, cake mixes, on and on and on. /26

Judy: Everyone has some of those. /27

Karen: I think there's something else that everyone has some of. These all have been dealing with grains and things. But we mentioned before—Jerry did at the outset—about refining and processing having an effect on the nutritive value of food. On this we can look at one other processing agent, and that's *canning.* And that again, like Gary said, encompasses an awful lot of separate commodities. In those commodities there's the same kind of nutritive change that occurs in everything else we've been giving examples of. For example, in the processing of canned carrots, they lose about 65% of their potassium content; green beans lose about 60% of their potassium content; and tomatoes lose about 51%. And that same kind of list goes on through the rest of the vegetables and the rest of the vitamins. But I think that we ought to make one more thing clear in relation to this. In the book *Consumer, Beware* (1971), by Beatrice Hunter, she makes the statement that not only do these nutritive values come out during the canning process, but there are also chemical changes that may actually be harmful to the consumer. For example, in the canning of carrots, their sodium content is increased 45,000%; and that creates a vast danger to the consumer healthwise, in relation to hardening of the arteries and various other heart diseases. /28

Judy: OK. You seem to have labeled some of the potential dangers in the refining process, but this leaves me in an awful bind, an awful quandary. As an average American consumer, I think the refining process and the methods used in supplying food to the consumer are fantastic. I get the kind of foods that I want. Are we indicting the entire process as being a hazard to the American consumer? /29

Jerry: Not at all, Judy. I think we have to understand that in a country this size, with the population we have, that food has to be refined to a certain degree. It has to be processed. It's a practical matter. In order to get food to that many people, certain refinements are necessary. But what we want to point out is that there should at least be an awareness by the consumer that there is a nutritive loss in certain types of refinement, in processing—that the consumer should be aware of this nutritive loss. /30.

Judy: Then that would be the crux of the matter—the lack of knowledge? /31

Jerry: Right. /32

Judy: All right. This I could conceive as definitely a problem. You've shown me with specific evidence of such basic foodstuffs as bread and breakfast cereals and sugar, and even canned foods, that the consumer does have a very definite lack of knowledge about the refining process and what he is getting from it. But what about some real *harm?* Is there any real harm incurred through food quality? /33

Gary: I think that one of the important considerations as far as food quality is concerned is the *additives* that are put into food. There are many, many additives that go into our food—some for cosmetic purposes and others to add to the nutritional value and to help retard spoilage and such. In fact, we have over 2500 additives added to our food. And of those, less than half have been tested by the FDA. /34

Jerry: I think it's important to realize that according to Marine and Von Allen, in *Food Pollution and Violation of Our Inner Ecology,* the average American annually eats three pounds of these food additives, many of which cause genetic mutations, give us cancer, or simply make us sick. And so there are real problems with these additives in food. /35

Karen: Well, I think if we're going to indict additives, up to now we've been talking kind of generally as to how many there are and what they may or may not do. I think it's important that we take a look at some of the ones that may actually be coming to the consumer—that he may be ingesting into his system. And I think a good example is FD & C Citrus Red #2. It was reported in *Consumer Reports,* May of 1973. This particular additive is used as a coloring in the skin of oranges, the skin of potatoes to make them appear fresher, and in all candied yams to make them appear fresher. And this particular drug, through feeding tests, showed growth retardation and cancerous bladder changes in male rats and degenerative changes in female rats. And, ironically enough, it has been banned by the World Health Organization and by the Canadian Government. And yet, in the United States it's still used, and the FDA has made no attempt to warn the American public of just what the dangers may be.* /36

---

*Since this discussion was held, the FDA has, in fact, prohibited the use of a large number of these additives and artifical colorings.

Gary: Karen, unfortunately, that is not the only example we can cite. One example I found was monosodium glutamate. In May, 1969, a test by Washington University revealed that MSG or monosodium glutamate had caused brain damage in two- to ten-day-old mice. Now, this was revealed to the FDA in May of 1969, but it was over five months before they took it out of baby foods. /37

Judy: But this is specifically the FDA's jurisdiction, their problem. Ah—I mean, don't they *test*? Don't they *inform* the consumer? /38

Jerry: Judy, unfortunately, most of the time they don't test. Most of the time they have to rely on the information provided by the industry in evaluating its own product. They don't have the resources, unfortunately; and, as a result, the American consumer is consuming additives that have some question as to their safety. /39

Karen: I think, Jerry, not only are there questions about a lot of this, but the Food and Drug Administration is, in many cases, not even raising those particular questions. There is what they call a provisional list, and additives will be allowed to be put into food for consumption by the American consumer while they're being tested or until tests occur. One particular additive, FD Red #2—it's not the same one I mentioned before; it's a different title—was kept on the market for ten years, even though other countries had banned it, because the FDA had not begun to run its tests yet. /40

Jerry: I found there are a lot of people really concerned about this. One that I found specifically is Dr. James Crow, in *Medical World News* of 1968. He stated that potentially irrevocable genetic damage might be done without immediate warning by some of the more than 10,000 natural and synthetic chemical agents now produced commercially, or by the million or more additional agents that may have been isolated or synthesized by man. Fewer than 200 of these suspected mutagens have been systematically assayed. And according to Victor Cohen, in the *Washington Post,* we may already be experiencing some of the effects of these potential mutagens in the increased rate in birth defects in this country. /41

Gary: I think it's important that we realize in discussing additives that perhaps there are individual additives that are harmful, There may, of course, also be additives that are not harmful. But we have to realize that we really don't know what a *combination* of these individual additives can produce. And there's another danger right there. /42

Jerry: Yeah, I agree with that, Gary. The problem I think that we have is with the FDA, and a lot of times not only with the provisional list and with the additives that they've okayed for use in this country, but *enforcement* is a real problem. Unfortunately, the FDA has to depend on voluntary compliance by industry. And, in the MSG case, for example, it took them five months to get it off the market after there was a lot of static about it. Dan Gerber, of Gerber Baby Foods, stated to his shareholders that the testing, in his opinion, by the FDA—or by Washington University, I'm sorry—was incomplete, and he felt that MSG should be left on the market until it was proven dangerous. Thus, he wanted to reverse the law; and instead of proving something safe before it was put on the market, he wanted to make sure it was proven dangerous before it could be taken off. /43

Judy: You're speaking of "safe" and "dangerous." What I've gleaned so far is that there are basically two types of additives. There are those that enhance the nutritional value and preserve the product, and these benefit the consumer. Then, there are those cosmetic additives, it seems to me, those that are for the producer's benefit. /44

Jerry: That's correct, Judy. /45

Judy: Which one does the consumer get more of? /46

Jerry: Definitely the additives that are for cosmetic purposes; about 80% of them are for cosmetic purposes. For example, according to Marine and Von Allen, in the book *Food Pollution,* they noted that the Food Protection Committee lists 1622 additives currently in use. Of those, 1077 were used for flavoring; and as far as bulk is concerned, the vast majority of the additives we consume are for nothing but coloring. /47

Judy: But doesn't the FDA provide information on this? Don't they obey the Labeling Act? /48

Jerry: Well, no, they don't. Again they have to rely on, or at least they have been relying on, voluntary compliance. The Nader group, when they studied the FDA, found that in 1969 alone the FDA recommended 5052 label changes, but not one was adopted. /49

Karen: I would like to add just one more thing to that, Jerry, that would help to answer Judy's question; and that's the idea that the Fair Packaging and Labeling Act, which so many think protects us, doesn't really do that because there's no portion of that act which requires manufacturers to list how many or what type of additives are in a particular food product. In fact, often the FDA treats those additives as manufacturers' trade secrets. /50

Gary: Jerry, you mentioned these so-called cosmetic additives or additives added simply to increase or enhance the appeal of food or taste of it. I think a very common example of this is brown dye, called caramel coloring. This is added to enriched white, refined bread; and when this caramel coloring is added, it gives it the appearance of being whole-grain bread, 100% whole wheat bread, when in fact it is the regular white enriched bread just colored brown. /51

Judy: OK, then, with all of this in mind, again the underlying problem seems to be a lack of consumer knowledge. /52

Karen, Jerry, Gary: Yes. /53

Judy: Then, to me, obviously the food-quality problem manifests itself as a kind of a two-headed monster for the American consumer. In two ways he's ignorant—ignorant of the refining process and what it does to the food he is getting; and additionally, he's ignorant of potential harm-inducing elements added to food in the guise of, say, cosmetic additives for taste and coloring. Will you agree with me that this seems to be the essence of the problem we've been discussing? /54

Karen, Jerry, Gary: Yes! Definitely! Very definitely! /55

STAGE THREE

SUGGESTING SOLUTIONS

Judy: If, then, this is a problem that cries for a solution, what would be any criteria we would have to consider in proposing a solution? /56

Karen: Well, I think the most obvious criterion would be that we have to deal with the *cause;* and because we define government as federal government, we should have some sort of federal agency that would get at the cause. /57

Jerry: Judy, I think another criterion that we should keep in mind is that we don't want to diminish the *selectivity* of the American consumer. We don't want to take away his choices at the supermarket. /58

Gary: Going beyond what you're saying, Jerry, we have to remember that the consumer has eaten these processed foods for a long period of time. Now, if we're going to tell him that there are problems with these foods, that the consumer can in fact be eating food that is harmful to him, we're attacking some pretty deep-rooted *attitudes, values,* and *beliefs.* And we're going to have to consider that in our solution. /59

Judy: That seems to me the biggest problem we've got to face, and one that's going to be crucial to any of the solutions we may come up with—that, as well as the other two very pertinent criteria we have set up. What would be a feasible solution that would somehow include all of these? /60

Jerry: I think one solution comes to mind right away. We mentioned that 80% of the additives in our food are in there for commerical reasons; they aren't in there for the good of the consumer at all. I think that all of these should be eliminated from foods. /61

Karen: Well, I think, Jerry, in order to do that, we're going to have to deal with the government agency that I mentioned before. And that probably would be the Food and Drug Administration, because we said that they don't have standardization in their testing, and they don't have subpoena power to get information; they rely on voluntary compliance. So, it seems to me that in order to deal with that problem, we probably ought to *strengthen the Food and Drug Administration* so that it can do what it's supposed to be doing for the consumer. /62

Judy: Now, you're bargaining for quite a job there, because strengthening or reducing any bureaucracy is going to be a paramount problem. Why not just eliminate the FDA and start maybe somewhere else? /63

Karen: Why, I think it's fairly obvious that right now the Food and Drug Administration is all we have to work with; and as you mentioned before, we live in a bureaucracy. To start a completely new agency would probably be much more difficult than to simply strengthen an agency that has already made itself felt somewhat in our American society. /64

Gary: Judy, I think another thing that would have to be considered as a possible solution would be dealing with the consumer himself, dealing on the consumer level—that is, providing some type of information, some type of education-enlightenment, a realization that there is a problem with his food. Before any real change can be brought about, I think we have to *convince the consumer* that he does have a problem with his food. I would suggest that this could be done by utilizing the various consumer-information agencies from the federal, state, and down to the local level—getting them to supply information to the consumer and explain to him what the problem is and where it lies. I think also that using the FDA and the Department of Health, Education, and Welfare, public-service announcements could be made on national, state, and local media to try to inform the consumer. /65

STAGE FOUR
EVALUATING THE PROPOSED SOLUTIONS

Jerry: Gary, I think what you say makes a lot of sense. In the past we've seen problems with cyclamates, monosodium glutamate, and many other issues. The American consumer, when he's informed that there are dangers, has put the pressure on the politicians and the agencies that were supposed to protect him. So, I think consumer activity would be effective. /66

Judy: In other words, persuasion is preferred, but panic is more productive. /67

Karen *(as all laugh):*   Right. /68

Judy: OK, but I see a kind of weakness in all of this. It seems to be realistic, but it also seems to be *restrictive* to me as a consumer. /69

Jerry: Yes, I think in a sense it would be restrictive. The FDA may restrict the amount of poison you could eat each day. /70

Jerry *(amid more laughter):*   Then, they also may restrict you to eating steaks that are fresh, not just look fresh, but *are* fresh. It may diminish your selectivity a little bit, but I don't think you'd really complain about that. /71

Gary: Well, Jerry, I may take issue with this, in that you suggest that we eliminate all the cosmetic additives. Perhaps they do not serve any purpose as nutritive value, but I think we may have to keep in mind that the consumer has to be prepared—that when we eliminate all cosmetic additives, that means his margarine will be white instead of yellow, that his oranges may not necessarily be oranges' color, or that perhaps certain foods that he's used to seeing will be colored somewhat differently. /72

Karen: I think that there is one more thing that can answer part of your question—about restrictions of the consumer—and it deals with something we haven't mentioned yet. That's the idea of the refining processes and the canning processes that we sort of indicted at the beginning of this discussion. I think what we should remember is that in this particular area, again, we're dealing with *informing* the consumer. There's no way that we can get rid of the refining process, because it services the consumer. So, what we should do is inform the consumer as to what the potential dangers are and where he could possibly get more nutritive value for the food he is eating. /73

STAGE FIVE

*CHOOSING THE PREFERRED SOLUTION**

Judy: All right, then, if we were to state one general theme of our entire discussion tonight, it would be that the problem for the consumer, in food quality, is his lack of knowledge of just what he is getting. It seems he doesn't know what he's getting—rather, what he *isn't* getting as a result of processing—and what he's getting with additives. And our solutions suggest that *information,* whether from the FDA or from the consumer groups, would be the foundation for a resolution to the problem—one that's realistic, not prohibitive, and perhaps even beneficial; for it would mean removing harmful additives. *Enlightenment* here seems to be the critical element. And I hope it would make a difference to the average consumer, say, someone like Mrs. Starkey, a homemaker, who was once before congressional hearings on color additives. It was in 1960, and at that time she had made a statement: "The shopper, really informed and looking for a plain food, with nothing added and nothing taken away, is like Diogenes with the lantern, unable to find an honest man." But if solutions such as those brought forth here tonight were implemented, her task might still be a difficult one; but with knowledge as her lantern, her path would be well lighted. /74

---

*Note that on p. 455, the fifth stage of the decision-making or problem-solving discussion is "Deciding How to Put the Approved Solution into Operation." However, because of the nature of this group and the circumstances of the discussion, the final stage here is the choice of the preferred soltuion.

Reference Notes

[1] See Chapter 7, "Analysis of Reflective Thinking," in *How We Think* by John Dewey (Boston: D.C. Heath & Company, 1933).

[2] Harrison S. Elliott, *The Process of Group Thinking* (New York: Association Press, 1932), p. 89 ff.

[3] Permission to transcribe and edit this discussion was granted by Professor Carl M. Moore as agent for Kent State University. The authors and the publisher wish to thank also the students' coach, Dr. Linda Irwin Moore, and the audio engineer, Martin Gallagher, for their work.

Problems and Probes

1. Compare and contrast *small group discussion,* as defined in this appendix, with other types of interchanges—social conversations, interviews, arguments, or debates, etc. Consider such communication variables as *(a)* opportunities for interaction, *(b)* opportunities to gain information about other persons participating in the interchange, *(c)* opportunities to control the emotional and physical environment in which communication takes place, and *(d)* opportunities to reach mutually satisfying communicative outcomes.

2. Remembering that a good question for discussion should be stated briefly, clearly, and objectively, frame a question on each of the following subjects suitable *(a)* for a study group and *(b)* for a decision-making group:

The college grading system.	College curriculum decisions.
Governmental support of the arts.	The future of the automobile.
Public political lobbies.	Intercollegiate athletics.

3. Compare and contrast the processes of preparing for a discussion and for a speech. Write a short paper in which you evaluate your skills in each of these forms.

Oral Activities and Speaking Assignments

1. The class will be divided into groups of three to five persons, and each group will be asked to build an agenda on a topic suggested by the instructor. Take ten or fifteen minutes to build the agenda, and then reassemble as a whole class. Each group will then present its agenda so that all class members can compare and contrast the various approaches to agenda building. Formulate answers to the following questions: How were the agenda different? Why were they different? Does the exercise indicate to you ways in which the agenda reflects a group's biases or concerns? Can you see why agenda building is more than a formality?

2. Meet with four or five classmates. Select a nominal leader; choose a question; agree upon a format; gather information in accordance with a discussion plan; then present a discussion for the class as a whole. Other members of the class, as designated by the instructor, will criticize and evaluate the discussion after it is concluded and offer suggestions for improvement. If possible, the discussion should be audiotaped or videotaped for your subsequent personal analysis. Here are some subjects:

How effective is our freshman-orientation program?
How are American cities solving their traffic problems?
What makes a novel/play/film great?
What are the social and ethical implications of organ-transplant surgery?
How can we reconcile the demands of both the ecological and the energy crises in this country?
How well are American colleges and universities preparing students for life?
What can be done about America's child-abuse problem?
Is protest dead on the campuses of American colleges?
How should the basic speech communication course be taught?
Is it possible to put into law reasonable controls over pornography?
What has the United Nations accomplished?
Can individual citizens ever make their collective voices heard in Washington?

Suggestions for Further Reading

John K. Brilhart, *Effective Group Discussion,* 2nd ed. (Dubuque, Iowa: Wm. C. Brown Company, Publishers, 1974).
B. Aubrey Fisher, *Small Group Decision Making: Communication and the Group Process* (New York: McGraw-Hill Book Company, 1974).
Joseph Luft, *Group Processes: An Introduction to Group Dynamics,* 2nd ed. (Palo Alto, Calif.: National Press Books, 1970).
Lawrence B. Rosenfeld, *Human Interaction in the Small Group Setting* (Columbus, Ohio: Charles E. Merrill Publishing Company, 1973).

Index

Index

Some Suggestions for Using the

Checklist and Index for Evaluation and Improvement of Student Speeches

which appears on the Endsheet following this page

This chart, which identifies many of the factors contributing to effective public speech communication, may be used by both instructors and students in evaluating speech plans and manuscripts and also when reacting to speeches as they are being delivered. By using a plus (+) or minus (−) sign together with symbols keyed to specific items in the Checklist, the instructor may readily indicate point-by-point reactions to a speech or a speech outline. For example, a *plus* sign before SUBJ./7 indicates that the speaker has narrowed the speech subject satisfactorily, whereas a *minus* sign placed before the code ADAPT./24 suggests that further attention should be given to using the factors of attention, etc. Students will find the Checklist especially helpful when preparing oral and written assignments or reviewing for examinations. The parenthetical reference to specific pages in the textbook makes it possible to find relevant textual explanations quickly and easily.

Checklist and Index for Evaluation

(Suggestions for Using This Chart Appear on Page 492.)

ANALYSIS OF AUDIENCE = AN./

1. Audience accurately identified (67–71)
2. Audience analysis thorough (66–71)
3. Audience's presumed interests, beliefs, attitudes, and values carefully considered (61–62)
4. Audience's attitude toward speaker and subject correctly analyzed (61–62)
5. Occasion correctly analyzed (62, 77–81)

SPEECH SUBJECT AND PURPOSE = SUBJ./

6. Subject appropriate to audience and occasion (55)
7. Subject appropriately narrowed (55)
8. General speech purpose appropriate (56–59)
9. Specific purpose clear and attainable (59–63)

CONTENT OF SPEECH = CONT./

10. Major ideas adequately supported or explained by good:
    A. Use of explanation (103–105)
    B. Use of analogy/comparison (105–107)
    C. Use of illustration (107–108)
    D. Use of specific instances (108–109)
    E. Use of statistics (109–111)
    F. Use of restatement (261–263)
    G. Use of visual supports/aids (261–263)

ORGANIZATION OF SPEECH = ORG./

11. Major ideas properly established (174–177)
12. Speech plan clear (164–165)
13. Full and balanced coverage of subject (165)
14. Moves toward satisfying termination (165)
15. Major ideas systematically arranged (165–170)
16. Organization adapted to specific purpose (59–63)
17. Organization adapted to specific occasion (80)

DEVELOPMENT OF SPEECH = DEV./

18. Beginning (attention step) satisfactory
    A. Captures attention (151, 190–191)
    B. Well suited to subject/purpose of the speech (191)
19. Need step satisfactory
    A. Clearly developed (151–152)
    B. Strongly related to audience (152)
20. Satisfaction step well developed
    A. In a speech to inform (152, 279–281)
    B. In a speech to persuade (152–153, 305–307)
    C. In parallel with need step (153)
    D. To ensure clarity of proposal (298–299)
    E. To show proposal as workable/desirable (298–299)
21. Visualization step well handled
    A. Projects audience into future (155)
    B. Conveys reality and vividness (154–155)
    C. When positive method is used (155)
    D. When negative method is used (155)
    E. When contrast method is used (155)